INSIDERS' GUIDE® SERIES

INSIDERS' GUIDE® TO

WILLIAMSBURG AND VIRGINIA'S HISTORIC TRIANGLE

FIFTEENTH EDITION

MARY ALICE BLACKWELL, ANNE PATTERSON CAUSEY, AND JOETTA SACK

INSIDERS' GUIDE®

GUILFORD, CONNECTICUT
AN IMPRINT OF THE GLOBE PEQUOT PRESS

The prices and rates in this guidebook were confirmed at press time. We recommend, however, that you call establishments before traveling to obtain current information.

INSIDERS' GUIDE®

Text design by LeAnna Weller Smith
Maps by XNR Productions, Inc. © Morris Book Publishing, LLC

ISSN: 1541-454X
ISBN: 978-0-7627-4783-2

Printed in the United States of America
10 9 8 7 6 5 4 3 2 1

CONTENTS

Directory of Maps

Williamsburg and the
Virginia Peninsula

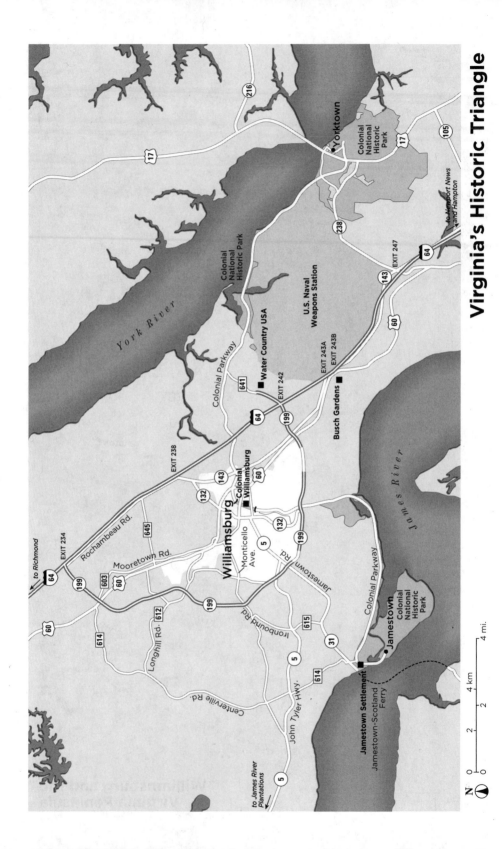

Virginia's Historic Triangle

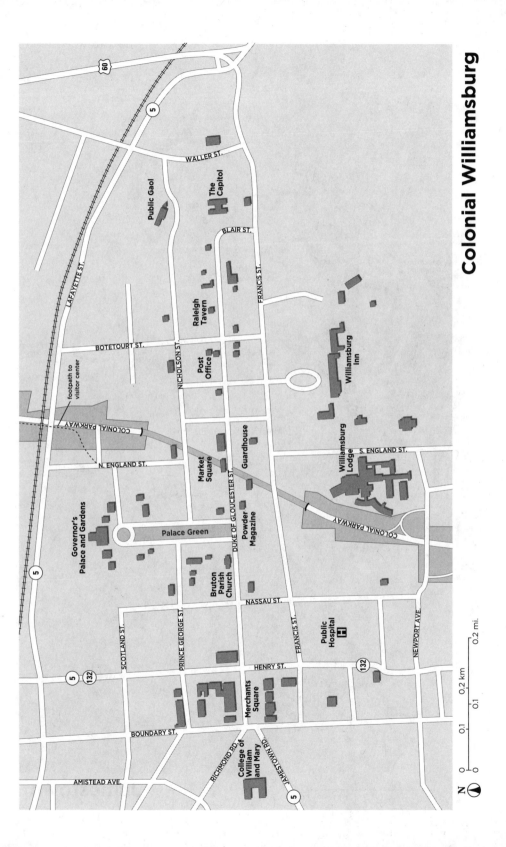

Colonial Williamsburg

N

0   0.1   0.2 km
0   0.1   0.2 mi.

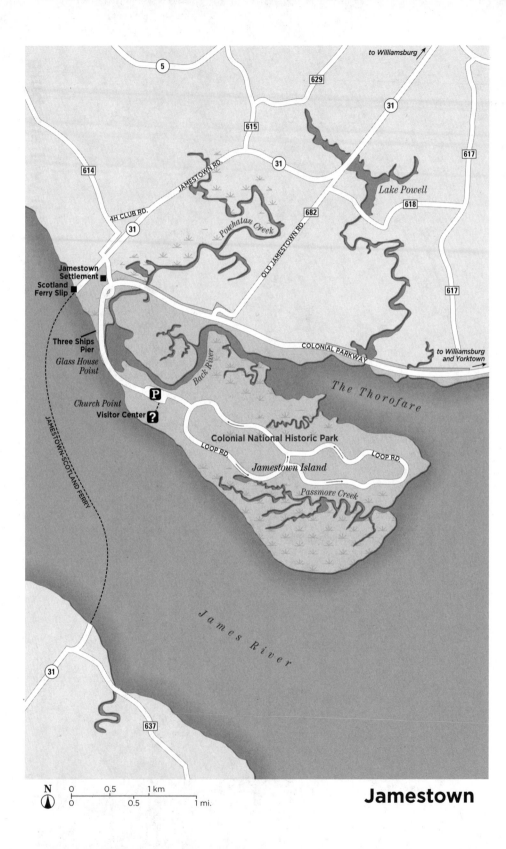

Jamestown

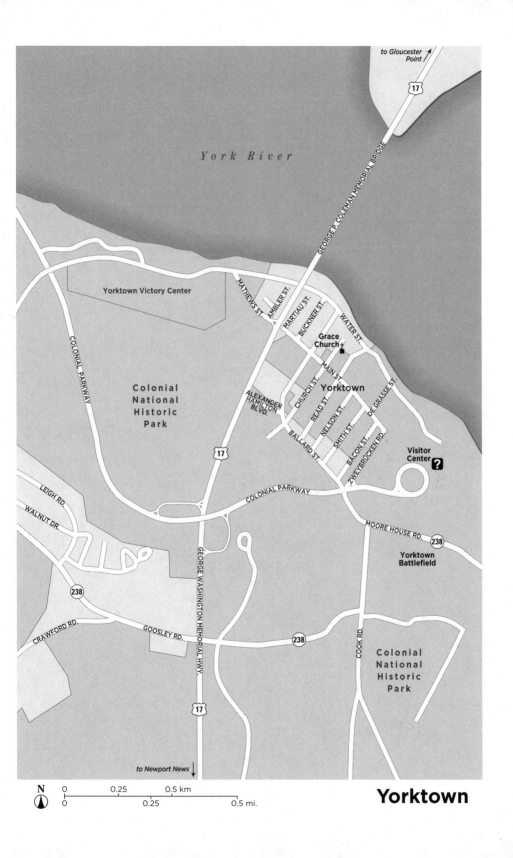

Yorktown

PREFACE

Vacationers who try to take in all—or even most—of the sights and riches of Virginia's Historic Triangle—Williamsburg, Jamestown, and Yorktown—in just one visit, probably come away a bit dazed. Like time travelers, they may feel enthralled yet confused by jumbled glimpses through the kaleidoscope of eras and attractions. In the morning they stroll down an 18th-century lane. Blacksmiths' hammers ring; horse-drawn carriages clatter by. By afternoon they find themselves on board a futuristic, inverted roller coaster at Busch Gardens. Come dinnertime, they face the same perplexing diversity in terms of menu: new American cuisine at The Trellis or distinctive colonial fare at Shields Tavern?

While hurried trips to the Williamsburg area are definitely not recommended, even those with luxurious amounts of time to spend in the Historic Triangle will find that paradoxical transitions between past and present abound. The Triangle includes, after all, Jamestown, where Captain John Smith and his determined crew landed in 1607 and arduously established the first continuous English-speaking settlement in North America. A bit up the road (and away from those marshy riverbanks) lies Williamsburg, capital of the Virginia Colony and center of Revolutionary War fervor. At Yorktown, site of the American Revolution's last battle, British General Cornwallis surrendered to forces led by Washington and French General Rochambeau. With so many historic sites so close to one another, it's small wonder the past not only echoes here but resounds and booms like cannon fire. The sights and sounds of the Historic Triangle can stir visitors' blood in the same manner that young Patrick Henry's speech denouncing taxation without representation must have inflamed the hearts and minds of his listeners in the Hall of the House of Burgesses.

Turn away from the Historic Districts now and step forward in time. Just across the street from the Williamsburg Historic District is modern, thriving "Billsburg," as locals affectionately call the city of Williamsburg. This area isn't just about tourism, after all: It's also an increasingly popular place to live, particularly among retirees. According to the 2006 census figures, Williamsburg boasts more than 11,800 residents within its city limits, including a college student population of more than 7,500. While those numbers may seem small, consider that the city is adjacent to the suburban populations of James City County and York County, which amount to more than 121,500 residents.

Increasing numbers of citizens bring with them more of everything else—more neighborhoods, services, and scores of new businesses, including antiques emporiums, bargain outlets, ethnic restaurants, and video stores. Thus, the present encroaches on the past in the Historic Triangle and vice versa. After a day spent renewing an acquaintance with the dramas, hardships, and dreams of 18th-century colonists, visitors can tap their feet to the contemporary rhythms of jazz or blues at J. M. Randalls Restaurant & Tavern or The Corner Pocket. Or you can head over to Water Country USA for a rousing ride on the heart-stopping Rampage or a family splash aboard a giant tube at Big Daddy Falls. Or, perhaps when darkness descends, you can join in a chilling, thrilling, Ghosts of Williamsburg night tour.

Such diversity of activities can entice, stimulate, and...overwhelm. Our guide exists to help visitors and newcomers stay out of the overwhelmed category. We've explored, researched, and compiled. What we offer here is a guide to the Historic Triangle's brightest and best of, well...just about everything.

So put on your walking shoes, fasten your seat belts, and come journey with us through the glories and, yes, the evils of past and present-day Williamsburg, Jamestown, and Yorktown. The glories of the past are self-evident—the colonists' struggle for freedom and independence, for example. The evils, you say? Well, slavery and massacre, to mention but two. History isn't all a laugh a minute, unfortunately. Then, neither is the present, as anyone who drives Richmond Road at rush hour during tourist season can tell you.

Take advantage of the decades of Insiders' experience we've accumulated while living, working, and learning in the area. Even those visitors who are returning for the third or fourth time will find our guide helpful, as exploration, research, and discovery are ongoing processes here. New museums and exhibits open; archaeological digs unearth new remnants of the past; new perspective on historical events is gained each year. Newcomers will find valuable information for helping them get acquainted with the area.

We wish you the most memorable of experiences in the Historic Triangle. We hope our book helps you feel right at home, right away.

HOW TO USE THIS BOOK

After months of research and writing, we proudly present to you the 15th edition of the *Insiders' Guide to Williamsburg and Virginia's Historic Triangle*. This venerable veteran certainly has seen a lot of changes over the years, but as they say, we're confident we're getting better rather than simply older.

This book will lay out the best sites to see, things to do, dining and lodging, kid stuff, and more. Watch for the ■—those Insiders' tips that let you in on the (shhh!) local secrets.

Recognizing that families are always on the lookout for adventures that will broaden their children's horizons, we've added more activities that can be enjoyed in the great outdoors to our Kidstuff and Parks and Recreation chapters. Likewise, Colonial Williamsburg offers a long list of programs designed to entertain and enlighten the entire family. It's a selection you can review with your children as you sit down and plan your vacation.

Other changes are less obvious, the result of considerable tweaking and polishing, while making sure our information is as up to date as possible. We're pleased with the results and hope you will be, too.

We have set up the book so that it flows in a logical sequence, though you probably won't be reading it from front to back. It's also organized so that you can flip directly to the topic that piques your interest. A quick glance at our Contents will take you directly to the topic you want to explore, and the first page of each chapter will give you an idea of how that chapter's organized. If a particular attraction or restaurant comes to mind, and you are unsure of its location, simply check out our alphabetical index at the back of the book for the appropriate page number.

We begin by giving you a detailed history of Virginia's colonial capital and telling you about its current economics and the many attractions you'll enjoy here. Next we give you information about transportation options for getting here and for getting around once you've arrived. As part of the Getting Here, Getting Around chapter, we also give you some tips on pronouncing some of the more unusual place names your tongue may trip over (more like a major stumble in some cases) as you encounter them.

To help you decide where to rest your weary head, our Accommodations and Bed-and-Breakfasts and Guest Homes chapters give you a choice of more than 100 places. (Truly, as long as you make reservations in advance, there should always be room at the inn.) You'll see quite a few changes in this section, as many of the older mom-and-pop motels have closed in recent years, giving way to bigger chain-owned hotels, and bed-and-breakfast inns are becoming even more popular. All entries are in alphabetical order within these categories and include a pricing key. Keep in mind that these are not meant to be comprehensive listings but a sampling of the area's best offerings.

In our Restaurants chapter, Williamsburg eateries, listed in alphabetical order, are divided between those owned and operated by Colonial Williamsburg and the dozens of eateries of all types located within Williamsburg and nearby areas. So you don't strain your budget, we have included an easy-to-use pricing guide.

A detailed guide to shopping is divided geographically, working from the center of the colonial city outward, so you can carefully plan your excursions in this true shopaholic's mecca. Our chapters highlighting attractions begin with Colonial Williamsburg in all of its 18th-century splendor. Our general Attractions

i A number of U.S. presidents have visited the historic Colonial Williamsburg area, including Franklin Roosevelt, Harry Truman, Dwight Eisenhower, Lyndon Johnson, Richard Nixon, Gerald Ford, Jimmy Carter, Ronald Reagan, Bill Clinton, and George W. Bush.

chapter follows, providing information on both the area's other side—the Busch Gardens theme park and Water Country USA—and more on its less well-known, but no less popular, historic destinations, from Jamestown and Yorktown to beautiful plantation houses and churches that are centuries old.

If there's a duffer in your party, peruse our chapter on Golf for the lowdown on all of our local courses and a sampling of fees you can expect to pay. Other outdoor pursuits are explored in Parks and Recreation, which directs you to places where you can hike, bike, swim, or drop that hook, line, and sinker in and around the Williamsburg area.

Our Day Trips chapter can tell you how to get to points of interest outside the Historic Triangle and what to do once you reach them. (In this chapter, inquiring minds also will find the answers to the following questions: Which locale is home to a world-famous brand of ham? Where did Dupont produce its first cellophane in 1930? Don't look here for the answers; that would make it far too easy—and give you less incentive to peruse our guide.)

As in previous editions, we have dedicated considerable attention and space to Newport News and Hampton, adjacent cities on the Virginia Peninsula that are just a short jaunt east of Williamsburg on Interstate 64. This in-depth chapter includes information on attractions, restaurants, accommodations, and shopping. In essence, it's a microcosm of the information we give you on Williamsburg and certainly gives enough data for planning a separate vacation to this area, dubbed the Lower Peninsula.

We also have provided special chapters on other topics of interest, including Virginia's Indian Culture, Myths and Legends (aka ghost stories), The Environment, Our Military Heritage, and Regional Cuisine and Wines. And our chapter on Relocation will give you some solid leads if you're considering pulling up roots and moving to the Williamsburg area.

We hope you enjoy using the guide as much as we enjoyed putting it together. From our perspective, at least, it was quite a learning experience. We trust that once you read over the information printed on its pages, you will say the same.

If you would like to offer any suggestions as to how we can improve the Williamsburg guide in future editions, we'd be delighted to hear from you. Contact us on the Web at www.insiders.com or write to us care of the Insiders' Guide to Williamsburg, The Globe Pequot Press, P.O. Box 480, Guilford, CT 06437-0480.

HISTORY

Williamsburg claims a long and fascinating history. In its three centuries, Virginia's former capital enjoyed both periods of great fortune and dramatic decline before reinventing itself through an unprecedented restoration process that began in the mid-1920s.

This successful effort at re-creating Williamsburg's past in a way it can be enjoyed in the present is what draws (and awes) vast numbers of visitors to the renowned and curious 18th-century buildings and brick-paved streets of the city from the first of January to December's final days. Most find themselves moved and inspired by this living, breathing example of America's earliest days spread out right in front of them. In town in the late 1990s to discuss his well-known documentary on Thomas Jefferson, filmmaker and historian Ken Burns called his visit to Williamsburg "the highlight of my professional life."

Speaking at a convention at the College of William and Mary several years ago, Pulitzer Prize–winning author David McCullough, whose biography of John Adams topped the New York Times best-sellers list, told why we should pay attention to the lessons taught by the past. History, he said, "is a source of strength because we learn by example." And although exploring the past may provide more questions than answers, McCullough noted, it is "an antidote to self-pity" because it teaches us that "no matter what, others have had it worse."

Of course, we don't think that for one minute you're here in Williamsburg to gloat over your forefathers' tough life and other misfortunes. We do believe, however, that if you have come to town to seek a little respite from the cares and speed-of-light pace of 21st-century life, you're in the right place. After all, to say it as succinctly as we can, Colonial Williamsburg is history.

WHY WILLIAMSBURG?

Did you ever wonder how it all began? Why the early colonists chose Williamsburg as the seat of government for Virginia? Believe it or not, you can thank the lowly mosquito for getting Williamsburg off the ground. When English settlers set foot on New World soil in 1607, they made their homes in Jamestown, which became the center of the Virginia Colony's government. But, as luck would have it, Jamestown lay on a low, marshy island that was also home to a well-established (and quite nasty) population of stinging and biting insects. Some settlers, fearing island conditions could lead to epidemics and finding the current site not grand enough for the capital city of America's largest colony, lobbied for relocation to a place called Middle Plantation, which was 5 miles inland. This settlement, which had grown up around a 17th-century palisade built as a defense against Indian attack, by 1690 was a small village composed of stores, mills, a tavern, a church, and an assortment of homes. In reality, there was nothing grand about it, but it sat on relatively high ground and had access to both the James and York Rivers via navigable creeks.

Serendipity for those who advocated moving struck in the form of fire, when the Jamestown Statehouse burned for the fourth time in 1698. Thus, the basically unformed village of Middle Plantation became the locus for colonists who envisioned a capital city equal to their aspirations. The name Middle Plantation, more rural than regal, was changed to Williamsburg in honor of William III, King of England, and building began.

The new capital was laid out in a distinctly geometrical fashion, dictated by the colonists' beliefs about proper urban planning. The Market Square, or town commons,

Governor's Palace, Colonial Williamsburg. JESSI DICK

and a main street stretching from the Capitol building to the newly established College of William and Mary were the key structural elements of the plan. The Capitol and the college, along with Bruton Parish Church, which lay west of the square, represented stability and continuity to early settlers. It's not hard to imagine why such symbols were important to colonists who had braved crossing the Atlantic Ocean, facing the unknown in their search for economic advancement and better living circumstances.

By the mid-18th century, Williamsburg was a thriving center of commerce and government. Close to 2,000 people, half of them slaves, called the city home on the eve of the American Revolution. Tailors, carpenters, bakers, gunsmiths, wheelwrights, merchants, clerks, and slaves all worked to form the support system for the capital city's growing

number of—what else—politicians and lawyers. While the latter two professions wielded power and enjoyed considerable prestige, there are those who would argue that the most important persons in town were the tavern keepers. Taverns were not just for drinking, after all; they were the political, social, and cultural heart of colonial life. If the walls of the Raleigh Tavern could speak, surely they would tell of the times Virginia's burgesses, disbanded by Lord Botetourt, held clandestine sessions there. They could also tell tales of a more scandalous and less heroic sort, for Thomas Jefferson didn't brand the town "Devilsburg" for nothing.

The prominent role Williamsburg played in events leading to the Revolutionary War is well known. In 1765 Patrick Henry delivered his rousing (some said treasonous) Stamp Act Speech at the House of Burgesses here. The

First Continental Congress was called from here in 1774. And, for all intents and purposes, the Revolution ended not a dozen miles away, with the surrender of Cornwallis to Washington on the fields of Yorktown in 1781.

FROM RICHES TO RAGS

But as the Revolutionary War wound down, Williamsburg's days as a center of government were over. In 1780, shortly after Jefferson was elected to succeed Patrick Henry as Virginia's governor, the capital city was moved to Richmond. Jefferson, who came from the western part of what is now the state of Virginia, had long advocated moving the capital west to lessen traveling distances for officials coming from the far reaches of the colony (then stretching as far as Illinois). Richmond also was judged a safer site, in terms of both climate and military defense.

As Richmond moved into the spotlight, Williamsburg suffered through a decline and loss of prestige and vitality. Taverns closed; public buildings fell into ruin. The number of residents dwindled to about 1,400. Shortly after the Revolution, the empty Governor's Palace and Capitol burned. Only two institutions of note remained: the college, with enrollment greatly diminished, and the Public Hospital for the Insane. (Town wags liked to say that the only difference between the two was that the latter required some proof of improvement before letting you leave.)

The Civil War did little to enhance Williamsburg's fortunes. Though most of the 18th-century buildings survived, Federal troops occupied the town for three years, and the college was forced to close after its Wren Building burned. In 1862 McClellan's Union forces battled through in their attempt to reach Richmond, the Confederate capital.

The arrival of the railroad in 1880 revived the town a little. The C&O's Fast Flying Virginian, also called the Cannonball Express, ran daily out of Newport News to the south, through Williamsburg, and on to Toledo, Ohio. (Dinner in the dining car cost less than a dol-

lar, and that included whiskey.) New houses sprang up near the C&O depot; roads were paved; and William and Mary added dorms, a library, and a gymnasium. But Williamsburg remained a quiet college town, rather insulated, until the mid-1920s, when a Rockefeller came to town.

AND BACK TO RICHES AGAIN

Luckily for Williamsburg, Dr. W. A. R. Goodwin, rector of Bruton Parish Church, was a man of vast imagination. He saw past the shabby exteriors of the many old buildings and dreamed of restoring the town's faded heritage. Goodwin also was a persuasive fellow and was able to interest philanthropist John D. Rockefeller Jr. in his vision of a vibrant Williamsburg. The two men teamed up, and in 1926 work on the restoration of the colonial capital began. Rockefeller not only provided funds but also personally devoted himself to the ambitious project by directing the measurements of buildings and spearheading research efforts.

Fittingly, the Raleigh Tavern was the first restored building opened to the public, in 1932. Soon the Governor's Palace and reconstructed Capitol also were ready for viewing. Colonial Williamsburg, repository of the American past, was well on its way to becoming the fascinating domain that it is today. Tourists arrived in small numbers at first, but after Queen Elizabeth's visit to the Historic Area in 1957, the public began coming in droves. Hotels, motels, restaurants, and shopping centers sprang up to serve them. Visitors to the area today find no lack of dining or lodging alternatives, from the superior to the merely adequate and pretty much everything in between.

Benefiting from the ready audience Colonial Williamsburg provided, a number of nearby Historic Triangle attractions decided in the 1960s and 1970s to put on the ritz. National Park Service properties at Jamestown and Yorktown were improved. Jamestown Festival Park (now called

A Williamsburg Chronology

1683: Bruton Parish completes its first church building.

1693: King William III and Queen Mary II grant a charter for the College of William and Mary in Virginia; bricks are laid in 1695.

1699: The colonial capital moves from Jamestown to Williamsburg, previously called "Middle Plantation." On June 7, 1699, the city officially is renamed Williamsburg when the General Assembly passes the act to build the statehouse.

1715: The second Bruton Parish Church structure replaces the first.

1765: Patrick Henry gives his Stamp Act Speech in the House of Burgesses.

1774: The First Continental Congress meets in Williamsburg.

1780: Thomas Jefferson becomes the elected Revolutionary governor; the capital moves to Richmond for better security.

1781: The "Frenchman's Map" of the city, later used in restoration of Colonial Williamsburg, shows the city streets and structures after Lafayette's troops help Revolutionary forces win the Battle of Yorktown.

1862: Williamsburg falls to Federal forces that garrison at the College of William and Mary.

1880: The C&O Railroad (now CSX) arrives in town, bringing with it some recovery from the economic damages of war and decline.

1924–1927: The Reverend W. A. R. Goodwin obtains John D. Rockefeller Jr.'s support in restoring Williamsburg's 18th-century heritage.

1932: The Raleigh Tavern, Colonial Williamsburg's first completed restoration, opens to the public. The Governor's Palace follows in 1934.

1957: Queen Elizabeth II tours the Historic Area; Colonial Williamsburg's Information Center and the Jamestown Festival Park (now Jamestown Settlement) open.

1975: Anheuser-Busch develops its Busch Gardens theme park.

1976: Network television carries the debate between President Gerald Ford and Democratic nominee Jimmy Carter, held at William and Mary's Phi Beta Kappa Hall.

1983: The Summit of Industrialized Nations meets here, bringing together heads of state from the United States, Japan, France, West Germany, Italy, Great Britain, Canada, and the European Economic Community. President Ronald Reagan serves as host.

1988: Democratic presidential candidates debate in Phi Beta Kappa Hall.

1993: The College of William and Mary celebrates the 300th anniversary of the year it was chartered in England.

August 1995: The College of William and Mary throws a 300th birthday party for the Christopher Wren Building, the nation's oldest academic building in continuous use, built two years after the college was chartered.

October 1995: Defense ministers from each of the 16 North Atlantic Treaty Organization (NATO) nations meet in Williamsburg. It is their first meeting in the United States in four decades.

December 31, 1998: Williamsburg begins its 300th anniversary celebration at annual First Night festivities.

1999: Williamsburg commemorates its 300th anniversary with special events throughout the year.

2001: Colonial Williamsburg celebrates its 75th anniversary with extended hours, reduced rates, and grand reopenings of several renovated properties.

2007: Jamestown puts on a yearlong party for its 400th anniversary.

Jamestown Settlement), adjacent to Jamestown Island, opened. Yorktown Victory Center opened in 1976. Anheuser-Busch arrived in the area, first with a brewery, then with the enormously popular Busch Gardens theme park, which celebrated its 30th anniversary in 2005. The Williamsburg Pottery Factory grew from a roadside stand into a vast and somewhat indescribable retail complex that draws millions of shoppers annually from across the nation. Water Country USA opened its doors in 1984 and was later purchased by Anheuser-Busch, and Old Dominion Opry, a country music and entertainment hall, arrived in the summer of 1991. Not one of these attractions has been content to rest on its laurels. Busch Gardens has been adding attractions nearly each year. The park's latest thrillers are Griffon, a mythical bird that is part eagle and part lion, which plunges riders down a 205-foot roller coaster at 70 miles per hour; Curse of DarKastle: The Ride, which sends guests aboard sleighs careening through the dark and mysterious corridors of a Bavarian castle; an expanded Wolf Habitat with an improved area for viewing the park's bald eagles; and a Bavarian "Oktoberfest" area with German-style shopping and dining. The Williamsburg Pottery Factory—a 200-acre complex of 50 factory outlets and 8,000 parking spaces—includes a Christmas shop and a spacious garden center. Water Country USA continues to add water slides and river rides to its 40-acre play park, the largest in the Mid-Atlantic area. Old Dominion Opry has reinvented itself as the Music Theatre of Williamsburg, offering a variety of shows from comedy to country music, and relocating to a new 20,000-square-foot theater on Richmond Road next to the Williamsburg Soap & Candle Company. Jamestown Settlement put on a major celebration in 2007 for its 400th anniversary as America's first permanent English colony, which included a visit from Queen Elizabeth II from Great Britain. A 10-year master plan brought a new education center, a visitor reception center, entrance plaza, commemorative monument, and the-

i In Virginia, if you are looking for the experience of living history, you'll find nearly every era represented at numerous special events and destinations year-round. For free brochures on African-American, Native American, and Hispanic heritage, call (800) 321-3244; on Civil War battlefields and sites, (888) CIVIL WAR.

ater and exhibition hall just before the year-long gala began.

Over the years, numerous groups have organized other special events to celebrate the city's heritage or to show off its many resources. Annual events such as the Williamsburg Scottish Festival and An Occasion for the Arts now are part of the regional fabric. Other celebrations—including First Night festivities and the Colonial Williamsburg Garden Symposium—have been added in recent years. And the list undoubtedly will continue to grow.

ABOUT THE ECONOMY

Although sometimes it may seem like it, attracting tourists isn't the only business of the Historic Triangle. Industry, commerce, and professional services have grown hand in hand with tourism, if not always at the same pace. Hard industry is represented by Ball Metal Container Corporation and Owens-Brockway Glass. Philip Morris USA employs thousands in nearby Richmond. Other major employers include the College of William and Mary, Anheuser-Busch, Colonial Williamsburg, the Williamsburg Community Hospital, and the Williamsburg Pottery Factory. Thanks in some measure to the large presence of the American military, unemployment in the area remains low, and job growth continues at a slow but steady rate.

When discussing economic development in the area, it's important to remember that Williamsburg is part of the greater Virginia Peninsula, a region that stretches to the south and embraces York and James City Counties as well as the cities of Hampton, Newport News, and Poquoson. The fortunes of these communities are inextricably linked, and the addition or expansion of a business in one locality is considered good economic news for the entire region. With that thought in mind, it's easy to recognize how the decision of Canon—a major Japanese enterprise—to move to the Peninsula in 1987 opened the door to subsequent international investment and provided a major boost to the economy of the whole area, which has struggled with serious ups and downs in the economic development arena.

The wonders of science are explored at the $600 million Thomas Jefferson National Accelerator Facility (Jefferson Lab for short) in nearby Newport News. It is here that scientists from around the world gather to further research on the mystery and potential of the atom. The city has developed a research park nearby to attract high-tech enterprises. Factoring in the NASA Langley Research Center, Hampton Roads claims the second-highest concentration of scientists and engineers in the country!

Tourism counts as industry, of course. In fact, Williamsburg recently ranked as one of the country's top five tourist destinations by the Travel Industry of America. In particular, special occasions and memorable attractions—and with a few centuries under its belt, Williamsburg has plenty of them—always seem to lure big crowds. In a typical year about four million people travel to the Williamsburg area, spending about $1 billion on hotel rooms, meals, and anything and everything remotely colonial.

Revenues and attendance continue to climb for Anheuser-Busch, which employs 1,000 people at its brewery, theme parks, corporate center, and residential and resort properties and boasts a payroll of more than $95 million. Many jobs at the Busch Brewery, by the way, are considered attractive because of decent wage scales, good benefits, and overtime potential.

i Most college graduates don't even show up for reunions. But 165 people from the 1949 graduating class at William and Mary pooled their resources in 1999 to present the college with a gift of more than $1 million. The money is earmarked for two scholarships and an expansion of the Earl Gregg Swem Library, which opened in 2005.

While not a traditional tourist attraction, the Williamsburg Pottery Factory lures two to three million customers each year, who spend as much as $60 million on peanuts, plants, and pottery. Smaller businesses, such as the award-winning Williamsburg Winery, featured in our chapter on Regional Cuisine and Wines, also find the economic climate of the area salubrious, as witnessed in the expansion of shopping centers and outlets on U.S. Route 60 west of the city. The upscale Prime Outlets of Williamsburg on Richmond Road, for example, has grown to become the largest outlet center in a 100-mile radius. And a 300,000-square-foot shopping center, called Monticello Marketplace, is located in James City County, not too far from the Williamsburg line. (See the Shopping chapter for list of tenants.)

Well-planned residential developments in and around Williamsburg continue to attract scores of retirees to the region. Among the newest is Stonehouse, a 5,700-acre community off Interstate 64 in western James City County. Other upscale developments in the Williamsburg area include The Governor's Land at Two Rivers, a vast, 1,444-acre community with private country club, golf course, nature trails, and sanctuary at the juncture of the James and the Chickahominy Rivers in James City County, and Holly Hills of Williamsburg, where strict architectural standards help maintain property values. And Kingsmill on the James and Ford's Colony, both golf-course communities, boast two of the region's most prestigious addresses.

All told, there are more than 130 neighborhoods in and around Williamsburg where home prices range from the low $100,000s upwards to several million dollars. House hunters have their choice of contemporary or historical designs, planned communities or rural, recluse-style living. And although the average price of a home is high—about $300,000 in 2007—the city of Williamsburg's tax rate is one of the lowest in the nation.

Residents of the Historic Triangle are blessed in other ways as well: The rich lessons of the past surround them, and the best of the present is just as close at hand. For those in need of a little R&R, Williamsburg hosts the Ladies Professional Golf Association (LPGA) Michelob ULTRA Open on Mother's Day weekend in early May. To get the word out that golf courses here rank with the best in the world, the Williamsburg Area Golf Association was formed a few years back. The association designs golf packages for visitors and offers a card to local golfers that provides discounts on play during the off-season.

If swinging a club isn't your bag, parks in the area offer boating, fishing, and hiking. Cultural activities abound—everything from the Virginia Shakespeare Festival at the College of William and Mary each July to an evening at the opera across the James River in Norfolk— but down-home fun isn't hard to find either.

For anyone interested in higher education, it is important to note that the College of William and Mary not only is considered an excellent university from an academic standpoint but also has been ranked as the third-best value in state universities nationwide by *Kiplinger's Personal Finance Magazine*. The ranking looked at everything from SAT scores to in-state tuition to the average debt of graduates. William and Mary annually educates more than 7,500 students on its historic (and gorgeous) 1,200-acre campus. Thomas Nelson Community College, a two-year school based in Hampton, has a satellite campus in James City County's Busch Corporate Center.

i The quality of life and a highly trained workforce have attracted more than 150 international companies to the Hampton Roads area.

GETTING A HANDLE ON GROWTH

While many (but certainly not all) would agree that growth is good, keeping up with the rapid pace of development is a challenge for those who plan and construct the region's infrastructure. A key component in Williamsburg's future is the completion of the Route 199 beltway around the city. First discussed by planners more than 30 years ago, the highway was completed in the summer of 1999, curving from the Lightfoot exit off I–64 west of Williamsburg to Route 5 and on to I–64 near Busch Gardens and Water Country USA in one giant loop around the perimeter of the city.

Once the road opened, transportation and local officials set their sights on other projects to improve traffic flow in and around the city. Construction is now completed on the Monticello Avenue Extension West, which begins at Monticello Marketplace and stretches 5 miles to Route 5 near Governor's Land.

So, as you plan your visit, we hope this introduction has whetted your appetite for all that this historic town and its environs have to offer. For much, much more, look ahead to our many other chapters and listings. While no city or region can really be contained within the pages of a book, we trust our guide will serve as a stepping stone for you during your visit to—or perhaps your life in—Virginia's Historic Triangle.

GETTING HERE, GETTING AROUND

Repeatedly, those of us who live in the greater Williamsburg area have heard complaints from visitors about how difficult it is to navigate around our town. Admittedly, it can be confusing, but it isn't impossible. In the last few years, the localities, in conjunction with the Virginia Department of Transportation, have made an effort to streamline and update road signage—much with the visitor in mind.

It is important to remember that Williamsburg, Jamestown, and Yorktown are small towns, and roads in the heart of the localities are actually paved versions of the early roads known to colonists. While these roads are of better quality than 300 years ago, they still are quaint, sometimes narrow, and—with three centuries of population growth—often congested. Take your time, drive slowly, and leave plenty of time to navigate unknown territory and still make it to your destination at the desired hour.

Our first bit of advice is, don't throw away those road maps. This chapter gets you here and helps orient you so that you'll have a sense of where things are in relation to each other. Finding a specific destination may require the appropriate map and possibly your willingness to admit that, yes, you're lost, and it's time to ask someone for assistance. When it comes to seeking help, don't think twice about asking for directions. Locals are accustomed to helping visitors find their way. We actually get a certain amount of satisfaction from knowing we can get you where you want to go. And the fewer confused motorists on the roads, the safer for all who travel them.

Before you can hope to find your way around, it's essential you get a brief geography lesson. The terms we'll be throwing at

you are enough to confuse many Insiders, let alone a visitor. To help you get your bearings, let's start small and work our way up. If you have a regional or state map handy, it might help to refer to it as we go through our explanation.

Williamsburg is the northwesternmost city in a region called the Virginia Peninsula. The Peninsula also includes the cities of Hampton, Newport News, and Poquoson and the counties of James City and York. Surprisingly, Gloucester County also has official status as a Peninsula municipality, even though it sits across the York River from Yorktown and, technically, is not part of the same peninsula.

Across the James River to the south lies an area Insiders call, appropriately enough, South Hampton Roads or Southside. This region encompasses the cities of Norfolk, Portsmouth, Chesapeake, Suffolk, and Virginia Beach. Taken together, the Virginia Peninsula and South Hampton Roads make up a geographic area dubbed Hampton Roads, which is also the name of the harbor at the mouth of the James River around which most of these cities are located.

Now, here's where it gets a little confusing. Hampton Roads is also the name given to our metropolitan statistical area (MSA). For close to a decade, the MSA included only those communities we've listed above. But in 1993, the MSA was expanded to include Matthews County to the north and Isle of Wight County and Currituck (that's "Curry-tuck") County, North Carolina, to the south. This came about primarily because of their employment ties to the rest of the region. Technically, that expanded Hampton Roads to include three additional municipalities, although locals haven't entirely gotten it straight just yet, and the viewpoint may change depending upon whom you ask. No matter. The bottom line is that Hampton Roads, with about 1.5 million people, is the nation's 27th-largest MSA, ranking right between Sacramento and Indianapolis, and the fourth-largest MSA in the southeastern United States.

GETTING HERE

By Automobile

Since we're near the southeastern corner of Virginia, most of our visitors travel here through Richmond, which we have to keep reminding ourselves is north of us. Actually, it is northwest, and therein lies some confusion for direction seekers. Because the Virginia Peninsula, on which we are located, runs northwest to southeast, it is helpful to think of Richmond as the northwest end of a diagonal line extending to Virginia Beach in the southeast. The line itself is Interstate 64, the backbone of motor transportation in the area. And I–64 is designated an east-west roadway.

Most visitors from the north and south head toward our area on Interstate 95. From there, they connect with I–64 East in Richmond, or the Interstate 295 eastern bypass around Richmond, which brings them closer to Williamsburg. Farther west, another major north-south connector is west of Charlottesville, where I–64 intersects Interstate 81 in the Shenandoah Valley.

i Route 199 helps motorists circumvent downtown traffic, making the trip from Busch Gardens, Williamsburg, or Water Country USA to the Williamsburg Pottery Factory area in record time. It is a limited-access highway, so drivers can exit at any number of points en route and hasten their trip into the heart of Williamsburg, too.

The speed limit on I–64 is 65 mph most of the way from I–95 to Williamsburg, but it can be a monotonous drive, often in heavy traffic. One alternative route is U.S. Route 60, which also intersects with I–295 and is a four-lane, virtually traffic-free highway. US 60 runs parallel and slightly to the south of I–64. A third option is Route 5, the old plantation route between Williamsburg and Richmond. Protected as a Scenic Byway, Route 5 is a two-lane road through some of our prettiest countryside. It is especially picturesque during autumn and provides a cooler, tree-shaded option during the heat of summer.

Traveling at legal speed on any of these three highways, you are within an hour of Williamsburg from downtown Richmond. A word of caution: The Virginia State Police often check for speeders using radar. If you travel above the posted speed limit, be aware that this can happen at any point along your route. You will be ticketed.

A Word about Routes

Since the chaotic days prior to the American Revolution, Virginians have been marching to the beat of their own drummers. That tradition continues today, it seems, even when it comes to naming roadways. Here in Virginia, state and national highways are referred to as "routes." Thus, if when asking directions, you simply inquire where to find Route 5, you'll get an answer immediately. But if you ask for Virginia State Highway 5, a designation you may read on your road map, you'll surely encounter serious hesitation. Therefore in this guide we use the term Route 5 for what you may see on your map as Virginia State Highway 5. U.S. highways are referred to as U.S. routes. Please pardon us this idiosyncrasy.

Enjoying the Colonial Parkway

If vacations were designed to help you relax, a visit to the Historic Triangle wouldn't be complete without a leisurely drive along the 23-mile Colonial Parkway. It provides ample opportunities to relax, walk the banks of the bustling James and York Rivers, and enjoy the view.

This charming roadway, which connects Jamestown to Yorktown with exits to Williamsburg in between, was designed to give motorists the feel of a colonial-era byway. Free of any commercial advertising and all trucks, it teems with wildlife. It is not unusual to see deer, squirrels, muskrats, and possums wandering across the road. The waterways you encounter are home to fish, crabs, egrets, and many waterfowl.

The drive, marked in kilometers and miles, is especially enchanting in spring, when the dogwood and redbud, two native flora, are blooming. But don't discount the drive in summer, fall, or winter. Each season brings a special feel to the parkway. And in all seasons you will see various boats, ships, barges, and navy vessels plying the waters of the James and York Rivers, which bound the parkway.

Along the route numerous turnouts with informative signs mark points of interest. These often give historical information not covered by visits to individual sites, so the drive will complement any touring you do of Jamestown, Williamsburg, or Yorktown. Above all, it demonstrates how history and the prosperity of the Historic Triangle are tied directly to two important waterways, from colonial times to today.

Our suggestion to you is to plan a slow, informal drive one morning. Pack a lunch and plan to stop for a picnic. You'll find plenty of places to pull over and enjoy some lovely Virginia waterside vistas as you down your repast.

We'll take you on a virtual trip down the road, beginning at Jamestown, and offer some highlights of what you'll encounter along the way.

Leaving Jamestown, you'll pass through some lovely woodlands, with silver maples, river birches, pine, and spruce trees galore. The James River will run along your right. You'll note dozens of duck blinds in the marshes and creeks. The river is a flyway for many ducks as well as Canada geese.

As the speed limit is 45 mph, you'll quickly encounter a turnout with two fascinating markers. Trust us: You should slow down, pull over, and read them. One notes the site of an early community called Archer's Hope, which was wiped out one day in 1622. The five inhabitants of Archer's Hope were among the victims claimed during the Great Indian Massacre of March 22, 1622, when a full quarter of the population of Virginia was killed by Native Americans. Among the dead were Archer Hope's inhabitants: John Fowler, William Richmond, Alexander Bale, William Fairfax, and a man known simply as "the Tinker."

At the same site another marker tells a very different story. Apparently, the earliest African-American national radio and television minister, who also served as an adviser to three American presidents, purchased the surrounding land in 1936. Elder Lightfoot Solomon Michaux established a farm and hoped someday to build a national memorial to the progress of African-American citizens in the United States. The first Blacks to come to Virginia are thought to have landed in Jamestown, perhaps in 1619.

A little farther down the road toward Williamsburg, you'll come across a turnout marker that notes the site of an early attempted settlement that actually predated Jamestown. In September 1570 a group of Spanish Jesuits attempted to establish a settlement a few miles downriver from Jamestown Island. Landing along College Creek, they crossed the peninsula to the York River, where they established a mission. But six months later all of them, except one young boy, were wiped out during an Indian massacre. The young boy survived in the woods until he was rescued by a relief expedition in 1572.

After reading that marker, turn around and look out across the James River. If it's a relatively clear day, in the distance along the right side of the opposite shoreline, you may spy several old United States Navy ships moored close to the bank. What you're looking at is "the Mothball Fleet," a collection of nearly 200 decommissioned naval ships that are anchored in the James River.

At this point you'll be driving inland, and the river will fall out of view. Fear not and move on as another great river, the York, will soon emerge into view. But first, you'll bypass Williamsburg, the colonial capital of the great Virginia Colony.

Moving along down the parkway, you're nearing Williamsburg now, and the speed limit lowers to 35 mph. Markers along the roadside point to several important sites. Time allowing, you may wish to stop and read them. Soon you'll pass through a tunnel that travels beneath Williamsburg's Historic Area. It's a two-lane, narrow affair, so you'll want to drive slowly and burn your headlights as you pass through it. When you emerge at the other end, Robertson's Windmill, dating from the 18th century, will be over your left shoulder. To stay on the Colonial Parkway, bear to your right and keep going straight.

Yorktown is only about 13 miles away via the parkway, but there'll be plenty to see before you get there, we promise! Without going into too much detail—after all, we want you to enjoy a leisurely drive and stop and read informative signs along the way—you'll come upon several markers. One is at the site of a Union Army advance on Williamsburg during the Civil War; another shows you Jones Mill Pond, a favorite local fishing hole. You'll pass by the sites of Ringfield and Bellfield Plantations. Once you pass over King's Creek, the banks of the majestic York River open up before you. On the left side of the river is Gloucester County, a place full of a history all its own.

But on this side of the river, plenty of excitement is about to unfold. For example, on your left is a long pier stretching far into the river. It's the loading pier of Cheatham Annex, an ammunition supply depot for the Norfolk Naval Base. It is not unusual to see anywhere from one to four or more supply ships tied up to the pier, taking on munitions.

Nearby is a marker that points out the place across the river where during Jamestown's early years, Chief Powhatan had his "chiefest habitation," called Werewocomoco, where Captain John Smith was held captive in 1607.

The York River, known as the Pamunkey by Native Americans, was renamed by colonists. First they called it the Charles and later the York, both in honor of the Duke of York. A total of 26 miles long, the York is a

continued

tidal river that flows over the deepest natural channel of any in the Chesapeake Bay tributary.

That is why a little farther downriver you'll come across another pier extending out into the York. This one is located adjacent to the Yorktown Naval Weapons Station, established in 1918 to support the Atlantic Fleet, home ported in nearby Norfolk. If you pull over into the Bracken's Pond turnout, you just may be lucky enough to see one or more large naval ships—anything from a supply ship to a cruiser—taking on supplies. If you see armed guards along the parkway, red lights on the pier, or a ship flying a red flag, you'll know that's the business at hand.

Within minutes you'll come upon a left-hand exit for the port town of Yorktown, site of the British surrender to the American Continental Army in 1781, when the American Revolution began to come to a close. If you choose instead to do a driving tour of the Yorktown battlefield, stay on the Colonial Parkway until it ends, which puts you right on the battlefield road.

The entire Colonial Parkway drive, with stops at roadside markers, won't take you more than a couple of hours. But it will provide you with some additional local color and a refreshing break from more structured touring of the Historic Triangle.

NOTE: The Colonial Parkway is a federal road, and the speed limits, which range from 25 mph to 45 mph, are strictly enforced. Getting a ticket means appearing in federal court, where few beat their offenses. The best idea, Insiders agree, is to simply observe the posted limits and enjoy the ride.

Northern travelers coming down the Delmarva Peninsula on U.S. Route 13 must take the Chesapeake Bay Bridge-Tunnel to Virginia Beach and follow signs for I–64. That crossing costs $12, a worthwhile investment because you avoid the traffic on I–95. It also is a majestic 23-mile drive. You pass alternately over several bridges and through a couple of tunnels as you traverse the Chesapeake Bay. The sights you may encounter include vistas of Virginian coastline, fishing trawlers going about their business, and large fish breaking the water. If you're lucky, you'll even encounter some navy ships heading out to sea.

Travelers on U.S. Route 17 from the north will have to cross the George P. Coleman Bridge over the York River from Gloucester County to Yorktown. This bridge can be the scene of maddening northbound commuter traffic on weekday evenings, though the southbound route is usually good to go except during morning rush hours. A $2 toll is collected from northbound motorists on the north end of the bridge. No toll is collected if you're heading south.

Travelers from the south on US 17 rarely have problems. James River Bridge traffic usually runs smoothly into Newport News. A scenic alternative approach from the south is to cross on the James River car ferry from Surry, Virginia (see our entry on the Jamestown-Scotland ferry in our Day Trips chapter).

For shore folk, there's no way around it: If you're traveling to Williamsburg from the east, you will have to cross water. That means bridges, tunnels, or a combination of the two, which also frequently means traffic delays. From Norfolk and the Virginia Beach resort area, the majority of visitors reach us through the Hampton Roads Bridge-Tunnel. There is no charge for this route, though you might pay a toll in time and patience. Delays are common due to accidents and slow-downs in the tunnel, especially on holiday weekends. The best alternative route is the Monitor-Merrimac Memorial Bridge-Tunnel, which is part of Interstate 664.

Be aware that from the Hampton Roads Bridge-Tunnel or from the Monitor-Merrimac Bridge-Tunnel to Williamsburg, I–64 is under-going widening and improvements in the Newport News and Williamsburg area. While a lot of roadwork is done overnight when traffic is light, some bottlenecks do occur. At some points the road narrows to one lane. Be patient: These stretches are short. In the summer, heavy traffic heading east toward the beaches can wreak havoc on anyone's plans. Always add "if traffic cooperates" after saying "We'll be there Friday evening early" to a Southside friend.

By Plane

Three commercial airports provide service to the area. All offer a choice of major airlines with a combined total of more than 350 flights daily.

Newport News/Williamsburg International Airport
900 Bland Boulevard, I–64, exit 255B
(757) 877-0221
www.nnwairport.com
The Newport News/Williamsburg International Airport (formerly "Patrick Henry International")

i It pays to have a destination in mind when you ask a local for directions. Most local directions are not given in terms of east or west, north or south. Instead they are given in terms of "toward" someplace, e.g., "Is that Route 60 toward the pottery or Route 60 toward Busch Gardens?" or "Are y'all looking for I–64 toward Richmond or toward Norfolk?"

and known locally as "New-New Willy") is only 17 miles from the heart of restored Williams-burg. A $26 million passenger terminal opened in the fall of 1992, housing loading bridges, service counters, and all the standard amenities of larger airports. The airport is serviced by three airlines. Included are Delta Connection, (800) 221-1212; U.S. Airways, (800) 428-4322; and AirTran, (800) 248-8726.

Once you're on the ground, you can catch a taxi (the fare will run about $30), or you can take the Williamsburg shuttle (757-877-0279, $26 one-way/$40 round-trip). Both options are located outside the terminal. It's about a 25-minute ride to Williamsburg.

Of course, you can also rent a car. Several car rental companies have desks in the airport terminal, including Budget, (800) 527-0700; National, (800) 227-7368; Avis, (800) 831-2847; Enterprise, (800) 261-7331; and Hertz, (800) 654-3131.

Norfolk International Airport
2200 Norview Avenue, I–64, exit 279
(757) 857-3351
www.norfolkairport.com
Norfolk's airport lies 45 miles southeast of Williamsburg. It offers major connections, par-ticularly to New York City. Expect an hour's drive from Norfolk to Williamsburg (allowing for traffic and roadwork). Insiders know, how-ever, to allow extra time when trying to make flights or pick up arriving passengers. Snarls at the Hampton Roads Bridge-Tunnel can wreak havoc if you're running on a tight schedule.

Norfolk is the major airport in southeast-ern Virginia and offers dozens of daily flights to all major destinations, and most minor ones. Flights come and go regularly, so you can make good connections at hubs.

Renovations to the Norfolk International Airport in 2001 brought the biggest change to the facility in 20 years. It included a renovated main terminal lobby and shopping and dining options; a three-story, 243,000-square-foot arrivals terminal; and a nine-story parking garage. An elevated pedestrian bridge with skylights, floor-to-ceiling windows, and moving

Close-up

Pronunciation Guide

The last thing newcomers need to add to their lists of things to do is to learn a foreign language. English is spoken here, of course, and for a longer period than it has been anywhere else in North America. Yet some Historic Triangle local talk may sound downright foreign at first. There are two main reasons for this phenomenon: American Indians and colonials. Many area geographical terms draw on the region's broad Indian heritage. And a goodly portion of the early settlers' Shakespearean English lingers stubbornly in the pronunciation of places and family names.

We've listed the words that are most likely to confuse, followed by tips for saying them like locals do and short explanations of origins.

Botetourt: BOT-a-tot. Lord Botetourt was the Virginia Colony's governor from 1768 to 1770. You'll see his name on area streets and the occasional room or hall of a public building.

Chickahominy River: chick-a-hom-i-nee. This Indian word means "land of much grain." The river is in New Kent County.

DOG Street: Students and locals use this acronym for Duke of Gloucester Street, Colonial Williamsburg's central pedestrian thoroughfare.

Fort Eustis: fort you-stess. An army base in northern Newport News. See our Newport News and Hampton and Our Military Heritage chapters for more information on this fort and its transportation museum.

Gaol: jail. At the Publick Gaol behind the Capitol on Nicholson Street in Colonial Williamsburg, visitors can see the small, dank cells where 18th-century criminals and debtors were incarcerated. The English are to blame for the funny spelling.

Gloucester: GLOSS-ter. This county north of the York River is named after an English city.

Isle of Wight: ile-of-wite. Named after an English island, this county lies south of the James River.

sidewalks connects it with the old terminal building and provides a scenic view of the Norfolk Botanical Garden.

Airlines servicing Norfolk International include American, (800) 433-7300; Continental, (800) 525-0280; Delta, (800) 221-1212; Northwest, (800) 225-2525; United, (800) 241-6522; Southwest, (800) 435-9792; and US Airways, (800) 428-4322.

Rental car companies have desks on the lower level of the airport near the baggage claim area. Among those represented are Hertz, (800) 654-3131; National, (800) 227-7368; Avis, (800) 831-2847; Dollar, (800) 800-3665; Thrifty, (800) 367-2277; and Budget, (800) 527-0700.

Ground transportation to Williamsburg from here includes several taxi services and a

Mattaponi River: mat-ta-pa-NI. The name of this York River tributary is derived from an Indian language.

Monticello: Thomas Jefferson's estate outside Charlottesville may be mont-a-CHEL-lo, but Monticello Road in Williamsburg should be pronounced mont-a-SELL-o.

Norfolk: NAW-fok. Even natives sometimes disagree about the right way to say this city's name, which is another borrowing from the British, who have a Norfolk County. No matter how you say it, be careful! The best advice probably is to say it quickly.

Pamunkey: puh-MUN-key. An Indian tribe whose reservation is in King William County.

Poquoson: puh-KO-sen. Derived from the Indian for "low ground" or "swamp," this Peninsula city (next to Yorktown) is actually quite a pleasant place to live.

Powhatan: POW-a-tan. This famous Indian chief, father of Pocahontas, might be surprised to see his moniker used not only on streets but also as a name for a time-share development.

Rochambeau: row-sham-BOW. This French general was Washington's ally at Yorktown during the Revolutionary War.

Taliaferro: TOL-liv-er. This old Virginia family, originally Italian, saw their name anglicized. General William Booth Taliaferro was a wealthy planter and greatly aided the devastated College of William and Mary after the Civil War.

Toano: toe-AN-oh. This city in James City County takes its name from an Indian believed to have been a member of Powhatan's tribe.

Wythe: with. George Wythe signed the Declaration of Independence, was William and Mary's first professor of law, and eventually became chancellor of Virginia. The Wythe House in Colonial Williamsburg was once his property.

ground shuttle service by Norfolk Airport Connection, (877) 422-1105.

Richmond International Airport
1 Richard East Byrd Terminal Drive
(804) 226-3000
www.flyrichmond.com
Richmond International Airport, exit 197A off I–64, is about the same distance from Williamsburg as Norfolk's airport. It is 50 miles west of Williamsburg and offers nonstop flights to 21 destinations and connecting flights to worldwide destinations. Nearly 3.3 million passengers used Richmond International Airport in 2006, and it has recently undergone a major expansion that added a new bi-level terminal, ticketing areas, baggage claim carousels, and 8,000 parking

spaces. Future plans call for a new 10,000-space parking garage. Some of the amenities at this airport include a teleconferencing center with fax services, telephones, Internet connections, copiers, and three meeting rooms available for rent.

The advantage of using this airport, especially if you're renting a car or can't abide a delay on the highway, is that it is a fairly quick, albeit benign, route to the Williamsburg area. The only delays are the occasional highway accident that ties up traffic. Even during rush hours in the morning and evening, this leg of I-64 moves along with few delays.

Airlines servicing Richmond International include AirTran, (800) 247-8726; American, (800) 433-7300; Continental, (800) 525-0280; Delta, (800) 221-1212; JetBlue, (800) 538-2583; Northwest, (800) 225-2525; United, (800) 241-6522; and US Airways, (800) 428-4322.

You'll find the rental car companies adjacent to the baggage claim area. Companies that serve this airport include Avis, (800) 831-2847; Budget, (800) 527-0700; Dollar, (804) 226-8852; Enterprise, (800) 736-8222; Hertz, (800) 654-3131; National, (888) 868-6207; and Thrifty, (800) 367-2277.

Ground transportation to Williamsburg from the Richmond airport includes several taxi services and a ground shuttle by Groome Transportation at (800) 552-7911. The shuttle to Williamsburg leaves every hour on the hour and costs $40, or $25 per person for two or more. While reservations aren't necessary if you're traveling from the airport to Williamsburg, it is best to call a day or two in advance to make a reservation for a return trip from Williamsburg to the Richmond airport.

Williamsburg-Jamestown Airport
100 Marclay Road
(757) 229-9256
www.williamsburgairport.com
Owners and pilots of private planes can land at Williamsburg-Jamestown Airport. This facility, only 3 miles from town, was greatly upgraded several years ago. A conference room is available, as are a pilots' lounge and a very good restaurant, Charly's, which serves lunch from 11:00 a.m. to 3:00 p.m. daily (see our Restaurants chapter).

Williamsburg-Jamestown has a 3,200-foot runway with a right-hand traffic pattern to runway 13 and a standard pattern to runway 31. Noise abatement procedures are in effect on 13. The airport subscribes to Pan Am Weather Systems and can be reached on radio frequency 122.8. Taxi service, car rental, catering, and air tours are available. The airport staff, always congenial and willing to assist, is happy to provide information on aircraft rental and flight instruction, or just give friendly advice about the area. Commercial, corporate, and charter flights will pay a minimal landing fee upon arrival.

By Railway or Trailway

Amtrak
The Williamsburg Transportation Center
468 North Boundary Street
(757) 229-8750, (800) 872-7245
www.amtrak.com
Many of our visitors choose to come here by train. The Amtrak terminal, housed in what is now called the Williamsburg Transportation Center, is just 3 blocks from the Historic District. If you're energetic and travel light, it's even possible to walk from the train station to some nearby hotels, though taxi service, provided by several companies, is available.

Two trains arrive daily at the station, and a third on Friday. The service is part of Amtrak's Northeast Corridor 2 run, which originates in Boston and makes stops in major cities, including Washington, D.C., Richmond, and Williamsburg. From here it travels to Newport News and Virginia Beach.

Amtrak provides good connections through Washington, D.C., to all points north and west. Connections to the north and south are frequent from Richmond as well.

Westward trains depart from Williamsburg with stops in Richmond and Washington, D.C. Departure and arrival times change every six months. Call or check online for a current schedule. Amtrak's rates are surprisingly affordable. A one-way fare from Williamsburg to Washington, D.C., starts at $34, for example. The fare to Philadelphia runs about $56; to New York City, about $77; and to Boston, about $86. Children 2 to 15 travel for half-fare. Club-car seating is available on some weekend trains, but advance reservations are required for these seats. Senior discount tickets are available for those who are 62-plus. AAA and active military also have discount options.

A final word of advice for train travelers: The major car rental companies' offices are some distance from the station. However, B&W Rental & Colonial Rent-A-Car Inc., a locally owned company, has an office in the Transportation Center. If you make a reservation with them, a company representative will meet your train with keys and a contract for a rental car in hand. Their services may save visitors taxi fare to hotels and an overnight wait for a car. Call (757) 220-3399 or (888) 220-9941 for specifics.

Greyhound/Trailways Bus System
The Williamsburg Transportation Center
468 North Boundary Street
(757) 229-1460
www.greyhound.com

Greyhound/Trailways offers nationwide service to and from the Williamsburg area. Arrivals and departures are from the Williamsburg Transportation Center. Buses heading to major destinations such as Washington, D.C. ($32 one-way), Philadelphia ($52 one-way), and New York City ($65 one-way), leave throughout the day with as many as six departures in a 24-hour period. No reservations are required, but passengers are asked to arrive at the station at least half an hour ahead of departure time to allow ample time to buy tickets, stow baggage, and get ready for boarding. Tickets purchased more than seven or 14 days in advance are discounted.

By Motorcoach

Just about all major motorcoach companies offer charter service and specialized tour packages to the Historic Triangle. Large groups can

contact these companies to arrange visits that focus on special interests, and there are many standard tour options that last from three to eight days. Each company offers something a little different to highlight its tours—visits to Busch Gardens, the Williamsburg Pottery Factory, the Norfolk Harbor Cruise, free-time days, or colonial-plantation dinners, for example. Many include the cost of a pass to Colonial Williamsburg in their package prices.

Listed below are names and numbers for some of the major tour companies servicing the Historic Triangle.

Collette Tours/Rhode Island
(401) 727-9000

Mayflower Tours/Illinois
(630) 960-3430

Paragon Tours/Massachusetts
(508) 379-1976

Star Tours/New Jersey
(609) 586-6080

Local tour companies also specialize in assisting groups of tourists or individual visitors. Itinerary suggestions, tours, step-on guides, airport transfers, shuttle service to attractions, and help with bus maintenance are some of the services provided by the following enterprises.

Carey/VIP & Celebrity Limousines of Williamsburg, (757) 220-1616
Colonial Connections, (757) 258-3122
Groome Transportation, (800) 552-7911
Maximum Guided Tours Inc., (757) 253-2094
Newton Bus Service Inc., (757) 874-3160
Oleta Coach Lines Inc., (757) 253-1008
Tidewater Touring Inc., (757) 872-0897
Tourtime Martz, (800) 544-3389
Williamsburg Limousine, (757) 877-0279

By Boat

It's ironic that the most historic way to arrive in the Triangle—by water—is the least accessible today. While owners of pleasure boats do dock at Yorktown, Jamestown, Smithfield, Hampton, or Norfolk to undertake tours of the region, few cruise ships now come to call.

While the *Queen Elizabeth II* has stopped in Newport News on occasion on its way from New York to San Juan, this is not a regular occurrence. All cruise ships, including Carnival Cruises, instead dock in Norfolk at Nauticus, the National Maritime Center.

Hampton has a number of boating options—all in the form of short cruises of the bay, such as the daily narrated harbor cruise of the Norfolk Naval Base taken by the *Miss Hampton II*, (757) 722-9102; and the *Venture Inn II*, a 62-foot yacht that offers winter whale watching and evening adventure and nature cruises seasonally, (757) 850-8960. There's always the Harbor Link Ferry that leaves from Hampton (docks at the public pier behind the Hampton Visitor Center) and goes to Norfolk (the dock is adjacent to Nauticus on Waterside Drive). The ferry makes several trips daily from Hampton with return rides from Norfolk. Call for a current schedule, (757) 722-9400. (See our Newport News and Hampton chapter for more about individual cruises.)

Norfolk also has several short cruises of the harbor, as well, all leaving from Norfolk Waterside. There's the *Spirit of Norfolk*, which offers two-hour lunch and three-hour dinner cruises with live musical entertainment year-round, (757) 627-7771. Or, climb aboard a ship that harkens back to the bygone days of tall sailing ships. The *American Rover*, a 135-foot-long, three-masted topsail passenger schooner, inspired by 19th-century cargo schooners, can carry 149 passengers on two-hour morning harbor cruises, three-hour afternoon harbor cruises, and two-hour sunset cruises in the spring, summer, and fall, (757) 627-SAIL. There's also the Carrie B Harbor Tours, a cruise of the Elizabeth River aboard a replica of a 19th-century Mississippi River paddle wheeler, (757) 393-4735. If you have additional questions about travel around Norfolk, call the Visitor Information Center at (800) 368-3097.

i Travelers on I–64 who must cross the Hampton Roads Bridge-Tunnel from Norfolk will find it helpful to call (757) 727-4864 or tune their car radios to AM 610 before approaching the bridge. These services might recommend saving time by crossing on the I–664 Monitor-Merrimac Memorial Bridge-Tunnel (The M&M), a $400 million, state-of-the-art harbor crossing named for the ironclads that dueled near its northern end during the Civil War. I–664 connects with all major Southside destinations.

Coming up the James River from either the ocean or the Intracoastal Waterway, private boaters will find a dearth of public marinas convenient to Williamsburg. The Downtown Hampton Public Piers on the Hampton waterfront has floating transient slips available for $1.25 a foot per night. Call (757) 727-1276. Bluewater Marina (formerly Hampton Roads Maria) also provides transient slip rental for $1.25 a foot per night and has plans in the works for a full-service marina, complete with a restaurant and a pool, (757) 723-6774. In Williamsburg there are Queen's Lake Club, (757) 229-0973; and Jamestown Yacht Basin, (757) 229-8309. Both rent slips to transient boats. Note that crafts visiting Jamestown need to be able to clear an 11-foot, 6-inch stationary bridge.

ONCE YOU'RE HERE

There is no better orientation to the area than that provided at the Colonial Williamsburg Visitor Center, roughly at the center of a cross formed by important routes. The Colonial Parkway, the upright portion of the cross, has Yorktown at the top and Jamestown at the bottom. US 60, the crossing arm, has Toano, Lightfoot, and the outlets to the left and Busch Gardens to the right. For getting around Williamsburg on your own, it might help to orient yourself by thinking of US 60 as the spine of the city, since there is no motor travel on Duke of Gloucester Street until late in the evening. Toward the north and west from downtown Williamsburg, US 60 is named Richmond Road, the major commercial artery. From the William and Mary campus eastward, it travels Francis Street to York Street, where it turns east and is the route to Busch Gardens. A parallel Bypass Route 60 north of the center of town features several major motels and restaurants and is a good route for avoiding traffic when traveling from Busch Gardens to Richmond Road locations.

The fastest way to get around town is Route 199, which will get you from I-64 near Busch Gardens across Williamsburg to the Williamsburg Pottery Factory side of town in record time. The completed Route 199 opened in the fall of 1999 and has streamlined travel around the area. It is a limited-access highway, so motorists can get off and on at a number of points along the way. For instance, you can access it from US 60 west of Busch Gardens and take it to Jamestown Road without getting involved in downtown historic area traffic. It exits also at Route 5, Monticello Avenue, Longhill Road, and US 60 West near the pottery factory. It also connects I-64 at Busch Gardens on the east side of Williamsburg with I-64 on the far west side of town near Lightfoot. Sound confusing? It's not really. It is faster.

For additional advice about getting around, try the Williamsburg Area Convention and Visitors Bureau on 201 Penniman Road. Open Monday through Friday from 8:30 a.m. to 5:00 p.m., the bureau can be reached at (800) 368-6511 or (757) 253-0192; www. visitwilliamsburg.com.

Automobile Rentals

Don't be fooled by what seems to be a short distance between the Historic Triangle's three corners—it's roughly 23 miles from end to end—or by the fact that many attractions must (and should) be explored on foot. A vehicle is mandatory for a full experience of the area's wealth. Several nationally known car rental companies have offices in Williamsburg or at area airports. Local rental agencies include the following:

Avis Rent A Car, (800) 831-2847
Enterprise Rent-A-Car, (757) 220-1900
Hertz Rent A Car, (757) 877-9229
National Car Rental, (757) 877-6486
Thrifty Car Rental, (800) 367-2277

Buses

A car is an invaluable asset in enjoying the full scope of the area, but parking limitations can make it more of a liability when touring Colonial Williamsburg. Note that the city police take parking restrictions seriously and regularly patrol all signed parking areas and lots in and around the historic area. Parking fines are an expense you can avoid by parking in the Visitor Center lots provided by Colonial Williamsburg.

Or, if Colonial Williamsburg is your main focus, the easily accessible CW bus service, which leaves the Visitor Center and circulates throughout the restoration from 8:30 a.m. to 10:00 p.m., is a great advantage for ticket holders. And another bus system, described below, rounds out your options for traveling to and within the Historic Triangle.

Williamsburg Area Transport
109 Tewning Road
(757) 259-4093
www.williamsburgtransport.com

For those among you who are intrepid and adventuresome, there is the Williamsburg Area Transport. The route connects the Williamsburg Pottery Factory in the western part of the area to Busch Gardens and Water Country USA in the east with multiple stops in between. En route you will encounter many restaurants, outlet malls, downtown shops, attractions, restaurants, and more. It has its advantages, not the least of which is that you don't have to worry about parking or paying for parking at any attraction at which you stop.

The fare is $1.25 plus 25 cents to transfer from another line. Students from William and Mary or local schools ride free if they show identification. Senior citizens and disabled passengers with Medicare cards ride for 50 cents. The transit runs every hour from 6:00 a.m. to 10:00 p.m. in the summer, and until 8:00 p.m. the rest of the year.

ACCOMMODATIONS

The pineapple was the colonial symbol of hospitality, and it still signifies gracious accommodation. For area hoteliers today it signifies the high standard to which they hold themselves and their properties. You will find that your hosts and hostesses go the extra mile to extend Southern hospitality at its finest—from the moment you arrive until you prepare for departure.

Today you'll have a much easier time finding welcome here than did the British, French, and Continental armies, and later the Civil War's Yankee soldiers. They boarded at the colonial inns and taverns in the Historic Area, the true antecedents of today's hotels, motels, and inns. Your stay should be much more comfortable.

You'll be pleased to know that your sleeping arrangement will be nothing like that pictured in Colonial Williamsburg's movie, *The Story of a Patriot,* in which wealthy planter John Frye resides in a dreary room and shares his bed with a huge, snoring, vermin-infested "slugabed." Nowadays you will enjoy privacy, spaciousness, and comfort, with such amenities as indoor plumbing, which the good Mr. Frye could only dream about.

The Williamsburg area offers more than 10,000 hotel and motel rooms in a wide range of prices, so you should have no difficulty finding accommodations that suit you. If you're coming at Christmas, however, we recommend that you make your reservations well in advance.

In any case, you'll have no problem wondering in which city you're awakening. Most of our fine accommodations truly carry on the best traditions of Christiana Campbell's Tavern, the Raleigh Tavern, and the King's Arms Tavern, which, in their heyday, offered the best service and accommodations possible.

A toll-free reservation service, (800) 211-7165, or (800) 446-9244 for same-day bookings, is operated by the Williamsburg Hotel/Motel Association and can advise you on a choice of accommodations as well as make your reservation with member properties. Reservations for accommodations and many attractions may also be made through their Web site, www.gowilliamsburg.com. Most accommodations, in turn, will make dinner reservations for you, and tickets to Colonial Williamsburg and Busch Gardens can be purchased at many of the check-in desks. Or visit www.visitwilliamsburg.com to explore all the options and make reservations.

Remodeling and variations in services take place frequently at lodgings in the Historic Triangle. We recommend you determine your specific requirements for satisfaction and discuss them with the host's representatives when you phone for reservations.

A timely inquiry can make a big difference in your satisfaction when you arrive in town. While we give you up-to-date details on amenities at the time of publication, some things can change abruptly. In recent years quite a few properties have changed ownership and changed names, or shut down, and this trend will likely continue for the foreseeable future as more hotel chains move into the area. Where possible, we've noted a new hotel's former name or affiliation.

To ensure your satisfaction, we strongly recommend you ask about details on specifics, such as access to rooms, elevators, nonsmoking rooms, separate heating and cooling controls, mattress sizes, showers or tubs, age of the establishment, whether your four-footed family members are welcome, and provisions for cable TV service, when you make your reservation.

You might also inquire about proximity to highways, CSX railroad noise, and even the condition of the room or rooms you are offered. Other considerations to ask about are distance to your local touring destination and directions from Interstate 64 or whichever route you plan to travel.

When making a reservation, also inquire about special discounted rates for AAA members, children, senior citizens, members of the military, and government travelers, and package and commercial rates under various conditions. That is also the time to inquire about changes in pricing between in-season and out-of-season times. These periods are defined by the individual lodging, but generally in-season or peak season is from late March to November and again during the winter holiday season. Off-season months are generally January, February, and much, if not all, of March, though this can change, depending on when Easter Sunday falls. We cannot stress enough that reservations made well in advance are almost a necessity in peak season.

The accommodations listed below accept major credit cards unless otherwise noted. And, unless we tell you differently, assume that the lodgings allow smoking and children, and that the facility is wheelchair accessible. Although it's certainly possible to find a pet-friendly hotel or motel in the Historic Triangle, it's not the norm. If pets are not mentioned in a hotel's description, assume that you and your family are welcome there, but pets are not.

HOTELS AND MOTELS

Price Code

Based on information available at the time of publication, we offer the following price code as a general guide, with the warning that fluctuations in price and availability, and even chain allegiance, of lodging often occur. The figures indicate an average charge for double occupancy during peak season.

$.	**Less than $50**
$$	**$51 to $75**
$$$	**$76 to $100**
$$$$	**$101 to $150**
$$$$$	**More than $150**

Colonial Williamsburg

Lodging in one of Colonial Williamsburg's properties offers many advantages—especially if you've come to town to tour the Historic Area and wish to immerse yourself in the full colonial experience. For instance, these hotels and motels are the closest to the Historic Area, so you can park upon arrival and either walk or ride the CW bus for free to get around. You can charge anything you buy—from tickets to tri-corner hats or just about anything else—to your room and pay for everything when you check out. All Colonial Williamsburg hotel properties offer concierge service.

In addition, your children can participate in special summer activities held for guests only and need only pay a nominal fee. Adults can use the Tazewell Club Fitness Center (with only a small charge for guests lodging at the Woodlands or Governor's Inn). But the three best perks are priority for tee times, priority for dining reservations, and the convenience that anything you purchase during your stay will be delivered free to your room, so you don't have to carry packages around all day. Need we say more? Check out details about the following six properties on the Internet at www.colonialwilliamsburg.com.

Colonial Houses $$$$$
Check-in: 136 East Francis Street, at the
Williamsburg Inn
(800) HISTORY
www.colonialwilliamsburg.com/visit/stay
WithUs/colonialHouses

i A babysitting service is provided for all guests staying in the Colonial Williamsburg lodgings. However, guests must call two weeks prior to arrival in order to arrange for the service. Call (757) 229-1000.

If you've ever wished you could wake up in the 18th century in a colonial residence, the colonial houses offer the closest fulfillment of that wish you're likely to find. These 28 original and reconstructed colonial houses, taverns, and outbuildings are the only accommodations within the restored area, and they can comfortably accommodate two to a room. These unique houses, scattered between Duke of Gloucester and Francis Streets, Waller House and the Palace Green, were featured in a lavish article in the June 2001 edition of the upscale magazine *Architectural Digest*. Furnishings vary; some rooms have fireplaces, and some have canopy beds. Some have private gardens. All rooms are furnished with antiques and period reproductions and afford recreation privileges at the Williamsburg Inn. Since these offerings are part of the Historic Area and are very popular, we recommend that you inquire very early about availability and about the accommodations unique to each. There are 73 rooms total, and many book as much as a year in advance for Christmas and Thanksgiving.

The Governor's Inn $$–$$$$
506 North Henry Street
(800) HISTORY
www.colonialwilliamsburg.com/visit/
stayWithUs/governorsInn

This 198-room motel—formerly a Sheraton—is a convenient 4-block walk from Merchants Square between the Historic Area and the Colonial Williamsburg Visitor Center. Offering shuttle bus service to its guests, the Governor's Inn is a good economical option among the Colonial Williamsburg hotel properties. Other amenities in the recently refurbished motel include tennis privileges, golf, a pool, and a babysitting service (see Insiders' Tip), as well as a continental breakfast bar, game room, minigolf, shuffleboard, and a gift shop. For additional adult guests, there is an $8 charge for a roll-away bed.

Providence Hall Wings $$$$$
136 East Francis Street,
adjacent to the Williamsburg Inn
(800) HISTORY
www.colonialwilliamsburg.com/visit/stay
WithUs/providenceHallWings

In this elegant accommodation, next door to the Williamsburg Inn, you will find spacious suites decorated with a blend of 18th-century and Oriental decor. Rooms are well suited for families and include either one king-size bed or two queen-size beds, a sleep sofa, and a separate vanity and dressing area. Private concierge service is among the amenities afforded guests in the 43 rooms, and they also enjoy the same privileges extended to guests of the Williamsburg Inn.

The Williamsburg Inn $$$$$
136 East Francis Street
(800) HISTORY
www.colonialwilliamsburg.com/visit/hotels/
williamsburgInn

This is arguably the premier accommodation in Tidewater, justly proud of its fine tradition of excellence. The main structure—with its grand Regency design—is in a dignified, beautifully landscaped setting with the Historic Area and The Golden Horseshoe Golf Course on its periphery.

The Williamsburg Inn has received numerous high ratings in the travel industry. It is listed on both the National Register of Historic Places and in *Travel and Leisure*'s "Top 100 Hotels in the Continental United States and Canada." Rooms typically cost at least $300 a night.

When the inn opened in 1937, it was immediately an icon among American luxury hotels. John D. Rockefeller Jr., benefactor of Colonial Williamsburg, and his wife, Abby, took an interest in the details, personally approving the furnishings of the guest rooms. Today an extensive renovation to the historic hotel has refurbished the public areas, adding significant upgrades to the interior, and returned the hotel to the number of guest rooms in Rockefeller's original plans, reducing it from 95 to 62. The yearlong project enlarged the guest rooms to create luxurious bedrooms with generous seating areas that include a large writing desk, and bathrooms reconfigured in marble and enlarged to include dual vanities, a bathtub, and a separate shower. In addition, larger televisions, minibars, in-room safes, and two telephone lines with Internet access were installed in every room. The newly renovated rooms average 500 square feet, the size most requested by the inn's guests. While there were extensive mechanical, electrical, and plumbing upgrades, the inn's exterior remains the same, as do the elegant, Regency-style furnishings and handsome window treatments. A new tearoom and bar lounge replace the upper dining room.

The renovations brought modest alterations to the Regency Dining Room, including improved wheelchair access.

Three golf courses, a bowling green, a croquet court, tennis courts, a pool, babysit-ting, wheelchair-accessible accommodations, a gift shop, and meeting and banquet rooms are among amenities you will find here. We refer you to our Restaurants chapter for information on dining here, but please excuse us if we whisper just three words on that subject now: "The Regency Room." Enough said.

The Williamsburg Lodge $$$$–$$$$$
310 South England Street
(800) HISTORY
www.colonialwilliamsburg.com/visit/williamsburgHotels/williamsburgLodge
This hotel is very popular for tourists and for conferences and other large gatherings. It is across South England Street from the Craft House and the Abby Aldrich Rockefeller Folk Art Museum. (Enjoy the beautiful sunken garden there. It's one of our favorite settings for a quiet stroll.) The Golden Horseshoe Golf Club course and clubhouse also are across

Renovated in 2001, the Williamsburg Inn is regarded as one of the country's top hotels. JOETTA SACK

the street, and the Powder Magazine and the center of the Historic Area are within a short block's distance. While the arrangement of the lodge's accommodations suggests an intimate scale, the facility is much larger than it seems. Its 323 rooms are in a beautiful, rambling structure representing several periods of growth. The lodge recently underwent a two-year renovation and expansion that was completed in early 2007.

In 2005 the Inn opened its Ashby and Custis Guesthouses, which have 30 rooms each. Those luxury rooms feature wireless Internet, cordless phones, televisions with DVD players, in-room safes, coffeemakers, and refrigerators.

The Conference Center is in the main building of the lodge and offers a total of 50,000 square feet of meeting and banquet space. The 480-seat auditorium features a communications center equipped for television or motion picture projection, radio and television broadcasting, and multilingual translation.

Indoor and outdoor pools, a health club, a fitness facility, and wheelchair-accessible rooms are other conveniences.

Many of Colonial Williamsburg's recreation facilities are available to lodge guests, and so are very fine-dining facilities in the Bay Room restaurant (see our Restaurants chapter). In cool weather it's a treat to sit in front of the lobby's fireplace and enjoy quiet conversation. In cold weather, the warm, cozy piano bar is a must.

Woodlands Hotel and Suites $$$$–$$$$$
102 Visitor Center Drive
(800) HISTORY
www.colonialwilliamsburg.com/visit/
stayWithUs/williamsburgWoodlands
This three-story facility, with brick and glass exterior, is set in a 40-acre pine forest. The hotel is adjacent to the Colonial Williamsburg Visitor Center, and its completion is Phase I of the $100 million renovation of Colonial Williamsburg hotels and the visitor center.

The lobby and front desk area include a separate space for a continental breakfast buffet. The 202 guest rooms each have two full-size beds, a seating area with table, two chairs, and a comfortable lounge chair. The 98 suites have king-size beds, a sitting area with a queen-size sofa bed and upholstered chairs, a desk, TV, and a kitchen area with a small refrigerator, microwave, and sink.

There's an outdoor swimming pool, and the popular Woodlands recreational amenities, including miniature golf, horseshoes, volleyball, badminton, table tennis, and shuffleboard, remain. The Huzzah! restaurant, a family-friendly place famous for pizza, is also located here.

Other Favorites

Bassett Motel $$
800 York Street
(757) 229-5175
http://bassettmotel.com
At this motel you are 3 short blocks from the eastern end of the Historic Area. Being 2 miles away from Busch Gardens, it is also very popular with those planning to spend time there. The 18 large, clean rooms provide individual heat and air-conditioning controls and full-tile baths and showers. The motel is open all year.

Colonel Waller Inn & Suites $–$$
917 Capitol Landing Road
(757) 253-0999, (800) 368-5006
Families like the inexpensive, all-suite configuration of this 28-room motel's large, comfortable offerings, conveniently located near the eastern edge of the Historic Area. After supper, if you have a ticket, you can wander over to the Colonial Williamsburg Visitor Center and catch the bus into Merchants Square for an ice-cream cone or fresh-roasted Virginia peanuts. The outdoor pool will take your mind off your sore feet while you review your day's touring. Senior citizen, AAA, and other discounts are offered, except on holidays. There are refrigerators in all the rooms.

i Some area dry cleaners pick up at local hotels and then return clothes when they are done. It's cheaper than having clothes cleaned by the hotel. Check the Yellow Pages for listings.

Comfort Inn–Central $$–$$$
2007 Richmond Road
(757) 220-3888, (800) 221-2222
www.choicehotels.com
An indoor, heated swimming pool is available for guests of this motel, as are a sundeck and two restaurants, the Fireside Chophouse and Old Mill Waffle and Pancake House. There are 128 comfortable rooms waiting for you, some with a Jacuzzi and some with king-size beds. Wheelchair-accessible facilities can be arranged, and nonsmoking rooms are also provided upon request. The facility is 5 minutes by car from the Historic Area and outlet shopping and a 10-minute drive from Busch Gardens and Water Country USA. Senior citizen and other discounts are offered.

Comfort Inn–Historic Area $$$
706 Bypass Road
(757) 229-9230, (800) 358-8003
www.choicehotels.com
There are 157 rooms in this four-story hotel that is a short drive from all area attractions, especially the Colonial Williamsburg Visitor Center. The indoor-outdoor heated pool, exercise equipment, Jacuzzi, sauna, and lounge are highlights, and the rooms have HBO and cable for those who need a rest after a day of touring. Jacuzzi suites and combinations of connecting and meeting suites can be obtained upon request. Wheelchair-accessible rooms are also offered. The hotel offers a free continental breakfast, and all rooms have free wireless Internet. Senior citizen and other discounts are offered.

Country Hearth Inn & Suites $–$$
924 Capitol Landing Road
(757) 229-5215, (800) 368-8383
www.countryhearth.com

This motel offers 58 guest rooms, all with data ports. An outdoor pool, free phone calls, wheelchair-accessible rooms, nine suites with full kitchens, a game room, and picnic area with grill are additional features. A free continental breakfast is included. This part of the city does not have the highway-strip character of Richmond Road, and its quieter and slower pace may be attractive to you. Children younger than 17 stay free with their parents.

Country Inn & Suites by Carlson, Williamsburg East $$$
7135 Pocahontas Trail
(888) 201-1746, (757) 229-6900
www.countryinns.com
Formerly the Park Inn by Carlson, this 88-room property has been completely renovated and is located only one and a half miles from Busch Gardens. It's entirely smoke free and offers a complimentary continental breakfast; however, if you're looking for a heartier meal, Sammy & Nick's Pancake House is on-site. The hotel also offers an outdoor pool, wading pool, fitness room, business center, and video game room. High-speed Internet and premium cable television are also complimentary.

Country Inn & Suites by Carlson Williamsburg Historic Area $$$
400 Bypass Road
(757) 259-7990, (800) 456-4000
www.countryinns.com
This modern, 66-room hotel is fast becoming a favorite for families who need a little extra space. In addition to standard guest rooms—all with country-style decor—the hotel offers a variety of suites that work well for families or larger groups. The hotel also offers special-rate seasonal packages, some of which are geared toward children. Kids will love the indoor pool and Jacuzzi, and their parents can check out the fitness room. The hotel also provides a free continental breakfast, free newspaper, and free wireless Internet. Each room has a television with DVD player. Some

ℹ️ A beautiful secluded setting for conferences, receptions, and overnight lodging is Airfield 4-H Conference Center, south of the James River near Wakefield, about an hour from Williamsburg, including the ferry ride. The 218-acre site, operated by Virginia Tech University, features a variety of recreational activities including tennis, canoeing, paddleboats, and walking trails in the woods. Many summer 4-H camps are held here. Call (757) 899-4901 or write the center at 15189 Airfield Road, Wakefield, VA 23888, for information and reservations. Or see the Web site: www.airfieldconference.com.

restaurants are within walking distance of the hotel; most other attractions are just a short drive away. The Colonial Williamsburg attractions are just over a mile away.

Crowne Plaza Williamsburg at Fort Magruder Hotel and Conference Center $$$–$$$$
6945 Pocahontas Trail
(U.S. Route 60 East)
(757) 220-2250, (800) 333-3333
www.cpwilliamsburghotel.com

Formerly a Radisson hotel, this property underwent a $4 million renovation in 2005. With 303 rooms, this is one of the larger hotels in the area and an extremely popular conference location. The hotel is built on the site of a Civil War battle, the Williamsburg Battle of 1862. Visitors can gaze at an actual redoubt from the earthworks of Fort Magruder on the hotel's grounds and examine Civil War artifacts in the hotel lobby. Its public rooms honor the site's importance in the War Between the States. We like Lee's Redoubt and Grant's Redoubt as meeting-room names and especially like to watch first-time visitors react to the sign for Hooker's Redoubt—named for the Union general. All guest rooms have cable TV, high-speed Internet access, and Sony PlayStations. You'll also

find saunas, a gift shop, a fitness center, lighted tennis courts, a fine restaurant (the Veranda Room), and J. B.'s Tavern (see our Nightlife chapter). You will also enjoy the indoor pool, attractive landscaping, and proximity to the Historic Area and Busch Gardens. Children younger than 18 stay for free.

Days Inn–Colonial Resort $$$
720 Lightfoot Road
(757) 220-0062, (888) 345-3470

Hanging plants and wicker rockers give Williamsburg's newest Days Inn an inviting country-home feel. And that's just the front porch. Inside, the cozy lobby is equally inviting with a fireplace, comfy sofas, and a pot of freshly ground coffee. Just minutes away from the prime shopping outlets, this 120-room hotel features a Jacuzzi and indoor pool that opens to an outdoor sundeck. If you didn't get enough walking during the day, there is a treadmill in the fitness center. The younger ones will probably prefer the game room. This five-story inn opened in August 2000 with a meeting room, hospitality suite, and deluxe rooms with either double or king-size beds. Guests also have access to a coin-operated washer and dryer. You can sit back and watch cable TV with HBO in the evening and start your day off with a continental breakfast before hitting the shops. It's right across the street from the Pottery Campground.

Days Inn–Downtown Colonial $$
902 Richmond Road
(757) 229-5060, (800) 743-4883

This two-story, 100-room Days Inn is very popular due to its location within walking distance of both the Historic Area and the College of William and Mary. Park in the motel's spacious lot and walk to Colonial Williamsburg, Merchants Square, or anywhere on the William and Mary campus. Renovated in 2005, it also has the amenities expected from this national chain—clean rooms, friendly service, cable TV, an outdoor pool, meeting rooms, and a complimentary continental breakfast. It's a good choice if your destination is any of the in-town attractions. It's also a short drive to all area attractions. Nonsmoking rooms and wheelchair-accessible rooms are available. Children younger than 18 stay for free, and senior citizen discounts apply.

Days Inn–Historic Area $$–$$$
331 Bypass Road
(757) 253-1166, (800) 759-1166

Free coffee, tea, and cookies all day are a nice touch at this 120-room motel, just a short drive from the Historic Area, Richmond Road shopping, Busch Gardens, and Water Country USA. AARP members receive a 10 percent discount. Other amenities include small group meeting rooms, a heated outdoor pool and Jacuzzi, a game room, restaurant, volleyball court, and even a cozy lobby with a fireplace. At this hotel, guests also find cable TV, wheelchair-accessible rooms, and nonsmoking rooms. The entire fourth floor is a penthouse with a king-size brass bed in the master bedroom. Several popular dining choices and a shopping center are close by. A complimentary continental breakfast is included with your stay, and several restaurants are within walking distance of the hotel.

Econo Lodge Central $
1800 Richmond Road
(757) 229-2781, (800) 828-5353
www.choicehotels.com

This motel offers an outdoor pool, free continental breakfast, Internet, cable television, and newspaper. It is close to the Richmond Road outlets and restaurants, and it is within a 10-minute drive to the Historic Area and a 5-minute drive to the Williamsburg Pottery Factory. Children younger than 18 stay for free. Senior citizen and other discounts apply.

Econo Lodge Colonial $–$$
216 Parkway Drive
(757) 253-6450
www.choicehotels.com

Just off Colonial Parkway and a half mile from the Historic Area, this property has an outdoor pool and free continental breakfast, and

i Want to hear about firsthand experiences with hotels from fellow travelers? There are several good Web sites available to post reviews and share experiences—good and bad. One of our favorites is www.tripadvisor.com. The travelers' insights offer a wealth of information and can help you choose the perfect hotel or bed-and-breakfast—or perhaps steer you away from a bad experience. And after you travel, be sure to add your own review!

a car rental agency on-site. Some rooms include a kitchenette with microwave and refrigerator.

Econo Lodge Parkway/Historic Area $$
442 Parkway Drive
(757) 229-7564
www.choicehotels.com

This hotel is located within walking distance to many restaurants and close to the Historic Area. It has an outdoor pool, free continental breakfast, and a guest laundry. Each room includes high-speed Internet, cable television, and a microwave and refrigerator.

Embassy Suites–Williamsburg $$$$
3006 Mooretown Road
(757) 229-6800, (800) 333-0924
www.embassysuites.com

One hundred percent satisfaction is guaranteed at this plush suites–only hotel. Tucked away behind the Kingsgate Greene (Kmart) Shopping Center, this hotel enjoys quiet seclusion but quick access to all attractions and shopping. The 168 suites here feature a king-size bed or two doubles in the bedroom and a sleep sofa, wet bar, refrigerator, and microwave in the living room. A cooked-to-order breakfast and a daily evening manager's reception are included in the rate. You also can enjoy the whirlpool adjacent to the indoor heated pool. Wheelchair-accessible suites, a lounge, a full workout room, and a restaurant also are on the premises. A laundry facility and a meeting room for parties of up to 65 people are available. The hotel is 5 minutes from the Historic Area and 10 minutes from all other attractions around the city. Group, corporate, military, AARP, and government rates are available. Children younger than 17 stay for free.

Fairfield Inn and Suites $$$
1402 Richmond Road
(757) 645-3600, (800) 228-2800
www.fairfieldinn.com

This hotel, which opened in 2005, is centrally located in Williamsburg. As part of the Marriott chain, it shows off a new decor with luxury features such as down pillows in each room. Rooms also have such staples as coffeemakers, irons and ironing boards, cable TV, and wireless Internet. The hotel has 148 rooms and suites on four floors with elevators. It has an indoor swimming pool, whirlpool, and fitness center, and it offers a free continental breakfast. No pets are allowed.

Fairfield Williamsburg at
Kingsgate Resort $$$$
619 Georgetown Crescent
(877) 782-9387, (757) 220-5702
www.wyndham-vacations.com

This elegant, 456-room time-share property offers one-, two-, and three-bedroom condominiums, most with fully equipped kitchens and washer/dryer, decorated elegantly in colonial-period style. There's also indoor and outdoor pools, tennis courts, miniature golf, a video game arcade, recreation center, and masseuse on-site. While it's quickly becoming a favorite of families that are looking for an upscale experience, there are usually requirements to stay a minimum of three nights, and you will likely be solicited to buy a time-share.

Family Inns of America $$
5413 Airport Road,
at U.S. Route 60 West
(757) 565-1900, (800) 521-3377
www.familyinnsofamerica.com

A quick drive from the Richmond Road shopping attractions and 2 miles west of the Historic Area, this motel has 63 rooms. Cable TV, meeting rooms, and a swimming pool are provided, and Jacuzzis, water beds, kitchenettes, and suites are available. Rail traffic on the adjoining CSX tracks may require some adjustment for light sleepers, but our visiting relatives—the severest of critics—attest that the rooms are acceptably quiet. Senior citizen and military discounts are offered. Pets under 20 pounds are permitted for $10 per pet per night. Coupons are sometimes available on the corporate Web site.

Four Points by Sheraton $$$–$$$$
351 York Street
(757) 229-4100, (800) 962-4743
www.starwoodhotels.com

There are 143 deluxe guest rooms and 56 two-bedroom efficiencies here, all a very short walk from the eastern end of the Historic Area. Busch Gardens and Water Country USA are within a five-minute drive. You will enjoy the indoor heated pool, Jacuzzi, game room, dining room, and lounge. (See Bones Grand Slam Eatery and Sports Bar, listed in our Nightlife and Restaurants chapters.)

Three meeting rooms can accommodate up to 250 people for banquets or meetings. Four Points also offers wheelchair-accessible rooms. Children younger than 18 stay for free. Senior citizen and other discounts are offered. The two-bedroom suites, which can accommodate up to six people, each have three color TVs, VCRs, and a full-size living room and well-equipped kitchen. This arrangement is particularly good for visitors planning extended visits.

Great Wolf Lodge $$$$$
549 East Rochambeau Drive
(757) 229-9700, (800) 551-WOLF
http://williamsburg.greatwolflodge.com

This new hotel—complete with indoor and outdoor water parks—is about the most unique stay you'll find in this typically colonial area. It's a four-story contemporary log lodge, with an enormous stone fireplace, massive wood beams, and wild animal decoys. There are a variety of luxury rooms and suites, all with modern amenities and all clad in a burgundy and forest green decor with rustic pine furniture. Many have fireplaces, whirlpools, and vaulted ceilings. Some have log forts or tent areas—complete with televisions—within the rooms for children to sleep in.

With all that this Wild West–themed complex offers, you may never make it outside. The 55,000-square-foot indoor water park includes eight water slides, an interactive tree house, a wave pool, two 7,000-gallon hot tubs, water basketball court, and rock-climbing wall. An outdoor pool, open only in summer months, has water "geysers" that kids love to splash through. There are more than 60 lifeguards on duty throughout the complex. If parents need a decidedly different type of getaway, the Elements Spa Salon at the hotel offers a variety of salon and spa services, including 12 different types of massages. There are also several restaurants on the premises, ranging from fast-food and snack types to the Loose Moose Cottage, which serves a breakfast buffet and a la carte lunch and dinner. The Camp Critter Bar and Grill is reminiscent of a camping retreat: Diners eat on picnic tables and benches set within a "forest" of maple and oak trees. Three times a day, the animated clock tower puts on a nature-inspired show for children, and the Northern Lights arcade is also a favorite spot. The lodge also features many special seasonal events for children, such as a two-week Halloween festival in October where kids can dress in costume and go trick-or-treating each night.

Reservations must include a deposit of the first night's charge, plus tax, and reservations cancelled up to 72 hours before the stay incur a $25 charge. Reservations cancelled within 72 hours will incur a charge of the first night's rate.

Hampton Inn & Suites–Williamsburg $$$
1880 Richmond Road
(757) 229-4900, (800) 346-3055
http://hamptoninn1.hilton.com

One of the more convenient hotels in town is this imposing property on Richmond Road at the edge of the city. Aside from a choice of 100 rooms and suites, this property gets high marks for its convenience to local dining, shopping, eating, and sightseeing. Standard rooms offer queen- and king-size beds, as do all the suites. There is an indoor pool and exercise room available for use by guests year-round. The motel offers a deluxe continental breakfast each morning from 6:00 until 10:00 a.m., and wheelchair-accessible rooms and nonsmoking rooms are available for those who prefer them.

Hampton Inn–
Williamsburg Center $$–$$$
201 Bypass Road
(757) 220-0880, (800) 289-0880
http://hamptoninn.hilton.com

This inn offers an indoor pool, Jacuzzi and sauna, free continental breakfast, free wireless Internet and local calls, and contemporary decor. It is also a convenient drive (within 10 minutes) to the Historic Area, Busch Gardens, Water Country USA, and—in the other direction—the Richmond Road outlets and the Williamsburg Pottery Factory. There are 122 rooms with cable TV and free HBO. Discounts are offered.

Hampton Inn & Suites
Williamsburg Historic District, VA $$$
911 Capitol Landing Road
(757) 941-1777
http://hamptoninn.hilton.com

The newest Hampton Inn, which opened in August 2006, is already getting good reviews for its clean, well-equipped rooms and amenities. It offers 109 rooms and suites, some with kitchens and living rooms, and all include a hot breakfast buffet, free high-speed Internet, and cable television. There's also a fitness room, outdoor pool, guest laundry, and business center.

Hilton Garden Inn $$$$
1624 Richmond Road
(757) 253-9400, (800) HILTONS
www.hilton.com

This imposing four-story structure on Richmond Road is in the heart of town. A lot of thought went into designing this hotel, which offers everything to make a family or business traveler right at home.

There are 119 rooms, including 17 suites, all offering 25-inch color TVs with built-in cable TV, free HBO, and video games for the kids; refrigerator, coffeemaker, microwave, hair dryer, iron and ironing board, wireless Internet, and two phones. Guests can use the hotel's 24-hour business center, which provides fax, copier, printer, computer with modem, and phone lines. Also on the property are wheelchair-accessible rooms, an indoor heated pool, whirlpool, separate fitness room, and a gift shop. Ideal for family reunions, the inn also offers a meeting room able to accommodate up to 100 people (it can be split in half if needed). The restaurant on premises serves breakfast only. A local favorite, The Seafare of Williamsburg, provides evening room service, and a Red Hot & Blue barbecue restaurant is located in front of the hotel.

**Holiday Inn–Downtown
Williamsburg & Busch Gardens** $$–$$$
814 Capitol Landing Road
(757) 229-0200, (800) 856-7815
www.holidayinn.com

This hotel features a "Holidome," with indoor pool, exercise room, sauna, and whirlpool, that's been a perennial favorite of families for many years. Video games, shuffleboard, and a putting green also are offered. If you're in the mood for a stroll, the eastern end of the Historic Area is a short walk away. The 137 rooms, all with free Internet access, cable TV, and in-room coffee, include wheelchair-accessible provisions. Modern and colonial decor, seven meeting and banquet rooms, a lounge (Ledo Pizza and Pasta Restaurant for lunch and dinner), and an on-premises restaurant (E. J.'s Restaurant for breakfast)

are other conveniences for guests. Package accommodation rates and a family plan are offered, so inquire about them when making reservations. Senior citizen and other discounts also are offered.

**Holiday Inn Patriot and
Conference Center** $$–$$$
3032 Richmond Road
(757) 565-2600, (800) 856-7815
www.holidayinn.com

This inn is on the western border of Williamsburg and very convenient to the outlets and the Williamsburg Pottery Factory. It is a short drive to Colonial Williamsburg and to Busch Gardens as well. Inquire about family rates for the 160 rooms. The hotel offers access to babysitting services, and you will find golf and tennis privileges, seven meeting rooms, The Sports Bar and Grille, and the Plantation Dining Room. An indoor pool and hot tub also are available to guests. Microwaves, refrigerators, wireless Internet, and wheelchair-accessible rooms are available also. Senior citizen and other discounts are offered, and children younger than 19 stay for free.

**Holiday Inn Hotel & Suites–
Williamsburg Historic Gateway** $$–$$$
515 Bypass Road
(757) 229-9990, (800) 856-7815
www.holidayinn.com

Here's another new addition to the Williamsburg hotel scene that opened in October 2006. It offers first-class amenities and 96 rooms and suites, including several two-bedroom suites. All rooms have refrigerators, microwaves, and free high-speed Internet. Hotel amenities include an indoor pool and whirlpool, fitness center, guest laundry, business center, convenience store, and a restaurant, Bistro 515. There are also meeting rooms on-site.

Homewood Suites by Hilton $$$$–$$$$$
601 Bypass Road
(757) 259-1199, (888) 892-9900

This property prides itself on being "a hotel

that's like home," and it is. This unusual, attractive property features 61 rooms, all true suites, with "rooms within each room," including one- and two-bedroom suites with queen- and king-size beds, separate dressing areas, and residential-style bathrooms. In addition, each suite features a fully equipped kitchen with microwave, refrigerator, and dishwasher as well as TVs in the living area and the bedroom. Honeymoon suites offer Jacuzzis. A well-equipped fitness center features an indoor swimming pool. Also on the premises is a shop where guests can buy anything they might need while in residence, including groceries. Guests are invited to a daily pantry breakfast and "Manager's Reception," with a light meal and beverages Monday through Thursday from 5:00 to 7:00 p.m. by the pool or on the patio deck. Wheelchair-accessible rooms are available, as are nonsmoking suites. A full laundry facility is provided. This property is conveniently located on the U.S. Route 60 bypass, about a mile from the city's Historic Area, Merchants Square shopping, and the College of William and Mary. AAA and AARP discounts are available.

Kingsmill Resort $$$$$
1010 Kingsmill Road
(757) 253-1703, (800) 832-5665
www.kingsmill.com

The setting and design of this accommodation is truly stunning and unique as area offerings go. In addition, the four-diamond property offers a large ballroom-banquet room, spa, and sports club. The structure overlooks the beautiful James River on one side, and the famous Kingsmill golf courses surround the property, something to consider if you plan to visit during the annual Michelob Championship (see our Golf and Annual Events chapters). As a guest of the resort, you will have access to any of the three 18-hole golf courses. All area attractions are a short drive away, but Busch Gardens is the closest. The center offers 418 rooms, including one-, two-, and three-bedroom suites, some providing working fireplaces with complimentary wood during the winter.

Kitchenettes, babysitting (children younger than 18 stay for free), swimming, tennis, racquetball, other health facilities, billiards, card room, lounge, meeting rooms, and five restaurants and grills are available to guests. A marina with boat slips available for visitors opened in 1999, so guests can cruise to Williamsburg via the James River and dock at Kingsmill. Various packages are also available, so inquire about them during your initial contact. We say without reservation—no pun intended—that this is one of the most pleasant accommodations in the Williamsburg area.

La Quinta Inn $$$
119 Bypass Road
(757) 253-1663, (800) 283-1663
www.lq.com

Quick in and quick out with all the conveniences of home is what this renovated motel, formerly Holiday Inn Express, is all about. Conveniently located on the edge of town, Bypass Road offers a quick route to the Historic Area and Richmond Road shopping as well as Busch Gardens and Water Country USA. The 131 rooms feature cable television and high-speed Internet access, and some have refrigerators and microwaves. Guests are treated to a free continental breakfast and newspaper each morning. Wheelchair-accessible rooms and an outdoor swimming pool also are featured. Pets under 25 pounds are free; for larger ones, there is a $30 flat rate.

Marriott's Manor Club at Ford's Colony $$$$–$$$$$
101 St. Andrews Drive
(757) 258-1120
www.marriott.com

Nestled in the woodlands of Virginia's rolling countryside, but still within a short drive to historic Williamsburg, is the exclusive Marriott's Manor Club at Ford's Colony, a graceful resort set within a planned community designed to "reflect the spirit of eighteenth-century America." At Ford's Colony Country Club, you'll have access to 54 holes of championship golf, the Dining Room at Ford's Colony Country Club, and jogging and hiking trails.

The imposing, Georgian-style resort offers 111 accommodations. There are one- and two-bedroom villas, with limited fairway or garden views. All the villas have a full kitchen with cookware and tableware, DVD player, washer/dryer, dining and living room area, oversized tub, shower, fireplace, sleeper sofa, and an enclosed balcony or patio. The guest rooms have a king-size bed, sleeper sofa, microwave, and small refrigerator. All rooms and villas have wireless Internet access. Special rates and packages are offered on the Marriott Web site.

Patrick Henry Inn $$–$$$
249 York Street
U.S. Route 60 East
(757) 229-9540, (800) 446-9228
www.patrickhenryinn.com

This hotel, the closest to Colonial Williamsburg's easternmost edge, is especially convenient to Busch Gardens as well. Formerly a Best Western, it came under new ownership and management in 2007 and was undergoing renovations. The Patrick Henry Inn and Conference Center, with its meeting and banquet rooms for groups of up to 480 people, might be perfect for your business or party requirements. More than 300 rooms are available, with suites and king or whirlpool rooms upon request. You will find convenient, safe, wheelchair-accessible accommodations here. Other amenities include free deluxe continental breakfast, coffeemakers, irons, and in-room safes. Also on the premises are a heated outdoor swimming pool, game room, laundry, babysitting, dining room, and lounge. Vacationing pets are welcome in designated rooms (if accompanied by their masters, of course), for a one-time fee of $15. Special discounted rates are available on the hotel's Web site.

Quality Inn at Kingsmill $$$–$$$$
480 McLaws Circle
(757) 220-1100, (800) 296-4667
www.choicehotels.com

This hotel is convenient to I–64 as well as to Busch Gardens, Water Country USA, and the Historic Area. There are 111 rooms, including wheelchair-accessible facilities. Continental breakfast, indoor and outdoor pools, a game room, some king-size beds, refrigerators, microwaves, and an adjacent restaurant are among the amenities at this hotel. Children younger than 18 stay for free. Senior citizen and other discounts are offered.

Quality Inn–Colony $$–$$$
309 Page Street
(757) 229-1855, (800) 228-5151
www.choicehotels.com

This small yet charming motel offers 59 rooms with shower baths and remote-controlled TVs. An outdoor pool provides a spot for relaxation in warm weather. All rooms are modestly furnished but clean and well kept, and include free high-speed Internet. The continental breakfast starts the day well. Wheelchair-accessible rooms are available, as are refrigerators and whirlpools in some rooms. Senior citizen and other discounts are offered. After a day of touring, the quiet you find here is a blessed welcome!

Quality Inn Historic Area $$$
600 Bypass Road
(757) 220-2800, (800) 444-4678
www.choicehotels.com

This 135-room hotel is a few blocks' walk from the eastern boundary of the Historic Area, a short drive from the Colonial Williamsburg Visitor Center, and within easy driving distance of Busch Gardens and Water Country USA. This hotel offers a free continental breakfast, indoor and outdoor pools, sauna, and whirlpool, as well as wheelchair-accessible rooms.

Children younger than 18 stay for free, but also inquire about the family plan. Senior citizen and military discounts are offered.

Quality Inn–The Lord Paget $$$
901 Capitol Landing Road
(757) 229-4444, (800) 537-2438
www.choicehotels.com

The 94 rooms, including suites, in this hotel are furnished in colonial and traditional decor. The inn is a 10-minute walk from the Historic Area. You will find a putting green and fishing lake as options for your entertainment, and a coffee shop is on the property for your convenience. Wheelchair-accessible rooms are offered, as are an outdoor pool and complimentary continental breakfast. Senior citizen and other discounts are offered.

Quality Suites–Williamsburg $$$
1406 Richmond Road
(757) 220-9304, (800) 444-4678
www.choicehotels.com
This accommodation is near the intersection with Bypass Road and all of the Richmond Road shopping. Microwaves and refrigerators are available in some of the 118 two-room suites at this lodging, and there is a restaurant adjacent. Also offered are wheelchair-accessible rooms, executive suites, and indoor and outdoor swimming at a shared entertainment facility. A full buffet breakfast is included. Senior citizen and other discounts are offered. Pets under 40 pounds are allowed to stay in upper-floor suites, which have two double beds, for a fee of $10 a day.

Quarterpath Inn $$
620 York Street
(757) 220-0960, (800) 446-9222
www.quarterpathinn.com
This independently owned inn offers 130 rooms a short walk from Colonial Williamsburg's eastern boundary and five minutes by car from Busch Gardens and Water Country USA. It's been known as a good value for travelers on tight budgets, and it has seen many repeat visitors over the years. The wheelchair-accessible rooms, an adjacent restaurant, free coffee, outdoor swimming pool, king suites, and whirlpool tubs make the Quarterpath Inn a comfortable place to stay. Senior citizen and other discounts are offered. Small pets are welcome at no charge.

Ramada Williamsburg–Outlet Mall $$
6493 Richmond Road
(757) 565-1111, (800) 272-6232
www.ramada.com
This newest Ramada hotel is just steps away from the Williamsburg Outlet Mall and Williamsburg Pottery Factory, and a short drive to other attractions. There's a complimentary continental breakfast and outdoor pool. Guests will find free high-speed Internet access, and cable television and refrigerators in their rooms.

Residence Inn by Marriott $$$$–$$$$$
1648 Richmond Road
(757) 941-2000, (800) 331-3131
This elegant, conveniently located hotel offers 108 rooms—all of them suites with fully equipped kitchens. Guests can select from studio suites with king-size beds or one- or two-bedroom suites with a choice of a king- or two queen-size beds. Other guest amenities include a daily breakfast buffet, evening "hospitality socials" with beverages and appetizers, high-speed Internet access, outdoor pool, and fitness room. While there is no restaurant on the premises, this lovely property is within easy walking distance of several local or chain family-style restaurants, and a quick drive away from Merchants Square eateries and the city's Historic Area taverns. Pets are allowed with a $75 nonrefundable fee and $6 daily fee. AARP discounts are available, so be sure to ask when you make reservations. Nonsmoking rooms are available.

Roadway Inn $$
1413 Richmond Road
(757) 229-3400
www.choicehotels.com
Nothing fancy here, just 40 clean, efficient rooms in a highly convenient area, close to shopping, touring, the college, the Historic Area, and many family restaurants. Amenities include an outdoor pool for guests to enjoy in warm weather.

Rochambeau Motel $
929 Capitol Landing Road
(757) 229-2851, (800) 368-1055
www.motelrochambeau.com

Let's not forget the French general whose assistance to General Washington ensured victory at Yorktown! This locally owned, 22-room motel offers its guests free wireless Internet, cable television, and a picnic area. Guests can also use a pool at the motel's sister property, the White Lion Inn, across the street. Small pets can be accommodated. AAA and senior citizen discounts are available.

Rodeway Inn & Suites $$–$$$$
7224 Marrimac Trail
(757) 229-0400
www.choicehotels.com

This 32-room hotel gets praise from families on a budget for its large, no-frills suites and its location near Busch Gardens and Water Country USA. It offers a free continental breakfast, has an outdoor pool, and each room has a microwave.

Sleep Inn Historic $$–$$$
220 Bypass Road
(757) 259-1700, (888) 228-9698
www.choicehotels.com

This attractive motel has a pristine roadside appearance—with its handsome stucco exterior and neatly landscaped gardens. It also offers fine accommodations in a range of prices. In addition to 65 rooms, this property offers two Jacuzzi rooms, each with two king-size beds and, yes, a Jacuzzi for two. All rooms here provide guests with cable TV, high-speed Internet, phones, alarm clocks, walk-in showers, and tasteful, traditional decor. Everyone who stays here is treated to a full continental breakfast. And the indoor swimming pool and exercise room are open year-round. Wheelchair-accessible rooms are available, and they feature queen-size beds. Most rooms are for nonsmokers, though a few rooms have been set aside for those who do smoke. While there is no restaurant on the premises, several good family restaurants are literally steps away. No pets are allowed. AAA and AARP discounts are available.

Spring Hill Suites by Marriott $$$
1644 Richmond Road
(757) 941-3000, (888) 287-9400

This pristine yet moderately priced all-suites property is located conveniently on Richmond Road. It offers guests a choice of 120 rooms, all suites, with sleep sofas and a choice of two queen-size beds or one king-size. The rooms have separate eating areas and a pantry with a refrigerator. Other amenities include a deluxe continental breakfast, an indoor pool, whirlpool, and exercise room.

Super 8 Colonial Downtown $$
1233 Richmond Road
(757) 253-1087, (800) 800-8000
www.super8.com

It's small and not particularly fancy, but you can't beat this motel's location, less than a mile from the Historic Area. A few years back, it even served as housing for some William and Mary students whose dorm burned. Today, this motel is open to visitors and offers 66 rooms, cable TV, a continental breakfast, king-size or double beds, nonsmoking rooms, senior citizen and other discounts, and an outdoor swimming pool. Children younger than 12 stay for free. Small pets can be accommodated for a $10 per night fee.

Super 8 Motel–Williamsburg/Historic Area $$–$$$
304 Second Street
(757) 229-0500, (800) 800-8000
www.super8.com

This recently renovated property is a half-mile from Colonial Williamsburg and only a short drive to all the Williamsburg attractions. Its

> **i** Many hotels require a two-night minimum stay during the peak season, which in Williamsburg is June through Labor Day and also the holiday season in November and December.

104 guest rooms have microwaves, refrigerators, irons and ironing boards, and cable TV. It has an outdoor pool and grills for guests' use, and it also offers a continental breakfast. The South of the Border and Second Street Tavern restaurants, as well as several fast-food restaurants, are within walking distance.

Super 8 Williamsburg/Pottery $$–$$$
6488 Richmond Road
(757) 565-0090, (800) 800-8000
www.super8.com

If you're a shopaholic, this 68-room lodging has a view of the Williamsburg Pottery Factory in one direction and the Williamsburg Outlet Mall in the other. And within a square mile, there's more shopping than anyone could handle in an entire weekend. The hotel offers an outdoor pool, continental breakfast, covered parking, and wheelchair-accessible accommodations. Best of all, you can shop till you drop and be within crawling distance of your room. There are several restaurants within a block in either direction, though you'll have to drive to the finer dining establishments. Children younger than 17 stay for free.

Travelodge–Historic Area $$–$$$
120 Bypass Road
(757) 229-2000, (800) 544-7774
www.travelodge.com

Guests here enjoy one of the area's largest heated outdoor pools and Jacuzzis. It also has volleyball and picnic areas, laundry facilities, and a small game room. Nonsmoking and wheelchair-accessible rooms are available, and so are efficiencies with microwaves and refrigerators.

Travelodge King William Inn $–$$$
834 Capitol Landing Road
(757) 229-4933, (800) 446-1041
www.travelodge.com

This motel is a half-mile from the Historic Area and is very convenient to Busch Gardens and Water Country USA. The 108 rooms have microwave ovens, refrigerators, and in-room safes. A free continental breakfast is offered

as well. An outdoor pool and an adjacent restaurant make this a comfortable home base for a stay in the Historic Triangle. Wheelchair-accessible rooms are available. Children younger than 18 stay for free, and senior citizen and other discounts are offered.

White Lion Motel $–$$
912 Capitol Landing Road
(757) 229-3931, (800) 368-1055
www.whitelionmotel.com

Some of the 38 rooms at this independently owned motel have kitchenettes. It's a 10-minute walk to the eastern boundary of the Historic Area and about the same in driving time to Busch Gardens and Water Country USA. The outlet shopping and the Williamsburg Pottery Factory west of the city are a 15-minute drive, if you use I–64 west. There is an outdoor pool, picnic area, and continental breakfast. Ask about discounts if you belong to AAA. Children 2 and younger stay for free.

Williamsburg Courtyard by Marriott $$$$
470 McLaws Circle,
Busch Corporate Center
(757) 221-0700, (800) 321-2211

You can enjoy the indoor/outdoor pool here after playing at Busch Gardens or touring the Historic Area, each a short drive away. The restaurant is convenient and good, and a visit to the lounge in the evening is a pleasant way to end your day. Courtyard's 151 rooms are popular for individuals conducting business with Anheuser-Busch or with any of the companies in the growing Busch Corporate Park, which surrounds the facility. If you are visiting for the Ladies Professional Golf Association (LPGA) Michelob ULTRA Open, this choice is desirable, particularly for its proximity to Kingsmill and amenities. Wheelchair-accessible rooms, meeting rooms, nearby dining and shopping, and quick access to I–64 are special attractions here. Senior citizen and other discounts are offered, and if your children are younger than 17, they stay for free.

Williamsburg
Hospitality House $$$–$$$$$
415 Richmond Road
(757) 229-4020, (800) 932-9192
www.williamsburghosphouse.com
This stately hotel with 297 rooms is directly opposite the College of William and Mary's football stadium and Alumni House, which makes it popular with visiting parents and team fans as well as those visiting the area attractions. Inside, all is quiet elegance and deeply polished woodwork. You'll enjoy efficient attention to your needs. It is a 2-block walk to Merchants Square and a 10-minute drive to Busch Gardens and Water Country USA to the east or to the outlets and the Williamsburg Pottery Factory to the west, but shoppers should also check out the gift shop, The Mole Hole, for unique souvenirs. An outdoor swimming pool is offered. Meetings of up to 750 people can be accommodated, and free parking is provided in the attached garage. The restaurant's atmosphere is refined, traditional, and comfortable (see Papillon: A Bistro and 415 Grill in the Restaurants chapter), and the lounge is popular with students and townsfolk alike. Senior citizen and other discounts are offered (based on availability), and children younger than 18 stay for free.

Williamsburg Marriott $$$$–$$$$$
50 Kingsmill Road
(757) 220-2500, (800) 228-9290
www.marriott.com
If Busch Gardens is your destination, you couldn't get closer. There are many amenities at your disposal. Racquetball, indoor and outdoor swimming, a health club, saunas, and a Jacuzzi all cater to your workout needs, and a fine restaurant and lounge are featured here. Guest rooms have large desks and high-speed Internet access. Tennis courts, meeting rooms, and wheelchair-accessible rooms are also offered. The hotel has 295 rooms, some of which are suites. The excellent on-site restaurant, The Harvest Grille, lives up to Marriott's reputation for fine food, and Pitchers is a friendly, entertaining lounge. The Williamsburg Cafe offers sandwiches and lighter fare. If you are visiting for the Michelob Championship, this is a very convenient lodging. Senior citizen and other discounts are offered.

BED-AND-BREAKFASTS AND GUEST HOMES

The greater Williamsburg area offers visitors more than 10,000 hotel and motel rooms in a variety of price ranges. Yet no accommodation offers a more intimate glimpse into the life of people who inhabit the Historic Triangle than our cadre of bed-and-breakfast inns and guest homes. While a contemporary hotel/motel room may meet your lodging needs, staying in a tastefully appointed bed-and-breakfast, especially one with colonial flair, sets the tone for your Historic Area visit.

In the early days of the Historic Area restoration, which was launched in the late 1920s, there were no hotels in town. The response was to do what folks in the 'Burg always have done: open our doors to visitors and offer them hospitality. You soon will find that in Virginia, there is a history to everything, and it's certainly true in this case. If you lodge with Williamsburg residents, you are continuing a tradition dating back more than 200 years, when, during "publick times" twice each year, the legal and governmental business of the colony took place, and the city was as crowded with visitors as you're likely to find it today.

A few savvy locals opened their homes to visitors, many of whom had heard about the restoration project and came to take a closer look. These guest homes were, for many years, the only lodgings available to out-of-towners. The elegant Williamsburg Inn opened in 1937, but few could afford to stay there. And it wasn't until the 1940s that a couple of "motor courts" opened. During the years before the establishment of drive-up motels, the local homes handled accommodations for the lion's share of visitors—and they learned their business well.

Today, Williamsburg has a well-established roster of exquisite bed-and-breakfasts, some of them world-class, national-award winners. Each has a unique decor and personality all its own. Each offers different amenities. Some are close to the Historic Area, while others are as far afield as Charles City County. Yet don't discount an inn because of distance—you could stay in a true southern plantation house dating from colonial times, if you're willing to drive a bit.

Keep in mind, too, that the bed-and-breakfast establishments offer some of the finest food served in the area. Breakfasts take on grand proportions in some of the lodgings, and no, you don't have to sit at a large table with a bunch of strangers in all cases. "That's one thing we learned over the years," said Sandy Hirz, who along with her husband, Brad, runs the lovely Liberty Rose Bed and Breakfast. "We discovered that some people simply prefer to enjoy a quiet, private breakfast at a table for two."

That spirit epitomizes the best part about our B&Bs. They cater to their clientele. People who run these inns are a breed unto themselves. They're gregarious, charming, and ready to go the extra mile to ensure their guests thoroughly enjoy their stay. By the nature of their size, hotels and motels simply can't be equally responsive to their guests.

Your hosts today will not require you to sleep three or more to a bed and to bring your linen—and your meals—as was customary in colonial times. Rather, you will find privacy in clean, comfortable, and gracious settings where you can make yourself at home. Most houses date from the Colonial Revival of the 1920s onward. The City of Williamsburg's Architectural Review Board in 1993 designated several of the houses as "historically significant" in helping define the city's character and representing architectural styles and cultural periods from the city's past: Applewood, Colonial Capital, Liberty Rose, and Williamsburg Manor. The West Williamsburg Heights Architecture Preservation District includes some of the listings, and you may wish to discuss the architectural importance of the area with your hosts. Each of the residences listed below offers charm unique to its hosts and history, with special collections or furnishings for you to enjoy. What could be more "inside" than a short stroll home after a day in the Historic Area?

Most of the homes take their own reservations. But many of the bed-and-breakfast owners also have joined the Williamsburg Hotel-Motel Association, which offers a toll-free number, (800) 211-7165, and Web site, www.visitwilliamsburg.com, for bed-and-breakfast reservations.

Most establishments accept American Express, Visa, and MasterCard. We've noted where this is not the case. If you plan to use another credit card, a personal check, or traveler's checks, we suggest you check with the inn when you make your reservation. Wheelchair accessibility can be tricky at bed-and-breakfasts. We recommend you discuss any special needs with your host ahead of time.

Many bed-and-breakfasts also offer special seasonal packages, particularly romance packages, where guests can stay two or more nights and receive extras such as gift certificates to dinner or flowers and champagne in their room for a special price. Often, this information is listed on their Web site, but you might inquire if you're making a reservation for a special occasion. Some of the larger residences also host weddings and other events as well.

It is important to note, too, that some of the bed-and-breakfasts also sell tickets to local attractions. Be sure to ask your hosts when you make your reservation if they provide this added-value service.

Price Code

The dollar signs in each entry indicate a range of rates for double occupancy (two persons)

per night. Please be aware that, during peak season (generally anytime other than January, February, and March), rates may vary from those indicated. Also, some establishments offer lower rates for single occupancy, and some may require a minimum two-night reservation on select weekends. Please confirm your rate with your hosts at the time you book your visit.

$ . . . . $75 or less
$$ . . . . $76 to $125
$$$ . . . . $126 to $175
$$$$ . . . . $176 to $250
$$$$$ . . . . More than $250

BED-AND-BREAKFASTS

Alice Person House $$–$$$
616 Richmond Road
(757) 220-9263,
(800) 370-9428/Access Code 41
www.alicepersonhouse.com
Even George Washington couldn't book accommodations such as these in Williamsburg, because 18th-century accommodations simply didn't offer such understated elegance.

Innkeepers Jean and Harry Matthews are as inviting as their charming Colonial Revival home, which is located within easy walking distance of the College of William and Mary and the city's Historic Area. The Matthewses also have perfect personalities for operating a bed-and-breakfast establishment—they're gregarious, articulate, and knowledgeable about the city and its environs. Add to that their Southern charm and, well, your stay here is destined to be memorable.

Built in 1929, the lovely house is reminiscent of early-20th-century Williamsburg accommodations, replete with high ceilings and spacious rooms, furnished with antiques and Oriental rugs galore. It is located on one of the city's main streets, once lined with stately old homes and venerable old trees. Today, homes in the area are a mix of traditional and contemporary. The house features a formal parlor with a fireplace on the first floor, where guests are welcome to sit and read, and three guest rooms, each with private bath, cable TV, and VCR.

The Queen Room features a queen-size, four-poster bed, while the King Room offers just that: an extra-large, king-size, four-poster bed, as well as an antique chest-on-chest. If you would prefer more room, the Capitol Suite is available.

The bathrooms feature plush, white towels, while European linens are used on the beds. The result is accommodations that are so inviting you just might miss time otherwise spent touring the old town.

Guests won't go hungry here, either. Enjoy a full breakfast of Southern family recipes that can include biscuits, quiche, crepes, and waffles served with Virginia sausage or bacon, seasonal fresh fruits, yogurts, fresh-ground coffees, and teas.

Off-street parking is available, but no pets and no smoking, please. Children 10 and older are welcome.

Applewood Colonial Bed and Breakfast $$–$$$
605 Richmond Road
(757) 810-4656
www.williamsburgbandb.com

It doesn't take long to see where the name of this elegant home comes from: The owners' colonial-era apple print collection in the parlor immediately provides a point of interest, bringing individual charm to a romantic setting.

Located only 4 blocks from the city's Historic Area, Applewood is a convenient walk to both Colonial Williamsburg and the College of William and Mary campus. But it is this home's distinct charm that makes it a B&B to enjoy and remember. A brick walkway leads up to the Georgian doorway and into the home's front parlor. Built by a Colonial Williamsburg craftsman, the house dates from 1929 and features Flemish bond brickwork, colonial decor, fireplaces, and canopy beds in the four guest rooms, each with a queen-size bed and private bath, and each named for a colonial variety of apple.

The Col. Vaughn Suite is a large first-floor wing accommodation with private breakfast room and entrance from the patio, and features a tub and shower. The Gilliflower Room is a spacious and romantic second-floor accommodation with a shower-bath. The Margil is a cozy, romantic second-floor room with a private bath featuring a tub and shower. The Golden Pippin Suite is a private, quiet, third-floor room with a private bath and shower.

Guests enjoy a full breakfast by candlelight in the home's elegant dining room. Each repast offers such treats as spinach pie, ham quiche, blueberry flan, eggs, and meat, all served at an antique pedestal dining table. Complimentary refreshments include scrumptious apple pie.

The Applewood can provide tickets to many area attractions. The innkeepers also are happy to book your dining reservations and tee times upon request.

Also available here are special occasion Applewood baskets—ask the innkeepers about them at the time you book your reservation, or e-mail them at info@williamsburgbandb.com.

Children can be accommodated in several of the rooms. This is a nonsmoking house, with air-conditioning to further ensure your comfort. On select holidays and certain college-event weekends, a two- to three-night minimum stay is required.

A Boxwood Inn of Williamsburg $$–$$$
708 Richmond Road
(757) 221-6607, (888) 798-4333
www.boxwoodinn.com

This extensively renovated 1928 home has won accolades from guests for its peaceful garden setting. It features luxurious king- or queen-size beds, pristine private baths, whirlpool tubs, TVs, antiques, a cozy fireplace, a spacious sunroom, and Williamsburg's "nicest back porch." It is located in the Architectural Preservation District within walking distance of historical Colonial Williamsburg, and it is 2 blocks from the College of William and Mary. Garden lovers will be impressed with the inn's perennial gardens, which have won several local awards, including the 2005–2006 Williamsburg Beautification Award.

The inn features three rooms, which are named after U.S. presidents who attended the College of William and Mary, and a carriage house suite. The rooms are decorated with traditional cherry furnishings. The inn also offers the Washington Carriage House, a separate retreat that features an in-room fireplace and Jacuzzi tub for two. Innkeepers Sandi and Steve Zareski serve a full breakfast each day on a 9-foot-long cherry Shaker farm table made expressly for the Inn.

The Inn does not permit children or pets.

The Cedars $$$–$$$$$
616 Jamestown Road
(757) 229-3591, (800) 296-3591
www.cedarsofwilliamsburg.com

We are particularly taken with the front-garden approach to this house, a pleasure to view from Jamestown Road or the front windows. Canopy or four-poster beds, most in queen- or king-size, ensure your comfortable rest at The Cedars, which is across from William and Mary and a short walk from Merchants Square. Antiques and 18th-century reproductions throughout the house convey an elegant, historic ambience, fitting to the place known as "Williamsburg's oldest and largest guesthouse," which has operated since 1935.

Varied accommodations are provided at The Cedars. For complete privacy, cottage suites with working fireplaces are offered in a quaint separate Country Cottage. A two-room suite, the William and Mary, is in the main house. The George Washington Suite provides a queen-size canopy bed in the bedroom and a daybed in a sitting room, as well as a private bath. The William and Mary Suite has two rooms joined by a bath and is furnished with a four-poster bed in one and twin beds in the other. The other six sleeping rooms all have private baths.

When you inquire about a bed-and-breakfast or guest home, our advice is to ask lots of questions! If you have particular desires regarding decor, air conditioning, type of breakfast, shower or bathtub availability and location, dietary needs, check-in or cancellation policies, provision for children or pets, or even the kind of bedding you will have, just ask. When phoning, you are likely to be speaking to one of the hosts, and the rapport you establish at this time may be an indicator of your satisfaction later.

Brace yourself for a day of touring with a full gourmet breakfast featuring fresh-baked muffins, a hot entree that might include oatmeal pudding with brandied raisins or smoked salmon flan, and coffee, tea, juice, and fruit. The Cedars is a nonsmoking house. You'll find off-street parking in the rear.

Colonial Capital Bed and Breakfast $$$
501 Richmond Road
(757) 229-0233, (800) 776-0570
www.ccbb.com

Three blocks from the Historic Area and opposite William and Mary's Alumni House and football stadium, Barbara and Phil Craig have opened their three-story Colonial Revival home, built about 1926, to guests. A 1989 renovation left many original fixtures throughout the house. The zoned central air conditioning is especially welcome in summer. There are antique furnishings and Oriental rugs throughout the house.

You'll find a pleasant setting in the plantation parlor on the main floor, kept cozy by a wood-burning fireplace in winter. In-room phones have been added for the convenience of guests, as well as dedicated fax lines. Incoming voice calls for guests should be received at (757) 229-7430. You can enjoy the outdoors on the deck, patio, or screened side porch. Smoking areas outdoors and nonsmoking guest bedrooms and bathrooms are offered. In the afternoon, tea and wine are available for your refreshment and relaxation. Bicycles also are provided at no charge, including an old Western Flyer tandem (built for two), regarded by locals as "the friendliest bike in Williamsburg."

Any one of the five large guest rooms (each with private bath) will make you feel right at home. The Chesapeake features a pencil-post, queen-size bed handcrafted by Barbara's father and an unusual corner sink. The James has canopied, four-poster twin beds handcrafted from a single tree by master craftsman Fred Craver. The third-floor Pamlico has windows on three sides and can be combined with the sitting room across the hall with its half-bath and sleeping accommodations for two, making the entire floor a private suite. Terry robes are provided here for the private hall bath. The Potomac Room has an en suite bath and a private porch with rocking chairs and features a king-size bed with canopied half-tester. The York is a favored room for honeymoons (package plans available) and anniversaries, with its queen-size, turned-post canopied high rope bed and en suite bath with original claw-foot tub. All rooms have remote-controlled ceiling fans, TVs and VCRs, and "Cozy Canopy" beds that get a nightly turndown with a pillow mint.

Breakfast is a decadent affair with French toast, western omelets, soufflés, and a variety of casseroles. Colonial Capital received America's Favorite Inn award for its hospitality, food, and accommodations.

Pickup from Newport News/Williamsburg International Airport and Williamsburg Transportation Center is available upon request. Children older than 8 years old with well-behaved parents are welcome. Single occupancy rates are available from January to the middle of March.

Colonial Gardens Bed & Breakfast $$$
1109 Jamestown Road
(757) 220-8087, (800) 886-9715
www.colonial-gardens.com
Close to the Historic Area and Merchants Square shopping, this split-level brick home sits on a quiet two acres that conceal its proximity to the center of Williamsburg.

The gardens are an ongoing project for hosts Scottie and Wilmot Phillips, who are always adding to the work done by previous owners. The North Carolina rhododendron garden is simply stunning in bloom. You will notice right off, however, that the Colonial Gardens' name reflects the interior as well as the exterior: An abundance of fresh seasonal flowers fills the house constantly. The Phillipses' combination of family heirloom antiques with treasures from 35 years of collecting completes the furnishings beautifully and sets off Wilmot's own selection from his original paintings.

A combination of four suites and guest rooms named for blooms in the garden have private baths and telephones, as well as TVs with VCRs. As an added convenience, the Phillipses offer a library of videotapes.

The Rhododendron Suite features a king-size bed, a marble-topped Empire dresser and chest, and a sitting area in a sunny alcove overlooking the garden for which it is named. The Azalea Suite provides a plantation rice-carved, canopied queen-size bed and a magnificent 19th-century ornate English dresser. Its sitting room holds comfortable chairs for relaxation. If you enjoy antiques, don't miss the early-19th-century painted New England cottage dresser in the Primrose Room. The Library Room is a handy first-floor guest room that features the home's original built-in bookshelves.

Breakfasts change seasonally to provide the best start for the day according to the weather. The sunroom overlooking the landscaping is the favorite for afternoon refreshments, and in winter months, the warmly decorated formal dining room is the place to start the day. An 1830s hunt board in the foyer displays the city's dinner offerings on its posted menus, but you may wish to ask your hosts for their suggestions to suit your appetite. The living room's game table will provide you with an enjoyable evening's leisure.

Plan on placing a one-night prepaid deposit when making your reservation, with the balance due two weeks prior to arrival. A two-night minimum reservation is required for weekends; some holidays require a three-night stay. Colonial Gardens accepts children older than 14, but is unable to accept pets. It is a nonsmoking inn.

Edgewood Plantation $$$–$$$$
4800 John Tyler Memorial Highway
(Route 5), Charles City County
(804) 829-2962, (800) 296-3343
www.edgewoodplantation.com

You will enjoy the historic plantation trail (Route 5 west from Williamsburg) that leads through forests past this superb Carpenter Gothic house, built in 1849, located a quarter-mile west of the entrance to Berkeley Plantation. In countryside filled with the formalities of Georgian and Colonial Revival architecture, this is a truly refreshing lodging for you to consider.

The mansion, with its double spiral staircase and 10 fireplaces, is a National Historic Landmark. A gristmill on the property dates from 1725.

On one bedroom window upstairs, Elizabeth "Lizzie" Rowland wrote her name with a diamond. Legend has it that she died of a broken heart waiting in vain for her lover to return from the Civil War. She reportedly still waits, watching from Lizzie's Room. (You can learn more about Lizzie in our Myths and Legends chapter.)

Don't let the Edgewood ghost intimidate you, however. You will find comfort, relaxation, and a good night's sleep in any one of the seven bedrooms or Prissy's Quarters, a cabin behind the main house. *Gone with the Wind* lovers will enjoy the third floor, with its sitting and common area rooms, Scarlett's Room and Melanie's Room. If Christmas is your favorite season, you will be amazed at the 18 Christmas trees at Edgewood. There is also a large collection of period clothing decorating the rooms.

Special features include king- and queen-size canopy beds, formal gardens, a swimming pool, and a candlelight full breakfast, which varies from day to day. It may include fresh fruit, orange juice, crepes, quiche, croissants filled with fruit and cheese—or sometimes a country breakfast of Smithfield ham biscuits and fried apples. Special features available upon request include Victorian teas and tours, including a haunted tour, luncheons, and weddings. Smoking is allowed outside and in the kitchen only.

Williamsburg is a pleasant 25-minute drive to the east; Richmond and Petersburg are about the same distance to the west. If you're looking for a place to rest and collect special memories, this is one excellent option.

For Cant Hill Bed & Breakfast $$$
4 Canterbury Lane
(757) 229-6623

Two guest rooms are available in the charming home of Martha and Hugh Easler. In one room you will find a comfortable mahogany four-poster bed, and you'll enjoy the private bath, television, and air conditioning. A second room provides the same amenities with twin beds. Guests can enjoy lovely Lake Matoaka from the house, which is a 15-minute walk to the Historic Area. Bikes and a tennis court are available to guests. A full, homemade breakfast is provided as well as candy in each room, and wine for anniversaries and honeymoons. Telephone and fax services are also available in the home.

Fox & Grape Bed & Breakfast $$–$$$
701 Monumental Avenue
(757) 229-6914, (800) 292-3699
www.foxandgrapebb.com

Your hosts, Pat and Bob Orendorff, offer four guest rooms, each with a private bath. Two of the rooms have queen-size canopy beds. Breakfast can include pancakes, waffles, or egg dishes and meats with fresh breads served in a charming dining room decorated with handcrafted regional decoys. You may also choose to enjoy your coffee on the spacious wraparound porch. The cup plate collection, Pat's counted cross-stitchery, and

Bob's stained glass, walking sticks, and folk art–style Noah's arks—available for sale—are especially interesting conversation openers. A minimum stay of two nights is required on weekends. The house is only 5 blocks north of the Capitol building in the city's Historic Area. Smoking is prohibited.

Governor's Trace $$$
303 Capitol Landing Road
(757) 229-7552, (800) 303-7552
www.governorstrace.com
This Georgian brick house was built during the restoration of Colonial Williamsburg and features all the same fine details including Flemish bond brick. This is the earliest of our listings to open specifically as a bed-and-breakfast rather than a guest home. Conveniently located in town, it is just steps from the eastern end of the Historic Area and is closest to the Capitol building and the taverns. This house occupies more than a half-acre of a former peanut plantation that extended the length of what is now Capitol Landing Road. Nearby, 13 of Blackbeard's pirates were hanged. The *Washington Post* has touted it as Williamsburg's "most romantic" bed-and-breakfast.

Today's visitors receive a much more cordial welcome than the pirates did. Hosts Sue and Dick Lake are happy to tailor a touring itinerary to help you make the best use of your time. Shuttered windows, brass candlelight lanterns, and a fireplace are featured in one room with a waist-high, four-poster king-size bed. Another room offers a private screened porch, four-poster colonial-style canopy bed, gingham, country florals, and pastels against a background of family antiques. Private baths adjoin the rooms, which are air-conditioned.

One guest room is reminiscent of *Gone with the Wind*'s Tara, according to some guests. Honeymooners love this room, which also can be combined with the adjacent room to turn the entire second floor into a suite for two couples traveling together. It offers a queen-size antique-brass bed. The

bathroom, done in brass, features a large glass shower enclosure.

Governor's Trace serves breakfast in the rooms and provides cozy robes so guests need not "dress" for breakfast. A leisurely candlelight breakfast in your room might be just the perfect unusual touch to make your stay memorable. This is a nonsmoking accommodation. It offers off-street parking. No pets are allowed.

Hite's Bed and Breakfast $$
704 Monumental Avenue
(757) 229-4814
We like the attractive Victorian decor of Faye and James Hite's Cape Cod home, just a seven-minute walk from Colonial Williamsburg. Both rooms are large and nicely furnished with antiques and interesting collectibles, and have private baths, cable TV, phones, radios, and coffeemakers. A suite with a large sitting room is particularly inviting, and the claw-foot bathtubs in both bathrooms will entice you to relax and refresh yourself. Robes, hair dryers, and other nice touches ensure your convenience, and you can enjoy the old-fashioned yard swing while admiring the birds, squirrels, and the goldfish pond. A beautiful old pump organ and hand-crank Victrola will entertain you in the parlor. A leisurely full breakfast, including stuffed croissants, eggs, juice, coffee, muffins, apple turnovers, sausage, and different goodies every day, is served in the privacy of your room or in the dining room as you choose. Pets are not allowed. This is a nonsmoking lodging; no credit cards.

The Inn at 802 $$$
802 Jamestown Road
(757) 345-3316, (888) 757-3316
www.innat802.com
This lovely bed-and-breakfast in town is a charming brick Cape Cod inn, where relaxation and charm are the order of the day. Innkeepers Joe and Cathy Bradley offer four exquisite, carefully appointed rooms, each with private bath renovated in 2005. The

i In true Southern hospitality, when bed-and-breakfasts are booked, many of the innkeepers will refer you to one of their "competitors." To make it even easier for visitors, 20 of the Williamsburg area bed-and-breakfasts have formed a network to help you find a place to stay. Just click on the network's Web site at www.bandbwilliamsburg.com and find up-to-date information on lodging and room availability.

home is meticulously decorated in the colonial style and furnished for comfort. Located across from the campus of the College of William and Mary, the house is an easy 12-minute walk from Colonial Williamsburg.

Common areas of the house include a large living room and well-stocked library, both with fireplaces; a formal dining room; and a glass-enclosed sunroom that overlooks a manicured garden.

Breakfast here is served in the formal dining room, where the table is set with fine crystal, china, and silver to set off the sumptuous homemade breakfast. Prepared daily, this repast, served by candlelight, includes fresh fruit, juice, coffee, tea, hot chocolate, assorted entrees, bacon, sausage or ham, and homemade pastries.

The King George Room, located on the first floor, features a king-size, rice-carved four-poster with goose-down comforter and full private bath with tub and shower. The Duke of Gloucester Room, also located on the first floor, has a pencil-post queen-size bed with goose-down comforter and a full bath.

The Lafayette, located on the second floor, is a spacious guest room with a queen-size, rice-carved bed and a full-size bed, as well as a full private bath with tub and shower. This room can easily accommodate three guests. The Francis Nicholson, also located on the second floor, is the largest guest room in the inn. It features a king-size walnut bed with a feather mattress and goose-down comforter, and a twin bed.

This magnificent bed-and-breakfast is appointed to make your stay user-friendly in a high-tech world. In addition to wireless Internet and central heat and air-conditioning, each guest room has a ceiling fan, radio, and TV with remote control. Guests may use other on-site amenities including the barbecue grill, guest phone, CD player, copy machine, fax machine, computer, and conference room.

Children older than 8 are welcome. This is a nonsmoking inn.

The Legacy of Williamsburg Bed and Breakfast $$$
930 Jamestown Road
(757) 220-0524, (800) 962-4722
www.legacyofwilliamsburgbb.com

After checking out life in Colonial Williamsburg, check in to the Legacy and live the part. This modern home was designed with an 18th-century tavern in mind, and innkeepers Joan and Art Ricker will make you feel like you have stepped across the threshold of time.

From the crown molding lining the ceiling to the wooden and brick floors, the Legacy of Williamsburg Bed and Breakfast has the feel of an 18th-century inn. Throughout the house, candlelight adds a soft glow to the hardwood pine floors, and six fireplaces will keep you warm in the cooler months.

If you fancy a game of chance before you retire, stop by the Billiard Room and play on the red-felt table that was built in England. If you would rather relax after a long day on your feet, cozy up to a good book in the library.

Careful attention was given to all the furnishings, as each piece was reproduced in the 18th-century style.

Each of the three suites and one guest room feature a queen-size poster bed with canopy and a private bath complete with comfy terry-cloth robes.

Wingback chairs face the oval fireplace in the Williamsburg Suite, while a love seat sits opposite the taller brick fireplace in the Nicholson Suite. The Grand Suite is well named, having its own selection of books above the elegant wooden mantel. The Brush

Everard Room also offers a curtained canopy bed with chairs and window dressings in an appropriate matching shade of colonial blue.

Guests also have access to a few of the more modern amenities, including a TV, an iron and ironing board, and a hair dryer.

Breakfast by candlelight in the Keeping Room includes sizzling bacon and homemade baked goods.

The Legacy is only 4.5 blocks from the Historic Area, so leave your car in one of the private off-street parking spaces and enjoy a stroll to Colonial Williamsburg or the College of William and Mary.

This nonsmoking bed-and-breakfast does not allow pets or children younger than 12.

The Legacy was named the United States, Canada, and Worldwide's Inn of the Year in 1997. In 2002, *Arrington's Bed & Breakfast Journal* listed it as one of the top-15 romantic inns in the United States.

Liberty Rose
Bed and Breakfast $$$$–$$$$$
1022 Jamestown Road
(757) 253-1260, (800) 545-1825
www.libertyrose.com

We're struck by the romantic interior design offered at the Liberty Rose, and if you are planning a honeymoon or an anniversary in Williamsburg, you might give this home special consideration. Since 1986 Sandra and Brad Hirz have completely renovated this 1920s house made from Jamestown brick and white clapboard. The house, on a hillside covered with beautiful old trees, is a mile from the Historic Area. Recently the Hirzes have given additional charm to their backyard with gardens, courtyards, and old-fashioned swings from the old oak trees.

The Hirzes' efforts have achieved high recognition: For 1999 Liberty Rose was one of two Virginia bed-and-breakfast inns placed by American Historic Inns in the top-10 most romantic out of 13,000 inns in the United States and Canada.

Inside you'll find English, Victorian, French country, and colonial antiques. Rich fabrics

and wallpapers contribute to the romantic mood. A grand piano and fireplace in the salon and gratis soft drinks at any time on the glassed-in breakfast porch are particularly inviting. Each guest room has its own name, and Rose Victoria, Magnolias Peach, Savannah Lace, and Suite Williamsburg are accurate indicators of their charm. All rooms offer telephones, TVs, VCRs, movies, lush bathrobes, bubble bath, a silk rose for the lady, a bowl of chocolates, alarm clocks, and gold miniature flashlights. The amenities seem never to end: Mention the famous chocolate chip cookies, and they will be baked up fresh for an evening's snack.

If decorating is a hobby for you, consult your hosts, as they are fountains of advice: They did all of the professional-quality sewing, papering, sawing, hanging, refinishing, and final touching that make this such a charming setting.

Breakfast here is not to be missed. It includes such delicacies as stuffed French toast with marmalade and cream cheese, fruit, juices, and everything from apple-cinnamon pecan pancakes to eggs, toast, and the like.

Liberty Rose does not accept pets or children. It also is a nonsmoking lodging.

Newport House $$$
710 South Henry Street
(757) 229-1775, (877) 565-1775
www.newporthousebb.com

If you came to immerse yourself in a colonial atmosphere, this might be your choice. A five-minute walk from the Historic Area, the building is a reproduction from a 1756 design by colonial architect Peter Harrison, whose buildings spanned the British empire from America to India and who was the architect of the Williamsburg Statehouse rebuilding in 1749. The building is furnished entirely with English and American period antiques and reproductions (even guests' blankets are historically authentic), and most of these furnishings are available for sale—to guests only.

Each bedroom has a private bathroom and contains two four-poster canopy beds (an extra-long queen-size and a single). Each is air-conditioned. Breakfast is usually accompanied by an interesting historical lecture by your host, John Fitzhugh Millar. He is a former museum director and captain of a historic full-rigged ship, as well as author and publisher of many books of history. Your hostess, Cathy Millar, is a registered nurse whose hobbies include gardening, beekeeping, needlework, and making reproduction 18th-century clothing.

On Tuesdays at 8:00 p.m., you may participate in colonial country dancing in the ballroom of the house. Beginners are welcome to join in or watch during these occasions. A harpsichord is available for guests' enjoyment, and with a few days' advance notice, guests may rent colonial clothing either for their entire stay or for dinner at one of the colonial taverns. Newport House accepts no pets and is a nonsmoking house. With advance notice, it may be possible for your hosts to pick you up at Williamsburg's train/bus station or at the Newport News/Williamsburg International Airport.

Breakfast is based on 18th-century recipes and includes Rhode Island johnny-cakes, a 1650s bread, scuppernong jelly, baked goodies, and more. Pancakes and waffles are served with honey from the owners' own beehive, and fresh berries and apples—when in season—come straight from the property's garden.

Although credit cards cannot be used for payment, they can be used to hold a reservation.

North Bend Plantation $$
12200 Weyanoke Road
Charles City County
(804) 829-5176
www.northbendplantation.com

One of the truly old bed-and-breakfast structures in the area (built ca. 1819 and enlarged in 1853), North Bend Plantation is on the National Register of Historic Places and also is designated a Virginia Historic Landmark. The National Park Service features it on its Civil War and birding trails. Your hosts here are Ridgely and George Copland, the fifth generation of the family to own the home, which was built for Sarah Harrison, George's great-great-aunt and sister of William Henry Harrison, the ninth president of the United States.

The main house's Greek Revival design will meet your expectations of a plantation house and educate you concerning the changes in architecture on antebellum plantations. It is situated on 500 acres just east of Charles City Court House and 1 mile off Route 5 on Weyanoke Road, about a 25-minute drive west of Williamsburg in James River plantation country.

The Civil War (in these environs, you might better refer to it as The War between the States) has close associations with this residence. In 1864, Union General Phil Sheridan headquartered at North Bend, as you will see upon examining the plantation desk he used at that time. Union breastworks from the war still exist intact on the grounds. This is not Yankee territory, however: A direct ancestor of the owner fired the first shot at Fort Sumter in April 1861, the initial engagement of the conflict.

Possessions still treasured and displayed by the family are worth your interest: A fine collection of old and rare books, colonial antiques from related early James River plantation families, and an antique doll collection are special features. As in many guest homes, smoking is limited to designated areas. In recompense, a fine swimming pool, a billiards room, croquet, horseshoes, volleyball, and a full country breakfast—for once you may take this literally—more than make up for that restriction. Breakfast fills your plate with fresh fruit, juices, waffles, omelets, bacon, sausage, and biscuits.

Accommodations include varying combinations of bed sizes and styles, and all rooms feature private baths, VCRs, and TVs. The Magnolia Room features a canopied queen-size rice bed and a shower. The Sheridan Room features a high queen-size tester bed (ca. 1810–40) that belonged to Edmund Ruffin,

George Copland's great-great-grandfather. The headboard was shot out in the Civil War. General Sheridan's desk and a sitting area are in the room. The Federal Room features an iron-and-brass queen-size bed. The Rose Room has a queen-size canopy bed, a fireplace, and a sitting area. The Maids Quarters connects to the Magnolia Room and has a double bed. An upstairs sunporch (one of three) is available for guests' enjoyment.

Guests are treated with refreshments on arrival: cookies and lemonade or hot cider, depending on the season. A choice example of Southern cooking in a pleasant historic setting is available nearby at Indian Fields Tavern (see our Restaurants chapter); reservations can be made for you at North Bend. Children 6 and older are welcome, but pets are not. Senior citizens receive a 10 percent discount. North Bend is available for weddings and receptions.

Piney Grove at Southall's Plantation $$$
16920 Southall Plantation Lane
Charles City County
(804) 829-2480
www.pineygrove.com

A 12-mile drive west of Williamsburg is Southall's Plantation and Piney Grove. The Gordineers welcome discriminating travelers to their home, which is a Virginia Historic Landmark and is listed on the National Register of Historic Places.

The Chickahominy Indians first occupied the property. Piney Grove was built around 1800 on the prosperous 300-acre Southall's Plantation, and today it is the oldest and best-preserved example of log architecture in Tidewater Virginia. Also on the property is Ladysmith, a modest Greek Revival plantation house built in 1857. Both houses have been meticulously restored to their original appearances and include every modern convenience for guests.

The four spacious guest rooms—each with a private bath, working fireplace, small refrigerator, and coffeemaker—are tastefully appointed with family heirlooms as well as antiques and artifacts that chronicle three centuries of habitation on the property. The rooms include one suite with a double bed in one room and a single twin in another, a second room containing a double bed and a twin bed, and two other rooms with standard double beds.

Guests may enjoy the parlor library with its books of Virginia history; walks on the nature trail along Rippon's Run are also inviting, as are the gardens and pool. Mint juleps, hot toddies, Virginia vintages, Virginia sparkling cider, and nightcaps of Virginia apple brandy await you no matter what the season. The weather does determine, however, whether guests at breakfast will be serenaded by residents of the aviary or warmed by a roaring fire.

Piney Grove cannot accept pets. It is also a nonsmoking home. Children are welcome, however, and there are no age restrictions. Young guests will particularly enjoy the barnyard full of farm animals. No credit cards.

A Primrose Cottage and Williamsburg Cottage $$$
706 Richmond Road
(757) 229-6421, (800) 522-1901
www.primrose-cottage.com

Few homes are as inviting as the charming white Cape Cod, Primrose Cottage, which has a perennial garden of rainbow colors that draws praise from all who walk or drive by. Here is the place for visitors who enjoy regional flora and fauna. You'll find primroses—hence the name—abloom in spring, and pansies galore in cooler weather. You can watch native birds feed outside the breakfast-room window. Nature is cleverly brought indoors, too, as you'll find the verdant garden's wildflowers painted on the kitchen walls.

Owner Inge Curtis welcomes guests with hospitality and charm to this cozy, two-story home. Primrose Cottage features spacious, bright rooms, with free wireless Internet, in a desirable location within easy walking distance of the city's Historic Area and the William and Mary campus.

A collection of antique furnishings, including original paintings, helps set the tone for your visit to the colonial capital. The lodge offers four large rooms, each with a private bath, two with whirlpools, each room with a television, and queen- or king-size featherbeds with down quilts, cozy desks, and comfortable chairs. A quiet sitting room, decorated with wicker, has a telephone for guests. A harpsichord, built by the innkeeper, is available for those guests who care to play. Central air conditioning and heating keep these accommodations comfortable year-round.

Your stay includes a full breakfast. Inge bakes almost every morning, and the aromas from her kitchen are the best wake-up call you could ask for. "Dutch Babies" are the specialty of the house, though you'll also find apple pancakes, bread pudding, soufflés, quiche, and scones among the fresh-baked goods offered guests. Herb tea, juice, and fresh fruit help get you off to a good morning's start.

The house is about a nine-minute walk from Merchants Square and features off-street parking and a quiet atmosphere. Primrose Cottage is a nonsmoking home, and pets cannot be accommodated.

A few miles away, Curtis has opened Williamsburg Cottage, a self-catering facility on the banks of the Chickahominy River. This cottage can host up to four people and is available to rent by the week or month.

War Hill Inn $$
4560 Longhill Road
(757) 565-0248, (800) 743-0248
www.warhillinn.com

Set on a bucolic 32-acre estate, this house was built in 1968 for hosts Shirley and Bill Lee under the guidance of a Colonial Williamsburg architect. Crickets, frogs, owls, and Angus cattle are the closest neighbors, and it is easy, upon awakening, to imagine yourself having traveled 200 years back to a peaceful setting in the colonial period. Among War Hill's attractions is a reproduction colonial cottage, the Washington Cottage. It offers a canopy bed for a comfortable rest, a private bath, and a whirlpool tub for your relaxation and enjoyment. The Jefferson Cottage also features a fireplace, whirlpool bath, and kitchenette. Four other rooms in the main house all have private baths, antique furnishings, and TVs. Inquire whether the accommodation you are considering has queen-size, double, or single beds, as all are offered.

Children are welcome here, and smoking is not allowed in the house.

This accommodation is 4 miles from downtown Williamsburg in James City County. Don't let that daunt you. It's worth investigating.

Williamsburg Manor
Bed and Breakfast $$–$$$
600 Richmond Road
(757) 220-8011, (800) 422-8011
www.williamsburg-manor.com

A five-minute walk from Merchants Square and steps away from the College of William and Mary is this lovely 1929 Georgian brick Colonial Revival manor house. Innkeepers Laura and Craig Reeves opened it to guests in 1992 and offer a wealth of experience and expertise to ensure a wonderful stay.

Previously director of catering at Ford's Colony Country Club, Laura has decorated the house tastefully with fine antiques, reproductions, and collectibles throughout, and the mood is gracious and warm, reflecting the traditions of Southern hospitality maintained by the hostess. She still operates the Catering Company of Williamsburg.

Five comfortable bedrooms—all with private baths, televisions, and central air conditioning—are offered to guests. Four rooms offer queen-size four-poster beds, and one two-room suite offers two twin beds and a queen. It will be difficult to remain in bed in the morning no matter how comfortable you are, knowing that your hosts will be serving you a culinary masterpiece for breakfast. They provide a lavish presentation of regional foods prepared to perfection, such as pear cobbler, individual quiches with shiitakes and oven-roasted tomatoes and asparagus, and stone-ground grits with chicken stock and heavy cream.

Williamsburg Manor is available to cater weddings, private parties, anniversaries, and other special occasions. It is a nonsmoking house where children are welcome and wheelchairs can be accommodated. Off-street parking is available to guests.

Williamsburg Sampler
Bed and Breakfast $$$–$$$$
922 Jamestown Road
(757) 253-0398, (800) 722-1169
www.williamsburgsampler.com

Across the street from the College of William and Mary and within a ten-minute walk of Merchants Square, this stately brick home in the style of an 18th-century plantation manor house is decorated throughout with antiques, books, a magnificent pewter collection, other Americana, and—how did you guess?—a host of wonderful samplers that innkeeper Ike Sisane has collected and displays for your enjoyment.

Excellence is a hallmark of the Sampler, and it has been widely recognized. In 1995 George Allen, the former governor of Virginia, officially recognized Williamsburg Sampler as the Inn of the Year in the Commonwealth of Virginia and said, "I call its significance to the attention of all our citizens."

Williamsburg Sampler was listed as "Best Breakfast in 2003" in *Arrington's Bed & Breakfast Journal.* The home, once featured on the CBS TV show *This Morning,* boasts a wealth of authentic colonial details, a lovely keeping room, a rich dining area, graceful wooden staircases, pegged hardwood planked floors, and a reception foyer. A welcome noncolonial touch, however, is central air-conditioning.

The guest rooms offer a variety of accommodations, including four bedrooms or suites with fireplaces. King-size, rice-carved four-poster beds are available, and Thomasville furnishings, a private bath, and a comfortable sitting area with wing chairs or daybed are features of every guest room. Two two-room suites open up to a rooftop garden overlooking a garden and woods below. Television with premium cable is offered in each room.

Breakfast at the Williamsburg Sampler has been rightfully dubbed the "Skip Lunch" breakfast. Fine china and pewter grace the Rooster's Den dining room, where the hearty fireside meal—including fresh coffee and muffins and, frequently, "the best waffles in the USA" (a German guest's comment)—is sure to please. Beautiful grounds at the rear invite a morning or afternoon stroll just downhill from a replica of Colonial Williamsburg's 18th-century Coke-Garrett Carriage House. Or you can work off that breakfast in the fitness center in the carriage house. Off-street parking is provided at this nonsmoking house. Children 13 and older are welcome. No pets, please.

Although credit cards cannot be used as payment, they can be used to hold a reservation.

A Williamsburg White House $$$
718 Jamestown Road
(866) 229-8580, (757) 229-8580
www.awilliamsburgwhitehouse.com

This unique bed-and-breakfast treats visitors as though they are the president of the United States—and as a matter of fact, it's decorated in themes celebrating the nation's presidents. Visitors from near and far rave about the warmth and hospitality of innkeepers Deborah and John Keane. Their two-story, 100-year-old colonial home sits just four blocks away from all the Historic Area attractions.

Its four suites, complete with private baths, are named after past presidents: Lincoln, Washington, Jefferson, and Theodore Roosevelt, all with unique and distinguished appointments befitting of the presidents themselves. The Roosevelt Suite celebrates Teddy's love of train travel with a queen-sized railroadlike berth.

Each morning, guests are treated to a sumptuous selection of made-to-order breakfasts, served on fine china in the Reagan Dining Room. Afternoon sweets, tea, and cocktails are served in the Diplomatic Reception Room.

Literary types and history buffs will certainly appreciate the extensive JFK Library, which is stocked with historical, political, and special themed books.

And the nonpartisan nature even carries over to the parking lot: the inn has signs for "Democrats only" and "Republicans only" spaces!

The inn also offers its one-and-a-half-acre lawn for weddings, and elopement or vow renewal packages are available.

York River Inn Bed & Breakfast $$
209 Ambler Street, Yorktown
(757) 887-8800, (800) 884-7003
www.yorkriverinn.com

Discriminating visitors will enjoy the colonial ambience of this inn, the only Williamsburg-area B&B with a waterfront location. This charming lodge overlooks the York River and Coleman Bridge. The philosophy of innkeeper William W. Cole is that the inn "is more of a home with frequent guests than a small hotel," and he carries out that philosophy in every detail, from the warm greeting you receive to the elaborate breakfast. The inn provides cable TV in each room, fresh flowers, plush bathrobes, fax services, and other amenities for guests' enjoyment and comfort. Your host's experience in the museum field, including 19 years with Colonial Williamsburg and four as director of the Waterman's Museum, and his detailed knowledge of the area will help you spend your time here wisely and enjoyably.

The first-floor public area has a panoramic view of the York River and Coleman Bridge, augmented by the deck at this level, which opens the view considerably. Virginia antiques from the innkeeper's family and his own collection of Virginia furnishings are features of the dining and living areas on this level.

Upstairs are three accommodations. The Presidents' Room on the second floor features an open deck overlooking the river. The queen-size bed and two comfortable lounge chairs are accented by the interesting display of items associated with seven Virginia-born presidents. Facing the land on this floor, the Pocahontas Room also offers a queen-size bed and other amenities. The items in this room, as might be expected, relate to Virginia's famous Native American princess. On the third floor, the Washington Room is the inn's largest, and is graced with a Victorian bedroom suite from the innkeeper's family. There are two seating areas, one overlooking the York River. The Jacuzzi is a special treat after a day of touring the area. You will find Yorktown's victorious general well honored in the decor of his namesake room.

This establishment claims to serve the largest and best breakfast of all the area bed-and-breakfasts. Goodies can include a clam casserole, three-cheese quiche, fresh honey-dew-pineapple-kiwi salad, and pecan waffles with blueberry sauce.

This is a nonsmoking inn, and neither pets nor children can be accommodated.

To reach the inn from U.S. Route 17, turn onto Route 1001 (Mathews Street) and then immediately right onto Ambler Street. Proceed 1 block to the inn, which will be directly ahead of you.

PRIVATE GUEST HOMES

Most of our guest homes do not accept credit cards but do take personal checks or cash. We have noted the exceptions in their entries.

Forest Hill Guest Home $
15 Forest Hill Drive
(757) 229-1444
www.visitwilliamsburg.com/forest_hill.htm

Mr. and Mrs. Cliff Gauthier offer a first-floor, single room with king-size bed, cable TV, microwave, and refrigerator, table for two, private bath, and private entrance in a quiet, secluded wooded setting within walking distance of Colonial Williamsburg. Children cannot be accommodated.

Goswick-Whittaker Guest Home $
102 Thomas Nelson Lane
(757) 229-3920

Two miles from Colonial Williamsburg in the Skipwith Farms neighborhood, this ranch

Guest homes offer the quaintness of bed-and-breakfasts at a more modest price.

Guest homes are nestled within many of Williamsburg's most established neighborhoods.

home offers two rooms with double beds, semiprivate bath, and television for guests to enjoy, as well as central air conditioning. The home accepts children and is convenient for those visiting the Richmond Road outlets and the Historic Area.

Hughes Guest Home $
106 Newport Avenue
(757) 229-3493

Across Newport Avenue from the Williamsburg Lodge, Genevieve O. Hughes offers three rooms for you to enjoy in her large two-story home decorated with family antiques. One double-bed room features a private bath, and a suite with one double and two twin beds has a shared bath. It is a two-minute walk to the restored area. This is a nonsmoking home, and pets cannot be accommodated.

Johnson's Guest Home $
101 Thomas Nelson Lane
(757) 229-3909

Your host, Mrs. Wallace C. Johnson, has opened her home to guests for more than a decade. Canopy beds grace two of the three guest rooms and twin beds are in the third. Private and semiprivate bath arrangements are offered, along with televisions. Combinations of rooms upstairs can be arranged for families or other groups.

King Guest Home $
307 Cary Street
(757) 229-7551

You will find three nice, clean rooms with a refrigerator, private bath, and private entrance. The beds are either double size or twins. Off-street parking is available here. The hospitality is inviting, and the location convenient: It is 5 blocks from the Historic Area and close to shopping. This is a nonsmoking guest home, and it does not allow children.

REGIONAL CUISINE AND WINES

While the South doesn't have a monopoly on good food, the land that lies 'neath the Mason-Dixon Line certainly can lay claim to its share of mouthwatering delights. Indeed, the words Southern and cooking go together like buttermilk biscuits and country ham. Or like fried flounder (usually caught fresh that day) and hush puppies. Or how about a slice of melt-in-your-mouth pound cake and home-made iced tea?

Well, you get the picture. So when you pull your chair up to a table in a Williamsburg eatery, bring a hearty appetite. Drop that napkin in your lap and prepare to have your senses delighted by a smorgasbord of Old Dominion favorites including chicken, skillet fried to a golden brown, crab cakes chock-full of the sweetest backfin meat, freshly shelled black-eyed peas and butter beans accompanied by warm-from-the-oven corn bread or hush puppies. Add in a big bowl of hearty Brunswick stew, and you'll have a dinner fit for any famished family, no matter where its members call home.

Since this is southern Virginia, more than likely you'll wash it all down with a gallon of sweetened iced tea (though unsweetened tea. is available to those who prefer no sugar), but if you have more "spirited" taste buds or just want to celebrate, order a bottle of Virginia wine. The Old Dominion is home to nearly 100 wineries, including several just outside Williamsburg and many others just a couple of hours' drive away. We profile a few later in this chapter.

The Williamsburg area won't disappoint when it's time for dessert. For a true taste of the South, try a wedge of sweet-potato or pecan pie. Especially good is the region's version of pecan pie—made with peanuts instead. But if you're a certified chocoholic—and who isn't?—stop off at Williamsburg's celebrated Trellis restaurant, where the dessert menu includes sinful creations with names such as Chocolate Temptation, White Chocolate Balloon, and Death by Chocolate.

THE FOOD

Virginia's tradition of hospitality began here in the Historic Triangle, where early settlers cheerfully shared their victuals with neighbors and strangers alike. Once the more genteel plantation society was well established, sheer culinary extravagance became the standard. Of course, it was pretty easy finding good things to eat. Fish crowded Virginia's waterways, wild game roamed the forests, English vegetables and fruits flourished in the moderate climate, and pigs and other farm animals made themselves right at home here.

Settlers learned about a small miracle called corn from the Native Americans. Ground, it turned into a meal for bread; crushed, it gave them hominy, used to make grits. Distilled? Well, corn whiskey, ancestor to bourbon, was the happy result. The uses of corn were seemingly endless. Thirsty settlers even contrived to brew beer from green cornstalks. But mostly they made corn bread, hoecakes, ashcakes, and pone, staples in the diet of poor and planter alike. The hominy they combined with Virginia-cured bacon.

In colonial times kitchens occupied separate buildings so that the heat and smells of cooking wouldn't invade the house. Food preparation—slaughtering, plucking, skinning, skewering—was hard labor and largely the burden of slaves. Baking took place on the wide hearths of chimneys lined with hooks holding heavy iron cooking pots. Spits for roasting joints stood by the fire. While early fare was plain and plentiful, by the 18th century the colony was prosperous enough to support its share of feasts. Bounteous Williamsburg landladies and plantation housewives provided guests with "groaning boards": Early settlers' dining tables were literally boards set on trestles that "groaned" under the weight of the food that was heaped upon them.

Meals were lavish, dishes sometimes exotic, or so they seem to us today. Stuffed cockscombs, ragout of hogs' feet and ears, and fricassee of rabbit are some of the recipes recorded in period cookbooks. Favorite foods of colonists included Virginia ham, roasts of all varieties, venison, meat pies, stews, oysters, crabmeat, jellies, tarts, fruits, and cheeses.

Good food and pleasurable dining are as easy to come by in the Historic Triangle today. Browse through our Restaurants chapter for more suggestions on the best places to find the regional fare we describe, as well as your own favorite dishes. With all the fine food the region has to offer, we feel there are only two words left to say on the subject: Bon appétit!

In a Stew

A number of regional specialties that evolved from the early bounty of Virginia's fields and rivers are proudly prepared and heartily consumed in the Historic Triangle today. Local restaurants serve Brunswick stew by the gallon. While the original version of this savory dish called for a couple of freshly shot squirrels and rabbits, contemporary recipes are a tad tamer. The meat you find in today's dishes typically is chicken, with a little beef or ham tossed in for good measure. Onions, celery, corn, okra (if it's available), lots of tomatoes, potatoes, butter beans, and generally whatever else is ripe in the garden are added, as are vinegar, sugar, salt and pepper, even ketchup. And to get it just right, this thick concoction must be simmered all day in a big iron pot. By the way, you may have heard some apocryphal tales about the true origins of Brunswick stew. Brunswick County, North Carolina, claims it, along with several other East Coast Brunswicks. But we believe Virginia lore, which says intrepid hunters back in the early 1700s created the dish in the Old Dominion's Brunswick County, relying on resourcefulness and whatever happened to cross their paths out in the wilds. In other words, squirrels and rabbits were all the game they bagged that day.

Frequently, you can find Brunswick stew on sale at any number of outdoor festivals or church bazaars. But to assure yourself of getting a stew of the highest quality, check out the Old Chickahominy House at 1211 Jamestown Road, (757) 229-4689. (See the Restaurants chapter for more on this wonderful eatery.)

As we noted before, you'll probably see this regional specialty paired with another local delectable—ham biscuits. (An Insider who knows Southern cooking swears that the biscuits at the Old Chickahominy House are the best in the area.)

Hamming It Up

We must note here that Virginia's most famous meat is ham, and you'd be missing something if you left town without sampling this treat. Its popularity dates from colonial times, when hog and hominy were an essential part of the early settlers' diets. Ham was easy to preserve—an important quality in a time before refrigeration. After slaughter, pig meat was smoked, dried, sugar-cured, even pickled. Virginia ham became so well known that it was soon being exported to the North and even abroad.

Before we go any further, let's clear up the great Virginia/Smithfield/Williamsburg/ country ham confusion. On local menus you may see entrees prepared with Virginia ham, Smithfield ham, Williamsburg ham, or sometimes simply country ham. While all of these pork products are similar in that they are salt-cured, there are some important differences among them. The one basic difference between Virginia hams and other cured hams is that Virginia hams are dry salt-cured before smoking. Technically, only hams cured in Smithfield, a small town across the James River and a little ways east from Williamsburg, can be called Smithfield hams. These hams, left in the skin and aged for up to a year, have a stronger, smokier taste than younger Virginia hams, sometimes known as Williamsburg or country hams. Smithfield hams are coated with pepper during the curing process, which enhances the hams' flavor. You may see these hams hanging in burlap sacks in local stores. They require overnight soaking before cooking, but don't make the mistake one Pennsylvania woman did upon her first encounter with a Smithfield ham. After years of preparing only the sugar-cured variety, she received a Smithfield ham from a generous son-in-law and proceeded to boil it hour after hour "to tone down the salty taste." The result: a stringy, inedible addition to the trash pile and a very dismayed son-in-law.

Once your Smithfield ham is prepared correctly (a knowledgeable Insider recommends soaking it for at least 24 hours, simmering it for about 20 minutes per pound, then baking it in a 350-degree oven for 20 to 25 minutes, basting frequently), it should be consumed sparingly, thinly sliced. Typically, it is nestled in a buttermilk biscuit, but like its Italian sibling prosciutto, Smithfield ham works well as an appetizer, wrapped around melon, for example.

Get a 'Cue

It's obvious that pigs don't stand much of a chance in the Old Dominion. If it's not bacon or ham, it's barbecue, also known around here as Bar-B-Que. Make that a jumbo, please, but hold the coleslaw and hand over the hot sauce. Southerners don't have to be told how to eat their barbecue: that knowledge is instilled when they cut their first teeth. Non-Southerners probably won't notice or care about the finer distinctions between varieties of this pit-cooked, chopped-pork delight, but there are differences. Virginia barbecue tends to have a delicate, smoky flavor. The sauce adds a tang, not a kick. Down in the Carolinas,

they make their barbecue with a stronger vinegar base, and you'll sometimes see references to pulled barbecue, which is more strip-like than chopped. We like our barbecue any which way and find that a little Texas Pete never hurt either a Virginia or a Carolina pig.

Where to Find It

Here in the Tidewater area of Virginia, there's plenty of debate over who makes the best barbecue. We've listed a few of our favorite barbecue restaurants so that you can try them all and cast your vote.

County Grill & Smokehouse
1215-A George Washington
Memorial Highway, York County
(757) 591-0600
A literal hangout for barbecue lovers, County Grill has beef and pork varieties available in sandwiches and platters. Tables are decked out in butcher paper and equipped with half a dozen different barbecue sauces. You can wash it all down with one of the microbrews you'll find on tap. Daily specials are available. This spot has been a favorite of *Daily Press* readers for several years running. It's open seven days a week.

Pierce's Pitt Bar-B-Que
447 East Rochambeau Drive
Williamsburg
(757) 565-2955
www.pierces.com
A trip to Pierce's is mandatory for all barbecue lovers who come to Williamsburg. Be prepared for a big crowd and long lines. Pierce's, which is open daily, is virtually an institution among locals.

Queen Anne Dairy Snack
7127 Merrimac Trail
(Route 143), Williamsburg
(757) 229-3051
If you're in the mood for takeout, pick up a pint of this popular Carolina-style barbecue to take home with you. (Chopped barbecue sandwiches also are available if you prefer

your food more ready to eat.) Although Queen Anne's is typically open seven days a week, you may want to call ahead on Sunday, when the restaurant occasionally closes at the owner's discretion.

Rocky Mount Bar-B-Q House
10113 Jefferson Avenue, Newport News
(757) 596-0243
In the restaurant business longevity pretty much says it all. Rocky Mount has been cooking North Carolina–style 'cue for more than 40 years. Tuesday is a great day to bring the kids—they get to munch out for free. One child per paying adult, please. The restaurant is closed Saturday and Sunday.

Salute to Seafood

Of all our regional specialties, seafood is the undisputed king. Virginia's rivers were so full of fish in colonial days that tales have come down about giant crabs, fish that literally jumped into boats, and 12-foot-long sturgeon. Herring, shad and shad roe, mussels, oysters, clams, and crab were some of the seafood most pleasing to early Virginians' palates. Sadly, civilization and development have brought some decline from past abundance. Sturgeon are hard to find now, and oyster beds are disappearing. But area fishermen still reel in plenty of blues, croakers, shad, spot, pike, bass, crappie, and other varieties of freshwater and saltwater fish.

On local piers you're likely to see weekend anglers patiently baiting their lines for crabs. Virginia's most common crab is the blue crab, or *Callinectes sapidus*, which translates as "savory, beautiful swimmer." This ornery-looking creature lives two or three years and periodically molts, shucking off its exoskeleton. For a short stretch of time after molting, the blue crab is soft and vulnerable, but a new, hard shell quickly forms. Commercial crabbers harvest this tender prey to sell as soft-shell crab, considered a delicacy locally but apt to make the noninitiate ask, "You mean I'm supposed to eat it legs and all?" Hard crabs are harvested too, of course,

and come in a variety of stages and forms. Stopping off at area fishing docks, you may overhear talk about peelers, jimmies, sooks, sponge crabs, busters, and doublers.

While commercial fishermen work from their boats, dropping large baited crab pots made of specially treated steel wire into area waterways, there is a simpler way to catch a crustacean dinner. Adults and children like to tie chicken necks or fish heads to kite string, grab a dip net, and head for the shallows. The trick to this method of crabbing is to gently lure a nibbling crab close enough to net him from underneath. Crabs are smart enough to be frightened by abrupt movements or a sudden play of shadows on the water, such as a body blocking the sun. But they're not smart enough to stop coming back for more, so don't give up. Crabs often turn up when you're not expecting them and, believe it or not, some fishermen don't want them. (One Insider, trying to fill up her cooler with spot and croaker on a hot July day of pier fishing, kept on pulling in tenacious crustaceans, too few to eat, but enough to quickly deplete her bloodworm supply.) You also can buy small crab pots for use from piers in local sporting goods stores. Crabbing is a time-honored way to spend a leisurely morning in eastern Virginia.

Cooking Up Crab

This quirky crustacean, so important to the culture and economy of the Hampton Roads area, has captured the imagination of cooks and consumers, spawning an endless variety of recipes from the humble crab cake to Crab Imperial. Backfin crabmeat is considered the tastiest and is often served simply—sautéed with butter or chilled with mayonnaise. You'll also see crabmeat served chilled, as a stuffing for avocados, tomatoes, or mushrooms. Heated, it combines with shrimp, lobster, and other seafood for a variety of baked dishes and casseroles.

Local cooks spar to create the best crab cakes, with feuds developing over whether corn meal, cracker crumbs, or bread and eggs provide the most suitable base. Deviled crab comes in several varieties, too—some swear by horseradish, some by chili powder. You may even see something called a crab burger on area menus. And backyard crab feasts, where determined partygoers stand around tables covered with newspaper and pick at hard crabs from a bushel basket, are a common summer's evening occurrence around the area.

As we mentioned before, soft-shell crab is prized locally, but no longer is it only fried and stuffed in a bun or simply sautéed with butter and lemon. Marcel Desaulniers, chef and co-owner of the Trellis restaurant on Duke of Gloucester Street, (757) 229-8610 (see our Restaurants chapter), includes several innovative dishes made with soft-shell crabs in his *Trellis Cookbook*. Grilled soft-shell crab with cucumbers, dill-butter sauce, shiitake mushrooms, and country ham is one such offering, but even more imaginative is Desaulniers's recipe for marinated soft-shell crabs, using vinegar, dry white wine, and jalapeños.

By the way, fresh soft-shell-crab season runs roughly from May to early fall. If you see the dish offered at other times of the year, you're probably getting a frozen product, which is not recommended.

Crab bisques, soups, and gumbos (both hot and chilled) are perennial favorites around here as well. Hampton crab bisque is made with cream, Tabasco, and sherry. Crab soups are sometimes based on fish stock, sometimes tomato broth. She-crab soup, which combines sauterne or sherry with whipping

cream, butter, and lots of crab, including the roe, is just too good to miss. Unfortunately, this succulent soup is infrequently seen on menus. We wonder if this is because all of it is consumed in restaurant kitchens.

Where to Find It

Some popular local eateries that serve up delicious crab cakes and other crab dishes are noted here. For a more complete listing, turn to our Restaurants chapter.

Crab Shack on the James
7601 River Road, Foot of the James River Fishing Pier, Newport News
(757) 245-2722
If you mosey on down toward the Lower Peninsula in pursuit of the ultimate crab dinner, drop anchor at the Crab Shack. An Insiders' favorite when guests are in town, the Crab Shack serves up some of the best hard-shell crabs on the Peninsula. And the crab cakes—chunky yet delicate and a mile high—are a beauty to behold. Even if you're not in the mood for seafood, the setting—a long, closed-in porch jutting out over the James—makes the trip from Williamsburg worthwhile. The Crab Shack is open daily.

The Dining Room at Ford's Colony
240 Ford's Colony Drive, Williamsburg
(757) 258-4107, (800) 334-6033
www.fordscolony.com
This extremely posh restaurant serves outstanding seafood. Although menu selections may vary, Ford's Colony has featured such delights as crab cakes topped with shiitake mushrooms and a delicious bisque that pairs roasted red peppers and crabmeat. The restaurant is closed on Sunday and Monday.

Dudley's Farmhouse Grille
7816 Richmond Road, Toano
(757) 566-1157
www.dudleysfarmhousegrille.com
Chef Jim Kennedy uses fresh, local ingredients to create a simple but sumptuous dining experience in a 1905 farmhouse—his motto

i Don't leave town without sampling Virginia's crunchy, roasted peanuts. After all, more than 30 percent of the 93,000 acres of peanuts planted in the state are in nearby Suffolk and Isle of Wight Counties. Two of the best places in Williamsburg to check out this treat are The Peanut Shop of Williamsburg, (757) 229-3908, on Merchants Square; or The Whitley Peanut Factory, (757) 229-4056, at 1351 Richmond Road.

is, "where great food doesn't have to cost a lot." The lunch menu includes soups, salads, and sandwiches, topped off with an assortment of homemade desserts. Dinner is composed of fresh seafood selections and choice cuts of meat. Kennedy, the local planning commission chairman and a restaurateur, spent months restoring the home and recreating the bygone era before opening for business in summer of 2007. In warmer months enjoy a casual dinner on the farmhouse porch, or inside, there's a cozy, romantic dining room. (The namesake of the restaurant, by the way, is a 14-year-old Silver Dapple, blue-eyed dachshund named Dudley.) Lunch is served Monday to Saturday from 11:00 a.m. to 2:00 p.m. Dinner is 5:00 to 9:00 p.m. The restaurant is closed Sundays. Reservations are recommended for dinner.

Welcome South Restaurant
8558 Richmond Road, Toano
(757) 566-8255

While this restaurant has wonderful barbecue and fried chicken, we recommend it here for its crab cakes. Believe us when we tell you they are grilled to perfection! Welcome South is closed on Monday.

Happy as a Clam

Although crab is king in the Williamsburg area, brother clam has muscled his way in for a share of the limelight. Most people eat these shellfish raw or steamed, but if you're a soup lover, you might want to try Chesapeake Bay clam chowder. Unlike the New England version, with its creamy base, or the Manhattan recipe, which calls for a tomato broth, this savory chowder has a clear base made with clam stock to which onions, celery, potatoes, and a variety of herbs have been added. Bacon is sometimes thrown in for added flavor.

VIVE LE VIN!

While visions of Virginia vineyards aren't exactly what comes to mind when one thinks about fine wines, it's definitely time to recon-

sider. A record number of wineries opened in Virginia in 2005. At last count there were more than 90 vineyards in the Old Dominion, up from 75 in 2001. That's an astonishing number when you realize that in 1979 there were a scant half-dozen. The business of growing grapes has been going so well in this southeastern state that *Wine Spectator* magazine has singled out Virginia as "the most accomplished of America's emerging wine regions." Indeed, the commonwealth is making something of a name for itself in circles where the grape is served and celebrated. In 1993 Virginia wines were served to former Soviet Premier Mikhail Gorbachev at a 200th birthday bash for Thomas Jefferson. The following year, Old Dominion wines reaped awards and medals at the San Francisco Fair National Wine Competition, San Diego National Wine Competition, and INTERVIN International Wine Competition.

Several factors contribute to the flowering of this most pleasant of industries: Virginia's moderate climate, American consumers' increasing interest in wine, enactment of laws providing incentives for wineries, and state funding of marketing and promotional programs. Today, Virginia wines are served, consumed, praised, and awarded around the world. Ronald Reagan gave a bottle of Virginia Seyval to Gorbachev (the gentleman certainly seems to appreciate fine wine) at the 1988 Moscow Summit. Locally, the Williamsburg Winery Ltd., set on more than 300 acres of farmland close to the James River, has garnered a number of awards, including the 1989 Governor's Cup for the best Virginia wine. Throughout the 1990s the winery has also

i Wines from Virginia vineyards, some of which have won numerous national awards, can be found across the state in retail outlets and restaurants and at festivals and other special events. Wines can also be purchased directly at the wineries. For more information, go to the Virginia Wineries Association's Web site, www.virginiawines.org.

When driving to Virginia's wineries, make sure you have a detailed Virginia road map, as many are in rural areas and are off back roads. Also look for the distinctive grape cluster highway signs pointing the way to the winery. Many of these signs also tell how many miles to go before reaching the winery.

earned a number of critic's choice awards from *Wine Spectator* magazine. This coveted award is bestowed annually on just 200 wineries throughout the world. In 2005 the James River Wine Cellars in nearby Glen Allen, Virginia, made a name for themselves by winning the Governor's Cup for their dessert wine, Dolce Vino.

Times weren't always so good for growers of the grape in the Old Dominion. Early colonists used hardy native American grapes such as the scuppernong to produce wines at Jamestown and other colonial outposts. But these wines had a strong, "foxy" flavor European settlers found unpleasant. Some brought cuttings from French, Italian, and German vineyards in an attempt to create more palatable vintages. Then, Thomas Jefferson summoned a wine expert from Italy, Philip Mazzeo, to advise him on the vineyards near Monticello. The Italian was enthusiastic about Virginia's potential as a wine-producing region, and soon Jefferson was experimenting with European varietals on his estate. Until the 1850s, the Charlottesville area was known for its excellent claret. Unfortunately, cold winters, insects, and diseases destroyed most early vineyards. Civil War battles also extensively damaged them. Meanwhile, California vintners had captured the domestic wine production market. In the 1920s prohibition delivered the crowning blow to what little wine industry remained in Virginia.

The climate of the Old Dominion seems especially well suited to cultivation of the Chardonnay and Cabernet Sauvignon varietals

as well as hardier hybrids. But throughout Virginia you also will find Rieslings and Gewürztraminers, Vionier and Pinot Noir, Merlot and Pinot Grigio, Barbera and Chenin Blanc.

An agreeable by-product to all this viticultural enterprise is the vineyard tour. While most Virginia vineyards cluster around Charlottesville, Culpeper, the Middleburg-Leesburg area, and the Shenandoah Valley, visitors to Williamsburg now have the option of touring as many as eight vineyards within a 50-mile radius.

The Virginia Wineries Association, which represents most of the wineries in the state, has produced a "Passport" guide that visitors can pick up at any participating winery and have stamped as they visit different wineries. Those who visit a certain number of vineyards within a year receive discounts and are eligible for prize drawings.

As part of the regional tours, six wineries have formed the Northern Neck Wine Trail, which snakes up Route 3 near the Potomac River, beginning about 30 minutes east of the Williamsburg area. For more information, go to www.northernneckwinetrail.com.

Readers interested in finding out more about wineries in the state also might want to pick up a copy of the *Insiders' Guide to Virginia's Blue Ridge*. Included in this book is a chapter detailing the numerous Blue Ridge wineries.

As one of the expressions we have heard over the years advises: Life is too short to drink bad wine. We heartily concur.

The Virginia Wineries Association advises visitors to call a winery before visiting, especially the small, family-owned operations, as they may be closed unexpectedly. Also, if a group of eight or more is planning to visit, always call ahead of time to help the winery prepare for your visit and to make sure they can accept groups.

Winemaking

Patrick Duffeler II laughs when he talks about his first winemaking experience.

"It was an eighth-grade science project," he said with a good-natured smile. "My family was in the winemaking business, so I thought, 'Why not?'"

So the determined youngster went to the grocery store and bought some grapes.

"I crushed them all up and made this cloudy, murky, nasty stuff," he said.

Still, the proud little winemaker packed up his project and headed off to class.

"It was confiscated," he said, "because you can't bring booze on school grounds."

Knowing his subject thoroughly, Duffeler advised his teachers to keep his wine in a cool environment. Apparently, more concerned that the brew didn't end up in the wrong young hands, the teachers stored Duffeler's project in a safe place—inside the school's safe.

"The temperature in there got to 90 degrees and the wine bubbled out," he said with a dramatic pause, "and, of course, they had set my wine right on top of the PSAT tests.

"Needless to say, I was persona non grata the rest of my junior high school days...and that was the last time I ever made wine."

Even though he went on to do an internship with winemakers in Bordeaux, France, after college, Duffeler is quite content with sticking to the marketing end of winemaking. Today, he is the vice president of Williamsburg Winery Ltd., the company founded by his father. The once painfully shy young Duffeler has evolved into a top-notch promoter of his family's business.

"When my family moved here, there was nothing here but a couple of abandoned barns," Duffeler said. "They weren't sure what they wanted to plant...soybeans, corn, maybe some other crop."

But after a visitor mentioned grapes, the Duffelers—Patrick and Peggy and their two young boys—put in a few Chardonnay vines. What started in a weed-filled plot turned out to become one of the most successful wineries in the state. In fact, one out of every four bottles made in Virginia today bears the Williamsburg Winery name. Their Governor's White, a light, easy-to-drink blend for even the novice wine taster, is the top-selling wine in the state.

For more information on the tours and tastings at Williamsburg Winery, call (757) 229-0999 or visit their Web site, www.williamsburgwinery.com.

The Williamsburg Winery and Gabriel Archer Tavern

A 320-acre farm owned by Patrick and Peggy Duffeler and known as the Wessex Hundred (the same name it had in colonial times) is the site of the state's largest winery (the Williamsburg Winery produces more than 60,000 cases a year). The winery got off, or perhaps we should say in, the ground when the first Chardonnay vines were planted in spring 1985. Two years later, the first wines were bottled. One of their very first wines, the 1988 Chardonnay, won the Virginia's Governor's Cup, the top prize in the prestigious Virginia wine competition. Today more than 60 acres are in cultivation, and Williamsburg wines are both sold throughout Virginia and exported to various countries in Europe. Indeed, growth has been so healthy that the winery underwent a major expansion, adding Wessex Hall, a 3,800-square-foot room designed to hold large gatherings, as well as a new barrel cellar that doubles production and storage capacity.

Tours and Tastings

To get an Insiders' peek at this popular winery, you can enjoy a guided tour that begins in the retail store and leads to the 18th-century-style brick building that holds a banquet room, underground cellars, a bottling room, warehousing space, and offices. Tour guides explain the winemaking process and point out interesting objects associated with the winery, including pictures of a 17th-century skeleton found here during a dig and founder Patrick Duffeler's collection of more than 300 18th-century wine bottles dating as far back as 1710. Duffeler (who was born in Brussels, Belgium, and organized car races and consulted for a large cosmetics company

before becoming a vintner) co-owns the winery with 30 investors. He takes an approach to viticulture that combines traditional winemaking methods with modern technology. Currently the winery makes a number of different varietals aged in the 600-plus French and American oak barrels you'll see lined up in the temperature-controlled cellar where the woody aroma of fermentation greets guests. Stainless-steel fermenters also are used here, mostly in the creation of blends.

Williamsburg is a large operation for the state as far as wineries go; one out of four wines made in Virginia is made here. By Virginia law, varietals—wines named after the grape from which they are produced—must contain at least 75 percent of that particular grape, such as the Chardonnay, Merlot, Cabernet Sauvignon, or Riesling. However, the Williamsburg Winery uses 100 percent varietal grape in its Chardonnays, including the John Adlum regular bottling; the Acte 12 Chardonnay, named for the Virginia House of Burgesses 1619 act calling for the planting of vines by settlers; a Vintage Reserve Chardonnay, entirely barrel fermented; and Ratcliff Vineyard Chardonnay. An altogether different bottling, the Gabriel Archer Reserve, is a Bordeaux-style blend of Cabernet Franc, Cabernet Sauvignon, and Merlot. The winery also makes two Cabernet Sauvignons and a Cabernet Sauvignon Reserve, a Merlot and Merlot Reserve, and James River White, a blend of Chardonnay and Seyval. The Governor's White, a mix of Riesling and Vidal grapes, is the best-selling wine made in Virginia. Other blends include Two Shilling Red, a light-bodied blend of Ruby Cabernet and Merlot meant to be served lightly chilled, and Plantation Blush, made from Riesling and Seyval.

Since 1996 the company has released a half-dozen labels made at its Dominion Wine Cellars, a former wine cooperative in Culpeper that was purchased by the Williamsburg Winery a few years back. These include Johannisberg Riesling, Lord Culpeper Seyval Blanc, and Filippo Mazzeo Reserve, a Cabernet Sauvignon and Nebbiolo mix. Some won-

i The Williamsburg Winery's spiced wine is created in the tradition of the mulled wines famous in the early days of Jamestown or in the taverns in Williamsburg. It's best served warm or even hot in a mug with a cinnamon stick.

derful dessert wines—a raspberry Merlot, a blackberry Merlot, and a Late Harves Vidal—round out the Dominion label offerings.

After your tour you will be invited to participate in a tasting, which will include samples of seven of the wines mentioned above. The tour and tasting also includes a short film and a souvenir wine glass, all for $7 a person. Or, for a real treat, call ahead to arrange for the Reserve and Library Selections tasting, which includes 12 special reserve wines from the wine library and an oversize Schott-Zwiesel German glass, all for $25.

Once your palate has been thoroughly tempted, you can browse through the retail store, which sells winery products, international wines, replicas of 18th-century wine bottles that were handblown in the traditional manner by artisans who work at Jamestown Glasshouse, fancy corkscrews, and other accessories for the wine connoisseur. The winery also offers a collection of authentic salt-glazed pottery coasters, pitchers, wine cups, and coolers—designed with a grape motif by Duffeler. Prices for a bottle of wine range from about $10 to $24. Discounts are offered on orders of six or more bottles, and shipping is available within Virginia. Credit cards are accepted.

Gabriel Archer Tavern

If it's time for lunch, you're in luck. The Gabriel Archer Tavern, which opened in 1996 and is named for an explorer who is believed to have chosen a landing site somewhere on the winery property, serves cheese and pâté platters, smoked meats, specialty breads, and wines by the glass, complete with a vineyard view "right in the Merlot." The tavern is open from 11:00 a.m. to 4:00 p.m. daily and from 6:00 to 9:00 p.m. Thursday through Monday for dinner. Why not work lunch in with your winery tour? Reservations are recommended for groups of eight or more for meals at the tavern. Or, if you'd like to reserve space for a private dinner or wine tasting, the Williamsburg Winery makes its facilities available every day year-round. Relying on the expert-

ise of local caterers, the winery can accommodate both large and small groups for just about any private function.

Special Events

Throughout the year, the winery hosts a number of festivals and special events. These include occasional celebrations of wine and food featuring regional chefs. In September, the Williamsburg Scottish Festival brings the sight of kilts and the sound of bagpipes to the vineyards. Throughout the year, musical events featuring such celebrated groups as the Virginia Opera and the Virginia Symphony are offered.

Getting There

To reach the winery from Interstate 64, take exit 242 onto Route 199 and take a left turn onto Brookwood Lane. Turn left again onto Lake Powell Road, and you'll soon see the winery sign. From Colonial Williamsburg, travel Route 132 south (North Henry Street) through the Historic Area until you reach the junction with Route 199. Take a right onto Route 199 going west and take the next right onto Brookwood Lane. At Lake Powell Road, turn left and follow the signs. (The state's highway sign for vineyards, a cluster of grapes, will help guide you to the winery, too.) The winery's formal address is 5800 Wessex Hundred; the phone number is (757) 229-0999, and the Web site address is www.williamsburgwinery.com. Hours of operation for tours are Monday through Saturday from 10:00 a.m. to 6:00 p.m. and Sunday from 11:00 a.m. to 6:00 p.m. The wine shop is open the entire time. (If members of your party are under 21, they can take the tour free of charge, but may not, of course, imbibe!)

Ingleside Vineyards

5872 Leedstown Road
Oak Grove, VA 22443
(804) 224-8687
www.inglesidevineyards.com
Ingleside Vineyards is part of a 3,000-acre estate that has been owned by the Flemer

family for over 100 years. There you'll find 70 acres of vineyards owned by Doug Flemer, a great-great-grandson of Charles Flemer, the original owner. The roots of the winery go back to 1960, when the Flemers started with an experimental vineyard of French-American hybrids before turning to commercial wine-making in 1980. Back in 1834, the property housed Washington Academy, a boarding school, and later it served as a garrison for Union troops during the Civil War. Today it boasts one of the older wineries in the state, producing prize-winning wines in what had once been an old dairy barn. Its new court-yard and fountain enhance Ingleside's new European ambience. In fact, the courtyard and pavilion have been used for weddings, receptions, and business meetings. The win-ery also has a gift shop and a museum with Native American artifacts.

Using state-of-the-art equipment, Ingle-side produces 20 different wines, including a delicate, dry Chardonnay; a Cabernet Sauvi-gnon and a Cabernet Sauvignon Reserve; a claret, its Chesapeake Claret, which is a mix of Seyval, Chardonnay, and Sauvignon Blanc; and a number of innovative blends, such as the Blue Crab Red, made with Vidal and Cabernet grapes. Two semisweet wines include Blue Crab Blanc, a blend of Seyval and Vidal grapes, and Virginia Rose, a dessert wine made with a blend of French hybrids. October Harvest Vidal is a slightly sweet dessert wine with intense apricot flavors, while relatively new red wines include a Mer-lot and the medium-bodied spicy red Caber-net Franc. Among other wines are Pinot Grigio, Viognier, Sangiovese, and Colonial Red, a semisweet dessert wine. Ingleside is one of only a few Virginia wineries to make a sparkling wine; making champagne is labor-intensive, and the availability of Virginia Brut changes from year to year.

Tours and Tastings

Tours and tastings are free to the public and are conducted Monday through Saturday from 10:00 a.m. to 5:00 p.m. and Sunday from noon to 5:00 p.m. You can combine a winery tour and tasting with a river cruise, too (see Getting There, below). In the retail store and gift shop, you'll find Ingleside wines with prices ranging from $8 to $25, books about area history, gourmet foods, and Virginia arts and crafts.

Special Events

Every year the winery hosts a series of special events, including spring and fall barrel tast-ings, a Cabernet Sauvignon tasting, summer bluegrass, jazz concerts, and a Christmas open house. A Northern Neck Seafood Extrav-aganza, introduced in 1994, brings a festival atmosphere to the winery each October. For a cover charge of about $38, patrons enjoy a tour and tasting and sample seafood from one or more participating restaurants. Of course, you'll also have the chance to quaff wines deemed suitable for the seafood of your choice. Reservations are required for this and other Ingleside events.

Getting There

Directions to Ingleside Vineyards in Oak Grove on Virginia's Northern Neck may seem a bit complicated to Williamsburg visitors. The win-ery can be reached by traveling Interstate 95 north of Richmond to Route 3, then south on Secondary Route 638 until you see the entrance signs; or by taking U.S. Route 17 across the York River, up to U.S. Route 360 and across the Rappahannock River, north on Route 3 to Route 638.

From May to October a third alternative is to drive via US 17, which you pick up south of Williamsburg on I–64, to Tappahannock. Once there, look for the signs for the Rappahan-nock River Cruise, which is right on US 17, Tappahannock's main drag. The cruise offers a winery tour, wine tasting, and lunch, catered by the Mount Holly Steamship Inn and served at the winery. The cruise runs from 10:00 a.m. to 4:30 p.m. every day, and reservations are required. The cruise alone costs $24 for adults, and $14 for children 13 and younger. The cost of the lunch is $10.95 for adults and

$8.95 for children. Call (804) 453-2628 or check the Web site at www.tangiercruise.com for cruise information.

Belle Mount Vineyards

2570 Newland Road, Warsaw
(804) 333-4700
www.bellemount.com

Just down the street from Ingleside is another new winery, Belle Mount, founded in 2002 by winemaker Ray Petrie and his wife, chief of operations Catherine Petrie. The duo produce between 1,000 and 3,000 cases of hand-crafted wines each year, and want to keep their operations small so that they can focus on producing high-quality wines from carefully nurtured varietals of grapes. They are proud to use sustainable, or environmentally friendly, techniques to grow and harvest the grapes and enrich the soil for the next year's crops. They have recently produced reds, including a Merlot and Cabernet Franc, and whites including a Chardonnay and Vidal Blanc. A rosé-style blush, named Lighthouse Rouge, makes a good picnic wine.

The winery hosts several special events during the year, but reservations are required for tastings and tours. Please call for more information and for directions.

James River Wine Cellars

11008 Washington Highway, Glen Allen
(804) 550-7516
www.jamesrivercellars.com

This family-owned winery started small but now produces 13 varieties of grapes. Its 2004 version of its dessert wine, Dolce Vino, won the prestigious Governor's Cup for Best Virginia Wine of 2005.

The business opened in 2001 when Ray Lazarchic, who also owns a large landscaping management business, put in an acre of grapes on his property here. With another 14 acres in Montpelier, he and his partners had enough grapes to create the first vintage. Under the watchful eye of winery manager James Batterson, James River Wine Cellars bottled five types of wines: Cabernet Sauvi-

i Virginia Governor Mark R. Warner awarded James River Wine Cellars with the 2005 Governor's Cup, the highest honor in Virginia's wine industry, for its 2004 Dolce Vino.

gnon, Merlot, Chardonnay, Chardonel, and a popular Gewürztraminer.

James River also has a gift shop and a scenic picnic area for those who would like to bring their lunch baskets. The winery doesn't have a restaurant, but the staff does offer light gourmet fare, including the perfect wine complement, cheese.

Tours and Tastings

The winery is open seven days a week, from 11:00 a.m. to 5:00 p.m. Sunday and Monday, and from 10:00 a.m. to 6:00 p.m. Tuesday through Saturday. There is a $1 tasting fee, $3 if you would like to keep a souvenir glass.

Special Events

Relax, sip some wine, and savor live music at "Fridays on the Patio" the third Friday of every month from May through October. The cost is $12 and includes a wine glass. Other events include Powhatan's Festival of the Grape in July and wine and cheese weekends in the spring. Call or check their Web site for an up-to-date calendar of events.

Getting There

If you are traveling from Williamsburg, go west on I–64 to I–95 near Richmond. Take exit 86 at Atlee/Elmont and head west on Route 656 for 0.6 mile. Turn right onto Washington Highway, also known as Route 1, and you should see the entrance after 1.2 miles. It is on the right, just past a driving range.

Chatham Vineyards & Winery

9232 Chatham Road
Machipongo
(757) 678-5588

This small winery opened in 2005 on a 400-year-old working farm on Virginia's Eastern

Shore. The land was patented in 1640, and the acreage includes a federal-style brick house built in 1818 and several historic out-buildings and barns that recently have been renovated. The winery produces about 3,000 to 5,000 cases annually, and offers complimentary tours and tastings from 10:00 a.m. to 5:00 p.m. Thursday to Monday, and noon to 5:00 p.m. on Sunday.

Getting There

To get there, take the Chesapeake Bay Bridge-Tunnel from Virginia Beach to Virginia's Eastern Shore. Follow Route 13 about 25 miles, , then make a left onto Wilsonia Neck Drive. Go 3.5 miles and make a right onto Bayside Drive, make a quick left onto Church Neck Road, then follow signs to the winery.

RESTAURANTS

Whether you spend a couple of days or a week in the Historic Triangle, you'll spend as much time selecting restaurants and dining as you will touring points of interest. For that reason, we offer you a listing of some of the more notable eateries in the area. You've come to town at a high point in its long culinary history, which dates back several hundred years.

The original public establishments here were the taverns you now will find in the city's Historic Area. Each offers distinctive colonial fare and a unique atmosphere. Then the Regency Room at the Williamsburg Inn made its debut. It maintains the same high standards today that made it the focus of national recognition in 1937. (It proved so popular, in fact, that about 25 years ago, Colonial Williamsburg decided to add the lower dining room to meet demand.)

That was pretty much it for the local "restaurant scene" until the 1940s, when some small mom-and-pop places opened. It wasn't until 1957 (the year of the 350th celebration of the landing at Jamestown) that more restaurants opened. From then onward, Williamsburg has offered a selection of restaurants from which to choose, though many—not all—were mediocre. Luckily, with the recent influx of chain restaurants, local restaurateurs realized they had better improve their job of catering to their dining public. As a result, the food and service is better than it's ever been before—and the variety and scope of eateries is on the rise as well.

In recent years, the number of ethnic restaurants has increased significantly, and now includes Chinese, Vietnamese, Japanese, French, Indian, Greek, Italian, and more. That's in addition to fine continental and nouvelle cuisine dining spots—and those that serve down-home-style Southern cookery. Whether you're in the mood for a slab of succulent Black Angus prime rib or a colonial game pie, we can accommodate. Prices, as do menu options, vary widely. So read on and take note.

While we would like to recommend each establishment where we have had a good meal, that might be a book in itself. Instead, the listings are our favorite representatives of the variety available to visitors and townsfolk.

Our entries begin with the Colonial Williamsburg dining options. An alphabetical listing of neighborhood haunts, favorite delis, out-of-the-mainstream locations, and nationally acclaimed dining rooms follows. We also list other establishments offering some unique items of cuisine or special values we feel you ought to consider during your stay. Unless they are particularly good or offer something of special note, however, we do not list chain restaurants. Neither do we list hotel or motel dining rooms unless we know that Insiders seek them out or that visitors recommend them for a particular reason.

You'll find an extended article on food in our chapter on Regional Cuisine and Wines, but it's in order now to mention what you're likely to find in many of our restaurants. You non-Southerners are in for a treat as you discover regional favorites like spoon bread, crab cakes, and grits (they're not just for breakfast, y'all). Hush puppies are omnipresent companions to seafood in this area, usually appearing on your table in a heaping basket shortly after you order and often included in the price of your meal. As you try different restaurants, you'll discover that area chefs make their particular hush puppies a point of pride.

Another regional custom, surprising to many visitors, is that iced tea is the drink of choice to accompany all Southern meals. Those folks in Boston may have thrown their tea into the harbor, but Southern colonials and their progeny love their tea and maintain that sugar, not salt, is the best companion for the Oriental leaf—and plenty of it! Remember to ask for your tea unsweetened if that is your preference.

You'll also notice that we mention Sunday brunch quite often in our listings. It sometimes seems that no one cooks the big Sunday meal at home anymore—and why should they with all of the delectable brunches available locally? You'll be standing in line with many of our townsfolk no matter which brunch you select.

One more thing frequently asked about: Often you'll see "ABC on/off" as part of a Virginia restaurant's advertising. The Commonwealth's Alcoholic Beverage Control (ABC) regulations require this designation for establishments serving beer, wine, or spirits for consumption on or off the premises. Liquor stores are commonly referred to in Virginia as ABC stores.

With visitors and tourists comprising the majority of diners, casual dress is appropriate. Where there are exceptions, we indicate such.

Nearly all restaurants in this chapter offer diners a nonsmoking section. Those that do not, or those establishments that do not permit any smoking, are so noted.

Hours vary seasonally and on special weekends, so we note only particular deviations from what you might expect, and we recommend that you call your chosen establishment to be sure of its current hours of operation. And since the area is host to literally millions of visitors, you can find lines at most restaurants during peak dining hours in season. Off-season dining is far more leisurely, and you rarely, if ever, encounter lines at local eateries.

Finally, enjoy yourself! That's the whole point of your stay here, isn't it? Good eating.

Price Code

Area restaurants almost universally accept Visa and MasterCard, so we only note exceptions. If you're using another card, you should inquire whether it will be accepted.

The state charges a tax on meals, and localities charge a minimal meals tax.

The following code indicates the average price of two entrees only—without appetizer, dessert, beverages, tax, or gratuity. Keep in mind that may fluctuate and rates may be higher in season (generally from mid-March to November and during the winter holidays).

$	Less than $20
$$	$21 to $35
$$$	$36 to $50
$$$$	More than $50

COLONIAL WILLIAMSBURG RESTAURANTS

A centralized reservation service, (757) 229-2141 or (800) TAVERNS, makes it simple and easy to ensure a seating at any of the Colonial Williamsburg taverns, the Williamsburg Lodge, or the Williamsburg Inn. We strongly suggest you make use of this service, particularly when making dinner plans. Call for information on what options are available at the time you have selected, and a helpful representative will be happy to accommodate your party. You can also peruse all the restaurants' menus at www.colonialwilliamsburg.com. If you have overlooked making a reservation for dinner and are feeling lucky, walk-ins at each site are welcomed if seating is still available. At all the taverns in the Historic Area, you will find a costumed host or hostess who will place your name on a list for the first available table. Each restaurant has its own particular charm, so consider all of the options before making your selection. Smoking is not permitted in any of the taverns.

Chowning's Tavern $$
100 East Duke of Gloucester Street
(757) 229-2141, (800) TAVERNS
Chowning's Tavern is a perennial favorite with visitors to the city, both for its ideal location—right in the center of the Historic Area—and for the 18th-century ambience the reconstructed

building provides. The furnishings are simple and rustic, and the pewter table service and costumed staff contribute to the impression that you truly have gone back 200 years to take your refreshment. You cannot make reservations here, so plan ahead and arrive in enough time to await your turn to be seated.

The menu is a blend of food found in English pubs and standard American favorites. At lunch a selection of sandwiches includes pulled-pork barbecue and other Virginia favorites on large sandwich rolls. If a bowl of stew is more to your liking, the house-special Brunswick stew is always a favorite. At dinner, the stew remains on the menu, along with barbecued pork ribs, beef loin steak, lamb shanks, and roasted hen. Favorites include Brighton chicken wings and bubble and squeak (fried puffs of mashed potatoes and cabbage). Stick around for dessert—peanut pie or cider cake, to name only two.

After 9:00 p.m., Chowning's staid propriety is put aside—in colonial fashion—for the Gambols, rowdy 18th-century entertainment provided by costumed balladeers, magicians, minstrels, and various other rogues. Board games are provided, Virginia peanuts and various colonial "liquid refreshments" accompany light snacks, and soon the crowd is singing along to tunes that frequently reflect a side of colonial life not mentioned in the history books. Cover is $3.

Christiana Campbell's Tavern $$$
Waller Street
(757) 229-2141, (800) TAVERNS
George Washington favored meals at this establishment opposite the eastern end of the Capitol building. An enjoyable midday meal is Mrs. Campbell's brunch, providing a selection of omelets, waffles, and skillet-fried chicken. At dinner, enjoy regional favorites such as crab cakes or Carolina fish muddle (a dish of fresh fish, shrimp, scallops, and clams mixed with tomatoes, sweet peppers, and noodles), or try the Gloucester dinner—soup, half a chicken crisply coated with Colonial Williamsburg's own seasonings, Smithfield ham, and your choice of ice cream. Parking in

the rear makes access convenient, and the authentic colonial ambience and strolling musicians contribute to a memorable time. Make reservations to ensure convenient seating, and in season don't be surprised to find a brief wait. If this should come to pass, fret not. Sitting on the wide porch is a pleasant prelude to your meal.

Golden Horseshoe
Golf Club House Grille $$
401 South England Street
(757) 229-2141, (800) TAVERNS
A block from the Powder Magazine and across from the Williamsburg Lodge is the clubhouse for Colonial Williamsburg's fine golf course. One grill faces the famous Golden Horseshoe fairways; the other overlooks the Green Golf Course. Light lunches are available from 11:00 a.m. until 4:00 p.m. daily, dinners from 6:00 to 9:00 p.m. Wednesday through Sunday (seasonally). At lunch you are likely to see city business and professional people enjoying the excellent sandwiches, soups, and salads, always up to the standard for which Colonial Williamsburg is noted. This place also is known locally for serving the best hamburgers in town. The seasonal dinner offerings are just as high in quality. We recommend reservations for dinner.

King's Arms Tavern $$$
Duke of Gloucester Street
(757) 229-2141, (800) TAVERNS
In its decor and its menu, this restaurant reflects the refined tastes of the colonial gentry who dined here. Virginia ham, filet mignon stuffed with oysters, peanut soup, and Sally Lunn bread are house specialties, and we recommend the colonial game pie for an unusual and authentic taste of early Virginia fare. Another good choice is the cavalier's lamb roast.

Shields Tavern $$$
Duke of Gloucester Street
(757) 229-2141, (800) TAVERNS
Operated by James Shields in the 1740s for a clientele of planters and the well-to-do, this

tavern is the most recent one to be reconstructed. It has been carefully appointed to serve visitors authentic colonial Virginia foods in a setting antedating the other taverns by 25 years. Foods based on recipes in 18th- and early-19th-century cookbooks are available on the bill of fare: chicken roasted on a spit, crayfish soup, greengage plum ice cream (yum!), and other unusual items provide an education on the dining habits of the early 18th century. Liquid refreshments are equally unusual. Syllabub is a period drink of cream, white wine, sherry, sugar, and lemon that separates into a meringuelike topping with the wine and sherry at the bottom of the glass.

The Shields Sampler may be the best choice for your first taste of colonial cooking: Indian corn pudding, crab cakes, sippets with potted Virginia ham. Breakfast, lunch, and dinner are available. In an attempt to cater to more modern taste buds, the tavern has added a few low-fat and vegetarian dishes, including a grilled portobello stack with potato hash, baby spinach, and vegetable demiglacé.

The Williamsburg Inn
Regency Room $$$$
136 East Francis Street
(757) 229-2141, (800) TAVERNS

One of the finest restaurants in the Tidewater area, the Regency Room is consistently recognized with fine-dining awards—and with good reason. Listed as a Mobil Four-Star and AAA Four-Diamond facility, the Regency is featured in the *Guide to Distinguished Restaurants of North America* and is the recipient of *Wine Spectator*'s Award of Excellence for its wine list.

Executive chef Calvin Belknap and his staff offer a rare and pleasant experience with classic continental dishes and regional specialties. Elegant appointments surround you while an attentive service staff works unobtrusively to provide your requirements. Breakfast, lunch, and dinner seatings are available. Gentlemen are required to wear a jacket and tie. Dinner reservations are the only way to ensure seating at your preferred time.

The Williamsburg Lodge Bay
Room and Cafe $$$
310 South England Street
(757) 229-2141, (800) TAVERNS

Fine breakfasts, lunches, and dinners are available in the Bay Room every day of the week, but two meals are worthy of special acclaim. Williamsburg Insiders return again and again to the brunch on Sunday, which offers made-to-order omelets and a buffet with fine breads, pastries, fruits, and hot dishes. Every Friday and Saturday evening, the Chesapeake Bay Seafood Feast offers a bounty of fresh seafood consistently favored by residents of the area. We recommend reservations for all Bay Room dinners, but especially for these two meals.

The cafe provides quick, excellent meals also. The setting, menu, and price are scaled down somewhat from the Bay Room, and the mood is less formal. But the food is well prepared, well served, and tasty. You must at least consider the desserts.

ADDITIONAL FAVORITES

A. Carroll's Bistro, Martini & Wine Bar $$
601 Prince George Street
(757) 258-8882
www.a-carrolls.com

A. Carroll's brings new vitality to the city's Triangle Block, located near Merchants Square and one street over from Richmond Road. Locals and visitors looking for comfortable dining will enjoy the clean, fresh decor of warm and simple colors, the simply prepared bistro food, and the quick yet friendly service. Repeat customers are recognized and welcomed. Cigars are welcome in the bar (check out the humidor). The lunch menu is casual, with a selection of soups, salads, stews, potpies, sandwiches—even a blue plate special. Lunch is served 11:00 a.m. to 2:00 p.m. Dinner begins at 5:30 p.m. and runs to 9:00 p.m. Tuesday through Thursday and to 11:00 p.m. Friday and Saturday. Sunday brunch is also served 11:00 a.m. to 2:00 p.m., and the restaurant is closed on Monday. The dinner

A variety of restaurants can be found on Merchants Square. JOETTA SACK

menu is imaginative, especially when it comes to appetizers and desserts, so be sure to save room. Entrees include the only imported corn-fed, Midwestern beef in town. Also featured are fresh tuna and yummy lump crab cakes. Entrees and vegetable sides are BIG, but you're encouraged to share with a friend.

Aberdeen Barn $$
1601 Richmond Road
(757) 229-6661
www.aberdeen-barn.com
Known for its aged steaks, prime rib, lamb chops, seafood, and combinations, this restaurant opens nightly for dinner. The decor is rustic, subdued, and candlelit. The kids' menu makes everyone in the family happy. The service is attentive, and the food is good. It is very popular, so we recommend you make reservations. Aberdeen Barn opens at 5:00 p.m. for dinner.

Aroma's Fine Coffees, Teas,
and Bake Shop $
431 Prince George Street
(757) 221-6676
Right behind Merchants Square sits this charming little java spot offering coffee, tea, omelets, and other breakfast items, sandwiches, desserts, and a limited dinner menu.

The Backfin Seafood Restaurant $$$
3701 Strawberry Plains Road
(757) 565-5430
www.backfinrestaurant.com
This is among the most popular local restaurants for a lot of reasons. The comfortable, come-as-you-are atmosphere enhances the experience. Open daily for lunch and dinner, the menu features a variety of baskets, sandwiches, salads, soups, and appetizers, as well as low-cost children's entrees. Insiders love the crab cakes (offered as a sandwich at lunch

The Indians taught the Jamestown colonists the secret behind the famous Virginia cured ham. Their methods of salting, smoking, and aging venison were adapted by the Europeans. Today, the distinctive taste of salt-cured ham is achieved by following essentially the same process used by the early settlers.

or on a platter at dinner); the backfin skins (potato skins stuffed with crabmeat and topped with melted cheddar and bacon); the hot crab dip; and the raw bar selection of steamed shrimp, oysters, clams, and crab legs. Like pasta? They'll add shrimp, scallops, or crabmeat (or all three, if you prefer) to a basic linguine in Alfredo sauce. Don't eat seafood? Fear not, the burgers here are among the best in town. The good news here is that anything you order will please. Be sure to check the chalkboard for daily lunch and dinner specials. A final word: Save room for a slice of their homemade key lime pie. You'll be glad you did. Lunch is served from 11:00 a.m. to 3:00 p.m. with dinner from 4:30 to 9:30 p.m.

Berret's Seafood Restaurant and Taphouse Grill $$$
Merchants Square
199 South Boundary Street
(757) 253-1847
www.berrets.com
Berret's location on Merchants Square can't be beat. In good weather, the raw bar is popular with young professionals as well as tourists and college students. In addition to the usual raw-bar fare, it offers grilled steaks, chicken, and fish. Inside you'll find tasty, fresh Chesapeake Bay seafood and a wide selection of other choices served in a pleasant, upbeat atmosphere. The seafood chowders and fresh soups of the day are always wonderful. Ask for the specials of the day, as they are usually based on what is available locally. A children's menu is available. Reservations are recommended. Smoking is not permitted.

Big Apple Bagels $
1222 Richmond Road
(757) 253-8456
Bagel aficionados, listen up! This charming, informal eatery adjacent to Williamsburg Shopping Center features about three dozen flavored bagels, all baked fresh daily. Especially good—and unique—is the enchilada bagelata. More traditional fare includes bagels with anything from roast beef and turkey to Nova Scotia salmon, corned beef, pastrami, salami, and more. Want to sample a variety? Try the Bit O' Bagel: a platter of bite-size bits of bagels with three types of cream cheese on the side. Also offered are a variety of coffees and juices. Gift baskets are also available. But don't plan to come here for dinner: Big Apple opens at 6:00 a.m. and closes at 4:00 p.m. Monday to Saturday; Sunday hours are 7:00 a.m. to 3:00 p.m.

Black Angus Grille $$
1433 Richmond Road
(757) 229-6823
www.blackangusgrille.com
In spring 2005, chef Bobby Mageras shocked the local restaurant scene when he changed the name of The Prime Rib House, a time-tested favorite, to Black Angus Grille. Mageras, who trained at the Culinary Institute of America in Hyde Park, New York, thought the name change would be more indicative of the restaurant's casually upscale atmosphere, variety of menu items, and the upgrade to prime angus beef. He has not disappointed. The Black Angus Grille still offers an imaginative selection of other specialties including veal, chicken, lobster, shrimp, and Eastern Shore seafood. Magerus welcomes vegetarians, and offers them original entrees using locally available, seasonal ingredients. The dessert list is equally tantalizing, so save room. This is a popular, locally owned and operated restaurant, which was recently renovated and expanded from 100 to 200 seats. Dinner reservations are recommended unless you want to chance a wait. If you do make a

reservation, be prompt. After 10 minutes, you'll be sent to the back of the line.

Bones Grand Slam
Eatery and Sports Bar $$
351 York Street
(757) 229-4100
This popular local restaurant inside the Four Points by Sheraton Hotel features Black Angus prime rib, barbecued baby back ribs, spit-fired rotisserie chicken, and a wide selection of fresh seafood. The atmosphere is relaxed, but the tempo picks up during the evening once happy hour begins. The drinks are good, the food special, and it is, overall, an experience worth savoring. Live entertainment is offered some evenings, and karaoke happens every Thursday. Along with its dinner fare, Bones also serves breakfast from 6:30 to 11:00 a.m.

Candle Factory Restaurant $-$$
7521 Richmond Road
(757) 564-0803
In spite of its location away from the city, this restaurant draws residents who drive out for its good and plentiful family-style meals. It's not fancy, and it's not expensive, but it is good food. Specialties include freshly made soups, prime rib, barbecued pork ribs, and scallops. Visitors to the shops attached to the Candle Factory consistently rate the restaurant here as excellent. The restaurant closes at 4:00 p.m. every day. Groups larger than four may have a short wait unless they make reservations in advance.

Captain George's
Seafood Restaurant $$$
5363 Richmond Road
(757) 565-2323
www.captaingeorges.com
Don't be startled by the tall ship splitting this restaurant. It's your landmark from the highway. The all-you-can-eat buffet inside is a sight to see and a challenge to even the hungriest members of your party. Dozens of baked, broiled, and fried seafood entrees are com-

plemented by separate salad and dessert bars. The full menu offers more than 70 items, including seafood and beef. A children's menu is available, and there are banquet rooms for large parties. With seating for 2,000, this is the largest restaurant in town. The line moves quickly, so don't anticipate a long wait. Dinner is served Monday through Friday beginning at 4:30 p.m., Saturday beginning at 4:00 p.m., and Sunday, when doors open at noon. Throughout the summer, a production of the Haunted Dinner Theater is offered at Captain George's on various evenings. For more information, turn to our Nightlife chapter.

Charly's $$
Williamsburg-Jamestown Airport
100 Marclay Road
(757) 258-0034
Here's a unique restaurant you might not find unless you fly directly into Williamsburg. It's well worth seeking out even if you arrive by land. Homemade breads and desserts, a chef's salad piled with meats, fresh homemade soups, and other salads are very tempting and complement the careful preparation of the main courses. We recommend the seafood bisque and the French onion soup, crusted with cheese and topped with croutons from the homemade bread. The menu is varied and satisfying, with the most unusual ambience in the area: The restaurant and its patio have a clear view of the runway, and it's fascinating to watch the takeoffs and landings while dining. On Sunday, a $10.95 prime rib special is served along with the menu items from 11:00 a.m. until 4:00 p.m.

The Cheese Shop Cafe $
Merchants Square
410 Duke of Gloucester Street
(757) 220-0298
If you stop a local resident on Merchants Square to inquire where you can get a reasonably priced, outstanding sandwich, chances are you'll be directed to The Cheese Shop. Its fine reputation for super sandwiches was built on an outstanding freshly sliced roast beef

special, served on fresh-baked French bread with a secret house dressing. This sandwich is a meal! The cafe menu also offers fresh salads, quiche of the day, and an array of sandwiches including smoked turkey, barbecue, an assortment of cheeses, baked ham, liverwurst, Nova Scotia salmon, and more. Assorted beverages, both alcoholic and soft, are available, as is a mouthwatering selection of desserts. Place your order, and they'll call you when it's ready, usually within minutes, except at peak lunch hours. Then step outside and eat under gaily colored umbrellas in the flower-encircled outdoor cafe, or take your order to enjoy on one of the Merchants Square benches. Don't forget to offer the crumbs to the birds.

A Chef's Kitchen $$$$
501 Prince George Street, #102
(757) 564-8500
www.achefskitchen.biz

If you're an aspiring gourmet—or just enjoy cooking classes—you'll want to make time for this cooking school, which demonstrates and serves five-course dinners from Wednesday through Saturday evenings. Dinners begin at 6:30 p.m. with champagne and hors d'oeuvres, followed by the five-course meal, paired with three glasses of wine or your choice of beverage. Menus vary seasonally—the fall menu might start with Thai golden squash soup and jumbo lump crab with mango and avocado and chilled sweet corn salsa, while the summer menu could feature butter-sautéed diver sea scallops with fried capers and roasted whole garlic. The experience typically lasts about three hours. The cost is $69.50 per person, and no gratuities are accepted. Reservations are a must, and a credit card number or advance payment is needed to confirm the reservation. There is a 72-hour cancellation policy; any cancellations within that time or no-shows will be charged the full amount.

Chez Trinh $$
157 Monticello Avenue
(757) 253-1888
www.cheztrinh.com

Chef Minh Giang has described Vietnamese cuisine as "among the most outstanding on earth," and here's a fine opportunity to test his judgment. In the Williamsburg Shopping Center near Peebles Department Store, this restaurant might be a well-kept secret if it weren't for the high recommendation of Insiders. It's a cuisine distinct from the familiar Chinese. Taking from the best of classic Oriental and French food preparation techniques, Vietnamese dishes have their own distinctive appearance, flavors, and delights, and the kitchen staff is skilled in presenting them at their finest for lunch and dinner. For a good introduction, we recommend the fixed-price banquet menu for a minimum of six guests, featuring the most popular house specialties, such as steamed shrimp with herbs. If you're in a rush, Chez Trinh offers take-out meals.

Cities Grille and Wine Shop $$–$$$
Governor's Green
4511C John Tyler Highway
(757) 564-3955
www.citiesgrilles.com

The atmosphere of this popular bistro is as inviting and comfortable as the menu, and the wine list is intriguing. As the name implies, the menu here pays tribute to the regional cuisine of different American cities. You can order here as you might order were you in, say, New York, Seattle, or Washington—depending on what cities are featured on the menu, which changes three times a year. The taste sampling is formidable, thanks to the talent of CIA-trained chef Hunter Stegall, who makes lunch as much of a culinary event as dinner. The lunch menu features a variety of tasty sandwiches—consider the Aspen grilled chicken, pecan fried catfish, or BBQ chicken Reuben—as well as special salads and daily specials, such as shrimp and salmon with penne pasta. Yum! At dinner, the entrees are so varied and so evocative as to make selection a delightfully painful process. Some of the favorites from past menus include Peachy Pecan Catfish, in honor of Charleston, South Carolina, and Vinney's Kamano, celebrating Lahaina, Hawaii.

Kamano, by the way, is Hawaiian for salmon. If you are in the mood for a little of the flavor of Baltimore, check out the Tornado Hunter Stegall, a grilled portobello mushroom, tenderloin of beef, and crab cake with tomato hollandaise and crispy onions. Cities Grille also is expanding its menu with Hikapachi Chops, for a taste from Australia.

The Caesar salads here can't be beat, and dessert is a must. The restaurant's wine list has won the *Wine Spectator* magazine's Award of Excellence. Wine is available by the bottle or glass.

The Coffeehouse $
Williamsburg Shopping Center
Route 5 at Route 199
(757) 229-9791

This bright addition to the restaurant scene features more than 40 varieties of coffees and 17 varieties of loose teas. Regional and estate coffee beans from the Americas, Africa, Southeast Asia, and the Pacific are roasted on the premises, ensuring coffee lovers the freshest, most tasteful brews. Espresso, espresso macchiato, cappuccino, cafe mocha, cafe latte, and cafe au lait, along with a selection of teas, top the excellent variety of hot and cold beverages you may enjoy; Italian sodas and cream sodas are alternatives. Your beverage selection can be complemented with the perfect baked treat from an extensive list of French pastries baked on premises and other home-baked cakes, cheesecakes, muffins, and other delights. We're particularly partial to the Triple Fudge Brownies, but you'd better check both display cases before making your choice. The Coffeehouse offers authentic fresh-baked French bread daily. Lunch is also served. Of course, all coffees and teas are prepared for you to enjoy on the premises or at home. The Coffeehouse is open 7:30 a.m. to 6:00 p.m. Monday through Saturday and 10:00 a.m. to 4:30 p.m. Sunday.

College Delly $
336 Richmond Road
(757) 229-6627

Across from the college and 2 blocks from Merchants Square, this restaurant is a longtime favorite with students, townsfolk, and tourists looking for a good deli meal or pizza accompanied by a selection from the wide assortment of beverages in the wall cooler. Reading the sandwich ingredients from the menu will certainly fire up your appetite, and the freshly made Italian and Greek dishes (especially the souvlaki and shish kebab) are delicious and filling. Insiders are particularly fond of the Hot Holly: roast beef, cheese, turkey, bacon, lettuce, tomato, and pickle on a toasted roll. The College Delly offers limited delivery service in the evenings until 1:00 a.m., and the hungry night owls among us find the hours to our liking: The restaurant is open from 10:30 a.m. until 2:00 a.m. weeknights and Saturday, and until midnight on Sunday.

The Colonial Pancake House $
100 Page Street at Penniman Road
(757) 253-5852

You can find traditional Southern cooking at this restaurant whether you come for breakfast or lunch. The fried chicken is worth writing home about and the steaks, seafood, and Italian dishes are delicious and carefully prepared. This is a casual family restaurant, established in 1955, and local businesspeople and college faculty have made it a regular informal clubhouse at lunch. Smoking is not permitted. The Colonial is open daily from 7:00 a.m. to 2:00 p.m.

The Corner Pocket $
4805 Courthouse Street
(757) 220-0808
www.thecornerpocket.us

Here's an alternative to humdrum eating. The Corner Pocket is Williamsburg's upscale billiards club, but Insiders also know that it offers excellent sandwiches and light entrees for dinner, with daily specials. The chef, formerly with the renowned Trellis, brings such specials as flash-fried calamari with mixed greens and grilled mako shark with caramelized pineapple rice pilaf. If you're going to the nearby movies, this will be a great before- or after-movie choice for a bite. Not your typical pool hall by any means, The Corner Pocket welcomes casual attire, and an adult must accompany children under 18. Check out whether there is live entertainment on the menu while you're in town. This establishment likes the blues and imports some of America's finest blues performers. The Corner Pocket is open from 11:30 a.m. until 2:00 a.m. Wednesday through Saturday, until 1:00 a.m. Sunday through Tuesday.

Courtyard Cafe $–$$
Williamsburg Crossing Shopping Center
5251 John Tyler Highway
(757) 253-2233

This cafe with a relaxed atmosphere has a small dining room that is often packed—evidence that the food and service are excellent. While casual in demeanor, the restaurant serves very fine grilled and baked entrees, with fresh fish, meats, and pastas, as well as burgers, a creative children's menu, and super desserts from the Carrot Tree Kitchen, a popular local bake shop. Note that it is a favorite of those coming or going to the seven movie theaters around the corner. Open for lunch and dinner Monday through Saturday, it is usually busiest just before and after the evening movies. Insiders know not to leave without inquiring what freshly baked goodies are on the dessert list for the day.

Cracker Barrel Old Country Store $
200 Bypass Road
(757) 220-3384

Anyone who has traveled in the southern United States is familiar with this chain. The Cracker Barrel features an extensive menu of authentic country fare—from barbecued ribs and grilled steaks to country fried steak and chicken and dumplings. Vegetarians will delight in the sumptuous though very low-priced vegetable platter special that allows you to select from nearly a dozen vegetables and side dishes. Especially good are the hash brown cheese casserole, whole baby carrots, and real mashed potatoes. Note that this is one of the most popular stops in town, and it's often crowded; expect a wait for breakfast or dinner.

Doraldo's $–$$
1915 Pocahontas Trail
The Village Shops at Kingsmill
(757) 220-0795

Cozy and casual, this Italian restaurant offers a traditional menu and serves up tasty, authentic cuisine. Chef and owner Frank Alosa offers an extensive menu featuring a combination of northern and southern Italian dishes—including veal, fish, eggplant, chicken, seafood, beef, and a glorious array of pastas and, of course, pizzas. The food is so good, in fact, that the small dining room fills up fast. And since food is prepared to order, plan to sit and relax. Doraldo's is open 11:00 a.m. to 2:30 p.m. for lunch and 5:00 to 10:00 p.m. for dinner.

Fat Canary $$$
410 West Duke of Gloucester Street
(757) 229-3333

When this upscale yet casual restaurant opened in 2004, it almost immediately became the top choice of locals for special occasions. Now, visitors are discovering it as well. Chef Tom Power Jr. offers a variety of carefully crafted seafood and meat dishes—for a local flavor, try the fresh Virginia Littleneck clams appetizer, served with chorizo, tomato, basil, and trofie pasta. The crispy Carolina catfish and Rappahannock oysters, served with black-eyed peas and collards, give an upscale twist to a classic Southern dish. For the more cosmopolitan palates, there's low-roasted duck with udon noodles in Chinese black bean sauce, or a braised lamb shank with gorgonzola polenta. There's an extensive wine list as well. It's open 5:00 to 10:00 p.m. daily, and reservations are encouraged.

415 Grill $
Williamsburg Hospitality House
415 Richmond Road
(757) 229-4020
www.williamsburghosphouse.com/
415grill.shtml
This unique eatery is famous for its burgers
and business lunches. Its collection of memorabilia will entertain families as well. The
copper-topped tables and brass-lined bar
add to the tavern's appeal. It's open daily
from 11:30 a.m. to 11:00 p.m. for lunch and
dinner. 415 Grill shares the same building
and phone number with Papillon: A Bistro.

**Gabriel Archer Tavern
at the Williamsburg Winery** $
5800 Wessex Hundred
(757) 229-0999, ext. 117
www.williamsburgwinery.com
If you're looking for a quiet, inexpensive lunch
in a wholly pleasant setting where a glass of
wine is proffered along with made-to-order
entrees, drive out to the Williamsburg Winery.
This place is, indeed, special. The menu is limited—smoked salmon, selected pâtés, Italian
prosciutto, a wonderful fresh mozzarella and
roasted red pepper sandwich on basil focac-
cia, and the like—but it is tastefully, carefully
prepared and nicely served. But you're getting more than just a good meal for the
money. You'll dine in a quiet setting amid
grape orchards. Gentle breezes keep you cool
on the veranda, or you can opt for the air-
conditioned dining room. The service is attentive but low-key—and since this place is a little off the beaten track, it's rarely noisy or
busy. Along with your meal, enjoy a glass of
Governor's White or John Adlum Chardonnay.
Other wines are offered as well. Top off your
meal with a tour of the winery and a visit to
the gift shop across the lane from the tavern.
   (For more on the winery, see the Regional
Cuisine and Wines chapter.) The tavern is
open for lunch 11:00 a.m. to 4:00 p.m. Monday through Saturday and for dinner 5:30 to
9:00 p.m. Thursday through Saturday, April
through October.

**The Gazebo House
of Pancakes and Waffles** $
409 Bypass Road
(757) 220-0883
www.thegazeborestaurant.com
This bright, airy restaurant is convenient to all
lodgings on Bypass Road and is popular for
both breakfast and lunch. There are 21 pancake and waffle dishes and complete Virginia
country breakfasts offered all day. A variety of
specials and fresh sandwiches are available at
lunchtime from Monday through Friday, when
area businesspeople join tourists to relax
while enjoying the indoor garden environment. We suggest you call ahead to check on
daily specials. The restaurant is open 6:00
a.m. to 2:00 p.m. daily.

Giuseppe's Italian Cafe $–$$
Ewell Station Shopping Center
5601 Richmond Road
(757) 565-1977
www.giuseppes.com
The enticing aroma of delicately blended olive
oil and fresh garlic tells you immediately that
this is real Italian food at its finest. We love it!
Chef Daniel Kennedy and host Joe Scordo offer
a pleasing blend of carefully prepared fine
food, a comfortable, upbeat dining room, and
friendly service in their trattoria, with al fresco
dining in season. An unusual and varied menu
with a wide variety of prices offers such treats
as several vegetarian entrees, an outstanding
lentil and sausage soup, as featured in *Bon
Appétit* magazine, and contemporary versions
of old Italian standby desserts such as spumoni
and cannoli. Everything is made to order; yet
the small kitchen churns out meals quickly, so
there's no waiting between courses. Because
of the fine quality of the food, this is an
extremely popular restaurant with Insiders for
both lunch and dinner. Giuseppe's only takes
reservations for parties of six or more.

Green Leafe Cafe $
765 Scotland Street
(757) 220-3405
www.greenleafe.com

This is where the College of William and Mary students and other young folk congregate. In addition to its proximity to the college campus, it offers a menu that can fill the bill whether you're looking for something simple (burgers and the like) or something a little more exotic (some super Greek and American specialties). Also check out the homemade desserts. The bar offers cocktails and bottled and draft beer. *USA Today* rated Green Leafe Cafe as one of the top 10 bars in the country for its beer. Note that this place can be crowded, lively, and loud, but the food is good and the atmosphere is fun. The cafe serves food from 11:00 a.m. until 1:30 a.m.; the bar is open until everyone is happy or 2:00 a.m., whichever comes first. (For more on Green Leafe Cafe after the sun goes down, turn to our chapter on Nightlife.)

The Grille at Ford's Colony $
240 Ford's Colony Drive
(757) 258-4100

Bistro fare—pastas, entrees, and traditional grill items—is the specialty of this alternative to the more formal Dining Room at Ford's Colony. The Grille serves lunch and dinner in an intimate atmosphere and brunch from 11:00 a.m. to 2:30 p.m. on Sunday. The menu is varied and the food is excellent. The grilled salmon is particularly wonderful. Note that this establishment is closed Monday.

Hayashi Japanese
Restaurant & Sushi Bar $$
5601 Richmond Road
(757) 253-0282
445 Prince George Street
(757) 253-0458
www.hayashijapanese.com

Hayashi offers traditional Japanese cuisine as well as a full sushi bar, and it recently opened a second location to accommodate its growing popularity among locals. The decor is understated, and the atmosphere makes for an enjoyable, serene, and memorable repast. If you're squeamish about the sushi, a few pasta and chicken dishes are offered just for you. Lunch is served Monday through Saturday, while dinner is served weeknights until 9:30 p.m. and weekends until 10:30 p.m.

IHOP $
1412 Richmond Road
(757) 229-9628

Yeah, yeah. We know we're not supposed to list chain restaurants. But this International House of Pancakes is the only restaurant in Williamsburg that remains open 24 hours on Friday and Saturday; otherwise it remains open until 1:00 a.m. Breakfast is served anytime. Lunch and dinner also are served. A children's menu is offered. IHOP is big enough to accommodate large groups and banquets. A word of caution: The entrance is at a busy intersection along Richmond Road. Be very careful turning into and out of this establishment.

Indian Fields Tavern $–$$
Route 5, Charles City County
(804) 829-5004

Halfway between Williamsburg and Richmond is this superb restaurant in a remodeled, late-19th-century farmhouse. You can dine inside or outside, in favorable weather. The menu is varied, and specials are offered daily. This place is known for its lump crab cakes that only get better year by year. It is open for lunch and dinner and on Sunday for brunch from 11:00 a.m. to 3:30 p.m. It is a superb stop when you're touring the Route 5 plantations, as it is just minutes from Sherwood Forest, Berkeley, Shirley, and Evelynton. Reservations are strongly recommended, particularly for dinner.

J. M. Randalls
Restaurant & Tavern $$
4854 Longhill Road
(757) 259-0406
www.jmrandalls.com

Combine your favorite grill fare and specials

i With rare exceptions, such as the Regency Room at the Williamsburg Inn, dress is casual at most Williamsburg area restaurants. If in doubt, call ahead and inquire about any dress requirements.

with the music offered here, and you've got a hit. Especially popular among locals who frequent the small eatery, it's known for good home cooking and fun. Acoustic, blues, jazz—you'll find it all live, and the place swings until 2:00 a.m. seven days a week. Sunday brunch features NFL football on five screens, and the same screens get another workout for Monday night football. Also featured is NTN interactive trivia. The restaurant opens at 7:00 a.m. for breakfast, lunch, and dinner.

The Jefferson Restaurant $$
1453 Richmond Road
(757) 229-2296

Since 1956 this restaurant has been delighting patrons with delicious steaks, fresh seafood, and other choices from the wide variety on the menu. With waiters dressed in colonial attire, The Jefferson's charming English country decor invites a leisurely meal with cocktails and a selection from the wine list. We recommend reservations—and dessert—here. It's open daily 3:00 to 10:00 p.m.

Jimmy's Oven and Grill $
7201 Richmond Road
(757) 565-1465

Locals pack this place on weekends and often on weeknights, testimony to the fact that the pizza is authentic and the pastas are made to order. This small eatery is known for super pizzas (any style) with standard toppings, as well as traditional pasta entrees. The menu also features seafood and steaks. The restaurant is open daily from 11:00 a.m. to 10:00 p.m.

Kingsmill Restaurants $$–$$$
1010 Kingsmill Road
(757) 253-3900
www.kingsmill.com

There are several options here to suit your mood or your needs, and each of them affords wonderful views of the James River. The Bray Bistro, on the main level of the Conference Center, offers a menu of special selections each evening as well as wonderful fresh seafood, veal, or beef. A wine list capable of

pleasing the finest palate is available, as are delicious desserts. A beautiful view of the James River is the backdrop. This room is a very popular location with townsfolk for its Sunday buffet brunch of unusually fine selections. We think it's the best in town. The Bray Bistro is closed Sunday evenings. Eagle's is Kingsmill's upscale interpretation of a traditional steak house, serving smoked beef and exquisite salads and side dishes.

For drinks in a casual setting, try Moody's Tavern on the top level of the Conference Center, which specializes in Anheuser-Busch products and cocktails.

We recommend reservations for dinner or the Sunday brunch. Smoking is not permitted in any of these establishments.

The Kitchen at
Powhatan Plantation $$$
3601 Ironbound Road
(757) 253-7893
www.kitchenatpowhatan.com

If you're in the mood for a special night out and a superb dining experience in an atmosphere unlike any other in the area, this is the place to go. Located in a small outbuilding in the shadow of the restored 18th-century Powhatan Plantation house, this restaurant is quaint but exquisite. Enjoy a limited but excellent menu featuring fresh seafood, wild game, and regional favorites in a colonial setting. An extensive wine list and excellent desserts and specials are offered nightly. The dining room is very small, so reservations are a must.

Kyoto Japanese Steak &
Seafood House & Sushi Bar $$–$$$
1621 Richmond Road
(757) 220-8888
kyoto2.com

In a town where family dining is a major draw, this restaurant has hit on a combination sure to entertain youngsters and delight their parents as well. Formerly the Dynasty restaurant, this attractive eatery offers typical Japanese steak house fare as well as sushi (yes, even for beginners) and other entrees that have been prepared to please an American audience. Trust the Liu family to do it right. After you select your entree, watch the teppan showman chef prepare it. Things get downright fun if you're willing to applaud your chef, who is spurred on by appreciative guests. All meals come with soup, salad, hibachi shrimp appetizer, vegetables, rice, and hot tea. Entrees include teriyaki chicken, hibachi shrimp or steak, bonsai scallops, sukiyaki steak, or Teppanyaki filet mignon. Delicious house specialties feature specially prepared combinations of meat, poultry, and seafood—even a surf and turf of steak and lobster called the Kobe King Special. Vegetarian and children's meals are also offered. It's best to call for reservations here, and bring your credit card: No personal checks are accepted. The restaurant, which also offers carry-out and delivery, is open 4:00 to 11:00 p.m. daily for dinner. The hours are extended in summer and for holidays.

La Tolteca Mexican Restaurante $
5351 Richmond Road
(757) 253-2939

135 Second Street
(757) 259-0598

This popular, locally run Mexican restaurant has two locations, one on either side of town. Both offer tasty, authentic Mexican food. Homemade tamales, chiles rellenos, chalupas, chimichangas, enchiladas, and burritos are among the dishes prepared fresh each day. If you don't eat meat, or want something lighter, you can choose from the vegetarian menu. Imported beer and cocktails are served on request. Is it any wonder why Insiders like these places? Both restaurants are small, so don't be surprised to find a line at the Richmond Road location. Hint: You'll rarely encounter that problem at the Second Street location.

Ledo Pizza $
814 Capitol Landing Road
(757) 220-3791

Ledo is the home of the square pizza. The folks at Ledo's say they make their pizzas square "because they don't cut corners." Ledo's moved to its Capitol Landing location just a few years ago, but these pizzas have been famous in the Washington, D.C., area since the 1950s. They feature homemade sauce served on fresh dough made from scratch and come in three sizes. Plus there is also an assortment of soups, salads, subs, and pasta. The casual atmosphere makes it a favorite with the locals, big and small. Ask about the children's meals. Ledo Pizza is open for lunch and dinner from 11:00 a.m. to 10:00 p.m. Monday through Saturday, and closes at 9:00 p.m. on Sunday. The hours are extended to 11:00 p.m. during the summer. Carry-out is available.

Le Yaca $$$
The Village Shops at Kingsmill
1915 Pocahontas Trail
(757) 220-3616
www.leyacawilliamsburg.com

This is one of the area's finest restaurants, offering creative French cuisine in a country French atmosphere. Le Yaca's carefully prepares all lunch and dinner selections, and the proper wine to accompany each meal is available on the extensive wine list. Whether you opt for a five-course dinner or something a little lighter, do not miss the delicious onion soup—the soup you've always imagined existed somewhere in this country. The house specialty is a delightful garlic- and herb-crusted lamb loin roast. At least once you must order the marquis au chocolate for dessert. As you can expect, the wine list, like the food served here, is exquisite. We strongly suggest reservations. Lunch is served 11:30 a.m. to 2:30 p.m. Monday through Friday. Dinner is available from 5:45 to 9:30 p.m. Monday through Saturday. Le Yaca is closed Sunday.

Mama Mia's Pizza & Delicatessen $
521 Prince George Street
(757) 253-2225

Dine in or carry out from this deli, which is open daily from 11:00 a.m. to 11:00 p.m. and located a block from Merchants Square. The selection of food includes pizza, stromboli, gyros, and souvlaki as well as steaks and seafood. A good selection of beer and wine is provided. Limited delivery is offered. The deli does not have a nonsmoking section.

Mama Steve's House of Pancakes $
1509 Richmond Road
(757) 229-7613

A landmark along Richmond Road that also draws many locals, this restaurant offers breakfast and lunch every day of the week in a casual, inviting atmosphere. Mama Steve's is known for its creamed chipped beef, corned beef hash, and Plantation Platters, a tasty bargain at less than $10. Parking is plentiful, and the Historic Area and the outlets are just minutes away. Mama Steve's is open until 2:00 p.m. daily. No credit cards.

Manhattan Bagel $
1437 Richmond Road
(757) 259-9221

If you're in the mood for authentic New York bagels, this is the place. Diners can select from among 22 different flavored bagels, baked continuously throughout the day, which are offered along with myriad accompaniments. Most popular selections include their deli sandwiches. Also available are gourmet coffees, including espresso and cappuccino. Jumbo gourmet muffins, cinnamon rolls, pastries, and other sweets are featured as well. The atmosphere is casual yet inviting, and this place is always impeccably clean. It's open from 6:30 a.m. to 3:00 p.m. every day.

Maple Tree Pancakes & Waffles $
1665 Richmond Road
(757) 220-3544

What is it about being on the road that makes you crave a hearty breakfast—especially pancakes and waffles? In a town where there is more than your usual selection of pancake houses, this tidy little restaurant holds its own

nicely. The menu offers an extensive selection of pancakes and waffles—from small silver dollar pancakes to jumbo flapjacks, and a mouthwatering selection of waffles—fancy or plain. Someone in your group not in the mood? There's also a selection of other breakfast fare—available from opening till midday closing—including assorted egg dishes, sausage, ham, bacon, and corned beef hash, as well as cereals and more. The restaurant is open daily from 6:30 a.m. until about 2:30 p.m. Lunch specials are available from 11:30 a.m. to 2:30 p.m. No credit cards.

Marino's Italian Cuisine $–$$
1338 Richmond Road
(757) 253-1844
www.marinosofwilliamsburg.com

There is an all-you-can-eat salad bar here that includes all the spaghetti you can eat in the bargain. Deals don't get much better than this! Diners also can select from a full menu of dishes including steaks and seafood. A children's menu is available. Marino's is open from 3:00 to 11:00 p.m. daily.

Maurizio (formerly Sal's by Maurizio) $
Festival Marketplace
264 McLaws Circle
(757) 229-0337

There are three Sal's restaurants in Williamsburg, all of which at one time were owned by the same family. Not true anymore. This location near Busch Gardens is owned and operated by a chef who once worked at Sal's by Victor, located in town. The menu features a variety of traditional Italian favorites, as well as a real pizza. Looking for a good linguine with white clam sauce? A good, Italian-style chicken in lemon? Fresh bread, a good glass of wine? Look no further. Nightly specials are offered. It's open daily from 10:30 a.m. to 11:00 p.m.

Milano's Italian Family Restaurant $$
1635 Richmond Road
(757) 220-2527
www.milanosofwilliamsburg.com

The all-you-can-eat spaghetti, soup, and salad bar is only one attraction at this restaurant. Your host personally prepares all meals, and the service staff is equally attentive to guarantee your satisfaction. The sauces here are delicious, and offerings include northern Italian dishes that otherwise are hard to find in this area. The menu is extensive and service is prompt. Milano's also offers a children's menu.

Miyako Japanese Restaurant $$
153 Monticello Avenue
(757) 564-0800

This charming restaurant offers diners the unique opportunity to sample authentic Japanese cuisine—from sushi to sashimi—in a casual, upbeat atmosphere. The list of appetizers, entrees, and yes, even desserts, includes traditional favorites such as shrimp or vegetable tempura, steamed or fried dumplings, teriyaki steak and seafood, and much more. There is sushi for beginners and those accustomed to the vinegar rice rolls. The restaurant's smoke-free regulation enhances the experience. Beer and wine are served on the premises. Miyako's is open for lunch 11:00 a.m. to 2:30 p.m., and dinner 5:00 to 10:00 p.m. Monday through Saturday; it is closed on Sunday.

Mr. Liu's Chinese
Restaurant & Lounge $$
The Village Shops at Kingsmill
1915 Pocahontas Trail
(757) 253-0990

In The Village Shops at Kingsmill, between the Historic Area and Busch Gardens, this restaurant is popular with tourists and townsfolk alike. Rick Liu and his staff present excellent Hunan, Szechuan, Mandarin, and Cantonese cuisine in a quiet, modern setting accented by beautiful examples of Chinese art. The preparation and presentation of every dish, whether traditional or a house specialty, are attended to with great care. Beef with broccoli, for example, isn't just beef and broccoli, but a carefully placed ring of broccoli filled with tender, meticulously seasoned beef. If you are in a hurry or would prefer to take your meals with you, carry-out orders are welcome. There is also limited delivery service available.

National Pancake House $
Festival Marketplace, 264 McLaws Circle
(757) 220-9433
7105 Pocahontas Trail
(757) 220-9433

This restaurant features homemade Belgian waffles, pancakes, country fresh eggs, and healthy alternatives, as well as a soup and sandwich lunch menu. It is open 7:00 a.m. to 2:00 p.m. daily.

Nawab Indian Cuisine $$
204 Monticello Avenue
(757) 565-3200
www.nawabonline.com

The dining room is small, but crisp white linens, ceiling fans, and nicely attired, attentive waiters set the stage for your East Indian meal at this excellent restaurant. The extensive menu offers something to please everyone—from the seasoned diner to those who've come to taste Indian cuisine for the first time. The menu is so extensive that making a choice is the most difficult thing you'll face here. In addition to appetizers, soups, and salads, the menu offers a variety of tandoori specialties—all cooked in a clay pit oven fueled by charcoal—including chicken, lamb, beef, shrimp, and fish options. As you would expect, there are curries galore—with the temperature adjusted to your preference. Indian staples, such as raita, mango chutney, and specialty breads including naan, roti, and pratha are featured. First timers might want to order the Nawab Special, a sampler of Indian foods that includes soup; tandoori chicken; lamb kabob; a choice of lamb, beef,

i We enjoy our Virginia peanuts—any style, any time. If a restaurant's menu offers a selection with peanuts, try it! Local favorites include peanut soup and yummy peanut pie.

or chicken curry; vegetable korma, basmati rice, and naan bread. Remember, however, that when you order anything, specify if you want it prepared mild, medium, hot, or Indian hot. There is a difference!

New York Deli $
6546 Richmond Road
(757) 564-9258
www.newyorkdelipizza.com

The name of this popular deli—which recently moved to a bigger location a few blocks up Richmond Road—should pay tribute to the delicious Greek food available here. Yes, you can get the standard New York deli fare: good corned beef and Swiss on rye, piled-high roast beef, pastrami, kosher dills, smoked turkey and ham, coleslaw, assorted beverages, and more—but try some of the Greek specialties if you want a taste treat. This place is informal, but the food is something special. It doesn't offer a nonsmoking section, however. No credit cards.

Old Chickahominy House
Restaurant & Antiques $
1211 Jamestown Road
(757) 229-4689

This restaurant is extremely popular with locals, who keep it hopping during off-season. But any other time of the year, the place is packed with visitors who remember a good thing and return again and again. The restaurant, which has a fixed menu, celebrated its 50th anniversary in 2005. Located on Jamestown Road a few blocks south of the Historic Area, this traditional Virginia plantation house is decorated in the style of a colonial tavern, but the real attraction is the reasonably priced and excellent breakfasts and lunches. They include fresh chicken and dumplings, our favorite version of the traditional Virginia ham biscuit, and Brunswick stew. Miss Melinda's Special is a sampler plate we recommend to first-time guests. We strongly recommend that you save room for a slice of one of the delicious, homemade pies. They all are special, and making a choice is

difficult. However, if you can force yourself to turn down the coconut pie or a slice of the delicious semisweet chocolate pie, try the buttermilk—it is excellent and not commonly found in this area. Upon arriving, be sure your name is added to the seating list, and then enjoy examining the antiques and other items for sale in the shop. Tired? Have a seat on the large front porch and watch the passing parade. The restaurant is open for breakfast and lunch only—but don't leave town without sampling it. The restaurant is open 8:30 to 10:30 a.m. for breakfast, and 11:30 a.m. to 2:30 p.m. for lunch each day.

Old Mill House of
Pancakes & Waffles $
2005 Richmond Road
(757) 229-3613

Insiders really like this inviting little place, perhaps because you are greeted by the charming smile of Miss Irene, a local celebrity. Open for breakfast and lunch daily, this restaurant presents 20 varieties of pancakes and waffles in an airy, cheerful atmosphere. Particularly good are the French strawberry pancakes and cheese blintzes, which are unlike any you'll find anywhere else in the world. There are also club sandwiches and burgers for the lunch crowd. The Plantation Breakfast is a must for hearty eaters, and the daily (except Saturday) luncheon specials are popular with townsfolk. Smoking is not permitted.

Padow's Hams & Deli $
Williamsburg Shopping Center
1258 Richmond Road
(757) 220-4267

This is a great place to go for delicious made-to-order deli sandwiches—more than 40 varieties of them. The deli, which is open until 7:00 p.m., also offers fresh soups and salads and a good selection of desserts. The friendly folks at Padow's will be glad to box your favorite sandwich, drink, and other side orders if you are on the go. If you want to take a little more home with you, Padow's offers whole Smithfield hams, smoked turkeys, Virginia peanuts, and gift baskets.

Papillon: A Bistro $$
Williamsburg Hospitality House
415 Richmond Road
(757) 229-4020
The comfortable decor in this room provides a relaxed but elegant setting in which to enjoy a meal. This is an upscale but comfortable restaurant with an excellent menu for breakfast and lunch. The breakfast buffet is especially good. Breakfast is served from 6:30 to 11:00 a.m., except Sunday, when the hours are 7:00 a.m. to noon. Papillon is located in the same building as 415 Grill.

Paul's Deli Restaurant & Pizza $
761 Scotland Street
(757) 229-8976
www.paulsdelirestaurant.com
Fresh "New England–style" pizza is this deli's featured dish, but you will also find Greek and Italian dishes on the menu. A large selection of imported and domestic beers and wines is available to complement your choice or to help you cheer as you follow the action on one of the nine televisions located throughout the place. Just off Richmond Road across from William and Mary's football stadium, this is a popular spot with students. It's open for lunch and dinner daily from 10:30 a.m. until 2:00 a.m., and delivery to area lodgings is available.

Peking and Mongolian Grill $–$$
Kingsgate Greene Shopping Center
122 Waller Mill Road
(757) 229-2288
www.peking-va.com
Three popular local restaurants have merged to form one great dining venue. Here you'll find one kind of barbecue that's news, even in the South! If you wish, you can order from the traditional Chinese menu. Or you can opt for the Mongolian barbecue or Japanese hibachi and sushi. After enjoying one of the wonderful soups, move to the curved buffet line and select the ingredients for a fresh salad. We recommend the peanut dressing. After your salad, return to the buffet and fill a bowl with Chinese noodles and selections from the fresh-cut vegetables, meats, chicken, lamb, or seafood and top off your selections from a variety of sauces and herbed oils. At that point, the show begins. Hand your bowl to the cook behind the curved buffet and watch as he sizzles it, walking slowly in a circle around the huge round grill, stirring your meal with what have to be the world's largest chopsticks. There is a tasty dessert section at the buffet if you have any room left.

Pierce's Pitt Bar-B-Que $
447 East Rochambeau Drive
(757) 565-2955
www.pierces.com
Here's a true bit of local history: When highway construction on I-64 restricted access to the restaurant, Pierce's barbecue fans parked their semis, cars, and vans on the new highway's shoulders in order to get their "cue." The highway department put up a fence. No problem. What's a little ol' fence to a determined barbecue connoisseur? It was knocked down and scrambled over more than once by folks determined to get to Pierce's. Take the pottery exit off the interstate and look for Lowe's. The restaurant is a little more than a mile down the road on your right. You are almost certain to have a short wait in line, but the pulled-pork barbecue made right on the premises (you can follow your nose to Pierce's on a clear day), onion rings, and other selections are worth the wait. Just ask beachgoers and other travelers from all over the state who make the pilgrimage regularly. You also can get food to go if you're in a hurry. But it's worth the effort, trust us. Hours are 10:00 a.m. to 9:00 p.m. each day.

Pitchers Sports Bar $–$$
Williamsburg Marriott
50 Kingsmill Road
(757) 220-2500, ext. 7719
Looking for a casual, relaxed yet upbeat place

to kick back, enjoy a light repast, a game on TV, and a few, well, pitchers? This place steps out of the mold of hotel taverns and sets a new standard for enjoyment. Quesadillas, nachos, dip 'n' eat spinach, crab cakes, chili, burgers, seafood, etc. Whether you want to eat light or heavy, they can meet your demands. Looking for some game action? Twenty-three televisions are always tuned in. Pitchers is open until 2:00 a.m., with the last call at about 1:30. See you there!

Pizzeria Uno Chicago Bar & Grill $–$$
205 Bypass Road
(757) 220-5454
A taste of Yankee pizza right here in south-eastern Virginia: That's what this restaurant is all about. The extensive, entertaining menu features authentic, hit-and-run traditional Chicago-style deep-dish pizzas with a variety of toppings. Also offered are sumptuous appetizers, ample entrees, and tempting desserts—and that's just for starters. The menu also offers a variety of fresh salads, sandwiches, burgers, and pastas. Perennial favorites include baked chicken Spinoccoli, chicken fajitas, and cooked-to-order sirloin tips. A full bar is on the premises. The hours are 11:00 a.m. to midnight Friday and Satur-day and 11:00 a.m. to 11:00 p.m. the rest of the week.

The Polo Club Restaurant and Tavern $$
135 Colony Square Shopping Center
1303 Jamestown Road
(757) 220-1122
www.poloclubrestaurant.com
This restaurant is a very popular place with local folk at lunch and dinner. The tavern area is sufficiently separate from the dining areas to keep the moods distinct for those wanting a quiet meal. Later in the evening, the place becomes crowded with young pro-fessionals. The drinks are good, the food var-ied and always very tasty. Nightly specials include beef, chicken, and seafood entrees as well as special, and tasty, soups and appe-tizers. Our favorite burger creations in the

city are here, but other options on the menu and the daily specials frequently tempt us as well. A kids' menu is sensitive to their limited taste preferences, and the portions are scaled to their appetites.

Queen Anne Dairy Snack $
7127 Merrimac Trail
(757) 229-3051
Pulling up to this establishment is a retro visit to the 1950s era of walk-up window service. Though the building has seen a better day and only has a couple of old outside picnic tables and benches on which to sit, don't be put off. This little place serves some of the best fried shrimp, fried chicken, barbecue, and burgers in this part of Virginia. To top it off, order one of their old-fashioned shakes, sundaes, or malts. (All together now: I scream, you scream...) You can spend a lot of time making your selection from the variety posted in the window. The price is right, and if you're in the mood for a touch of tasty nostal-gia, this is the place to visit. No credit cards.

Sal's by Victor $
Williamsburg Shopping Center
1242 Richmond Road
(757) 220-2641
www.salsbyvictor.com
This in-town location has been a popular eatery for residents and students for years. It has undergone an expansion and a bright new remodeling, and the menu has been expanded to include delicious new dishes. This may just be the best pizza in town—probably because a native-born Italian makes it. Running the kitchen is chef Vittorio Minichiello, who hosts his guests with friendly warmth and enthusiasm. One sign of the authenticity of the cuisine is the homemade cannolis (pastry desserts), which are a deli-cious way to end your lunch or dinner—if you saved room. The veal dishes here are particu-larly delicious. The fresh pastas are unbeat-able, and the espresso creations are outstanding. Be sure to check the chalkboard or ask your server about daily dinner specials,

Nick's Seafood Pavilion, located on Water Street on the York River waterfront in Yorktown, is now owned and operated by the Yorktown Education Foundation. Dine here for the best seafood meal in York County—and know that the proceeds go toward improving the quality of public education in this part of Virginia.

because they often are too good to pass up. This is truly a family restaurant, and children are not only welcome, they have a section of the menu devoted especially to them. FYI: Sal's delivers after 5:00 p.m., for free. After a busy day of touring or playing, the pizza here cannot be beat—especially when it is delivered freshly made and hot. This Sal's is open 11:00 a.m. to 11:00 p.m. with a midnight close on Friday and Saturday.

Sal's Ristorante Italiano $
835 Capitol Landing Road
(757) 221-0443

This restaurant offers a Greek twist on Italian favorites. Excellent hot and cold appetizers and "the largest sandwiches in town" complement a wide selection of pastas and pizzas. Pastas and breads are fired in the brick hearth, which imports a special, smoky flavor that is unmistakable. Located across from the International Village, it is often busy with European students who come to Williamsburg in season to work at Busch Gardens and Water Country USA. Children are welcome. This location is a quarter-mile from the Historic Area and the Information Center.

The Seafare of Williamsburg $$$
1632 Richmond Road
(757) 229-0099

Lobster, served any number of ways, is a specialty here. But look beyond lobster for some other delicious options. The seafood is very well prepared as you would expect. For dryland diners, options include milk-fed veal, prime beef dishes, and tableside gourmet

preparations. A wine steward will help you select a vintage to enjoy with your meal, and cocktails also are available. You might select one of the flambé desserts to top off a pleasant dinner. The restaurant is open for lunch on Sunday and dinner daily until 11:00 p.m.

Seasons Cafe Restaurant $$
Merchants Square
110 South Henry Street
(757) 259-0018

Seasons has captured a loyal audience of Insiders since its opening in the old post office on Merchants Square in 1993. The restaurant seats 350, with nearly one-third on an awning-covered patio outside. But the restaurant is divided into several rooms and small areas to provide a sense of intimacy. The theme is most definitely Southern (check out the plantation mural), but the cuisine is varied and delicious: Linguine with spicy peanut sauce and fresh swordfish are favorites. We recommend you don't overlook the salad bar with its creative seafood and other salads, and the grilled sandwiches on sourdough bread. The smoked barbecued ribs are national-award winners. Lunch specials and a terrific Sunday brunch offer lots of variety. For $13.95, the brunch (served until 3:00 p.m.) is a bargain, with seafood Newburg, beef Burgundy, and breakfast items such as flavored waffles. Flavored cappuccinos from the bar will round out an enjoyable meal.

Second Street Restaurant and Tavern $$
140 Second Street
(757) 220-2286

The sports center at this recently remodeled local hangout, with its 7 television screens, is popular throughout the year but especially during football season. The mood is very casual, and when the college is in session, you may have to wait for a seat. Don't let the exuberance of the crowd daunt you—you'll soon be in a party mood yourself. A menu of steaks, seafood, munchies, sandwiches, salads, and soups complements the full range of beverage offerings. This is not an adults-only establishment: A children's menu is provided. The grill is open and munchies are available for lunch and dinner until 11:15 p.m., and the bar is open until 2:00 a.m. daily.

The Sportsman's Grille $$
Marketplace Shopping Center
240 McLaws Circle
(757) 221-8002

With menu headings such as Starting Line-up, American All-Stars, and Spring Training, you know you're in a sportsman's paradise at this restaurant. That's no simple pita sandwich, it's a "catcher's mitt." Breadsticks are Louisville sluggers, and the kid selections are teamed under Little League. Pasta dishes, salads, barbecue, and pot roast complement the standard grill fare. For dinner, The Main Event offers entrees with salad or soup and daily entree and dessert specials. Insiders are particularly fond of the birdie chicken salad, which pairs chunks of boneless, skinless whitemeat chicken with chopped pecans and zesty chutney on a bed of greens with thin, crunchy slices of garlic toast on top. Yum! And you don't have to be a sportsman to appreciate the cozy, inviting decor and friendly service. We love this place! It's closed on Sunday.

The Trellis $$$
Merchants Square
403 Duke of Gloucester Street
(757) 229-8610
www.thetrellis.com

Ah, The Trellis! Please excuse us, but it's hard for Insiders to be casual when attempting to inform visitors about this nationally acclaimed restaurant. To dine here, whether for lunch or for dinner, is to experience a unique and wonderful combination of elegant but understated atmosphere, efficient and pampering service, and, well, the menu. It's unforgettable, that menu. But a warning is in order: This is not a restaurant to collapse into with hungry kids after a day of touring Colonial Williamsburg. All meals are lovingly made to order and sometimes that means a wait. An alternative during warm weather is the outdoor cafe, with its more casual menu and faster service.

A seasonal selection of creations by nationally renowned executive chef Marcel Desaulniers, a star graduate of the Culinary Institute of America, features mesquite-grilled fare and regional items such as Chesapeake Bay seafood and Smithfield ham prepared with gourmet accents such as shiitake mushrooms, fine sauces, and unusual relishes. The soups and salads are equally fresh, creative, and appealing. The menu is re-created each season, and the featured dinners and daily chef's selections are always unique. Listening to the service staff preview them at your table is an effective appetizer in itself. The perfect wine to complement your dinner is certain to be on the extensive list of European and American vintages. If you are not familiar with Virginia's—and particularly Williamsburg's—wines, the staff can advise you in making a selection (and you can also read about them in the Regional Cuisine and Wines chapter). You might wish to complete your dinner with something sweet: The desserts are as unique as the other dishes, and a love affair with one or another is entirely possible. You might think twice about ordering something called Death by Chocolate, but from experience we'd respond, "O Death, where is thy sting?" about a dessert more immortal than mortal. If you're not prepared for such a glorious demise, other tasty pastry specials are available, as are homemade ice creams, sorbets, and fresh fruits. Chocolate lovers may wish to obtain chef Desaulniers's books—Death by Chocolate, Desserts to Die For, An Alphabet of Sweets, The Trellis Cookbook, or Cooking with the Burgermeisters—as gifts or enticements for the cooks at home.

We suggest that you make reservations early to ensure the seating time and room you desire. The more formal Garden Room offers a fine "window on the world" of Merchants Square. The Vault Room is especially intimate. All the dining spaces are lovely. Attire is nice casual and beyond. The Trellis also offers a special take-out service menu for sandwiches, salads, and desserts from 11:00 a.m. to 3:00 p.m. for lunch, and again with the addition of entrees for supper from 5:00 to 9:30 p.m.

Welcome South Restaurant $–$$
8558 Richmond Road, U.S. Route 60 at the Route 30 intersection
(757) 566-8255

Insiders LOVE this place! When we visit this restaurant, located 9 miles west of Williamsburg, and we do so often, we see right many townsfolk, all having found or heard that it's worth the drive to enjoy a delicious meal. The kitchen specializes in "affordable Southern cooking with a light gourmet touch," and that includes entrees cooked over charcoal and smoked with mesquite and hickory. Owner Anna Liguria offers steaks and chicken with wonderful pasta creations and tasty variations on side dishes. Only fresh, local, seasonal veggies are prepared in a variety of delectable ways. Insiders are particularly fond of the blackened salmon—always perfect! The only problem here is that the nightly specials are so good, it's difficult to decide whether to pass up menu regulars, which are out of this world. This is home cookin' like Mama only dreamed of! The service is friendly, attentive, and helpful, and the food is worth the drive. Oh, and you'd better save room for one of the generous helpings of homemade desserts offered with the requisite gourmet spin; our favorite is the chocolate French silk pie. The restaurant serves lunch and dinner. On weekend nights, make reservations if you want to avoid a wait; seats are in demand.

The Whaling Company Seafood Restaurant $$
494 McLaws Circle
(757) 229-0275
www.TheWhalingCompany.com

You can catch a glimpse of this restaurant from U.S. Route 60 east on the way to Busch Gardens. It offers fresh seafood prepared in an incredible variety of ways—steamed,

> The Trellis's mocha chocolate chip cookies are the richest we've ever tasted . . . grab some for a quick snack in Merchants Square.

broiled, poached, and grilled. Specialty steaks, lemon herb chicken, soups, and salads round out the menu. But the best part about this restaurant is that if you don't see something prepared the way you would like, say so. Usually the chefs can accommodate your tastes and prepare something special to order. A children's menu offers youngsters the old standbys that make them smile: fish, hamburgers, shrimp, chicken fingers. Add to that some attentive service and, well, it adds up to a pleasant, memorable dining experience at reasonable prices. We recommend reservations for dinner.

The Whitehall Restaurant $$$
1325 Jamestown Road
(757) 229-4677
www.thewhitehall.com

This upscale restaurant with two dining patios features Italian cuisine along with other European specialties. The focus here is on delicious veal and chicken dishes, fine wines, and delectable desserts—all served in an atmosphere conducive to memorable dining. Owner Karen Moor prides herself on her restaurant's elegant but laid-back atmosphere and adventuresome yet classic cuisine. Soups of the day vary from the classic fish soup to the more contemporary crab and spinach. Specialties of the house are Wiener schnitzel and flounder Whitehall, which combines sweet flounder fillet with prawns and fresh spinach in a pink sauce, all surrounded by real mashed potatoes. Pasta lovers must try the pasta du jour. Finish your repast with any one of the fine desserts listed on the menu: a special tiramisu, chocolate raspberry torte, Italian cheesecake, or crème caramel. The extensive wine list includes appellations from Italy, France, California, and Virginia. With the exception of one small room, no smoking is allowed. Attire is nice casual and beyond. Reservations are recommended. Open daily for dinner.

Yorkshire Steak & Seafood $$–$$$
700 York Street
(757) 229-9790
This was Williamsburg's first nonsmoking restaurant. It's a great place for fine beef, succulent seafood, and attentive service in a smoke-free environment. Prime beef and fresh seafood are favorites on the dinner menu, with beef shish kebab the house specialty. Insiders know, however, that the seafood shish kebab is equally delicious but requires a mammoth appetite. Opened and operated by a local family, this establishment has a large local and repeat visitor following, despite its understated location and ambience. Excellent cocktails and fine wines and beers are available. Banquets can be accommodated, and there is a children's menu. Reservations are in order. Yorkshire is open 5:00 to 10:30 p.m. daily.

NIGHTLIFE

Grammy Award–winner Bruce Hornsby is, without a doubt, one of Williamsburg's favorite sons. It's a sentiment the master ivory tickler undoubtedly returns. But if your timing isn't right to catch Bruce Hornsby on a Williamsburg stage, don't despair. Although this isn't a rowdy, rocking kind of town, there is enough variety for just about everyone to find something fun to do once the sun goes down.

While now and then you still can find DJs who spin loud, throbbing dance music, the local bar scene these days is decidedly more low-key. Rock 'n' roll has taken a backseat to the soulful sounds of jazz and blues, and taverns that offer a quiet, restful place to sip microbrews and enjoy friendly conversations have elbowed out glitzier nightclubs. Fewer nightspots have live music, but those that do, choose their acts carefully and make sure their patrons are properly entertained. There also are growing numbers of sports bars and a variety of unusual twilight diversions—from candlelit walking tours to rowdy dinner theaters to 18th-century-style concerts—right in the heart of Colonial Williamsburg.

If you're in the mood to quaff a few, keep in mind that Virginia's legal age to buy, possess, or consume alcohol is 21, and that a picture identification is required as proof of age. If you do choose to imbibe, it's always best to designate a nondrinking member of your party as chauffeur for the evening.

Because Williamsburg is a college town, there's always something happening at Phi Beta Kappa Memorial Hall on the William and Mary campus. To find out what's on the agenda at the hall, you can call (757) 221-2655 and listen to the list of voice mail options. Or better yet, drop by during your tour of the colonial capital: Upcoming events are posted in the lobby.

If you're in the mood for a bit of Broadway or an evening of opera and have the whole night to spare, you might want to plan a trip to Norfolk, about an hour's drive east on Interstate 64. Or, if you're looking for big-name musical acts, check out the schedules at the coliseums in Hampton and Richmond or the Verizon Wireless Amphitheater in Virginia Beach. We give you all the information you need to map out your itinerary in our Out-of-Town Nightspots section near the end of this chapter. For ticket information and availability, call the numbers listed or contact Ticketmaster at (757) 872-8100 or visit www.ticketmaster.com.

The best way to find out what's happening in and around Williamsburg is to check the *Virginia Gazette* (published in town on Wednesday and Saturday) or the *Newport News Daily Press* (particularly Friday's "Ticket Weekend," featuring entertainment news; and the "Sunday Ticket" section, which offers a guide to arts and leisure activities). Or you can visit the *Daily Press*'s entertainment Web site at www.hrticket.com.

Other sources for entertainment news include *Williamsburg Magazine* (a free monthly publication you can pick up just about anywhere) and *Colonial Guide* (a seasonal publication available free at numerous locations around the greater Williamsburg area). *The Richmond Times-Dispatch* (published each morning) lists happenings and entertainments in the greater Richmond area. To find out what a particular evening's offerings include in and around the Historic Area, consult listings at the Colonial Williamsburg Visitor Center.

Considering the volatile nature of nightspots, whose popularity waxes and wanes with the lunar cycle, don't be afraid to ask residents their opinions. Chances are you'll learn about the brightest and best that Williamsburg has to offer from those who speak from personal experience.

While we're confident you won't have any trouble finding a suitable venue for passing an enjoyable, memorable evening in Williamsburg, we offer the following list of possible options for an evening out. Happy hunting!

MUSIC AND MUNCHIES

What follows is a list of typical nightspots. They offer music—either by band, DJ, or jukebox; big-screen TVs to catch the game; and libations and a bite to eat well into the evening. Stop by and give in to those late-night cravings.

A. Carroll's Bistro, Martini & Wine Bar
601 Prince George Street
(757) 258-8882

This swank, sophisticated restaurant offers live jazz every Friday evening and the last Saturday of every month. There are also 29 different martinis to choose from, everything from the sweet tart and watermelon to gin blossom martinis. The airy, open atmosphere and original artwork make this a refreshing place to relax and unwind after a day of touring. Cigars are welcome in the bar. A. Carroll's is one street over from Richmond Road.

Bones Grand Slam Eatery
and Sports Bar
351 York Street
(757) 564-7109

If the words *play ball* are music to your ears, check out this local sports bar. Open seven nights a week, Bones offers 18 televisions—including one big screen—so you can tune in to any sporting event that strikes your fancy. (Lacrosse, anyone?) You also can test your expertise in the interactive trivia contest or fine-tune your hand-eye coordination at the dartboard. Dinner is served from 5:00 to 10:00 p.m. (occasionally 11:00, if there's a crowd), with light munchies available until the 2:00 a.m. close. There's karaoke every Thursday. Attire for the evening is casual.

Green Leafe Cafe
765 Scotland Street at Richmond Road
(757) 220-3405

Open since 1974, this is—without question—the most enduring nightspot in town. (It even says so in the *New York Times* review framed and hanging on the wall.) The Green Leafe is a veritable institution in Williamsburg, equally popular with tourists, locals, and students from the College of William and Mary, which is located across Richmond Road. Good food, diverse conversations, and occasional live music characterize this rather Spartan hangout. Solid-wood chairs and tables—impervious to the generations of partiers who have frequented this place—are crowded together, though not uncomfortably. This place rocks until 2:00 a.m. and offers an exceptional array of adult beverages. At last count, the selection included a 30-tap draft system (with almost daily rotations among selections) and more than 100 varieties of bottled American microbrews. "We really try to do the whole American beer experience," notes one long-time employee. But the assortment of spirits doesn't end there. Green Leafe also offers 12 to 15 single-malt Scotches and a number of single-barrel bourbons and high-end tequilas. For vino lovers, about 20 different wines—everything from Chardonnay and Cabernet to a bit of the bubbly—are sold by the glass or bottle, depending on the wine. There's also a small bar-top humidor where cigar aficionados just might locate that prized hand-rolled stogie from Nicaragua or Honduras. Join the long line of locals who have helped close the place down night after night (365 times a year), either in the roomy front area or in the more intimate bar in the rear.

J. B.'s Tavern
Crowne Plaza Williamsburg at
Fort Magruder
U.S. Route 60 East
(757) 220-2250

This is a place where you can kick back, watch a baseball game on one of five TVs, shoot a round of pool, and listen to tunes on the jukebox any night of the week. The attire is casual, the bar is full, and sandwiches, salads, and pizza are available until closing at midnight.

J. M. Randalls Restaurant & Tavern
Old Towne Square, 4854 Longhill Road
(757) 259-0406
www.jmrandalls.com
Since opening in 1995, this nightspot has developed quite a reputation for its blues and jazz offerings. "We've hosted 13 Grammy winners," says owner Randall Plaxa. As one local musician notes: "They're real professionals, and they have the best music room in town." Open until 2:00 a.m. seven days a week, J. M. Randalls features regional, national, and international acts Tuesday through Sunday. An occasional informal jam session provides aspiring musicians with an opportunity to play with the pros. Big-screen football is a popular Sunday- and Monday-night option, and NTN interactive trivia has really caught on in recent years. ("I have one 81-year-old woman who comes here who is ranked 16th in the country," says Randall.) The tavern also boasts an acclaimed kitchen, turning out perennial favorites like bourbon-marinated steak, honey molasses barbecue ribs, and pierogies, a Polish dish that takes Randall back to his Pennsylvania roots. If our description conjures up an image of a smoky blues joint in your mind, erase it. Randalls is a popular family spot where kids are encouraged to listen to the first set and cultivate their love of music. "Two-thirds to three-fourths of my people are here three to six days a week," says Randall, "and four out of six of them are eating dinner at the bar."

Paul's Deli Restaurant & Pizza
761 Scotland Street
(757) 229-8976
A popular destination of the college crowd, Paul's occasionally offers a variety of progressive, alternative, and acoustic music on Wednesday nights. Call ahead to find out who's on the agenda when you're in town. For those who like a little armchair (or barstool) quarterbacking, nine television screens will take you to the action. This lively spot is open until 2:00 a.m. and serves some of the best pizza in the 'Burg.

Pitchers Sports Bar
Williamsburg Marriott
50 Kingsmill Road
(757) 220-2500
If you like to munch a great burger or snack on some tasty nachos while tuning in to Monday Night Football, a visit to this casual hotel tavern is in order. Pitchers, which features 23 televisions for your viewing enjoyment, is open until 2:00 a.m., with last call at 1:30 a.m. Pitchers also has pool tables, darts, and games. Food service stops at midnight.

Second Street Restaurant and Tavern
140 Second Street
(757) 220-2286
www.secondst.com
There's enough happening in this popular watering hole to keep even the most kinetic partier happy for an entire evening. This is, without a doubt, one of the most popular after-hours haunts in the Williamsburg area. With the bar open until midnight daily and the late-night grill cookin' until 45 minutes before closing, this is a good place to go after taking in a show or concert. A sports center features more than a half-dozen TV screens, offering hard-core sports fans an optimum vantage point from any of the numerous tables in the place. (And if you're in the mood to sink your teeth in some beef, locals have deemed Second Street's burger the best in the 'Burg since 2001.)

LET THE GAMES BEGIN

The first two establishments are a bit of a twist on the traditional nightspot. The owners will still feed you and offer you a drink, but they may also ask you to take your turn in a game or two.

AMF Williamsburg Lanes
5544 Old Towne Road
(757) 565-3311
www.amf.com/williamsburglanes
If bowling is your bag, don your funkiest shirt—you know, the one with somebody else's initials that you picked up for a buck at a yard sale—and head to this popular alley on Friday or Saturday night for a round of "Xtreme Bowling" for a chance to bowl 'neath black lights and a disco ball. As the hour grows later, the lights are turned down, the music is pumped up, and you're ready to roll. Times may vary, so call beforehand. If you return on a more staid evening—Sunday through Thursday—the lanes are open until midnight

Chowning's Tavern
100 East Duke of Gloucester Street
(757) 229-2141, (800) TAVERNS
This authentic colonial Virginia alehouse, in the heart of the city's Historic Area, comes rambunctiously alive each evening at 5:00 p.m. when the Gambols, colonial tavern games, begin. You'll be seated at big wooden tables side by side with visitors from across the country as you listen to impromptu serenades by costumed troubadours (be prepared: some are designed to bring a blush to the cheek of the fair maid or shy gentleman) and participate in 18th-century board games. The mood is extremely lively, accurately reflecting our forefathers' enthusiasm for the bawdy side of life. You may rethink your understanding of American history when you see how those proper folks in the staid paintings were wont to behave at their leisure!

Ale and beer—including Chowning's own label—are available, and there's an assortment of colonial spirits, beverages, and light menu fare. Guests are welcome to join in the fun or to relax and take in the entertainments. Casual clothing is fine here after the dinner hour.

The Corner Pocket
4805 Courthouse Street
(757) 220-0808
If you have always had a hankering to wield a pool cue and say, "Rack 'em up!" to your partner, head on over to The Corner Pocket and put a unique spin on your evening activities. This upscale billiards parlor is not your stereotypical pool hall: An 18-years-or-older policy (unless accompanied by a parent) and a dress code are enforced (among other things, that means, gentlemen, your shirts must have collars). There are eight 8-foot tables and three 9-foot tables (Ventana brass pool tables). If you take a break from shooting pool, you can enjoy the large murals, the televisions, or the conversation about the armadillos. No, you're not seeing things, and yes, we said armadillos. Don't ask us, we'll just shrug; ask Lynn Allison, the owner.

The Corner Pocket offers a daily menu of light meals featuring soups and unusual, creative entrees. The restaurant/billiards parlor opens every day from 4:00 p.m. to 2:00 a.m., except Sunday, when it's open from 11:30 a.m. to 2:00 a.m. Popular menu items include jambalaya, chicken burritos, a weekly pasta special, and a rotating selection of microbrewery beers. Lynn also has begun experimenting occasionally with live music. Seven times a year she brings in a blues, jazz, or zydeco act. Tickets for these evenings, which follow no predetermined schedule but are publicized in the *Virginia Gazette,* start at $15 on average and can go up to $25, depending upon the act. "The music is very special," says Lynn. "We've had some unbelievable nights here."

LEND ME YOUR EARS

The fun doesn't stop in Williamsburg when the sun goes down. There are plenty of tours, concerts, and performances reserved especially for after hours.

Summer Breeze Concert Series
Merchants Square
(757) 259-3760
A unique and thoroughly enjoyable entry on the entertainment scene and an excellent early-evening option is the Summer Breeze Concert Series held Thursday in July and

August. Performances by artists from throughout the region are held in front of The Christmas Shop in Merchants Square and feature a variety of music from contemporary to traditional jazz, acoustic, folk, swing, and pop. Concerts start at 6:30 p.m. and run until about 8:30 p.m. Attendees are invited to bring folding chairs and blankets to the performances, and everyone is encouraged to get there early to get a space with a good view. This is a joint effort of the Merchants Square Association and the City of Williamsburg and James City County Parks and Recreation Departments. To find out who's playing any given week, simply call ahead or check the Merchants Square online calendar at merchantssquare.org/calendar.

Williamsburg Regional Library
515 Scotland Street
(757) 259-4070
www.wrl.org
If you think of a library as a place where the noise level never rises above a whisper, you're in for a surprise. At the regional library, the fall through spring evening concert series is crammed full of entertaining sounds. Although the lineup varies, you can count on a diverse array of performers: In its Dewey Decibel Concert Series, music runs the gamut from folk, bluegrass, and country to traditional and jazz. Past performances have included John McCutcheon, Tommy Emmanuel, and Stephen Bennett, as well as a free concert by the Langley Winds (a woodwind quintet from the U.S. Air Force's Heritage of America Band). And if you're wondering about the seating arrangements and acoustics, we're happy to inform you that the regional library has a full 266-seat theater complete with stage lights and an excellent sound system. Hampton Road's *Daily Press* named the theater "Best Small Venue" in its Sound Check Musical Achievement Awards.

Concert dates vary, but most start at 8:00 p.m. Some concerts are free, but for the most part ticket prices range from $10 to $15, or $5 to $7 for those younger than 16. Call ahead to have tickets held for you at the door. Tickets can be reserved as far as two months in advance with advance payment either by telephone with a credit card or in person with cash, check, or credit card.

MAGIC, MAYHEM, AND MYSTERY

In recent years an array of dinner theaters has opened, tempting audience members with the promise of medieval mischief making, the allure of special effects, and the chance to test their skills as super sleuths.

Haunted Dinner Theater
Captain George's Seafood Restaurant
5363 Richmond Road
(757) 258-2500
www.wmbgdinnertheater.com
Offered from June through the end of December, this two-and-a-half-hour hair-raising experience combines a 71-item all-you-can-eat buffet dinner with a full-length play complete with music, magic, and some pretty awesome special effects. Past programs have included *Ding Dong the Witch Is Dead* and *Lights, Camera, Shoot!* Even though this dinner theater bills itself as "haunted," its low-key spookiness is family friendly. Tickets cost $39.95 for adults and $28.95 for children 6 through 12. Reservations can be made online or by phone, and all shows start at 7:00 p.m. and run different days each month.

i If you like chamber, organ, or choral music, the Bruton Parish Church on Duke of Gloucester Street hosts free concerts at 8:00 p.m. on Saturdays throughout the year and Tuesdays and Thursdays from March through December. The church also presents some special evening concerts throughout the year.

A free-will offering is collected at each performance. For more information call (757) 229-2891 or go to www.bruton parish.org.

Mystery Dinner Playhouse
The Days Inn Hotel
201 Water Country Parkway
(888) 471-4802
www.mysterydinner.com
If you're a sleuth at heart and are in the mood for a good "whodunit," check out this lively dinner theater option. While enjoying a delicious meal, audiences can chat with the play's characters and look for clues to solve the mystery. At the end of the show, everyone gets a chance to take a "stab" at fingering the bad guy. Those who guess right win a prize. The playhouse scores points for having its programs planned well in advance. During past seasons, the mysteries to solve included *The Game Show Murders* and *Here's Killing You, Kid*. Performances are Wednesday, Friday, and Saturday at 7:30 p.m., with Monday and Thursday shows added sometimes during the busy summer months. Tickets for dinner and the show cost $39.95 or $29.95 for children 12 and under. Senior citizen, group, and other discounts are offered, and the Web site often offers coupons.

Rosie Rumpe's Regal Dumpe
Quality Inn
1402 Richmond Road
(757) 565-4443, (888) 767-9767
www.ontheline.com/group/
This three-hour dinner theater is billed as "Music, Magic & Medieval Mayhem at King Henry VIII's Favorite Tavern." Introduced in the spring of 1997, it's actually a lively (and somewhat bawdy) combination of acting, revelry, and singing set in a 16th-century London pub run by Rosie, of course. There's plenty of audience participation with a variety of "saucy serving wenches, minstrels, and court fools" (as well as Rosie and good old Henry himself). Oh, did we forget to mention all this is merely a side dish to the five-course meal served at your table? Served and consumed as part of the show, the meal includes soup and salad; a choice of entrees (prime rib, half a baked chicken, and marinated grilled tuna steak are the current selections); all the potatoes, veg-

etables, and homemade bread you can eat; coffee or tea (soft drinks are a single additional charge with unlimited refills); and dessert. Appetizers and bar drinks may be purchased separately.

If you're in need of multiple belly laughs (and a very full belly), call for show times and make a reservation. The cost is $37.95 per person and $23.95 for children 12 and younger, but check the Web site for coupons. Shows are typically offered on Friday and Saturday beginning at 7:30 p.m., with additional shows on Tuesday nights in May and June and sometimes Thursday nights during the peak summer season. "We like to say it's the most fun you've ever had...sitting down," says owner, director, and actor George Hasenstab. "Of course, we're going to embarrass you, but it's not done maliciously. We've found people love to play along." (We think it's obvious from the name alone, but we'll tell you point blank—if you decide to visit Rosie, leave younger children with a sitter.) The shows are rated PG-13, so parental discretion is advised.

AT THE MOVIES

In the past few years, movie options for residents have quadrupled. Not only have several multiplex theaters opened, but the Kimball Theatre on Merchants Square features foreign and arts pictures, much to the pleasure of area film lovers. Since the video revolution, which has allowed us to turn our living rooms into private viewing palaces, new movie rental stores seem to have popped up each week. Since they don't always last, we've listed below only the movie theaters in the area.

Kimball Theatre
428 Duke of Gloucester Street
(757) 565-8588
www.kimballtheatre.com
After an extensive renovation was completed in September 2001, this chandelier-lit, 538-seat theater appeared essentially as it did when it opened in 1933 as the Williamsburg Theatre. Even at that time it was state of the

art: The theater was equipped with the latest projection equipment, an air-conditioning system, and comfortable, cushioned seats. The current restoration was made possible by a $3 million gift from benefactors Bill and Gretchen Kimball of Belvedere, California. The theater is owned by the Colonial Williamsburg Foundation. It features Colonial Williamsburg evening programs, year-round artsy films, performing arts events, community lectures, and concerts. The box office is open from 1:00 to 9:00 p.m. daily.

ALTERNATIVE ACTION

For those who prefer the great outdoors once night falls, Colonial Williamsburg offers a number of historic and sometimes haunted evening tours. So put on your walking shoes and check these out.

Colonial Williamsburg Evening Tours
Historic Area
(800) HISTORY
www.history.org/visit/eventsAndExhibits/
colonialPerformances/
Special programs are offered every evening in Colonial Williamsburg to entertain and educate visitors. Colonial performances in the past have included "Williamsburg's Most Wanted," where visitors got to debate the guilt or innocence of some of the most notorious murderers in colonial times; "The Military by Night," where visitors experience camp life and battlefield situations, in the dark; the popular "Cry Witch," the dramatic trial of a "real" Virginia witch (Grace Sherwood), in which the audience participates in deciding her guilt or innocence; "Remember Me When Freedom Comes," a program of spirituals, work songs, and storytelling as the enslaved community brought to life the memories of a slave named Paris. Other programs included an 18th-century play, The Haunted House, and a re-creation of an 18th-century traveling circus and vaudeville show. Keep in mind that not all shows are appropriate for young children.

Evening tours require a fee above the price of your Colonial Williamsburg ticket, and prices vary depending on the performance. Tickets must be purchased prior to the event at any of the Colonial Williamsburg ticket locations, including the Visitor Center, Merchants Square ticket office, or Lumber House ticket office at the end of the Palace Green. To learn what's happening during your visit, check listings in your Colonial Williamsburg Visitor's Companion, a weekly publication available at the Visitor Center.

The Original Ghosts of Williamsburg Candlelight Tours
Historic Area
(757) 565-4821, (877) 62-GHOST
www.wmbggrouptourservices.com
When can the past make you gasp? At 8:00 p.m. every night of the week, if you choose to participate in a "ghosts" tour offered by a local tour company. Based on the book by L. B. Taylor Jr., the one-and-a-half-hour tour introduces you to legendary ghosts, folklore, and legends of the colonial capital. It actually is great fun and a nice alternative to the club scene. About 85,000 people take the spooky trek each year. Cost of the tour is $10; children six and younger participate without charge. Group rates are available, and reservations are required.

OUT-OF-TOWN NIGHTSPOTS

Hampton

Hampton Coliseum
1000 Coliseum Drive
(757) 838-4203
www.hamptoncoliseum.org
You never know what you'll find going on inside the coliseum, easily visible as you head east on I-64, about 30 to 40 minutes from Williamsburg. One week, The Beach Boys are in town. The next it's the Trans Siberian orchestra. And, if you come in February, you can catch clowns, big cats, and trapeze artists in the "Greatest Show on

Earth." To find out what's happening for the dates you plan to be in town, call the box office.

Norfolk

Harrison Opera House
160 East Virginia Beach Boulevard
(757) 877-2550, (866) OPERA-VA
www.vaopera.org
The Harrison is home to the Norfolk-based Virginia Opera, which was formed in 1975 and performs regular series in Norfolk, Richmond, and northern Virginia. Recent Norfolk operas have included *La Bohème, West Side Story, Othello, Porgy & Bess, Madame Butterfly, The Elixir of Love, The Tender Land, Il Trovatore,* and *H.M.S. Pinafore.* The opera house formerly was the Center Theater, which underwent a total restoration in 1993.

Norfolk Scope and Chrysler Hall
415 St. Pauls Boulevard
(757) 664-6464
Just a few blocks from the waterfront, the Norfolk Scope Cultural and Convention Center is really two venues that share the same address. The 13,800-seat dome-shaped Scope houses sporting events and big-name musicians. Old Dominion University plays many of its basketball games here, while Admirals hockey games and ice shows are also popular events. The circus usually makes an annual stop here, too. The more majestic Chrysler Hall is home to the Virginia

Symphony, and the Broadway Touring Company makes frequent visits, usually beginning in October. Among the more memorable performances have been *Grease* and *Jesus Christ Superstar.* For a schedule of Virginia Symphony events, call (757) 892-6366 or go to www.virginiasymphony.org.

The Norva
317 Monticello Avenue
(757) 627-4547
www.thenorva.com
Music has returned to this renovated building on Monticello Avenue. In the 1920s it served as a movie palace and home for vaudeville shows. Today this three-floor concert hall across from the MacArthur Center has hosted some of the top old and new names in the music business. Past performances have ranged from Motorhead and Pat McGee to A.F.I. and Suzanne Vega. One of the favorite spots to view the action is from the second-level balcony. There is limited off-street parking, but valet parking is available at the MacArthur Center mall.

Richmond

Classic Amphitheatre on Strawberry Hill
600 East Laburnum Avenue
(804) 345-7223
This outdoor arena on what used to be the state fairgrounds is now part of the Richmond Raceway Complex. Although it used to host the likes of Virginia's own Dave Matthews Band and country crooners Vince Gill and Alabama, there haven't been as many concerts lately. It's still a good idea to check out the local papers if you are in town because it is an enjoyable arena. The racetrack is the big draw. It hosts about a half-dozen races each season, including two Nextel NASCAR events. Its colorful history dates from its dirt-track days in the 1940s. Richard Petty's father, Lee Petty, won the first NASCAR-sanctioned race here in 1953. Today, drivers on the D-shaped oval travel in excess of 125 mph.

Southeastern Virginia can lay claim to some landmark places and occasions in rock 'n' roll history. Did you know, for instance, that Fort Monroe was the birthplace of country-rock renegade Steve Earle, or that rockabilly giant Gene Vincent (think "Be-Bop-A-Lula") hails from Norfolk? How about the fact that Missy "Misdemeanor" Elliott, one of America's hip-hop princesses, was born in Portsmouth and recorded her solo debut album at Master Sound Studio in Virginia Beach?

Richmond Coliseum
601 East Leigh Street
(804) 780-4970
www.richmondcoliseum.net
This is the place in Richmond to catch major sporting events and a variety of shows. Sports teams that call the coliseum home include the Richmond Renegades, an ice hockey team; and Richmond Speed, an indoor professional football team that debuted in 2000. Recent entertainers performing at the coliseum have included the Dixie Chicks, Aretha Franklin, and Shania Twain. For more information, you can call the box office, typically open 10:00 a.m. to 5:30 p.m. Monday through Friday, or Ticketmaster at (804) 262-8100.

Virginia Beach

Verizon Wireless
Virginia Beach Amphitheater
3550 Cellar Door Way
(757) 368-3000
www.livenation.com
It may be a bit of a drive (about 90 minutes on a good day), but this dazzling amphitheater draws the really big acts to Hampton Roads. New in 1996, the outdoor arena's first year brought Jimmy Buffet, The Eagles, James Taylor, and Sting to town. If you want comfort and a reserved seat under the pavilion, you will pay more. Lawn seats are the biggest savings, sometimes cutting the cost by as much as $20. But go early to claim your spot. The amphitheater has 7,500 reserved seats, with room for about 12,500 on the lawn. Don't worry, two giant screens on either side of the stage will get you a good view. Refreshments are available at every show. To purchase tickets by phone, call Ticketmaster locally at (757) 872-8100 or (757) 671-8100.

SHOPPING

While the Historic Triangle is known first and foremost for its venerable history, it is quickly building a reputation as an outlet-shopping mecca along the East Coast mega-lopolis. It is unique in that it offers shoppers myriad retail options—from outlet malls to quaint colonial shops selling items that, while familiar to people 300 years ago, are unusual and unique today.

The Williamsburg Pottery Factory, which has been drawing visitors since 1938, today pulls in nearly five million shoppers a year. It may be the granddaddy of retail outlets locally, but it faces competition from a growing number of stores offering visitors diversion.

What follows is a listing of most available shopping, though new stores open regularly, so be on the lookout. To make it as easy as possible for readers, we'll work from the colonial center of the city outward, disregarding restaurant, hotel, and motel gift shops unless we know of some special case. In general, you'll find specialty shops offering unique fine-quality items grouped in the heart of the city as well as in shopping centers scattered on the periphery and beyond.

If you're looking for manufacturers' outlet stores, head westward out Richmond Road (U.S. Route 60), where individual brand-name stores give way to multiple-outlet centers and finally to the famous Williamsburg Pottery Factory and its attached brand-name outlets. (See the Attractions chapter for more on the pottery.)

We caution you against thinking that all the fine shops are in the center of the city. Exquisite items and specialty purchases can be found in the small, private concerns scattered in shopping centers and among the large outlets, taking advantage of their high visibility and traffic. These shops cater to vis-itors who come to the city, but their existence depends upon the return clientele of Insiders they have developed over the years by offering quality, dependability, and good, friendly service.

Tidewater residents and shoppers from as far away as Washington, D.C., make regular visits to Williamsburg for special-occasion shopping throughout the year and especially at Christmas, taking advantage of the shipping service provided by most of the shops. If you don't see a sign indicating this service at a particular shop, be sure to inquire.

Don't take for granted, either, that "outlet" means "inexpensive." There are hundreds of bargains to be had, true, but only dedicated shopaholics (and you know who you are) will uncover the real finds combining high quality with low price. Of course, that's what makes shopping so much fun: the thrill of the hunt, the tension of competition, the joy of discovery, and the bragging rights when the trophies are brought home for display. Okay, we'll buy it if you tell us that it's not the money one spends, but the money one saves that provides the satisfaction. Sure.

From our own experience and from what we observe through the windows of automobiles departing the area, there's an awful lot of shopping satisfaction happening in Williamsburg.

THE HISTORIC AREA

Along Duke of Gloucester Street are several shops where colonial men and women made their purchases. Some are designed for the sale of items crafted on the premises by the artists and crafters you can observe hard at work. The Golden Ball Shop offers a variety of large and small metal-craft items, including

An open-air market in the Historic Area features flower bulbs and baskets. JOETTA SACK

ladies', gentlemen's, and children's fine jewelry in silver and gold, which can be engraved to order. The Colonial Post Office, a functioning branch of the U.S. Post Office, carries handmade papers, leather-bound books, maps, marbled paper, prints, and cartoons. The Raleigh Tavern Bakery (just follow your nose) provides oatmeal and ginger cookies, breads, apple "pasties," and refreshing cider. M. Dubois Grocer's Shop offers Smithfield hams, jams, relishes, and other colonial fare. General merchandise shops include Prentis

Store, Tarpley's Store, and Greenhow Store, carrying pottery, hats, games, toys, baskets, candles, pipes, handwoven linens, leather and wooden crafts, jewelry, and many more items. These shops are open year-round and are the places to find the perfect memento of your visit or the unique gift for a special occasion. The Colonial Nursery, an open-air market across from Bruton Parish Church, sells 18th-century plants, seeds, bulbs, and some pottery. An interpreter will be on hand to answer questions about 18th-century gardening. You can obtain other information about shopping in Colonial Williamsburg shops by calling (757) 229-1000. Also, see our chapter on Colonial Williamsburg.

THE CITY'S CENTER: MERCHANTS SQUARE AND ENVIRONS

Merchants Square, which centers on a block of Duke of Gloucester Street that today is closed to traffic, has a fascinating history all its own. When it was established in 1935, it really was the city's "shopping center." It was founded to allow for the relocation of businesses formerly scattered throughout the Historic Area. It catered primarily to locals and the small tourist trade of the day. It was formally named Merchants Square in 1964.

As Williamsburg and the surrounding counties grew, more businesses opened outside Merchants Square. At that point, Merchants Square businesses decided to focus more on providing goods and services demanded by the burgeoning tourist trade.

Designed to resemble a late 18th-century village, Merchants Square features brick walkways dotted with inviting wooden benches and shaded areas to rest, along with a combination of adjacent and satellite parking. It contains a fascinating mix of more than 40 shops, galleries, upscale clothiers, fine-food outlets, and several good restaurants. Hours are normally 10:00 a.m. to 6:00 p.m. Monday through Saturday and 12:00 to 5:00 p.m. on Sunday. Ample parking is provided in lots in the center of each block and on streets at the periphery. Parking behind the shops is free, but time limits are strictly enforced and tickets are regularly issued. Another option is the metered parking lot across Francis Street.

The shops are leased to independent merchants by the Colonial Williamsburg Foundation, which operates several businesses of its own on the square. The merchants operate under the guidance of the foundation in conjunction with the Merchants Square Association, established in the late 1960s and composed of retailers and business representatives that do cooperative advertising and sponsor a variety of promotions to draw shoppers and visitors to the area.

There's a wide variety of shops and eateries within Merchants Square, and every few months another new store pops up. Here's a roundup of some of our time-tested favorites; check merchantssquare.org/shops/ for a complete listing, addresses, and phone numbers.

Antique and contemporary quilts, high-quality traditional handcrafts, fabrics, and quilting supplies are for sale at **Quilts Unlimited**. You'll also find a selection of fine jewelry, clothing, toys, and Virginia handicrafts.

A welcome addition to Merchants Square has been the **Nancy Thomas Gallery**, featuring the internationally renowned work of folk artist Nancy Thomas of Yorktown. For more details see our entry in the Jamestown and Yorktown chapter.

While the **Campus Shop** offers gifts and apparel featuring the logo of the College of William and Mary, King's Treasure features a selection of small souvenirs of your stay in Williamsburg as well as gifts, stationery, and greeting cards.

Classic Cravats specializes in quality neckwear at affordable prices, including long ties, bow ties, pocket handkerchiefs, silk squares, and men's jewelry and accessories.

Shirley Pewter Shop, one of the longest-standing businesses on Merchants Square, offers pewter gifts, many of them made by hand in Williamsburg at their workshop on Jamestown Road. Engraving is done on the premises and often can be done the same day.

Aromas, a coffeehouse offering numerous blends and coffee-based drinks as well as light fare, is excellent for breakfast, lunch, dinner, or simply dessert or coffee after a show or movie.

The Colonial Williamsburg–owned **Craft House**, located at the corner of Merchants Square and Henry Street, sells authorized Williamsburg reproductions, including furniture, glassware, accessories, and other items whose prototypes are on display in the

There is a fascinating variety of shops on Merchants Square. JOETTA SACK

Historic Area. (The original Craft House is still open for business adjacent to the Williamsburg Inn.) Downstairs you'll find Sign of the Rooster, a pleasant little shop that features folk-art reproductions, stationery, small linens, and other gift items.

J. **Fenton Gallery** focuses on fine, contemporary American crafts. The emphasis is on unusual individual pieces by American artists, many from Virginia. The selection includes stained-glass fireplace screens, fountains, kaleidoscopes, pottery, handpainted clothing, puzzle boxes, and jewelry.

If you want to take a little of Colonial Williamsburg home with you, stop by **Everything Williamsburg.** You'll find sweatshirts and other CW-labeled apparel, jewelry, exclusive Colonial Williamsburg tavern china and accessories, and delicious specialty food products such as cider, jellies, and sauces.

At the **Carousel**, clothing and accessories for infants through preteens are the specialties. One-of-a-kind outfits, hand-smocked dresses, and clothing lines of small manufacturers are featured as well as a baby shower registry.

G. Bates Studio Workshop features seven tastefully appointed rooms in an enchanting display of decorating ideas. You'll also find gifts you'd normally have to travel the world to find.

Only the most self-disciplined can walk away from **Wythe Candy and Gourmet Shop** without at least one of its sweets or specialty foods. The homemade fudge is always excellent, but you'll also find candies and gourmet foods aplenty. Can't eat sugar? Fear not! The shop has a wonderful selection of sugar-free goodies, too.

The familiar 31-plus flavors, waffle cones, and soft drinks are available at **Baskin-Robbins Ice Cream & Frozen Yogurt** when you're ready for a treat. Sugar-free and 97 percent fat-free ice cream provide nice alternatives.

The range of foreign and domestic toys at **The Toymaker of Williamsburg** is amazing. Observe the crowd at the windows: The items on display captivate as many adults as children. The Toymaker sells Steiff, Brio, Galt, Playmobil, and many other name-brand items for children of all ages.

Birkenstock Footprints offers shoppers an array of footwear, including the world-famous sandals that made the company a household name.

Top designer fashions and other quality clothing for ladies are the specialties at **Binn's of Williamsburg**.

It's the happiest of seasons year-round in **The Christmas Shop**, which offers unusual Christmas ornaments and decorations.

Stop by Scotland House Ltd., which displays imported ladies' and gentlemen's apparel, tartan, heraldry, and gifts.

The Cheese Shop has cheeses, wines, picnics, and specialty foods galore. At lunchtime, Insiders like to buy one of the wonderful sandwiches from the take-out counter,

i Little boys go nuts over the wooden, old-fashioned popguns that can be found at The Toymaker of Williamsburg at Merchants Square.

select one of the many unusual beverages in the shop, and enjoy both while seated on one of Merchants Square's many benches. (See the Restaurants chapter for more details.)

The Silver Vault Ltd. offers a variety of treasures in silver and crystal, including unusual jewelry and accessories.

R. Bryant Ltd. offers traditional men's and boys' clothing with a flair for fresh designs in classic items. This locally owned shop has an on-premise tailor.

The Peanut Shop of Williamsburg sells crunchy home-style peanuts prepared in a variety of ways as well as Virginia hams and bacon and selected gifts.

At Merchants Square is the College of William and Mary Bookstore–**Barnes and Noble Bookstore** on the corner of Henry and Duke of Gloucester Streets. The block-long book-lovers paradise includes a cafe plus music and DVD selections upstairs, a William and Mary Spirit Shop and general reading materials on the main floor, and a floor devoted to textbooks on the lower level.

And if you need some cash for shopping, the main branch of **Sun Trust Bank** is located at the corner of Duke of Gloucester Street at Henry Street. Also, an ATM can be found 1 block north at Henry and Prince George Streets.

MORE DOWNTOWN SHOPPING

Within 2 blocks to the north and west of Merchants Square are other shops offering unique wares and services. Not affiliated with the square's merchants, these stores are equally worth investigating.

The Flower Cupboard
205 North Boundary Street
(757) 220-0057
www.flowercupboard.net
This florist specializes in beautiful 18th-century

arrangements, like those seen throughout the Historic Area, but they can also box up a dozen roses with the best of them.

Massey's Camera Shop
447 Prince George Street
(757) 229-3181

A full-service camera store, Massey's has an assortment of equipment and supplies as well as fine-quality developing services.

Mermaid Books
421-A Prince George Street
(757) 229-3603
www.mermaidbookswilliamsburg.com

Here you'll find a nice selection of used, out-of-print books and collectibles.

Parlett's Card and Gift Boutique
421 Prince George Street
(757) 229-7878

This long-established boutique sells traditional and creative greeting cards for every occasion, wrapping paper and ribbon, local crafts, colonial-style pierced-tin lanterns, and many unusual gifts.

Prince George Graphics
437 Prince George Street
(757) 229-7644

Beautiful prints, graphics, and posters from Prince George Graphics grace many of Williamsburg's homes, and the custom framing done in the shop is of the highest quality.

This Century Gallery
219 North Boundary Street
(757) 229-4949

As might be deduced from the name, the gallery displays contemporary crafts and art pieces. Frequent shows feature new artists' works. In a city devoted to its past, this is a refreshing place to shop. Gallery openings are an occasion for the city's art lovers to meet, socialize, and enjoy the featured artists' works.

Webster's Incredible Gifts
435 Prince George Street
(757) 253-8816

Webster's is the place to go if you're looking for just the right unusual gift or accent item. This little shop offers a great selection of high-quality items, often whimsical and sure to please.

ALONG JAMESTOWN ROAD

Old Chickahominy House Restaurant & Antiques
1211 Jamestown Road
(757) 229-4689

We love this place! The eatery part is covered in our Restaurants chapter, but the gift shop is worth investigating on its own merits. Antique furniture, 18th-century clocks, Dresden china, prints and oils, a Christmas shop with antique ornaments, and other gift items all are available in several quaint showrooms. The outside appearance belies the size of this establishment. Don't plan a quick visit or you'll be sorry.

Colony Square Shopping Center
1303 Jamestown Road
(no phone)

Located just west of Route 199, this busy, popular center draws most of its traffic from townsfolk and students because it is the most convenient center for Jamestown Road area neighborhoods. The busiest tenants are Eckerd drugstore, The Fresh Market, and The Polo Club Restaurant and Tavern (see Restaurants). Williamsburg Jewelers designs and creates exquisite items on the premises and offers excellent gifts and collectibles. Morrison's Flowers & Gifts provides FTD service and charming arrangements as well as special sales on cut roses. The Book Exchange of Williamsburg has more than 35,000 used paperbacks at half the cover price. You'll also find Hair Dimensions, Kinks, and Quirks and Caffeine (a wonderful gallery shop).

Bookpress Ltd.
1304 Jamestown Road
(757) 229-1260

A bibliophile's dream, Bookpress Ltd. offers antiquarian books, old prints, and maps. The staff is also helpful in locating and obtaining rare books. In a college town like Williamsburg, items related to the college are popular with students, alumni, and visitors alike. This is another shop where you'll kick yourself if you don't plan ahead and leave ample time to browse and enjoy.

Vernon Wooten Studio & Gallery
1315 Jamestown Road, Suite 204
(757) 253-1953

This small but important studio is open by appointment only. It's worth making that appointment, however, to view Wooten's originals in oil, watercolor, and acrylic. Framed and unframed limited editions of his prints are available. Limited editions are collectors' items.

TK Oriental Antiques
1654 Jamestown Road
(757) 229-7720

A showroom full of Eastern items awaits you at TK's. You'll want to visit often since new pieces come in all the time. They don't just house and sell their collection—restoration of antiques and fine items is their specialty.

Carrot Tree Kitchen
1782 Jamestown Road
(757) 229-0957

Talk about mouthwatering! At one time Debi Helseth operated a wholesale bakery out of her kitchen, but at last it found a site open to the public as part of the Carrot Tree Lodging. The carrot cake is popular with many Insiders, but our favorite is the coconut cake. You'll have to try them both and all the others as well. But there's more than baked goods here. A small dine-in seating area allows you to try their soup of the day, salads, ham biscuits, and other goodies. We bet you'll return.

ON JOHN TYLER HIGHWAY (ROUTE 5)

Trevillian Furniture and Interiors
3301 Venture Lane
(757) 229-9505

If you're looking for home furnishings and accessories, check this place out. It offers fine furnishings and interior decorating services as well as a popular moving and transport service (they are especially skilled with antiques and prized items).

Five Forks Shopping Center
4490 John Tyler Highway
(no phone)

This is a small center serving the developments that have sprung up around it. The outparcel is home to a branch of Chesapeake Bank. Center businesses include Amory Music, where local musicians go for supplies, scores, and instruments, Two Sisters Pizza, and Williamsburg Realty.

Governor's Green
4511 John Tyler Highway
(no phone)

This small but busy strip center offers a variety of basic services for locals—but it also draws lots of visitors. The anchor store is the Winn Dixie Marketplace. This super grocery also has a pharmacy, photo center, on-site restaurant, and catering service. Centura Bank and McDonald's occupy two outparcels. Also located here are Master Cleaners, Cities Grille (see Restaurants chapter), Margeaux's Florist, Margeaux's Party & Cards, Supercuts (no appointment needed), Eckerd drugstore, and Ace Hardware.

Williamsburg Crossing Shopping Center
5251 John Tyler Highway
(no phone)

Williamsburg Crossing, as locals refer to this center, anchors the intersection of Route 199 and Route 5. Along the front of the center, you'll find an enlarged and refurbished Food Lion grocery store, with its deli and bakery. At the other end of the center is the seven-screen Carmike Cinemas. Other tenants include Berkeley Pharmacy, Hair Essentials, The Coffeehouse, The Corner Pocket (billiards and light food fare), Courtyard Cafe, Dairy Queen, Mail Boxes Etc., Papa John's Pizza carry-out, Laney's Diamonds & Jewelry, Scrapbook Crossing (children's art and educational supplies), Subway deli sandwiches, Taco Bell, Video Update, Walls Alive, Nail Uptown, The Framery, Nam's Cleaners & Tailor, Top's China carry-out, and Merle Norman cosmetics.

ON AND OFF BYPASS ROAD

Bassett's Classic Christmas Shop
207 Bypass Road
(757) 229-7648
Fans of the holiday season find Bassett's an excellent store to hunt for ornaments, trees, Madame Alexander dolls, and other fine gift items.

Cracker Barrel Old Country Store
200 Bypass Road
(757) 220-3384
Attached to a restaurant familiar to travelers in the South, the gift shop here offers an eclectic assortment of items from clothing and candles to candies, all in keeping with the establishment's country (and the emphasis is on mountain country) theme. Can't make up your mind about an item? Have a bite to eat, then decide.

Kingsgate Greene Shopping Center
120 Waller Mill Road
(no phone)
Big Kmart is the most visible store you see from the street, but there are other noteworthy shops here as well. In the center of the

i For a restful interlude on a sunny day, get a Cheese Shop sandwich and soft drink to eat on a bench at Merchants Square. Then feed the crumbs to the chimney swallows that gather for a handout.

"L," three popular restaurants have merged. Enter Peking and Mongolian Grill, which also serves Japanese cuisine (see our Restaurants chapter). Other occupants of the center include Movie Scene, Domino's Pizza, and The Hair Cuttery.

ON U.S. ROUTE 60 EAST

Festival Marketplace
264 McLaws Circle
(no phone)
Located just east of the Route 199 intersection, this small but bustling strip center is home to Maurizio, the National Pancake House (both also covered in the Restaurants chapter), the Tidewater Virginia AAA office, Pro Temps, Kingsmill Jewelers, GSH Real Estate, PostNet: Postal & Business Services, and The Hair Shop.

Marketplace at Kingsmill
240 McLaws Circle
(no phone)
This busy little shopping center in the round is abuzz with a variety of retail shops, service businesses, and one particularly popular restaurant. Also located here are Sir Speedy Printing, Shear Creations, Kingsmill Food Mart (a deli and wine shop), Swan Cleaners, Marketplace Texaco (with a quick and cheap car wash), Circus Train Ltd., Colony Insurance Agency, Molly Maid, Sue Mayberry Travel, Inc., Starbucks Coffee, Riverside Plastic Surgery, Family Dentistry, and Liberty Mutual Insurance. It's also home to the always-popular The Sportsman's Grille restaurant (see the Restaurants chapter), which kids love as much as adults. The sports-themed menu is as fun as the food is delicious and the service attentive.

The Village Shops at Kingsmill
1915 Pocahontas Trail
(757) 873-2020
The charming and varied shopping center, gives the impression of a small village whose narrow lanes are lined with shops and services. Its feeling is European rather than Ameri-

can colonial, more in keeping with nearby Busch Gardens than with Colonial Williamsburg. The items for sale are first quality, and there are many one-of-a-kind selections. Insiders shop at The Pottery Wine & Cheese Shop for the low prices on those items and the variety of gourmet foods on display. Other tenants include Performing Arts Limited, Cambridge Exchange, Baggs of Thrift Avenue, The Lemon Twist, The Art of Photography, East Baker Street, Virginia Capital Advisors, C. Ritz Interiors, The Trimble Collection, Mr. Liu's Chinese Restaurant & Lounge, Eastern Virginia School for the Performing Arts, Le Yaca French restaurant, Oriental Textile Arts, Doraldo's Italian restaurant, American Harvest, Village Jewelers, The Great Entertainer, Silent Sparrow Framing, Haus Tirol—The Stitching Well, Cattails, Two in a Zoo, Lightfoot Manor Shoppe, U-Travel Service, A Logo for You, The Personal Touch, Michelle's Potpourri, the Williamsburg Hotel-Motel Association, Village Flower Shop, High Cotton Ltd., Antiques, and Lankford & Company.

Carter's Cove
8758 Pocahontas Trail
(757) 220-0386
The totem poles in front of this trading post make it easy to spot. Inside you will find Native American art and crafts created by artists of various tribes throughout the nation. We especially like the pottery and jewelry, but the staff is extremely helpful in advising you on some of the more unusual items such as drums and pipes. Carter's Cove also serves as a camp store for the adjoining campground, offering a game room and a variety of sodas, snacks, and camping gear for its campground guests.

ON MERRIMAC TRAIL

Williamsburg Farm
Fresh Shopping Center
455 Merrimac Trail
(no phone)
The anchor here is the huge Farm Fresh Super Store, which is open all night. In addition, there is a variety of stores in its two adjacent sections.

James York Plaza
701 Merrimac Trail
(no phone)
The Dollar General Store and Eckerd drugstore are the big draws at this shopping center on Merrimac Trail.

ON AND OFF RICHMOND ROAD (U.S. ROUTE 60)

Master Craftsmen
255 Richmond Road
(757) 253-2993
This fine artisan's shop offers high-quality, handcrafted jewelry, hand-spun pewter, and a variety of beautiful keepsakes in silver and gold. They also provide engraving services.

Williamsburg Shopping Center
157 Monticello Avenue
(no phone)
This was the first "modern" shopping center in the city, developed in the 1960s. Together with the adjacent Monticello Shopping Center, it is the heart of commerce for the residents of Williamsburg and students at the College of William and Mary. Stores include Stein Mart Department Store, carrying clothing, jewelry, accessories, and household items; Bloom Grocery, Ace Peninsula Hardware, CVS drugstore, Radio Shack, Books A Million with its own cafe called Joe Muggs Coffee, an ABC store, and Fashion Bug & Fashion Bug Plus. Also you'll find a variety of dining options: Chez Trinh (Vietnamese cuisine), Sal's by Victor (Italian), Miyako Japanese Restaurant, and Padow's Hams & Deli. (Please see our Restaurants chapter for more detailed information on several of these.) Kinko's Copy Center is open 24 hours and offers copying, printing, publishing, and other business support services. Blue Ridge Mountain Sports provides complete outfitting for outdoor adventurers.

Monticello Shopping Center
218 Monticello Avenue
(no phone)

Located 1 block off Richmond Road, the four screens at Carmike Cinema 4 are a popular attraction. This shopping center faces Williamsburg Shopping Center across Monticello Avenue. Other tenants here include the Children's Hospital of the King's Daughters Thrift Shop, Nawab Indian Cuisine, Staples, Pet World, Pizza Hut Carry Out, and Big Lots.

Monticello Marketplace
Monticello Avenue
(no phone)

One of the area's crown jewels of shopping is this bustling shopping center, located off the Monticello Avenue extension. The anchor stores are two: Target and Ukrop's, the latter a regionally famous, multiservice grocery and everything-except-alcoholic-beverages store under a single roof. Alcohol can be purchased in the center at the state-run ABC store. Outparcels here include Burger King, Ruby Tuesday, and Chick-Fil-A restaurants and two banks: Wachovia and First Union Bank. Other tenants include T. J. Maxx, Parcel Plus, Discount Cleaners, California Closets, wear else, The Mole Hole, GNC Nutrition Center, TCBY, Blimpie Subs & Salads, The Wine Seller, dentists, Hallmark Cards, School Crossing, Wild Birds Unlimited, Goodman & Sons Jewelers, Mattress Discounters, Heaven & Earth, Bike Beat, Perfect Edge Salon & Spa, 20/20 Eyecare, Blockbuster Video, Dollar Tree, Rack Room Shoes, A&N, Williamsburg Bagels, Bakery & Cafe, and Shacklefords II Restaurant, a full-service restaurant, serving lunch and dinner.

Auto Parts and Supply Inc.
225 Monticello Avenue
(757) 229-3580

Adjacent to the Carmike Cinemas at Monticello Shopping Center sits this small but helpful auto parts supply store. If they don't have what you're looking for, they'll gladly order it for you—and at a reasonable price.

Williamsburg Professional Pharmacy
1302 Mount Vernon Drive
(757) 229-3560

This long-standing drugstore is conveniently located across Monticello Avenue from Williamsburg Community Hospital. Full pharmacy and drug services are available.

Whitley's Virginia Peanuts and Peanut Factory
1351 Richmond Road
(757) 229-4056

You'll find delicious "home-cooked" Virginia peanuts, Virginia hams, gift baskets, and other goods from the Commonwealth, all available for you to carry out or mail order back home.

Civil War and Native American Store and Gallery
1441 Richmond Road
(757) 253-1155

At first glance this mix under a single roof seems odd. Civil War items for sale include pewters, replica guns, pistols, swords, and other memorabilia and collectibles. You can also find limited-edition prints and paintings and flags. Native American arts and crafts, jewelry, pottery, dolls, and more—the vast majority made by Native Americans—are also sold here.

Jefferson Walk
1505 Richmond Road
(no phone)

This little cluster of shops offers a variety of goods and services popular with locals and visitors. Located here is Action Electronics, Souvenirs N' Stuff, and Shear Perfection hair salon.

Edwards' Virginia Ham Shoppe of Williamsburg
1814 Richmond Road
(757) 220-6618

This mouthwatering little shop sells Surry hickory-smoked hams and bacon direct from the family smokehouse, plus a variety of Virginian specialty foods, including jellies, jams, flours, cake and pie mixes, craft items, and more. They'll wrap and ship, too, at your request.

The Christmas Mouse
1991 Richmond Road
(757) 221-0357
www.christmasmouse.com

Chock-full of goodies for everyone's favorite season, The Christmas Mouse is open all year. Through their windows you'll see dozens of trees lighted and decorated with unique items. Inside you'll find more things associated with the holidays than you ever imagined possible. A second store is just past the Pottery in Norge.

Attic Collections
2229 Richmond Road
(757) 229-0032

This minimall in a single building includes several individual shops. Don't let the size of the building fool you. More than 4,000 square feet of treasures reside here, including the useful and the whimsical, the elegant and the amusing. The largest items are furniture pieces, but there is glassware from the 18th century forward (including Depression glassware), buttons, marbles, books, postcards, prints, paintings, posters, lamps, kitchenware, toys, vintage clothing, accessories, and jewelry. Attic Collections is closed Tuesday and Wednesday. Upstairs, you'll find Forget-Me-Nots and Sugar and Spice, which carry consignment clothing for adults and children, respectively.

ALONG U.S. ROUTE 60 WEST

Patriot's Plaza Outlets
3044 Richmond Road
(757) 258-0767

The first of the outlet malls you'll find as you shop your way westward, this plaza offers a variety of premium stores, including Lenox, Dansk Factory Outlet, Izod, the Polo Ralph Lauren Factory Store, Plow & Hearth, Villeroy & Boch, Leather Loft, Totes, and Fila.

Carolina Furniture of Williamsburg
5421 Richmond Road
(757) 565-3000
www.carolinafurniture.com

This shop, with its large selection of furniture in varied styles and price ranges, is known for high quality and excellent service. Don't miss their scratch and dent and remnant room in the little building to the left of the main store. You buy it, and they'll ship it anywhere you want.

Carolina Carpets
5425 Richmond Road
(757) 565-3006

A sister store to Carolina Furniture, Carolina Carpets is the Williamsburg outlet for Karastan goods, offered at discounts of 40 to 60 percent. Broadloom carpeting and one-of-a-kind Oriental rugs also are discounted—another reason to stop in. Countrywide shipping service makes this store convenient to your home, wherever you live.

Williamsburg Brass, Lighting & Textiles
5425 Richmond Road
(757) 565-4545

This wonderful store features Virginia Metalcrafters and Baldwin Brass products along with period lighting fixtures, wallpaper, and fabrics you can select to create a Williamsburg feeling to your decor.

The Pennsylvania House
Collector's Gallery
5425 Richmond Road
(757) 565-3535

Specializing in comfortable solid cherry, oak, maple, or pine furniture, The Pennsylvania House offers at least 40 percent off the suggested list price.

Ewell Station Shopping Center
5609 Richmond Road
(757) 565-4526

This well-maintained shopping center mainly serves residents in the western end of the area and saves them the drive into town for basic services. Visitors and townsfolk enjoy Peking Restaurant, with its fine cuisine. Giuseppe's Italian Cafe is an extremely popular trattoria, providing delicious and creative dishes. Among other tenants are Bloom grocery store, Rite Aid Pharmacy, Swan Cleaners, The Hair Shop, Prime Time Video, Subway, Hayashi Japanese Restaurant & Sushi Bar, Community Care, Bed Crafters, CI Travel, and Doctors Vision Center.

Prime Outlets at Williamsburg
5699 Richmond Road
(757) 565-0702
www.primeoutlets.com

This expanded outlets mall, which faces Richmond Road on your left as you head west, features the top of the line in designer and fine name brands. There are great savings ranging from 20 to 70 percent on items in these shops. Tenants include Aeropostale, Ann Taylor Factory Stores, Anne Klein Factory Store, Banana Republic Factory Store, Bass Outlet, Ben & Jerry's, Bombay Outlet, BOSE Factory Store, Brooks Brothers Factory Store, Carter's Childrenswear, Clarks Bostonian, Coach Factory, Cole-Haan, Cosmetics Company Store, Crabtree & Evelyn, Dana Buchman, Designer Fragrance & Cosmetics Company, Dooney & Bourke, Eddie Bauer, Etienne Aigner, Fragrance Outlet, Gap Outlet, Geoffrey Beene, Guess? Factory Store, Gymboree Outlet, Haggar Clothing Co., Harry and David, Hush Puppies, IZOD, J. Crew, Jockey, Jones New York, Jones New York Sport, Kasper A.S.L., Kitchen Collection, Koret, Le Creuset, L'eggs-Hanes-Bali-Playtex Express, L. L. Bean Factory Store, Le Gourmet Chef, Liz Claiborne, Maidenform, Michael Kors, Mikasa Factory Store, Motherhood & Maternity Outlet, Movado Company Store, Naturalizer, Nautica, Nike Factory Store, Nine West Outlet, Oakley, OshKosh B'Gosh, Perfumania, Reebok Factory Direct Store, Rockport Factory Direct Store, Rocky Mountain Chocolate Factory, Samsonite Company Store, Saucony, SEIKO: The Company Store, Strasburg Children, Stride Rite/Sperry/Keds, Sunglass Hut/Watch Station International, Tahari, Timberland Outlet Store, Tommy Hilfiger Company Store, Sunglass World, Ultra Diamond & Gold, Under Armour, Van Heusen Direct Store, Vans, Waterford Wedgwood Outlet, Wilson's Leather Outlet, and Zales Fine Jewelry Outlet.

IN LIGHTFOOT

Candy Store Factory Warehouse Outlet
6623 Richmond Road
(757) 565-1151

You can't miss the big barn-shaped building across the street from the Pottery. If any young ones are in the car, they won't let you. The Wythe-Will Distributing Company has stocked the shelves of this specialty shop with many of the fine chocolates that it stocks at both the Henry Street Chocolatier and the Wythe Candy and Gourmet Shop in Merchants Square. There is everything from saltwater taffy to Ghirardelli chocolates. Here's a warning: It will be hard to leave without a sample of the homemade fudge. The Candy Store also carries a line of Virginia-made products, including wines, peanuts, hams, jellies, and apple butter.

The Colonial Town Plaza Shops
6965 Richmond Road
(no phone)

This strip center, which has been around for years, is a collection of several buildings housing a variety of shops. You'll find The Williamsburg Brass Shop, Brand Name Sofa Outlet, Fort Cherokee, and Music Land.

The Gallery Shops at Lightfoot
6580 Richmond Road
(no phone)

Our favorite shop here is A Touch of Earth, Williamsburg's oldest American crafts gallery, offering highly prized American craft work by

i Pop into the College of William and Mary Bookstore on Duke of Gloucester Street for a cozy sweatshirt if the evenings are too nippy for you.

There's nothing that perks up a gloomy day better than a special "Gloom Chaser" from A Touch of Earth in The Gallery Shops—we've seen them in homes around the country!

fine artists in many media. (Be sure to take a "Gloom Chaser" home!) In this popular center, you'll also find Boyers Diamond & Gold outlet (featuring custom designs and wholesale prices on finest-quality items), N.Y. Deli, Kwik Kopy/Ardsen Printing, and Sugar & Spice consignment apparel.

Lightfoot Antiques Mall & Country General Store
7003 Richmond Road
(757) 229-8759

The masked pumps out front indicate that this once was the site of a small gas station. Today the building, located adjacent to the Colonial Town Plaza Shops, is home to myriad antiques, collectibles, and assorted attic treasures. The showroom is packed with lots of goodies, from used skis and old furniture to mantelpieces, lanterns, musical instruments, picture frames, weathervanes, glassware, needlework, and old-timey telephones. If you have a couple of hours to spend digging through the stacks, you just might find that special something you've been looking for but couldn't find elsewhere.

Piano-Organ Outlet
6315 Richmond Road
(757) 564-9592

This freestanding shop is very visible on the north side of the highway as you approach Lightfoot. The keyboard selection in this store is extensive, and prices are very reasonable.

Pottery Factory Outlets
U.S. Route 60 West
(757) 564-3326

Located on US 60 west on the grounds of the Williamsburg Pottery Factory, these outlets include Pfaltzgraff Pottery, Glass Elite, Oneida Silversmiths, Totes, Christopher's Leather, King Neptune's Treasures, Out of Africa, The Pecan Factory, Rolane Factory Outlet, Black & Decker, Banister Shoes, Westport Ltd., Peanut Shack, Tobacco Outlet, Mr. Peepers Sunglasses, Pens Plus, Rug Gallery, Silver Dragon, and Van Heusen. See the Pottery section of the Attractions chapter for more details.

Williamsburg Antique Mall
500 Lightfoot Road
(757) 565-3422
www.antiqueswilliamsburg.com

Tucked away off US 60 in Lightfoot (but visible from Route 199) is this incredible collection of 400 dealers of antiques and collectibles. This place is unique in that you wander freely, picking up goodies you wish to buy (they supply handy baskets to hold your newly found treasures), and then you leave via a central checkout area. You'll find just about anything from furniture, jewelry, glass, old photos, clocks, pottery, frames, clothing and decorative textiles, boxes, toys, cameras, and more. Open seven days a week.

Williamsburg Outlet Mall
6401 Richmond Road
(757) 565-3378, (800) SHOP-333

There are more than 50 factory outlet stores and plenty of benches for tired shoppers' companions in Williamsburg's only enclosed mall. The single-story structure is arranged in a cross shape, with food courts in the center and the long portion extending away from the highway frontage. The shops offer from 20 to 70 percent off regular retail prices.

Tenants include Antiques & Estate Jewelry, Avon, Bass Shoe Outlet, Bon Worth, Bruce Alan Bags, Capacity, Claire's Boutiques, Crafter's Market, Dexter Shoes, Diamonds Unlimited, Dockers Outlet, Dress Barn Woman, Famous Brands Housewares, Famous Footwear, Farberware, Gold Toe, Jockey, L'eggs-Hanes-Bali-Playtex, Levi's Outlet, Linen Barn, New Concept Gifts, Newport News Outlet, Oreck Vacuums, The Paper Factory, Rack Room Shoes, Rue 21, S&K Menswear, Silver

i If you have a green thumb, stop in at the landscaping nursery at the Williamsburg Pottery, where you will find everything from trees and shrubs to herbs and flowering plants.

Stream, Sunglass World, Swank, Totes, Toy Liquidators, Vitamin World, Watch World, We R Nuts, and Zap Electronics.

Williamsburg Pottery Factory
US 60 West
(757) 564-3326
www.williamsburgpottery.com
A shopping mecca that is featured in its own section in the Attractions chapter of this book, the Pottery is in a class by itself. There are 39 buildings and 8,000 parking spots waiting for shoppers at this monumental business, less a factory than a bazaar with an international array of goods displayed along miles of shelves. Between two and four million visitors a year shop at this area landmark, coming in bus caravans from all over. Don't miss this "shop 'til you drop" experience. For more details, flip to the Attractions chapter.

IN NORGE

Williamsburg Clocks
110 Peninsula Street
(757) 564-0107
This charming shop, located in an old Victorian house 1 block west of US 60, is a must for collectors. Insiders know this is the place in town to look for clocks—old and new—or have your family heirloom repaired. The showroom is filled with grandfather clocks, mantel clocks, antiques galore, and more. The surprise here, however, is the incredible collection of music boxes for men, women, and children. Services include repair and restoration of music boxes, too. Owners Keith and Louise Clayton-Kastenholz provide service with a personal touch. Can't get to them? They'll come to you. Just give them a call.

Williamsburg Doll Factory
7441 Richmond Road
(757) 564-9703
You can watch production of Lady Anne Porcelain Dolls during your visit here. The Doll Factory also offers dollhouses galore, doll supplies of all kinds, fine stuffed animals, and, of course, a huge selection with just the right doll to join your family.

Williamsburg Soap & Candle Company
7521 Richmond Road
(757) 564-3354
You can observe soap and candles being made in the Candle Factory, the anchor store for this cluster of shops. The Candle Shop has hundreds of unique candles and soaps crafted on-site. From the observation room, you can watch the candles and soaps being made and even view a video on the candle-making process. The specialty stores around the "factory" offer a complete shopping experience, so plan to spend some time here. The Christmas House is full of novelties for the holiday season. Barney's Country Store has a variety of country-living items. Emporium offers a selection of international gifts and greeting cards. The Tapestry Outlet features throws, wall hangings, pillows, table runners, and other textile home accessories. Needlecrafts sells quilts, fabrics, needlework supplies, and quilting accessories. Candle Factory Restaurant is popular with locals for breakfast, lunch, and dinner (see the Restaurants chapter).

The Williamsburg Wicker and Rattan Shoppe
7422 Richmond Road
(757) 565-3620
A charming Victorian house shop features many fine lines of wicker and rattan, including

i The candles used in the 1998 film *Practical Magic*, starring Sandra Bullock and Nicole Kidman, were manufactured at the Candle Factory on Richmond Road.

Henry Link, Lane Venture, Lloyd Flanders, and Ficks Reed. Shipping is provided.

IN TOANO

Basketville of Williamsburg Inc.
7761 Richmond Road
(757) 566-8420

A tisket, a tasket...If you've lost your Easter basket, make a trip to this sprawling shop that sells several hundred kinds of baskets from around the world, along with wicker furniture, dried flowers, and home accessories in wood and wicker, as well as sundry other items.

Charlie's Antiques and Repairs
7766 Richmond Road
(757) 566-8300

Called "the largest in the area," this unique shop offers a selection of American and imported antique and reproduction furniture, much of which is hand-carved solid mahogany. The continental antiques are unusual in an area so replete with English

items. Shipping and wholesale and retail prices are offered. Closed Tuesday and Wednesday.

The Farm House
7787 Richmond Road
(757) 566-8344

You can't miss this store—there's a selection of items sitting out front along the highway. Inside is an assortment of furniture for house, porch, and garden at extremely attractive prices. Clean out the trunk—you must transport what you purchase. Closed Sunday.

Toano Toy Works
8003 Richmond Road
(757) 566-0171

All the toys made here are wooden, and the selection is overwhelming. These are keepsake items certain to be prized through the years. Noah's arks, rocking and stick horses, games, cars, trains, and boats are among the many creative items you'll find displayed. These unique treasures make excellent gifts for youngsters, particularly of preschool age.

VIRGINIA'S INDIAN CULTURE

In the early 1600s the wilds of Virginia represented a brave New World to the English colonists struggling to start a new life along the region's exotic shores. But there already was one civilization that was hundreds of generations old and thriving—that of the Virginia Indians.

Nomadic hunters had occupied the region from as early as 10,000 B.C. After 5000 B.C., Woodland Indians established more permanent settlements and began cultivating the land. When European settlers came, they found Algonquian Indians, thought to have arrived around A.D. 1000, living in longhouses, hunting, fishing, and growing crops, notably corn. Some 32 different tribes, ruled by Chief Powhatan, inhabited the area in the early 1600s.

However, this thriving culture couldn't withstand European diseases and the other stresses that came with colonization. As the Virginia colony flourished and settlers continued to arrive, the indigenous peoples were deprived of more and more of their ancestral land. Within 100 years the population of Virginia Indians dropped by 85 percent. By 1700, their numbers had dwindled to 15 percent of what it had been 100 years earlier.

But the influence of the native tribes can be seen in the culture of the Historic Triangle today. The stories of Powhatan (whose real name was Wahunsonacock) and his daughter Pocahontas, the Indian princess who married Englishman John Rolfe and went to live in London, are part of the region's historic lore. Place names derived from the Indians are omnipresent; throughout southeastern Virginia, there are Powhatan and Pocahontas parkways, motels, condominiums, and stores. While the Algonquian language, never written, has vanished, a number of Algonquian words—squash, succotash, opossum, tomahawk—are now part of everyday American English.

Artifacts uncovered during archaeological digs in the Historic Triangle have provided a mother lode of information about the lives of the earliest inhabitants of Virginia. A dig at Governor's Land at Two Rivers, for instance, produced new data about the Pasbehegh Indians, whose village was the first to be destroyed by Jamestown settlers. Finds at the site, which may date from 1500, include ceramics and a burial pit containing copper beads. At Jamestown Island and Jamestown Settlement, there are statues, displays, and living-history programs that focus on the role of Virginia Indians in the settlement of the New World. Across the York River in Gloucester County, archaeologists from the College of William and Mary have found what was likely the principal residence of Powhatan and his village. The owners of a farm on the York River found artifacts and notified archaeologists, who after extensive digging discovered a massive concentration of artifacts that indicate that the site was a substantial village settlement dating from colonial times. The finding was announced in May 2003.

But what about the descendants of these tribes of yore who met, traded with, sometimes massacred, and ultimately were overpowered by the European settlers? In Virginia eight different tribes dating from at least 200 years ago are recognized by the state. Census data from 1990 show that about 21,172 people living in the Old Dominion call themselves Virginia Indians, and that several remnant tribes of the Powhatan Confederacy live within an hour or so of Williamsburg. Until very recently the lives of Virginia's contemporary Indians often seemed obscured by our fascination with history and stereotypes, not to mention Hollywood myth. While Virginia's Indians, including those living on reservations, are largely assimilated into mainstream society, the preservation of heritage is of vital importance to them. The information we've listed below about the region's Indians and their programs, events, and ongoing traditions is proof that their culture is alive and thriving here today. You can call the phone numbers listed to learn more about the tribe; the number given is not necessarily that of the chief, whose name is also included with each entry.

TRIBES

Chickahominy
Charles City County
(804) 829-2027
www.chickahominytribe.org
Chief Stephen Adkins
The name Chickahominy means "coarse-ground corn people." Close to 1,000 Chicka-hominy Indians live in the United States, with the largest concentration in Charles City County. The Chickahominy have never been reservation Indians; at the heart of their active community are the Samaria Baptist Church and Charles City Primary School.

While the Chickahominy are largely assimilated into mainstream American society, tribe members maintain strong ties with each other and work at passing on their traditions. The fourth Saturday and Sunday of every September, the Chickahominy Indian Fall Festival and Powwow is held on the tribal grounds, with activities including traditional dances and handmade jewelry exhibitions. Many of the traditional dances are performed by the Chickahominy Redman Dancers.

To find out more information about the First People of Virginia, write the Virginia Council on Indians, P.O. Box 1475, Richmond, VA 23218, call (804) 225-2084, or visit www.indians.vipnet.org.

Eastern Chickahominy
New Kent County
(804) 966-2719
Chief Marvin "Strong Oak" Bradby
About 150 members of this division of the Chickahominy tribe became residents of New Kent County, 25 miles east of Richmond, in 1925. This relatively new organization carries on the responsibility of educating and administering to the religious needs of members. The Eastern Chickahominy church is Tsena Commocko Baptist in New Kent.

Mattaponi Reservation
Off Route 30 at Route 626, West Point
(804) 769-7745
Chief Webster "Little Eagle" Custalow
The name Mattaponi is an Anglicized version of the original *Mattapanient,* which may mean "landing place." Of the 500 members of the tribe, some 63 Mattaponi Indians live on a 125-acre reservation established in 1658 north of the Pamunkey River. These residents are the descendants of Indians who once served and worshipped the Great Spirit, their god of the heavens, sun, moon, and stars. Today the members of this tribe are Southern Baptists who have made their church a center of their community's activities. In the 17th century, Powhatan and his successor, Opechaneough, are said to have visited here. Today the tribe is self-governed by a chief and council. A pottery now occupies the old reservation schoolhouse; potters fashion both traditional and nontraditional objects, using clays from the riverbanks and from commercial sources. Visitors may purchase these handmade pieces. The Wahun-sunakah Drum Group, which performs traditional drumming, operates out of the reservation. The reservation—situated on the banks of the Mattaponi River—welcomes visitors from 2:00 to 5:00 p.m. Saturday and Sunday.

Pamunkey Reservation
Off Route 30,
King William County
(804) 843-4792, (804) 843-2032
Chief William P. "Swift Water" Miles

While the Pamunkey were once the most powerful people in the Powhatan Confederacy, today fewer than 100 live on their 1,200-acre reservation in King William County. The Great Chief Powhatan and his daughter Pocahontas once lived among the Pamunkey empire of 10,000 people. Indeed, Chief Powhatan governed territory that spread from Washington, D.C., to North Carolina. The reservation in King William County is now on the Virginia Historical Landmarks Register. Pamunkey women founded a potters' guild in the 1930s, and today they're dedicated to preserving the traditional coil-and-pinch method of making pots, using clay collected from the banks of the Pamunkey River. Etched bowls, vases, jugs, pipes, and other handcrafted items are sold at the reservation. The reservation is about 40 minutes from Williamsburg, along Secondary Route 633 off of Route 30. Visitors are welcome anytime.

Upper Mattaponi
Off Route 30,
northwestern King William County
(804) 769-0041
Chief Kenneth Adams
www.uppermattaponi.org
The Upper Mattaponi Indians, an urban, non-reservation group who trace their origins to both the Mattaponi and Pamunkey Reservations, reside in northwestern King William County. The tribe is developing a new cultural village across from its house of worship, the Indian View Baptist Church.

The Upper Mattaponi Tribal Center is on Route 30, about a mile southeast of Route 360. The tribe holds its meetings at the center. The tribal center is housed in a brick building that tribal forefathers had helped

i One of the oldest shad hatcheries in the nation has been replaced with a newly equipped one at the Mattaponi Reservation in West Point. In 2004 the tribe returned eight million endangered shad to the Mattaponi River.

build and that had once been a school. The Upper Mattaponi has its annual Native American Powwow and Spring Festival on the Saturday of Memorial Day weekend on the tribal grounds across the street from the tribal center. This event offers Native American dancing and drumming, storytelling, arts and crafts, children's games, native food and refreshments, miniature-horse rides, and more. Cost is $5 for adults, $3 for children younger than 12. The Powwow runs from 10:00 a.m. to 5:00 p.m. Visitors are encouraged to bring lawn chairs. Write to the center for more information about the Upper Mattaponi, at P.O. Box 182, King William County, VA 23086, or go to www.baylink.org/mattaponi.

OTHER TRIBES

There are several other Indian tribes that are recognized by the Commonwealth of Virginia. They include the Monacan, whose 1,400 members primarily live in Amherst County, the westernmost of the state's eight recognized tribes. For information, call the Monacan Indian Nation Headquarters at (434) 946-0389, or go to www.monacannation.com.

The Nansemond have about 300 members living in the cities throughout south Hampton Roads; call (757) 986-3354, or go to www .nansemond.org. Approximately 250 members of the Rappahannock live in King, Queen, Caroline, and Essex Counties. Call the Rappahannock Tribal Office at (804) 769-0260, or write HCRI Box 402, Indian Neck, VA 23148.

MUSEUMS

Hampton University Museum
American Indian Collection
Huntington Building
Frissell Avenue, Hampton
(757) 727-5308
www.hamptonu.edu/museum
More than 1,600 objects of art and artifacts from 93 tribes constitute the large American Indian collection at Hampton University Museum. The collection became available for

public viewing in October 1998, when its move to the Huntington Building from the now-closed Academy Building of 1881 was completed. Established in 1868, most of the collection was gathered between that year and 1923 by faculty, friends of the school, and Native American students sent by the federal government to receive an education at Hampton University. Most artifacts are from Plains Indians, but some pieces of contemporary Pamunkey pottery are also part of the collection. By the way, the museum's central collection of 19th- and 20th-century African-American paintings, sculptures, and prints is one of the country's best. Museum hours are 8:00 a.m. to 5:00 p.m. Monday through Friday and noon to 4:00 p.m. on Saturday, closed Sunday and major holidays. Admission is free. To reach the museum from Williamsburg, take Interstate 64 east to exit 267 in Hampton and follow the signs.

Jamestown Settlement
Route 31 and
Colonial Parkway, Jamestown
(757) 229-1607, (888) 593-4682

At this popular museum, explored thoroughly in our Jamestown and Yorktown chapter, the Powhatan Indian Gallery is devoted to the tribe that inhabited coastal Virginia when the English arrived in 1607. Visitors to the gallery are greeted by life-size figures of a Native American family and can listen to a recording of a dialect of Algonkin, the language of the Powhatans. Detailed exhibits examine the life, religion, social structure, government, trade, and food of the tribe. An outdoor Powhatan Indian village—complete with costumed interpreters—gives kids and grownups alike a taste of life as it was lived by the original Americans. Admission to the settlement is $11.75 for adults and $5.75 for children 6 to 12.

The settlement is open from 9:00 a.m. to 5:00 p.m. daily (until 6:00 p.m. from mid-June to mid-August). It is closed Christmas and New Year's Day.

Mariners' Museum
100 Museum Drive (exit 258A off I-64)
Newport News
(757) 596-2222, (800) 581-SAIL
www.mariner.org

The Chesapeake Bay Gallery of this world-renowned museum, described in detail in our Newport News and Hampton chapter, features a dugout canoe from 1630, one of the few Indian vessels ever discovered. Admission is $12.50 for adults, $7.25 for children 6 to 17, and free for those younger than 5. The Mariners' Museum is open 10:00 a.m. to 5:00 p.m. Monday to Saturday and 12:00 to 5:00 p.m. on Sunday. Closed Christmas and Thanksgiving.

Mattaponi Indian Museum and Minnie Ha Ha Educational Trading Post
1409 Mattaponi Reservation Circle, off Route 30, West Point
(804) 769-2194

The Mattaponi Indian Museum, built here in 1954, features tribal artifacts, including a stone necklace worn by Pocahontas and the tomahawk used by Opechaneough in the battles of 1622 and 1644. Some ancient artifacts on display date from 5000 B.C. Classes in Mattaponi history, beadwork, cooking, Indian medicine, crafts, dance, and lore are taught at the nearby trading post. The museum is open on Saturday and Sunday from 2:00 to 5:00 p.m. or by arrangement. Admission is $1.00. Arrangements must be made in advance for classes at the trading post. The fee for each two-hour program participant is $2.50.

i If you want to take home some Native American pottery, drums, pipes, or clothing, stop in at the Fort Cherokee Trading Post, 6929 Richmond Road. The trading post, (757) 220-1010, carries wonderful examples of the arts and crafts fashioned by members of various tribes from across the country.

Powhatan Indian village at Jamestown Settlement. LYNN ZELEM

Pamunkey Indian Museum
Lay Landing Road off Route 30 and Route
133, King William County
(804) 843-4792
On the Pamunkey Reservation is the Pamunkey
Indian Museum, designed to resemble traditional longhouse Indian dwellings, with displays
of artifacts, replicas of stone tools, and the
ongoing tradition of pottery-making in the
centuries-old manner of the Pamunkey women.
Many of the pieces made at the museum can
be purchased in the gift shop. Museum hours
are 10:00 a.m. to 4:00 p.m. Tuesday through
Saturday and 1:00 to 5:00 p.m. on Sunday.
Admission is $2.50 for adults, $1.75 for seniors, and $1.25 for children.

MYTHS AND LEGENDS

Before we begin, let's set the mood. Think back to when you were 9 or 10. It's a dark, moonless night. You and a bunch of friends are out in the backyard with nothing but the glow of a flashlight to illuminate your faces. You're sitting in a circle, and someone starts whispering a ghost story. As the tale escalates, your heart begins to pound. The sound of that heartbeat grows louder and louder until it seems to fill the very air around you. Your feet itch to run for the safety of your house, but you can't move. Who knows what evil lurks between you and the back door? You are, in a word, terrified.

Okay. I think your pulse rate is high enough for us to unveil our ghost stories. After all, Williamsburg seems to have more than its share of spooky specters and appalling apparitions.

The tales that follow about the colonial

capital and the rest of the Virginia Peninsula aren't exactly backed up by years of historical research, but they sure are fun to recount. So sit back and enjoy as we raise a goose bump or two. Perhaps before you leave our historic city, you'll have a tale to add to our list. If so, don't hesitate to share it. Unlike some things that go bump in the night, we don't bite.

The author who perhaps has best chronicled the area's ghosts is L. B. "Bob" Taylor Jr. of Williamsburg, who for more than 20 years has written numerous books on the subject. (See the Close-Up, "Virginia's Ghostwriter.") A couple of the tales in his regional volume *The Ghosts of Williamsburg* are summarized below. Throughout this chapter you also will find a number of popular tales frequently recounted by local residents.

THE TRIPLE GHOSTS OF WESTOVER

In his book Taylor recounts the tales of three ghosts that reportedly haunt Westover Plantation in Charles City County. There's the benevolent spirit of Evelyn Byrd, a beautiful young woman who made a pact with close friend Anne Carter Harrison that whoever should die first would return to visit in a way that would not frighten anyone. As legend has it, Evelyn died of a broken heart after her father forbade her to see the suitor she loved. Anne, of course, was the first to see Evelyn's spirit, but as years passed, others reported seeing an ethereal figure dressed in white in rooms throughout the house and floating over the lawn.

Another spirit that haunts Westover is thought to be the ghost of Elizabeth Carter Byrd, wife of Evelyn's brother, William Byrd III. William apparently was a gambler and a

i If you'd like to get up close and personal with some of Williamsburg's ghosts, consider joining in on the Original Ghosts of Williamsburg, a candlelight walking tour that starts in Merchants Square at 8:00 p.m. each night. During the tour you'll be treated to folklore, legends, and ghost stories, but nothing terribly scary. More than 85,000 people annually take part in the tour. Reservations are required and tickets may be picked up at the Williamsburg Attraction Center in the Prime Outlets mall on Richmond Road at least two hours before the tour. Or you can charge tickets by phone and get them from a guide minutes before the tour begins. The tour costs $10 per person and is free to children 6 and younger. Call (757) 253-1058 or (877) 62-GHOST for more information.

womanizer, and Elizabeth's life with him was miserable. Reportedly, at the urging of her much-hated mother-in-law, Elizabeth tried to search for evidence of her husband's infidelities in the drawer of a huge chest in an upstairs bedroom. As she tried in vain to reach the top drawers, the chest toppled over and crushed her to death. Ever since that day, servants at Westover have told of hearing high-pitched calls for help coming from that bedroom. Although most surmise that the cries are from Elizabeth, another theory says it is the disturbed voice of the mother-in-law, who regretted the role she played in Elizabeth's death.

The third and final Westover ghost is that of William Byrd III himself, who, just six months after Elizabeth was buried, married a Philadelphia woman. Although the couple was happy together, William, true to form, eventually squandered the family fortune and took his own life in his favorite room of the house. More than a century and a half later, a guest who spent the night in the room reported that, at the stroke of midnight, the door opened, a crash resounded through the house, and a shadowy presence seemed to glide through the room, suffusing the atmosphere with the chill of death. The apparition, said the visitor, was the spitting image of the portrait of William Byrd III that hangs at Westover.

THE STRANGE SAGA OF AUNT PRATT

The elegant Shirley Plantation, a colonial mansion halfway between Williamsburg and Richmond that is profiled in our Attractions chapter, is noted for its fine collection of family portraits. One of those paintings is of Aunt Pratt, reportedly a late-17th-century resident of the plantation, although little is known about her life. For a number of years after Aunt Pratt died, her portrait occupied a suitable place in a downstairs bedroom until it was banished to the attic after a new generation took over the house and redecorated. It

seems Aunt Pratt, despite being dearly departed, as they say, did not like the idea of her portrait being moved. Residents and guests at the mansion reported hearing a rocking chair in the attic, but those who summoned up the courage to climb the stairs to the attic never discovered the source of the sound. Eventually, the rocking became so disturbing that the house's occupants retrieved the portrait and returned it to the bedroom wall. Once that was a fait accompli, the strange rocking sounds never were heard again. The tale of Aunt Pratt's portrait doesn't end there. According to one employee at Shirley, every time the portrait was moved to a room other than the downstairs bedroom, it simply fell off the wall. Aunt Pratt, it seems, has mastered the art of throwing otherworldly temper tantrums.

THE MOTHER-IN-LAW TREE

This Jamestown legend concerns the "mother-in-law tree" that grew between two tombs next to Jamestown Church. The tale begins when 17-year-old Sarah Harrison broke off her engagement to one young suitor and married James Blair, cofounder and first president of the College of William and Mary. James had quite a few years on Sarah, and her mother, disapproving of the match, tried to have their marriage annulled. As the legend goes, Sarah's mother was struck by lightning and killed before she accomplished her plan. Sarah, who was shunned by her family, later died and was buried in a separate area from the rest of her family in the Jamestown Church cemetery. Upon his death, Blair was buried at her side. Soon, however, a sycamore tree sprouted between the couple's graves, breaking the tombstones and pushing Sarah's grave over toward the family plot, away from her husband. So, it is said that Blair's mother-in-law ended up having the last word after all. The old tree died several years ago, but a new sapling sprang up in the same place.

WILLIAM AND MARY'S PRESIDENT'S HOUSE

Poor James Blair just can't rest in peace. He also happened to be the first inhabitant of the College of William and Mary's President's House, which is said to be haunted. This house is the setting of a number of strange phenomena. For a long time, a certain bedroom closet door in the house wouldn't stay shut. No one could figure out why. Then, workmen making repairs in a ceiling crawl space found a skeleton embedded in the wall. (No, it wasn't Blair's mother-in-law.) Once the skeleton was removed, the closet door stopped popping open.

But the ghost purportedly occupying the house can't be so easily expelled. Footsteps, supposedly those of a French soldier who died in the house during the Revolutionary War, can be heard mounting and descending an upper staircase. A number of the college's past presidents have reported visits from the spirited fellow. During the final weeks of the Revolutionary War, the house was used as a hospital for Lafayette's soldiers. Legend has it that one of these soldiers who now haunts the President's House died in a small back room on the third floor.

THE BRAFFERTON

Perhaps the French soldier's ghost is trying to get out of the President's House to head over to The Brafferton building across the college yard, where the spirits of Native American boys who once attended the old Indian school are said to still be in residence. Many folks have reported hearing hair-raising sounds emanating from The Brafferton late at night, including sobs, shuffling footsteps, moans, and the beating of tom-toms.

The Brafferton building was built on the campus of William and Mary in 1723, erected specifically as a school for Native American boys, to train them in the ways of civilization, teach them English, and to "bring the Gospel to the Indians." After the death of the school's headmaster, the building was full of unhappy

i Over the years, Jane Polonsky of Hampton and Joan Drum of Williamsburg have collaborated on three books of regional ghost stories. Their latest, *Hampton's Haunted Houses*, is available at the Casemate Museum, (757) 788-3391, at Fort Monroe, and at The Virginia Store at 555 Settlers Landing, (757) 727-0600, in downtown Hampton.

boys, many whose fathers had been killed, and others who had been brought to Williamsburg against their will. Not only did they have trouble with the townsfolk, who weren't keen on having the young Indians around, the boys came from different tribes and had difficulty communicating with each other. Homesick and lonely, many of them tried to escape, so they were locked in the building at night. The building stopped being used as a residence for the American Indians in 1736, but the anguished cries and angry sounds are still reported today.

THE PEYTON RANDOLPH HOUSE

In the Peyton Randolph House on Nicholson Street, numerous guests who have stayed in the oak-paneled second-floor bedroom have reported waking up in the middle of the night to see a wispy figure of a woman at the foot of the bed. Dressed in 18th-century nightclothes, complete with a cap, she wrings her hands, then quickly disappears. Those who have seen her feel sure she is there to warn them of impending tragedy. For, although the Peyton Randolph House has an esteemed history, built in 1715 and inhabited by Sir John Randolph, a respected lawyer and clerk of the House of Burgesses, its later history took a tragic turn. Once the house was sold out of the Randolph family in 1824, its history is less known, except for the fact that it saw many untimely deaths, including the sad deaths of several children, two or more suicides, and the agonizing last days of a promising young man who passed away from tuberculosis. The

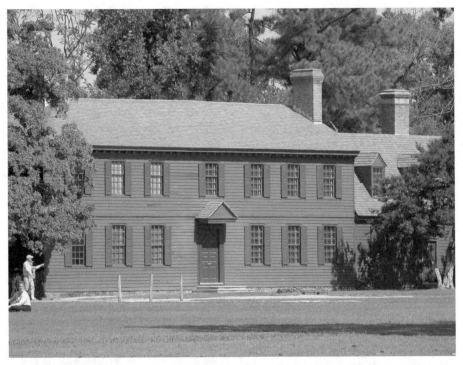

The Peyton Randolph House is known locally as a place of sorrow. JESSI DICK

anguished apparition has contributed to the building's reputation as a house of sorrow.

THE WYTHE HOUSE

The Wythe House, behind Bruton Parish Church, is said to be haunted by a beautiful woman wearing a splendid ballroom gown and brilliant red slippers. She appears at midnight and sometimes runs upstairs. She is wearing only one high-heeled slipper, having lost the other in her dash across the palace green toward Wythe House. The shoe clicks distinctively on the broad stairway as she ascends. Legend identifies this hurried phantom as the fiery-tempered Lady Anne Skipwith, who once fled a palace ball in a fit of jealousy over her husband's attention to another woman. At other times, the apparition is said to exit a closet from a certain

room, glance at herself in the mirror, and then disappear.

TALES OF RUTH HANKINS

Many past and present residents of the Williamsburg area have their own haunting tales to tell. In 1984 Ruth Hankins, whose husband was a member of an old James City County family, shared her ghostly recollections for a local oral-history project. In one of her reminiscences, Mrs. Hankins, who was 86 at the time, described the origins of the "witch doors" that were part of many early Williamsburg and Jamestown houses. These heavy, wide doors carried the image of a cross and a section shaped like an open Bible. Every house was supposed to have at least one, according to Mrs. Hankins, and its purpose was to ward off witches and evil spirits.

As long as the witch door was closed, no evil apparition could enter the room behind you.

In another of her tales—one a little closer to home—Mrs. Hankins spoke about the ghost that took up residence with her family. It first made its presence known when her sons were young. The family was gathered in one room, where the children were doing their homework. Suddenly, a yellow pencil rose into the air and began scribbling on a sideboard, before falling to the ground. Mrs. Hankins and her children ran to see what was etched in the dust on the sideboard but found nothing.

Another time, Mrs. Hankins was working in her house when she heard a voice say, "Good afternoon." Without thinking, she said, "Well, it isn't afternoon yet. I haven't had my lunch," before realizing that there wasn't another soul anywhere nearby. A fairly rational woman, she was ready to explain the voice away as a product of her imagination, until she glanced over at her little dog, who looked petrified and was staring bug-eyed into space. For a long while after the incident, Mrs. Hankins noted, her dog avoided the area from which the ghostly voice had emanated.

CARTER'S GROVE

In a downstairs parlor at Carter's Grove plantation, George Washington proposed marriage to Mary Cary, and Thomas Jefferson proposed to Rebecca Burwell, though both women refused the offers. In the room where the refusals took place, a ghost has been rumored to appear, reportedly tearing up flowers that had been left in the room. Legend implies that the ghost is one, or both, of the women, who later came to regret the decision not to marry her famous suitor. Then again, perhaps the rejected suitors are to blame for the shredded blossoms.

Another Carter's Grove legend, that of Colonel Banastre Tarleton's charge on horseback up the entry staircase during the Revolutionary War, is widely disputed. Some still hold, however, that the indentations on the banister are from Tarleton's saber.

EDGEWOOD'S LIZZIE ROWLAND

When Dot Boulware bought Edgewood Plantation in 1978, one of the first stories she heard was the sad tale of Lizzie Rowland. It seems Lizzie, one of four children and the only daughter of the man who had built the three-story Gothic house in 1849, was 19 when she fell in love with a young man who most likely lived at Berkeley Plantation, a quarter-mile away. He began courting her, riding right up to the doors of Edgewood on a very spirited horse. Because the horse had a loose shoe, Lizzie always could tell when her sweetheart was coming, and she would run to the window to watch his approach. The couple eventually became engaged but, before they could wed, the young man went off to fight in the Civil War, but did not return. Lizzie Rowland died of a broken heart.

To this day, Lizzie's first name can be seen clearly etched in tiny letters (she reportedly used a diamond ring) on the glass of an upstairs window. And it seems, says Dot, that the young woman's spirit freely roams throughout the house. Dot recalls that shortly after she bought the house, she was sitting in the dining room with a group of 11 friends when the talk turned to Lizzie Rowland. Everyone was eager to know if the young "spirit" had ever made her presence known. One woman, however, pooh-poohed the idea, loudly announcing that she didn't believe in ghosts. A brass plate held snug in a plate holder chose that instant to roll from its perch atop a cupboard and hit the woman. "Within 15 or 20 minutes, all of my friends had left," recalls Dot.

On another occasion two Civil War reenactors came to the house on horseback, and Dot snapped a picture of them, with the house in the background. When developed, it clearly showed the image of a young, frail woman in an upstairs bedroom window, even though, according to Dot, there was no other woman in the house at the time. A few years later when a wedding ceremony was held at Edgewood, a photo of a horse and carriage

Close-up

Virginia's Ghostwriter

There is probably no one who knows more about Virginia's ghosts than Williamsburg author L. B. "Bob" Taylor Jr. For more than 20 years, Taylor has researched and chronicled hundreds of terrible and traumatic ghost tales from throughout the Old Dominion. His eerie narrations include everything from the "Mad Escapades of the Powhatan Poltergeist" to the "Green-Eyed 'Monster' of Richmond."

Taylor, who is in his 60s, became interested in ghosts after a chance assignment from Simon & Schuster to do a book on haunted houses. "In doing the research, I came across so much material I couldn't use in the book," he said. He decided to put the stories to good use and pen his own manuscript on Virginia's specters. Ten more books have followed. Five of these are on the general topic of the ghosts of Virginia; others deal with regional hauntings: ghosts of Williamsburg, Richmond, Tidewater, Fredericksburg, Charlottesville, and Lynchburg (Taylor's hometown). Taylor also has conjured up some wartime ghosts in his *Civil War Ghosts of Virginia*, which was released in 1995, just in time for Halloween.

Taylor's research demands considerable legwork. "I do a lot of digging in archives, old county histories, and, for the Civil War book, magazines dating back to the early 1900s," he noted. Taylor also tries, whenever possible, to interview folks who have had firsthand encounters with Old Dominion ghosts. He gives a number of talks throughout the area on the subject of ghosts, and afterward, he says, "people come up to me and tell me their stories." After following up on those leads and checking out the tips he gets via cards and letters from throughout the state, he soon has enough material to begin a new book.

The author admitted that a ghost has never visited him, although it's an experience he said he would welcome. As for believing in apparitions? Until he began writing about ghosts, he said, he never really thought that much about them. "But I've talked to so many people who are so sincere in their encounters that I tend to believe there's something there," said Taylor.

To obtain a copy of any of Taylor's books, you can write the author at 108 Elizabeth Meriwether Street, Williamsburg, VA 23185. Also, look for copies of his books in area bookstores and at the Williamsburg Attraction Center at Prime Outlets at Williamsburg. And, who knows? You just might glimpse the ghost of a colonial American during your stay in Williamsburg and have a tale or two of your own to tell to the folks back home.

again with the house as a backdrop showed a similar image of a woman in the window of a locked, third-story bedroom.

Over the years Dot has become very comfortable with the idea of sharing residency with the spirit of Lizzie Rowland. "She's a ghost, but she's a good ghost," notes Edgewood's owner.

THE GRAY LADY

Sherwood Forest, an impressive 300-foot-long mansion, built in 1730 and bought in 1842 by President John Tyler, sits quietly on the banks of the James River. Unbenownst to many visitors, this historic house has its own dark tale of restless spirits. One particular ghost has haunted the mansion since the late 18th century. She is the "Gray Lady," called such because those who have seen her say she wears gray, like a servant of that time period. She is thought to have been a governess who had cared for a small child, whom she would carry from the first-floor bedroom, known now as the Gray Room, up a hidden staircase to a second-floor nursery, where she rocked the child in her lap. As the story goes, the child became ill and died.

Residents of the house, including descendants of President Tyler who still own the old house, have encountered the Gray Lady. Several report hearing her footsteps going up the hidden stairway and the sound of her rocking her small charge in the Gray Room. Others claim that they have even seen her walk through their bedrooms at night!

THE LEGEND OF BRUTON PARISH VAULT

Williamsburg residents have long been familiar with stories about ghosts said to inhabit some of the town's historic buildings, but several years ago, the rest of the nation got to hear one, too. It involved a cemetery, a grave desecration, mysterious manuscripts, and secret tunnels. Some locals called the publicity much ado about nothing, but we call it the Legend of Bruton Parish Vault.

It all began, according to believers, in the 17th century, when Nathaniel Bacon came to the New World to flee the persecution of King Charles. The legend goes that Bacon brought with him precious documents: a Utopian blueprint for a peaceful world in the 21st century, original versions of the King James Bible and Book of Saint Peter, and manuscripts proving that Sir Francis Bacon, his father, authored

Shakespeare's plays and sonnets with a little help from a few friends. These priceless pages were first buried at Jamestown. Then, in 1674, through tunnels from the George Wythe House, Geddy Foundry, and William and Mary's Wren Building, a large vault containing the documents, along with gold chalices, was conveyed in secret to a spot beneath Bruton Parish Church property. At some later date, presumably, an original draft of the U.S. Constitution was slipped into the vault.

Time passed and the vault slumbered until 1938, when Marie Bauer Hall of Los Angeles decoded a book written by George Withers in 1635. It's not clear how Withers knew where the vault was buried before it was indeed, supposedly, buried, but symbols in his book led Hall to the Williamsburg churchyard in search of the blueprints for Utopia. Since the tunnels allegedly had been filled with cement by the Colonial Williamsburg Foundation, Hall obtained permission from church officials to dig in the cemetery. Nine feet down, past foundations of the original church, she hit a coffin with brass tacks, and church officials stopped her.

Hall continued to believe in the existence of the vault, however, and founded an organization called Veritat, which pressured the church to allow excavation. Limited authorized testing of the site with radar in 1985 and 1986 brought inconclusive results, rekindling interest in the vault theory. Was it really there, or was it all a midsummer night's dream?

Enter Marsha Middleton of Santa Fe, who calls herself a New Age Christian mystic and believes that she was Saint Peter in a previous incarnation. In 1991 Middleton, along with her group, Ministry of the Children, conducted two illegal midnight digs in the churchyard. She, her husband, and a third conspirator were charged with trespassing and vandalism. To flee or not to flee, that was the question for the Francis Bacon fugitives. They fled back to more mystic-friendly New Mexico to avoid facing charges. But all that under-cloak-of-darkness activity brought the national spotlight to focus on Bruton Parish. In January 1992 the *Wall Street Journal* poked gentle fun at the whole undertaking in a front-page article, further upsetting church leaders.

The comedy of errors was far from over. Under continued pressure from the Veritat vigilantes and other interested groups to allow excavation, Bruton Parish caved in during the summer of 1992. No, the church didn't fall down, but the vestry agreed to let Colonial Williamsburg archaeologists investigate. That August they dug a 20-by-20-foot site, uncovering mud, water, graves, and pieces of bone from a corpse apparently damaged during the earlier digs. Alas, poor Yorick.

A geologist from the College of William and Mary undertook further tests, drilling holes some 20 feet deep around the site with a hand auger. He, too, found mud, but no sign of disturbed earth, no elusive vault. Church officials are satisfied they've proved beyond the shadow of a doubt that nothing unusual is buried in their cemetery. What do Hall, Middleton, and others believe? They may think the Virginia Shakespeare Festival should be renamed the Virginia Bacon Festival, but they apparently—at least for the time being—have decided to let sleeping artifacts lie.

YORKTOWN GHOSTS

Yorktown has its own ghostly apparitions. A British soldier who was killed during the last days of the Revolutionary War is said to sometimes make his presence known in the historic Nelson House. And the Moore House, a property restored and operated by the National Park Service, is believed by many to contain a young ghost, Augustine Moore Jr., who also may have been killed during the Revolutionary War. This particular spirit doesn't make appearances, but leaves impressions on bedcovers and a chair where he likes to sit, or so employees have claimed.

POCAHONTAS AND JOHN SMITH

Perhaps the oldest and most famous area legend surrounds Pocahontas, who was an adolescent at the time English settlers arrived in Jamestown. The story goes that Captain John Smith had ventured too far into Indian territory and was taken prisoner. The Indian Chief Powhatan was ready to have the captive beheaded when his favorite daughter, Pocahontas, threw herself on the Englishman's body, pleading for his life. Powhatan, a doting father, acquiesced, and a grateful and relieved John Smith was allowed to return to Jamestown.(A much romanticized version of this legend, as anyone with small children knows by now, was made into the 1995 Walt Disney movie *Pocahontas*.)

THE WHITE LADY OF FORT MONROE

Jane Polonsky of Hampton, coauthor of three books about the region's ghosts, has a favorite tale among the many she has heard and recounted over the years. It concerns a young woman who went to live at Fort Monroe in Hampton with her husband after the Civil War. "She did not like Fort Monroe," notes Polonsky. "She found it stodgy and stuffy." To ease her boredom the woman—considered flirtatious and a bit unstable by her peers—began an affair with a dashing young officer. The two thought they were being very secretive about the relationship, but soon everyone around them—including the woman's husband—knew exactly what was going on. One night the lovers planned to meet in the woman's quarters inside the moat after her husband went out of town. But the husband, having gotten wind of the planned assignation, showed up unexpectedly, picked up a dueling pistol lying beside the bed, and, instead of killing the lover, shot his wife dead. It is her ghost—clad all in white—that now roams the grounds of Fort Monroe. Although seen only once every 20 years or so, the "White Lady" leaves quite an impression, says Polonsky. "Several people have seen her, including a bunch of kids playing hide-and-seek at sundown," she notes. "They saw her up in a tree barefoot and wearing a long white dress."

COLONIAL WILLIAMSBURG

Have a hankering to hobnob with Thomas Jefferson? Or perhaps you'd like to share a little tea and conversation with Martha Washington? If you're in luck, George might just happen by and chime in with the gossip of the day. And if all this talk of taxes, politics, and religious freedom (forget small talk) stirs up an appetite, you can bid adieu to your illustrious companions and stroll over to a local tavern for a fine repast of Cavalier's lamb, peanut soup, and game pie.

A visit to Colonial Williamsburg is like leafing through the pages of a history book—only better, since you get to employ all of your senses. Indeed, there is probably nowhere else in America where the sights, sounds, tastes, and even smells of the past come alive in the present as they do in Williamsburg. Reconstructed with a meticulous eye for authenticity, Colonial Williamsburg offers 301 acres of 18th-century history along with a full slate of lectures, concerts, theatrical performances, and militia exhibits year-round. The city is portrayed at the eve of the American Revolution, when the air is tense with rumors of rebellion, espionage, and possible war. Known as America's oldest and largest outdoor living-history museum, Colonial Williamsburg was rated the "Favorite Historic Site" for five straight years by readers of *Southern Living Magazine*. Throughout the Historic Area, costumed interpreters toil at their trades like their kinsmen of yore. In colonial taverns, balladeers serenade their audiences with the bawdy tales that were popular with previous generations while learned gentlemen of the time discuss the political issues that were at the forefront of everyone's mind.

With 88 original structures, 300 major reconstructions, 40 exhibition buildings, and 90 acres of gardens and greens, Williamsburg isn't a city you can see in a day—or even two. It's a place to be savored, so make sure you allow enough time to listen to an evening reveille, dance in the candlelit House of Burgesses, and participate in a military drill. The memories you'll come away with are unlikely to be duplicated anywhere else. To start you on your trip to another era, we begin with a comprehensive look back at how it all began.

HISTORICAL OVERVIEW
Promising Beginnings

Williamsburg served as the capital of England's oldest, largest, richest, and most populous colony from 1699 to 1780 and, during that time, grew from a small settlement to a thriving, sophisticated urban center, reflecting the city's prominent role. By the mid-18th century, the population was nearing 2,000; slaves accounted for roughly half of that number. When courts convened, Williamsburg's population more than doubled, with citizens from the far reaches of the vast Virginia Colony arriving to participate in the fairs, festivities, and fancy dress balls of Publick Times.

American ideals of democracy and liberty took root here in the 1700s, as colonists began to question, and finally repudiate, British rule. Patrick Henry inveighed against taxation without representation in the House of Burgesses in 1765. The First Continental Congress was called from Williamsburg in 1774. The Declaration of Rights, soon to become the foundation for the first 10 amendments to the Constitution, was penned here by George Mason. Thousands of Continental Army soldiers were billeted in Williamsburg, which bustled with revolutionary fervor. In 1780, however, Thomas Jefferson's campaign to move the capital to Richmond succeeded, and Williamsburg, no longer the heart of social, political, and economic life in Virginia, entered an era of sleepy decline. Population waned, and businesses were forced to close. While it continued to function as county seat, 19th-century Williamsburg was mostly a market town for area farmers, disturbed only by Union General George McClellan's 1862 Peninsula Campaign during the Civil War.

The College of William and Mary and the Public Hospital remained the only institutions of much size or importance. Some public buildings fell into neglect and burned (the Palace in 1781), but most of the 18th-century homes and structures continued to be used simply because there was little reason to build anew. While interim uses were at times less than noble (Prentis Store survived in the early 20th century as a gas station; the Magazine once served as a stable), the structures were saved from destruction.

Two Men and a Dream

Williamsburg might still be a sedate spot on the map if not for the actions of two men who conceived of a grander future for the once-great city. The Rev. W. A. R. Goodwin, rector of Bruton Parish Church, dreamed of restoring the heritage of Virginia's colonial capital. He was successful in raising enough money to restore his own church, but in 1908 left Williamsburg to become rector of a Rochester, New York, church. In 1923, however, he returned as professor of religion at the College of William and Mary. As luck would have it, the college chose Goodwin as its representative at a 1924 Phi Beta Kappa dinner in New York. Also attending the dinner was John D. Rockefeller Jr., philanthropic heir to the Standard Oil fortune.

This meeting led to the Rockefellers' 1926 visit to Williamsburg, during which negotiations for the restoration of certain 18th-century buildings began. Planning was carried out in a highly secretive manner. Measurements of buildings were taken under cover of dark. Rockefeller insisted on signing documents pseudonymously as "Mr. David." Town residents felt understandably apprehensive and mystified as they watched their rector buying up land. Rumors spread, and real estate values took off. Soon it was necessary to reveal to Williamsburg citizens the nature of the restoration plan. Initially, not all were pleased; some balked at the idea of their town being "sold." Others were skeptical about the practicality of such a scheme. As the restoration process began, however, the economic benefits of the project became clear. Tenancy agreements allowed most residents of 18th-century buildings to occupy their homes for life.

A Reconstruction Frenzy

Though Rockefeller at first intended to subsidize the restoration of a small number of structures, his enthusiasm and ambitions grew as research turned up more and more pertinent data. Drawings, maps, and records culled from libraries and museums in Europe and America revealed a trove of historical details. Teams of architects, led by William Graves Perry, worked to authentically restore original 18th-century sites and to reconstruct others on original foundations. Hundreds of more modern buildings were razed or removed. Eighteenth-century building and brick-making techniques were painstakingly researched so that a restored or reconstructed building would resemble the original as closely as possible.

The success of Goodwin's and Rockefeller's grand vision is well documented today. About a million visitors tour Colonial Williamsburg (or CW, as Insiders like to say) each year. They step out of their 21st-century lives into an authentic, engrossing 18th-century world. The Historic Area contains hundreds of restored public buildings, residences, outbuildings, dependencies, shops, and hostelries, plus acres of formal and informal gardens, pastures, and lanes.

While in one sense the restoration Goodwin and Rockefeller envisioned is complete, the Colonial Williamsburg Foundation continues to pursue its vision—or perhaps we should say revision—of the past. In recent years, Colonial Williamsburg has redirected its focus somewhat. Previously, restoration efforts and programs at Colonial Williamsburg concentrated on the lives of an elite group—colonial governors, revolutionary leaders, and prominent citizens. Today, in the Historic Area and its museums, you will find more space given to the 18th-century community as a whole. Slaves, indentured servants, women, tradespeople, the typical family of the period, and other "middling" folk are increasingly featured in interpretive programs that more accurately reflect the complexities of 18th-century history.

One program, for instance, explores the paradoxical issue of freedom in a society that fought to win its independence from the British Crown while practicing and condoning slavery. Colonial Williamsburg also has used grant monies to improve and more fully assimilate interpretation of the 18th-century African-American experience into its presentations. The role religion played in the daily lives of colonists is being more fully explored and interpreted for the benefit of visitors through lectures, tours, and concerts. Each year, black history, women's history, music, and religion are observed with special programming. Reenactments and re-creations of historical events—from a day of fasting, humiliation, and prayer in response to the Boston Tea Party to a mock trial and burning of Britain's chief minister, Lord North—occur on a regular basis throughout the Historic Area.

Starting in 2003, for the first time, costumed tradespeople at nearly 20 sites throughout the Historic Area invited visitors to roll up their sleeves and assist them with their 18th-century trades, whether shoemaking, basket weaving or silversmithing. In addition, Thomas Jefferson, Patrick Henry, and other founding fathers now engage visitors with compelling discourse on such topics as democracy, slavery, marriage, and the "Mother Country" of England.

The best way to find out what's on tap when you're in town is to consult your *Colonial Williamsburg Visitor's Companion,* a free publication available at the Colonial Williamsburg Visitor Center or wherever Colonial Williamsburg tickets are sold. It's updated weekly and contains a map and information on sites, special programs, lodging, shopping, and dining within Colonial Williamsburg.

CHANGE IS IN THE AIR

In recent years the winds of change have begun blowing a little more forcefully down the dusty streets of Williamsburg. The bid for tourists' time—and money—is a competitive business, and the Colonial Williamsburg Foundation has grown increasingly concerned in recent years over declining attendance figures. In the 1980s the number of tickets sold annually regularly hit the 1.2 million mark, but for the first half of the 1990s, they were stuck around 950,000 or so. Thanks to creative educational programming, aggressive marketing, and the addition of more actors to the living-history streetscape, the number of paying visitors began climbing once again in the mid-1990s, peaking at 995,000 in 1999.

But attendance in the first years of the 21st century declined significantly, attributed to a combination of horrific events that kept would-be visitors at home (the terrorist attacks on the World Trade Center and Pentagon in September 2001, the sniper shootings that paralyzed Washington, D.C., in the fall of 2002, and the ongoing war in Iraq). That trend reversed in 2006, however, when 767,000 visitors arrived, up from 710,000 in 2005 and 707,000 in 2004. Colonial Williamsburg officials are confident that, when final tallies are in, 2007 will see an even bigger attendance, with more visitors coming to the area for Jamestown's 400th anniversary celebration.

Certainly, the rising level of private contributors indicates great confidence in a promising future for Colonial Williamsburg. The number of annual donors reached a record 115,000 in 2006. Annual donations rose to $14 million—significantly higher than the $10.7 million in 2001.

"I am heartened by the continued and growing support for Colonial Williamsburg demonstrated by our donors," said Colin G. Campbell, president and chairman of the Colonial Williamsburg Foundation.

A major physical change in recent years in the Historic Area is the relocation of the Armistead House from Duke of Gloucester Street to the 300 block of South Henry Street. Until November 1995 the house was the sole Victorian frame house left amid its older brethren along the restored street. Built in 1890 by Cary Peyton Armistead, the house was maintained as a family residence until 1984. Then the Association for the Preservation of Virginia Antiquities operated it as a museum until 1993. The museum was finally closed because of declining attendance. Now, with the house relocated and restored to its original color (a creamy peach), Colonial Williamsburg most likely will rebuild an 18th-century coffeehouse or tavern on this prime site next door to the Capitol after it finishes its in-depth archaeological studies.

Visitors to Colonial Williamsburg will also see a newly renovated Bassett Hall, the 18th-century frame house where the Rockefellers lived. In addition to the home, located at 522 East Francis Street, the 585-acre property includes a teahouse and three original out-buildings: a smokehouse, a kitchen, and a dairy. The house reopened in December 2002 following an extensive renovation that includes a new exhibit of the history of the Rockefellers in Williamsburg as well as an updated house tour.

A few years back CW opened the $37.2 million Bruton Heights School Education Center, which has significantly expanded the organization's research capabilities. Located just outside the Historic Area, the center includes facilities for the John D. Rockefeller Jr. Library, with its collection of 65,000 books, 43,000 manuscripts, 12,000 rare books, and 50,000 architectural drawings; the DeWitt Wallace Collections and Conservation Build-

ing, which houses up to 20,000 reserve objects from CW's fine- and decorative arts collection; an audio-video production area; and other departments that previously had been scattered in various locations throughout Colonial Williamsburg.

As a way to acknowledge and offer more services to CW contributors, the Colonial Williamsburg Foundation has opened the Saint George Tucker House Donor Reception Center on Nicholson Street next to the Palace Green. This hospitality center is open daily from 9:30 a.m. to 4:30 p.m. for annual donors of $100 or more. Volunteers staff the center, which offers VIPs light refreshments, entertainment, and special assistance with reservations and visit plans. Each year more than 50,000 donors support Colonial Williamsburg's educational mission. From a historical standpoint, the Tucker House was the site of the first Christmas tree in Williamsburg and was owned by the Tucker family for more than 200 years, until 1993. The $1.1 million renovation was funded by—what else?—donations.

In 2001 Henry and "Jimmy" (June deH.) Weldon of New York donated their $5 million collection of rare English pottery to the Colonial Williamsburg Foundation. The collection of 725 pieces dates from the mid-17th to early 19th century. Regarded as one of the finest collections of its kind in private hands in North America and possibly the world, it consists primarily of salt-glazed stoneware and refined earthenware.

And speaking of changes in the air, a growing number of interpretive programs portray the lives of African Americans and Native Americans in 18th-century colonial Virginia. At the Peyton Randolph House site, home of the first president of the Continental Congress, provocative and compelling African-American programs are taking place in the recently reconstructed kitchen.

Several court trials, held in the Courthouse on Duke of Gloucester Street, reenact scenes from actual criminal cases that involved slaves, and not all had a happy outcome. During these trials, packed wall to wall with visitors, the air is thick with tension at times as onlookers observe the humiliation heaped on the African-American defendant.

Families with children will benefit from the 50 percent increase in family and children's programs that was instituted in 2003. Youngsters now have more opportunities to see, touch, smell, and hear about the 18th century. Children are able to make stitch books, play hoops, master a colonial ball-and-cup game, polish silver with the silversmiths, and tread mud with the brick makers. At the Benjamin Powell House, families will have the opportunity to participate in the daily activities of a successful 18th-century builder and his household.

In "Papa Said, Mama Said," guests journey back in time to learn how 18th-century enslaved Africans and their descendants created an oral culture through storytelling. "Remember Me When Freedom Comes" takes place through the eyes of an enslaved man and his slave-quarter community, who tell the story of the quest for freedom.

These expanded offerings go a long way toward fulfilling Colonial Williamsburg's key educational mission: "That the future may learn from the past."

CELEBRATING 75+ YEARS

In 2001 Colonial Williamsburg observed the 75th anniversary of the original restoration project started by John D. Rockefeller Jr. In conjunction with the anniversary was the restoration of several Colonial Williamsburg facilities, all part of a $100 million renovation of Colonial Williamsburg hotels and the Visitor Center. The Visitor Center experienced a major renovation, as did the adjoining Woodlands Hotel. The old 1957 single-story hotel, a premier facility of its time for the growing automobile-traveling public, was torn down, and a new 300-room facility constructed in its place, featuring a new outdoor swimming pool, and a pedestrian promenade to the Visitor Center. The renovation of the Visitor Center, which was enlarged and its interior

upgraded, and the hotel represent Phase I of the renovation project, which was completed in 2003. Other facilities renovated in 2001 were the popular Governor's Palace Maze and the Kimball Theatre in Merchants Square (formerly Williamsburg Theatre), which opened in the fall of 2001 as a place for Colonial Williamsburg evening programs and other community performances.

The most breathtaking was the extensive renovation of the world-famous Williamsburg Inn. The makeover didn't touch the exterior of the grand building, but it reduced the 95 guest rooms to 62, reverting to Rockefeller's original vision when he opened the inn in 1937. Rooms were enlarged to create luxurious bedrooms with generous seating areas, and bathrooms were reconfigured in marble and enlarged to include a bathtub and separate shower. Guests will be happy to know that there were extensive mechanical, electrical, and plumbing upgrades as well.

As part of the 75th anniversary celebration, the Colonial Williamsburg Foundation kicked off its first comprehensive fund-raising campaign and largest single undertaking since the original restoration effort. The original goal was to raise $300 million by December 2002, but organizers revised that goal to $500 million by 2007 to ensure Rockefeller's original vision by supporting Colonial Williamsburg's educational mission. By mid-2006, they had surpassed that goal with $510 million in donations. Fund-raisers focus primarily on planned preservation, educational programming, and a strengthened workplace environment. The fund-raising is critical; Colonial Williamsburg is a private living-history museum that receives no regular state or federal support.

HANDS-ON HISTORY

During your stroll through colonial times, we urge you to get involved in what is happening all around you. The teaching of history is a primary goal in Colonial Williamsburg, and folks here do it as well as most classroom teachers.

ℹ️ When it comes to providing jobs to the local population, the Colonial Williamsburg Foundation is in a class unto itself. The Foundation employs 3,500 year-round workers and 700 to 800 volunteers.

To engage visitors as fully as possible, Colonial Williamsburg offers a variety of lively, hands-on learning presentations. Interactive programs such as the trials of the "Virginia Witch" and other courtroom dramas allow visitors to enjoy a living-history experience. Children and parents will find programs that deal with family issues—and possibly have the chance to help Grandma Geddy (mother of eight) with the laundry—at the Geddy House, home of a working-class, 18th-century family. You also will have the opportunity to meet many of the other women of Williamsburg—from Grissell Hay, a widow and "Gentlewoman of Note," to Venus, daughter of Old Paris, one of the Carter's Grove slaves. Other notable "persons of the past" are George Wythe, a gentleman and scholar, and Lewis Tyler, enforcer and practitioner of the law.

Martha Washington, who became part of the colonial cast in 1995, has proved to be a perennial favorite as she sips tea with Sunday guests in the Williamsburg Inn. Portrayed as a 28-year-old during her first two years in Williamsburg, Martha finally has caught up in age to her historical brethren. A few years back, a more "mature" interpreter took over the role and transformed our original First Lady into the 43-year-old wife of a newly elected member of the House of Burgesses. Other CW characters include the Coopers, a free black family; Ann Wagner, mistress of the Bray School for Negro children; and Lydia Broadnax, an enslaved cook.

And, in response to visitors' requests, CW has recruited more children and youth volunteers to portray characters in the Historic Area during the summer months when they are out of school. Most of the youngsters are in costume—whether they're doing their lessons, sewing a sampler, or studying religion—

and they are responsible for only two four-hour shifts a week.

A CONTINUING COMMITMENT

Colonial Williamsburg's commitment to authenticity remains strong. Historians, archaeologists, and researchers continue to uncover documents and artifacts that reveal new aspects of the past and make possible more exact interpretations of history. As we mentioned earlier, excavation work has been ongoing at the former site of the Armistead House. In the first year or so of digging, researchers unearthed evidence of the porch to a coffeehouse from the 1760s and uncovered more than 15,000 artifacts, including broken wine glasses and bottles, smoking pipes, and tavern mugs. These painstaking efforts ensure that America's heritage will continue to be preserved and enriched for future generations. It is this sense of ongoing discovery that makes history seem alive here and motivates visitors to keep returning across the miles and centuries to a place called Williamsburg.

GETTING STARTED
Visitor Center

The Visitor Center, on Visitor Center Drive (132-Y), should be the starting point for any tour of Colonial Williamsburg. Follow the green-and-white directional signs placed around town, and park in one of the center's 2,000 parking spaces. Parking in the lot is free.

Once you've committed yourself to a day at Williamsburg, head straight to the Visitor

ℹ️ The Colonial Williamsburg Foundation's teacher development programs provided learning opportunities for more than 1,000 teachers in 2005, both on-site and through virtual field trips. During the 2005-06 school year, more than 1,600 schools in 46 states participated in Colonial Williamsburg's Electronic Field Trips program.

Center to purchase tickets and obtain sight-seeing information, maps, guidebooks, and some excellent advice about touring the colonial capital. Reservations for special tours and presentations, for meals in Colonial Williamsburg's several taverns and restaurants, and for lodging at its hotel facilities can be arranged here as well. The renovation to the Visitor Center in 2001 relocated and enlarged the bookstore and a separate gift shop, added a comfortable seating area at the south end, and brought technologically upgraded ticket and reservation booths. The Visitor Center bookstore is well stocked with titles relating to colonial history, including sections on antiques, archaeology, crafts, gardening, decorative arts, and biography. Other sections hold books detailing the roles of African Americans, Indians, and women in colonial life. Souvenirs and gifts as well as postcards, film, and camera accessories also are for sale. The Visitor Center is open from 8:30 a.m. to 5:30 p.m. daily during the summer, although hours are shortened during the fall and winter months. Any and all questions you have about visiting Colonial Williamsburg attractions can be answered here, or by calling (800) 246-2099, (800) HISTORY, or (757) 229-1000. You can also log on to the CW Web site, at www.colonialwilliamsburg.com.

Tickets

You can feel transported back to the 18th century just by roaming the historic streets of Colonial Williamsburg free of charge. But we recommend purchasing a ticket to be fully immersed in the historical re-creation experience. Although walking the streets may be free, visitors need a ticket to enter exhibition buildings and historic trade shops, ride the buses provided by CW, or take part in guided walking tours. Tickets can be purchased at the Visitor Center, the Merchants Square Information Center on South Henry Street, the Lumber House ticket office on Duke of Gloucester Street in the restored area, the Gateway Building, or at the Secretary's Office, located at the foot of Duke of Gloucester next

to the Capitol. A one-day Capitol City pass is $36 for adults, $18 for children 6 to 17. Children 5 and under are free. Two-day passes are $49 for adults, $24 for 6 to 17, and a year-long annual pass is $59 for adults, $29 for children 6 to 17. But Colonial Williamsburg hotel guests receive a special discount: guest passes for $29 per adult and $15 for youth 6 to 17 (5 and under are free), good for the entire length of their stay. Every CW ticket includes admission to all exhibition buildings, daytime programs, and museums. Separate museum tickets and passes are an additional charge. Call for current details, or go to the Web site, www.colonialwilliamsburg.com.

Freedom Pass
$59 for adults, $29 for children and youth 6 to 17
Good for one year from the date of purchase, this option provides visitors with admission to all museums, exhibitions, trade sites, and Williamsburg by Night Programs. This option includes a 50 percent discount on evening programs except during the Christmas season.

Virginia Resident Freedom Pass
$49 for adults, $24 for youth 17 and under
Newcomers to the area should know that all Virginia residents are eligible for a Resident's Pass to Colonial Williamsburg. This pass provides all the benefits of the Freedom Pass at the price of the two-day city pass. You'll need a photo ID and proof of residency to obtain this pass, which is available at the Visitor Center guest services desk. Call (757) 220-7562 for more information.

Hours of Operation

Colonial Williamsburg is open every day of the year, including all holidays. The Visitor Center, where your tour should begin, is open from 8:45 a.m. to 5:45 p.m. daily during the summer, with reduced hours during other seasons. Most buildings in the Historic Area are open from 9:00 a.m. to 5:00 p.m. with some variations. During the summer, some buildings remain open until 6:00 p.m. In the winter, open hours are shortened to 9:30 a.m. to 4:30 p.m.

Transportation

A fleet of Colonial Williamsburg buses circulates through and around the Historic Area, stopping at major points of interest. They carry visitors to and from the Visitor Center continuously from morning until about 10:00 p.m. (this may change seasonally), and ticket holders may board at any stop. Special assistance and shuttle bus service is available to visitors with disabilities. If you need this service, inquire at the Visitor Center, Lumber House ticket office, or Merchants Square Information Center. As we mentioned in our Getting Here, Getting Around chapter, cars are more bother than they're worth when touring the Historic Area. Parking around the Historic Area is limited, and the streets are typically closed to vehicles from 8:00 a.m. to 10:00 p.m. Parking at the Visitor Center is free. All guests at Colonial Williamsburg hotels can rent bikes and strollers at the Tazewell Fitness Center in the Williamsburg Lodge if the weather is nice. Strollers rent for $10.50 a day. Bikes can be rented by the hour for $5.00, for a half-day (four hours) for $11.00, or for a full day for $18.00. Call (757) 220-7690 for more information.

HISTORIC AREA ATTRACTIONS

While it's impossible to absorb everything Colonial Williamsburg has to offer in a day or two, some visitors can't stay much longer. Even a short visit will be memorable if you take the time to plan your tour in advance. Before you visit, check out www.colonial williamsburg.com to get a general idea of what is happening during the time you plan to be in the area, or call (800) HISTORY for a free vacation planner. Then, when you arrive in Williamsburg, ask hotel personnel or staff at the Colonial Williamsburg Visitor Center for a copy of the weekly updated *Visitor's Companion,* a daily calendar and schedule that gives operating hours for Historic Area buildings, restaurants, tours, and events. This publication, without which we personally wouldn't step foot in Williamsburg, can help you decide on an agenda for each day.

Below, we highlight the major buildings and exhibits you won't want to miss, no matter how brief your stay. We recommend the escorted half-hour introductory tour Colonial Williamsburg offers as orientation for a leisurely self-touring vacation, or just as a very pleasant—if short—excursion into the world of 18th-century Williamsburg. You also will want to read through the *Official Colonial Williamsburg Guidebook and Map* (available at the Visitor Center), an excellent introduction to the diverse and sometimes complex experiences in store for you as you travel back in time. While we mention which buildings and exhibits require special reservations, it's always best to check at the Visitor Center the day you plan to tour a specific site, as hours of operation vary, and buildings occasionally are closed to the public.

The Buildings

Governor's Palace

Set on 10 acres of restored gardens, this elegant mansion housed a series of royal governors and the Commonwealth of Virginia's first two governors, Patrick Henry and Thomas Jefferson. The original construction began in 1706 and took 17 years to complete; alterations and redecoration continued until the December 22, 1781, fire that left only the palace foundation. At the north end of the Palace Green, the reconstructed mansion, with its entrance hall, parlor, ballroom, dining rooms, bedchambers, waiting areas, and even a wine cellar, is opulently furnished from an inventory of more than 12,000 items dating to the period of Lord Dunmore, Virginia's last royal governor. Lord Dunmore and his family lived in Governor's Palace in the early 1770s.

Children delight in trying to count the muskets mounted in a circle on the entrance hall ceiling. (We know how many are up there, but it's more fun if you guess before asking your guide.) Check out the incredible crown moldings and wall coverings (that's leather on the walls in the upstairs meeting room), and don't miss all the interesting details throughout the palace. The chairs in Lady Dunmore's upstairs bedchamber are made to simulate bamboo, there really were Venetian blinds on the windows, and the small statues lining the dining room mantel are the actual figurines representing the costumed characters from the masquerade ball commemorating King George III's 21st birthday.

In the 18th century the Governor's Palace was the scene of many get-togethers of early America's well-to-do. Dances, for example, were held about every three months in the palace ballroom, each typically lasting up to 18 hours, since many visitors had journeyed three or more days on horseback to reach Williamsburg, and it would have been exceedingly impolite to send them home too soon.

On the palace grounds you will find a stable and carriage house, kitchen, scullery, laundry, and hexagonal "bagnio" or bathhouse, a real frill in colonial times. Take the time to stroll through the formal gardens, similar to early-18th-century English gardens, which lead to informal terraces and a fish pond. Children love running and playing hide-and-seek in the boxwood maze. The palace, which opened to the public in 1934, is one of Colonial Williamsburg's most popular attractions, drawing 650,000 visitors annually.

Capitol

Prior to the Revolutionary War, the House of Burgesses and a 12-member council met in this ornate structure at the east end of Duke of Gloucester Street. Many important political events that involved Virginia in the Revolutionary War took place here. The most significant was on May 15, 1776, when Virginia's legislators adopted a resolution declaring independence from England, two months before the Continental Congress adopted the Declaration of Independence in Philadelphia. Once war began, and until 1780 when the capital was moved to Richmond, it housed the state government. Foundations were laid in 1701

for the H-shaped building, designed with two wings to hold the bicameral legislative bodies that made up colonial government. Like the Palace, the original Capitol building suffered fire damage, burning in 1747. Its replacement, neglected after the capital moved to Richmond in 1780, eventually burned also. What you see today is a reconstruction of the first Capitol, about which more architectural evidence was found. Here, you can tour the House of Burgesses, Council Chambers, and General Courtroom and join in a number of special evening programs. These include "Cry Witch," a popular re-creation of the dramatic trial of Grace Sherwood, the "Virginia Witch."

Public Gaol

Behind the Capitol on Nicholson Street is the Public Gaol (pronounced jail), with partially original walls and wholly authentic grimness. Shackles that were excavated while the gaol was under restoration are on display. Take a look in the small, dank cells hung with leg irons, and consider spending a winter night in such a place with only a thin blanket for cover. Among the 18th-century inhabitants of these cells were Blackbeard's pirate crew, runaway slaves, Indians, insolvent debtors, and, occasionally, mentally ill persons. During the Revolution British captives, accused spies, and Tory sympathizers were cordially allowed to use the gaol facilities. Part of the gaol has been refurbished to reflect its other function—home to the gaol keeper and his family. Furnishings are representative of those owned by a typical family of the period.

Raleigh Tavern

Revolutionary heroes like Patrick Henry and Thomas Jefferson gathered to discuss politics and reach important conclusions in this famous Duke of Gloucester Street tavern, the first of Colonial Williamsburg's reconstructed buildings to open for public viewing. Built around 1717, the Tavern was the axis around which 18th-century Virginia society, business, and politics revolved. George Washington dined here often and mentions the tavern in

The Magazine on Duke of Gloucester Street. JOETTA SACK

his diary. The Phi Beta Kappa Society was founded here in 1776. The tavern burned in 1859, but original foundations and drawings aided architects in the 1930s reconstruction. We were impressed by the billiard table: Its 6-foot-by-12-foot dimensions required that a room large enough to hold it be added onto the tavern. Behind the Tavern is the Bake Shop, where visitors line up for gingerbread, Shrewsbury cakes, sweet-potato muffins, and other home-baked goodies. The Tavern is on Duke of Gloucester Street near the Capitol.

Magazine and Guardhouse

Across Duke of Gloucester from the popular Chowning's Tavern is the octagonal Magazine, which was built in 1715, by order of Lieutenant Governor Alexander Spotswood, to store arms for the protection of the colony and for trade with the Indians, and a

Guardhouse, reconstructed in 1949. The Magazine played an important role during the French and Indian War (1754–63), when it became evident that the wooden stockade surrounding it served as woefully inadequate protection from enemies. In 1755 Peyton Randolph, Carter Burwell, John Chiswell, Benjamin Waller, and James Power were named as directors to hire workmen to build both a brick wall around the Magazine and a Guardhouse to protect this valuable weaponry storehouse. Although no one knows who actually erected the first Guardhouse and what it looked like, the original structure most likely consisted of a room for the officers, another for the men, and a piazza or porch for the sentry. It is believed that the reconstructed Guardhouse, following that formula, closely resembles the original.

Perhaps the biggest conflict surrounding the Magazine occurred before dawn on April 21, 1775, when British soldiers removed fifteen half-barrels of gunpowder from the storehouse, stirring a protest from Williamsburg's angry citizenry and fanning the fires that led to the Revolution. (Other arms and ammunition stored in the Magazine at the time included shot, flints, and military equipment such as tents.) After the Revolution the Magazine housed a market, meetinghouse, dance school, and livery stable. Humble as they seem, these interim uses probably saved the original building from abandonment and destruction.

George Wythe House

Together with outbuildings and gardens, this spacious original Georgian-style home affords an understanding of gracious living in 18th-century Williamsburg. The house, featuring two great chimneys and large central halls, was used as George Washington's headquarters before the battle of Yorktown. Owner George Wythe was the nation's first law professor and an influential teacher of Thomas Jefferson. During the last several years, the environmental and security systems were upgraded at the Wythe House and a $750,000 redecorating project was completed. The changes involved replacing marble fireplace mantels with more authentic ones of red sandstone and installing custom hand-printed wallpaper after a painstaking analysis revealed that the Wythe House most likely was wallpapered during Wythe's lifetime (1726–1806).

Behind the house you'll find symmetrical gardens, tree box topiaries, and an arbor of shady hornbeam. In reconstructed outbuildings, including a stable, smokehouse, laundry, kitchen, and lumber house, interpreters periodically demonstrate domestic activities such as cooking a batch of apple fritters over the kitchen's open hearth.

Peyton Randolph House

The Peyton Randolph House at Nicholson and North England Streets is among Williamsburg's oldest and finest 18th-century homes. The west wing of the house has stood at its current location since about 1715, sheltering the likes of General Rochambeau, the Marquis de Lafayette, and its namesake, the first president of the Continental Congress. Sir John Randolph purchased the west wing in 1721. A few years later he bought the adjacent one-and-a-half-story house that later became the structure's east wing. Sir John's son, Peyton, speaker of the Virginia House of Burgesses in the years leading to the Revolution, built a spacious and well-appointed two-story central section that connected the two houses via a hall and magnificent stairway. Today this well-preserved center section contains some of the best surviving paneling in Williamsburg as well as much of the original edge-cut pine flooring. The parlor doors have unusually fine brass hinges and locks. In addition to the three sections of the house, there was a full complement of outbuildings in back, including a coach house, stable, dairy, and two-story brick kitchen.

i A 1775 inventory of the Peyton Randolph House showed that the family owned 492 ounces of silver, which translates to the equivalent of 40 or so small silver teapots.

Colonial Williamsburg began restoring the Peyton Randolph House in late 1939 and finished a few months later. Further restoration was completed in the late 1960s. The center and west portions of the house opened for visitors in 1968. In recent years the house once again has been painstakingly restored. All of the work that was done was based on two decades of research and a remarkable room-by-room inventory of the house taken at the time of Peyton Randolph's death in 1775. Many of the outbuildings—including a smokehouse, dairy, storehouse, and 2,000-square-foot kitchen and covered way that attached it to the house—recently were reconstructed. These structures not only restore the historic site, but they also provide the opportunity to interpret the lives of the 27 slaves who lived and worked here.

Bruton Parish Church

On Duke of Gloucester Street west of the Palace Green, Bruton Parish Church is one of America's oldest Episcopal churches, in use since 1715. While Bruton Parish is owned not by Colonial Williamsburg but by congregation members, the public is welcome to tour the church from 9:00 a.m. to 5:00 p.m. Monday through Saturday and from 1:00 to 5:00 p.m. Sunday. The church was fully restored in 1940. Walls and windows are original. The stone baptismal font, according to legend, was brought from an earlier Jamestown church. The churchyard holds many 18th-century graves. Buried inside the church is Francis Fauquier, one of Virginia's royal governors. Evening organ recitals, chamber music performances, and choral concerts frequently are presented at the church. For more on the Bruton Parish Church, turn to the chapter on Attractions. And be sure to check out "The Legend of Bruton Parish Vault" in our Myths and Legends chapter.

The Gardens

While the one-of-a-kind buildings of Colonial Williamsburg intrigue the mind, the Historic Area's 100 or so gardens are balm for the spirit. Luckily, you will stumble upon them just about everywhere you turn. Rest assured, in addition to its beauty, each garden has been meticulously researched for style and accuracy in the Dutch, English, and southern traditions of the 17th and 18th centuries. Archaeological digs conducted on many sites often revealed the remains of walkways, brick walls, and fence lines, which served as blueprints for the gardens and outbuildings eventually erected on each lot.

Most of Colonial Williamsburg's gardens were planted from the 1930s through the 1950s and reflect the Colonial Revival style, which tends to be rather refined and elegant. Ongoing research suggests that this interpretation of our nation's colonial gardens may not be accurate; thus Colonial Williamsburg gradually is reworking its gardens in a simpler form.

As you stroll through these gardens, you will enjoy a profusion of greens, including English boxwood, hollyhock, and Yaupon holly. Seasonal flowers—everything from the wandering phlox to the purple crocus—provide a wash of color that changes with the passing months. Kitchen and vegetable gardens are yet another part of the Historic Area landscape. While corn, tobacco, wheat, cotton, and flax were grown in the fields, it was the much smaller kitchen gardens that provided the fruits and vegetables used at the table and for preserving.

As part of its regular programming, Colonial Williamsburg offers a guided Garden History Walk through its restored grounds. Consult your *Visitor's Companion* for tour availability.

Historic Meals

A visit to Williamsburg, no matter how short, should include at least one meal in one of the popular restored taverns. All Colonial Williamsburg taverns are furnished with an 18th-century flair, but each offers a different adventure in dining. All taverns also offer seasonal garden dining, a delightful option on a balmy spring or cool fall evening. Once you read the tavern descriptions and choose the

Close-up

Christmas in Colonial Williamsburg

In colonial times feasts and celebrations were the highlights of the Christmas season. Families and neighbors gathered together to celebrate with the best their tables could offer. In the 18th century the holiday season began on December 24 and culminated with a large celebration on the Twelfth Night, January 6.

These days, the holiday season is still one of the most popular times to visit Colonial Williamsburg. The first Christmas celebration organized for visitors took place in 1936, and the celebrations have gotten even grander in recent decades, adding modern touches to time-honored colonial traditions. It's a perfect time to see the village decked out in 17th-century holiday decor, take in a holiday concert, and taste some traditional Yuletide dishes.

The Christmas season is officially ushered in on the first Sunday in December with the Grand Illumination. Candles and cressets are lit around the Historic Area and musical and theatrical performances are held in several areas. Finally, three impressive fireworks displays take place over the Governor's Palace, the Magazine, and the Capitol.

Many of the restaurants offer special holiday menus, and one of the favorite culinary activities is a wine dinner with "Thomas Jefferson, Connoisseur of the Colonies." A reenactor lectures on Mr. Jefferson's travels through Europe as visitors feast on his favorite cuisine and wines. Visitors with sweet tooths won't want to miss a breakfast with the colony's pastry and culinary chefs, as they demonstrate cooking traditional holiday meals. The Shields Tavern and King's Arms Tavern also host scrumptious selections of holiday dinners.

Colonial Williamsburg guides will lead visitors through the streets to see the lovely decorations on all the buildings. Just outside the Historic Area, the Green Spring Garden Club hosts an annual Christmas homes tour of private residences that have been beautifully decorated as well.

And look for concerts of music played on 18th-century or reproduction instruments at the candlelit House of Burgesses or the Governor's Palace. In addition, the Fifes and Drums offer an annual concert of international military music and Christmas tunes.

Just be sure to make reservations early, as many hotels and restaurants book up weeks in advance. For more information, visit the Colonial Williamsburg Web site, www.history.org/Christmas, or call (800) HISTORY.

one that tickles your fancy, you can make reservations by calling (757) 229-2141 or (800) TAVERNS or by stopping in at the Visitor Center, where you can also find out about hours and seasonal openings. Reservations are recommended at all but Chowning's Tavern, which only offers a first-come, first-served option.

Take a look, too, at our Restaurants chapter for more information about tavern dining and entertainment. Recipes from the tavern kitchens as well as from other Colonial Williamsburg restaurants are published in books available at the Visitor Center bookstore. The *Williamsburg Cookbook* contains 193 recipes, traditional and contemporary, culled from the taverns and other restaurants in Colonial Williamsburg.

Chowning's Tavern

The public that frequented Chowning's Tavern on Duke of Gloucester Street were locals—farmers who sold produce at market, people with business at the courthouse, and bystanders with a little time to kill. From 11:30 a.m. to 5:00 p.m., head to Chowning's for reasonably fast casual fare, such as barbecue, hot dogs, ribs, corn on the cob, and veggie burgers. Food is available from the new Cider Stand from the garden bar located behind the tavern, facing Market Square, allowing guests to quickly return to the day's programs and pursuits. Seating is available under the grape arbor or inside the tavern. From 5:00 p.m. on Chowning's resembles a colonial alehouse and offers light fare, local ales and wines, rums, and Colonial Williamsburg's own draft root beer and ginger ale. The Gambols, a lively nighttime program, operates throughout the evening. Balladeers rouse guests in period sing-alongs and play popular games of the day.

King's Arms Tavern

In its original incarnation the King's Arms Tavern, also on Duke of Gloucester Street, catered to Virginia's gentry. Today the menu features recipes from English cookbooks of the 17th and 18th centuries. Choose from a variety of colonial favorites including peanut "soupe," Sally Lunn bread, oyster-stuffed filet mignon, roast prime rib of beef, Cavalier's lamb, or game "pye." Complement your meal with a selection from the extensive wine list and, for dessert, pucker up for a bite of sour cherry trifle.

Christiana Campbell's Tavern

Christiana Campbell's Tavern on Waller Street, where Washington also dined, specializes in fresh seafood, offering foods from all 13 original colonies. Specialties include New England clam chowder, Maryland crab cakes and oyster fritters, and fish muddle from the Carolinas, as well as crabmeat omelets, filet mignon, and grilled regional fresh fish. Entrees are complemented by longtime tavern favorites, such as Campbell's cabbage slaw, spoon bread, and sweet-potato muffins. Finish your meal off with a slice of black-bottom chocolate pecan pie. The tavern is closed Sunday and Monday.

Shields Tavern

The fourth and newest tavern operated by Colonial Williamsburg, Shields Tavern on Duke of Gloucester Street, served lower gentry in the middle 1700s. The menu here is inspired by early American cookbooks and incorporates seasonal changes using foods available locally. This includes roasted duckling, veal "birds," and roasted chicken with Virginia ham. If you're up for it, there's always the syllabub, a fortified dessert drink made with sherry, wine, and cream.

Trade Shops and Demonstrations

Scattered throughout the Historic Area are costumed craftspeople, journeymen, and apprentices practicing the various old trades that were part of life in the 18th century. At the Printing Office on Duke of Gloucester Street, visitors can see newspapers printed on an 18th-century press, learn about bookbinding, and watch periodic demonstrations of typesetting, papermaking, and decorating. At the James Anderson Blacksmith Shop, seven reconstructed forges operate, and smithing techniques are demonstrated. Silversmiths craft mote spoons—decoratively perforated and good for straining tea—at The Golden Ball, where you can also buy gold and silver jewelry. The Margaret Hunter Shop re-creates the atmosphere and activity of an 18th-century milliner's, with hats, gloves, purses, shoes, and embroidery pieces on the shelves.

Next door to the King's Arms Tavern, a wigmaker uses goat, horse, yak, and human hair to conjure up a few curls. (A few years ago, the wigmaker shop began an apprentice program that for the first time in CW history admits women.) Out on North England Street, you can visit Robertson's Windmill, where wind-driven sails power stones that grind corn. Nearby, coopers shape and assemble staves to form casks, piggins, and other wooden containers. In addition, harness and saddle makers, shoemakers, cabinetmakers, brass founders, gunsmiths, wheelwrights, carpenters, cooks, and basket makers go about their business in Historic Area sites.

Mercantile Shops

While some of the historic trade shops sell crafted items, several operating mercantile shops accurately re-create 18th-century business premises, offering wares and services representative of colonial times. Finest among these is Prentis Store, an original

building dating from 1740 that features reproductions of 18th-century wares. Tarpley's Store sells pottery, educational toys, and soaps, while the Greenhow Store's inventory includes candy, three-cornered hats, and fifes. These stores, along with the Mary Dickinson Store, which sells jewelry, toiletries, and women's accessories, and the M. Dubois Grocer's Shop, where you can pick up a bottle of tavern sparkling cider, can all be visited on Duke of Gloucester Street. At the Colonial Post Office you'll find an extensive collection of 18th-century prints and maps as well as postcards that can be hand-canceled using the original 18th-century Williamsburg postmark, while behind the Secretary's Office is Tickets, Treasures and Books, which sells Colonial Williamsburg tickets, children's items, and books relating to early American history. (For more details on these shops, see the Shopping chapter.)

Visitors enjoy carriage rides that pass by the mercantile shops. JOETTA SACK

Other Buildings and Exhibits

If you aren't pressed for time, you may want to explore more restored or reconstructed sites in the Historic Area, and there are a few we'd like to particularly recommend.

James Geddy House and Foundry

The James Geddy House and Foundry, on Duke of Gloucester Street just across the Palace Green from Bruton Parish Church, was home to a family of artisans who worked in bronze, brass, pewter, and silver. Visitors to the house can learn about the life of an 18th-century tradesman and his children by helping out at the foundry or assisting Grandma Geddy (mother of eight) with the laundry.

Thomas Everard House

The Thomas Everard House on the Palace Green is known for its carved woodwork. The yard is paved with original bricks found during excavation, and the smokehouse and kitchen are original restored structures. The Thomas Everard House was one of three buildings included in a $2.5 million renovation project that included state-of-the-art air conditioning and heating, fire detectors, security systems, and computerized humidity and temperature controls. While the restoration work was going on, historians had a rare opportunity to explore much of the building and readjust their thinking about its history. The house was built by John Brush, then occupied by Henry Cary, who extensively renovated it between 1730 and 1740. Thomas Everard moved in around 1770 and added wallpaper in the dining room and chamber. The Colonial Williamsburg tour focuses on the life of Everard, an immigrant and mayor of Williamsburg, and the lives of his family and 19 slaves.

Wetherburn's Tavern

Wetherburn's Tavern, an original building, was carefully refurnished using information gleaned from a detailed inventory left of Henry Wetherburn's estate and from artifacts uncovered during excavation at the site. Tours spotlight the lives of Wetherburn's family and slaves. The house is on Duke of Gloucester Street next to Tarpley's Store.

Courthouse

With its cupola, weather vane, and round-headed windows, the Courthouse is visible up and down Duke of Gloucester Street. It is one of three courthouses in Williamsburg, and the first to be built here. A series of special programs allows visitors to experience the day-to-day functioning of early American jurisprudence. Costumed interpreters and guides lead visitors through participatory scenes, such as trials and impromptu dialogues. Interesting furnishings include the chief magistrate's thronelike chair and cloth-bound docket books used by colonial clerks and sheriffs.

Beyond the Historic Area

Visitors lucky enough to have more than a few days to spend in the area, those on return trips, and those with special interests can enhance their appreciation of 18th-century history, arts, and related phenomena by visiting some of the properties operated by Colonial Williamsburg outside the Historic Area. Unless otherwise noted, entry to these attractions is included in a Colonial Williamsburg pass.

Bassett Hall
Off Francis Street
(757) 220-7724
Bassett Hall is the two-story, 18th-century frame house that was the Williamsburg home of John D. Rockefeller Jr. and his wife, Abby Aldrich Rockefeller. While earlier tours of the home focused on Mrs. Rockefeller's folk art collection, visitors now learn about the Rockefellers themselves and about their contribution to the creation of Colonial Williamsburg. Bequeathed to the foundation in 1979, the house is set on a 585-acre tract of woodlands, and the property includes a teahouse, called the Orangerie, and three original outbuildings: a smokehouse, kitchen, and dairy. Bassett Hall reopened in 2002 after undergoing

renovations that include a new exhibition of the history of the Rockefellers at Bassett Hall and a return of the extensive gardens to their 1940s appearance. It is open to the public 9:00 a.m. to 5:00 p.m. daily.

Abby Aldrich Rockefeller
Folk Art Museum

This museum closed in 2005, and its extensive collection of folk art is now showcased at a separate hall in the expanded DeWitt Wallace Decorative Arts Museum.

Abby Aldrich Rockefeller began collecting folk art early in the 20th century. By her death in the 1940s, she had amassed an impressive array of objects, more than 400 of which formed the basis for the Abby Aldrich Rockefeller Folk Art Museum.

Established in 1957 by John D. Rockefeller Jr. in honor of his wife and her love of folk art, it's one of the oldest institutions in the country dedicated solely to collecting and preserving American folk art.

Today the collection numbers more than 4,000 pieces and exhibits change seasonally. It is open from 10:00 a.m. until 7:00 p.m. from mid-March through December. Call for winter hours.

Public Hospital of 1773
Corner of Francis and South Henry Streets
(757) 229-1000

The somber building at the corner of Francis and South Henry Streets is a reconstruction of the first public institution for the mentally ill to be built in colonial America. Opened in 1773 and known as the Hospital for Lunaticks, this facility first treated its inmates more as prisoners than patients, as the early small cells indicate. Nineteenth-century scientific and medical advances improved methods of treatment, which the hospital's interpretive exhibits chronicle, but also on display are a number of devices used to treat patients, some of which resemble implements of torture. The hospital is open from 11:00 a.m. to 6:00 p.m. daily.

DeWitt Wallace Decorative Arts Museum
Corner of Francis and South Henry Streets
(757) 220-7724

Adjacent to the Public Hospital is a fascinating museum devoted to British and American decorative arts from 1600 through 1830. The contemporary two-tiered building, designed by internationally known architect I. M. Pei and completed in 1985, features exhibits of metal, ceramics, glass, prints, textiles, costumes, and other decorative objects from Colonial Williamsburg's permanent collections. The collection of Virginia furniture is the largest of its type in the world, and the collection of English pottery is more vast than any other on this side of the Atlantic. The museum features 11 galleries and 27,500 square feet of exhibition space, where more than 8,000 objects and works of art are on display. Among the finest pieces are a full-length portrait of George III, painted by English artist Allan Ramsay; a burled-walnut and gilt Tompion clock, which is among a handful of the most important pieces of English furniture in the United States; and a 1735 mahogany tea table, which had been owned by the Galt family for more than 200 years.

Changing exhibits have included *Identifying Ceramics: The Who, What, and Ware* and *Ordering the Wilderness*, which explores Virginians' relationship to both the land and the instruments used to survey and map the land.

It would be easy to spend the better part of a day browsing through the illuminating museum or lingering in the comforting natural light of the museum's glass-roofed courtyards. Fortunately, a cafe on the gallery's lower level serves lunch, tea, and light refreshments. A gift shop selling reproductions and decorative arts journals is also on the premises. The museum is open from 10:00 a.m. to 7:00 p.m. daily from mid-March to December 31, but hours vary outside those months and are subject to change without notice. Admission is included in any Colonial Williamsburg ticket. Call the gallery for information on tours and exhibits.

Take time to visit CW's Web site, www.colonialwilliamsburg.com, to peruse menus, plan your schedule, purchase tickets and passes, or book your hotel.

Carter's Grove, Wolstenholme Towne, and the Winthrop Rockefeller Archaeology Museum
U.S. Route 60,
8 miles east of Historic Area

On the James River, 8 miles southeast of Williamsburg, is Carter's Grove, a beautiful 750-acre plantation with a richly complex 400-year history. There is a reconstructed slave quarter on the site, uncovered by accident when archaeologists discovered a series of pits that slaves had dug for storing food under their dwellings. Gardens, corncribs, and chicken compounds were re-created here, along with three rustic domiciles that would have housed 24 slaves. Unfortunately, the Carter's Grove museums closed in 2003 for an assessment of the property and grounds. In December 2006, Colonial Williamsburg officials announced that they will sell the property. As of late 2007, they were collaborating with the National Trust for Historic Preservation and the Virginia Department of Natural Resources to develop rules for protecting the historic property from development.

The interpretation of slave life has moved to the downtown Historic Area. For more information, contact the Colonial Williamsburg Visitor Center, (757) 229-1000.

Winthrop Rockefeller Archaeology Museum

The Winthrop Rockefeller Archaeology Museum presents early-17th-century and Native American artifacts excavated from the Wolstenholme Towne site at Carter's Grove. Two tales are told in the 7,000-square-foot underground facility. First is the tale of ill-fated Wolstenholme Towne and the English colonists who lived there from 1619 to 1622,

when Powhatan Indians virtually destroyed the settlement. Second is the story of the rediscovery and excavation of Wolstenholme Towne by Colonial Williamsburg archaeologists in the 1970s. Hundreds of artifacts have been displayed here, but history has not been allowed to sit mute and remote behind glass. Audiovisual displays, reconstructive paintings, photographs from the excavation itself, and interactive opportunities, such as the diver's mask through which visitors have been able to watch the excavation of a shipwreck, have made for a dynamic museum experience.

At least 57 of Wolstenholme Towne's inhabitants were killed, and others were taken captive, on March 22, 1622, when once-friendly Powhatan Indians staged a regional uprising. Many questions remain about this massacre: How many exactly survived? What became of those the Indians took as captives? When was the fort burned? New settlers from England eventually did arrive at Wolstenholme to bolster the population, but the town never fully recuperated. Contagion and starvation left scarcely 30 occupants by 1625. Gradually the settlement disappeared from view, grown over and forgotten.

Wolstenholme Towne

Although up to half of the Wolstenholme site may have been lost already to shore erosion, it's almost certain that much more of our early history remains buried in the many fields of Carter's Grove. Whether future excavation will uncover answers to the mysteries of Wolstenholme or just more enigmas, only time will tell. Down the slope from the underground museum's tunnel-like exit is the partially reconstructed Wolstenholme site, including palisades, buildings, and fences.

Carter's Grove Mansion

On a bluff overlooking the river stands this lovely brick mansion, built in the 1750s by Carter Burwell, grandson of Robert "King" Carter, colonial Virginia's wealthiest planter. The plantation house was considered sophisticated in design and was elegantly furnished for the entertainment of Virginia aristocracy. The interior woodwork of soft Virginia pine is especially remarkable, as are the mahogany balustrade of the staircase, the fluted Ionic pilasters on the wall, and the intricate cornice work. The "Grove Farm" passed out of Carter family hands in 1838, however, after which a succession of owners made changes to the original Georgian structure, adding a Victorian veranda and painting over pine paneling. Then, in 1928, Archibald McCrea bought the property and a full-scale renovation of the mansion began. The result of the wealthy McCrea's "restoration" of Carter's Grove was a grand Colonial Revival–style plantation manor, often called America's most beautiful house. McCrea's restoration raised the roof, connected dependencies, and added modern plumbing but hid the toilets. The restoration revealed more about the romantic view of the past held by members of 1930s high society than about actual colonial history and Colonial Williamsburg, to which the mansion was deeded in 1969.

Once Colonial Williamsburg owned the property, the foundation at first sought to restore Carter's Grove as an authentic 18th-century plantation. Plans changed, however, and today Carter's Grove mansion largely reflects the McCreas' Revivalist tastes. This was done partially in deference to the interest in historic preservation in America that Colonial Revival enthusiasts like the McCreas helped spark. Nevertheless, some 18th-century details recall the mansion's original splendor, including the fine carved woodwork of the entry and mahogany staircase as well as pilasters and cornices created by English master artisan Richard Baylis in the 1750s. Furnishings reflect the mansion's mixed uses and ancestry—chintz

i Did you know that in 18th-century Williamsburg a married woman could take over her husband's business upon his death, but if she remarried, the business became the property of her new spouse?

sofas in drawing rooms and an assortment of 1940s objects juxtapose a spinning wheel and flatirons in the kitchen. Ghosts of 18th-century pirates reportedly haunt the wine cellar in the mansion.

Seasonal Programs and Special Tours

Each year Colonial Williamsburg tailors many of its programs around a special theme. One year CW's "Taking Possession" programs illustrated for visitors how three forces—free-born Virginians' interest in owning their land, the desire of native inhabitants to retain control of their ancestral homes, and the development of imperial policies—evolved during the 17th and 18th centuries. No matter what time of year you come to Colonial Williamsburg, you'll find an array of special tours and programs available, many of which coincide with the annual theme. Although the programs are constantly changed and updated, here are a few examples of what you may come across.

Family Programs

If you think a historical site is not a place to take children—and still have a good time—think again. Colonial Williamsburg offers a growing number of special programs designed to enrich every family's exploration of the past, and in fact, CW increased its family programs by 50 percent in 2003. Although there are literally dozens of programs designed specifically for family enjoyment and participation, we have highlighted a handful we're sure you will enjoy. There are some exceptions, but the majority of family programs are offered beginning in mid-June and continuing through the summer. During their visit children also have the opportunity to don colonial garb (available for rent in a tent next to the Powder Magazine on Market Square) and play with 18th-century toys and games. Since activities not only vary from day to day, but also from hour to hour, check that indispensable *Visitor's Companion* for specific times and locations.

Family Life Adventures

These activities take place at buildings throughout the Historic Area. At the Benjamin Powell site, families can engage in normal household tasks using objects straight from the 18th century. At the Wythe House they can congregate in the backyard and learn to make stitch books, create watercolor paintings, put together old-fashioned puzzles, or be instructed in the fine art of writing. At the Governor's Palace the activities are decidedly more genteel: Parents are encouraged to join their youngsters in a game of lawn bowling, hoops, pickup sticks, tops, or checkers.

At the Public Gaol, learn about the gaoler and his family and join them as they go about their daily activities, like sewing, singing, or dancing.

You Are There

In Colonial Williamsburg adults aren't the only ones who get to have all the fun. Several interpretive programs engage children, from reenactments of county and city court sessions to military encampments, where your child can experience 18th-century military life through marching, musket drills, and observing a cannon firing.

Song and Dance

To get into the rhythm of colonial life, families can participate in 18th-century dance demonstrations by costumed interpreters or enjoy a potpourri of 18th-century music along the Palace Green, especially recommended for families with children under age 12. In another program, "18th-Century Dance," costumed youth interpreters demonstrate, interpret, and help visitors learn about 18th-century dance in Virginia, as well as encourage visitor participation. CW's musical ambassadors, the Fifes & Drums, perform in parades and military music programs daily during the summer months.

Walking Tours

These unique walking tours focus on specific aspects of 18th-century life. On a garden walk you and your family can discover how the plants in the colonial area reflected the lives and ideals of the populace of the time, while "The Other Half" walk provides an in-depth look at the African and African-Virginian experience of the era. Or discover how artifacts in the Historic Area are processed and interpreted by taking the "Rubbish, Treasures, and Colonial Life" walking tour. All ticket holders must make reservations at any ticket sales location for the one-hour tours, which vary daily. All tours start at the Lumber House ticket office unless otherwise noted.

Cool Things to See and Do

As your family strolls through Colonial Williamsburg, attentive youngsters will be rewarded with the unusual sights, sounds, and opportunities afforded by the Historic Area. Where else would they get to help brick makers knead clay to mold into bricks, watch cooks stir up batches of 18th-century victuals, chat with Thomas Jefferson, George and Martha Washington, and Patrick Henry about events of the day, or form a bucket brigade on an 18th-century fire engine? For the animal lover in the group, there's also the rare opportunity to glimpse winged and furry creatures they may never see elsewhere—the English Leicester long-wool sheep, Red Devon milking cattle, and American Cream draft horses that were part of the landscape in the 1700s. In "Colonial Kids on Parade," guests can learn the history of Williamsburg through the eyes of its children, who take guests from the earliest days of the town's history through the Revolution.

Evening Events

The Colonial Performances, several of which are listed later, require a separate ticket and can be purchased at any ticket sales location, including the Visitor Center and the Lumber House ticket office. All performances except "Cry Witch" are $12.00 per person 6 and up, $5.00 for children 5 and under. Admission for "Cry Witch" is $15.00 per person 6 and up, $7.50 for children 5 and under (it is not recommended for young children, however).

Courtroom Reenactments

A crowd of tourists jams into the overheated Courthouse, slides onto smooth wooden benches, and waits for the court proceedings to begin, shushing the children.

In strut the magistrates, witnesses, deputy kings attorney, and chief justice. "Hear ye, hear ye, hear ye...All rise," shouts the chief justice, and as the crowd stands, he introduces the case: a capital crime involving the slave Moses.

Then Moses is let into the courtroom from a side door, and he shuffles to the defense stand, his head bowed low, his hands cuffed in front.

Nearly daily during the summer months, Colonial Williamsburg throws open the Courthouse doors and invites visitors to experience up close how the early legal system worked in this nation. Actors bring to life several actual court cases tried in Williamsburg and York County in the late 18th century. All deal with slavery in some way.

In this particular trial Moses is accused of assault and highway robbery of a woman, Elizabeth Dorin, late one night on a country road not far from town.

In those times enslaved people were tried in court when accused of crimes. Even though legally slaves were a form of property, they were held responsible for their actions. However, slaves had no right of appeal to a higher court and could not be tried by a jury. And, since they had no money, they couldn't hire an attorney and had to defend themselves. Even with the odds stacked against them, slaves who were brought to trial in York County Court were acquitted about a third of the time, according to John Greenman, an actor who played the role of chief justice.

The case of Moses also led to his acquittal, much to the relief of the audience, who cheered and applauded when the decision was announced. The jury of lawyers decided to let Moses go because there was no witness to the crime, and the victim, a Quaker, refused to testify for religious reasons. The lawyers denigrated Moses for having illegally married and fathered two children with a white woman, but gave him some credit: "Moses is no fool."

"I ain't got nothing but my word," Moses said during his brief testimony. "I didn't rob anyone. If you gonna steal, the last person you are going to rob is some Quaker!"

According to Greenman, some of CW's reenacted court trials involving slaves do not have a happy ending, and it's not always a comfortable experience for visitors. It helps that Greenway or another reenactor stands outside after the trial to answer visitors' questions and provide more background information on the actual cases.

Freedom Pass holders receive half off the ticket price.

As the capital of Virginia, Williamsburg was the cultural center of the colony. As such, the nights come alive with entertainment, including musical galas, colonial dancing, dramatic presentations, and riveting plays.

Check your *Visitor's Companion* for specific dates, times, and locations during the week you are visiting. As we noted earlier, programming changes frequently, so selections may be different during the time you are in town.

"CLANDESTINE MARRIAGE"

In this 18th-century play, two young lovers try to keep their marriage a secret, while their families plot to buy and sell their relations for their own wealth and respectability.

"CRY WITCH"

One of the most enduring of Colonial Williamsburg's programs, this is a highly enjoyable presentation of an early-18th-century witch trial, but it is not recommended for young children. Audience members may pose questions to witnesses and play the role of jury in the strange case of Grace Sherwood, accused of causing neighbors' crops to fail, bewitching folks, and turning herself into a cat. The location of this program sometimes varies, but it is typically held at the Capitol.

A GRAND MEDLEY OF ENTERTAINMENT

A 90-minute "variety show" done colonial style features music, magic, feats of strength, trained animals, and other amusements guaranteed to entertain young and old alike, in this re-creation of an 18th-century traveling show.

"JUMPIN' THE BROOM"

A young enslaved couple form a marriage union despite the uncertainty of slavery. While preteens may be enthralled by this drama, the mature subject matter makes it inappropriate for younger children

LEGENDS: GHOSTS, MYSTERIES, AND MYTHS WALKING TOUR

Here visitors travel to candlelit rooms throughout CW to hear colonial tales of mystery and the unexplained.

"PAPA SAID, MAMA SAID"

This presentation has guests journey back in time to learn how 18th-century enslaved Africans and their descendants created an oral culture through storytelling.

DANCE, OUR DEAREST DIVERSION

Find out about the role of dance in 18th-century society and join in the fun.

"REMEMBER ME WHEN FREEDOM COMES"

Step back in time and spend an evening with Old Paris as he recalls Africa and his enslavement. You also will watch and understand the spiritual and cultural ties and customs that helped Old Paris—and those like him—survive slavery.

"WILLIAMSBURG'S MOST WANTED"

Deliberate with other guests over the guilt or innocence of some of the most notorious accused murderers of Colonial Virginia.

Other Programs and Events

THE COLONIAL WILLIAMSBURG FIFES & DRUMS

Beating drums or trilling fifes, this colorful group makes regular marches down CW's Duke of Gloucester Street throughout much of the year. On various dates (which are always noted in your *Visitor's Companion*), visitors can enjoy the 18th-century ceremony of reveille in the morning at Market Square Green. In the early evening the corps does its retreat, a time when pickets are posted, flags lowered, and the soldiers relieved of their daily duties. All told, the corps performs in and around Colonial Williamsburg nearly 500 times during the year, in daily programs from April through

The Colonial Williamsburg Fifes & Drums Corps. LYNN ZELEM

October and during special programs on major holidays. In the spring and summer, the corps usually marches at 5:00 p.m. on Wednesday and 1:00 p.m. on Saturday, weather permitting.

Founded in 1958, the corps traditionally has been made up of boys 10 through 18. In 1999 the Colonial Williamsburg Foundation opened the corps to female applicants for the first time. Typically, applicants for this extremely popular program are placed on a waiting list around age 5 and must participate in the required training before they can become active members of the corps. Nearly 100 youths perform as members of the corps' two units: a junior corps and a senior corps. Over the years the corps has served as Colonial Williamsburg's musical ambassadors across the nation, performing at Macy's Thanksgiving Day Parade in New York, the

Pentagon in Washington, D.C., Independence Hall in Philadelphia, and the Art Institute of Chicago.

For specific Colonial Williamsburg Fifes & Drums performance times during your visit, consult your *Visitor's Companion.*

African-American Heritage

In recent years Colonial Williamsburg has begun to examine more fully the experiences of African Americans brought to the Virginia Colony in the 18th century. After all, during the 18th century, half of Williamsburg's population was black.

The foundation's black-history department was created in 1982 and in its early years included only one tour and a few music programs. But in 1988 the Department of African American Interpretation and Presentations was founded, and, for the last dozen

ℹ️ Over the last six decades, many of our nation's leaders have strolled down CW streets. Whether you know it or not, you are following in the footsteps of Presidents Franklin Roosevelt, Harry Truman, Dwight Eisenhower, Lyndon Johnson, Richard Nixon, Gerald Ford, Jimmy Carter, Ronald Reagan, and Bill Clinton.

years or so, this creative and ambitious group has put together dramatic interpretations depicting everything from runaway slaves to the relationship of Thomas Jefferson to his personal servant. To more accurately reflect the population of the time, a number of tours and programs dealing with these inhabitants' lives are now offered throughout the year.

Although it is not being offered at this time, one African-American program that focused national attention on Colonial Williamsburg was a controversial slave auction staged in October 1994. The program, which brought a crowd of thousands to Duke of Gloucester Street, recounted the selling of a pregnant slave and her husband to different masters as well as the sale of two other slaves along with land and farm equipment during an auction to settle estates and debts. It was the first such re-creation for the Colonial Williamsburg Foundation, and it brought protests from the NAACP and the Southern Christian Leadership Conference, a vote of acceptance from Jesse Jackson, front-page headlines in local newspapers, and praise and criticism from across the country. When

ℹ️ The Colonial Williamsburg Historic Area is kept safe from the intrusion of the modern world by a 3,000-acre greenbelt.

all was said and done, however, the program, which emotionally depicted the horrors of slavery, made the point it had set out to make in the first place. Whether the slave auction program will ever be revived is still a matter of discussion.

In 1999 Colonial Williamsburg debuted its "Enslaving Virginia" programs, which introduced visitors to the social, moral, and political realities of slavery in colonial Virginia. Set on the eve of the American Revolution, these programs carefully detailed slavery's development as well as its impact on the lives of all Virginians.

In 2001 the "Enslaving Virginia" program became a daily discussion with a CW historian about the African-American experience during colonial times. It also includes a daily guided walking tour, which explores the conditions that led to the development of slavery.

Annual Events

There are a number of celebrations that take place in the restored area throughout the year. Perhaps the most well-known—and certainly the most spectacular—is the Grand Illumination, which marks the beginning of the Christmas holiday season in Colonial Williamsburg. This decades-old tradition attracts thousands of revelers to the Historic Area the first Sunday of December to hear the cannon sound, see the thousands of candles that illuminate the windows in public buildings, and view the colorful explosion of fireworks. Other annual events include a February Colonial Williamsburg Antiques Forum; a Garden Symposium each April; Memorial Day ceremonies; Independence Day festivities with fireworks on July 4; and military reenactments held at various times throughout the year. For a complete and detailed rundown of these events and other yearly festivals and celebrations, please turn to our chapter on Annual Events.

ATTRACTIONS

In and around Colonial Williamsburg, boredom busters abound. Where else can you converse with colonial crusaders, relive the Revolution, or ride the Roman Rapids, all in the same day? And those are just a few of the highlights. Indeed, there's so much to see and do in the Williamsburg area, it's hard for visitors to decide what not to include on their itineraries the first—or even second—time around. After you've strolled through the Colonial Williamsburg Historic Area, seen the beginnings of American civilization as we know it at Jamestown, and followed in George Washington's footsteps on the Yorktown battlefield, there still are many, many historic treasures to tour. These include the James River plantations, along historic Route 5; the College of William and Mary, which celebrates its 315th birthday in 2008; and a number of Williamsburg churches that date back as far as 1715.

The other attractions profiled in this chapter are of the decidedly modern sort and make an exciting complement to historic sightseeing. High-flying thrills in the various "countries" of Busch Gardens await you, as well as the wet and wild exhilaration of tube rides at Water Country USA and the downright euphoric feeling of shopping at the sprawling Williamsburg Pottery complex just off U.S. Route 60.

We admit that stretching your time and budget to make room for all Williamsburg has to offer is difficult. Our best advice is to plan ahead, choosing the activities best suited to your interests. But we also think good vacations should allow room for a little spontaneity, a walk on the wilder side, if you will. So be flexible, be outrageous, and try something completely new. And most of all, make sure you mean it when you mail off those postcards

that proclaim to friends back home: "Having a great time in Williamsburg!"

HISTORIC ATTRACTIONS
James River Plantations

While Virginia's Historic Triangle offers visitors plenty to see and do, it also provides easy access to myriad attractions just a short drive outside the immediate Williamsburg area. Of particular interest to history and architecture buffs are the historic James River plantations in James City and Charles City Counties. For many whose vision of Southern plantations has been shaped by *Gone with the Wind*, these structures will be a surprise. Predating the era of Greek Revival columns and other such adornments, the refined Georgian architecture of the buildings, executed in rich red-brick or in white wood, is understated and takes its elegance from simplicity and tasteful detail. These were among the first mansions in the country, and their history is, in a sense, ours. These magnificent estates are located along the James River because that was the area's main artery when they were built. Luckily, many are open to the public. In cases where the houses are not open, visitors usually are welcome to tour the grounds. The trip on Route 5 from Williamsburg to Richmond to visit the plantations is gorgeous, passing through thick, overarching forests and wide open farmlands. It was colonial Virginia's premier land route and remains an Insiders' favorite route west, especially in autumn.

There is a Progressive Plantation Tour for groups, which includes guided tours of the grounds and houses at Piney Grove, North Bend, Edgewood, and Westover plantations. For more details on the Progressive Tour, call (804) 829-2480.

Belle Aire Plantation
11800 John Tyler Highway
(Route 5), Charles City County
(804) 829-2431
www.jamesriverplantations.com
Just off Virginia's scenic byway, Route 5, east
of the Charles City County courthouse complex, this charming and deceptively large mid-
17th-century frame house—the only one
known to still stand in the Commonwealth—
was built around 1670. While it was open to
the public for many years, unfortunately
today it is not, though the owners do open
their doors to group tours of 20 or more, provided they make reservations well in advance.
An admission of $10 per person is charged.
The tour includes a peek at four first-floor
rooms, three upstairs bedchambers, and the
grounds. (Belle Aire also is open during Historic Garden Week, near the end of April each
year.) Call for group rates.

Berkeley Plantation
12602 Harrison Landing Road,
off Route 5, Charles City County
(804) 829-6018
www.berkeleyplantation.com
This was the site of the first official Thanksgiving in North America, celebrated by English
settlers on December 4, 1619. It is on Route
5, halfway between Williamsburg and Richmond. Berkeley is one of Virginia's most historic plantations, as it was the birthplace of
Benjamin Harrison, a signer of the Declaration
of Independence, and his third son, William
Henry Harrison, who was the ninth president
of the United States. The plantation was
patented in 1618, and the stately Georgian
mansion, overlooking the James River, was
built in 1726 of brick fired on the site. It is said
to be the oldest three-story brick house in Virginia and the first with a pediment roof. The
handsome Adam woodwork and double
arches in the great rooms were installed by
Benjamin Harrison VI in 1790 at the direction
of Thomas Jefferson. The rooms in the house
are furnished with period antiques. As you
approach the site along Route 5 in Charles

City County, you'll have to follow a sharp
curve onto a side road that leads to the plantation drive.

Two tidbits of Berkeley history deserve
particular attention. "Taps" was composed
here by U.S. General Daniel Butterfield in 1862
during the Civil War while Union troops were
encamped on the site. And the first bourbon
whiskey in America was distilled here in 1621.

The plantation is open daily from 9:00
a.m. to 5:00 p.m., with the last tour beginning
at 4:30 p.m. Tickets for a garden and house
tour cost $11.00 for adults, $7.50 for students
13 to 16, and $6.00 for children 6 to 12. Dis-
counted tickets are offered for senior citizens,
military, and AAA members.

Edgewood Plantation
4800 John Tyler Highway
(Route 5), Charles City County
(804) 829-2962, (800) 296-EDGE
www.edgewoodplantation.com
You will enjoy the section of the historic plantation trail (Route 5 west from Williamsburg)
that leads through forests past this superb
Gothic Revival house (ca. 1849) in Charles City
County. With only a minimum of imagination,
you might envision Edgar Allan Poe passing in
a carriage in the other direction. (Indeed, the
house is reputed to have a ghost in residence!) In a countryside filled with the formalities of Georgian and Colonial Revival
architecture, this is a truly refreshing structure. Today the plantation is operated as an
opulent bed-and-breakfast inn, which we have
profiled in our Bed-and-Breakfasts and Guest
Homes chapter. Even if you choose not to go
in, you will see it clearly from the highway.

Edgewood arranges group tours with
advance notice of at least a week or two.
Luncheon and candlelight tours are the most
popular. Our choice is a tour and high Victorian tea, available for groups of 10 or more,
during which visitors don special period hats
provided by your hostess and enjoy delicate
cucumber, crab salad, and tomato basil sandwiches as well as homemade scones with
clotted cream, pound cake, and a variety of

other desserts in the plantation's beautiful tearoom. Cost of the luncheon tour or afternoon tea tour is $30 per person. At Christmas, the 17 or so trees in the house for the Victorian Christmas are dazzling. For standard tours without lunch or tea, the cost is $10, which includes a peek at the home's first and second floors and an adjacent tavern. The plantation also offers special themed dinners with reenactors. Call for reservations and details.

North Bend Plantation
12200 Weyanoke Road
Charles City County
(804) 829-5176
www.northbendplantation.com

The original plantation house was built in 1819 for Sarah Harrison, the wife of wealthy landowner John Minge and a sister to William Henry Harrison, our ninth president. In 1853 the house was doubled in size, and a total renovation was completed in 1982 by the Copland family, descendants of noted agriculturist Edmund Ruffin and current owners of the house. Even after all the changes, North Bend's main house survives as the best-preserved example of the academic Greek Revival style of architecture in Charles City County. Of special historic note is the plantation's 1864 occupancy by General Phillip Sheridan and his 30,000 Union troops.

Today, the plantation operates as a bed-and-breakfast (see our chapter on Bed-and-Breakfasts and Guest Homes for more information). Day and evening tours for groups of 10 or more are offered by appointment. The cost is $10 per person and either a box or catered lunch can be ordered in advance and enjoyed after the tour. If you just happen to be in the neighborhood, the 500-acre grounds are open daily from 9:00 a.m. to 5:00 p.m. for a self-guided tour. To begin your tour, simply stop in at the grounds kiosk and pick up a bright yellow brochure. A $3 donation is requested, and guests are on their honor. Points of interest include the smokehouse and dairy house,

both built around 1819, a slave quarters, and the site of the 1853 cookhouse. The tour ends just outside the house, where tables and chairs have been set up to give visitors an opportunity to sit awhile and take in the view. North Bend is about 25 minutes west of Williamsburg. To reach the plantation, take Route 5 to Highway 619, then travel about 1 mile to Weyanoke Road.

Piney Grove at Southall's Plantation
16920 Southall Plantation Lane
Charles City County
(804) 829-2480
www.pineygrove.com

Piney Grove was built around the year 1800 on the 300-acre Southall's Plantation, a property that was first occupied by the Chickahominy Indians and survives as the oldest and best-preserved example of log architecture in southeastern Virginia. In recent years Piney Grove, 8 miles north of Route 5 on Route 623 (which eventually becomes Route 615), has served the public as a beautifully appointed bed-and-breakfast inn. In 1994 the owners introduced a self-guided tour of the plantation grounds, which takes visitors along a splendid nature trail that begins beneath a century-old cedar, meanders around a swimming hole and past a gazebo, and then winds along the edge of a ravine where the trail is canopied by beech, hickory, and white oak trees. A short path leads down into the ravine to Piney Springs, where constantly flowing water eventually funnels into the Chickahominy River. Past the ravine the trail skirts a horse corral and pasture, offering a scenic view of Piney Grove, as well as a view of Moss Side Barn, once part of Southall's Plantation. The trail ends at Glebe Lane, originally called "The Old Main Road from Barret's Ferry to Charles City Court House."

The cost of the self-guided grounds tour, which is offered daily from 9:00 a.m. to 5:00 p.m., is $3 per person. Guided tours are offered for groups only, with advance reservation; for more information call (804) 829-2196. To find out more about Piney Grove's operations as a bed-and-breakfast inn, consult our Bed-and-Breakfasts and Guest Homes chapter.

Sherwood Forest Plantation
14501 John Tyler Highway
(Route 5)
Charles City County
(804) 829-5377, (800) 704-5423
www.sherwoodforest.org

Without a doubt, this is one of the loveliest homesteads in this part of Virginia. Sherwood Forest Plantation was the home of President John Tyler. It is about a 30-minute drive west of Williamsburg. Considered the longest frame house in America, it measures 300 feet along its front facade. Built about 1730, the original structure was altered and renovated by President Tyler in 1844. The house today looks very much like it did when Tyler retired here from the White House in 1845. He brought with him his new bride, Julia Gardiner of Gardiner's Island, New York. Since then, the plantation has been continuously occupied by members of the Tyler family and has been a working plantation for more than 240 years.

The house features a private ballroom 68 feet in length and is furnished with an extensive collection of 18th- and 19th-century family heirlooms. President Tyler's china, porcelain, silver, mirrors, tables, chairs, and other furnishings are still in use here. In the library are the books of Governor Tyler (President Tyler's father), John Tyler, and his son, Dr. Lyon Gardiner Tyler, who served as president of the College of William and Mary. The grounds are open daily, except Thanksgiving and Christmas, from 9:00 a.m. until 5:00 p.m. Themed house tours are $35, by reservation only. Tours of the grounds are available for groups of 10 or more, for $5 a person.

Shirley Plantation
501 Shirley Plantation Road
Charles City County
(804) 829-5121, (800) 232-1613
www.shirleyplantation.com

This fine plantation, off Route 5 on the banks of the James River about 35 miles from Williamsburg, is perhaps the most famous of Virginia's plantations. Designated a National Historic Landmark, Shirley was founded in 1613 and granted to Edward Hill in 1660. The present mansion house was begun in 1723 by the third Edward Hill, a member of the House of Burgesses in the Virginia Colony, for his daughter Elizabeth, who married John Carter, son of King Carter. It was finished in 1738 and is largely in its original state.

The house is a recognized architectural treasure. Its famous walnut-railed staircase rises three stories without visible means of support and is the only one of its kind in America. The mansion is filled with family portraits, furniture, crested silver, and other family heirlooms. George Washington, Thomas Jefferson, John Tyler, Teddy Roosevelt, and John Rockefeller were all guests at Shirley. Robert E. Lee's mother, Anne Hill Carter, was married to "Light Horse" Harry Lee in the parlor.

The house opens daily, except Christmas, at 9:00 a.m., and the last tour of the day begins promptly at 4:45 p.m. The grounds remain open until 6:00 p.m. or sunset, whichever comes first. Admission is $11.00 for adults, $7.50 for 6 to 18, $10.00 for seniors and AAA members, and $5.00 for active military (must show identification). Children younger than 6 get in free.

Westover Plantation
7000 Westover Road
Charles City County
(804) 829-2882
www.jamesriverplantations.com

During the colonial period, this exquisite plantation was the property of William Byrd, who owned extensive properties that stretched for many miles in each direction. Off Route 5 in Charles City County, it is adjacent to Berkeley Plantation. Situated on the banks of the James River, this palatial early Georgian house is sometimes described as the most elegant Georgian structure in the United States. The plantation features an outstanding Georgian boxwood garden and 150-year-old giant tulip poplars. William Byrd's tomb is also on the property. The gardens and grounds are open to visitors from 9:00 a.m. to 6:00 p.m. daily, but the house is not open to the public. The grounds tour is $2 for adults, 50 cents for children 6 to 16, and free for those younger than 6. For groups of 12 or more, a $1 fee is charged. The plantation house is open once a year for tours, during the Garden Club of Virginia's Historic Garden Week, held in late April each year.

College of William and Mary

The next entry on our list of historic attractions brings us back to Williamsburg, where you will find numerous noteworthy sites on the gracious campus of the College of William and Mary, which in 1993 celebrated the 300th anniversary of its February 19, 1693, chartering in England.

The college campus is at the western end of Duke of Gloucester Street between Jamestown and Richmond Roads, a landmark known locally as College Corner or by frequently frustrated motorists as "confusion" corner. Near this intersection you'll find the Sir Christopher Wren Building, which typically has served as the starting point for any self-guided walking tour. Information on the college is also published at its Web site: www.wm.edu.

As you approach the Wren Building, you'll notice the brick wall surrounding the triangular College Yard, which also holds two other pre–Revolutionary War structures: the President's House and Brafferton, formerly an Indian school.

While the college was chartered by the Crown in 1693 in response to a 1691 petition from Virginia's General Assembly, bricks weren't laid for the Wren Building (originally known as "The College") until two years later, making it the oldest academic building in continuous use in the United States.

Indeed, the building actually was the guest of honor for a major birthday bash in August 1995, complete with yellow and green balloons, cake, and a passionate speech by Pulitzer Prize–winning historian David McCullough on the significance of historic buildings to modern America.

But the mood pervading the Wren wasn't always so celebratory. For several years the building served as temporary headquarters to Virginia's colonial government. Then, in 1705 and again in 1859, fires destroyed portions of the building, which was twice rebuilt by using the remaining foundation and walls. Alas, in 1862, Federal soldiers set the building afire again. Despite such damage, the original exterior walls survived to be restored during the 1920s and 1930s, and the Wren Building visitors see today has the appearance of the pre–1859 fire structure. Today the Wren houses William and Mary's religion department. Visitors also will see early classrooms, the 1732 chapel—under which noted Virginians such as Sir John Randolph and Lord Botetourt are buried—and Great Hall, where the Burgesses assembled.

North of the Wren Building in the College Yard is the President's House, built in the early 1730s. Besides serving as a home to such famous college presidents as James Madison and James Blair, it also housed British General Cornwallis before his Yorktown surrender to Revolutionary forces led by Washington. The building is still in use as a residence for College of William and Mary presidents.

The third and smallest structure facing the College Yard is The Brafferton, now used for offices, but originally an Indian school. The Brafferton was built in 1723 with funds provided by an English scientist determined to bring Christianity to area Indian youths, who already were forced to attend a training school in Williamsburg. Apparently, the young boys were not at all happy about living in town, learning English, or wearing uniforms, and they longed for their villages and tribes. Legend has it that the spirits of these homesick lads still inhabit The Brafferton—footsteps, moaning, even drumbeats are said to be audible at times in the building (see our Myths and Legends chapter). Another William and Mary myth holds that one of these Indian stu-

The Wren Building at the College of William and Mary is the oldest academic structure still in use in America. JOETTA SACK

dents can sometimes be seen running quick as the wind across campus at night, as if trying to regain his freedom.

Don't worry—you probably won't encounter such ghosts while visiting the William and Mary campus. You can stroll in the Sunken Garden west of the Wren Building or through shady Crim Dell with its footpaths and small pond. Other buildings worth noting on campus include Phi Beta Kappa Memorial Hall, Earl Greg Swem Library, and the Muscarelle Museum of Art. Visitors are welcome at the Muscarelle, whose collections and programs are described in the Museums section of The Arts chapter.

Although you're surrounded by history as you stroll on the William and Mary campus, not all the buildings can lay claim to 200 or 300 years of existence. Tercentenary Hall, named to commemorate the college's 300th

anniversary in 1993, was dedicated during homecoming festivities in 1995. The four-story, Georgian-style structure houses the college's applied science program as well as classroom space for geology, physics, and computer science programs.

If you would like a few reminders of your walk through the grounds, stop by the College of William and Mary Bookstore–Barnes and Noble Bookstore. The shop has moved to a new location at 345 Duke of Gloucester Street in Merchants Square. It carries a variety of clothing items inscribed with William and Mary logos, along with an impressive collection of contemporary fiction, children's, and reference books as well as stationery, greeting cards, and art supplies.

There are a number of cultural events at the college that both students and locals may attend year-round. These are listed in detail in our chapter on The Arts. New Williamsburg residents who want to know more about educational opportunities at the college—a state-supported, four-year university with a prestigious reputation—should turn to our chapter on Education and Child Care.

Historic Churches

Bruton Parish Church
Duke of Gloucester Street, Williamsburg
(757) 229-2891
www.brutonparish.org
On Duke of Gloucester Street west of the Palace Green, Bruton Parish Church, in use since 1715, is one of America's oldest Episcopal churches. The church's history is rich: Its architectural features include the 1769 Tower; high box pews dedicated to Presidents Washington, Jefferson, Monroe, and Tyler, all of whom worshiped here; and a bronze lectern donated by Theodore Roosevelt. Fully restored in 1940, the church also boasts original walls and windows and a stone baptismal font said to have come from an earlier Jamestown church. The churchyard holds many 18th-century graves. Church tours are offered from 9:00 a.m. to 5:00 p.m. Monday to Saturday. No admission is charged for church tours, but donations are welcome. Bruton Parish holds services every Sunday, with noonday prayers on Monday. It also is a popular venue for choral concerts and small chamber ensembles, which are usually held at 8:00 p.m. every Saturday night, and Tuesdays and Thursday nights in the spring and summer months. The Bruton Parish Book & Gift Shop, (757) 220-1489, also is on Duke of Gloucester Street. Open 10:00 a.m. to 5:00 p.m. Monday through Saturday and 1:00 to 5:00 p.m. Sunday, it stocks not only religious books but also jewelry, stuffed animals, and other gifts.

The First Baptist Church
727 West Scotland Street, Williamsburg
(757) 229-1952
Another church of historic note is The First Baptist Church. One of the earliest Baptist congregations in the country, it is more importantly one of the first African-American churches in America, organized in 1776. Blacks had been allowed to worship in Bruton Parish Church, where they were seated in the North Gallery. Because they were not included in the worship service, they left the parish and built Brush Harbor on the Greensprings Plantation west of town, where they worshiped early in the morning, late at night, and sometimes in secret. This site was remote from the city, so they built a second Brush Harbor at Raccoon Chase, nearer Williamsburg, and sought spiritual fellowship there. A resident of Williamsburg, Jesse Coles, heard of these communities and made his carriage house available to blacks in the city. The group that met there organized in 1776 as The First Baptist Church. The church applied for admission into the Dover Association in 1791 and was accepted two years later.

For just more than a century, the congregation worshiped in a brick church building built in 1855 on Nassau Street, but that's now gone. In 1956 the congregation moved into its present structure at 727 West Scotland Street. In the lower level of this church is a fascinating display tracing the history of this important congregation; furnishings of the earlier church are used in various parts of the current edifice. Worship service at The First Baptist is at 11:00 a.m. Sunday.

Hickory Neck Episcopal Church
8300 Richmond Road, Toano
(757) 566-0276
www.hickoryneck.org
The Virginia landscape is dotted with small brick churches dating from the colonial period, many associated with plantations, others with small communities that vanished in the ensuing years. One worship site of historic interest is Hickory Neck Church on the western side of Toano. The edifice was built about 1740 and continues to be the worship place of an active Episcopal parish. On April 21, 1781, it housed militia opposing the

Close-up

Presidents Park

Know the names of all the U.S. presidents, but not their faces? A unique new attraction in Williamsburg should be able to help.

Presidents Park features larger-than-life sculpted busts of all 43 U.S. presidents and is becoming a favorite spot for school groups and history buffs. The park, which opened on Presidents' Day in 2004, features the work of sculptor David Adickes, whose work has been shown in 10 art museums across the country and internationally.

Sandwiched between Water Country USA and Busch Gardens, the park's mission is to promote a better understanding of the U.S. presidency, encourage visitors to get to know the presidents as individuals, and promote civic responsibility. Its directors hope that it will complement Williamsburg's rich colonial history with lessons that begin with George Washington's inauguration in 1789 and bring visitors to modern times.

Presidents Park also has a panel of educators and university scholars as its directors to provide guidance on how to best use the park as an educational tool. A museum building houses classrooms, meeting rooms, a gift shop, cafe, banquet room, and other amenities.

The busts, which range in height from 16 to 18 feet, also showcase personal facts about each president and his accomplishments. While the park is self-guided, tours on special topics such as the Constitution and Bill of Rights, religion, civil rights and slavery, and protecting the nation may be arranged. Special tours are available for school groups, and the park also hosts special days for students who are homeschooled.

The project was met with significant skepticism when it was first proposed in the early 1990s. Some historians and local Williamsburg residents worried that it would be a tacky commercial amusement. Some still aren't convinced of its merit. But one fan is former President George H. W. Bush, who was the only living president to sit for the sculpture of his bust.

The park is open year-round, except for Christmas and New Year's Day. The park opens at 9:00 a.m. each day, and closes at 8:00 p.m. from April through August and at 5:00 p.m. from September through March. Admission is $13 for adults, $12 for seniors 55 and older and military, and $8 for children 6 to 17. Group tours are available. For more information, go to www.presidentspark.org, or call (800) 588-4327.

British army. Later that year the militiamen fought in the siege of Yorktown. Standing with your back to busy U.S. Route 60, it is still possible here to glimpse a vista without 21st-century encroachments. If you're interested in attending worship services, they are held at 8:00, 9:00, and 11:15 a.m. on Sunday. Although there are no official tours, the church is always open.

THRILLS, CHILLS, AND A SHOPPERS' PARADISE

We may learn from the past, but we live in the here and now. While our earlier entries in this chapter focused on historic attractions, the information we provide here gives you all you need for a thoroughly modern good time. In this section we'll look at the lighter side of Williamsburg—the side that brings you Busch Gardens, Water Country USA, and the Williamsburg Pottery Factory.

Busch Gardens

Busch Gardens, which is located on US 60, 3 miles east of Williamsburg, turned 30 years old in 2005, yet its appeal remains ageless. No wonder; the diversions seem endless. Within Busch Gardens are more than 40 rousing rides and attractions, including a number of gravity-defying roller coasters; Escape from Pompeii, a fiery boat ride through replicas of ancient Italian ruins; the wet and wild Roman Rapids; nine 17th-century European theme villages where you'll find musical shows, feats of magic, and street entertainers; strapping Clydesdale horses and miniature animal breeds; resident and visiting craftspeople; and German oompah bands featuring a singing Burgermeister.

The park's many eateries offer a variety of international temptations for your taste buds—everything from barbecue and bratwurst to biscotti and Black Forest torte can be purchased and consumed within Busch Gardens's confines. (To get an idea of how ravenous park visitors can get, consider that more than 700,000 hamburger buns and 350,000 pizza crusts are created annually in the in-house bakery at Das Festhaus in the German village.)

While resident potters, woodcutters, glassblowers, and blacksmiths show off their talents at the park on a regular schedule, a variety of European artisans trek across the Atlantic each season to demonstrate their well-honed Old World skills. You can watch a master painter from Germany work magic on

The Big Thrills

Alpengeist
Apollo's Chariot
The Battering Ram
Big Bad Wolf
Corkscrew Hill
Curse of Darkastle
Da Vinci's Cradle
Escape from Pompeii
Le Scoot
Loch Ness Monster
Roman Rapids
Wilde Maus

a stein or an Italian artist brush a new face on a Venetian mask. In the past the park has hosted Waterford crystal master designer and sculptor Fred Curtis, a David Winter cottage master painter from Italy, and an M. I. Hummel figurine master artist from Germany. And, to top it all off, the park was voted "Most Beautiful Theme Park" by the National Amusement Park Historical Association for 10 consecutive years. While beauty is in the eye of the beholder, cleanliness is easy to assess. And we give Busch Gardens an A+ in that department. The grounds are practically litter free, and it's our experience that restrooms are as clean at 5:00 p.m. as they were when we first arrived that morning. You can contact Busch Gardens at their toll-free number, (800) 772-8886, or locally at (757) 253-3350, or visit www.buschgardens.com.

Full of Surprises

Busch Gardens has so much to offer that there's always something new, even for repeat visitors. The park welcomed Griffon in 2007, a roller coaster powered by a mythical bird that is part eagle and part lion that plunges, twists and turns its riders at speeds up to 70 mph. In 2001 the park opened its first new country in 20 years, Killarney, Ireland, featuring among other attractions its 4-D adventure ride, Corkscrew Hill. This state-of-the-art adventure is one of the first to combine large-screen 3-D digital projection, sensory special effects, and motion-based technology to create an incredible 4-D experience.

The 1999 season welcomed Apollo's Chariot, a coaster that takes passengers on the ultimate two-minute thrill ride during which they plummet a combined 825 feet. In 1997 park visitors enjoyed the debut of Alpengeist, a perennial crowd pleaser that, at 195 feet and reaching speeds of 67 mph, has been billed as "the world's tallest, fastest, most twisted inverted roller coaster." Land of the Dragons, a children's adventureland built around a three-story tree house and a central character named Dumphrey, offers gentle fun for little ones. This enchanting area features special rides for the pint-sized, a theater, and a wading pond with stepping stones and geysers that actually erupt.

Kids will beg moms and dads to let them return again and again, for there's plenty more for the pint-size crowd, from the carnival atmosphere with jugglers, puppets, and street characters to watching Grandpa ride the Big Bad Wolf roller coaster for the umpteenth time. For their part, adults enjoy the shows, the variety of fine foods, the looks of wonder on the children's faces, and the rides. Area residents cite the park's well-maintained grounds, courteous employees, and overall cleanliness as a drawing factor. Since its 1975 entry on the Williamsburg scene, Busch Gardens has been one of Virginia's most popular tourist attractions, partly because of the constant addition of new rides, musical revues, and theme villages. In fact, each year Busch Gardens plays host to more than three million guests, often 25,000 to 30,000 in a single day.

The entertainment park, a not-so-small world of its own, occupies 3,600 acres of woodlands bordering the James River just 3 miles east of Williamsburg. Many visitors to Colonial Williamsburg, Jamestown, and the other history-rich attractions in the area find that a trip to Busch Gardens provides a timely change of pace—a day or two of sheer, unadulterated vacation fun.

Because the many amusements can seem confusing, we've divided helpful information on Busch Gardens into five sections: Getting Inside, Getting Around Inside, Rides and Countries, Wildlife, and Entertainment and Dining. All you have to do is get in the car and go for it.

Getting Inside

Busch Gardens opens at 10:00 a.m. throughout its late-March to October season, but closing times vary greatly. At the end of March, it opens for weekends only through mid-May. In the peak summer season, mid-June to mid-August, the park closes at 10:00 p.m. all days, even staying open until 11:00 p.m. Saturday in July through mid-August. In late summer the park hours start winding down again, closing at 8:00 p.m. during the week and 10:00 p.m. Saturday and Sunday. It's best to call ahead for closing times, as a new schedule is made each year and is always subject to change.

To find Busch Gardens from Interstate 64, simply take the Busch Gardens exit and drive straight into the parking area. For the 2001 season visitors saw a new, larger entrance to Busch Gardens and a larger toll plaza to handle more guests simultaneously. The toll plaza grew from 6 lanes to 10 to expedite the process of getting visitors into the park, but sometimes traffic into the attraction is horrendous, especially during peak season. Parking is $8 to $10, depending on location; free for tour buses. One note of caution: During the summer months, the parking lots tend to fill up, leaving late arrivals to find their own alternatives. We recommend you plan to reach the park early so that you won't face this problem or the morning traffic backups that often occur on US 60 and Route 199 during peak season. Whatever you do, don't park along the shoulder of US 60, as police routinely ticket and tow cars that are illegally parked there.

On to the ticket booths. (Admission prices and packages offered are subject to change.)

You can expect to pay $54.95 for general admission for adults, $47.95 for children 3 to 9 (kids 2 and under are free). Special prices also are available for seniors and all active-duty military with a valid identification card, though they must be picked up at base offices and are not available at the Busch Gardens admission windows. Ticket holders are entitled to unlimited rides, the park's regular show lineup, in-park transportation, and other entertainment, but fees may be charged for arcade games, carnival games, and certain special events.

Busch Gardens offers discounts for multi-day, multipark tickets.

If you're also planning to wade over to Water Country USA, you might consider purchasing the Three Day/Two Park Ticket that provides unlimited admission to both parks on any three days, all for $69.95.

Another option is the 3-in-1 Wild Card, which provides admission to Busch Gardens, Water Country USA, and Colonial Williamsburg for three consecutive days for $115.90 for adults, $99.00 for children 6 to 17. Children under 6 are free.

Weeklong and season tickets are also available. Call for details as packages and prices vary.

For more information, inquire at the gate or call (800) 343-7946. You can try the interactive Web site at www.buschgardens.com. Be aware that admission and parking prices are subject to change.

Getting Around Inside

Tree-lined wooden walkways and arched bridges link the various villages and areas in the park, but the Aeronaut Skyride can take you from England to France to Germany on a 3,000-foot triangular route. Sit back in the aerial cable cars and enjoy panoramic views of the park and surrounding woods. Or hop aboard one of two steam locomotives, replicas of European trains, that chug along on a winding track around the attractions, crossing the Rhine on a trestle bridge and stopping in Heatherdowns, New France, and Festa Italia.

Even with the in-park transportation options, a tour of Busch Gardens can require a good deal of self-locomotion. Wear good walking shoes (we can't stress this enough) and bring strollers for infants and toddlers and perhaps hats or visors on hot, sunny days. Strollers and wheelchairs can be rented near the ticket booths, but the numbers are limited.

Rides and Countries

ENGLAND

Banbury Cross

This English theme village is home to a Big Ben–like clock tower and a replica of Shakespeare's Globe Theatre where shows are staged daily. Try English pastry or a scrambled egg breakfast at the Muffin Man, and visit Her Majesty's Fancy for English soaps and porcelain gifts. Have your likeness sketched by a sidewalk artist, research your family coat of arms at the Heraldry, and don't miss the Globe's "Pirates," a 4-D high-tech comedy adventure that takes you to the Caribbean isles and puts you right in the throes of the swashbuckling action. We won't give away any secrets, but, me maties, you may actually bring a little of the "high seas" out of the theater with you once you dock on dry land. "R. L. Stine's Haunted Lighthouse," a new 4-D film experience, opened in the spring of 2003 and can be seen at the Globe Theatre here.

SCOTLAND

Heatherdowns

Move on to Heatherdowns, a Scottish village easily spotted by the Loch Ness Monster roller coaster. "Nessie," one of the largest, daredevilest steel roller-coaster rides in the world, transports you into two minutes of pleasurable terror. You'll drop 114 feet, reach speeds of 60 mph, double loop upside down, and shoot over the quiet waters of the Rhine and through a dark cavern before the monster lets you loose.

Once you've recovered from Nessie, you can have your picture taken with the Anheuser-Busch Clydesdales, shop for a kilt in

🔍 Close-up

Thrills and Technology: A New Kind of Ride

Larry Giles, vice president of design and engineering for Busch Gardens, seems like a laid-back, down-to-earth kind of guy in a neat polo shirt and khakis. After obtaining his civil engineering degree from the University of Missouri in Rolla, the St. Louis resident moved to Virginia more than 20 years ago. He's the one in charge of overseeing the new "country" of Ireland, recently added to Busch Gardens, which means he also oversees things like the new state-of-the-art Corkscrew Hill.

"We're real excited about it. We think it's going to be the sleeper hit of the summer," Giles said at the opening celebration of the Killarney, Ireland, attraction.

Corkscrew Hill, an incredible 4-D experience, uses a 40-foot-wide-by-27-foot-tall screen. The ride uses stereoscopic preshow and digital stereoscopic projection. Digital projection allows for sharper imagery, higher pixel resolution, and images that are stable, unlike film projection. It also has motion-based technology provided by BA Systems of Tampa, Florida. The adventure was written and directed by Jeff Kleiser and Diana Walczak, who also designed the ride The Amazing Adventures of Spider-Man, a star attraction at Universal's Islands of Adventure Theme Park in Orlando, Florida. Kleiser-Walczak is an independent production studio.

But enough about software.

In this adventure the riders become the main characters, who must experience life in a world of giants. According to Giles, the riders/participants meet a guy who shrinks them, then takes them back to Ireland. They are found by two children who take them around Ireland and try to sell them. A witch tries to add them to her stew and pokes them with a fork; they meet poukas and banshees and are dumped into the ocean.

"We are excited. [The rider] doesn't see the hardware. The story becomes more of the focus," Giles said. "With the visuals, story, and motion, this is a fabulous experience. The effects pop right off the screen."

Tweedside Gifts, or climb aboard a steam locomotive at Tweedside Train Station and head to Festa Italia.

FRANCE

Aquitaine

Next it's Vive la France in Aquitaine, a quaint village reminiscent of Provence. Delicious food, a French preoccupation, is available here at Le Coq d'Or or in Le Grand Gourmet European dessert shop, where you can relax and satisfy your sweet tooth while bolstering your energy with a quick cup of espresso or cappuccino. To stimulate digestion, hop in one of the replica racing cars on the Le Mans Raceway and maneuver through a track of tunnels and bridges or shop for jewelry or a stylish hat at La Derniere Mode. If you're ready to sit for a spell, check out Le Palais Royal Theatre, with its 5,200 seats and special events ranging from a dazzling outdoor ice show to a Russian tumbling act to a laser light show against the backdrop of a summer evening sky.

New France

The French Canadian trappers' village you walk to next features homespun fun and crafts displays. Rustic log cabins and country music provide the background for a potter, blacksmith, and wood-carver demonstrating their trades. Smoked meats and barbecue are offered in the very popular Three Rivers Smokehouse, hand-thrown pots and bowls are on sale in the Caribou Pottery Shop, and you can have a tintype photograph taken of your family or group decked out in old-fashioned regalia in the photo studio. (One of these Insiders did this years ago when our older daughter was an infant, and she still has the photo of Mom and Dad as gun-slingers cradling a babe in arms on her bedroom wall.) The song-and-dance show Jukebox at the outdoor Canadian Palladium rounds out the entertainment, but the main attraction still is Le Scoot, a log flume ride with a 50-foot drop. On a hot summer day, it is truly a treat. Timberrrr!

GERMANY

Oktoberfest

Next stop Germany, where the Big Bad Wolf perches high above Oktoberfest's Bavarian village. The Wolf, a suspended roller coaster, is 5 acres big and bad and lunges over Bavaria at 48 mph. The finale to this ride is a 99-foot dive toward the Rhine. After you test your wits against Deutschland's metallic monster, stop off at the 2,000-seat Das Festhaus to recuperate (and perhaps learn to polka). At the Festhaus you'll find German food, beer, stage performances, folk dancing, and serenading by the Burgermeister, who has been with the park since its beginning. Beyond the Festhaus is a rides and games area featuring a wave swing; Der Autobahn bumper cars; and Der Red Baron, an airplane ride for kids.

Another Oktoberfest attraction is Wilde Maus, which debuted as Wild Izzy in honor of the 1996 Centennial Olympic Games and was renamed a year later. This single-car roller coaster simulates the motion of a mouse through a maze and, at 46 feet, with top speeds of 22 mph, is the smallest (but not necessarily the "gentlest") of Busch Gardens's coasters.

Rhinefeld

If you have young children along, you will not want to miss picturesque Rhinefeld, where you can take a scenic riverboat cruise down the Rhine while listening to an oompah band. Here, there are miniature versions of adult rides and an antique carousel that dates from 1819. Rhinefeld is also home to the place that the little ones love best—Land of the Dragons. This delightful adventureland features a three-story tree house inhabited by Dumphrey and his dragon playmates and several gentle rides.

While the tree house is a great place to climb, our favorite feature is the shallow wading pond with waterfalls and erupting geysers. After hours of walking, you may want to cool your tired feet here. But be advised: As a safety precaution, no one is allowed to walk barefoot through the pool (something we found out the hard way). Also in Rhinefeld are gift stores, where you can shop for beer steins, M. I. Hummel figurines, David Winter cottages, cuckoo clocks, and imported German chocolates. If you're feeling creative, you can record your own video at the Musik-macher. And, if you time it just right, you can follow the Boogie Band, keeping time with its seven one-of-a-kind musicians as they march, dance, and make music through the streets of this German hamlet.

Oh, but what is that lurking on the outskirts of Rhinefeld? It's Alpengeist, and the wild, twisted ride it offers isn't for the faint of heart. To begin the upside-down adventure of their lives, riders climb aboard a ski lift like no other ski lift on earth and head out into a heart-stopping blizzard of fright. Thrills include a half-dozen inversions from the Cobra Roll to the Flat Spin to the High-

Speed Spiral, which we could describe here but which really needs to be felt for the full effect. There's even an amazing 195-foot vertical drop that happens so fast that you're down before you even knew you were up. The Alpengeist spans Rhinefeld, Oktoberfest, Aquitaine, and New France and drifts over the scenic Rhine much of the time. The ride is fast and furious and the view probably is fantastic—if only we could keep our eyes open!

IRELAND

The 2001 season at Busch Gardens saw the opening of its first new country in 20 years: Ireland. When visitors pass through England and Scotland and walk over Brittany Bridge, they enter the Irish village of Killarney. This charming new locale is in what used to be the village of Hastings. The opening ceremony even saw a dedication from the real mayor of Killarney, Ireland. The new addition is a popular one because 43 million Americans claim Irish ancestry. Busch Gardens officials cited the European charm and mythical folklore of Ireland and its reputation for hospitality as a natural choice for the theme park. The attractions of this Irish village include the Abbey Stone Theatre, which resembles a stone castle inside, complete with climbing ivy twisting around columns. The fast Irish step-dancing show, Irish Thunder, is sure to be a favorite, similar to the quick step and rhythms of the popular Riverdance.

A surefire hit is the state-of-the-art 4-D adventure of Corkscrew Hill. This eight-minute ride is one of the first of its kind to combine large-screen 3-D digital projection, sensory special effects, and motion-based technologies to create an incredible 4-D experience. The high-tech-format, digitally projected stereoscopic ride film takes guests on a mystical Celtic journey through the land of the giants. The computer-generated animation propels the ride film, and the riders become the main characters in the story. Riders are shrunk into miniatures and encounter a witch, a magical stallion, and a huge beast that takes flight with the riders on its talons.

Another adventure sure to charm the young ones is the production at Castle O'Sullivan. Aaron is the young heir who has inherited this castle from his ancestors. An American, he is eager to auction it off, and the audience becomes a part of the show that involves dynamic music and special effects. The young heir discovers, with the help of a pushy leprechaun, that his ancestry is much more complex than he realized.

For adults there is the Anheuser-Busch Beer school, where those 21 and older can taste test a variety of preselected Anheuser-Busch beers, learn a little company history, and find out about the history of beer making. Students leave the "classroom" with their own beermaster's certificates. This free tasting is popular, so make reservations early near Grogan's Pub, an authentic Irish pub.

And there is plenty of shopping to be done at the new country. Visit the Emerald Isle Shop for fine Waterford crystal, Belleek china, Irish linens, and other handcrafted products. The Toys of the Leprechaun Shop is the place to go for a gift for the little ones. Don't forget the Pot o' Gold Magic Shop for a wide selection of magic tricks and mystical keepsakes.

After all that shopping stop for a bite to eat at Grogan's Grille, serving traditional Irish food such as corned beef sandwiches, Irish stew, mashed potatoes and soda bread, plus a variety of Anheuser-Busch beers.

Other touches that help bring the feel of the "Green" and give the kids a chuckle include the Killarney Sound Machine's resident leprechaun, who engages guests in witty conversation and entertains with his magical music machine. Strolling musicians and singers in the village square also charm guests with song, dance, and storytelling.

ITALY

San Marco

From Germany a long footbridge leads across the Rhine into the Italian village of San Marco, complete with red-tiled roofs, porticos, and a tiered piazza. Relax under leafy trellises and enjoy a slice of spicy Italian life. Save some room for pasta because it's available in abundance at the open-air Ristorante della Piazza. San Marco is the place to watch *Holiday in Roma*, a musical featuring a blend of modern opera and popular music, in Il Teatro di San Marco. Capodimonte porcelain can be purchased here as well. Summer nights bebop to the sounds of swing performed by the big band Starlight Orchestra.

Next to the San Marco piazza you'll see Da Vinci's Garden of Inventions, a rides area built as a kind of accolade to Leonardo da Vinci, the 15th-century artist, genius, and inventor. Da Vinci's Cradle, The Flying Machine, and The Battering Ram as well as special rides for children are located here. Don't be misled by the gentle look of the Cradle, which starts to rock slowly but soon takes off on a spin, round and round in a 360-degree circle until riders beg for the bough to break.

San Marco also is home to Escape from Pompeii, a three-minute ride that transports the daring through 75-foot-tall Roman ruins, where they are blasted with the sounds of Mount Vesuvius erupting amid fiery explosions. The action doesn't stop there. Statues and beams tumble around riders, who can feel the heat of the volcanic flames on their faces. It's all over when the door to the ruins opens, and riders plunge 50 feet into a pool of water. No sweat!

Festa Italia

These days, there are two words that best describe this Italian village—*Apollo's Chariot*. One look at this coaster and the only thing we felt was—fear. For the bungee-jumping, parasailing, hang-gliding crowd, it's the best thing since Jockey's Ridge and the cliffs of Acapulco. The coaster, named one of the "Top Ten Steel Coasters" by *Park World* and *Amusement Today* magazines, boasts nine pulse-quickening drops, the first of which plunges passengers down 210 feet of steel track. Riders "enjoy" a sensation of weightlessness as they race up and down a series of camelback humps at 70 mph. Another unique element of this new coaster is the seating. Passengers are elevated above the car's frame, which creates that "oh-my-gosh-I'm-flying-out-of-my-seat" feeling. Busch claims the ride plummets passengers more than any other coaster in the world, and with its 4,882-foot-long track, Apollo's Chariot offers a ride so breathtaking that no one who still can speak afterward will argue the point.

If you're not shaken up enough after climbing out of Apollo's Chariot—and assuming you still can walk—check out the Turkish Delight, a teacup spin, or enjoy the high-speed circular excitement of Tradewind. Festa Italia, where an Italian street carnival is re-created, also features the Roman Rapids, a raft expedition that sends riders swirling past ruins, through fog, and down the rapids for a wet and wild time. Watch out for the leaky aqueduct, and don't carry on anything that won't survive a good dousing.

Wildlife

In 2000 noted wildlife specialist Jack Hanna visited Busch Gardens for the opening of Jack Hanna's Wild Reserve and the introduction of its newest wild guests: six gray wolves. Visitors can view these majestic wild animals at Greystone Tower as trainers educate the public about the real wolf versus the myths regarding them. Watch as the young wolves show off their new training, and how they relate to their human trainers. The Wild Reserve is part of Busch Gardens's efforts in conservation and preservation of wildlife through educational programs. This area is a real treat for young and old alike as it provides a rare up-close view of endangered and exotic animals of all types. It was expanded in 2005 with better viewing areas.

Other areas to look for in the park are Eagle Canyon, a sanctuary for American bald eagles that have been injured in the wild; Feathered Follies Theatre, where staff show off rare raptors and exotic birds to illustrate the plight of endangered birds; and Reptales, a popular reptile education presentation. Then there's the amazing Lorikeet Glen, a

Busch Gardens is a big park, and its staff doesn't page for lost persons. Your best bet is to prearrange a central meeting place should members of your party get separated. Some suggestions: the Big Ben clock in Banbury Cross, in front of Das Festhaus in Oktoberfest, or the wine-stomping area in Italy.

large screened-in aviary that is truly interactive, as these brilliant green, red, and blue birds feel no qualms about flying onto your arm and nibbling at the notepad in your hand. They've been known to perch on your shoulders and even on your head.

Entertainment and Dining

Busch Gardens provides diverse entertainment for park guests, from ice shows, laser displays, and black-light puppeteers in Le Palais Royal Theatre to the traditional Irish dance of Irish Thunder. On summer nights enjoy the French circus production "Imaginique" at Le Palais Royal Theatre in Aquitaine.

Don't forget to visit Busch Gardens during the scariest month of the year. During October the park is transformed for Howl-O-Scream, featuring all sorts of fun for Halloween. During the day, in the Land of the Dragons, children can hear Halloween storytelling by friendly ghost characters and enjoy special themed shows and a children's maze. Once the sun begins to set, climb aboard the Transylvania Express, a haunted train ride through creepy cornfields and grave sites where all sorts of things lurk in the shadows. The park is transformed through the use of 1,200 tombstones, 300 skeletons, 20 coffins, 5 miles of cobwebs, more than 100 creepy corpses, 50 gallons of "blood" makeup, and numerous ghouls and zombies. "R. L. Stine's Haunted Lighthouse," an all-new 4-D film experience, debuted in March 2003. The adventure film is an original production written by R. L. Stine, the author of the popular *Goosebumps* series. State-of-the-art visual effects and multisensory surprises are wowing audiences in the Banbury Cross Globe

Theatre. The film stars actors Christopher Lloyd and Lea Thompson.

The park also sends its costumed street characters out to perform at various locations around the park. Sit down a spell with Beatrice Bloom, royal botanist, biochemist, and butterfly lover of Buckingham Palace, and listen to her daily readings for children in the Royal Preserve Petting Zoo. Gossip about Harriet Hartshorn and Harvey Hoosler, two truly tasteless American tourists who find themselves lost in Europe. Let the child in you delight in the misadventures of Dumphrey the Dragon, a favorite of both the young and young-at-heart. Savor the sounds of the gracious Burgermeister, as he sings a song or two while stepping lively to a German polka.

In addition, European artisans visit Busch Gardens each season to demonstrate their art, sign their work, and give visitors an opportunity to learn more about historic trades.

To provide authentic and delicious foods in the park's many restaurants, Busch Gardens sends its chefs to Europe to research and receive special training. You will taste the results of these trips when you sample such fare as the desserts at Aquitaine's Le Grand Gourmet, the pizza at La Cucina in Festa Italia, or spicy wursts and Black Forest torte in the German area.

The largest Busch Gardens restaurant is Das Festhaus, a 2,000-seat festival hall that serves authentic German cuisine, but there are 20 or so places to grab a bite to eat throughout the park. In the mood for a caramel apple just dripping with peanuts? Head to England's M. Sweets & Son. Kids want pasta? Then San Marco's Ristorante della Piazza is a must for your group. A 650-seat smokehouse restaurant features a mesquite-fired show grill, three dining areas, and a menu that includes barbecued ribs, chicken, brisket, grilled salmon, jambalaya, and roasted vegetables. LeMans Bistro in the France section offers crepes and paninis. But no matter what your taste buds are craving— from smoked beef brisket to corn dogs and french fries—we guarantee you'll find it somewhere in Busch Gardens.

If you packed a lunch, leave that picnic basket in the car. No outside food is allowed inside the park, although there are picnic tables scattered throughout the grassy areas of the parking lots. Be sure to get your hand stamped as you leave the park.

Groups of 40 or more can arrange for catered picnics in the Black Forest Picnic Village next to Das Festhaus. Reservations are required.

Water Country USA

Water, water everywhere—and Water Country USA has a genuine license to thrill. If you don't mind getting wet (you're going to if you come here), check out this combination of waterfalls, waves, and flumes, and get ready to make a big splash.

Opened in 1984 and purchased by Anheuser-Busch in 1992, Water Country USA sits on 40 acres of wooded land 3 miles east of Colonial Williamsburg on Route 199. The largest water theme park in the Mid-Atlantic region, Water Country now offers more than a dozen water rides as well as a pool, sunbathing, live shows, a variety of restaurants, arcades, and, of course, bathhouse facilities.

The theme at Water Country is 1950s and 1960s cool. The park is landscaped with palms, ornamental grasses, pines, and bold, bright flowers like hibiscus, hot pink geraniums, and blazing yellow marigolds. Bare feet abound, but we prefer to wear swim shoes or waterproof sandals for protection from hot pavement and stubbed toes. If you do don shoes and don't want to wear them on some of the rides, there are "sneaker keepers" at the base of many attractions. Some strollers, shaped like dolphins, of course, are available near the main concession area.

This family-friendly place boasts rides suited to all ages and all levels of swimming ability. Several pools and rides are temperature-controlled, a feature especially helpful for early-season splashing. And while thrills are the main business of this attraction, relaxation hasn't been forgotten. Beach bums can catch a wave at Surfers' Bay, then grab a few rays on the four-tiered sundeck. Parents can sit on deck chairs while the kids splash around in the supervised play area. All ages will appreciate "Jump, Jive, and...Duck!" a fun-loving musical revue that features park mascot W. C. Duck and his aquatic buddies. And visitors who are a tad anxious about all that water will be pleased to know Water Country USA has been rated among America's safest theme parks by Barclay & Associates, an independent risk-management firm. You can call the park at (757) 253-3350 or (800) 343-7946 or visit www.watercountryusa.com.

Getting Inside

Water Country USA is open from May 13 through September 1 and on some weekends in May and September. From mid-June through mid-August hours generally are 10:00 a.m. to 8:00 p.m., although the park typically closes at 6:00 p.m. both earlier and later in the season and at 7:00 p.m. in late August. On hot summer days we like to start early to get in as much water action as we can before the park gets really packed.

To reach the park from Interstate–64, take exit 243A and follow Route 199 for a quarter-mile to the entrance. Parking prices range from $8 to $13. For admittance into the park, expect to pay $38.95, or $31.95 for children 3 to 9. Children 2 and younger enter free. (Prices are subject to change.) Tickets may be purchased online, at www.watercountryusa.com, to avoid the lines at the ticket booth.

Another option is to consider a pass that gets you into Water Country USA and Busch Gardens for seven consecutive days for $79.95 for ages 3 and up. Call (800) 343-7946 between

> **i** More than 32 million gallons of water and 44,000 gallons of chlorine are used at Water Country annually. In spring the park uses artesian wells to help fill the pools, which are heated with propane in the fall and when temperatures dip in the summer.

9:00 a.m. and 5:00 p.m. Monday through Friday for information on other packages.

Unless you or a member of your group decides to sit the day out, we suggest you rent a locker. Since the lockers are centrally located, they're a good, safe place to keep funds (paper money, after all, isn't waterproof), as well as a dry set of clothes for when the frolicking is over. If you must carry cash with you, your best bet is to bring along or purchase one of those plastic cylinders that hangs from a cord around the neck. Need a little more persuading? We know of at least one thrill-seeker who is out 26 bucks because he kept his money in a sandwich bag stashed in his pocket. If you're like us and can't get by without sunglasses, they, too, should be worn on some type of head-hugging cord. One last word of advice: Take towels with you, and park them on lawn chairs at Surfers' Bay or one of the children's play areas. That way you'll have a home base to return to when you just want to sit awhile or test the waters in the wave pool.

The park has a fairly large supply of free life vests for nonswimmers and small children. Because you can find them on racks throughout the park, many people pick them up and drop them off as needed. We have found that after 2:00 p.m. it's rather hard to locate one of the smaller children's vests—it might be a good idea to hold onto one for your entire visit. Plastic swim diapers, required throughout the park, can also be purchased.

Water Attractions

Now that you've stashed your valuables and suited up, it's time for the main event. What follows are individual descriptions of each of the water rides and play areas.

ADVENTURE ISLE

One of Water Country's four pool areas, Adventure Isle's main event is a zany water obstacle course featuring agility ladders, rings, and inner-tube walks. Waterfalls, a children's waterslide, and several adult rides are here. The two enclosed tubular slides—Peppermint Twist and Lemon Drop—are popular with

the more adventurous. But more on those rides later.

AQUAZOID

If you like special effects, you'll love this 864-foot ride. Named for a 1950s mutant movie monster, Aquazoid's big black tubes have enough space for a family of four to pile in together and zip through curtains of water into a pitch-dark tunnel before splashing through yet another curtain of water at the speed of 11 feet per second. On your journey your senses will be assaulted by beams of light and howling sound effects as you escape from the Aquazoid's lair and plunge 78 feet into a splash pool.

ATOMIC BREAKERS

Meant to resemble a white-water river trip, this inner-tube ride takes you through churning rapids as well as tranquil pools, all connected by cascading waterfalls.

BIG DADDY FALLS

Get the whole family together and climb into a humongous inner tube for a wet and wild river-rafting adventure. This 670-foot water ride splashes through twists and turns, slips into a dark tunnel, then plunges into a slow-moving river alive with waterfalls before racing around the bend to a final splashdown. (The first time we tried this ride, we thought the waterfall effect was a little overdone until we realized it had started to rain buckets as we slid through the tunnel.)

COW-A-BUNGA

This children's play area features a 4,500-square-foot heated pool, an interactive speedboat with a water-skiing cow (what "udder" silliness), a curving water flume, a short but slick triple slide, and several fountains. There is plenty of deck seating for parents who want to watch the action from the sidelines.

H2O UFO

The park's newest and largest interactive children's play area has a sci-fi theme and features a fun combination of slides and spray jets. There's even a fairly long, scaled-down waterslide for kids (and their parents) who aren't quite ready to take a walk on the wilder side. Park your gear on one of the many lawn chairs and make a splash.

HUBBA HUBBA HIGHWAY

Covering 3.5 acres, Hubba Hubba Highway opened in the 2003 summer season and is the largest attraction at Water Country USA. It features a winding jet stream with a 2,000-square-foot lagoon entrance.

JET SCREAM

Everybody loves flume rides, and Water Country USA's is one of the longest and most exciting in the nation at 415 feet. Start 50 feet off the ground and streak down one of four twisting water slides at 25 mph into a splashdown pool.

KIDS' KINGDOM

Kids 12 and younger delight in this shallow play pool full of animal slides, huge floats, and inner tubes. Parents can sit on the surrounding sundeck and snap pictures to their hearts' content while their gleeful offspring slide down a pelican's pouch or a whale's open mouth. Kids' Kingdom also features Minnow Matinee, an outdoor theater that hosts magic and juggling routines and other types of entertainment for the whole family.

LEMON DROP

Next to the Peppermint Twist is this short but, dare we say it, awesome adventure. Two hydrochutes, one curved, one straight, rocket the rider down and drop him about 4 feet over the pool below. Maybe the fact that one Insider has nicknamed this ride "The Splat" gives you an idea of what we're talking about. Be prepared to make water contact with a major splash.

MALIBU PIPELINE

Opened in 1993, the Malibu Pipeline is a twisting, two-person tube ride through enclosed double flumes, complete with strobe lighting, waterfalls, and a splash pool at the bottom. The dark-as-night flumes made this one of our favorite rides, and our older daughter deemed it "wild, wild, wild."

MELTDOWN

This attraction is the fastest and steepest of all Water Country USA rides. This zoom-flume carries four people at a time along its icy waters. Grab three of your closest friends, get in the surf 'boggan raft, and you are ready for a high-speed glide through 180-degree turns. It will only take you 35 seconds to travel 701 feet, thanks to the 76-foot vertical drop. That's averaging about 22 feet per second!

NITRO RACER

If you like a little competition with your fun, this super-fast, slippery drag race is for you. After climbing to the top, six contestants (a great opportunity to grab bragging rights in a big family) race down a 320-foot-long slide to see who can reach the finish line first. Prepare your little ones before the drop: Big guys definitely have the advantage on Nitro!

PEPPERMINT TWIST

This is one of Water Country USA's most breathtaking rides. You'll plunge into a pool after spinning down a tangle of three curving tubes. Fast and fun!

RAMBLING RIVER

This ride is engineered to provide soothing relaxation for the whole family. Float your tube down the lazy river that surrounds Adventure Isle.

RAMPAGE

Grab your surf 'boggan, and speed down 75 feet of steep, slick Teflon slide. Then shoot across the long landing pool and try to catch your breath. This is one of the shortest and perhaps scariest rides in the park. One Insider was ready to climb back down after catching the view from the top until her young daughter took the plunge and shamed her into trying it for herself.

Comments made by riders (and would-be riders) at the Rampage: "My heart was just thumping"..."I can't do this, and no one is going to make me"..."I'm scared, but I'm going" (out of the mouth of the five-year-old)..."You mean I'm supposed to lean forward?". . ."That's a wild drop". . ."Never again". . ."Aaaaaaaaaaa!"

SURFERS' BAY

This is Virginia's largest wave pool, though it seems more like an ocean with its 650,000 gallons of water. Periods of mechanically produced 4-foot waves alternate with times of smooth surf for relaxation. Want to really chill out?

Stretch out in one of more than 1,000 lounge chairs on the wood sundeck surrounding the bay. Or, if you're looking for a little shelter from the elements, head for one of the bright canopied cabanas found poolside. Grab your seats early as they go fast.

WILD THANG

Take another walk on the wild side—with a companion—on this popular 500-foot-long double inner-tube ride past jungle scenes, under waterfalls, and through tunnels before splashing down.

Entertainment and Dining

Caban-A-Rama Theatre is the site for daily shows. "Island Quest" is a 20-minute extravaganza showing the talents of world-class acrobats, divers, and trampoline artists. Schedules are posted at the theater's entrance.

W. C.'s Hot Spot Cafe, the newest eatery in the park, offers an assortment of goodies to calm the I've-been-swimming-all-day munchies. In fact, Water Country's seven dining places sell an array of hot dogs, smoked sausages, chicken, pizza, pretzels, subs, fries, funnel cakes, ice cream, lemonade, sports drinks, and beer (which must be consumed in a single enclosed area). Snack bars are situated around the park and open for business as crowds dictate. Guests can eat purchased meals at shaded outdoor tables, and a catering facility may be reserved in advance for groups of 20 or more. Our Insiders' tip, since prices for park fare are a bit steep and service can be slow, is to bring a picnic. You'll have to eat it at tables on grassy areas in the parking lot, as no food or beverages may be brought into the park itself. But the tables are on

i If your adventures at Busch Gardens or Water Country USA leave you gasping from thirst, ask at any of the drink concessions for a cup of ice water. They will gladly oblige—free of charge.

grassy median strips and most are shaded by umbrellas, so it's both a cheap and pleasant alternative. There's also a shaded pavilion for picnicking off to the right of the park entrance if you prefer. Make sure to have your hand stamped at the gate so that you can get back inside the park.

Swimwear, gifts, souvenirs, sunglasses, and sunscreen are for sale at on-site surf and gift shops.

Safety Features

Water Country USA has an excellent reputation as a safe, fun place to enjoy water without hitting the beach. The park employs more than 80 certified lifeguards and stations supervisors at each ride and attraction. Lifeguards are trained in CPR, first aid, and accident prevention, and they participate in ongoing training programs and drills. Life vests and inner tubes are provided for free for anyone who would like one. Each year American Red Cross–certified volunteers offer swim lessons to area residents.

A first-aid station is open during all operating hours, walks are treated with salt to prevent falls, pool depths are clearly marked, and individual safety rules are posted at each ride. Children younger than 8 must always be in the company of a parent or other adult. This combination of rules and features at Water Country USA set the standards for safety among the nation's water parks. Precisely because the park is so safety-conscious, visitors can truly relax and enjoy a wet and wild adventure.

Williamsburg Pottery Factory

Imagine a building the size of eight football fields filled from floor to ceiling with fine crystal, plants, dried and silk flowers, baskets, microwave ovenware, folk art, woodwork, lamps, home accessories, glassware, pottery, and more—all on sale at wholesale prices or less. What you've envisioned is just one of more than a dozen such buildings that make up the Williamsburg Pottery Factory, a 1-million-square-foot retail complex that must be seen to be believed.

Just 5 miles west of Williamsburg, the Pottery draws between two and four million bargain-hunting customers annually, and as such it qualifies as one of the Williamsburg area's greatest attractions. It is Virginia's largest retail operation under single ownership at a single location, and it is unique in other ways as well.

The Pottery is open seven days a week and is closed only one day a year: Christmas. In the summer it is open from 9:00 a.m. to 7:30 p.m. Monday through Saturday, and 9:00 a.m. to 6:30 p.m. on Sunday. It closes at 5:30 p.m. during the winter. Hours, however, vary from season to season, so we suggest you call ahead at (757) 564-3326 to check the hours if you're planning to head to Lightfoot early or want to go later in the day. The Pottery also has a Web site: www.williamsburg pottery.com.

Getting There

It takes about 10 minutes to drive from downtown Williamsburg to the Pottery via US 60. An alternate route is to take I–64 to the Lightfoot exit and follow Route 199, where you will see signs directing you to the Pottery entrance.

Pottery Background

The Pottery is the ultimate American success story. Started in 1938 as a roadside stand where local potter James E. Maloney could sell his salt-glazed pottery made in 18th-century tradition, the Pottery evolved from a one-man operation to one of the largest bargain centers on the East Coast. The roadside stand has grown into a multisectioned retail complex. Its offerings have expanded and multiplied, and the Pottery is unlike anything you've seen or experienced.

The Pottery makes a lot of what it sells to avoid middlemen's profits. Small factories on the premises make cement gardenware, wood items, lamps, custom frames, trophies and plaques, etched glass, painted plasterware, floral arrangements, and other decorative items. You can also purchase unusual items here you won't find anywhere else. If the spirit moves you, there are Elvis Presley coffee mugs, black squid ink pasta, and life-size statues of bulldogs.

Simple buildings and a constant din create a carnival atmosphere as shoppers grab for, pore over, and wander amid aisle after aisle of assorted goods. While you'll find piles of junk or junque (as your tastes dictate), there's just no denying that this place offers some of the best buys on first-quality goods as well. The Pottery is almost always crowded (except first thing in the morning—a good time to do your serious shopping), and it's not unusual to arrive and find 25 or more buses lined up at the entrance (they're actually chartered from as far away as North Carolina, New York, New Jersey, and Pennsylvania). Fear not, there's plenty inside for everyone, and the stock is seemingly endless and constantly being replenished by the scores of workers who help keep the place humming.

Whether you're in a buying mood or not, a trip to the Pottery is a must while you're in the Williamsburg area. We must warn you that few visitors escape without succumbing to the urge to spend, and with good reason.

The Pottery is not fancy. Wear casual clothes and comfortable shoes. Be sure to block out several hours at least, and a full day if possible, to do the place justice. Remember that there are 32 or so buildings on the property. (A Christmas shop that sells just about everything for the holiday season is near Gate 1A, and a large Garden Center and adjacent greenhouse are at the entrance to Gate 5.) If you're willing to trek through miles of aisles, bargains do abound.

The Shops

The Pottery complex is split into two parts, bisected neatly by the CSX railroad tracks. On one side is the Pottery, with its ceramic factory, the Solar Shops, greenhouses, Buildings 21, 22, and 23, plus production and warehouse facilities. On the other side is a bevy of factory outlet stores, about 25 or so, plus Pottery production areas for cement gardenware and terrastone, a brass foundry, and a western shop.

If you plan to spend the day, you'll want to grab a shopping cart as soon as you can. This will come in handy once you accumulate an armload of packages. There are maps of the area available at the entrance gate. While it is always fun wandering around, discovering all the Pottery has to offer, the map is a useful time-saver. If you don't find one readily available, ask a security guard where you might pick one up.

To maximize your time, we suggest you arrive as early in the day as possible. The Pottery has a restaurant, a cafe, and a snack bar on the premises where you can eat breakfast, lunch, and a light dinner, if necessary.

The Solar Shops, so named because of the energy-efficient heating and lighting system installed when this building was constructed, are housed under a single, albeit gigantic, roof. Here you will find a great variety of household and decorating items, silk flowers, lamps, picture frames (a custom framing service is provided), mirrors, wooden accessories, imported crystal, baskets, prints, folk art, Oriental art, fine china, collector dolls, ribbon, Mexican imports, and more. Fine gold jewelry is sold here at about half the retail price.

Building 21 is where you will find a fresh bakery, gourmet foods, wine and spirits, kitchenware, a cheese shop, brass, candles, cushions, Oriental carpets and furniture, clocks, ceramics, linens, and other decorator items.

If you're in the market for nursery plants, trees, shrubs, flowering plants, vegetable seedlings, herbs, or decorative bushes, stop by the greenhouse or the landscape nursery near the 550-space Pottery Campground. Fine local, regional, exotic, and tropical plants in all shapes and sizes are sold. The Pottery grows many plants from seedlings and imports still more in bulk. All are sold at rock-bottom prices. You'll find bargains on gardening tools, accessories, and plant-care items. The shop even sells Christmas trees in season from its tree farm in the Virginia mountains.

Bargains from around the world are commonplace at the Pottery. At any one time you can spy goods from around the United States, the Orient, the Caribbean, South America, Europe, India, and elsewhere. Goods are purchased and sold in volume, with substantial savings passed on to the customer. Another key to the Pottery's success is its low overhead: Your purchases will be wrapped in newspaper and bound with masking tape, an inelegant but inexpensive system.

Another draw is the Pottery Factory Outlets, where you'll find a variety of items sold directly by the manufacturers at cost or slightly higher. These shops are open according to the Pottery's operating hours.

You could easily spend an entire morning in these shops alone; again, wise planning of your time is a must. Included among the outlets are shops offering sleepwear, outerwear, and sportswear for men, women, and children; hardware and small appliances; linens; sweaters; cosmetics and perfume; shoes galore; needlework accessories and supplies; designer clothing; and candy, ice cream, and nuts. See our Shopping chapter for more details.

Although more than 8,000 parking spaces are provided, parking can be difficult on busy days. We suggest that when you find a parking spot, stay there and walk from place to place. Parking is free, and lots are on all sides of the complex. We do warn you to observe strictly any no parking signs.

Visa, MasterCard, American Express, and Discover are accepted for purchases. Personal checks (even from out of state) are welcomed by most stores if accompanied by a picture identification card and two phone numbers.

JAMESTOWN AND YORKTOWN

In 2007 Jamestown marked the 400th year since English colonists first debarked from their three wooden ships after a four-month journey across the Atlantic and struggled to establish a settlement along the banks of Virginia's James River. The meeting of minds and cultures that followed, as the English met the Powhatan Indians who inhabited the region, laid the foundation for the rich cultural diversity that characterizes America as we know it in the 21st century.

Even as the enormous birthday bash takes place, life (in a sense) continues to stand still at Jamestown, where the English colonists' early years on American soil are brought to life and made meaningful through reenactments, interpretations, and displays. And, in nearby Yorktown, the National Park Service has preserved and restored Revolutionary War battlefields. It also stages recreations of colonial life in all its charm and adversity. In recent years archaeologists at Jamestown literally have dug up conclusive evidence that pinpoints the location of James Fort, the original colony fortification of 1607. In fact, continuing excavations at the original site of Jamestown, which are being conducted by the Association for the Preservation of Virginia Antiquities (APVA), have been called "the most exciting breakthrough in 17th-century archaeology in decades" by Dr. Thomas E. Davidson, senior curator for the Jamestown-Yorktown Foundation, which administers Jamestown Settlement. During the first four years of the digs—known collectively as the Jamestown Rediscovery Project—about 200,000 artifacts were unearthed. More recently, archaeologists have uncovered evidence of very early attempts at glassmaking and have found hundreds of cylindrical copper beads that most likely had been fashioned by English colonists for trade with the Powhatan Indians. These finds have led to a greater emphasis on industry and trade by the skilled interpreters who continue to bring Jamestown history to life for thousands of visitors each year.

Yorktown, too, is a work in progress. In May 1997 a newly built farmhouse opened at the Yorktown Victory Center. The 16-by-20-foot house was designed to show visitors the type of dwelling the typical Virginia planter of the period inhabited: a small, plain, even crude house with no formal entryway or individual rooms. New county administration buildings, including an eye-grabbing courthouse, have spruced up Ballard Street near the Yorktown waterfront, while a new riverwalk connects the Victory Center to Water Street.

But these are just a few examples of how Jamestown and Yorktown—two of the Historic Triangle's crown jewels—continue to reinvent themselves while making strides to enhance the authenticity of each and every visitor's journey back in time. Read on and learn all the details in this tale of two towns that once were—and still remain—such an integral part of our American heritage.

JAMESTOWN
History

Imagine leaving your home and country with little more than what few possessions you could carry in a small chest. Imagine boarding a vessel powered only by breezes (or gales for the more unfortunate) to cross the boisterous Atlantic Ocean. Imagine months at sea with no privacy, little fresh food, no heat or comfort of any kind, all in order to reach a land said to be inhabited by fierce native tribes where previous attempts at settlement had ended in disaster. Who would undertake such a journey? But imagine, too, dreaming of a fertile and bounteous land. Imagine dreaming of being free—from debt, from lack of opportunity, from city squalor, from whatever mistakes or burdens were part of your past. Imagine holding in your mind simultaneously the alternating hopes and forebodings of such an enterprise, and you can begin to fathom the experience of the Jamestown settlers.

In December of 1606 three wooden ships sailed from London for the New World. Southerly winds blew the 105 adventuresome members of the expedition to the Caribbean, where one of the men died. Here they obtained fresh provisions before voyaging again, this time up North America's eastern coast. Some four months and 6,000 miles after their departure from England, they found a swampy wilderness on the banks of the James River and pronounced it fit for settlement. Thus began the long and fascinating story of our country's beginnings.

The early years were difficult ones for the settlers of Jamestown, the New World's first permanent English-speaking colony. The climate proved hot and humid, the land marshy and mosquito-ridden. Several of the colonists' attempts at industry, including glassmaking, failed to create a solid economy. And the large native population of Indians, ruled by Powhatan, was understandably distrustful of these invaders from across the seas. The winter of 1609–10, known as the "Starving Time," was especially terrible for the colony. Only about 90 gaunt members of the colony still were alive when supplies and reinforcements finally arrived. Indeed, more than half of the colonists who came to Virginia in the colony's first seven years died. Ultimately, tobacco cultivation succeeded where all else had failed, ensuring survival. More and more settlers arrived, attracted by cash crop opportunities as well as the desire for a better life than that afforded by the rigidly hierarchical societies of Europe. Soon the Virginia Colony was flourishing; plantation society took firm root in its rich, sandy soils and lush woodlands.

Recently, Spanish documents have been uncovered that discuss the arrival of 20 or so Africans in Virginia in the summer of 1619. These written accounts suggest that the Africans reached Virginia soil aboard the Portuguese ship San Juan Bautista, which had sailed from Luanda, Angola, and was bound for the port of Vera Cruz, Mexico. In all likelihood, according to the Jamestown-Yorktown Foundation's Summer 1999 issue of its newsletter, Dispatch, the men were captured in skirmishes waged by Africans and their Portuguese allies against the kingdom of Ndongo.

Further research suggests that most of the few hundred Africans who came to the Old Dominion during the first half of the 17th century hailed from the regions of Angola. These men and women more than likely knew how to farm and had been acquainted with both Europeans and Christianity. About a third of these early arrivals and their children were or became free, notes the Jamestown-Yorktown Foundation, and some acquired their own land. The number of Africans in Virginia remained relatively small throughout the 17th century, accounting for only 2 to 3 percent of the non-Indian population in 1650, and about 10 percent by the turn of the century.

On July 30, 1619, the first representative legislative assembly in British America met at Jamestown. The community continued to thrive as the Virginia Colony's first capital until 1699 when, after the burning of the Statehouse, the seat of government was moved inland to Williamsburg for reasons involving health problems caused by insects in this low-lying marshland location. No longer a vital political and economic hub, by 1750 Jamestown ceased to exist as an actual community. Fortunately, much of the Jamestown story has been restored to us. Some genuine remnants of the famous settlement survive, including the bell tower of the church the colonists built and foundations of their simple homes. Archaeological discoveries (the highly acclaimed Jamestown Rediscovery Project, an ongoing archaeological dig, began in 1994), scholarly research, and a

Footbridge to Jamestown National Historic Site. JESSI DICK

number of organizations' dedication to understanding our nation's past have combined to produce the Jamestown historic experience today.

For purposes of this guide, we have divided our entry on Jamestown into two parts: historic Jamestown, coadministered by the National Park Service and the Association for the Preservation of Virginia Antiquities; and the delightful adventure of Jamestown Settlement, operated by Virginia's Jamestown-Yorktown Foundation. While these two attractions operate separately, they are but a mile apart and can be easily visited in

the course of the same day. This excursion back in time is well worth taking, and it's a large part of what makes the Historic Triangle such a popular tourist destination.

Getting There

To get to Jamestown from I-64, take exit 242A, Route 199, which brings you to the Colonial Parkway, where signs will lead you to Jamestown. If you're coming from Williamsburg, simply take Jamestown Road and follow signs from there. Visitors arriving from the south on Route 31 will cross the James River on the Jamestown Ferry, a pleasant excursion we profile in our chapter on Day Trips. Jamestown Settlement lies at the intersection of Route 31 and the Colonial Parkway, just up from the Jamestown Ferry docks.

Attractions

Jamestown National Historic Site
Western end of Colonial Parkway
(757) 229-1733, ext. 14
www.nps.gov/colo
At Jamestown a National Park Service employee will collect your admission fee at the park entrance (see prices that follow). Drive past the entrance to the reconstructed Glasshouse on your right and head straight to the larger main parking area, where a wooden pedestrian bridge through shady woods takes you to the spacious visitor center. Here you can view a 15-minute orientation film, *Jamestown: Where a Nation Began,* then join scheduled tours led by park rangers, pick up self-guiding leaflets if you prefer to go at your own pace, and view changing exhibits as well as an extensive collection of 17th-century Jamestown artifacts. Guided tours for groups are available, on a reservation basis, in spring, winter, and fall.

Begin your tour of the Old Towne Site at the Tercentenary Monument, a 103-foot shaft of New Hampshire granite that was erected in 1907 to mark the 300th anniversary of Jamestown's founding. River tides have washed away part of this early town site, but on your walking tour of Jamestown you can explore the 1639 Church Tower, the sole 17th-century structure still standing, and view ruins of the original settlement made visible by archaeological exploration. These include foundations of some of the early statehouses and ruins of the original glass furnaces built in 1608. Near the Church Tower along the James River waterfront is the Jamestown Rediscovery archaeological excavation site, where you can watch researchers sift through the remains of the James Fort, once believed lost forever, and talk to interpreters about the latest dig finds. Excavation on the site began in 1994 after archaeologist

i Jamestown is not only a drawing card for history buffs. Best-selling mystery writer Patricia Cornwell visited the island in the summer of 1999 to gather material for a novel. *The Last Precinct* was published in October 2000 and picked up where the heroine, Dr. Kay Scarpetta, left off in *Black Notice.* Cornwell also has donated $50,000 from the proceeds of the novel *Black Notice* to the Jamestown Rediscovery Project.

William Kelso led the team that discovered that the fort was not lost under the James River, as was formerly believed. It is estimated that about 85 percent of the fort still exists on land. Of that, about 20 percent has been uncovered so far. You'll also see statues of John Smith and Pocahontas as well as the Dale House, which sits near the seawall, just beyond the Confederate earthwork. The Dale House serves as an archaeological lab. In its visitors' gallery many of the recently uncovered artifacts of the Jamestown Rediscovery Project are on display. Along the way explanatory markers help those on self-guided tours understand the rich, multilayered history of the site.

Further progress was made in 2001, allowing visitors to get a feel for what the settlers would have seen inside or outside the walls of the fort. Partial sections of the south and east palisade walls, the southeast bulwark, an eastern extension, and gates were built last winter. Construction of the frame of a longhouse building discovered inside the fort area has recently begun to help visitors understand the dimensions and shape of the building.

Next, a pause at the Memorial Cross is in order. The cross marks some 300 shallow graves that were dug by the settlers during the so-called "Starving Time," the dismal winter of 1609–10. Walk to the other side of the visitor center, and you will find the New Towne Site, which contains reproductions of ruins built over original foundations, including those of the Ambler Mansion, a two-story home built in the mid-1700s. Also in New Towne is the Manufacturing Site, where a number of commercial endeavors—including brick making, pottery making, and brewing—occurred in the mid-1600s.

After you've toured the town site, take one of the loop drives around Jamestown Island. These 3- and 5-mile self-guided automobile tours through a wilderness of pine and swamp will bring you close to the vision early colonists must have beheld when they set foot in America—a natural environment at once beautiful and frightening. Herds of deer still roam the forested ridges of the island, sometimes coming close to the ruins under cover of dusk. Muskrats hide in the Jamestown marshes; you might glimpse one paddling leisurely through the swamp. A profusion of waterfowl, including ospreys, herons, and mallards, make seasonal stops. Roll down your windows, listen to the music of songbirds, feel the stillness all around you. We guarantee you'll feel an almost otherworldly peace in this place that, as one Insider likes to say, does not belong to us but to all of those who walked the land before us. If time permits—and you should make sure it does—you can pull over to read the markers inscribed with interesting historical and botanical data.

The next logical stop is at the reconstructed Glasshouse, where costumed craftspeople demonstrate 400-year-old techniques, making glassware much like that created and used by settlers. While hardwoods such as hickory and oak fueled the kilns in 1608, today natural gas heats the fiery furnace. No matter. The products, which register a red-hot 2,000 degrees when first pulled from the heat, are lovely. Clear and green goblets, bell jars, flasks, wineglasses, pitchers, and the like can be purchased here. A display case also shows off some of the glassblowers' after-hours work—the vases and such they make to perfect their skills long after you and I have gone home.

You may want to return to the visitor cen-ter for souvenirs before leaving. Reproductions of colonial stoneware, glassware made at the Glasshouse, a vast selection of books, videotapes, toys, games, and other keepsakes are for sale in the gift shop.

As part of the quadricentennial festivities, in the fall of 2006, Virginia's leaders unveiled a new 40,000-square-foot exhibition center, a cluster of buildings that includes visitor services, an interpretive introduction to the island, extensive exhibits, and a link to the James Fort and New Towne sites. Other improvements include changes in interpretive scripts to reflect the findings of recent research, a variety of site improvements, and a cafe at the Dale House.

Admission to Jamestown Island is $10 per adult, age 15 or older, and covers reentry for up to a week. Children 14 and younger are admitted free. Golden Eagle, Golden Age, and Golden Access Passports to the National Parks are accepted. Educational groups are admitted free of charge with advance notice and a written fee waiver.

Jamestown is open from 9:00 a.m. to 5:00 p.m. every day of the year except Christmas. Parking is free.

Interpretive Programs

To truly get a feel for the place and the era, children may participate in a number of special programs. These include the Pinch Pot program during the summer months, in which children can make their own pot of clay, and the Colonial Junior Ranger programs, where children 12 and younger can learn about Jamestown while enjoying a series of activities with their families. The Junior Ranger program, which is designed for family groups only, provides each child with a chance to earn a patch and a certificate. Other interpretive programs are offered seasonally, including ranger-led tours of the town site and living-history character tours. Preregistration is not required. Most programs are either free with admission or have a small materials cost per child.

Jamestown Settlement
Route 31 and Colonial Parkway
(757) 253-4838, (888) 593-4682
www.historyisfun.org

Known as Jamestown Festival Park until 1990, Jamestown Settlement is operated by the Jamestown-Yorktown Foundation of the Commonwealth of Virginia. The settlement blends an indoor theater and museum exhibits with an outdoor living-history program that re-creates both the early colonists' experiences and Native American habitats and customs. Here you'll also have a chance to board replicas of the ships that brought the English settlers to the New World in 1607.

The settlement underwent major renovations in preparation for the 2007 celebration, including an expanded gallery, more and larger classrooms, expanded offices, and an improved cafe with indoor and outdoor seating for 300.

Start off your visit, after purchasing your ticket in the entrance lobby, by watching a dramatic 15-minute film, *Jamestown: The Beginning,* in the comfortable 100-seat theater of the museum building. Narrated by an actor playing the role of colonist John Laydon, this docudrama familiarizes visitors with the origins of the Jamestown colony and also serves as an introduction to museum exhibits. It is shown every 20 minutes. After the film, make your way past the imposing brass statue of Chief Powhatan to the first of three distinct galleries that make up the indoor portion of Jamestown Settlement.

English Gallery

In the English Gallery you can examine artifacts, three-dimensional dioramas, reproductions, and graphics that explain British motivations for exploring and settling the New World. Some of the authentic artifacts include Spanish and Italian rapiers from the 1570s, armor from 1625, and 17th-century German muskets. There is also a one-quarter-scale model showing the framework of a 16th-century ship. The role of the British Crown in colonization and the founding of the Virginia Company, which sponsored Jamestown, are highlighted, as is the crucial role played by new navigational and ship-building techniques that made long ocean voyages feasible. There are replicas of the clothing worn by both the commoners and the well-to-do of the time and an explanation of the role wool production played in the economy of England. (In fact, British dependence on wool led to the common expression of the day that "England is a country where sheep eat men.")

Powhatan Indian Gallery

Chief Powhatan ruled 32 Algonquian tribes in coastal Virginia at the time of the Jamestown settlement. These tribes are now sometimes referred to simply as the Powhatans. You'll learn more about these people in the second exhibit gallery, the Powhatan Indian Gallery. Inside are life-size figures of a Powhatan man, woman, and child, plus a full-size replica of Powhatan's mantle. His ceremonial cloak is made from four deer hides and decorated with shell-bead figures. The original is in a museum in Oxford, England. Displays of originals and reproductions of tools, weapons, and fishing and farming implements, along with scenes of everyday life, offer a perspective on Native American culture during the period. Did you know, for instance, that Powhatan women built the houses for their tribe or that Indian babies were bathed daily in cold streams to make them hearty? Be sure to listen to the recording of an Algonquian dialect. While the Powhatan language is extinct, the tape is of an eastern Algonquian dialect used by tribes in Delaware and Pennsylvania. You also can touch treated samples of deerskin the Powhatans used as clothing. Probably even more famous today than the great Chief Powhatan is his daughter Pocahontas. There is a side gallery devoted to this young woman, including a bust, paintings, a marble statue, and a blue-onyx cameo brooch believed to have been given to her during her visit to England.

Jamestown Gallery

The Jamestown Gallery completes the triad of galleries here, depicting the growth of the settlement from its earliest rugged days to the bustling period when it served as the political and economic cornerstone of the sizable Virginia Colony. Tribulations endured by the first settlers are described, and the story of Captain John Smith is told. Also detailed are the roles played by tobacco, by Africans first brought to Jamestown in 1619, and by the church. There's the captivating story about Anthony and Mary Johnson, two Africans, who arrived as servants before slavery took hold. After working their way out of servitude, the two married, and by 1650 they and their two sons owned a 900-acre tobacco plantation in the Tidewater area.

If you are curious about the types of homes settlers built, you'll get a good idea by viewing the gallery's miniature replicas in wattle and daub, clapboard, and brick. Also on display are late-17th-century cannonballs and cannon barrel fragments, as well as numerous pieces of period furniture, representing the life of "the middling sort" and the well-to-do.

Although Jamestown Settlement's indoor exhibits are fascinating, your most vivid memories probably will come from the outdoor re-creations of 17th-century life. These offer a unique hands-on journey into our country's past. Not only do authentically costumed interpreters reenact the chores and amusements of daily life in colonial Virginia, they also encourage visitors to take a turn at many of these activities. Children especially like this aspect of Jamestown Settlement.

Powhatan Indian Village

In the Powhatan Indian Village, a short walk from the museum exit, you'll see several Native American houses (the British called them longhouses but the Algonquian word is *yahekan*) made of sapling frames covered with reed mats. These Native American dwellings are re-creations based on archaeological findings and the eyewitness drawings of a New World explorer. Walk around the ceremonial "dance face circle" made up of seven carved wooden poles created by an Indian artist and her husband. It is easy to get the feel for this place as you watch a historical interpreter costumed as a Powhatan Indian make tools from bone or smoke fish over a fire and cook it on a baking stone. Children can get a taste of American life in colonial times as they grind corn or play cob darts, a game of pitching dried corn ears through a hanging vine hoop.

Right outside the village, near the river, two costumed interpreters burn out a log to make a canoe, as they would have in the 17th century. Although the settlement staff could finish the project in 10 days, they slow the process for display purposes. Most of these canoes created at Jamestown are made for other museums. However, a recent canoe was large enough to keep for the settlement to use in demonstrations.

Three Ships

Follow the path down from the Indian village to the pier, where full-size replica ships, the *Susan Constant,* the *Godspeed,* and the *Discovery,* float in a recess of the James River. The *Susan Constant,* a replica that was actually built here at the settlement from 1989 to 1991, is brightly painted and fully rigged. It replaces an earlier replica built before the discovery of evidence that the original *Susan Constant,* probably built in 1605, had a 120-ton cargo capacity. Exploration of shipwrecked vessels of similar make and period also provided clues as to the appearance and construction of this remarkable craft. Go on board the 116-foot-long replica and imagine calling it home for nearly five months. Remember, including crew there were probably 143 men and boys aboard the three ships that reached Jamestown in 1607. You can climb down to the 'tween deck, where passengers were quartered, for an idea of just how cramped conditions were. When we remarked on the small size of the deck, one of the interpreters told us that conditions were even worse than we imagined: During the

The Susan Constant, *one of three full-size replica ships at Jamestown Settlement.* LYNN ZELEM

voyage from England, the deck probably was loaded with cargo waist high, then covered with mattresses, where most of the passengers spent many idle hours lolling about in utter boredom!

Take note that the *Susan Constant, Godspeed,* and *Discovery* are functional ships, and sometimes one of them sails off from Jamestown Settlement to participate in a maritime event or take part in an educational demonstration. One highlight of the 400th anniversary celebration, on May 12, 2007, the three ships sailed the James River and docked at the museum pier in a reenactment of the original docking. But visitors always have access to at least one of the ship replicas. Costumed crew members interpret life at sea, unfurling sails, dropping anchor, posting colors, and letting hardy souls try their hand at navigating or nautical knot tying. Children learn the role of 17th-century ship's boys and may be asked to ring the ship's bell or read directions on the compass. Other hands-on demonstrations may include rigging sails or operating a pulley (to show how simple machines work). A 20-by-50-foot pier shelter near the three ships is designed to resemble a waterfront building and is used for demonstrations, such as making hatch covers or sails. Visitors who might have trouble making the climb down the steep steps below deck on the *Susan Constant* also may opt to sit here under the sheltered pier and watch a videotape of what it's like below. Or, it's a cool spot to just stop in and rest a spell, out of the sun.

James Fort

When you're ready to stand on solid ground again, debark and head up to James Fort. Enter these stockade walls, and you'll experience the rough-and-ready life of early settlers— thatched roof, wattle-and-daub huts with rudimentary furnishings, the smell of wood smoke, the ceaseless worry and toil of survival. Inspect a cannon, try on armor, help a colonist tend the garden. Children delight in knocking down the wooden pins of a primitive bowling game, playing quoits (ring toss), or watching the periodic muster of the militia. Children can carry water the old-fashioned way—with a pole draped over their shoulders and heavy buckets attached to either end—toss food scraps to the chickens that roam the grounds freely, or help grind the pepper with a mortar and pestle. Male settlers may be engaged in the industries of Virginia, such as lumber manufacture or blacksmithing, or doing chores such as daubing a house, while the women are often cooking or demonstrating other domestic skills. A 50-foot barracks erected within the fort confines is the only building on the premises with a clapboard roof.

You may be amazed by what the reenactors tell you. We learned, for example, that while men couldn't marry until 19, girls of 13 were permitted to wed; that two or three entire families lived in a small 10-by-12-foot house; and that the punishment for failure to attend one of the two daily church services was no food for the day.

In addition to regular exhibits and activities, Jamestown Settlement sponsors a number of special programs throughout the year. These include a public lecture series; children's programs, always featuring hands-on learning activities; a November Foods and Feasts presentation that demonstrates how the early colonists prepared and preserved food; and traditional colonial Christmas festivities. (For more complete discussions, see the Annual Events chapter.)

Cafe and Gift Shop

After touring Jamestown Settlement, or if you need a break before plunging back into the 17th century, you can relax and get a bite to eat. The indoor-outdoor cafe is open from 9:00 a.m. to 5:00 p.m. and serves a variety of sandwiches, munchies, and ice cream. The Jamestown Settlement has wonderful gift shops that are open from 9:00 a.m. to 5:00 p.m. (6:00 p.m. during the summer months).

There are also snack and drink machines. In the settlement's gift shops, you can purchase reproductions of 17th-century glassware and pottery, commemorative coins, and

A Celebration in the Making

The year 2007 was a monumental birthday for the settlement of Jamestown—it reached the ripe old age of 400. The yearlong celebration, 10 years in the making, brought tens of thousands of visitors. More than 63,000—including Queen Elizabeth II of Great Britain, President George W. Bush, and Virginia's congressional delegation—-dropped by for the festivities that took place during the official anniversary weekend, May 11 to 13.

"The story of Jamestown will always have a special place in American history. It's the story of a great migration from the 'Old World' to the 'New.' It is a story of hardship overcome by resolve. It's a story of the Tidewater settlement that laid the foundation of our great democracy," President Bush said in a speech during his visit.

Numerous special events—from Native American heritage lectures to music concerts, took place over the year. In April 2007 the Jamestown Settlement's newly expanded museum opened the "World of 1607" exhibit, which put the settlers' lives into a global context, looking at innovation, culture, and the quest to expand during the time period. Museums, libraries, and private collectors worldwide lent some of their greatest treasures, including a copy of the Magna Carta from the 15th century. That exhibit will be open until April 2008.

Jamestown already had a great deal of practice throwing parties for every 50-year celebration, beginning with the settlement's 200th and 250th anniversaries in 1807 and 1857. And when Jamestown turned 300, the whole nation was invited to the 1907 Jamestown Exposition. Likewise, the 1957 Jamestown Festival brought folks from across the United States to the Old Dominion's Historic Triangle.

Planning for Celebration 2007 began with a 1996 mandate from the Virginia General Assembly designating the Jamestown-Yorktown Foundation as "the official entity of the Commonwealth charged with the planning and implementation of the 400th anniversary celebration of the Jamestown settlement."

Construction began in 1998 on a new complex that included an education center, theater, exhibition hall, and visitor's center to handle the expected crowds.

Jeanne Zeidler, executive director of the Jamestown 2007, the organization that led the planning of the events, said attendance to the site was up nearly 40 percent during the first half of 2007.

a variety of souvenirs, trinkets, and toys. If you have fallen in love with the settlement, you may want to pick up the 32-page *Jamestown Settlement: A Pictorial Guide,* which features dozens of color illustrations of the area.

Jamestown Settlement is open from 9:00 a.m. to 5:00 p.m. daily, with hours extended to 6:00 p.m. from June 15 to August 15. It is closed Christmas and New Year's Day. Ask about the guided tours that are offered throughout the day. Obviously, you don't want to go on a rainy day, unless you are interested only in the museum exhibits. Keep in mind that extreme heat and humidity may interfere with the pleasures of touring Jamestown Settlement during the height of summer, though river breezes help make all but the hottest of days tolerable. And try to allow two to three hours for a thorough exploration.

Admission to Jamestown Settlement is $13.50 for adults and $6.25 for children 6 to 12. It's possible to purchase a combination ticket for both the settlement and the Yorktown Victory Center, also run by the Jamestown-Yorktown Foundation. That ticket costs $17.75 for adults and $8.50 for children 6 to 12. Residents of York and James City Counties and Williamsburg are entitled to free entry.

YORKTOWN

History

There are scores—maybe hundreds—of American towns dozing gracefully along wide rivers, awakened occasionally by the passing of some historic event, then retreating into the quiet thread of their own affairs. At first impression Yorktown appears to be merely another one of these, and, in a sense, it is. Very few dates in its 300-plus years of existence are marked by anything of importance to outsiders. In fact, there's just one: October 19, 1781.

The small scale of this village on the bluffs overlooking the wide York River belies both its age and its importance. The history books tell another story. They tell it, of course, with all the proper names, dates, facts, and numbers. For us Insiders, however, and for the others who have walked its streets and fields in many seasons, there is something else here, something very much still alive and profoundly significant. Spend just a few quiet minutes overlooking the battlefield on an October evening, or at dusk on a hot summer day after the sightseers have departed, and you might sense that the spirit of the place is capable of overwhelming you.

The decisive victory of the long war for American independence from Britain was won here. The major British force in the colonies surrendered here. And, what had been rebellious colonies until then were, in fact and by their own will, freed here to seek their destiny on their own terms.

Compared to the battlefields of our own era, the place where the British empire's rebellious children came of age is compact, reflecting a combat situation of classic simplicity. The British under Lord Cornwallis were backed against the edge of the bluff and on the waterfront below it. The American and French forces surrounded them in an explosive arc of continuous cannon and musket fire. After the Comte de Grasse sealed the mouth of the Chesapeake Bay with the French fleet in the battle of the Virginia Capes, the British were cut off from reinforcement or retreat and faced inevitable defeat. In brief, fierce, hand-to-hand combat, the Americans and French captured the outlying British defenses—the redoubts—and the war ended.

The most significant moment must have come when the British troops filed out of the city, flags furled, to turn in their weapons at the Allied encampment while the humiliating tune "The World Turned Upside Down" was sounded by their own fifes and drums. Lord Cornwallis, pleading illness, had sent his representative, General O'Hara, to surrender his sword as acknowledgment of defeat. Disdaining the colonials, this proud British commander approached General Rochambeau, leader of the French troops on the Allied side, and attempted to offer him the sword. Rochambeau, with grace but firmness, refused. He indicated instead that the sword rightfully should be handed over to the other commander present, General George Washington. In turn, Washington, acknowledging O'Hara's inferior rank, directed that the sword be handed to his second-in-command, Major-General Benjamin Lincoln.

In that moment, with those gestures, the two greatest empires of the time—for whom this war had been merely one remote episode in their extensive and long-running quarrels—acknowledged that a new entity had come into its own. The American states, united in their desperate bid for independence, were, from then on, to be full and respected players on the field of history.

How wonderful it is that, more than 225 years later, we can stand on that spot in the profound peace and beauty of Surrender Field and ponder all that led to that moment and all that has proceeded from it. In many ways tiny Yorktown is both cradle and monument to events of immense significance.

Getting There

Although there are several ways to approach Yorktown, our preference and recommendation is via the Colonial Parkway, the backbone of the Colonial National Historical Park, as it stretches 23 miles from Jamestown Island to the Yorktown Visitor Center. The parkway was completed in 1957. From 1985 to 1995, an extensive three-phase restoration project included the replacement of construction pavement joints and the addition of steel-backed timber guardrails along the route.

But what visitors will notice most as they ride along the Colonial Parkway is the spectacular beauty. Scattered dogwood and redbud trees light bare woods in spring and a bright riot of oak and other foliage add color in the autumn. The modern world doesn't intrude on the parkway, thanks to careful landscaping and the maintenance of a greenbelt along its length. It also is closed to trucks and commercial vehicles. There is abundant

wildlife visible along the route. Turnouts on both sides of the three-lane roadway provide a stopping place to read markers, some accompanied by paintings, indicating the historic significance of each place and giving visitors a feel for the rich and varied life of the colonial planters and their descendants. The views of the James and York Rivers from the parkway are outstanding, and the pullouts are popular places to rest and reflect. Near the Yorktown end of the parkway, you can pull over and watch the ships as they are armed at the piers of Yorktown Naval Weapons Station, which extends much of the length of the York River between Williamsburg and Yorktown. As its name suggests, this installation is where ordnance used by the Atlantic Fleet is maintained and stored.

Our advice for sojourners on the parkway: Take your time and enjoy the ride, but keep an eye out for bikers and joggers, who enjoy exercising along the scenic road. For more on this scenic byway, turn to our Close-up "Enjoying the Colonial Parkway" in our chapter Getting Here, Getting Around. An alternative—but not nearly as picturesque—route to Yorktown is to travel east from Williamsburg on Interstate 64, exiting at the Naval Weapons Station in Lee Hall, then turning left onto Route 143, traveling to the first stoplight, and there turning left again onto Route 238. Proceeding on this road will bring you to the Yorktown waterfront.

The Town

In August 1991 Yorktown celebrated its 300th anniversary, but, of course, the history of the area goes back even further than 1691. The original settlers along this stretch of the York River were the Kiskiack Indians, who called the water the Pamunkey. Captain John Smith explored the area in 1607, but it was nearly 20 years before any large numbers of English settlers began to cultivate the rich land. The town itself was founded in 1691 by the "Act for Ports and Towns" passed by the Virginia General Assembly for the transport of the colony's lucrative tobacco crop to Europe via

England. This was also, in part, an attempt to force urban growth in the colony and centralize the water traffic among the numerous plantations spreading up the Chesapeake Bay. Taking advantage of the deep channel of the York, British ships could pull far enough upriver for shelter from the storms of the Atlantic Ocean and the Chesapeake Bay. The network of creeks that crisscrosses the Virginia Peninsula allowed access from the James River side as well.

The town takes its name from surrounding York County and the York River, which were so called around 1643 to honor the Duke of York, later King James II. Fifty acres of land on the plantation of Benjamin Read—including a wharf, ferry, store, and well—were set aside for a county seat that was intended to grow and prosper in commerce. Sheltered by the bluff, with a wide beach to hold the storehouses and other businesses of the sea trade, the site became busy and flourished throughout the colonial period.

The oldest house in the town is the Sessions House, built in 1692 by Thomas Sessions and a survivor of the siege of 1781 and later the Civil War. A courthouse has stood on the same site since 1697, and a new church for York Parish was built in the same year. After their construction the town's growth accelerated. By the mid-18th century, as many as 50 large trading ships would be in the vicinity of Yorktown at any given time, and the town had grown relatively prosperous.

In the latter half of the 1700s, however, the tobacco trade had shifted to the inland Piedmont region, and the shipping patterns shifted accordingly. A slow process of decline

began, and by 1776 the port was less important in commonwealth affairs. The battle of Yorktown hastened the decline of the community. The intense barrage of cannon fire from the Allied siege line and the fighting during the battle destroyed more than half of the town, and it never fully recovered.

Historic Buildings

Structures dating from the colonial period attest to the wealth citizens gained from Yorktown's prominence. Some of the most notable are listed here.

Archer Cottage
Water Street

This former waterfront tavern, originally built in the early 1700s and all but the stone foundation reconstructed after an 1814 fire, probably played a key role in Yorktown's early days as a bustling, hard-drinking port. The building belongs to the National Park Service and is used as an office. It is not open to the public.

The Augustine Moore House
Moore House Road, near the
Coast Guard Station
(757) 898-2410

This is the historic home where the terms of surrender were drawn in 1781. It has been restored and furnished to its 18th-century appearance. A living-history program tells the interesting story of the arguments that took place during the negotiations. The house is open from spring through fall. For specific dates and times, contact the National Park Service at the above number.

Grace Episcopal Church
Church Street
(757) 898-3261
www.gracechurchyorktown.com

In colonial times this church was known as the York-Hampton Church. It was damaged several times by war and fire, but the original walls have been standing since 1697 and have been incorporated into a number of reconstructions. It remains the place of worship for

i If bicycling is your preferred way to travel, you can try a trail that begins at Washington's Headquarters (in the encampment part of the Yorktown battlefield tour) and connects with a 5-mile bicycle loop in adjoining Newport News Park. Bring your helmet and remember to ride single file on the far right side of the road.

an active Episcopal parish. A bookshop on-site offers theological and devotional literature, selected gifts, and cards. The church is open for viewing from 9:00 a.m. to 5:00 p.m. Monday through Saturday.

The Nelson House
Main Street
(757) 898-2410

With its Georgian design, glazed Flemish bond brickwork, and lovely formal gardens, The Nelson House was home to one of the wealthiest of the town's families. The most notable scion of the Nelson family was Thomas Nelson Jr., a governor of Virginia, commander of the Virginia militia, and signer of the Declaration of Independence. It was this home that Cornwallis used as headquarters during the siege, and colonial cannonballs still are lodged in the wall facing the American siege line. Legend has it that Thomas Nelson Jr. himself gave the order to fire those cannons, even though it might have meant the destruction of his home and possibly his fortune, an act putting literal force behind his pledge in the Declaration of Independence. The Nelson House is open spring through fall. Admission is included in the $10 fee to the Yorktown Visitor Center and battlefield. The house is open in the summer from 10:00 a.m. to 4:30 p.m. and daily from 1:00 to 4:00 p.m. the rest of the year.

Old Custom House
410 Main Street
(757) 898-2410

Reputed to have been built by Richard Ambler in 1720 as his "large brick storehouse" and used by him while he served as customs collector, this sturdy monument to Yorktown commerce is administered by the Comte de Grasse Chapter of the Daughters of the American Revolution. Believed to be the oldest custom house in the United States, the Yorktown structure was named to the Virginia Landmarks Register in the spring of 1999. The custom house has an interesting history. Over the years it has been a dwelling, a store, the

headquarters of Confederate General John B. Magruder during the Civil War, and the medical offices of African-American physician D. M. Norton. Its restoration—at the hands of the Daughters of the American Revolution, who staged tea parties, cake sales, and masked balls to raise needed funds—is considered a milestone in the historic preservation movement. The museum and a gift shop are open Sundays from 1:30 to 4:00 p.m. Tours can be arranged at other times, and the site is available for rent for special events. Admission to the custom house is free.

Poor Potter Site
Read Street
(757) 898-2410

The remains of the entrepreneur William Roger's pottery factory in colonial America tells the story of how this industry flourished in Yorktown during the early 1700s. The site is preserved by the National Park Service, and archaeological surveys are still underway to find more clues about what is believed to be the largest known enterprise of its type in colonial America, which was greatly restricted from producing goods that competed with Great Britain. The site is a short walk from the visitor's center.

Celebrations

Although there is little evidence remaining, the Civil War brought renewed activity to the town. During the Peninsula Campaign of that conflict, Yorktown was one anchor of the Confederate defenses crossing the Peninsula to block Union progress toward Williamsburg; the fortifications of the Revolutionary War were renovated for that purpose.

Each year Yorktown observes two major celebrations related to its military history. Independence Day is celebrated with the rest of the nation, and crowds of people gather in and about the town to enjoy the traditional Fourth of July parade and the individual observations, entertainments, and celebrations at the museums, homes, and centers. The day culminates in a spectacular fireworks display on the York River, visible for miles around. On October 19 Yorktown again pulls out all the stops with exhibits, reenactments of military life, "tall ship" visits, naval reenactments, music, and other celebrations as Virginians and visitors celebrate with appropriate enthusiasm Washington's—and the United States'—victory.

(For more on yearly events in and around Yorktown, turn to the Annual Events chapter.)

Yorktown Today

The town of Yorktown is poised for dramatic change in the 21st century. A $9.4 million plan restored the historic face of this waterfront village. The long-awaited riverwalk opened in May 2005 and is decked out with granite curbs and landscaped with trees, flowers, and ornamental grasses and stretches about a half-mile along the York River. Other focal points of the revitalization include a relocated ferry terminal to house displays and exhibits; an L-shaped pier, designed to allow ships of different sizes to dock at the same time; a 50-foot observation deck to provide a stunning view of the York River; space for shops and a restaurant; and an extended free trolley run from the visitor center to the Victory Monument and then on to the Yorktown Victory Center.

Attractions

The Fifes and Drums of York Town
Main Street
(757) 898-9418
www.fifes-and-drums.org

Fifes and drums could be heard in the background as the British officially surrendered to General George Washington on October 19, 1781. In honor of our bicentennial, a fife and drum corps was revived in Yorktown in 1976. Today, the corps is nearly 60 strong, made up of boys and girls between the ages of 10 and 18. In order to wear the regimental uniforms reminiscent of the Continental Army, the young musicians must be able to read music, know a minimum of 24 songs, and be on call to march in frequent performances. During the summer months the corps gives free performances at 3:45 p.m. Sunday and 6:00 p.m. most Fridays at the National Park Service Visitor Center. Members also have performed at Carnegie Hall in New York and the Smithsonian Institution in Washington, D.C. For more information on the corps, e-mail corps@fifes-and-drums.org.

National Park Service Visitor Center
Eastern end of Colonial Parkway
(757) 898-2410
www.nps.gov/colo

The centerpiece of the National Park Service's presentation and interpretation of the Yorktown battlefield is here. We encourage visitors to make this their first stop before exploring the area because the 16-minute orientation film (shown every half-hour) and other information and exhibits bring to life the events that transpired in and around Yorktown in October 1781. George Washington's original field tents are a popular display, and youngsters of any age will enjoy a special children's exhibit of dioramas depicting soldier life from a young boy's point of view. Another treat is the chance to walk through a full-size replica of the quarterdeck of a British warship.

Guided 30-minute walking tours of the battlefield and Yorktown are offered seasonally. Or, if you prefer, you can pick up a free map of the park at the center, which will direct you on a 7- or 9-mile self-guided auto tour that winds through the siege lines and encampment areas of the 1781 battle. The battlefield is open to pedestrian access from the visitor center, and a one-way road travels from the British fortifications through the Allies' lines to the Moore House and Surrender Field, then back into town. It's a fascinating drive, and there are opportunities to get out of the car and inspect the earthworks (but please do not climb or walk on them) and vistas. Admission to the center, the battlefields, and the historic houses is $10 for adults for a seven-day pass. Children 15 and younger are admitted free. The center is open daily from 9:00 a.m. to 5:00 p.m., with extended hours

The battlefield at Yorktown. LYNN ZELEM

in the spring and fall. The Moore and Nelson Houses are open seasonally, so call ahead if you'd like to make these historic homes part of your itinerary. During the spring, fall, and winter, group reservations are accepted for guided walking tours. Please provide a 30-day notice.

U.S. Coast Guard
Reserve Training Center
Route 238
(757) 856-2270
www.uscg.mil/tcyorktown

Located on a small peninsula near the mouth of the York River, the Reserve Training Center site is rich in history, with the original village of Yorke located nearby in the early 1600s. In 1691 the port of Yorktown was chartered a few miles upriver. But Yorktown's moment in history, of course, was to occur on September 28, 1781, when an army of colonial and French soldiers set out from Williamsburg to lay siege to the British army that had fortified the seaport hamlet. Twenty-one days later Washington defeated British General Cornwallis and his regiments. The surrender of the British to American forces was signed in the Moore House, located just outside the entrance to the Reserve Training Center.

This site was first used for training when the U.S. Navy established its Mine Warfare School here in 1940. The Coast Guard took possession of the site in July 1959.

Annually, the training center offers more than 100 courses to more than 6,000 U.S. Coast Guard active duty, reserve, civilian, and auxiliary personnel, employees of numerous state and federal agencies, and members of allied nations. Additionally, teams from Yorktown provide training to coast guards and navies all over the world, visiting more than 50 countries a year. The schools that provide traditional resident training have grown from the original Officer Candidate and Marine Safety Schools to 17 schools, including the Contingency Preparedness School, Marine Science Technician School, Inspection and Investigation Schools, and others.

Victory Monument
Historic Main Street
(757) 898-2410

On October 29, 1781, a resolution of the Continental Congress made a call for a Yorktown Monument to the Alliance and Victory. It was to be a century, however, before the cornerstone was laid on October 18, 1881. The monument is the record of the centennial celebration that took place in the town that year. The stirring inscriptions around its base are worth investigating, and there is a convenient parking lot across the street so that you may walk over to do so. For information contact the Park Service at the number above.

The Watermen's Museum
309 Water Street
(757) 887-2641
www.watermens.org

Right on the York River, The Watermen's Museum preserves and interprets the long history of Tidewater Virginians' relationship with the water and its bounties. The museum features an excellent and growing collection of artifacts (jawbones from a right whale are the most recent additions). It also presents literature, exhibits, and photographs depicting crabbers, oyster harvesters, and clammers at work on the Chesapeake Bay and its tributaries, from the original Native American fishermen to present-day harvesters of the water's bounty. On the grounds you can see traditional watermen's equipment, a modified skipjack, and a Native American–style dugout canoe that was hand-fashioned by a local high school senior as a classroom project and donated to the museum. In early 2000 the museum introduced a boat-building living-display area, where skilled craftsmen can be observed making boats using the centuries-old methods and traditional tools of their forefathers. Programs, seminars, activities, and special events are available to the public throughout the museum's season, which runs from early April through mid-December.

The main building of the museum is a 1935 Colonial Revival house, a masterpiece of engineering that was floated 3 miles across the York River from its original site in Gloucester County in 1987. The house now is a handsome and fitting tribute to the generations of men and women in the area who gained their livelihood from the water. A later expansion added a second building overlooking the York River, designed for additional exhibits, public lectures, and educational programming. The renovated Carriage House, which also was brought from Gloucester to Yorktown and features an expansive dock overlooking the York River, can be rented for wedding receptions, private parties, and meetings.

At $4 for adults and $1 for students, admission to the Watermen's Museum is a bargain. Groups of 15 or more may make arrangements to visit any time—even during the off-season—by calling in advance. Discounted rates are offered for group tours. The museum is open to the general public year round. From April 1 to Thanksgiving, hours are 10:00 a.m. to 5:00 p.m. Tuesday through Saturday and 1:00 to 5:00 p.m. Sunday. From Thanksgiving to March it is open on weekends only. Later in the chapter you'll find information on the museum's outstanding gift shop.

Yorktown Trolley
Various locations
(757) 890-3840
www.yorkcounty.gov/tourism/
transportation.htm
Yorktown is small, but there's a lot to see, what with two visitor centers, a historic downtown area, a museum, and a beach.

A great option for getting around is the Yorktown Trolley. It operates daily from April 1 to October 31, from 10:00 a.m. to 6:00 p.m. The ride is free and begins at the National Park Service Visitor Center on the east side of town, proceeds to the Yorktown Victory Monument, then down the waterfront, to the Watermen's Museum, and on to the Victory Center, operated by the Jamestown-Yorktown Foundation on the west side of town. About every 20 minutes the trolley stops at one of seven locations in Yorktown during its 2-mile run.

Yorktown Victory Center
Old Virginia Route 238
(757) 887-1776
www.historyisfun.org
The history of the Revolutionary War and its culmination in the battle at Yorktown is told through a time line, thematic exhibits, and living-history interpretations at the center.

The events that led to the Revolution are chronicled along the "Road to Revolution," an open-air exhibit walkway that traces events leading to American independence. A timeline, together with quotes and illustrations, explores the changing relationship between Britain and the colonies from 1750 through 1776. It links four exhibit pavilions that focus on events and issues that led to the Revolutionary War.

The time line leads you into the center's lobby, where there is a replica of the Declaration of Independence, setting the stage for four indoor exhibition galleries.

Witness to Revolution

This gallery tells the stories of 10 ordinary men and women whose lives were greatly influenced by the American Revolution, including a slave who served in the army, a Mohawk chief, an army soldier, a native Virginian who was loyal to the king, and a southern planter and officer. Included in these riveting tales is Mary Jeminson, who told her life story to a doctor when she was 88 years old. Mary was captured at age 15 during the French and Indian War and was adopted by a Seneca tribe. She eventually married a warrior and had children. But during the Revolutionary War, her Indian home was attacked and she fled with her children.

A spotlight shines on dramatic statues of each person as an audiotape reveals his or her hardships. Also on display in this gallery are many artifacts of the time, including a hooded cloak worn by Captain William Wittier (1707-98), a British frock coat, a German snuffbox (ca. 1770), and a Mohawk "Two Roads" wampum belt (ca. 1775).

Converging on Yorktown

In this second gallery artifacts, maps, weapons, and documents relating to the Yorktown campaign convey how Yorktown became the setting for the battle that won American independence. Among the many artifacts are a flintlock pistol belonging to the Marquis de Lafayette (ca. 1776), muskets, officers' swords, a British Light Infantry cap, and brass hunting horns (ca. 1726). In this gallery visitors can view *A Time of Revolution*, an 18-minute film shown every half-hour in the 200-seat Richard S. Reynolds Foundation Theater. The film, set in a nighttime encampment during the siege of Yorktown, dramatizes recollections of soldiers and their officers.

Mathews Gallery

This, the third gallery, was so named in honor of generous Yorktown benefactors Nick and Mary Mathews. The exhibit, "A Soldier's Lot: Military Life and Medicine in the Revolutionary Era," relates the experiences of ordinary soldiers using military items and medical tools. Featured artifacts include a bone saw (ca. 1750), used for amputating arms and legs, a bleeding bowl, and a surgical kit (1782). Another exhibit in this gallery, "The Unfinished Revolution," recounts the steps that led to adopting the U.S. Constitution and Bill of Rights. On display is *A Collection of Constitutions of the Thirteen United States,* a leather-bound book printed in Glasgow in 1783.

Next to this gallery is the Children's Kaleidoscope Discovery Room, where youngsters can try on history by donning 18th-century-style clothing. There is a mirror to check out their garb, as well as a period backdrop for parents who want to snap some photos of their children in their historic fashions. The room also has tables of activities to amuse the kids, including woodcut rubbings, authentic hornbooks, and mystery objects. (Reach a hand into a hole to feel and guess what's inside. Open the lid to see if you guessed right.) Computers with touch screens will take young visitors "Around and About the Revolution."

Yorktown's Sunken Fleet

Visitors descend a walkway to reach the fourth gallery, which recounts the fascinating epic of British ships lost during the siege of 1781. A number of artifacts recovered during underwater excavations are included here. The re-created bow of the British supply ship *Betsy* serves as the exhibit's centerpiece. Included in the display are an 18th-century iron cannon recovered from the York River, a wood and pitch bucket, a 1772 copper coin and other coins, shoe leather, and several rats' skulls. As you walk through this dark exhibit area, stop at the small screen to watch the video and listen to the audiotape replay the story of the work of underwater archaeologists in excavating the cargo of the ship.

Continental Army Camp

Continue outside to see the re-creation of a Continental army camp that gives visitors a real feel for how soldiers lived and how war was fought in the 1700s. Examine the rows of simple tents, with simple furnishings and writing implements, as well as food at the camp fire. Costumed interpreters demonstrate military drills and musket and cannon firing, and would-be surgeons wield their medical knives as they would have on the Revolutionary battlefields, where shortages of medical supplies and unclean conditions made being wounded or ill even worse than it already was.

A sure hit with children as well as adults are the military drills. Drafted into service, visitors line up in military fashion, "fire" a wooden musket, and serve on the cannon crew. Interesting fact: Did you know many poor women followed their husbands in the army and lived in the military camps? They earned their keep by mending uniforms, doing laundry, and nursing the sick and wounded.

1780s Farm

After you've observed the exciting demonstration of a cannon firing, walk over to the typical 18th-century Tidewater farm, where year-round reenactments of life on a farm take place. After the American Revolution, most Virginians lived on small farms, usually less than 200 acres, and the typical planter grew and sold tobacco to make a living and grew corn for food.

This setting includes a tobacco barn, log kitchen, crop fields, and vegetable and herb garden. In 1997 a typical wood-framed, one-story house joined the agrarian landscape and, in 2001, a corncrib. Interpreters present farming methods, gardening, candle making, flax and wool preparation, and 18th-century games, often involving visitors in the activities.

Also on exhibit are the fabrics and dyes the farmers used. There are many hands-on activities here, from helping to clean house and do laundry to helping the farmer cultivate and till his crops, gather firewood, and grind spices. Children will get distracted too by the chickens, ducks, and turkeys that roam the farm freely. Intrigued visitors watch as interpreters do everything the way it was done in the 1700s—from starting fires with flint and stone, to using pails rather than hoses to water gardens, to chopping wood on the stump of a tree. Interpreters also use monthly journals kept by Yorktown's early farmers as a reference for growing crops, while the pottery pieces employed in the kitchen are authentic re-creations of the era. In fact, about 90 percent of the products used in demonstrations throughout the year are produced at the farm. Outside purchases include only seeds, supplemental food, some additional flax, animal feed, and a few spices.

In early 1995 the Yorktown Victory Center completed a major expansion and renovation that had begun two years earlier. The $3.86 million renovation of the main exhibit building included the design and fabrication of new exhibits to broaden the museum's theme to include the formation of a new government after the Revolution and to interpret the war from varied points of view.

After steeping in history all day, stop by the Victory Center gift shop to purchase a variety of souvenirs. Choose from Virginia peanuts, toys, whistles, jewelry, stuffed animals, pottery, and books, or reproductions of the Bill of Rights, Declaration of Independence, and the Constitution. The shop is open daily from 9:00 a.m. to 6:00 p.m.

The Victory Center is open daily from 9:00 a.m. to 5:00 p.m., with hours extended to 6:00 p.m. June 15 to August 15. It is closed Christmas and New Year's Day. For everyone except residents of Williamsburg and James City and York Counties, an admission fee is charged. The fee is $8.75 for adults and $4.50 for children 6 through 12. The best deal is to purchase the combination ticket—$17.75 for adults and $8.50 for children—also entitling you to enter Jamestown Settlement, which re-creates the life of the first English colony in the New World. Although you must tour the site where you purchase your ticket that day, your ticket for the other attraction can be saved for another day.

Restaurants

Price Guidelines

$ . . . . Dinner for two less than $20
$$ . . . . Dinner for two between $20 and $40
$$$ . . . . Dinner for two more than $40

Credit cards are accepted at these restaurants unless otherwise noted.

Carrott Tree Yorktown $
411 Main
(757) 246-9559
One of Yorktown's newest cafes located in one of its oldest homes, The Carrott Tree offers casual fare including sandwiches, salads, and fabulous desserts. It's open Monday through Saturday 8:00 a.m. to 4:00 p.m. and Sunday 10:00 a.m. to 4:00 p.m.

Yorktown Pub $$
540 Water Street
(757) 886-9964
This popular beachfront restaurant doubles as watering hole and social center for area folks, tourists, and the many military people stationed nearby. As a good beach pub should be, it's very casual, with plenty of

Tom Cruise and Steven Spielberg took in a few of the local sights in Gloucester, just across the bridge from Yorktown. Actually, they spent most of their visit working: Spielberg was directing Cruise in a scene for the film *Minority Report*. Although most of the movie was filmed near Washington, D.C., the two Hollywood celebrities spent several days in the area for the local shoot.

jeans in evidence, knotty pine walls, and worn wooden booths. A good assortment of food comprises the menu, with raw or steamed clams and oysters, steamed shrimp and other finger foods, salads and soups, and entrees such as prime rib sandwiches, scallops, and soft-shell crabs. Deli sandwiches and pub specialty sandwiches are also available, with late-night snacks served until midnight most nights and 1:00 a.m. on Friday and Saturday.

Accommodations

Credit cards are accepted at these lodging facilities unless otherwise noted.

Duke of York Motor Hotel
508 Water Street
(757) 898-3232
This three-story motel is the only one you'll find with rooms facing the beautiful York River. There's a nice swimming pool in the cool courtyard on the side away from the river. Connecting rooms can be provided upon advance request. In July the rate for a basic double is $70 to $140, very reasonable considering that you have a water view, beach access, all of Yorktown history to explore, and proximity to the beautiful Colonial Parkway with its scenic 20-minute drive to Williamsburg and Jamestown.

Marl Inn Bed and Breakfast
220 Church Street
(757) 898-3859, (800) 799-6207
marlinnbandb.com
This bed-and-breakfast is just 20 minutes from

Colonial Williamsburg. It has two rooms with double beds and private baths and two full suites, each with a kitchen, living room, bedroom, and bath. Innkeepers Seldon and Marcia Plumley encourage children, because each room is family-friendly with its own private entrance.

You won't want to sleep late here. The Plumleys serve up a full breakfast that just might include eggs Benedict. Complimentary bicycles are available for guests. Nightly rates are $95 for the guest rooms and $120 to $140 for suites.

York River Inn Bed & Breakfast
209 Ambler Street
(757) 887-8800, (800) 884-7003
www.yorkriverinn.com
On a high bluff overlooking the York River, this inn is the only waterfront bed-and-breakfast in the area. The colonial-style building is decorated with an impressive collection of period prints and maps relating to Virginia during the Revolutionary War. Rates are from $110 to $130 and include a full gourmet breakfast. All rooms have private baths, TVs, and VCRs.

Yorktown Motor Lodge
8829 George Washington Highway
(757) 898-5451
www.yorktownmotorlodge.com
On U.S. Route 17, the main highway leading into Yorktown, is this 42-room motel, which was remodeled in 2004. You will find pleasantly furnished rooms complete with a microwave and refrigerator. Outside, there's a pool for cooling off after a summer's day of sightseeing. Rates are reasonable, from about $70 to $120, and AAA and AARP discounts are offered.

Shopping

Gin Tail Antiques
114 Ballard Street
(757) 890-1335
Antiques lovers will enjoy this shop's gallery of Americana and folk art. It specializes in 18th- and 19th-century furniture and accessories,

including rugs, ceramics, and animal art. Gin Tail is open 10:00 a.m. to 5:00 p.m. Wednesday through Saturday and noon to 4:00 p.m. Sunday.

Nancy Thomas Gallery
145 Ballard Street
(757) 898-0738, (877) 645-0601
www.nancythomas.com

A master folk artist with a national reputation (Whoopi Goldberg once commissioned a set of 12 monthly plaques) and a presence in museums and films (her work can be seen in Jessica Lange's apartment in *Tootsie*), Nancy Thomas calls Yorktown her home. This fascinating shop is where you will find her acclaimed works on display: paintings, wood plaques and sculptures, freestanding whimsical animals, angels, trees, wreaths, Christmas decorations, and a variety of textiles and ceramics. The gallery also carries primitive antiques and a line of custom-upholstered furniture. A second Nancy Thomas Gallery is in Williamsburg's Merchants Square. Hours at the Yorktown store are Monday through Saturday from 10:00 a.m. to 5:00 p.m. and Sunday from noon to 5:00 p.m.

Period Designs
401 Main Street
(757) 886-9482
www.perioddesigns.com

Stop in and check out the wide variety of reproductions of 17th- and 18th-century decorative arts as well as some high-quality antiques from the same period. The shop—housed in the restored circa 1710 Mungo Somerwell House—was started by three friends, all William and Mary graduates. Michelle Erickson creates historically accurate ceramics for museums, while Virginia Lascara makes period frame moldings and floor cloths. Robert Hunter is an antiques dealer who also designs historical products. This shop carries fine floor coverings, ceramics, and furniture as well as items in tin, brass, leather, iron, and glass. Its framing service is museum quality. Period Designs is

i In the summer of 1999, Period Designs of Yorktown had a brush with fame when its owners were commissioned to make nearly 500 reproductions for the Mel Gibson film *The Patriot*. The pieces ranged from charts, maps, and 18th-century prints to tea sets and blankets.

open Tuesday through Saturday 10:00 a.m. to 5:00 p.m. and Sunday noon to 5:00 p.m., or by appointment.

Swan Tavern Antiques
300 Main Street
(757) 898-3033

This fine shop, housed in a charming re-created structure, offers one of the finest collections of antiques in the area. The collection concentrates on 18th-century English items and furniture, candlesticks, prints, and accessories. The items are of the highest quality, and each is a prize find. Swan Tavern also has a wide selection of miniatures that the owner has collected, plus boxwoods that he grew at his Lisburne home. Hours are Tuesday through Saturday from 10:00 a.m. to 5:00 p.m. and Sunday noon to 5:00 p.m.

The Watermen's Museum Gift Shop
309 Water Street
(757) 888-2623
www.watermens.org

This excellent shop on the museum's grounds offers a variety of interesting and unusual items, showcasing local artists and artisans and featuring items related to the water. You will find many pieces in here to be cherished as high-quality souvenirs or as gifts for those to whom Yorktown and the Chesapeake Bay are important. From April 1 to Thanksgiving, the museum and shop are open Tuesday through Saturday from 10:00 a.m. to 5:00 p.m. and Sunday from 1:00 to 5:00 p.m. From Thanksgiving to March 31, the museum and shop are only open on weekends.

The Yorktown Shoppe
402 Main Street
(757) 898-2984
www.yorktownshoppe.com
In this small shop you will find a number of items appropriate to the setting and period to which Yorktown is a monument. There are fine carvings and paintings, replica and whimsical houses, pierced lanterns, Old World Santas, special clothes, a variety of wrought-iron items, and the extremely popular Old World balance toys, in which a figure balances on a horizontal bar. The Yorktown Shoppe also is the exclusive holder of Marlene Whiting's series of Yorktown houses. Whiting's Brandywine Collectibles also includes the 16-piece Williamsburg set. The shop also carries Linda Bennett's unique-buttoned dresses, plus pewter ornaments carved by local artists. Hours are 10:00 a.m. to 5:00 p.m. Monday through Saturday and 1:00 to 5:00 p.m. Sunday.

OUR MILITARY HERITAGE

For hundreds of years this region known as Hampton Roads has been recognized throughout the nation for its military prowess. From the weapons of early Native American warriors to the stealth aircraft that stalk today's skies, the area not only has witnessed the most advanced weaponry and military power of each age but also has been instrumental in their development. In addition, hundreds of thousands of American servicemen and women have been stationed at one or another of the major military installations in the area, many eventually retiring to local communities. The air force, army, coast guard, marines, and navy still are very much a part of the local fabric, while numerous sites and monuments have been erected to commemorate the battles waged on our lands.

The earliest contacts between Native Americans and Europeans occurred, of course, in the early 1600s in and around Jamestown. Today at Jamestown Settlement (see our chapter on Jamestown and Yorktown), exhibits detail the culture of the Native Americans and the earliest settlers. A recreated Powhatan Indian village portrays the daily life of the people who originally lived on the land. Costumed interpreters there and at James Fort demonstrate the weapons and battle tactics of both groups during the early 17th century. And behind the scenes are the archaeologists and researchers whose discoveries continue to improve our understanding of this period.

DIGGING DEEPLY INTO HISTORY

Since 1994 researchers have been digging up even more information about Jamestown's battle-scarred past. Archaeologists working on the Jamestown Rediscovery Project on Jamestown Island continue to unearth conclusive evidence of the original fort erected in 1607. As researchers dig deeper into the past, they become more and more convinced that the structure of the fort was much more complex than anyone connected with the project had at first imagined. Indeed, when the James Fort project was begun more than 10 years ago, most scholars thought it an exercise in futility, believing the bastion had washed away into the James River decades ago. But noted historian and archaeologist William Kelso, who heads the project, has proved them wrong. Taking into account the evidence his team has uncovered, Kelso now estimates that at least 80 percent of the fort has survived on land. To date, more than 250,000 artifacts have been uncovered, including an intact Cabasset helmet (an elongated metal helmet constructed of two parts joined together at a center seam) and breastplate, pieces of cut-up armor, and matchlock muskets and dozens of other weaponry fragments. (For information on the Jamestown Rediscovery Project, visit www.apva.org.)

But don't think that Jamestown corners the market on archaeological treasures. Carter's Grove Plantation, where the Wolstenholme Towne site was the scene in 1622 of a massacre that wiped out the inhabitants there and nearly destroyed the fledgling colony, has seen its share of exciting discoveries. Earlier excavations of this site, originally called Martin's Hundred Plantation, uncovered the first two intact closed (face-covering) helmets found in North America. Since the Carter's Grove museums closed in 2003, some of the artifacts found there are now showcased in the Colonial Williamsburg museums.

18TH-CENTURY MILITARY CULTURE

The military history of the next century is revealed in many exhibits throughout the area. The Powder Magazine at Colonial Williamsburg is the focal point of 18th-century military interpretations. It houses a large collection of weapons of the 1700s, with an emphasis on the muskets used by the colonial militia. In Market Square at Colonial Williamsburg, period cannon are fired daily in demonstrations of the drill required to load, aim, and discharge the pieces. The military uniforms of the era are worn by costumed interpreters and the members of The Colonial Williamsburg Fifes & Drums, who demonstrate the martial music of the period in frequent parades on Duke of Gloucester Street. In the central hallway of the Governor's Palace, the display of firearms serves as a reminder of the power that both protected and controlled the British colony.

The most elaborate interpretation of 18th-century military culture is found at Yorktown. (See the Jamestown and Yorktown chapter.) The Yorktown Visitor Center displays uniforms, arms, and accouterments of the military forces that engaged there, and it includes a full-size reconstruction of a quarterdeck of a man-of-war of the era. The Yorktown battlefield provides an experience of the siege defenses of the period; interpretations in the center and mounted around the battlefield, particularly along the driving tour, will help you envision what warfare was like for soldiers of the day. At the Yorktown Victory Center at the other end of the fortifications, outdoor living-history presentations by costumed interpreters give visitors a memorable vision of the camp life of the common soldier in the 1700s. Inside the center are more exhibits that offer rich detail about the military experiences of the day.

ENTRENCHED IN CIVIL WAR

Two 19th-century periods of military interest are represented within easy driving distance of the Historic Triangle. In Hampton you will find Fort Monroe, the moat-surrounded fortification that served as an important Union base for campaigns throughout the Civil War. The Casemate Museum at the fort offers a rich interpretation of the military history and lifestyle of the early 1800s and of Fort Monroe in particular (see our Newport News and Hampton chapter). The fort, which, by the way, is still an active army post, played an important role in the Civil War, remaining in Union hands throughout the conflict and housing Jefferson Davis as a prisoner after the war. Nearby Fort Wool, accessible only by boat, dates from 1819 and was another Union stronghold throughout the Civil War. The first battle of ironclad warships took place offshore near Chesapeake Avenue in Hampton. Neither side emerged the victor, but the battle changed naval warfare forever; wooden fighting ships began to disappear from the world's navies and were replaced by better-armed metal successors. The battle engagement of the *Monitor* and *Merrimac* warships is honored by the name of the Monitor-Merrimac Memorial Bridge-Tunnel spanning the James River upstream from the site of the conflict.

In Newport News Park, just east of Williamsburg on Route 143, Dam No. 1 and Confederate gun positions, as well as remaining Union trenches, are evidence of the Peninsula campaign. The visitor center in the park interprets the action that took place there and offers literature on other sites nearby. At Lee's Mill, located along U.S. Route 60, just south of Fort Eustis in Newport News, the city has purchased six acres of Civil War earthworks and adjacent land for a small public park.

Also in Newport News you'll find some ongoing restoration of Civil War sites. The most notable is the transformation of Endview Plantation in northern Newport News into a $10 million Civil War interpretive center. The plantation was built in 1720 on a road that led to Yorktown and is the second-oldest house still standing in what was formerly Warwick County. The Virginia War Museum, located at the southern end of the city, has taken over the house and is hard at work recapturing its fascinating Civil War history. And what a rich history it is. During the war Dr. Humphrey Harwood Curtis recruited local residents, including nine of his own family members, to form the Warwick Beauregards. A farewell party was staged on the front lawn of Endview, and the Beauregards reported for active duty with the 32nd Virginia Infantry. Endview became an important campground for Confederate units, while the house was turned into a hospital during the Warwick-Yorktown siege. Later, during the Confederate retreat of May 3, 1862, the Union army occupied Endview and it, too, used the estate as a hospital. A couple of days later, Endview was visited briefly by Union General George McClellan while he was on his way to the battle of Williamsburg. Union and Confederate camps have been set up on the grounds of the historic plantation to make it easier for visitors to step back in time.

The Virginia War Museum also has restored Lee Hall Mansion, located in Newport News about a mile from Endview Plantation just off Route 143 on Yorktown Road. Built around the 1850s by a wealthy planter, the mansion was used as one of the headquarters for Confederate General John Bankhead (J. B.) Magruder during the Peninsula campaign. The mansion opened as a city-run museum in the fall of 1998. (For more on the Virginia War Museum, Endview Plantation, and Lee Hall Mansion, see the chapter on Newport News and Hampton.)

The Civil War left other vestiges in the immediate area. On and near the grounds of the Crowne Plaza Williamsburg at Fort Magruder Hotel and Conference Center on Pocahontas Trail are remains of the fort, which was active in the defense of Williamsburg. Several Confederate defense works remain on the banks of the James River, testimonials to the attempts of the Confederacy to block Union passage upriver. Near Jones Mill Pond on the Colonial Parkway are remains dating from the battle of Williamsburg in

1862. General Magruder reworked the defenses of the battle of Yorktown as the northern anchor of defenses crossing the Peninsula to prevent McClellan's Union forces from advancing on Richmond.

The Confederate secondary line at Williamsburg stretched from Queens Creek on the York River to College Creek on the James River, with Fort Magruder at the center (remains of the outer fort still exist near the swimming pool of the hotel there). Fourteen individual strongholds were located on the line, 12 of which still exist in varying states of preservation.

The Confederate withdrawal westward through Williamsburg on May 4, 1862, led to the battles that raged along that line from May 4 through 6. All in all, 3,900 men of both sides—about one-tenth of the combatants—were casualties in the fighting at Williamsburg.

Union troops eventually occupied Williamsburg on May 6, and, for a while, it was the closest Union-held city to Richmond. Full of Union troops and spies from both sides, the city of Williamsburg remained under martial law until the end of the war. On September 9, 1862, a former James City County lawyer, Confederate General Weiss, attacked Williamsburg and drove the Union forces back to Fort Magruder with a charge down Duke of Gloucester Street. The victory was ephemeral, however, lasting only one day. That afternoon a fire of unknown origin partially burned the Wren Building at the College of William and Mary. From that day on Union troops remained in control, though the citizens chafed under their rule.

The campaign passed westward. McClellan headquartered at Berkeley Plantation in Charles City County and conferred there with President Lincoln about the Peninsula campaign of 1862. McClellan's march up the Peninsula to Richmond was unexpectedly halted for 29 days along the Warwick River. Union General Daniel Butterfield during that campaign composed the haunting melody of "Taps" at Berkeley.

Within day-trip distance are the Richmond

and Petersburg battlefields as well as other sites significant to the Civil War, including several along Route 5 in Charles City County, just west of James City County. Historical markers alert motorists of their existence. In Richmond—about an hour west of Williamsburg on Interstate 64—Richmond National Battlefield Park and the Museum and White House of the Confederacy are great places to visit (see the Richmond entry in our Day Trips chapter). Monument Avenue, one of the most beautiful boulevards in the nation, honors the Confederacy's heroes with bronze statues at its major intersections.

The Siege Museum in Petersburg gives an extremely informative interpretation of the military actions that transpired in the area, and the exhibits put a human face on history. Farther to the west, Lexington is home to Virginia Military Institute and the tombs of Generals Robert E. Lee and Thomas "Stonewall" Jackson, which are shrines for many southerners and other admirers of those consummate tacticians. The battlefields at Manassas, Fredericksburg, Spotsylvania, New Market, and Cold Harbor are also close enough day-trip options for visitors to the Historic Triangle who are interested in the Civil War. To simplify the process of planning your trip, consider picking up a copy of the *Insiders' Guide to Civil War Sites in the Eastern Theater*. It includes 21 tours, covering nearly the entire state of Virginia and portions of Maryland, Pennsylvania, and West Virginia, as well as maps, personality sketches of figures who played key roles in the war, and chapters on accommodations and restaurants.

THE 20TH CENTURY

Military matters in our own century have left their marks on the area as well. The coastal gunnery fortifications at Fort Monroe are testimony to the developments in armaments that bridged the old and new centuries. The Civil War, after all, was America's first modern industrialized war. During that time this nation witnessed the first battle between ironclads,

the launching of two gas balloons, and the introduction of the first "coffee mill" gun, so called because of its rapid-fire technology. The Victory Arch in downtown Newport News and a Vietnam Memorial in Huntington Park outside the Virginia War Museum commemorate the millions of troops who sailed from here to France to fight in World War I as well as the citizens of the commonwealth who risked and gave up their lives in Southeast Asia in the 1960s and 1970s.

Northrop Grumman Newport News, formerly Newport News Shipbuilding, has been building America's mightiest warships since the Spanish-American War and continues that service today, as it designs and constructs nuclear-powered aircraft carriers for the U.S. Navy and provides life-cycle services for ships in the navy fleet. The company, located on 550 acres along the James River, has built 800 naval and commercial ships. In June 2001 the USS Nimitz, a nuclear-powered aircraft carrier, was released back to the navy after a three-year refueling and overhaul at Newport News Shipbuilding. First deployed in 1976, the ship is serving another 25 years.

Langley Air Force Base in Hampton is one of the pioneer sites of military aviation at about 80 years old. It is the headquarters for the U.S. Air Force's largest major command, the Air Combat Command, and the 1st Fighter Wing. The base played a central role in the Gulf War, and stealth aircraft from the base can be observed in the skies over our area.

TODAY'S MILITARY MUSCLE

And, despite Uncle Sam's downsizing and the privatization of many government functions, it seems you just can't take the military out of Hampton Roads. After all, more than 30 percent of our area's population is in some way connected to some branch of the service. Regionwide, the navy's presence remains particularly strong: Close to 100,000 active-duty sailors and marines serve in the area together with more than 40,000 navy civilians and retirees. Most of those on active duty, of course, are stationed at the Norfolk Naval Station, the world's largest navy base. To give you an idea of the size of Norfolk Naval, consider that it is homeport for 78 Atlantic Fleet ships, while its Chambers Field hosts 15 fixed- and rotary-wing aircraft squadrons. In addition, there are close to 54,000 active-duty sailors stationed at the base, while about 11,000 civilians work there.

And, reversing a nationwide trend of shrinking military installations, the Fort Eustis Army Base in Newport News was selected as the site for a new regional transportation headquarters that has brought another 500 jobs to the area in the past few years. Fort Eustis also is home to the Army Transportation Center and the 7th Transportation Group, factors that played a key role in the decision to consolidate the Eastern and Western Commands of the Military Traffic Management Command and relocate its headquarters to the Virginia Peninsula. Altogether, Fort Eustis has more than 5,000 military personnel and 2,500 civilian workers.

Jobs at Langley Air Force Base, located in Hampton, have also increased. An initial increase in positions was the result of the 71st Air Control Squadron relocating to the area from Moody Air Force Base in Georgia; additions to Langley's 1st Fighter Wing and 10th Intelligence Squadron; and the formation of the Air Combat Command Regional Supply Squadron, which has been formed to consolidate base-level supply functions.

If you are interested in exploring our military heritage in more depth, you will find the following major military installations, sites, and museums discussed in the chapters on their various localities. Many of the installations have museums open to the public.

In Jamestown, Jamestown Settlement will offer a rich insight into the military life of the period. Turn to our chapter on Jamestown and Yorktown.

In Yorktown and York County, check out the National Park Service's Yorktown Visitor Center and Yorktown battlefield, the Yorktown Victory Center, and the Coast Guard Training Center. See our chapter on Jamestown and Yorktown.

In Newport News, look up the Virginia War Museum, Endview Plantation and Lee Hall Mansion, the Mariners' Museum, the Newport News Park, and the U.S. Army Transportation Museum at Fort Eustis. See our chapter on Newport News and Hampton for more information. In the same chapter look for information on Hampton's attractions, such as Fort Monroe and its Casemate Museum, Langley Air Force Base, and the Virginia Air and Space Center. Also, do not overlook the real trove of information and artifacts pertaining to Native American life in earlier centuries at the Hampton University Museum American Indian Collection. Hampton National Cemetery, near Hampton University, holds remains from the Civil War to the present, and the Hampton Veterans Administration Hospital continues to serve the medical needs of generations of veterans.

In our Day Trips chapter, check out the Norfolk section for information on the Douglas MacArthur Memorial.

Not highly promoted, for obvious reasons, are several other large bases in the Yorktown and Hampton Roads area. The Department of Defense Armed Forces Experimental Training Activity at Camp Peary, off I–64 near Williamsburg, is otherwise known as Camp Peary. This base is closed to the public. The U.S. Naval Weapons Station in Yorktown is the site where the navy stores, maintains, and provides ordnance for the Atlantic Fleet, with the help of 1,000 military personnel and 2,000 civilian workers.

However, if you want to get your fill of big ships and guns, check out the Norfolk Naval Base Tour. This station sits on 3,400 acres in a peninsula known as Sewells Point. It is the world's largest naval station, with 78 ships and 133 aircraft that call the port home, along with 14 piers and 15 aircraft hangars. The Norfolk Naval Station is the home port to aircraft carriers, cruisers, destroyers, large amphibious ships, submarines, a variety of supply and logistics ships, various aircraft, and helicopters.

ℹ In June 1999 the NASA Langley Research Center in Hampton became the first federal employer to earn a "Star" certification in the Occupational Safety and Health Administration's (OSHA) Voluntary Protection Program. Its coveted "Star" status exempted Langley from surprise OSHA inspections for three years. The research facility earned the ranking because of its low accident rates, monthly safety meetings with employees, and on-site fire station.

Naval personnel guide visitors past the awe-inspiring ships and the Jamestown Exposition Homes of 1907, commonly referred to as "Admirals Row." This collection of restored historic homes portrays the distinguished architectural styles of the era. The Naval Tour and Information Center is open daily from 8:00 a.m. to 4:00 p.m., except Thanksgiving, Christmas, and New Year's Day. The 45-minute tour costs $7.50 for adults and $5.00 for children and senior citizens, and an identification with picture is required for adults. Tour times vary depending on the season, so call ahead, (757) 444-7955, or go to www.navstanorva.navy.mil/TOUR/ for information.

MODERN MILITARY

While you're visiting the Peninsula, take a moment and look around you. A glance across the James River reveals the navy's massive aircraft carriers. If you look up at the sky, you might see air squadrons from Langley Air Force Base flying in formation. And, if you stop off at a downtown Hampton restaurant for lunch, you'll probably see at least a few diners dressed in flight suits or fatigues. Hampton Roads, after all, is a military stronghold, a fact that becomes quite obvious once you have spent a little time here. This military community includes all branches of the service.

When you consider the region as a whole, the navy is dominant, with more than a dozen navy bases spread over 36,000 acres from Yorktown to Virginia Beach and a more than

$5 billion payroll. On the Peninsula, both the army and air force prevail. Of the three army bases in Hampton Roads, two—Fort Eustis and Fort Monroe—are on the Peninsula. Together, these installations provide jobs for more than 18,000 active-duty and civilian personnel and support an annual payroll approaching $500 million.

More than 10,000 personnel are based at Hampton's Langley Air Force Base, including 8,800 active military. The payroll for that installation tops $380 million annually. What follows is a breakdown of the military installations and related properties on the Middle and Lower Peninsula.

Newport News

Fort Eustis
Upper Newport News, exit 250A off I-64
(757) 878-4920
www.eustis.army.mil/
In upper Newport News, this is the army's command and training center for air, sea, rail, and land transportation. The base has about 4,500 military personnel and 2,400 civil service and civilian workers with a combined payroll of $761 million. On post are the Army Transportation Center, the 7th Transportation Group, and the U.S. Army Transportation Museum, which features more than 200 years of army transportation history depicted through models, dioramas, and life-size displays. (For more on the Transportation Museum, see our Newport News Attractions section in the Newport News and Hampton chapter.) The museum (757-878-1115) is just inside the main gate.

Hampton

Fort Monroe
Old Point Comfort,
southeastern Hampton
(757) 788-2238
www.monroe.army.mil/
At Old Point Comfort at the southeastern tip of Hampton, Fort Monroe is headquarters for the Training and Doctrine Command, the army's main think tank. The only active moat-

i In the warm weather months Fort Monroe in Hampton hosts "Fridays at the Fort" at the Bay Breeze Community Center. The public is invited to free activities including concerts, karaoke, billiards, or just to hang out on the beach. Happy hour specials on drinks and food are available from 5:00 to 7:00 p.m. For more information call (757) 788-2406.

surrounded fort on the army's roster, Fort Monroe can trace its history to Fort Algernourne, built on the site in 1609 to protect the first settlers. Present-day Fort Monroe was completed in 1834 and is recognized as the largest stone fort ever built in the United States. The fort has about 1,000 military personnel, 1,800 civilian workers, and a $113 million payroll. Of particular interest on the post are the Casemate Museum, (757-788-3391, where Jefferson Davis was imprisoned; the historic buildings dating from the early 19th century; and the coastal gunnery fortifications. A seawall surrounding much of the base offers a breathtaking view of boaters on the Chesapeake Bay. A covered bandstand on the well-kept lawn next to the Chamberlin Hotel is the site of Continental Army Band concerts during the summer. It is also a popular spot for military personnel to tie the knot: Visitors to the post grounds have been known to catch a full-dress wedding in progress. While Fort Monroe has generally been open to the public, increased security since the events of September 11, 2001, has resulted in significantly limited access. It is best to call ahead for up-to-date information.

To reach the base, follow Mercury Boulevard through Phoebus to its eastern tip at the Fort Monroe gate. For more information on the Casemate Museum, see Hampton's Attractions in our Newport News and Hampton chapter.

Hampton National Cemetery
Cemetery Road,
Hampton University Campus
(757) 728-3131

This cemetery dates from the Civil War, with many of the fallen from both sides interred here. Burials of veterans still are conducted in both the older and newer parts of the cemetery, and beautiful and fitting tributes to the servicemen and servicewomen interred here are presented each Memorial Day.

Langley Air Force Base
End of LaSalle Avenue
(757) 764-9990

This base has a history of operation beginning as Langley Field in the days when the flight line consisted of biplanes; for a while, military dirigibles were housed here as well. Today it's possible to see F-15 and F-16 fighter-bombers, stealth aircraft, and other planes taking off and making their landing approaches in the skies near the base. Home base to the combat air crews active in the Gulf War, Langley is headquarters for the 1st Fighter Wing and the Air Combat Command, which oversees all Air Force combat commands. Sharing the base property is the 787-acre NASA Langley Research Center, where the Mercury missions were conceived and where air and space flight research is conducted. Although the base does not have exhibits open to the public, periodic open houses and air shows afford an opportunity to visit. For information on the air shows, call (757) 764-2018.

Yorktown and York County

Coast Guard Training Center
End of Route 238
(757) 856-2270

This 154-acre campus is a key training center for the Coast Guard, providing classroom as well as shipboard instruction for men and women entering the service. Every year between 6,000 and 7,000 students train at the center's 17 schools, including the Maritime Law Enforcement School, the National Search and Rescue School, and the Utility Boat Systems Center. The training center is staffed by nearly 600 people, most of whom are active-duty Coast Guard personnel. No public tours of the training center are available.

Naval Weapons Station Yorktown
Route 143, Yorktown
(757) 887-4939

As the title suggests, this installation is where ordnance used by the Atlantic Fleet is maintained and stored. On Route 143, just west of Lee Hall, it extends much of the length of the York River between Williamsburg and Yorktown. Ships being armed can be seen at the station's piers from pullouts on the Colonial

Parkway near its Yorktown end. This view will have to do, as the weapons station is a closed base.

Navy Weapons Station, Cheatham Annex
York County
(757) 887-4939

This bulk storage facility in York County belongs to the Fleet and Industrial Supply Center in Norfolk. The center's loading piers in the York River are visible from the Colonial Parkway just where it turns inland from the river.

THE ARTS

The first performing arts theater in the Americas was located in Williamsburg on the edge of Palace Green. Long since gone, that early theater has not been reconstructed (though Colonial Williamsburg has flirted with the idea repeatedly over the last 20 years), but the tradition of presenting a variety of performing arts to the public has endured and, as expected, flourished in the intervening centuries.

When it comes to the arts, the Historic Triangle offers plenty to see, hear, and do. There are several museums and galleries in the greater Williamsburg area that display the visual arts. Live concert performances are an almost weekly occurrence, and dance is alive and well here.

Travel a bit east to Newport News, Hampton, and points south of Hampton Roads, and you'll find myriad museums with state-of-the-art IMAX movies, interactive exhibits, and other places to keep children as well as adults entertained for days. You'll also find performances by the Virginia Opera, Virginia Ballet Company, and other professional performing arts groups.

From fall through late spring, cultural events provide ample opportunity to enjoy the performing arts, and special shows and festivals feature both the visual and performing arts throughout the year.

Two especially popular and longtime festivals include An Occasion for the Arts, always held the first Sunday in October, and the Junior Women's Club Art Show, held each spring. Both are held downtown on Merchants Square. And growing in popularity is a performing arts event called First Night, an alcohol-free New Year's Eve celebration of the arts, with performances staged at several venues in downtown Williamsburg. (For information on this and other yearly events, we recommend you read the Annual Events chapter.) Here, all venues are in Williamsburg unless otherwise stated.

VENUES

Two Williamsburg venues are the sites of the majority of the fine performances produced in the city. Phi Beta Kappa Memorial Hall, facing Jamestown Road on the campus of the College of William and Mary, 2 blocks west of Merchants Square, has the larger theater and hosts many of the major performances on the arts calendar. The Williamsburg Regional Library has a small arts center and hosts various symphonic and dramatic events as well as a variety of other performances by classical and popular artists throughout the year.

Phi Beta Kappa Memorial Hall
College of William and Mary
Jamestown Road
(757) 221-2655,
(757) 221-2674 (box office)
www.wm.edu/theatre
This air-conditioned 750-seat hall is venue for a variety of performances, lectures, and forums of the highest quality, with the College of William and Mary the most frequent sponsor. William and Mary's theater department—whose graduates include Glenn Close and Linda Lavin—offers a high-quality season of performances here during the academic year, and the music and dance departments provide concerts of equally fine caliber. The William and Mary Concert Series held in the hall is a subscription series of performances by nationally and internationally acclaimed performers and groups presenting symphonies, ballet, chamber music, theater, and solo performances. Ticket sales are publicized in the fall. Think ahead—tickets go very quickly. The hall is wheelchair accessible and

has an electronic system for the hearing impaired.

**Williamsburg Regional
Library Art Center
515 Scotland Street
(757) 259-4040
www.wrl.org**
The library has done an extraordinary job of becoming, in effect, the community's cultural arts center. In the art center's lobby there are small ongoing exhibits by visual artists working in a variety of media. The auditorium, which seats 268, provides venue for lectures, debates, forums, and performances of all kinds, from symphonies, chamber concerts, and choral presentations to high school–band rock 'n' roll. Among the musicians who performed at the library recently is four-time Grammy-nominated folk singer and children's performer John McCutcheon. The library also hosted Fourum, members of the Scunthorpe Male Voice Choir, a children's play by the popular Rainbow Puppets, and the All Together Family Film Festival. The festival has looked into racial issues with films suited for the entire family. *Remember the Titans* and *Corrina, Corrina* were among the films viewed and discussed during the Sunday afternoon series. The art center's emphasis is on providing enriching, educational programming for the community. Events held here are typically free, but occasionally an event organized by an outside group will charge a minimal fee. The library also hosts a number of national acts that require a cover charge ranging from $5 to $15. (See the Nightlife chapter for more information.)

PERFORMING ARTS

Music

Symphonic, operatic, and recital performances by touring professionals and virtuoso students from the College of William and Mary's music department are presented throughout the year at Phi Beta Kappa Memorial Hall. Williamsburg also is home to several professional and skilled amateur musical groups, each presenting a varied program throughout the season. The venues differ depending upon the performance. The best way to get timely information is to monitor the *Virginia Gazette*'s arts and performance sections.

**College of William and Mary
Phi Beta Kappa Memorial Hall
Jamestown Road
(757) 221-2655,
(757) 221-2674 (box office)
www.wm.edu/theatre/generalinfo.htm**
Throughout the academic year the college offers outstanding talent both from within its ranks and from among the best performers throughout the world who come to campus with touring companies. The varied offerings are most frequently offered at Phi Beta Kappa Memorial Hall, but occasionally performances are at other venues. It's best to check the *Virginia Gazette*'s arts and performance listings or call the numbers given above to obtain accurate details on particular performances. Ticket prices vary widely depending on whether the performance involves students, local talent, a touring company, or professionals, but they typically run between $10 and $29.

During the academic year the first-class William and Mary Concert Series hosts nationally and internationally renowned performing groups. Over the years performances have included the New York City Opera National Company, the Alvin Ailey American Dance Theater, Jazz at Lincoln Center, and a variety of other performers from around the world. This

i More than 30,000 residents and visitors celebrate An Occasion for the Arts each year on the first Sunday in October. The event is a multifaceted tribute to local craftsmen, musicians, and performers in the Merchants Square area of downtown. It's limited to 100 artists to ensure that visitors can choose from the finest quality items and entertainment. There is also a unique selection of food vendors at the event.

is a subscription series, but seats are sometimes available the day of the performance. To get information on these seats for a particular performance, call the number listed.

The college itself hosts its own fine musicians year in and year out. William and Mary boasts four large ensembles: the Concert Band, the Concert Choir, the Women's Chorus, and the Symphony Orchestra, and a dozen small ensembles.

The William and Mary Symphony Orchestra performs all types of music, with an emphasis on music by contemporary and master American composers. For the schedule of the symphony's concerts, call (757) 221-1089 or go to their Web site, www.wm.edu/so/orchestra/.

The 73-voice William and Mary Concert Choir, conducted by James Armstrong, performs during the fall and spring semesters, and The Botetourt Chamber Singers, a 20-voice ensemble from the choir, performs numerous concerts throughout the region.

The 52-member William and Mary Women's Chorus, conducted by Jamie Bartlett, also presents a rigorous concert schedule.

The William and Mary Jazz Ensemble is an 18- to 21-piece big band that plays at college functions, conventions, and the annual An Occasion for the Arts (see the Annual Events chapter) festival. The William and Mary Concert Band, founded in 1929, joins wind, brass, and percussion instruments to play selections from 400 years of music from around the world. For information on the jazz ensemble and concert band, call (757) 221-1086.

The Ewell Concert Series, featuring visiting performers of note and William and Mary faculty musicians, offers a little bit of everything, from jazz and classics to traditional Virginian music. Contact Judy Zwerdling Zwelling, Ewell Concert Series Manager, at (757) 221-1082 (voice mail) or Sophia Serghi, Ewell Concert Series Chair, at (757) 221-1076 for more details.

The Sinfonicron Light Opera Company, a student group, offers its single production in January, typically a Gilbert and Sullivan light operetta. These are wonderful and particularly good for families with young children. For the schedule, go to www.wm.edu/so/sinfonicron/home.html.

Colonial Williamsburg
Various locations
(757) 229-1000, (800) HISTORY
Throughout the restored area Colonial Williamsburg entertainers provide a variety of musical diversions on an almost nightly basis. You'll find more information in our Nightlife and Colonial Williamsburg chapters, but, if your taste runs to music in a historical context, you might want to give special consideration to the following offerings. The number listed is the general information number for Colonial Williamsburg; it can provide you with current information on performances, times, and venues, including the restored Kimball Theatre. The *Colonial Williamsburg Visitor's Companion,* available throughout the Historic Area and at the Colonial Williamsburg Visitor Center, also is an invaluable aid in identifying and selecting fine-arts offerings.

A popular entertainment is to hear a chamber concert or see costumed dancers perform 18th-century dances during special programs in the candlelit hall of the Governor's Palace. Throughout the restored area wandering minstrels regale guests with songs that were familiar to 18th-century inhabitants of the colonial capital city. Troubadours, magicians, and other entertainers also delight visitors at nightly gambols in select Historic Area taverns. From time to time special performances by soloists, chamber groups, and other Colonial Williamsburg artists are offered. The area is alive with the sound of music (sorry, just couldn't resist), so be sure to check with the Visitor Center or scan a copy of the *Visitor's Companion.*

Summer Breeze Concert Series
Merchants Square
(757) 220-7751
A popular and informal arts offering is the Summer Breeze on the Square, which fea-

tures performances of America's original art form on Wednesday nights in July and August. Attendees are invited to bring folding chairs, blankets, and picnics for these outdoor performances, held on Merchants Square, that usually begin at 6:30 p.m. Get there early, though, to get a good spot. A temporary stage is set up in front of The Trellis restaurant and the whole spectrum of music, from folk to jazz, delights listeners. Summer Breeze on the Square is a joint effort of the Merchants Square Association, the City of Williamsburg, and James City County.

Williamsburg Choral Guild
P.O. Box 1864, Williamsburg, VA 23187
(757) 220-1808
www.williamsburgchoralguild.org
The Williamsburg Choral Guild is an established and esteemed mixed choral group made up of about 100 area volunteer singers. Under the direction of John Guthmiller, artistic director and conductor, guild members rehearse from late August through early May, presenting three subscription concerts during that time. Their first annual performance is presented during the annual An Occasion for the Arts outdoor festival, held the first Sunday each October. In addition, the guild presents an annual holiday season Messiah sing-along. The third seasonal concert is held in the spring.

Williamsburg Symphonia
312 Waller Mill Road
(757) 229-9857
www.williamsburgsymphonia.org
The Williamsburg Symphonia offers five concerts by subscription in Williamsburg. In addition, the orchestra performs special holiday and family concerts annually. The symphonia is noted throughout the region for the excellence of its programs. Maestro Ruben Vartanyan directs the professional chamber orchestra, with whom a number of outstanding solo artists perform for specific programs. Most performances are at Phi Beta Kappa Memorial Hall, but some occur elsewhere in the area. The Williamsburg Symphonia also is

Community members can get on the William and Mary Cultural Events Calendar mailing list. For information about college-sponsored arts happenings, call (757) 221–4000, the college's general information number.

helping to cultivate new generations of music lovers with three Young People Concerts that open classical music performances to students in area schools. Single-event tickets are $37 for first tier, $27 for second tier, and $7 for students (must be purchased at the door). Tickets may be purchased by calling (757) 229-9857, on the Web site, or at the Kimball Theatre in Williamsburg.

Williamsburg Women's Chorus
(757) 564-7875
www.williamsburgwomenschorus.org
The Williamsburg Women's Chorus is an all-volunteer group of 40 women who come together to sing in a variety of musical styles from Baroque to Broadway. The chorus performs several public concerts a year throughout the greater Williamsburg area, and a concert schedule is available on their Web site. Auditions are required of aspiring new members.

Theater
Williamsburg enjoys Shakespeare's plays during an annual summer festival held each July honoring the bard. There are also very high-quality classic and contemporary plays available throughout the year, compliments of the Williamsburg Players, who perform in their playhouse on Hubbard Lane. The William and Mary Theatre also offers an excellent season of drama and comedy.

Virginia Shakespeare Festival
Phi Beta Kappa Memorial Hall
Jamestown Road
(757) 221-2659
vsf.wm.edu
This series has developed an enduring audience over the last 25-plus years. Sponsored each July by William and Mary's theater

ℹ Musician and Grammy
Award–winning pop artist Bruce
Hornsby, who was born and raised in
Williamsburg, still lives in town with his
wife and two sons. He often can be seen
at local sports events—particularly basketball games—restaurants, and simply
walking about town with his family, taking in the sights like everyone else.

department, the festival season of two Shakespeare performances in repertory offers a
variety of the bard's works. The plays are performed alternately so that those in town for
only a short period can attend a performance
of each. The schedule varies, but shows are
usually held from Wednesday through Saturday at 8:00 p.m., and there are also 2:00 p.m.
matinees on Sunday and some Saturdays. Call
or check the Web site for an updated schedule. The cost is $20 per show, season tickets
for three shows are available for $45.

William and Mary Theatre
Phi Beta Kappa Memorial Hall
Jamestown Road
(757) 221-2655,
(757) 221-2674 (box office)
The college's theater, speech, and dance students stage four full-scale plays in addition to
many smaller productions during the academic year. Season subscribers may see all
four shows for the price of three. Matinees
are at 2:00 p.m., and evening curtain is at
8:00 p.m. In addition, plays performed, written, and directed by students are presented
in the Premiere Theater. The department usually stages one or two performances per
semester. Past performances include *A Little
Night Music* by Stephen Sondheim. Ticket
prices vary, and some performances are free.

The Williamsburg Players
200 Hubbard Lane
(757) 229-1679
(757) 229-0431 (reservations)
www.williamsburgplayers.org
From September through June the Williams-

burg Players produce plays of extraordinary
quality in their cozy playhouse. The season
usually consists of five plays, mixing little-
known and more-famous works, with emphasis on modern and contemporary authors.
The casts are all volunteers, but the players
draw upon more than 30 years of experience.
Their staging and performances, thanks to
their willingness to risk breaking conventions
to advance their art, consistently receive the
highest reviews and accolades. There are only
115 seats in the theater, and tickets go fast.
General admission is $15, senior citizens and
students pay $12, and children younger than
12 pay $8. We recommend the season tickets
as a guarantee of seating.

Dance

Dance is alive and well locally. Whether your
tastes run toward the classics or contemporary
dance, ballet, or tap, you'll find fine dance performances presented in and around Williamsburg. The College of William and Mary hosts
performances by national and international
dance troupes throughout the academic year,
and news of these performances is available
through the local media. In addition, the local
dance companies listed below have entertained many an enthralled audience with excellent productions, offered year-round. Venues
and dates change from year to year, however,
so it is best to check the *Virginia Gazette* for
performance information or call the companies
for updates on scheduled events.

The Chamber Ballet for
the Institute of Dance
3356 Ironbound Road, Suite 201
(757) 229-1717
Since 1968 The Chamber Ballet has offered
professional training for all ages. The curriculum provides expert and experienced instruction to ensure students the finest development
of their skill in ballet, offering classes in creative dance, tap, jazz, floor gymnastics, character, and ballet. Several productions are
staged during the year and are very popular
in the community. *The Nutcracker* at Christ-

mastime is a long-standing local tradition. Another performance is staged during the spring.

**Eastern Virginia School of
the Performing Arts
1915 Pocahontas Trail
The Village Shops at Kingsmill
(757) 229-8535**

We can't say enough about the talent, creativity, and enthusiasm exhibited by the staff and students at this wonderful school of the performing arts. Dr. Jane Bonbright, executive director of the National Dance Education Association, hailed EVSPA as "one of Virginia's best kept secrets," as it has become a role model for performing arts education in the United States. The school's philosophy is to give each child correct information at age-appropriate levels about the art forms. EVSPA uses the Standards of Arts Education as its core, and offers an added bonus of providing a professional standard through the experience of the school's directors, former professional opera singer Ron Boucher and prima ballerina Sandra Balestracci, a registered dance educator. Boucher and Balestracci cofounded the school in 1996.

Under the direction of Balestracci, the Dance Division offers the highest quality of instruction and performance. The Vaganova technique is used to develop the dancer and is a full, eight-year program, beginning at age 7. The division also offers instruction in modern, jazz, tap, and lyrical dance.

Boucher heads the Theater and the Voice Division and, with instructors, guides students through a balanced program of strong technique and application. Young people, 3 to 6, benefit from the school's special early childhood development program. It ensures that students will be given age-appropriate information and personalized instruction to prepare for the discipline required for theater, voice, and dance.

The educational program is augmented by the school's outstanding productions, featuring original full-length ballets such as The

i The Chamber Ballet's annual Christmas season performance of The Nutcracker is so popular that the company has had to add performances from year to year. Call (757) 229-1717 for information and an early choice of tickets.

Emperor and the Nightingale, The Littlest Angel, and *Les Patineure,* all choreographed by Kirov Academy's instructor and international choreographer Adrienne Delles.

VISUAL ARTS

Museums

**DeWitt Wallace Decorative Arts Museum
Corner of Francis and
South Henry Streets
(757) 220–7724**

It is difficult for visitors who have been in this gallery to reconcile its size and scope with the structure one sees from Francis Street in the Historic Area. Although the entrance is through the lobby of the reconstructed Public Hospital, this fascinating museum, designed by world-renowned architect I. M. Pei, is housed mostly underground. It displays prized pieces of Colonial Williamsburg's permanent collection—furniture, textiles, maps, prints, paintings, metals, and ceramics dating from the 1600s to the 1830s—in exhibits designed to instruct viewers in the aesthetics and tastes of the colonial period. Perhaps the largest collection and premier interpreter of objects from the households of early America, the gallery mounts special exhibits for several years at a time to allow large numbers of visitors to view them. Thorough research precedes each showing, and the results are presented in understandable and memorable ways. The overall effect on gallery visitors is an understanding of each object in the context of its function, design, and use.

The museum recently expanded further to house the Abby Aldrich Rockefeller folk art collection in a new gallery. Admission is included in all of the Colonial Williamsburg passes. The gallery is generally open 10:00 a.m. to 7:00 p.m. from March through December, but the hours vary seasonally. There is a cafe on-site, open from 11:00 a.m. to 4:00 p.m., and the entire museum is wheelchair accessible. Read the chapter on Colonial Williamsburg for more information.

Hampton University Museum
Huntington Building
Frissell Avenue, Hampton
(757) 727-5308
www.hamptonu.edu/museum/

This museum, the oldest African-American museum in the nation, is just down the road in nearby Hampton. The collections include more than 9,000 items related to fine arts, Hampton history, and African, Native American, Hawaiian, and Asian cultures. The African collection alone consists of 3,500 pieces, including 400 Kuba art objects collected by William H. Sheppard. A Hampton alumnus, Sheppard collected the works while he served as a missionary in the Congo from 1890 to 1910. The museum's archives include what is believed to be one of the nation's largest collections—eight million documents and 50,000 photographs and negatives—of items on the history of African Americans and Native Americans. A museum shop on the first floor carries handcrafted art objects, books, posters, and jewelry. The museum is open 8:00 a.m. to 5:00 p.m. Monday through Friday and noon to 4:00 p.m. Saturday. There is no admission fee. For more details on the Hampton Museum, turn to the Newport News and Hampton chapter.

Muscarelle Museum of Art
Jamestown Road
(757) 221-2703, (757) 221-2710
www.wm.edu/muscarelle/

In the evening this museum, just west of Phi Beta Kappa Memorial Hall on the William and Mary campus, is easy to spot. Multiple columns of color are lighted along one exterior wall, and the effect is quite startling when viewed from Jamestown Road for the first

time. The museum, designed by famed local architect Carlton Abbott, offers lectures, films, and tours, but the holdings are the major draw. The permanent collection includes works by European Old Masters as well as modern works, and a special holding is the collection of colonial-period portraits of Virginians. The museum also hosts several changing exhibits throughout the year. The museum is open from 10:00 a.m. to 5:00 p.m. Tuesday through Friday and noon to 4:00 p.m. Saturday and Sunday. It is closed on Mondays. Be sure to obtain a permit from the museum entitling you to reserved parking in the lot in front of the building. Parking spaces are at a premium on campus, and you risk having your vehicle towed otherwise. There is a $5 admission fee; admission is free for children under 12 and William and Mary staff and students.

The Watermen's Museum
309 Water Street, Yorktown
(757) 887-2641
www.watermens.org

Virginia's watermen, generations of them, are the focus of this small but lively museum located on Yorktown's waterfront and housed in a Colonial Revival manor house. Five galleries and a variety of outdoor exhibits chronicle the story of generations of Virginians whose livelihood stemmed from the waters of the Chesapeake Bay and its tributaries. Here visitors see ship models, paintings, photographs, nautical artifacts, and tools in permanent and rotating exhibits on this ancient trade.

The museum hopes to preserve the heritage of the watermen and to interpret their culture and their contributions to the region in an effort to provide and support educational opportunities and preserve and enhance the environment of the fragile bay. All generations are represented, from the original Native American fishermen to today's working men and women. On the grounds you can see some of the workboats and other traditional equipment once so common on

i Internationally known artist Georgia O'Keeffe received her first honorary degree from William and Mary. Although her two brothers attended college here, women were not allowed to enroll when the family moved to Williamsburg in the early 1900s. In honor of her honorary degree in 1938, the college put on an exhibition of her work, including eight paintings selected by O'Keeffe's husband, Alfred Stieglitz. Another, *White Flower*, was donated to the event by Abby Rockefeller. It was O'Keeffe's first show in the South, and it remained on view for six days. In 2001 the Muscarelle Museum of Art re-created her exhibit with eight of the original nine paintings. (One was too fragile to travel.) The new O'Keeffe show was on display for five months and also included letters, documents, and a six-and-a-half-minute home movie of her visit to William and Mary to accept her honorary degree.

our waters. The museum provides a variety of programs, seminars, activities, and special events to the public.

Admission is $4 for adults and $1 for children. The museum is open year-round, from April 1 through Thanksgiving hours are 10:00 a.m. to 5:00 p.m. Tuesday through Saturday and 1:00 to 5:00 p.m. Sunday. From Thanksgiving through March the museum is only open on Saturday and Sunday. The museum is closed Monday except Memorial Day and Labor Day. The Watermen's Museum Gift Shop features works by more than 40 local artists and crafters with unusual original works that will be cherished by those who appreciate folk art. The gift shop is at (757) 888–2623.

Galleries

Andrews Gallery
Jamestown Road
(757) 221-1452
www.wm.edu/andrewsgallery/
This exhibition gallery for the Department of

Art and Art History at the College of William and Mary is behind the Phi Beta Kappa Memorial Hall. Periodic exhibits of traveling shows and of faculty and student art make the gallery an interesting window on the art scene. Hours are from 10:00 a.m. to 5:00 p.m. Monday through Friday.

Kinks, Quirks, and Caffeine
1303 Jamestown Road
(757) 229-5889
www.kinksandquirks.com
Drop in for a latte and you'll find yourself surrounded by some curious, captivating original works by a variety of American craftsmen and artists. From fine jewelry, glass ornaments, lamps, pottery, and handcrafted bookmarks to gigantic neon wall treatments, this place offers an eclectic collection of fine crafts and art from around the country. If you're looking for some very special children's gifts, check out the unusual toys and wall pieces designed with kids in mind. You'll also find some clever and unusual office gifts and home accessories. Hours are 10:00 a.m. to 6:00 p.m. Monday through Saturday and noon to 5:00 p.m. Sunday. A second location, called Kinks and Quirks, recently opened at Riverfront Landing in Yorktown.

Nancy Thomas Gallery
Merchant's Square
145 Ballard Street, Yorktown
(757) 259-1938
(757) 898-0738
www.nancythomas.com
A master folk artist with a national reputation and a presence in museums (and in films—her work can be seen in Jessica Lange's apartment in Tootsie), Nancy Thomas calls Yorktown home. This fascinating shop is where you will find her works on display: paintings and sculptures, freestanding whimsical animals, angels, trees, wreaths, Christmas decorations, and much more. You are likely also to find Thomas herself displaying a new item or ready to discuss any of the wonderful things you might find interesting. In

It's not necessary to visit a gallery to see refreshing original art in Williamsburg. Sip a martini, listen to cool jazz, and gaze at the big paintings at A. Carroll's Bistro on Prince George Street. The owners are dedicated to showcasing contemporary art from around the region.

addition, you will find antiques and other original works and prints. Hours are Monday through Saturday from 10:00 a.m. to 5:00 p.m. and Sunday from 1:00 to 5:00 p.m. See the Shopping entry in the Jamestown and Yorktown chapter for more information. Note, too, that Thomas has a second gallery in Williamsburg's Merchants Square, adjacent to the city's Historic Area.

This Century Gallery
219 North Boundary Street
(757) 229-4949
www.thiscenturyartgallery.org

As the name indicates, the focus of this gallery, established more than 40 years ago, is work by contemporary artists, local, regional, and national. Shows featuring all media change on a regular basis, with an occasional Christmas crafts show in November/December

and spring crafts exhibition. The gallery, an affiliate of the Virginia Museum of Fine Arts in Richmond, displays traveling exhibits of that museum. Hours are from 11:00 a.m. to 5:00 p.m. Tuesday through Sunday, closed Monday.

A Touch of Earth
The Gallery Shops at Lightfoot
6580 Richmond Road
(757) 565-0425

Owned and operated by Lianne Lurie and Paul Pittman, this gallery, which opened in 1977, features fine decorative and functional crafts by more than 200 contemporary American artists and craftspeople. With a concentration on unusual works appealing to many senses, the selections include pottery, wind chimes in both clay and metal, glassworks, jewelry, lamps, musical instruments, kaleidoscopes, candle holders, and textiles—many of them signed one-of-a-kinds. The basic collection of lovely hand-built and wheel-thrown stoneware and fine porcelain includes the unique "Gloom Chasers," intricately decorated and pierced stoneware lanterns. A Touch of Earth is open from 10:00 a.m. to 5:00 p.m. Monday through Saturday, noon to 5:00 p.m. Sunday, and by appointment.

ANNUAL EVENTS

If you enjoy planning a vacation around a special event, a trip to the Historic Triangle offers plenty of options. While a summer excursion virtually guarantees a jam-packed itinerary of historic tours, sun-soaked shopping, and theme park rowdiness, the three other seasons can be just as glorious. And although the local festival season doesn't swing into high gear until April, you'll find a smattering of activities to choose from during the year's first quarter, a good time to visit if you don't like to fight crowds.

If you schedule your visit during spring break or later, your choice of fun activities pretty much runs the gamut. From the ever popular performances of Shakespeare's plays to the rousing sounds of Scottish bagpipes to the exquisite lights of Christmas, the Williamsburg area gives you a diverse menu of events and activities from which to choose.

Below, we've listed the major—and a few more low-key but fun—celebrations that take place in and around the Williamsburg area. For those of you willing to drive a little farther for a good time, we've also included some of our favorite celebrations that take place in other pockets of Hampton Roads. The annual events and festivals are listed month by month to make your vacation planning a little easier. The prices we provide are subject to change, but they should give you a solid ballpark figure to use when tallying up that vacation budget. We noted where events in the Colonial Williamsburg Historic Area are included in your ticket purchase.

For more information turn to the chapter on Colonial Williamsburg. But before you do, take the time to read through the listings and highlight any and all that strike your fancy.

EVENT SCHEDULE

February

Antiques Forum
Williamsburg Lodge Conference Center
South England Street, Williamsburg
(800) 770-5930
In early February the Antiques Forum comes to Colonial Williamsburg, bringing collectors and experts who share their knowledge in seminars, attend lectures given by Colonial Williamsburg's curators, take special tours, and socialize. The forum, which celebrated its 60th year in 2008, brings together scholars, collectors, and antiques buffs to reexamine past judgments about American decorative arts. The multiday event costs $530, which includes all lectures, tours, special programming, opening receptions, and continental breakfasts, coffees, and afternoon teas. Register well in advance: Registration begins in September.

Mid-Atlantic Quilt Festival Week
Hampton Roads Convention
Center, Hampton
(215) 862-5828
www.quiltfest.com
Explore an American art that has developed and grown with the nation. The Mid-Atlantic Quilt Festival Week is a compilation of four exciting quilting, fiber-arts, and wearable-art shows and is the perfect place for quilters and wearable, textile, and fiber artists of all levels and ages to explore these arts. In all, more than 500 quilts, clothing items, dolls, and textiles are on exhibit; workshops, lectures, and special activities are held in late February.

March

Williamsburg Film Festival
Holiday Inn Patriot and Conference Center
3032 Richmond Road, Williamsburg
(757) 565-2600, (800) 446-6001
Here's something special for movie and classic TV aficionados. Celebrating its 12th anniversary show in 2008, this three-day festival in early March features showings of old movies and television shows. The first festival brought character actor Gene Evans, television actor Dale Berry, and Willie Phelps of the Phelps Brothers to Williamsburg. Peter Boone, son of Richard Boone, displayed some of his father's movie memorabilia. The 2004 event featured stunt man Joe Canutt, who doubled for Charlton Heston in the Ben-Hur chariot race, and TV actor Alex Cord. The festival staff is planning autograph and photo sessions with the stars. Legendary actors and directors are honored at the Saturday Night Dinner Show. Daily admission is $20 per person, dinner show tickets are $25, and all tickets must be purchased on site.

St. Patrick's Day Parade
Granby Street
Ocean View section of Norfolk
(757) 587-3548
www.norfolkparade.com
This particular wearin'-of-the-green event may not take place in Williamsburg, but if you're in the mood to celebrate your Irish heritage or simply wish to get caught up in the revelry, check out Norfolk's St. Patrick's Day Parade and Festivities. The parade, held the Saturday closest to St. Paddy's Day, is the area's oldest and largest. (And, no, we don't know if they serve green beer.) The route typically begins at 10:00 a.m. at Northside Middle School on Granby Street (about 45 minutes from Williamsburg on Interstate 64 east on a good day) and winds up on West Government Avenue, although that is subject to change. You don't have to pay to watch the parade, but food concessions and rides are available at points near or along the route. Knights of Columbus Council 3548 is the sponsor.

April

Gloucester Daffodil Festival
Main Street, Gloucester
(804) 693-2355
Considered the opening event in the busy Hampton Roads festival season, the Gloucester gala celebrates what else but spring's harbinger, the sunny daffodil. Held on the first Saturday in April, this free festival features food, arts and crafts, musical entertainment, bus tours, children's events, games, historic displays, and the crowning of the Daffodil Festival Queen. Bring your pet along. Anyone is welcome to sign up for the Magnificent Mutt Show. To get to Gloucester, follow Route 17 north from Yorktown over the Coleman Bridge. For shuttle parking stay on the Route 17 bypass to the fourth stoplight. Turn left onto Short Lane and park at Gloucester High School. A bus shuttle ($1 per person) will take you right to the fun. (Parking fees, by the way, benefit the local Literacy Volunteers of America.)

Art on the Lawn
Muscarelle Museum of Art
Jamestown Road, Williamsburg
(757) 221-2703
This annual festival, typically held on a Saturday in mid-April, celebrates the arts with live music, food, and a student artwork display. Art activities, games, and museum treasures help keep the kids entertained. The event is free and open to the public.

Historic Garden Week
Various locations
(804) 644-7776, (757) 229-7516,
(757) 258-3553
www.VAGardenweek.org
Sponsored by garden clubs throughout Virginia, this special week celebrating nature's beauty (and the decorating skills of a number of homeowners) is held the third week in April. On Tuesday of that week, the Williamsburg Garden Club sponsors its garden week tour of both the gardens and interiors of four or five homes in the Williamsburg area. In addition, a walking garden tour of portions of

the Colonial Williamsburg gardens is offered. Tickets range from $10 to $35 per event and may be purchased online from late January until 10 days before the event. Visit the Web site for a schedule and more details. Tickets may also be purchased the day before the event at either the Colonial Williamsburg Visitor Center, the Williamsburg Lodge, or at the door of any of the houses the day of the event. Since the chairperson of the local event changes annually, your best bet for more information is to contact the Historic Garden Week headquarters at the above numbers, which should have updates. For statewide information, the Historic Garden Week headquarters is the first number listed. Beginning in February, you can get a guidebook about the state's next event by sending $6 payable to Historic Garden Week, 12 East Franklin Street, Richmond, VA 23219.

Norfolk's International Azalea Festival
220 Boush Street, Norfolk
(757) 282-2801
www.azaleafestival.org
Norfolk has celebrated its annual International Azalea Festival since 1953, when it was started as a salute to the new NATO's Allied Command Atlantic unit and the international community it brought to the city. The festival was designed to build friendships, facilitate cultural exchange, honor the military, and pursue new lines of trade between Norfolk and the rest of the world. More than half a century later, the event now includes the crowning of a queen, a dinner and ball, a flag-raising ceremony, a golf tournament, and lectures and other educational activities. It takes place in late April each year.

Virginia Arts Festival
200 Boush Street, Norfolk
(757) 282-2800
www.virginiaartsfest.com
Introduced in 1997 as a way to provide locals and tourists with a more varied cultural menu, the festival has been deemed "an unprecedented flowering of the arts" by a writer in the *New York Times*. The festival begins in late April and runs until early June, with a lineup that includes dance, theater, and a range of music, with more than two dozen performers and companies from as far away as Chile and Germany. Performances truly are world-class —participants have included Itzhak Perlman, the National Symphony Orchestra with Leonard Slatkin, The Boys Choir of Harlem, the Stuttgart Chamber Orchestra, the Russian National Ballet, and modern dance's innovative Mark Morris Dance Group. Although most events are held at sites throughout Norfolk, several are staged in Williamsburg or elsewhere on the Peninsula. Each of the more than 100 events are ticketed; in the past prices have ranged from a free concert by the U.S. Continental Army Band to a $150 orchestra seat for the Gershwin World Gala Celebration. Other performances included La Bohème and Herbie Hancock.

May

Colonial Williamsburg Garden Symposium
Hennage Auditorium, DeWitt Wallace Museum, South Henry and Francis Streets, Williamsburg
(800) 603–0948
Colonial Williamsburg's three-day crash course on cultivating a green thumb, held in late April or early May, celebrated its 62nd anniversary in 2008. If you want to know how to make your garden grow, join more than 200 horticulturists and gardening enthusiasts for a host of lectures, tours, and master classes. One year the theme was "Garden Earth: A Partnership," offering a look at vegetables, conservation, garden designs, and pest control. Registration typically costs about $325 per person, but varies depending on the number of days and activities chosen. Special lodging rates are available at Williamsburg properties.

Children's Festival of Friends
Newport News Park, Jefferson Avenue Newport News
(757) 926-1400

A popular destination for families with young children, this one-day festival is held on a Saturday in early May. The fun includes entertainment with pint-size appeal, hands-on activities, games, and a variety of rides. Admission is free but expect to pay about a $3 parking fee.

Greek Festival
Annunciation Greek Orthodox Cathedral
7720 Granby Street, Norfolk
(757) 440-0500
If you like Greek food—and don't mind rubbing elbows with tons of others who like Greek food just as much or even more—Norfolk's annual Greek Festival is the place for you to be the second weekend in May. Held from Thursday through Sunday, this event has grown by leaps and bounds in the past decade or so. Highlights include live Greek music and dancing, lamb feast dinners, and an a la carte menu of an array of Greek delicacies. Food is served cafeteria style and the lines are long, but all the camaraderie and good cheer make the wait seem brief. Festival events are free. Visit artists and vendors in the marketplace; food items are priced individually. And the festival is easy to find: Just follow I–64 to exit 276, which dumps you right onto Granby Street. The goings-on will be about a mile down the road on your left.

Ladies Professional Golf Association (LPGA)
Michelob ULTRA Open
Kingsmill Resort, James City County
(757) 253-3985
www.michelobultraopen.com
Previously home to the PGA Michelob Championship every October, Kingsmill now hosts the LPGA Michelob ULTRA Open in early May, with the inaugural event held in 2003. The first year attracted 49 of the country's 50 top women golfers with a $1.6 million purse. Tickets range from $10 to $30.

Jamestown Landing Day
Jamestown Settlement
Route 31, Jamestown
(757) 253-4838, (888) 593-4682
Held in Jamestown Settlement in early May, Jamestown Landing Day commemorates the anniversary of the 1607 founding of America's first permanent English colony with sailing demonstrations and interpretive activities that show the effects of contact between English settlers and the native Powhatan Indians. Participation in events is covered by the price of admission to the Jamestown Settlement museum: $13.50 for adults, $6.25 for children 6 through 12.

Confederate Attack on
Fort Pocahontas at Wilson's Wharf
Route 5, Charles City County
(804) 829-9722
www.fortpocahontas.org
This is a living-history reenactment of the action of Wilson's Wharf, known as Fort Pocahontas. In an effort to preserve this once-forgotten fort, a two-day reenactment of the Civil War battle that took place here on May 24, 1864, has been staged. It was the first major land-naval clash between the U.S. Colored Troops and General Robert E. Lee's Army of Northern Virginia. The weekend events include a living-history encampment, an evening lantern tour, military demonstrations, and two battle reenactments. Sutlers—men and women salespeople dressed in period attire—offer plenty of wares for sale. Admission is $10 for adults and $8 for students per day, or $15 for both days. For groups of 10 or more, daily admission is $7 per adult and $5 per student.

Stockley Garden Arts Festival
Stockley Gardens Park,
Olney Road and Stockley Gardens Road,
Norfolk
(757) 625-6161
www.hope-house.org/stockley.html
This lovely location in Norfolk's historic Ghent area is the setting for a weekend-long festival the third weekends of May and October, attended by more than 25,000 visitors. As you stroll among 150 exhibitors, you will see everything from painting and sculpture to

jewelry and photography. Don't hesitate to bring the children. There's plenty of music and food tailored just for the younger set. Admission is free, but you may have to hunt for side-street parking.

Annual Beach Music Weekend
Atlantic Avenue and Twenty-Ninth Street
Virginia Beach
(757) 491-7866, (800) 822-3224
www.vbfun.com
Feel like jammin' in the sand? Then head over to "The Beach" for three days of free concerts on a huge stage anchored right on the beach at Twenty-Ninth Street. The festival, held each year in mid- to late May, is free. Past performers have included the Chairmen of the Board, the Embers, and Bill Deal and the Rhondels.

Pungo Strawberry Festival
Princess Anne Road and
Indian River Road, Virginia Beach
(757) 721-6001
www.pungostrawberryfestival.info
As its name suggests, this event celebrates the splendid strawberry. Usually held the last weekend in May, the festival offers crafts by area artisans, carnival rides, children's games, and strawberries—and strawberry dishes—galore. More than 120,000 come to sample strawberry pies, tarts, jellies, and jams, plus a wide range of activities. There's live music on three stages, a jousting match with costumed knights of old, more than 100 arts and crafts booths, even clowns and pony rides for the kids. Entrance to the festival is free, but a parking fee is charged.

To get to the festival, take I-64 east to Route 44, the Norfolk–Virginia Beach Expressway. At the Birdneck Road exit, turn right and follow to General Booth Boulevard. Turn right onto General Booth, which eventually changes to Princess Anne, and follow until the intersection of Indian River Road. Look for festival signs along the way.

June

Newport News Greek Festival
Saints Constantine and Helen Greek
Orthodox Church
60 Traverse Road, Newport News
(757) 872-8119
www.newportnewsgreekfestival.org
When more than 12,000 folks decide to have dinner at the same place, you know the food must be good. If you're in town during the first weekend in June, you just might want to join the crowd at this annual Hellenic festival for a few traditional Greek favorites—moussaka, souvlaki, pastitsio, gyros, baked chicken, and rice pilaf—and enjoy the live entertainment. If you thought ahead and tucked a credit card in your pocket, stop in at the *plaka*, or marketplace, which sells everything from artwork and fine jewelry to Greek provisions such as filo, orzo, olives, and cheeses. Admission and parking are free. Meals typically are sold a la carte.

Harborfest
Town Point Park
Waterside Drive, Norfolk
(757) 441-2345
www.festeventsva.org
Norfolk's humongous waterfront bash is now 30 years old. This three-day event begins on Friday, when a parade of ships sails into Norfolk's harbor. The fun continues throughout the weekend with nationally known entertainment, fireworks, and an area set aside just for children.

Harborfest typically is held in early June in Town Point Park and along the Norfolk waterfront. It attracts about a quarter-million people annually, so the place is a zoo. Many Insiders won't miss it. If you truly love a party and can handle a mob scene, check it out. To get to downtown Norfolk, take I-64 east to Interstate 264 and follow the Waterside Drive exit. Parking is available in several area garages, but it is at a premium, so claim your spot early. And one final teaser if you're deciding which day to go: The fireworks on Saturday night are spectacular!

Boardwalk Art Show and Festival
Oceanfront Boardwalk, Virginia Beach
(757) 425-0000, (800) 822-3224

Art lovers won't want to miss these seascapes. More than 400 artists and craftspeople participate in the annual Boardwalk Art Show. It's no wonder that this four-day event in mid-June has been one of the most popular outdoor art festivals on the East Coast. With the Atlantic Ocean as a backdrop, this art show stretches for 12 blocks along the famous oceanfront boardwalk. What's better, it doesn't cost a thing to see some of the finest paintings, crafts, sculptures, and photography. But bring a little extra cash in case you are tempted to go home with a memorable souvenir.

Bayou Boogaloo & Cajun Food Festival
Town Point Park
Waterside Drive, Norfolk
(757) 441-2345
www.festeventsva.org

If you like your food spicy and your entertainment hot, hot, hot, head over to Norfolk's Town Point Park for the Bayou Boogaloo & Cajun Food Festival. Held each year over a weekend in late June, the festival combines étouffée, jambalaya, and catfish with Cajun and zydeco music and such activities as Cajun Critter Races, pepper-eating challenges, and Cajun cooking demonstrations. This event has grown tremendously popular because it often imports some of the South's legendary performers. In the past, the Bourbon Street Players, Dr. John, Papa John Creech, Little Feat, and Bela Fleck & The Flecktones were among those who appeared. So bring a blanket or comfortable chair and plan to sit out the duration of live performances. The event costs about $5 per person per day, or $10 for a three-day pass, with children under 12 admitted free. (Our advice: Bring along plenty of pocket change for beverages.)

Hampton Jazz Festival
Hampton Coliseum, exit 263B off I–64
(757) 838-4203
www.hampton.gov/coliseum/jazz/index.html

If you like jazz, you'll love this popular Hampton festival. How much will you love it? Let us count the ways: (1) Aretha Franklin, (2) Isaac Hayes, (3) Stevie Wonder, (4) B. B. King, (5) Gladys Knight, (6) Boney James, and (7) George Benson. Not all in the same weekend, of course, but there's usually a couple of major headliners performing each year. The festival typically is held in late June. Tickets can be purchased through Ticketmaster by calling (757) 671-8100. The cost for each concert is $52.50 plus service fees. To find out more, call after April 1.

July

Independence Day Celebration
Main Street, Yorktown
(757) 890-3300

Family-oriented festivities are the order of the day at the Fourth of July celebration at Yorktown. Activities include a foot race, parade, arts and crafts, musical entertainment, and, of course, a magnificent display of fireworks. Satellite parking is provided away from the waterfront, but free buses will get you to the heart of the daylong festivities. The free celebration is sponsored by the Yorktown Fourth of July Committee.

Annual Independence Day Ice Cream Social
Wren Building Courtyard
College of William and Mary
Williamsburg
(757) 259-6079

It's July and the operative word is hot. Enjoy a refreshing double dip at this annual July 4 event, sponsored by the Williamsburg Community Hospital Auxiliary. Held from 5:30 to 8:00 p.m. (to help you cool off and settle in before the fireworks), the event offers more than just ice cream. There are hot dogs, homemade cakes, drinks, entertainment, and games for the children. Even better, 500 chairs are set out on the courtyard lawn so that your tired feet can get a much-needed rest. You are welcome to bring your own chairs or a blanket if you prefer. The sitting part is free; food items are priced individually.

Independence Day Festivities
Colonial Williamsburg Historic Area
Williamsburg
(800) HISTORY

The day typically begins with a fife and drum salute to the 13 colonies on the Courthouse steps. At noon the Declaration of Independence is read at the steps of the Courthouse. The day also includes a garden party at the Governor's Palace and ends with a 9:15 p.m. fireworks display. The programs may change annually. Admission is included in your ticket to the restored area.

Fourth at the Fort
Waller Field at Fort Monroe, Hampton
(757) 727-3151, (757) 737-3302

Celebrate Independence Day on an active army post with the Continental Army Band, food, children's games and rides, and a fireworks display. The setting can't be beat: Fort Monroe overlooks the Chesapeake Bay. Admission is free.

Virginia Shakespeare Festival
Phi Beta Kappa Memorial Hall
Jamestown Road
(757) 221-2659
vsf.wm.edu

The Virginia Shakespeare Festival has been a highlight of the Williamsburg summer since its inception in 1978. Two performances typically are held throughout July in the 750-seat Phi Beta Kappa Memorial Hall on the campus of William and Mary. Professional directors from around the world work with an acting staff of both student interns and professional Shakespearean-trained performers. Recent performances include *Henry VIII, Love's Labour's Lost, Romeo and Juliet, The Merry Wives of Windsor, Twelfth Night,* and *Hamlet.* Curtain typically is at 8:00 p.m., with an occasional 2:00 p.m. matinee. Tickets, which go on sale in June, are $20 for one play, $45 for the season.

August
James City County Fair
Upper County Park
180 Leisure Road, Toano
(757) 566-1367

This free event has been growing like gangbusters since its beginnings more than 30 years ago as a tomato-growing contest. The two-day fair, held on a Friday and Saturday in early August, features rides, exhibits, crafts, music, and foods. Vendors will be on hand. To keep the fair's local flavor firmly intact, anyone selling goods must live or work in James City County, Williamsburg, or the Bruton District of York County. Satellite parking costs $1 at Toano Middle School, with buses shuttling you to the fairgrounds.

Hampton Cup Regatta
Mill Creek, Hampton
(757) 265-0964
www.hamptoncupregatta.org

If you're an armchair speed freak, head to Hampton in early August for the oldest and largest inboard hydroplane powerboat race in the United States. The summer national championships, which are sanctioned by the American Powerboat Association, include 11 classes of boats (including the Grand Prix hydroplanes, billed as the fastest piston-powered craft in the world) and speeds that top 170 mph. There's also live entertainment and food. The races, which run for three days at Fort Monroe's Mill Creek, celebrate their 80th year in 2006. Admission is free, but get there early to grab a prime viewing spot, as race sponsors expect about 160,000 thrillseekers to show up.

September
Rock 'n' Roll Half Marathon and American Music Festival
(800) 822-3224
www.eliteracing.com

Here's a hip twist to the usual marathon race: Pound the pavement to the sounds of rock 'n' roll, blues, reggae, and jazz. This 13.1-mile

i If you're in the area in late September or early October, you might want to motor up to Richmond for a good, old-fashioned time at the State Fair of Virginia. This 11-day event offers everything from live-animal exhibits and crafts displays to top-name entertainers and all the food you can eat. Gate admission is $11 on weekdays, $13 on weekends, but the price goes down to $8 after 5:00 p.m. from Monday to Friday. However, rides will cost extra. The fair is held at the Richmond Raceway Complex, 600 East Laburnum Avenue, which is a straight shot west on I–64 from Williamsburg. For information call (800) 588–3247 or go to www.statefair.com.

Labor-Day-weekend race draws 21,000 runners and walkers. An $80,000 prize purse attracts some of the world's fastest feet. In addition to the exciting road race, live bands are staged every mile of the course. More than 50 acts get the crowds dancing on the boardwalk and on the beach, with past acts including The Spinners, The Commodores, REO Speedwagon, and Counting Crows. Most concerts are free, but some are ticketed. Tickets are available at Ticketmaster and the Virginia Beach Visitor Center. For American Music Festival information, call (757) 491-7866 or go to www.beacheventsfun.com.

Bay Days
Downtown Hampton
(757) 727-6122
www.baydays.com
During the first weekend after Labor Day each September, the city of Hampton celebrates the heritage of the Chesapeake Bay with its three-day Bay Days bash. Admission to the Bay Days site is free, but there is a nominal fee for some special events, and parking—whether in city lots or private makeshift lots set up for the occasion—runs around $10. (Satellite parking and shuttle service are available at the Hampton Coliseum lot just off exit 263B of I-64.)

Featuring everything from hands-on Bay education activities for the kids to rides, crafts, food, and a juried art show, Bay Days has something for everyone. For those on the daring side, there's even an Extreme Arena that showcases everything from stunt bicycling, skateboarding, and in-line skating to laser tag, bungee jumping, and a rock-climbing wall. Continuous entertainment is staged at various locations throughout the celebration, which takes place along the Hampton waterfront and in the closed-off streets and parking lots of downtown. The Saturday night explosion of fireworks is a must-see. The festival concludes Sunday evening with a headline performer. Past entertainers have included country stars Patty Loveless and Deana Carter.

Williamsburg Scottish Festival
Jamestown Beach Campground
James City County
(888) 445-2738
www.wsfonline.org
This popular annual event, which celebrated its 30th year in 2007, takes place at the campground on the fourth weekend in September. Festivalgoers can watch or participate in Scottish games, Highland dancing, and athletic events, witness a parade of the clans and a war-cry rally, and, of course, listen to the bagpipes skirl. Individual drumming, piping, and band competitions also are held, but participants must preregister. The athletic events alone are worth the drive. When's the last time you saw athletes "toss the caber"? That's a 120-pound log that measures 20 feet long. Children also get involved with their own mock athletic games, plus a few of the good old-fashioned races—a sack race and an egg-and-spoon dash. At past festivals, border collies have demonstrated their sheepherding skills, and Scottish crafts and imports—books, jewelry, weaving, woolens—have been on display. Performances by demonstration bands are among the highlights of the day's events. Visitors can sample Scottish cuisine—everything

from pasties and bridies, a meat-filled popover, to shortbread and Scottish candy—or fill up on barbecue and fish and chips. Scottish soft drinks and beer are sold. Festival tickets are $12 for adults, $6 for children 6 to 12, and free for those 5 and younger. Parking at the campground is $5. Each year following the festival, there is an Evening Ceilidh (pronounced kay-lee). If you would like to attend the Scottish party of song and dance, stop by the information tent at the festival to purchase tickets for $8.

Fall Festival and Powwow
Chickahominy Tribal Ground
Charles City County
(804) 829-2261, (804) 966-7043

The Chickahominy Tribe hosts its annual festival at nearby Charles City County the last weekend of September, drawing 3,000 to 5,000 visitors. Each year the powwow features Native-American dancing, singing, and drumming. Not only is it an educational event for young and old alike, it's also an opportunity for shopping. There is an array of beautiful handmade Indian jewelry, pottery, and beadwork, plus books, tapes, and food. Fish sandwiches and chicken dinners are on the menu, but don't pass up a chance to try the Indian fry bread. It's a real treat. There is no admission fee, but donations are accepted. Special seating is provided for senior citizens; all others should bring their own lawn chairs or blankets. Please, leave the pets at home.

October

An Occasion for the Arts
Merchants Square, Williamsburg
(757) 258-5587

October in Williamsburg means An Occasion for the Arts, with outdoor exhibits and entertainment on Duke of Gloucester Street and Merchants Square. Held the first Sunday in October, this annual free autumn salute to visual and performing artists boasts the oldest juried invitational art show in Virginia, limited to 100 artists and craftspeople. The juror

typically is a respected area arts professional. In addition to the art show, entertainers—magicians, musicians, dancers, mimes—are on hand, performing on a number of different stages. The festival begins at 10:00 a.m., with entertainment running until dark. Most performances last from 30 minutes to an hour. Food and beverages are on sale. As a finale, a professional band or musical group gives a 5:30 p.m. concert on the festival grounds. This concert, often held in the Wren Yard at the foot of Merchants Square, is dubbed "the Capper" by organizers, and typically lasts about an hour.

First held in 1969, An Occasion for the Arts now draws about 30,000 people over the course of a single day. Artists and participants may park in designated lots a few blocks away. Visitors are encouraged to park on the William and Mary campus just off South Boundary Street, although other campus parking is usually available.

Fall Festival of Folklife
Newport News Park, Jefferson Avenue
Newport News
(757) 926-1400
www.nnparks.com/festivals.php

Somehow, the sun always manages to shine for this two-day festival held in the wooded environs of Newport News Park. This free event, held on the first full weekend in October, features crafts galore (we've purchased many one-of-a-kind Christmas gifts here). And, for a crafts festival, it's a fairly kid-friendly environment. There's always a children's area with stage shows and hands-on crafts. There's also a folk dance stage, where spectators can see Native-American, African, international, and square dancing presented in the round. The event draws about 70,000 visitors, warranting two bits of advice: Arrive early because on-site parking (which costs about $5) can be an extended ordeal; and eat early, as lines at the 30 food vendors tend to get really long, leaving you ravenous by the time you get a chance to dig into your pit-cooked steak sandwich and butterfly fries.

Poquoson Seafood Festival
Poquoson Municipal Park
830 Poquoson Avenue, Poquoson
(757) 868-3580, (757) 868-3588
www.poquosonseafoodfestival.com
If you're in the area in mid-October and in the mood for seafood and the type of fun that's part of small-town living, head down I–64 for the three-day Poquoson Seafood Festival. The fun is free (there's a $5 or so parking fee) and features music, fireworks, dance exhibitions, arts and crafts, children's events, the "Catch of the Day" baby pageant, and, of course, plenty of succulent seafood. Started in 1981, the event is a tribute to the working watermen of Hampton Roads and has become a tradition in the region. To get to Poquoson, which is a bit off the beaten path, take I–64 east to exit 256-B to Route 171 and follow signs for shuttle parking. Or, if you think you'll get lucky and find a parking place at the festival site, follow Route 171 for about 5 or 6 miles and follow signs to the parking area. Enjoy!

Yorktown Victory Day Celebration
Yorktown Victory Center
Route 238, Yorktown
(757) 253-4838, (888) 593-4682
On October 19, 1781, British General Cornwallis and his forces surrendered to the Americans at Yorktown; the American Revolution was essentially over, though the signing of treaties came later. This momentous day is commemorated each year with a two-day celebration of parades, fanfare, and reenactments. An encampment of Revolutionary War reenactors presents tactical demonstrations at both the Victory Center and on the Yorktown battlefield. Admission is $9.25 for adults and $5.00 for children 6 through 12 and includes entrance to center exhibits.

November

Urbanna Oyster Festival
Urbanna
(804) 758-0368
www.urbannaoysterfestival.com

Held the first full weekend in November in scenic Middlesex County, this festival's main attraction is, of course, oysters served just about any way you can think of—raw, roasted, stewed, fried, or frittered. If you tire of oysters (or, gasp, don't actually like the bivalves), you can sample the clam chowder, crab cakes, or steamed crabs. Or, if you prefer just about anything to seafood (although that makes us wonder why you're in Urbanna in the first place), you can always plunk down a few bucks for a hamburger, hot dog, or ham biscuit. While the food is the main attraction here, it isn't the only one. A variety of entertainment—including parades, visiting tall ships, fine arts, an oyster-shucking contest, live music, children's events, ship tours, pony rides, and the crowning of the festival queen—is all part of the two-day celebration. The Urbanna Oyster Festival began in 1957. To get to this somewhat out-of-the-way spot, take I–64 to Route 33 east (the West Point exit). Follow to U.S. Route 17, where you will turn left and follow the signs for Urbanna. An alternate route is to take US 17 north from Yorktown across the Coleman Bridge to Gloucester then north to Urbanna and once again follow the signs.

Thanksgiving at Berkeley Plantation
12602 Harrison Landing Road, off
Route 5, Charles City County
(804) 829-6018
www.berkeleyplantation.com
In early December 1619 a company of Englishmen arrived to settle a grant of Virginia land known as Berkeley Hundred. Their sponsor had instructed that the day of their arrival be "a day of Thanksgiving," so the settlers celebrated and gave thanks, more than a year before the pilgrims who landed at Plymouth, Massachusetts, in 1620 first did. Either a reenactment of the first Virginia Thanksgiving or a commemoration of the event has taken place the first Sunday in November since 1958 at Berkeley Plantation in Charles City County.

There is always some sort of celebration, although it varies from year to year. There is

no charge to take part in the simpler commemorative ceremony. A small fee is charged
during the years in which the reenactment is
scheduled. Sandwiches, Brunswick stew, and
other goodies are available for purchase after
the event in the Coach House Tavern. If the
weather is temperate, the venue combined
with activities makes for a poignant and lovely
afternoon.

Food & Feasts of Colonial Virginia
Jamestown Settlement
Route 31, Jamestown
Yorktown Victory Center
Route 1020, Yorktown
(757) 253-4838
This three-day event, held in late November,
illustrates how the Powhatan Indians and
Jamestown's earliest colonists prepared and
preserved foods nearly 400 years ago, including the processing of a whole hog. The festival typically draws about 5,500 visitors over
the three days. Admission to both sites is
included with the purchase of a combination
ticket that costs $19.25 for adults and $9.25
for children 6 through 12.

Mistletoe Market
Bruton Parish Hall
Duke of Gloucester Street
(757) 259-6079
Sponsored by the Williamsburg Community
Hospital Auxiliary, this get-in-the-mood-for-
Christmas event is held from 10:00 a.m. to
4:00 p.m. the weekend before Thanksgiving.
Expect to find just about anything at this free
market—from knitted sweaters, artwork, and
other handmade items to baked goods and
floral centerpieces.

i Planning to visit Williamsburg during December? Before you arrive
call (800) HISTORY and ask for a copy of
the Colonial Williamsburg Christmas
Companion, which will provide you with
a detailed account of all the goings-on
during the busy holiday season.

December

A Colonial Christmas
Yorktown Victory Center
Old Virginia Route 238, Yorktown
(757) 887-1776
www.historyisfun.org
This event, which typically runs from 9:00
a.m. to 5:00 p.m. daily throughout the entire
month of December at Yorktown Victory Center, allows you to take part in a variety of
18th-century-Virginia holiday activities in the
re-created farm and re-created Continental
Army encampment. Costumed interpreters
prepare traditional Christmas fare (visitors
sometimes even receive a special recipe!) and
tell stories of the holiday season. Participants
also will be invited to dip a candle to take
home. Cost is included in the center admission price of $9.25 for adults and $5.00 for
children 6 through 12.

Williamsburg Community
Christmas Parade
Richmond Road
(757) 229-6511
As the official start to the holiday season, the
Williamsburg Area Chamber of Commerce
sponsors its annual Christmas Parade the first
Saturday in December, the day preceding
Colonial Williamsburg's Grand Illumination
(see next entry). The ever popular parade,
which began in 1964, typically draws 100 or
more floats, marching bands, and other
entrants. The parade route begins at 9:00
a.m. in the Historic Area and proceeds down
Richmond Road to William and Mary Hall.

Williamsburg's Grand Illumination
Colonial Williamsburg Historic Area
(800) 447-8679, (800) HISTORY
On the first Sunday in December, Colonial
Williamsburg kicks off the Christmas season
by lighting candles in hundreds of windows in
Historic Area buildings. Cressets and bonfires
also illuminate the evening. Locals come in
droves, usually about 30,000 people attend,
and visitors love this splendid and energetic
Yuletide event, which includes performances

As you ooh and aah over Colonial Williamsburg's Christmas finery, consider this: It takes 16 carpenters, designers, and assistants 4 days to decorate 50 exhibition buildings, trade shops, taverns, and offices in the Historic Area. Meanwhile, the residents of nearly 85 homes within the 173-acre Historic Area put up their own decorations. Among the materials used to decorate Colonial Williamsburg are more than 5 miles of white-pine roping, 1,500 white-pine and Fraser fir wreaths, 15 bushels of apples, 9 bushels of lemons, and 6 bushels of oranges.

by the Junior and Senior Colonial Williamsburg Fifes & Drums; the firing of cannons on the town green; dancing, caroling, and carousing at four stages scattered throughout the restored area; and fireworks displays at three locations—the Governor's Palace, the Capitol, and the Magazine.

Candlelight tours are held and 18th-century plays and concerts are performed; tickets are required for some events. Outdoor activities start at noon and are free to the public. Arrive early to avoid parking hassles and bring a flashlight. When it comes to holiday programs, the Grand Illumination is the star atop the tree, so to speak. Throughout this season, the Historic Area is adorned in holiday finery and bustles with candlelit concerts, decorating workshops, 18th-century plays, Yuletide banquets, and numerous other programs. Carolers sing on the steps of the Courthouse at twilight during the season, while exhibits and holiday programs at the DeWitt Wallace Museum, (757) 220-7724, draw visitors indoors where it's warm.

Newport News Celebration in Lights
Newport News Park, Jefferson Avenue
(757) 926-1400
Remember when you were little and your parents would pile you in the car and drive up and down the neighborhood streets to look at all of the splendid and not-so-splendid Christmas lights? Whether they were terrific or tacky, they all served to spark a little holiday magic. Since 1993, Newport News has re-created and magnified that magic about a million times over with its annual Festival of Lights from Thanksgiving through New Year's. Two miles of animated scenes, featuring more than 650,000 lights, dazzle folks driving through Newport News Park. Cost is $8 per car or $50 per bus.

A Colonial Christmas
Jamestown Settlement
Route 31, Jamestown
(757) 253-4838
Held from December 1 to December 31, this tradition introduces visitors to the Jamestown Settlement with 17th-century Yuletide traditions. An audiovisual program and special guided tours compare and contrast English Christmas customs of the period and how the season may have been observed in the difficult early years of the Jamestown colony. Admission is included in a ticket to the settlement, which costs $13.50 for adults and $6.25 for children 6 though 12.

Yorktown Tree Lighting Festivities
Historic Main Street, Yorktown
(757) 890-3300
One evening in early December, area families are invited to hold aloft candles and walk down Main Street to participate in the annual holiday tree-lighting fun. There's caroling and background music by the Fifes and Drums of York Town. Light refreshments are served. There's even a guest appearance by jolly old Saint Nick himself.

Community Christmas Tree Lighting
Market Square Green
Colonial Williamsburg
(757) 229-1000, (800) HISTORY
On Christmas Eve, beginning at 5:00 p.m. each year, Williamsburg residents gather for a special celebration of this physically cold, yet spiritually warm, season. A huge tree stationed at

Market Square Green near the Magazine is festooned with white lights, a tradition that dates from 1935. Members of the community circle around, holding lighted candles and singing carols. A short speech is delivered, and the festivities begin, including a presentation of the story of the area's first tree, which was decorated by a German professor living in the St. George Tucker House. Colonial Williamsburg and the Kiwanis Club of Williamsburg cosponsor this free, 90-minute event.

Festival of Lights
301 Monticello Avenue, Williamsburg
(757) 259-6079

This Christmas tree lighting, a Williamsburg Community Hospital Auxiliary fund-raiser for more than 20 years, is held on the grounds of the hospital the first Thursday in December. The lights, purchased in honor or memory of loved ones, are switched on at 5:30 p.m. by a guest dignitary.

First Night of Williamsburg
various locations
(757) 258-5153
www.firstnightwilliamsburg.org

This alcohol-free New Year's Eve celebration of the performing arts, introduced in 1993, is an event for the entire family. The First Night concept originated in Boston in 1976 and has since spread to more than 170 cities throughout the United States, Canada, and Australia. The local celebration is held from 6:00 p.m. to midnight in downtown Williamsburg, on the campus of the College of William and Mary,

> **i** If you like your Christmas holiday as bright as possible, you might want to traverse I–64 from Virginia Beach to Richmond for the new "100 Miles of Lights." Throughout the month of December, drive-through light shows will be set up in Richmond, Newport News, Norfolk, and Virginia Beach, with additional holiday programs—everything from music and dance performances to parades and historic reenactments—featured along the way. Three-, four-, and five-day vacation packages centered around the "100 Miles of Lights" are available, beginning at about $150 per person. For more information call (888) 493-7386, ext. 100.

and in locations bordering the Historic Area. More than 450 artists perform, including actors, dancers, singers, musicians, jugglers, puppeteers, storytellers, and clowns. The evening's grand finale is a spectacular fireworks display. While guests can easily reach the First Night grounds on foot, complimentary buses also travel a circuit around the area and connect to ample satellite parking. The celebration typically attracts 50 acts and a crowd of about 7,000. Food and beverages are available from churches, businesses, and civic groups located along the site. The fete is open to anyone—from 2 to 102—but all but the youngest participants (5 and younger) must wear commemorative buttons, which cost $10 in advance and $15 on December 31.

DAY TRIPS

While Williamsburg is one of a kind, other pockets of Hampton Roads have plenty to offer the would-be wanderer. If time permits—and you are an explorer at heart—make it a point to check out the neighboring country-side. The Old Dominion, after all, is a land of vast diversity. Where else can you hobnob with the dolphins and starfish of Virginia Beach one day, then wander amid Richmond's Civil War battlefields the next? Indeed, your day-tripping options seem limitless.

What we've outlined below are some of our favorite adventures, places you can go by simply hopping behind the wheel and heeding our directions. Whether you ferry across the James River, grab some R&R on Tangier or Smith Island, stroll along the historic streets of downtown Smithfield, or splash in the surf of Virginia Beach, you get to call the shots. You are, in a sense, master of your fate, captain of your dear old day-tripping soul. All of these Insider favorites are worth a good 8 to 12 hours of your time and most (with the exception of the islands) take under two hours of driving time (if you can avoid traffic). So what are you waiting for? Adventure beckons. And remember: Area codes vary depending upon where you're heading. In Richmond it's 804; on Smith Island 410; and for the rest of our day trips it's 757, just like Williamsburg. (No need to memorize the codes, however. We note them in each of the entries.) Got all that straight? Then let's start exploring!

Jamestown-Scotland Ferry
End of Jamestown Road
(800) 823-3779

The mercury hovers at 95 degrees and your tired dogs cower at the thought of making contact with sizzling pavement. What you would rather do is relax and luxuriate in a cool breeze, preferably with someone else in the driver's seat. Why not cruise to Scotland, tour the rural landscape, and savor some of the best authentic regional cooking available? No, we're not crazy; just check your map (if you didn't leave it back in your hotel room). It's entirely possible to schedule a free, fresh-air cruise to Scotland, something both locals and visitors do regularly aboard the Jamestown Ferry.

While the ferry isn't your destination, it's still a wonderful and scenic outing, which is why we give it a separate listing here. This state-run service, the last of a once-thriving ferry commerce in Hampton Roads, crosses the James River from Jamestown to Scotland Wharf in Surry County in Southside (many contend that the South doesn't really begin until one is securely below the James). For a large number of residents, this scenic ride is a twice-daily commute, either to the Surry nuclear power plant across the river or to jobs on the Peninsula. For many others, especially on weekends in good weather, it's a favorite day trip. You can reach the ferry by traveling either Jamestown Road or the Colonial Parkway to its southernmost end, near Jamestown Settlement. We prefer the parkway route, which is less direct but much more scenic, offering beautiful views of the expanse of water you are about to cross. If you haven't done so already, you might also want to visit Jamestown Island first: There, you'll see landmarks you'll view later from the ferry. Be sure to note the ferry schedule, posted on a large sign on the right side of Jamestown Road as you approach its end, and plan your trip to allow time for a convenient return trip. There are four different ferries that make the trip across the James: the *Pocahontas*, the

Jamestown-Scotland Ferry. JESSI DICK

Williamsburg, the *Surry,* and the *Virginia.* The schedule varies with the season and the time of day. Typically, in the summer you can hop aboard every 20 minutes to half an hour from 5:00 a.m. to 11:00 p.m. and every hour from 11:00 p.m. to 5:00 a.m. Monday through Thursday. The ferry gets under way every 30 minutes or so from 5:00 a.m. to 11:00 p.m. Friday, Saturday, and Sunday. It runs every hour through the rest of the night. Winter, spring, and fall service is slightly more limited in the evenings, with ferries typically running on the hour after 8:00 p.m.

While on the concrete dock waiting to board, you'll notice the three restored ships of Jamestown Settlement to your left: the *Susan Constant,* the *Godspeed,* and the *Dis-*covery. You don't get a better waterside view of all three ships than this, and your wait might be a prime opportunity to pull out the camera. The trip takes a little less than 20 minutes from castoff to docking and offers beautiful views, especially on clear autumn days or during late-summer sunsets.

Once you have boarded one of the ferries of the fleet, you may leave your vehicle (being careful, of course, not to ding your neighbors' car doors) and enjoy the view from the railing or from bow or stern. There is a small cabin upstairs with water fountains and restrooms as well as good views, but there is no seating on most of the ferries.

The unique experience of riding a ferry is periodically threatened with extinction by studies that call for a replacement bridge spanning the river, either here or upstream. Each year about 936,000 vehicles use the ferry service.

SURRY COUNTY

After you're across the James and docked at Scotland Wharf, you'll drive off into Surry County. Many Insiders choose to go directly down Route 31 to the Surrey House (yes, that's the spelling) or Edwards' Ham for delicious Southern cooking. Others prefer exploring Smith's Fort Plantation, traveling to Bacon's Castle, or going to Chippokes Plantation State Park and Chippokes Farm and Forestry Museum. Whatever your choice, you'll find that a voyage across the James is a trip into the quiet, rural Southern landscape of Surry County that offers a last picture of what the Peninsula used to be. Miles of farmland and two-lane highways separate small, historic communities. Weathered tobacco barns, more tall than wide, occasionally are visible in fields where prized Virginia peanuts are now the major crop. It's a world away from generic fast-food restaurants, hotel chains, and the sometimes frantic pace of an established tourism industry. In Southside, life is savored.

Attractions

Bacon's Castle
465 Bacon Castle Road (Route 617), Surry
(757) 357-5976
www.apva.org/baconscastle
Williamsburg may have a palace, but Surry has its own castle—Bacon's Castle on Route 10. You might think you heard all about the Virginia colonists' rebellion as you toured Williamsburg, but did you know that, 100 years before the Revolution, another rebellion occurred? In 1676 Nathaniel Bacon began the colony's first act of insurrection against Governor William Berkeley's harsh rule. The struggle spread to Surry County, and, on September 18, Bacon's commander, William Rookings, captured this building, home to Major Arthur Allen, in a siege.

Major Allen built the house in 1665, and now, more than 340 years later, it is the oldest documented brick house in English North America. Architecturally, it is of extreme interest. Unlike its surviving, typically Georgian, contemporaries, the building has curving Flemish gables and triple chimneystacks. Its front and rear facades also are unusual in that they are broken midpoint by an entrance-and-porch tower in front and a corresponding stair tower in back. This gives the building a cruciform shape, the first house in the colony so designed. A formal garden has been excavated and restored, giving the whole estate a sense of antiquity and a peace that contrasts with its most famous historical event. From April 1 to October 31, the house is open 10:00 a.m. to 4:00 p.m. Tuesday through Saturday and noon to 4:00 p.m. Sunday, but it is closed on Monday. It is open only on weekends in November and March, and closed in January and February. Admission is $7 for adults, $5 for senior citizens, and $4 for students 6 to 18. Tickets for both Bacon's Castle and Smith's Fort can be purchased for $10 (adults), $8 (seniors), or $6 (students). Group tours can be arranged by appointment.

Chippokes Plantation State Park
695 Chippokes Park Road,
Secondary Route 634 off Route 10 east,
Surry
(757) 294-3439, (757) 294-3625
The 1854 manor house at Chippokes Plantation State Park might be a welcome change from the Georgian architecture on which this part of Virginia prides itself. Formal gardens surround the house and contain one of the largest collections of crepe myrtles on the East Coast. This plantation, named after a Native American chief friendly to the settlers, has been continuously farmed for more than 370 years, which makes the model farm and the adjacent Farm and Forestry Museum a fitting part of the state park. There are biking and hiking trails, picnic shelters, a swimming pool, and fishing. Some folks on the Peninsula are unaware of the fine public swimming pool,

Party at the Plantation

You're going to have to work a little to get there, but if you like a festival that has something of an Old World feel to it, don't pass up Plantation Christmas at Chippokes in Surry County. This three-day event, which typically takes place the last weekend in October, offers a unique array of crafts, a diverse assortment of food, and some truly unusual entertainment.

A relatively new celebration (it was started in 1997), Plantation Christmas is a juried invitational crafts festival that delights visitors with original offerings. Exhibitors show handcrafted wares that range from 18th-century furniture reproductions, exquisite wooden vases, and hand-braided rugs to marionettes, wooden toys, and children's clothing. To create an inviting atmosphere, vendors' booths are set up along curving paths that either front the James River or encircle the Chippokes Plantation mansion (which also is open to festival visitors for tours).

Many craftspeople work their trades while selling their wares, and most are pleased to have visitors come up and ask questions. At a recent festival one particularly inquisitive seven-year-old not only helped swirl paint on a porcelain dish, she also attempted to compose a tune on a handcrafted hammer dulcimer.

Also contributing to its "place-out-of-time" feel, the festival hosts strolling musicians. The Stowehaven Strings, for instance, is a trio that walks the grounds throughout the event, pausing to play holiday and traditional entertainment on violins and viola, while the Colonial Christmas quartet wear traditional colonial garb and raise pints of "ale" as they serenade festivalgoers with 18th-century holiday music.

The food, too, is a bit unusual. While you still can purchase typical festival fare like Italian sausage and foot-long hot dogs, those with more adventuresome palates can sample vegetarian crepes, smoked turkey legs, sweet-potato fries, and peanut raisin pie. Our favorite taste treat: a buckwheat crepe brimming with spinach, mushrooms, and tomatoes, then slathered with a light basil-garlic sauce. (We recommend washing it down with the homemade mint iced tea sold at the same food booth.)

General admission to the festival is $5.00 for adults and children older than 10. Parking is free, and group rates are available. To get to the festival, board the Jamestown Ferry at Jamestown and take it to Scotland Wharf in Surry County. Upon debarking follow Route 31 to Route 10. Head east on Route 10, then follow Secondary Highway 634 (and the signs) to Chippokes Plantation State Park. For more information call (757) 294–3728.

but Insiders know that a day trip to swim here is well worth the effort. Swimming fees run about $2 to $4.

If you would like to lengthen your outdoor stay, the park also has 32 campsites with water and electrical hookups, plus additional primitive campsites. Camping is open from March through October and costs $24 a night for sites with water and electricity. If you prefer a less rugged stay, Chippokes also has three air-conditioned cabins. It's a good idea to make plans well in advance if you want to camp. To reserve a spot, call (800) 933-PARK, or go to the Virginia Department of Conservation's Web site at www.dcr.virginia.gov/state_parks/index.shtml.

The park is the site of the Steam and Gas Engine Show in June; the Pork, Peanut, and Pine Festival in July; and Halloween at Haunted Chippokes and the Plantation Christmas in late fall, all of which draw huge crowds from around the region for a variety of activities that primarily focus on food and fun. (For more on the Plantation Christmas celebration, please turn to the Close-up in this chapter.) The manor is open from 1:00 to 5:00 p.m. Saturday and Sunday in April and May. From June through August visitors can tour the house from 1:00 to 5:00 p.m. Wednesday through Sunday. Admission is $3.00 for adults and $1.50 for children 6 to 12. In April and May the Farm and Forestry Museum is open from 10:00 a.m. to 5:00 p.m. Saturday and Sunday. From June to August the hours are 10:00 a.m. to 5:00 p.m. Friday through Monday. Admission is $2 for adults and $1 for children 6 to 12. Parking in the manor and museum lot is $3 most weekends and $2 during the week and on Saturday and Sunday during the winter. Both the museum and manor house are open for group tours by special request. Since seasonal hours may vary, call ahead for an exact schedule.

Smith's Fort Plantation
Route 31, Thomas Rolfe Lane, Surry
(757) 294-3872
www.apva.org/smithsfort

You may be surprised to note that the Smith in the name of this historic plantation is none other than Captain John Smith, who built a fort on high land at nearby Gray's Creek in 1609 as protection for Jamestown, directly across the river. The land has other famous connections as well, having been part of Chief Powhatan's wedding gifts to Pocahontas and John Rolfe. The building currently on the site was built in 1765 and is considered a fine example of a Georgian brick manor house with its typical one and a half stories and central entrance. It can be toured Tuesday through Saturday from 10:00 a.m. to 4:00 p.m. and Sunday from noon to 4:00 p.m. Admission is $7 for adults, $5 for seniors, $4 for students 6 through 18, and free for children under 6. Tickets for both Bacon's Castle and Smith's Fort can be purchased for $10 (adults), $8 (seniors), or $6 (students). The manor is open on weekends only during November and is closed January through March.

S. Wallace Edwards & Sons
11381 Rolfe Highway (Route 31), Surry
(757) 294-3688, (800) 222-4267 (for mail order)
www.vatraditions.com

If you like ham, plan to stop in at S. Wallace Edwards & Sons, just down the street from the well-known Surrey House and the source of the ham served at the restaurant. For three generations the Edwards family has been creating some of the finest hams you can find anywhere in Virginia. Their smokehouse offers a fascinating glimpse into how the curing process, taught to settlers by Native Americans, has become a modern art. Each ham, selected for its high quality, is hand rubbed with a special dry cure then aged perfectly. A notable mahogany color is achieved with days of exposure to hickory smoke and supervised aging. While some long-cut hams are aged for a year, the company's most popular hams are ones that have aged between four and six months.

Edwards' hams have a wide following. The company has its own mail-order catalog and also receives orders from mail-order merchandisers like Williams-Sonoma, Harry & David, Winterthur, and Neiman-Marcus—especially during the busy holiday months. They won a top honor from Gourmet magazine in 2005, and every September those same hams capture blue ribbons at the state fair in Richmond. Surry's most famous pork products have even earned a stamp of approval from none other than celebrated chef and cookbook author Julia Child.

We recommend that you spend some time in the retail shop: Your taste buds will demand it. If you can't make it to Surry, check out Edwards' Virginia Ham Shoppe of Williamsburg, (757) 220-6618. Located at 1814 Richmond Road, it's open 9:00 a.m. to 9:00 p.m. seven days a week.

Restaurants

Surrey House Restaurant
11865 Rolfe Highway, Surry
(757) 294-3389
www.surreyhouserestaurant.com
Somehow it wouldn't seem right if you left Surry County without stopping in at the Surrey House Restaurant, a favorite destination for Williamsburg residents, especially on a sunny Sunday after church. Established in 1954, the Surrey House specializes in ham, seafood, pork, and poultry dishes as well as other regional fare—it's Southern cooking at its best! We recommend that you begin your meal with peanut soup, a creamy delicacy full of chunky bits of world-famous Virginia peanuts. As a main dish, the Surrey House Surf and Turf is typically Virginian, featuring a combination of a rib-eye steak and crab cakes. Other regional dishes include apple fritters, delicious ham hocks, great Southern fried chicken, and homemade desserts. For the latter, we prefer the peanut raisin pie, a proudly served local variation on the South's ubiquitous pecan pie. It's delicious. Entrees range from about $9 to $20. This restaurant has a waiting list on weekends and holidays, so we recommend reservations. Just tell them what ferry you'll arrive on, and they'll tailor your reservation to meet your arrival. The restaurant is open Tuesday to Sunday from 8:00 a.m. to 8:00 p.m. It is closed Monday.

SMITHFIELD

While you're over in Southside, you might want to head to Smithfield in Isle of Wight County, the true home of the world-famous Smithfield ham. While ham has placed Smithfield on the map in recent years, the town actually grew up around the trade and commerce that flourished on the Pagan River. Its rich past provides Smithfield with much to tempt the day-tripper. The city's charming downtown is a National Historic District, and the restored pre–Revolutionary War homes that line Main Street are a delight to behold. In recent years a downtown improvement project has added new brick sidewalks, old-fashioned street lamps, and attractive landscaping.

While Smithfield isn't exactly next door to Williamsburg, it's just down Route 10 from Bacon's Castle and Chippokes Plantation. Take the ferry to Scotland Wharf, then follow Route 31 to Route 10 in Surry County, where you'll turn left. Drive down this road for another 18 miles or so until you come to a stoplight. Turn left, and you'll be on Smithfield's Main Street. If you hit the ferry at the right time, the whole trip should take about 50 minutes. (One word of advice: As you approach Smithfield on Route 10, disregard the signs that direct you to the Smithfield business district. This is a roundabout route that takes you past the area's meatpacking plants. Following these directions, you'll reach downtown much more quickly.)

Smithfield and Isle of Wight Convention and Visitors Bureau
335 Main Street
(757) 357-5182, (800) 365-9339
www.smithfield-virginia.com
To start your visit, stop by the old Isle of Wight Courthouse and pick up brochures and a walking map from the county tourism bureau. The courthouse was built in 1750 and

is owned by the Association for the Preservation of Virginia Antiquities. If you follow the walking tour guide, you'll stroll past dozens of gorgeous old houses, actually a blend of 18th-century Colonial, Federal, Georgian, and Victorian period houses sitting side by side. There are more than 65 structures on the tour—and they really are within comfortable walking distance of one another—including the Oak Grove Academy at 204 Grace Street, which was built in 1836 as Oak Grove Academy for Young Ladies. You'll also see the Keitz-Mannion House at 344 South Church Street, which was erected in 1876 as the Methodist parsonage and was originally located across the street from where it now stands. Other points of interest are Smithfield Academy, 205 South Mason Street, once a private school for young men; and Christ Episcopal Church, 111 South Church Street, which was built in 1830. Its bell was said to have been tendered to the Confederate Ordnance Department in 1862 during the Civil War.

Isle of Wight County Museum
103 Main Street
(757) 357-7459

This museum, housed in a former bank built in 1913, offers archaeological displays that highlight county history. It features imported marble and tile and an impressive Tiffany-style dome skylight. Exhibits include Civil War displays, a video presentation on Isle of Wight County's past and present, and a country store, complete with old post office boxes, a potbellied stove, a checkerboard, and old pharmacy and hardware supplies. The newest addition to the museum is a fully furnished miniature colonial plantation house patterned after an existing plantation in Surry County. Other exhibits focus on Smithfield's famous meatpacking industry and archaeological digs that have been conducted throughout the county. The museum is open Tuesday through Saturday from 10:00 a.m. to 4:00 p.m. and Sunday from 1:00 to 5:00 p.m. Admission is free.

Fort Boykin Historic Park
7410 Fort Boykin Trail
(Secondary Highway 673)
(757) 357-5182, (800) 365-9339

Out in the country along the banks of the James River sits Fort Boykin Historic Park, which was created in 1623 to protect the settlers from Indians and raiding Spaniards. The fort, shaped in a seven-point star, has been involved in every major military campaign fought on American soil and still retains earthworks dating from the Civil War. According to legend, the guns of Fort Boykin sunk two British men-of-war in 1813. A gazebo overlooks the river, and a picnic area is available. The fort is a tad off the beaten path, so your best bet is to pick up a brochure and map at the Smithfield Convention and Visitors Bureau. Its regular hours are 8:00 a.m. to dusk seven days a week. Admission is free.

Saint Luke's Shrine
14477 Benns Church Boulevard
(Route 10)
(757) 357-3367
www.historicstlukes.org

As you leave town and head about 2 miles east on Route 10, you'll come to Saint Luke's Shrine. Built in 1632 and nicknamed "Old Brick," this Episcopal church is the country's only original Gothic church and the oldest church of English foundation in America. The church features its original traceried windows, stepped gables, and a rare mid-17th-century communion table. Since 1957 Saint Luke's has been home to the oldest intact English organ in America. Constructed circa 1630, the organ recently had its beautifully painted doors restored. This National Shrine is open Tuesday through Saturday from 10:00 a.m. to 4:00 p.m. and Sunday from 1:00 to 4:00 p.m. The shrine is closed during January; admission is free.

Restaurants

C. W. Cowling's
1278 Smithfield Plaza
(757) 357-0044

Located in a shopping center just east of downtown, Cowling's has everything for lunch and dinner, from Cajun specialties and seafood pasta dishes to fajitas, steaks, chicken, and ribs. A variety of burgers and sandwiches—from catfish to chili cheese dogs—round out the menu. Dinners range from $7 to $16. A kids' menu has a number of options—all for less than $5—and desserts include such temptations as fried apple pie and a chocolate peanut butter pie topped with whipped butter frosting. Cowling's is open seven days a week.

Ken's Bar-B-Q
Route 258
(757) 357-5601

Ken's is a popular and friendly roadside restaurant that serves up great barbecue and ribs. If you love beef, the pit-cooked steaks are a good choice and come in regular and large sizes (for the heartier appetite). But even if you order the regular size, portions are huge and prices reasonable (an average entree is less than $10). Ken's is open 11:00 a.m. to 9:00 p.m. Tuesday through Friday, 8:00 a.m. to 9:00 p.m. Saturday, and 8:00 a.m. to 8:00 p.m. Sunday.

Smithfield Confectionery
& Ice Cream Parlor
208 Main Street
(757) 357-6166

A family-run business since 1982, this old-fashioned ice-cream shop sells subs, deli sandwiches, salads, and, of course, ice-cream dishes. Belly up to the traditional soda fountain counter and please your palate with a banana split or triple scoop of chocolate chip mint. If you'd like to chow down on a sandwich or salad instead, you can expect prices to run from $3 to $7. The shop is open 9:00 a.m. to 7:00 p.m. Monday through Saturday and 11:30 a.m. to 5:00 p.m. Sunday.

Smithfield Gourmet Bakery and Cafe
218 Main Street
(757) 357-0045

Since the spring of 1993, this delightful little eatery has served up tasty and unusual sandwiches to an adoring public. All breads are Smithfield Gourmet recipes, baked fresh daily. Cold pasta dishes and salads also are served. A variety of fresh-baked items—cookies, pies, cinnamon rolls, muffins, and a cake of the day—are available. Cheesecakes, in just about any flavor imaginable, are a house specialty. The cafe is open from 8:00 a.m. to 5:00 p.m. Monday through Saturday and 9:00 a.m. to 5:00 p.m. Sunday.

The Smithfield Inn & Tavern
112 Main Street
(757) 357-1752
www.smithfieldinn.com

This elegant dining spot in the heart of downtown Smithfield was built in 1752. Fine food—seafood, pork, lamb, beef, and chicken—is served in an atmosphere of candlelight, flocked wallpaper, and crisp linens. Entrees run $18 or more, and lunch is served Monday through Sunday from 11:30 a.m. to 3:00 p.m., dinner Tuesday through Saturday, from 5:30 to 9:00 p.m. Reservations are advised. There's also a tavern that serves appetizers and light fare, open from 4:00 p.m. to 10:00 p.m. Monday through Thursday, and until 11:00 p.m. on Friday and Saturday.

Smithfield Station
415 South Church Street
(757) 357-7700
www.smithfieldstation.com

A popular destination for boaters, Smithfield Station is one of our favorite haunts. It sits at the foot of a small bridge overlooking the Pagan River. The restaurant serves seafood, pork, pasta, and daily specials for lunch and dinner (entree prices start at about $19). We especially like the house salad, which is prepared with a slightly sweet Italian-style dressing and baby shrimp. The stuffed flounder also comes highly recommended. After dining, stroll out on the deck that surrounds the restaurant and connects it to the marina or mosey along the boardwalk. Hours are 11:00

a.m. to 9:00 p.m. Monday to Saturday, and a Sunday brunch is served from 8:00 a.m. to 12:00 p.m.

TANGIER ISLAND

http://tangierisland-va.com

An excursion to fancifully named Tangier Island makes for an enjoyable day trip from Williamsburg. It was Captain John Smith who chartered this remote island in 1607, naming it for the Moroccan region he thought it resembled. Twenty miles from the mainland and only 1 mile wide by 3.5 miles long, Tangier Island actually is part of Accomack County on the Eastern Shore.

During the Revolutionary War the British used Tangier as a base for raiding American ships. Pirates also frequented the island, finding it a great hideaway from enemies. After the war the island's population began to swell as more and more people settled down for the long haul and began working the Bay. Today, Tangier Island is home to some 700 inhabitants, most of whom rely on the Chesapeake Bay for a living. You'll hear the accents of 17th-century Elizabethan English here, as isolated residents have retained some of their ancestors' ways of speaking.

A variety of boats will get you to Tangier Island. The *Captain Eulice Tangier* passenger ferry leaves Onancock, Virginia, at 10:00 a.m. daily from Memorial Day to October 15. Tickets are $25 for adults and $13 for children 6 through 12 (no credit cards are accepted). Call (804) 453-4434 for information and tickets. If by chance you want to take this trip from Maryland's eastern shore, the *Steven Thomas*, a 300-passenger ship with an air-conditioned cabin and snack bar, leaves from Crisfield, Maryland, at 12:30 p.m. daily from May 15 through mid-October. Tickets are $25 per person. Call (800) 863-2338 for information.

As you approach the dock via the water, take the time to look around you. You will see dozens of crab farms, neat little sheds rising above the water on stilts. In small wooden pens inside these farms, crabbers hoard their catch until the crustaceans have molted and can be sold as soft-shell crabs. The work is tedious, as the pens must be checked every three hours around the clock throughout the entire season. A missed "peeler," as the soft-shells are called, turns into a quick meal for fellow captives.

Once on the island, you will have several hours to sightsee, take a golf cart or bike tour (there are only a handful of cars on the island), and grab lunch before it's time for departure. The island's pathways lead past charming white frame houses, and you'll probably notice only one school, which serves about 170 youngsters from kindergarten through high school.

Restaurants

Hilda Crockett's Chesapeake House (757) 891-2331

When you start hunting down a place for lunch, you'll find your choices are limited. But as long as you like seafood, you can't go wrong trying out Hilda's, which serves an all-you-can-eat breakfast, then a family-style lunch and dinner with crab cakes, clam fritters, Virginia ham, vegetables, potato salad, coleslaw, applesauce, homemade rolls, pound cake, and endless refills of iced tea. Breakfast is served from 7:00 to 9:00 a.m. for $7 per person. Lunch begins at 11:30 a.m., the last seating for dinner is at 5:00 p.m., and either meal costs $19 per person, $10 for children 6 to 12, and $5 for children under 5. The restaurant is closed November through April 15.

SMITH ISLAND

www.smithisland.org

Smith Island in the Chesapeake Bay is actually a chain of marshy islands with a fascinating history. Pirates once hid their boats in the tricky waters surrounding this archipelago, waiting to raid passing ships. Dissenters from the Jamestown colony settled here, eventually forming the three villages of Ewell, Rhodes Point, and Tylerton. Today, Ewell, the island's largest town, is sometimes referred to as its capital. Here, commercial fishermen catch hard- and soft-shell crabs and send them to the mainland to serve markets throughout the world. Life for these islanders is often harsh but is guided by a strong religious faith. Joshua Thomas established the Methodist church here and on several other Chesapeake Bay islands during the late 1800s; it continues to be the only organized religion on the island today.

Once you get to the island, go to the Smith Island Center, (410) 425-3351, and ask for a copy of the brochure describing the island. The pamphlet includes a detailed self-guided walking tour of Ewell, along with maps, historical information, and important tips on island etiquette (for example, the island is dry, meaning islanders don't appreciate public consumption of alcohol). At the center you can watch a 20-minute film featuring the people of Smith Island and view a number of exhibits on the history, environment, watermen, women, and church. Admission to the center, which is open from noon to 4:00 p.m. daily May through October, is $2.50 for those 13 and older; younger children enter free. Cruises to Smith Island leave from the Chesapeake Bay/Smith Island KOA Campground in the Smith's Point area of Reedsville. To reach the KOA from Williamsburg, take the Colonial Parkway east to Yorktown. Follow U.S. Route 17 north to Saluda, then Route 33 to Route 3 and Kilmarnock. From here follow Route 200 north to U.S. Route 360, which leads to Route 652. Go east on Route 652 until it becomes Route 644, then turn northeast on Route 650. It sounds complicated, but signs for the Smith Island cruise provide adequate directions. The drive takes about an hour and 45 minutes.

The cruise, aboard the Captain Evans, leaves the dock at 10:00 a.m. and pulls in at Ewell around 11:30 a.m., allowing visitors several hours to roam at will and grab lunch before departing around 2:00 p.m. or so. Current round-trip rates for the Smith Island cruise are $25 for adults and $13 for children

3 to 12. Children younger than 3 ride free. Reservations are required; for more information call (804) 453-3430.

If you decide to spend the night in one of the campground's 11 rustic, air-conditioned cabins, you'll have access to a swimming pool and pavilion, a bathhouse with private showers, canoe and bike rentals, and a number of planned weekend activities, including hayrides, lollipop hunts, pet shows, and crab races for the kids. Cabin rental rates start at $40 for a cabin for two. KOA discounts apply. For more information about the campground, call (804) 453-3430.

Once you arrive, the main attraction, of course, is the island itself. The leisurely pace of life here is a welcome change from the hustle and bustle of mainland existence. This is a place where you can put your feet up on a back porch railing and enjoy the soft breezes off the Chesapeake Bay. If it's spring, you might catch the fragrance of blossoming fig, pear, mimosa, and pomegranate trees, which grow in all of the island's towns.

Once you're rested, there is plenty to do and see. A walking tour of Ewell will take you past Cape Cod–style homes, rustic country stores, and the sunken remains of the Island Belle I, one of the earliest island ferries. Goat Island, across Levering Creek, is home to a herd of about 20 formerly domestic goats. Natives rely on the goats' migration to the water's edge to obtain salt from the marsh grasses as a sign that rain or snow is imminent. Other attractions include Pitchcroft, the island's first settlement, and the wooden keel remains of the 60-foot bugeye sailboat C. S. Tyler, built for islander Willie A. Evans.

You can also tour, by foot or bicycle, Rhodes Point, the island's center for boat repair. This small town originally was called Rogue's Point because of the pirates who frequented the area. Here you'll see boats being made and repaired and see the ruins of some of the earlier vessels that plied their trade on the Bay.

During your visit you also may notice how friendly everyone seems. Islanders in cars and trucks honk their horns and wave to greet every vehicle and pedestrian they meet. This hospitality also is extended to a hefty population of stray cats, which seem to be everywhere, but look especially well fed and comfortable despite their rather nomadic existence.

Restaurants

Bayside Inn
4065 Smith Island Road
(410) 425-2771
Located on Ewell's Harbor, this charming restaurant serves up a bountiful buffet from 11:00 a.m. to 4:00 p.m. daily. A typical menu includes a vegetable crab soup, crab cakes, baked ham, clam fritters, baked corn pudding, stewed tomatoes, macaroni salad, coleslaw, homemade rolls, iced tea, and homemade pie.

Ruke's Seafood Deck
Caleb Jones Road
(410) 425-2311
This very casual eatery is open seven days a week in the summer for lunch and dinner. Choose from crab cakes, soft-shell crabs, and a few other sandwiches. Your meal will be served on a screened-in deck. Payment policy is cash only, and you can expect a seafood platter to cost about $10. Ruke's closes at 4:30 p.m. every day except Saturday, when it's open until 11:00 p.m.

RICHMOND

The Old Dominion's capital certainly is worth a day of your time, particularly if you are a Civil or Revolutionary War buff or someone who enjoys the beauty of a large Southern city. The architecture here is splendid to behold. Trees and parks are everywhere, and an abundance of street festivals, outdoor concerts, garden and flower shows, and cultural events can keep you busy throughout the year. Although Richmond is well-known for its significant role in the unfolding of American history, you may not know that the city was the site of America's first hospital, built in 1611. Richmond was where military "aircraft" (tethered balloons actually) first were used for aerial reconnaissance during the Civil War. Richmond was chosen as the second home of the Confederacy, which Confederates liked because of its proximity to Washington. Richmond was home to the first electric streetcar in 1888, and it was where Dupont produced its first cellophane in 1930. And, the first beer to be packaged in tin-plated steel cans (Krueger Ale of Newark) was test-marketed here in 1935. But there's much, much more to the Old Dominion's capital than this.

Richmond truly is an inspired city, architecturally speaking, and no place illustrates this better than the famed Fan District. Named for the layout of its streets, which fan out toward the western part of town, the Fan is a historic district composed of Victorian-era homes, most of which have been renovated. This is the kind of neighborhood you should explore on foot, especially if you appreciate architectural beauty and urban gardens. Shops and restaurants abound here as well as some unusual art galleries. The Fan is bordered by Monument Avenue, a broad, tree-lined promenade marked with statues of notables such as Stonewall Jackson, Robert E. Lee, and Arthur Ashe. Another slice of Richmond life is Shockoe Slip, a quaint riverside area of downtown Richmond that bustles with restaurants and unusual boutiques. Between Twelfth and Fourteenth Streets on East Cary Street, Shockoe Slip is the cobblestone warehouse district of old Richmond, with many structures dating back a century or more.

In recent years, Richmond has been sprucing up its riverfront. In the spring of 1999, the George Washington Canal opened. Visitors can tour the restored canal waterways (which flow into the James River) on bateaux-like boats that seat 8 to 10 people. The opening of the canal is just one phase of long-range plans that call for walkways, hotels, shops, and boutiques to enhance a 1-mile riverfront corridor from the historic Tredegar Iron Works site east to Seventh Street.

The quickest way to reach Richmond from Williamsburg is to head west on Interstate 64 and keep going for about 50 miles. As you approach the city, take the Fifth Street exit to Broad Street and begin your city tour at that point. If you'd rather meander a bit and take the scenic route (which is what we advise), hop on historic Route 5 and wander along this two-lane road through James City, Charles City, and Henrico Counties. The speed limit on this road is lower than on the interstate, so the drive will take you a bit longer, but you'll wind past stately old homes and historic plantations. In fact, this old road, which at points is shaded by overhanging trees, is reminiscent of byways familiar to travelers from an earlier era. Route 5 eventually will intersect with Broad Street, and you can proceed from there.

The places below are just a few of our favorite places in the capital city. For more information on the area, check out the Web site www.richmondva.org, or pick up a copy of the *Insiders' Guide to Richmond*.

Richmond Metro Convention and Visitors Bureau
401 North Third Street
Richmond, VA 23219
(804) 782-2777, (888) RICHMOND
www.visit.richmond.com
Before you arrive you may want to orient yourself to Richmond's wonderful museums, historic neighborhoods, and excellent restaurants. If so, call ahead or write to the visitors bureau and ask for brochures, a map, and information on key points of interest. Or, if you prefer to wait until you actually arrive in town (what a free spirit!), stop in at the Richmond Metro Visitors Bureau off Interstate 95 at Third and Clay Streets for literature and assistance. This center, one of three in the city, is open daily from 9:00 a.m. to 5:00 p.m.

Attractions

Agecroft Hall
4305 Sulgrave Road
(804) 353-4241
www.agecrofthall.com

Originally built in England more than 500 years ago, Agecroft Hall was moved to Richmond and reconstructed brick by brick in the 1920s. Situated on 23 acres overlooking the James River, this Tudor estate is a wonderful example of pre-Elizabethan architecture. Inside you will find period furniture, tapestries, everyday objects from the 16th and 17th centuries, and British military artifacts. Outside, the grounds and gardens are gorgeous to behold. A gift shop on the premises offers items with a decidedly British flair: everything from books on the gardens of the era to Shakespeare T-shirts and Henry VIII mouse pads. Agecroft is open Tuesday through Saturday from 10:00 a.m. to 4:00 p.m. and Sunday from 12:30 to 5:00 p.m. Admission is $7 for adults, $6 for seniors, and $4 for students. Admission includes an introductory film and a guided tour of the house. The garden tour is self-guided.

Children's Museum of Richmond (CMOR)
2626 West Broad Street
(804) 474-CMOR, (877) 295-CMOR
www.c-mor.org
If you have youngsters along, you'll want to spend a few hours at this popular kids' hangout, which expanded early in 2000, moving to exciting new quarters adjacent to the Science Museum of Virginia. Indeed, we would rank this as a must-do on your itinerary if you have children of any age. (The museum is geared for kids 6 months to 12 years.) CMOR offers 42,000 square feet of hands-on exhibits, environmental discovery settings, and interactive artworks and sculpture. Exhibits are divided into eight different learning environments plus a 6,000-square-foot outdoor learning garden, multiuse classroom and lab facilities, and changing gallery. To make certain young visitors are getting a well-rounded taste of what the world has to offer, the museum melds the arts, sciences, humanities, technology, and the environment in a multidimensional learning experience. Start off with an interactive CMOR Machine, view an artist's demonstration, relax by a stream, or join a parade. "How

It Works" allows children to help operate solar collectors in its sky cube. In "Our Great Outdoors," kids can work off some of their energy by climbing to the treetops and settling into an eagle's nest that is roomy enough for 10!

If you want to check out CMOR, stop in from 9:30 a.m. to 5:00 p.m. Tuesday through Saturday or from noon to 5:00 p.m. on Sunday. The museum is open weekday hours on Monday between Memorial Day and Labor Day and on holidays that fall on Monday throughout the school year. General admission is $7 ($4 after 4:00 p.m.), with infants under 1 year admitted free. Seniors receive $1 off the admission price. There is plenty of free parking adjacent to the museum.

Edgar Allan Poe Museum
1914 East Main Street
(804) 648-5523, (888) 21E-APOE
www.poemuseum.org

The Poe Museum, which actually occupies five small buildings, pays tribute to the life and career of the famous writer, a native son of Richmond who was born in 1809 and died just 40 years later. At the center of the museum is Richmond's oldest structure, the Old Stone House, built circa 1737. Behind the Old Stone House lies the Enchanted Garden, awash in the color of the flowers and plants favored by Poe during his lifetime. The museum documents Poe's accomplishments with pictures, relics, and, of course, verse. A museum shop sells books, prints, postcards, and T-shirts. The museum is open Tuesday through Saturday from 10:00 a.m. to 5:00 p.m. and Sunday from 11:00 a.m. to 5:00 p.m. It is closed Christmas Day. Admission is $6 for adults, $5 for senior citizens and students; children younger than 8 are admitted free.

Lewis Ginter Botanical Gardens
1800 Lakeside Avenue
(804) 262-9887
www.lewisginter.org

At Richmond's celebrated botanical gardens, spring is always in the air. And no wonder! Something is always blooming in the 15 acres of gardens here. Displays include one of the most diverse perennial gardens on the East Coast, an elegant Victorian garden, an Asian garden, and a children's garden. When you have completed your tour, a gift shop and the Garden Cafe are open in the visitor center for your shopping and dining pleasure. Or, if you prefer, you can enjoy a light meal in the Robins Tea House, which overlooks a lake and the gardens and is open daily from 11:30 a.m. to 2:30 p.m. The gardens themselves are open daily from 9:00 a.m. to 5:00 p.m. with extended hours on Thursday in April and July through September. Admission is $10 for adults, $9 for seniors over 55, and $6 for children 3 through 12.

Maymont
2201 Shields Lake Drive
(804) 358-7166
www.maymont.org

If you haven't had your fill of flowers (does anyone ever?), then check out this fabulous, turn-of-the-20th-century estate, which is adorned with 100 acres of Japanese, Italian, English, and herb gardens. Maymont House, the restored Victorian mansion on the premises, overlooks the James River and is decked out in opulent Gilded Age finery. Also in Maymont's parklike setting are a nature center that opened in 1999, wildlife habitats, and a children's farm and carriage collection.

The 25,000-square-foot nature and visitor center features a 20-foot waterfall and 13 aquariums filled with river otters, fish, and turtles. Programs abound for young and old alike. Recent offerings for the young ones ranged from "One Fish, Two Fish," which blends hands-on fun with math and fish, to "If You Please: The Lost Art of Good Manners." Adults also have a variety of choices, including breakfast garden walks and craft workshops. A popular music series, Musical Mondays, brings community ensembles to Maymont for free weekly family concerts in the summer.

The grounds, gardens, and visitor center are open daily from 10:00 a.m. to 5:00 p.m., while exhibits in the Maymont House, the nature center, and children's barn are on view from noon to 5:00 p.m. Tuesday through Sunday. Weather permitting, you can catch a ride on the Maymont Tram, which runs every 20 minutes, for $3, $2 for children.

Maymont also offers carriage rides from noon to 4:00 p.m. Sunday. The cost is $3 for adults, and $2 for children. From June through August you can step back in time with an old-fashioned hayride. If the weather is nice, the hayrides run from noon to 4:00 p.m. Saturday and Sunday. The cost is $3 for adults and $2 for the younger riders.

Although there is no admission fee, suggested $5 donations for Maymont House and the nature center are graciously accepted. Special programs charge an additional fee and most require advance registration.

Museum and White House of the Confederacy
1201 East Clay Street
(804) 649-1861
www.moc.org

For more on the War Between the States, schedule a visit to this museum and house, home of Confederate President Jefferson Davis from 1861 to 1865. Deemed "perhaps the finest Civil War museum in the country" by the *Chicago Tribune*, the museum houses the world's most comprehensive collection of Confederate artifacts, including more than 500 flags from the Confederate army, navy, and government; Robert E. Lee's Appomattox sword and personal items from his field headquarters; and the plumed hat of J. E. B. Stuart, the Confederacy's most famous cavalryman. Here you also will find General Stonewall Jackson's sword, epaulets, and death mask; and the revered painting *The Last Meeting of Lee and Jackson,* arguably an icon of the Old South.

.A new permanent display at the museum, "African Americans in Confederate Service," examines the roles played by African Americans in the Southern army during the Civil War. The display includes a collection of arti-

facts, photographs, and documents. Before you go, you might want to check out the Haversack store, where you can pick up unique gift items ranging from pewter cups to wooden toys reminiscent of the 19th century.

The White House, located on a hill overlooking Shockoe Valley, is a gray stuccoed mansion that has graced Richmond's historic Court End neighborhood with its presence since 1818. Besides being the home of Jefferson Davis, the White House functioned as the social, political, and military center of the Confederacy. Thanks to extensive restoration efforts, it looks much as it did in the mid-19th century.

Both the museum and the White House are open from 10:00 a.m. to 5:00 p.m. Monday through Saturday and noon to 5:00 p.m. Sunday. Admission to the museum is $8 for adults, $7 for seniors, and $4 for children 7 to 13. White House fees are the same rates. If you have time and would like to save a few dollars, invest in the block ticket for both attractions. Adults gain entry into the museum and get a guided tour of the house for $11. It's $10 for senior citizens and $6 for children 7 to 13. Those younger than 7 are admitted free.

Paramount's Kings Dominion
16000 Theme Park Way, Doswell
(804) 876-5000
www.kingsdominion.com

It's not exactly in Richmond, and we wouldn't advise planning a day trip that included both an amusement park and a major city, but if you have a whole day to spare and are in search of an amusement park, this is a good one. Located 23 miles north of Richmond on I–95 near Ashland, Kings Dominion, which opens daily June through August and on weekends during much of the spring and fall, offers more than a hundred rides and attractions.

The granddaddy of them all is the Hyper-Sonic XLC, the eleventh roller coaster in this 400-acre theme park. Billed as the "world's first air-launched coaster," the HyperSonic rockets its riders 165 feet straight up, reaching a top speed of 80 mph. But, what goes up, comes straight back down—165 feet at a 90-degree angle, creating the ultimate in free-fall sensation.

Also opening in 2001 was 7th Portal, a 3-D ride simulator based on the popular animated online superhero series of the same name. Water World added three new rides in 2007: Tidal Wave Bay, Tornado, and Zoom Flume. You can also dip into the 650,000-gallon wave pool, experience the fun-house effects of Surf City Splat House, or ride the tubes in Pipeline Peak. (There's no extra charge to Water World, but you will want to bring your bathing suit.)

Meanwhile, back on dry land, more coaster fun awaits. There's Volcano; The Blast Coaster, called the fastest suspended roller coaster; and an indoor coaster, The Outer Limits: Flight of Fear, which twists you through 25 compound horizontal curves in complete darkness. And that's just the beginning. There are also rides with names like Grizzly, Anaconda, Shockwave, Hurler, and the classic wooden coaster, Rebel Yell. The younger set can join in the excitement over in KidZville, with Taxi Jam, billed as a young child's first coaster. And, of course, there's Nickelodeon Central with a plethora of interactive shows, attractions, food, and fun.

To get to the park from Williamsburg, take I–64 west to Interstate 295 west to I–95 north. Get off at exit 98. Admission to the park is $51.95 for visitors 3 to 62, $29.95 for seniors or those under age 3.

Richmond National Battlefield Park
Civil War Visitor Center at Tredegar Iron Works
Fifth and Tredegar Streets
Richmond Canal Walk
(804) 226-1981

Located at the site of the largest Southern hospital during the Civil War, this is the perfect first stop for military enthusiasts. The center, which is free and open daily, has three floors of exhibits, a film, and knowledgeable employees to guide you toward the city's

numerous battlefields and their visitor centers. The National Battlefield Park contains 10 park units that offer one-of-a-kind insights into this tragic period of American history. Make sure you ask about the battle sites, cemeteries, and markers east of downtown Richmond in Chesterfield, Hanover, and Henrico Counties. Specific Civil War sites from 1862 include the Chickahominy Bluff, Beaver Dam Creek, Gaines Mill, and Malvern Hill. The 1864 sites include Cold Harbor and Fort Harrison. The center is open daily from 9:00 a.m. to 5:00 p.m. All activities are free.

Science Museum of Virginia
2500 West Broad Street
(804) 864-1400, (800) 659-1727
www.smv.org

Another popular destination for the young and young-at-heart is Richmond's science museum, which offers hands-on fun in everything from aerospace and astronomy to chemistry, crystals, and computers. Housed in the old Broad Street Train Station, the museum contains more than 250 exhibits as well as an IMAX theater that features both films and planetarium shows. The museum has "expanded beyond its walls" with the restoration of the historic butterfly train canopies and four railroad tracks. Future plans also call for the renovation of a 1918 streetcar that will carry visitors on a loop around its Discover Park. For now, however, there is more than enough to keep young minds racing, especially in Cosmic Corner, Lunar Landing, and Zoomzone, an activity area where kids try out some of the fun things they have watched on the PBS show Zoom.

The museum is open Monday through Saturday from 9:00 a.m. to 5:30 p.m. and Sunday 11:30 a.m. to 5:00 p.m. The IMAX Dome theater and planetarium are open until 9:00 p.m. Friday and Saturday. Admission is $10.00 for the museum, $8.50 for the film only, and $17.50 for a combination ticket for anyone 13 to 59. For seniors 60 and older, the cost is $9.00 for the museum, $8.50 for the film, and $16.50 for both; for children 4 to 12, the cost is $9.00 for the exhibits, $8.50 for the film, and $16.50 for both. Planetarium shows are included in the exhibit fee.

Valentine Richmond History Center
1015 East Clay Street
(804) 649-0711
http://richmondhistorycenter.com

The Valentine collects, preserves, and interprets the life and history of Richmond through its permanent and changing exhibits and innovative programming. Founded in 1892, the Valentine maintains the South's largest collections of costumes and textiles as well as extensive holdings in photos, documents, industrial artifacts, and decorative arts.

If you get hungry, the Valentine also offers a garden cafe, or if you are looking for a special gift, the museum shop sells everything from books and jewelry to unusual children's items. The museum is open Tuesday through Saturday from 10:00 a.m. to 5:00 p.m. and Sunday from noon to 5:00 p.m. Admission is $10 for adults, $7 for students and seniors, $7 for children 4 to 18. Children under 4 are admitted free.

Virginia Museum of Fine Arts
2800 Grove Avenue
(804) 340-1400
www.vmfa.state.va.us

This is one Richmond attraction you shouldn't miss. This first-rate museum showcases 5,000 years of mankind's artistic achievements. The museum's gallery holds the largest public collection of Fabergé items outside Russia, including five imperial Easter eggs, as well as outstanding collections of art nouveau, art deco, India art, contemporary impressionists, and British sporting art. Artists you will see represented on the museum's walls include Monet, Renoir, Degas, Picasso, and Warhol. Here you also will find treasures from ancient Egypt, Greece, and Rome, as well as an abundance of medieval and Renaissance art.

Beginning in 2005, the museum embarked on a $122 million expansion that will add 165,000 square feet to the 320,000 existing structure, and will make it easier to navigate the gallery space. The project is expected to be completed in mid-2009, but until then, some galleries and exhibits may be moved or temporarily closed. Call or check the Web site for the most current information.

If you would like to catch a bite to eat, there are two cafes, one located in the museum's impressive Sculpture Garden. The dining is casual in the Arts Cafe and Cappuccino Bar.

There is also an on-site gift shop. Museum galleries are open from Wednesday through Sunday 11:00 a.m. to 5:00 p.m. A donation of $5 is suggested. Additional fees are charged for occasional special exhibitions.

Restaurants

Deciding where to eat is a delicious quandary in Richmond. Whether you're in the Fan District, Carytown, Shockoe Bottom, or near Virginia Commonwealth University, you'll find plenty of places that serve great food. We hit a few of the high points here.

Border Chophouse & Bar
1501 West Main Street
(804) 355-2907
www.borderchophouse.com

You want a steak, you go to the Chophouse, where high-quality meats are hand cut daily. Favorites include pork chops, blackened portobello cheesesteak, and a New York strip sandwich. As a side dish try a bowl of the Chophouse chili. Entrees range from about $10 to $25; sandwiches and salads start at about $5. The Chophouse is open seven days a week for lunch and dinner.

Cabo's Corner Bistro
2053 West Broad Street
(804) 355-1144
www.cabosbistro.com

With its eclectic menu, nightly live music, and extensive wine list, Cabo's truly does have something for everyone. House specialties include a number of steak, seafood, and pasta dishes (entrees range from $15 to $25).

Cabo's is open for dinner Tuesday through Saturday.

Crab Louie's Seafood Tavern
13502 Sycamore Square
Shopping Center
(804) 275-2722
www.crablouies.com

A popular destination for locals since 1981, Crab Louie's is the perfect place for a luncheon or dinner celebration. Located in the historic Sycamore House, this seafood restaurant serves great she-crab chowder, crab cakes, and homemade breads and relishes. With old wooden floors and a decor featuring antiques, Crab Louie's is a step back in time. The average cost of an entree is about $20. Lunch is served daily from 11:30 a.m. to 4:00 p.m. Dinner is offered from 4:00 to 10:00 p.m.

Europa
1409 East Cary Street
(804) 643-0911
www.europarichmond.com

If you're in the mood for something a little different, slip into Europa in Richmond's historic Shockoe Slip. The innovative menu here features Mediterranean dishes, including a large selection of Spanish tapas and the traditional Spanish dish paella served up in a variety of ways. Entrees range from $15 to the low $20s. The wine list is both exotic and long, and you have a choice of two distinctly different seating areas: the lively upstairs or the quieter downstairs Bodegas Room. Lunch is served at Europa from 11:30 a.m. to 2:30 p.m. Monday through Friday. Dinner hours are 5:30 to 10:00 p.m. Sunday through Thursday and 5:30 to 11:00 p.m. Friday and Saturday. There's a DJ on Thursday, Friday, and Saturday.

Joe's Inn
205 North Shields Avenue
(804) 355-2282
www.joesinn.com

Since 1952, Joe's Inn has been a perennial favorite with locals, serving up generous portions of a variety of American and Greek food. The dress code is casual, the atmosphere is friendly, and, with most dishes running less than $10, the price is right. Drop in anytime. Joe's serves breakfast, lunch, and dinner.

Sam Miller's Warehouse Restaurant
1210 East Cary Street
(804) 644-5465
www.sammillers.com

Pretty much a Richmond institution, Sam Miller's offers a clublike setting where patrons can enjoy Chesapeake Bay seafood, Maine lobsters, prime rib, and other fresh-cut beef dinners for between $20 and $40 per entree. The restaurant, located in a historic building dating from 1850, is open daily for lunch and dinner.

The Tobacco Company
1202 East Cary Street
(804) 782-9555
www.thetobaccocompany.com

This historic restaurant, located in a former tobacco warehouse in Shockoe Slip, has been serving up a varied menu of hand-cut steaks, veal, fresh seafood, and chef specials since 1977. The slow-roasted prime rib of beef has been a house special for the past 19 years. It's no wonder this dish has been a favorite for hearty eaters. Seconds are served on the house. Expect to pay between $20 and $30 for a dinner entree here. A lunch menu is offered on the first floor from 11:30 a.m. to 2:30 p.m. Monday through Saturday. Dinner is served from 5:30 to 10:00 p.m. Monday through Thursday, from 5:00 to 10:30 p.m. Friday and Saturday, and from 5:30 to 9:30 p.m. Sunday. The Tobacco Company also has a tasty brunch on Saturday and Sunday from 11:00 a.m. to 2:30 p.m.

NORFOLK

On the eastern edge of Hampton Roads in the world's largest natural harbor, Norfolk has been a sailors' city for more than 200 years. Norfolk Naval Base is the world's largest navy base, and the numerous posts and bases that support it have been a temporary home to thousands of men and women over the years, particularly during World War II. While Uncle Sam has always played a key role in the city's economy and demographics, Norfolk also serves as the region's financial hub: Within a 2-block radius of downtown Norfolk are the Hampton Roads headquarters for all of the state's major banks. But business often takes a backseat to culture, as Norfolk also is home to the area's four dominant arts organizations: the Virginia Stage Company, the Virginia Symphony, the Virginia Opera, and the Chrysler Museum. (See the Nightlife chapter for more information.)

During the past 15 years or so, the city has undergone a renaissance of sorts, transforming a decaying waterfront into an attractive gathering spot with the addition of the Waterside Festival Marketplace and new hotels, parks, and office buildings.

Although Williamsburg residents tend to turn toward Richmond for employment and for large-city conveniences, many residents commute to Norfolk for jobs, and still others make the trip for an evening out.

The approach to Norfolk from the Historic Triangle is stunning by any criteria: I-64 moves out over the mouth of Hampton Roads on a bridge-tunnel that affords a breathtaking view of the harbor and the navy base on the far shore. To get downtown once you've crossed the water, follow I-64 to Interstate 264 west, then take I-264 until it becomes Waterside Drive. The Waterside Festival Marketplace will be on your left, and parking will be to your right. If you're feeling adventuresome or just want to see a little more of Norfolk, an alternate—and more direct—route is to take the Granby Street exit from I-64, then follow Granby Street (a six-lane highway for much of the drive) through the neighborhoods of Norfolk until Monticello Avenue splits off to the right. Follow Monticello downtown. Several downtown garages offer public parking.

The drive takes about an hour from Williamsburg, longer if traffic is backed up at the tunnel—a frequent occurrence during rush hour, on summer weekends, and on holidays. Signs along the interstate refer travelers to a radio band for traffic advisories well before the tunnel, and an alternate route to Southside via the James River Bridge is marked with checkered attachments to highway signs. Interstate 664, which also spans the James River via a tunnel and a bridge, is a scenic—though somewhat roundabout—route into Norfolk.

There are special times of year when a trip to Norfolk has added interest. In late April through early May, the Virginia Arts Festival brings world-class music, dance, theater, and visual arts to the Norfolk waterfront; the late-April International Azalea Festival is staged amid the blossoms at Norfolk Botanical Garden; and, during the first weekend in June, you can join a crowd of thousands for Norfolk's annual Harborfest celebration, which brings music, food, and entertainment to the downtown waterfront for three days of fun in the sun. For more on these festivities, turn to the Annual Events chapter.

Before venturing south to Norfolk, you may want to pick up a copy of the *Insiders' Guide to Virginia's Chesapeake Bay* for more detailed listings of restaurants, accommodations, and attractions. (Or you may want to purchase the *Insiders' Guide to Virginia Beach*, which will have the same information.)

Norfolk Convention & Visitors Bureau
9401 Fourth View Street
(757) 664-6620, (800) 368-3097
www.norfolkcvb.com
Norfolk's main bureau is the best place to stop in during weekday business hours for brochures and pamphlets. Or call the number above and ask to have a visitor's guide sent to you. The bureau also operates a Visitor Information Center just off I-64. Take exit 273, the second exit after you come east through the Hampton Roads Bridge-Tunnel. The center offers brochures and a hotel reservation service; staff members there can answer all your questions. The center is open 9:00 a.m. to

5:00 p.m. Monday through Friday. If you're already downtown, there are three satellite offices that offer basic visitor's services as well: 232 Main Street, across from the Norfolk Waterside Marriott; One Waterside Drive, at the entrance of Nauticus; and MacArthur Center, at the first level customer service desk. Hours at these locations vary depending on the season, but they are usually open weekdays and weekends.

Attractions

Once you drop anchor in Norfolk, you will wish you'd reserved an entire day to take in all this seafaring city has to offer. Many of the city's attractions are in the heart of downtown, but along its western fringe is an area known as Ghent, the place where the downtown crowd likes to hang out. It's no wonder. Colley Avenue, the main corridor in Ghent, is home to many small specialty shops, some very good restaurants, and a bona fide old-fashioned movie house. Another Norfolk neighborhood is Ocean View, with 7.5 miles of public beaches bordering the Chesapeake Bay. Especially popular from the turn of the 20th century to the 1950s, Ocean View's three city beaches offer a place to swim, sun, and picnic. Ocean View is one of the first areas of Norfolk you'll come to after crossing the Hampton Roads Bridge-Tunnel; an exit is marked for it on the interstate.

The Chrysler Museum
245 West Olney Road
(757) 664-6200
www.chrysler.org
If you appreciate visual arts, this is the cream of the crop in Hampton Roads. The Chrysler is considered one of the top 20 art museums in the country. Its collection contains more than 30,000 pieces from all time periods. Holdings include works by Renoir, Matisse, and Gauguin, and its art library is the largest in the southeastern United States. The Chrysler also is known for its 8,000-piece glass collection, which includes

the works of Tiffany, Lalique, and other masters; its superb collection of 19th-century sculpture; and its well-recognized collection of photographs. Changing exhibits are excellent: In the past few years, the museum has hosted a gorgeous display of original illustrations from children's literature; "Rembrandt and the Golden Age," on loan from the National Gallery of Art; and the widely acclaimed "Hot Glass and Neon," which helped redefine the limits of sculptural glass.

On average, The Chrysler brings 15 special exhibitions to Norfolk each year. The outstanding collections have ranged from "Rodin: Sculpture from the Iris and B. Gerald Cantor Collection" to "The Art of Andy Warhol."

All told, the award-winning museum houses 60 galleries, the library, auditorium, gift shop, and a restaurant. The Chrysler hours are 10:00 a.m. to 5:00 p.m. Thursday through Saturday, 10:00 a.m. to 9:00 p.m. Wednesday, and 1:00 to 5:00 p.m. Sunday. The museum is closed Monday, Tuesday, and major holidays. Admission is $7 for adults, $6 for AAA members, and $5 for teachers, senior citizens, and members of the military. Children younger than 18 and college students with an ID get in free. On Wednesday everyone is admitted free; contributions are requested.

d'Art Center
208 East Main Street
(757) 625-4211
www.d-artcenter.org
Wander through this cooperative center and enjoy the creations of the 36 or so artists who sometimes will work their magic before your very eyes. You'll see painters, sculptors, and jewelry makers in their studios and can negotiate with most of the artists to purchase what catches your fancy. The center has been open since the late 1980s. Summer art classes are offered for adults and children.

Hours are 10:00 a.m. to 5:00 p.m. Tuesday through Saturday and from 1:00 to 5:00 p.m. on Sunday. Admission is free.

Douglas MacArthur Memorial
City Hall and Bank Street
(757) 441-2965
www.macarthurmemorial.org

For those intrigued by our nation's military history, the Douglas MacArthur Memorial honors the life and times of General MacArthur. The controversial general is entombed here, and his signature corncob pipe and the documents that ended the war with Japan are on display in the galleries. A 25-minute film featuring newsreel footage of MacArthur is shown in the memorial's theater, and the gift shop even displays the general's shiny 1950 Chrysler Crown Imperial limousine. Other exhibits include one on segregated military forces and another on female prisoners of war during World War II. No admission is charged for any of the exhibits, but donations are requested. The museum is open from 10:00 a.m. to 5:00 p.m. Monday through Saturday and 11:00 a.m. to 5:00 p.m. Sunday.

Harbor Park
150 Park Avenue
(757) 622-2222
norfolktides.com

Just a baseball throw from Waterside is Harbor Park, home base for the Norfolk Tides, a Triple A farm team of the New York Mets. Designed by the same firm that built the Baltimore Orioles park at Camden Yards, Harbor Park is seen as one of the best minor-league stadiums in the country. Catch the boys of summer in action from early April through Labor Day. Tickets cost $11.00 for box seats, $9.50 for an adult reserved seat, and $8.00 for reserved seats for children up to 8, seniors, and military with ID. Tickets can be purchased at the park, or you can order them through Ticketmaster by calling 757-872-8100.

Historic Ghent
Colley Avenue and Twenty-First Street

About a mile from downtown, this intriguing neighborhood is a mix of cafes, boutiques, and a bona fide old-fashioned movie house called the Naro, 757-625-6276 or www.naro cinema.com. This is where the folks who work downtown like to mix and mingle on any given evening. Join the crowds and enjoy a little people watching while you sip espresso in an outdoor cafe!

MacArthur Center
300 Monticello Avenue
(757) 627-6000
www.shopmacarthur.com

We have to admit—we don't usually think of a mall as an attraction. But in the case of Norfolk's MacArthur Center, we just have to make an exception. For one thing, the center, which opened in March 1999, is a destination in its own right. You can spend hours and hours browsing through this three-level land of wonder and still not see everything. The 70-foot atrium is a good place to start and maybe meet if you get lost from your traveling companions. All told, MacArthur houses more than 150 stores, 21 eateries and coffee shops, and a movie theater with 18 screens. In fact, once you get here, you don't even have to shop. Instead you can chat with a friend at a quiet corner cappuccino bar, unleash energy with the kids at a picnic-themed play area with giant foam hot dogs and cupcakes, or collapse into one of the overstuffed chairs in the lobby lounge and read a book. Other center amenities include valet parking, package carry-out, complimentary strollers and wheelchairs, and three ATMs. MacArthur Center also is the site of Virginia's first Jeepers!, an innovative pint-size amusement park right in the heart of the mall. As for the stores? The list includes Nordstrom, Dillard's, Abercrombie & Fitch Co., Pottery Barn, Restoration Hardware, and Williams-Sonoma, to name a few. Mall hours are 10:00 a.m. to 9:00 p.m. Monday through Saturday and noon to 6:00 p.m. on Sunday. Parking is available in the attached garage.

Nauticus
One Waterside Drive, Downtown Waterfront
(757) 664-1000, (800) 664-1080
www.thenmc.org

The National Maritime Center, more commonly

called Nauticus, opened in the spring of 1994 on the western edge of the downtown waterfront, adjacent to Town Point Park. And with the arrival of the battleship, the USS *Wisconsin,* one of the last and largest battleships of the U.S. Navy, things have only gotten bigger.

The 120,000-square-foot science center showcases more than 150 exhibits, including everything from the latest interactive computer technology to a touch-tank with sharks! The center was designed to have an equal appeal for both adults and children with displays focusing on maritime commerce, the navy, exotic sea creatures, and the weather. The Changing Gallery even houses the bridge from the USS *Preble,* while three theaters show films that help explain the maritime experience.

If you just want to drop in for a bite to eat at The Galley Restaurant or for a peek into the Banana Pier Gift Shop, you can enter the museum's ground floor for free. Access to the Hampton Roads Naval Museum, which moved from the Norfolk Naval Base to Nauticus and is operated by the U.S. Navy, is also free. The city of Norfolk took over operation of the facility in January 1997 and has been rethinking its approach to exhibits. The USS *Wisconsin*—an 887-foot battleship that earned five combat stars during World War II—set down anchor in its permanent berth right beside Nauticus. Now visitors go on board and can stand beside the massive 16-inch guns and take self-guided or audio tours of the historic ship's main deck.

In conjunction with the free ship's tour, Nauticus has created three exhibits of its own to honor one of the last battleships built by the U.S. Navy. "Design Chamber: Battleship X" lets you race against top designers to create a battleship. "City at Sea" shows what life was like on board the *Wisconsin,* while "Battle-Scopes" takes you on a virtual tour of the impressive vessel that survived kamikaze attacks and went on to assist in Desert Storm.

Nauticus and the *Wisconsin* are open from 10:00 a.m. to 5:00 p.m. daily from Memorial Day to Labor Day. The rest of the year, they're open 10:00 a.m. to 5:00 p.m. Tuesday through Saturday and noon to 5:00 p.m. Sunday. The ship will not have tours on Thanksgiving, Christmas Eve, or Christmas Day. You can tour the ship's deck for free, but admission to Nauticus is $10.95 for adults; $9.95 for senior citizens, AAA members, and military personnel; and $8.50 for children 4 through 12.

Norfolk Botanical Garden
6700 Azalea Garden Road
(757) 441-5830
www.norfolkbotanicalgarden.org

The great outdoors in all its splendor beckons at the Norfolk Botanical Garden near the Norfolk International Airport. This 155-acre garden began in 1938 as a Works Progress Administration grant. Today it boasts more than 12 miles of pathways and thousands of trees, shrubs, and flowering plants arranged in both formal and natural gardens. There are more than 20 themed gardens, including the 3.5-acre bicentennial rose garden, healing and herb gardens, and the fragrance garden for the visually impaired. We think the best time to go is in spring when the more than 250,000 azaleas are so spectacular they take your breath away, but there's something blooming just about any time of year. (Even during the winter months you can enjoy camellias, witch hazel, wintersweet, and colorful berries.) Newer gardens include the Bristow Butterfly Garden, a perennial garden, a wildflower meadow, and a renovated Japanese garden. There's even a "surprise" garden with changing blooms that always offer a hint of color and something new for visitors. One of the best ways to view the gardens during the warm-weather months is by a 30-minute

i The tiger swallowtail is Old Dominion's state insect. This beautiful yellow and black butterfly, which feeds on buddleia, honeysuckle, bee balm, and sunflowers, is one of many that can be found in plentiful supply at the Bristow Butterfly Garden, which opened in 1998 at Norfolk Botanical Garden, 6700 Azalea Garden Road, Norfolk. For more information call (757) 441–5830.

boat or tram ride. The gardens are open from 9:00 a.m. to 7:00 p.m. April through mid-October and until 5:00 p.m. the rest of the year. The cafe is open for a light lunch and snacks. Admission to the gardens is $7 for adults, $6 for seniors, $5 for youth 3 to 18, and free for children 3 and younger if accompanied by a paying adult. Tickets to the boat rides are sold separately. The boat tour costs $4 per adult, $3 per child. The tram ride is free with your paid admission to the garden. The Botanical Garden offers family programs throughout the year.

Virginia Zoo
3500 Granby Street
(757) 624-9937
www.virginiazoo.org

If you like to take a walk on the wild side—and if you have small children along—a stop at the Virginia Zoo is a must. Situated on 55 acres along the Lafayette River, the zoo is small but certainly charming. It is home to some 340 animals, including reptiles, nocturnal animals, rare Siberian tigers, primates, llamas, rhinos, and a pair of elephants who like to toss around tires and douse each other with water. A few years back, the zoo was singled out for praise by former Attorney General Janet Reno for making its facility more accessible to persons with disabilities. The zoo is in the midst of a 10-year, $15 million improvement plan that has resulted in a new entry and educational complex and the beginnings of an African Okavango River Delta exhibit. In the summer of 1999, the zoo opened its doors for a pair of gelada baboons—Joe-Joe and Tommy—as the first residents of the new African exhibit. Joe-Joe and Tommy have since welcomed a third baboon to the zoo, Hoss. Also opening with the baboon habitat was the Xaxaba village, which features structures similar to those found in the Okavango Delta in Botswana. The focal point of the African village is the Xaxaba Restaurant, which offers traditional fast food and specialty items such as catfish and chicken-fried steak. In 2007 the zoo's lioness gave birth to two cubs named Zola and Mramba, the zoo's first large carnivore birth in 35 years. The birth—which happened while the mother was on exhibit—actually came as a surprise to the zookeepers because she did not show obvious signs of pregnancy. The zoo's long-range plans are to include a North American walkway around the duck pond, a butterfly house, and South American, Asian, and Australian exhibition areas.

Special children's programs are offered year-round. Zoo hours are 10:00 a.m. to 5:00 p.m. daily. Admission is $7 for anyone older than 11, $5 for children 2 to 11, and $6 for seniors 62 and older.

Waterside Festival Marketplace
333 Waterside Drive
on the Elizabeth River
(757) 627-3300
www.watersidemarketplace.com

No trip to Norfolk is complete without a visit to Waterside, the city's festival marketplace overlooking the Elizabeth River. In fact, sometimes this is the only destination visitors have in mind when they come to Norfolk. Since opening in June 1983, the marketplace has provided the downtown waterfront with a colorful mix of retail shops and restaurants. The marketplace is constructed of steel and glass on two levels and is connected to a parking garage across the street by a second-level walkway.

A few years ago Waterside shifted its focus from a tourist attraction to an entertainment destination, welcoming a number of new tenants, including Jillian's, a vast entertainment complex that includes a hibachi grill restaurant, a sports video cafe, a blues and jazz club, a dance club, a sit-down restaurant, and an area where adults can play virtual-reality games. Other restaurants include Outback Steakhouse, Joe's Crab Shack, Bar Norfolk, Have a Nice Day Cafe, and a fast-food court.

Retailers include gift shops and boutiques, including Erin's Irish Imports, Earth's Treasures, Dollar Tree, and All About Virginia. In season, boat tours leave daily from the premises, and an attached marina makes the place convenient for pleasure sailors. From Waterside it's an easy stroll to Nauticus, Harbor Park, and other downtown attractions. The marketplace is open from 10:00 a.m. to 9:00 p.m. Monday through Saturday and noon to 6:00 p.m. Sunday, with extended hours during the summer and for special events. Restaurants and nightclubs maintain their own individual hours. Admission to the marketplace itself is free.

Restaurants

While Norfolk has pretty much anything your heart—and palate—desires, we have a few favorite haunts we want to mention. If you're looking for a satisfying meal in appealing environs, you can't go wrong with any of the eateries listed here.

Baker's Crust
The Palace Shops, 330 West Twenty-First Street
(757) 625-3600
www.bakerscrust.com
Sandwiches, salads, and homemade breads—we're talking more than 20 varieties from fat-free baguettes, boules, batards, and country loaves to challah, brioche, fruit and nut and pan foccacia. The soup of the day will come served in a bread boule on request, and a complete repast of rotisserie-roasted chicken is available. There also is a crepe bar that serves up just about anything that can be wrapped in these delicate, tasty pancakes. If you come at noon, be prepared to wait, as this is a very popular lunch destination for the local crowd. Dinner will run you between $8 and $19, with most entrees around $12. Baker's Crust is open Sunday through Thursday from 8:00 a.m. to 10:00 p.m. for breakfast, lunch, and dinner. It is open Friday and Saturday until 11:00 p.m. Smoking is permitted only in the outdoor patio seating area.

Doumar's Cones and Barbecue
20th Street and Monticello Avenue
(757) 627-4163
www.doumars.com

We couldn't decide if this was an attraction or a restaurant, but since you'd be hard-pressed to drop in and leave without eating, we've listed it here. What makes Doumar's so special? For one thing, it is one of the only remaining Hampton Roads eateries that still has carhops. For another, it has been at the same location since 1934. But, perhaps most interestingly, restaurant founder Abe Doumar invented the ice-cream cone back in 1904 during the St. Louis Exposition. Doumar's serves up outstanding, inexpensive pork barbecue, burgers, fries, and milk shakes in old-fashioned soda fountain glasses. And the limeade is superb. In 1999 Doumar's was a James Beard Award winner, recognized as one of America's eight regional classics that are "timeless, grass-roots restaurants that serve memorable food and are strongly embedded in the fabric of their communities." The restaurant is closed on Sunday but is open 8:00 a.m. to 11:00 p.m. Monday through Thursday and 8:00 a.m. to 12:30 a.m. Friday and Saturday. Doumar's does not accept credit cards.

Painted Lady Restaurant and Tea Room
112 East Seventeenth Street
(757) 623-8872
www.thepaintedlady.com
This Norfolk eatery is easy to spot—its bright pink paint job grabs the eye before you even know you're looking. Located in Victorian digs just off Granby Street, the Painted Lady offers seafood, beef, and pasta dishes and lighter lunch specialties. Dinners range from $15 to $28. Afternoon tea is available Tuesday to Sunday, and live piano music often sets the mood. The restaurant serves lunch Tuesday to Sunday, dinner Tuesday through Sunday, and brunch on Sunday. It is closed on Monday.

Rajput Indian Cuisine
742 West Twenty-First Street
(757) 625-4634
http://rajputonline.com
The name of this eatery refers both to royalty and to a region in western India. But the food

here is surprisingly diverse, including seafood and vegetarian dishes; a Tandori mixed grill with chicken, lamb, fish, and shrimp; and a smattering of curry offerings. Locals who've visited this restaurant give it nothing but rave reviews.

Todd Jurich's Bistro
150 West Main Street
(757) 622-3210
www.toddjurichsbistro.com
This award-winning restaurant serves some of the most creative fare in town. Innovative creations by chef/owner Todd Jurich include free-range Piedmont boneless sirloin with crispy buttermilk onion rings. Much of the menu, however, will vary with the season. A dinner for two—entrees only—will set you back about $50. The bistro serves lunch and dinner Monday through Friday and dinner only on Saturday and Sunday.

VIRGINIA BEACH

You say you're from western Ohio, central Pennsylvania, or some other landlocked region and the last time you saw the Atlantic Ocean was on a postcard sent to you by a vacationing friend? Well, then by all means schedule a day trip to Virginia Beach. After all, it isn't every day you get to dip your toes in the ocean, bury your spouse in the sand, or sip a piña colada while watching the waves break on shore.

A day at the beach also is the perfect addition to your itinerary if you have small children. In fact, it may be the only opportunity you have to stretch out in the sunshine as the kids frolic in the surf and sand. (We advise you to keep a very close eye on the little ones. The surf may, on occasion, appear gentle, but the ocean's undertow is unpredictable.)

The route to the beach is pretty direct. Hop on I–64 and head east through the Hampton Roads Bridge-Tunnel until you hook up with I–264, which heads either to Norfolk or Virginia Beach. Follow I–264 toward Virginia Beach, staying on the highway until it ends. Continue to head straight until you intersect with Atlantic Avenue. Turn right and you're cruising the beachfront. (The entire trip should take about ninety minutes.) You'll find there's plenty of parking space—both free and metered, depending on how close you are to the water—on side streets all up and down the beach, but they fill up fast. There's also paid parking in a number of municipal lots. Your best bet is to get to the beach early on a weekday so that you can grab prime spots for parking and sunning.

Virginia Beach prides itself on being a family destination, and over the last several years has backed up its claims with a $94 million modernization of both the boardwalk and Atlantic Avenue that includes new landscaping, whimsical sculptures, attractive signs, streetlights, and a special bike-riding lane along the boardwalk. City officials also are putting the finishing touches on an extensive beach erosion and hurricane protection project that has widened and reinforced the shoreline to withstand storms like Hurricane Isabel in 2003, which brought high winds and devastating rainfall to the region.

As part of the five-year plan, the city began pumping in more sand—an extra 3.2 million cubic yards—to turn Virginia Beach into one of its widest, sandiest beaches in recent memory. The last time the city's beach measured 300 feet wide was in 1700. To get an idea of how much sand Virginia Beach is bringing in, imagine a football field stacked 1,920 feet high with sand. That's one and a third times as tall as the Empire State Building.

If you prefer to plan your visit around a special event, you're in luck. In mid-June the city hosts its annual Boardwalk Art Show and Festival, which brings close to 400 artists to the oceanfront to display and sell the fruits of their creative endeavors. In mid- to late September, the Neptune Festival salutes summer's end with free musical entertainment, a world-famous sandcastle contest, and a military air show; and around Christmastime the boardwalk is ablaze with more than 200 displays of 450,000 lights as part of Holiday

If you're a lover of the great outdoors, why not try one of these Virginia Beach back-to-nature excursions: dolphin-watching boat trips sponsored by the Virginia Marine Science Museum, (757) 425–FISH or www.vmsm.com; nature tours aboard the 50-passenger *Coastal Explorer*, a pontoon boat that travels Owls Creek Salt Marsh near the marine science museum, (757) 437–BOAT; or a guided kayak tour in some of the scenic waterways, (757) 480–1999.

Lights at the Beach. Or, you can always take in a concert at the VerizonWireless Virginia Beach Amphitheater. The outdoor complex brings big-name entertainment to the "Beach" throughout the warmer-weather months. Of course, there's always the possibility that you may not want to do much more than lie in the sand. But, if you have a hankering to take in some of the sights, there are a number of places to visit along the waterfront and its side streets.

Virginia Beach Visitor Center
2100 Parks Avenue
(800) VA-BEACH
www.vbfun.com

If you'd like to find out exactly what this city on the ocean has to offer, call the toll-free number above or visit Virginia Beach on the Internet. The Web site is particularly helpful as it offers a convenient "trip planner," a feature that helps would-be vacationers customize their itinerary.

Attractions

Association for Research and Enlightenment (A.R.E.)
Sixty-Seventh Street and Atlantic Avenue
(757) 428-3588, (800) 333-4499
www.edgarcayce.org

This intriguing attraction is the headquarters for the work of the late psychic Edgar Cayce, who resided in Virginia Beach and was best known for falling into a trance and diagnosing

and prescribing cures for medical ailments. Each year A.R.E. hosts thousands of international visitors and researchers who have an interest in Cayce's remarkable talents. There are free lectures, video and film presentations, ESP demonstrations, and daily tours. There's even a meditation room overlooking the ocean and a bookstore with overflowing shelves. A.R.E. is open 9:00 a.m. to 8:00 p.m. Monday through Saturday and 11:00 a.m. to 8:00 p.m. on Sunday. Admission is free, but donations are accepted. Take care to park in the lot and not on the road as the local police are quick to ticket, especially in summer.

Atlantic Waterfowl Heritage Museum and deWitt Cottage
1113 Atlantic Avenue
(757) 437-8432
www.awhm.org

This museum interprets the heritage of wildfowl—everything from ducks and geese to songbirds—through art exhibits, interactive displays, and special demonstrations. The museum's five galleries feature artwork and decoy carvings, including some that date from the turn of the nineteenth century. Overlooking the ocean, the museum is located in the 1895 deWitt Cottage, the last remaining oceanfront cottage from the late nineteenth century. The museum is open Tuesday through Saturday from 10:00 a.m. to 5:00 p.m. and Sunday noon to 5:00 p.m. Admission is free, although donations are accepted.

First Landing State Park
2500 Shore Drive
(757) 412-2300, (800) 933-PARK

This 2,770-acre campground and sanctuary has more than 336 species of trees and plants, a self-guided nature trail, and a visitor center with books for sale and exhibits. Nine trails, including one that is wheelchair accessible, cover 19 miles and are part of the National Scenic Trails System. Located in the park is the Chesapeake Bay Center, an environmentally focused, interactive visitor information center that also offers aquariums, environmental exhibits, and a touch-tank developed by the Virginia Marine Science Museum. A 5-mile bike trail connects to the city's bike trails.

The camp store has all types of rental items, including bikes, fishing poles, umbrellas, chairs, four-wheelers, and two-person tents.

If you would like to extend your stay, First Landing has ample camping facilities with 213 sites along the Chesapeake Bay to pitch your tent—an inexpensive alternative to the cost of a hotel. You can even rent a cabin, if you prefer not to deal with tent stakes, but don't delay, the cabins are hot commodities. If you are interested in cabin rentals, call the Reservation Center at (800) 933-PARK. There also are places here to picnic, so if you're planning a visit, you might want to pack a lunch.

Francis Land Historical House and History Park and Nature Trail
3131 Virginia Beach Boulevard
(757) 431-4000

This eighteenth-century plantation home was designed by Francis Land, a wealthy landowner and political activist, and retains some of the original architecture and family heirlooms. Costumed tour guides help transport visitors to a time when the plantation was bustling with family members and the servants that helped keep the farm running. As an extension of the plantation, visitors trek along a scenic trail that offers glimpses of the city's once vast wilderness. Interpretive signs help make the journey an educational experience, while native plants and the wildlife of the woodland provide opportunity for year-round discovery. Admission to the Francis Land House is $4 for adults, $3 for seniors, and $2 for children 6 through 12. Park admission is free. Hours are 9:00 a.m. to 5:00 p.m. Tuesday through Saturday and 11:00 a.m. to 5:00 p.m. on Sunday.

Old Cape Henry Lighthouse
Fort Story, extreme north end of Atlantic Avenue
(757) 422-9421

Construction of this lighthouse was authorized by George Washington and was completed in 1791 at a cost of $17,500. The edifice continued to guide mariners until it was replaced in 1881. The stone used in the structure came from the same Virginia quarry that supplied the White House, the Capitol, and Mount Vernon. Over the years the edifice has become the official symbol of Virginia Beach. The lighthouse is open from 10:00 a.m. to 5:00 p.m., beginning in mid-March and continuing through October. From November 1 to early December and again from early January through mid-March, the lighthouse closes at 4:00 p.m. It's closed December 5 to January 4. The lighthouse is located on Fort Story military base, and anyone over 18 will need an ID to enter the base. The admission is $4 for adults, $2 for children 3 to 12, and free for children 3 and younger and military in uniform.

Old Coast Guard Station
Oceanfront on Twenty-Fourth Street
(757) 422-1587
www.oldcoastguardstation.com

A former U.S. Life-Saving/Coast Guard Station built in 1903, this simple wooden structure is reminiscent of an earlier, simpler oceanfront era. Inside, two galleries give glimpses into the history of the people who risked their lives to save strangers during shipwrecks. A perma-

i Horse-racing fans can trot up I–64 to Colonial Downs, a racetrack in New Kent County, about 25 miles west of Williamsburg. The track offers two seasons of equestrian racing. Harness season typically starts in late spring and ends in midsummer. Thoroughbred racing starts on Labor Day and continues through the first week or so of October. General admission is usually $2.00, $5.00 for a box seat. To reach Colonial Downs take I–64 west to exit 214. Turn left and the racetrack will be on your left. For more information call (804) 966–7223 or (888) 482–8722.

nent display focuses on the impact of World Wars I and II on Virginia Beach. A TowerCam, a roof-mounted video camera, can zoom in on passing ships spied on the Virginia Beach horizon. The camera transmits its pictures to a 27-inch television monitor, providing visitors with the same view crewmen had from the station tower almost a century ago. The museum is open Tuesday through Saturday from 10:00 a.m. to 5:00 p.m. and Sunday from noon to 5:00 p.m. From Memorial Day to October 1 the museum also is open Monday. Admission is $4 for adults, $3 for seniors and military personnel, and $2 for children 6 through 18.

Group tours and rates are available with advance notice.

Virginia Beach Sportsplex
2181 Landstown Road
(757) 427-2990
The Sportsplex is America's first stadium built specifically for soccer, but it is also used for football, rugby, and lacrosse. Home to the Mariners and Piranhas, a women's professional soccer team, the $10.5 million facility seats 6,000 spectators, but can be expanded to hold 30,000. Features include an 18-by-20-foot instant replay screen behind one goal and a high-tech sound system that can monitor the noise level of the stadium crowd and adjust the volume level accordingly. Ticket prices for soccer games range from $7 to $18. Rugby tournaments are held here also, and those tickets are $10 and up.

Virginia Legends Walk
Thirteenth Street
(no phone)
This outdoor monument between Atlantic and Pacific Avenues pays tribute to famous Virginians who have made significant contributions to the country and the world. When the walk was dedicated on July 19, 1999, thirteen of the original twenty-four inductees were represented at the ceremony, including representatives for Arthur Ashe, Pearl Bailey, Patsy Cline, Ella Fitzgerald, Patrick Henry, Robert E. Lee, Douglas MacArthur, James Madison, George

i If you decide you just can't "do" Virginia Beach in one day, you have plenty of sleepover options. The city has more than 11,000 hotel and motel rooms—5,000 of them on the oceanfront. A central reservation service is available at (800) ROOMS VB.

C. Marshall, Edgar Allan Poe, Bill "Bojangles" Robinson, Captain John Smith, and Woodrow Wilson. Each year nominations are accepted for future honorees. The plaques on the walk are lit from above so that it can be viewed at night. Future plans call to expand the walk across Atlantic Avenue to the oceanfront boardwalk. There is no admission fee.

Virginia Marine Science Museum
717 General Booth Boulevard
(757) 425-FISH
www.vmsm.com
An extremely popular destination for the entire family, the marine science museum completed a $35 million expansion in 1996. This fine facility—which continues to draw huge crowds throughout the year—features three buildings and dozens of exciting exhibits, from the Atlantic Ocean Pavilion, which showcases schooling fishes, sharks, and other deep-sea creatures in a 300,000-gallon aquarium, to the Family Channel IMAX 3-D Theater. Visit the Owls Creek Marsh Pavilion, where you can view a live river habitat and outdoor marsh bird aviary. Dozens of hands-on exhibits give children the opportunity to tong for oysters or make a few waves. And, by all means, stop and pet the rays, which may look a tad odd but are as friendly as any well-loved puppy. Plans are in the works for an additional facility that will highlight animals and plants from both the ocean and coastal regions. This facility also will house the museum's stranding program, which rescues endangered dolphins, seals, fish, and coastal birds. The museum is open 9:00 a.m. to 7:00 p.m. daily during the summer, and until 5:00 p.m. the rest of the year. Admission for the museum only is $11.95 for

adults, $7.95 for children 4 through 12, and $10.95 for senior citizens. Admission to the IMAX theater is $7.50 for adults, $6.50 for children, and $6.75 for seniors. Combination tickets are $16.95 for adults, $12.95 for children, and $15.95 for senior citizens.

Restaurants

All that splashing around in the ocean is sure to work up an appetite. While "the Beach," as locals call it, has a well-rounded selection of restaurants for your dining pleasure, we've singled out a handful sure to please.

Beach Bully Bar-B-Que
601 Nineteenth Street
(757) 422-4222
www.beachbully.com

For some of the best barbecue in town—for lunch or dinner—stop in at Beach Bully. Grab a half-chicken platter for $6.99, or dig into a beef platter for about $1.00 more. The restaurant is open seven days a week, and the dress code is casual, so just come as you are after a day in the sun and the surf. It's open from 10:00 a.m. to 9:00 p.m. Sunday through Thursday, an hour later on Friday and Saturday.

Duck-In Restaurant & Gazebo
3324 Shore Drive at Lynnhaven
Inlet Bridge
(757) 481-0201
www.vbeach.com/duck-in

This long-standing Chesapeake Bayfront institution serves up a variety of local seafood for lunch and dinner seven days a week, including an all-you-can-eat seafood buffet. The dress code is casual, and the average cost of an entree is $15. Breakfast is served Sunday from 9:00 a.m. to 2:00 p.m.; lunch and dinner are served daily, beginning at 11:00 a.m. Friday nights, however, belong to the beach party crowd and go late. You'll find live entertainment here in the summer.

The Jewish Mother
3108 Pacific Avenue
(757) 422-5430

Lunch and dinner are offered at this kid-friendly restaurant, a Virginia Beach landmark since 1975, which serves up an incredible array of sandwiches (most in the $7 range), wonderful desserts, and more than ninety different varieties of beer. Breakfast dishes are available all day long, and there's nightly entertainment.

Pasta E Pani
1069 Laskin Road
(757) 301-7488

If you like Italian, you'll thoroughly enjoy this restaurant and deli shop, whose name translates to pasta and bread. Both are homemade and delicious, making this restaurant a perennial favorite of Insiders who come here for lunch or dinner. A dinner for two should run about $25 to $30. Lunch is served weekdays from 11:30 a.m. to 2:30 p.m. Dinner is from 5:30 to 9:00 p.m. The adjoining deli and shop are open 10:00 a.m. to 6:30 p.m.

KIDSTUFF

Local kids know what events anchor each season. The Chamber of Commerce Christmas Parade, held the first Saturday in December along Richmond Road, officially opens the holiday season. The Community Christmas Tree Lighting on Market Square Green in the city's Historic Area, sponsored by the Kiwanis Club of Williamsburg, means singing carols by candlelight on Christmas Eve. Egg hunts galore usher in Easter. In fact, there are so many egg hunts scheduled locally, kids check the local newspapers to plan ahead of time which ones they want to attend. If it's time for the James City County Fair, summer is winding down. And An Occasion for the Arts, a huge street festival held in and around Merchants Square, means it's fall.

A few years back, community leaders worried that there really wasn't much locally for youngsters to do. That's no longer the case. Aware that kids need more than a venerable history to excite and inspire them, the community took steps to ensure that youth, including teenagers, would have multiple options for spending their spare time. More movie theaters opened and the bowling became better than ever, but kids, especially teens, needed more.

Kidsburg, a community-developed children's playground, opened in 1994 at Mid County Park on Ironbound Road near Route 5. Three years later, the James City County–Williamsburg Community Center was expanded and renovated. With a renewed focus on youth, it offers teens a drug-free, alcohol-free gathering place off Longhill Road. For a quick overview of what's on tap at any given time, you can call the Activity Hotline at (757) 259–4200.

With a little advance planning, creative options abound.

Let's begin with the major ones. Flip back a few pages and check out the detailed sections on Busch Gardens and Water Country USA in the Attractions chapter. The first stop requested by most kids upon arrival is Busch Gardens or Water Country USA, both owned and operated by Busch Entertainment Corp.

Colonial Williamsburg, also keenly aware that they needed to attract and entertain people of all ages, has created programs and events especially for young visitors. The Benjamin Powell site re-creates the daily life of a colonial family, and participants learn how they might have lived in the 18th century by performing tasks as well as observing (see Family Life Adventures in the Colonial Williamsburg chapter). Colonial games are played at several locations, including on the Palace Green and at the James Geddy House, in the Historic Area. Here kids can try their skill at trundling the hoop, stilt walking, jumping rope, lawn bowling, ninepins, leapfrog, blindman's bluff, and other games—assisted by young costumed interpreters. At Robertson's Windmill, at the corner of North England and Scotland Streets, visiting children help with seasonal farm chores. During the summer hands-on activities there include repositioning the windmill.

Several activities in the Historic Area are sure to get your children's imaginations racing. In the summer, take them to the site off Nicholson Street, where young helpers have the chance to stomp clay in a pit in preparation for brick making.

Especially popular with young visitors is the opportunity to rent a colonial costume, which they can wear during their visit. Costumes rentals are available in the visitor's center at Colonial Williamsburg. For more details about what the Historic Area has to offer, see the chapter on Colonial Williamsburg; check the information in the *Visitor's Companion,* a free, weekly publication distributed at the Colonial Williamsburg Visitor Center; or call (800) HIS-TORY to inquire about a given day's activities.

The Jamestown-Yorktown Foundation has plenty of exciting exhibits year-round at its museums, but it is during summer in particular that it offers special activities for youngsters at Jamestown Settlement and the Yorktown Victory Center. Programs change annually and vary according to age group, but young visitors always can find something of interest amid the array of entertaining, educational programs offered primarily from late spring through late summer.

Programs at Jamestown Settlement have offered kids opportunities such as following animal tracks through the Jamestown woods, building with colonial-style wattle and daub, or games where they jump into a bunk aboard ship, open a sea chest, and roll a barrel. Preschool programs at Yorktown Victory Center have included a day on an 18th-century farm and the opportunity to don colonial garb and join the Continental Army. Also at the Yorktown Victory Center, children can visit the Children's Kaleidoscope Discovery Room, where they can travel back in time as they try on 18th-century clothing, copy from a hornbook, make crayon rubbings of 18th-century woodcuts, play the African game mancala, and investigate the identity of artifacts.

Programs for first- and second-grade students have included hands-on crafts projects, stories, and other activities that make history at the two sites fun. In recent summers Jamestown Settlement has offered a time-travel adventure, a sewing program that allowed kids to try on garments like those worn by colonial-era youngsters, and one that emphasized use of the colonial language of settlers and Native Americans. Yorktown Victory Center programs included one that allowed youngsters to meet and spend time with members of the Washington family, while another program re-created a husking bee.

Third-, fourth- and fifth-graders got a different look at early American life during five-day programs geared to their learning level. Jamestown Settlement offered a program that celebrated the arrival of Sir William Berkeley as royal governor, and a hands-on workshop that emphasized the use of colonial-era construction tools. Yorktown Victory Center also sponsored a five-day program called Family Footsteps, which over the week focused on an early Virginia family, its attic treasures, its ancestors, and the everyday objects used on their farm. For more information on programs, see the Jamestown and Yorktown chapter or call (888) 593-4682.

If your youngsters are in need of a more in-depth experience of history, the Jamestown-Yorktown Foundation has set up extensive structured educational programs designed to meet Virginia's Standards of Learning for the second through eleventh grades. These two-hour curriculum-based, hands-on guided tours introduce students to daily life in the colony. They will learn more about life at Jamestown, getting hands-on experience with such activities as open-hearth cooking and 17th-century weaponry; the cultures of the Powhatan Indians in the re-created Indian village; the experiences of men and women during the American Revolution; and the practice of medicine in Revolutionary America—when they mix 18th-century herbal remedies. Reservations for these group programs are required. Call (757) 253-4939 at least two months in advance for fall and winter trips, four months in advance for trips in the spring.

Those are the major kid attractions. Below is a compilation of other attractions kids especially will enjoy.

AMUSEMENT PARKS AND MINIGOLF

Go-Karts Plus
6910 Richmond Road
(757) 564-7600
www.gokartsplus.com
If the kids are demanding something exciting,

try Go-Karts Plus. This thrills-and-spills park, located a softball's throw west of the Williamsburg Pottery Factory on U.S. Route 60, features enough rides and attractions to keep kids of all ages busy for hours. This park obviously rates highly with kids and teens because it's always packed. Attractions here include waterfall minigolf, four stock-car tracks, super stock cars, a crank 'n' roll train for little ones, Formula One racers, a figure-eight racetrack, bumper cars, bumper boats, and myriad game machines—to name a few enticements. There are age and height requirements; for instance, a child must be 12 before getting behind the wheel of a super stock car. Most rides in Kiddie Land are geared for children 3 to 8.

Admission and parking, which is ample, are free. Rides are paid for with $1.50 tickets purchased at a counter, with discounts for large quantities. The park is open daily from mid-March through late October. Hours Memorial Day through Labor Day are 11:00 a.m. to 11:00 p.m. Spring and fall hours vary, so call in advance to avoid disappointing the troops.

Kidsburg
Mid County Park, 3793 Ironbound Road
(757) 229-1232

Kidsburg is the best deal of all when it comes to finding a place where little ones can burn off some energy and let loose without fear of breaking something in the motel room.

This James City County park was built in 1994 when more than 1,000 volunteers pitched in and turned an empty grassy site into a kid-size version of Jamestown. Most days you'll find the park swarming with kids enjoying the mock-ups of the Jamestown Settlement's ship *Susan Constant*, the James Fort Tot Lot, the George P. Coleman Memorial Bridge, and two theaters. Admission to the park is free. Hours are from sunrise to dusk.

Mini-Golf America
1901 Richmond Road
(757) 229-7200
www.minigolfamerica.com

Nestled in an oasis of calm along one of the city's busiest streets is this lovely "putter's paradise." This eighteen-hole, par 40 course is as attractive as it is challenging. It is beautifully landscaped with 40-foot cascading waterfalls, ponds, and creeks stocked with goldfish, frogs, and turtles. Afraid of the sun? Fear not: More than 2,000 annuals and perennials make it lush and shaded. Included are hundreds of flowering shrubs, azaleas, and rosebushes. It is a bargain to boot. The first round is $6 for all players; round two is $3. Or you and your family can play all day for $11 per person. Group rates are also available. The park includes a picnic area and ice-cream stand. Open from April 1 through October, the park hours vary by season, but summer hours are generally 10:00 a.m. to midnight daily.

Pirate's Cove Minigolf
2001 Mooretown Road
(757) 259-4600
www.piratescove.net

You can't miss this minigolf extravaganza. Just look for the "mountain" rising up from the road next to the Big Kmart near Kingsgate Greene Shopping Center. This park has a fun, nautical theme, with its wooden walkways, rope fences, and ship's bow sticking out of the ground as if it had been sunk by Blackbeard himself. A waterfall flows down one side of the mountain rock, and two courses run through the caves inside. Pirate's Cove has thirty-six holes on three courses. Blackbeard's course is $7.95 for adults, $6.95 for children; the Captain's course costs $7.50 for adults, $6.50 for children; and the Challenge course (both the Blackbeard's and Captain's courses combined) costs $11.95 for adults, $10.50 for children. Pirate's Cove is open March through October, 10:00 a.m. to 11:00 p.m.

THE GREAT OUTDOORS

If your youngster likes to fish, paddleboat, canoe, hike, picnic, or simply spend time outdoors getting exercise, the Historic Triangle boasts many fine parks and recreation areas. See the Parks and Recreation chapter for specifics on what Williamsburg and James City and York Counties offer. Below you also will find listings for additional venues younger visitors will find entertaining.

James City County–Williamsburg Community Center
5301 Longhill Road
(757) 259-4200

When it comes to offering kids a variety of entertainment options, this place fills the bill. From preschool art days, offered January through April, to ballet, jazz, basic baton for youth 6 and older, arts and crafts classes for kids of all ages, plus spectator softball, baseball, and soccer games in season on several fields, this place has plenty to keep kids busy.

Families and youth are welcome to use the pool and whirlpool when they're not in use by aquatic programs, swim meets, and classes, dates and times of which are posted in the lobby and on the pool deck bulletin board. Pool inflatable structures, including a slide and hound dog, also are available for you to enjoy. Swimming classes for people of all ages from 6 months and older are offered, as well as classes in competitive racing skills for swimmers 5 to 7 and 8 to 15, water aerobics, aquacise, aquatic back therapy, and in-water kick-boxing sessions. Looking for more water activities? The center offers challenge swims for people 8 and up, private lessons, basic water safety classes, lifesaving, scouting water safety, and water safety instructor classes.

Prefer to stay out of the pool? No problem. The center offers before- and after-school care programs for elementary and middle school kids, a spring break program for kids in kindergarten through fifth grade, and a summer recreation camp program for youth.

Special programs for middle school kids featuring basketball, games, contests, food, and prizes are offered throughout the year. Special skiing and snowboarding activities are scheduled, as well as trips to the Chesapeake Skate Park for skateboarding and in-line skating.

Teen activities also abound here. High school students can opt for such winter pro-

i Kids will enjoy the Colonial Williamsburg experience all the more if they dress the part. Costumes are available for daily rental at the Colonial Willamsburg Visitor's Center. Call (757) 229-1000 for more details.

grams as bowling, a climbing extravaganza, shopping trips to northern Virginia outlet malls, or day trips to the Smithsonian Institution. Spring break events include a skating trip, tour of a Virginia fish hatchery, long-distance biking tours, or jaunts to Little Creek Reservoir Park for a day of canoeing, fishing, and a barbecue.

The center is open 6:00 a.m. to 9:00 p.m. Monday through Thursday, 6:00 a.m. to 8:00 p.m. Friday, 9:00 a.m. to 6:00 p.m. Saturday, and 1:00 to 6:00 p.m. Sunday. Resident members can choose between an annual, semiannual, or quarterly membership fee. Although the center is primarily for people living in the community, nonresidents are permitted to use the facility for a $11 charge a day for nonresident adults, $4 for children 5 to 17. There are also nonresident annual and semiannual membership fees.

Yorktown Waterfront
Water Street, Yorktown
(no phone)

On a warm, sunny day, what child doesn't enjoy a trip to the beach? And a trip to the small, yet inviting, Yorktown waterfront offers a wonderful change of pace for traveling families. The beach stretches about 2 miles along the York River. A large picnic area is located east of the beach, so carrying lunch is an option. Several restaurants within walking distance also are open during the day should hunger strike. Public restrooms are available at the west end of the beach and are open from early morning until after supper. Several trees can offer escape from the midday sun and a boardwalk, really a sidewalk, can take you from one end of the beach to the other. Lifeguards are on duty from Memorial Day to Labor Day.

HORSEBACK RIDING

Offer a kid the opportunity to ride a horse and chances are he or she will jump at the opportunity. The Historic Triangle has embraced this venerable Virginian tradition. Many local stables welcome children, who can take classes and, in many cases, sign up for summer riding camps. Generally, these places require children to be at least 6 or 7 years old, depending on temperament, and both boys and girls are welcome. Some require that the young equestrian be accompanied by an adult at all times; others provide adult supervision. Rules vary from place to place, so it's a good idea to call ahead and find out what gear is required as well as days and hours of operation.

Carlton Farms
3516 Mott Lane
(757) 220-3553

Cedar Valley Farm
2016 Forge Road, Toano
(757) 566-2621

Stonehouse Stables
2116-A Forge Road, Toano
(757) 566-0666
www.stonehousestables.com

CAMPS, CONCERTS, AND CLASSES

AMF Williamsburg Lanes
5544 Olde Towne Road
(757) 565-3311
When it comes to showing kids of all ages a good time, this place is tops. No bowler is too young, no party too big. Kids are invited to celebrate birthdays here—with special perks provided, including free bowling passes and a bowling pin given to the birthday boy or girl. If the bowler is a novice, the nice people here gladly pull up the bumpers in the gutters so everyone has a good time—and a decent score at the end of a game. While the place is wildly popular and often crowded with league play, kids are welcome anytime. But it might be a good idea to call ahead and make sure there won't be too long a wait for a free lane. If you should experience a wait, the game room and snack bar are sure to keep youngsters occupied until it's their turn to step up to the line. The center also hosts Xtreme bowling—where the lights are low and music is loud. Call for times and prices. The center also has summer and fall youth leagues.

The Chamber Ballet for the Institute of Dance
3356 Ironbound Road, Suite 201
(757) 229-1717
www.theinstitutefordance.org
This dance school has been on the local scene for more than twenty-five years—and performances throughout the year by its students have become traditional and welcomed events. Chamber Ballet performs during the city's annual First Night event, a nonalcoholic celebration of the New Year featuring myriad programs by local performing arts groups. Chamber Ballet also appears during the annual An Occasion for the Arts, a festival of the visual and performing arts held the first Sunday each October in and around Merchants Square. While the Chamber dancers do other performances throughout the year, their most popular event is *The Nutcracker*, held each December in Phi Beta Kappa Memorial Hall at the College of William and Mary. It draws thousands of local schoolchildren in addition to the general public. For more information on this wonderful school and its many opportunities for youngsters interested in a variety of types of dance, call the number listed above.

Eastern Virginia School of the Performing Arts (EVSPA)
1915 Pocahontas Trail
The Village Shops at Kingsmill
(757) 229-8535
www.evspa.org
EVSPA offers a summer performing arts program in dance, theater, and voice, as well as

ℹ️ Want to do something a little different with the kids? Take them from Jamestown to Scotland on the ferry. It runs every thirty minutes, more often during peak times, daily year-round. It's free and it's fun. Kids can't help but want to feed the flock of gulls that tags along behind the ferry as it plies the waters of the James River for the fifteen-minute crossing. A word of caution: If you must feed the gulls, offer them popcorn, crackers, or pieces of bread—but only from the back of the boat.

programs the rest of the year for students of all ages. The early-childhood program for ages 3 to 4 and ages 5 to 6 is a special one, using dance, creative play, and musical instruments. Here, children are introduced to three disciplined art forms. Their creative potential is nurtured through the use of stories, rhymes, music, games, crafts, and instruments. The school also offers classes in ballet, modern dance, jazz, and folk dance to children 7 and older and to teens as well. (Check out The Arts chapter for more information.)

James City County
Parks and Recreation
5249-C Olde Towne Road
(757) 259-4200

James City County's Parks and Recreation Office plans and sponsors numerous programs for our young residents—from preschoolers to high school seniors. Summer playgrounds offer fun things to do for toddlers, while Total Rec camps for 6- to 14-year-olds offer full-day programs of activities including field trips, swimming, reading, sports, games, arts and crafts, and special events. Specialty camps, ranging from arts and science to sports, for children 5 to 16 focus on specific themes that are studied with a hands-on approach. Registration opens in the spring, and slots fill early. For information on other recreation and sports programs, check out the Parks and Recreation chapter, or call the number listed here.

Muscarelle Museum of Art
Jamestown Road
(757) 221-2703
www.wm.edu/muscarelle

Art is for everyone—especially children! And nowhere else in town are youngsters considered more enthusiastically during scheduled programs and workshops than at this wonderful, small museum.

Each year the Muscarelle Museum of Art at the College of William and Mary offers gallery/studio classes during the fall, winter, spring, and summer, with students in elementary through high school. Each class uses art on display in the museum as inspiration for its activities, many of which are wholly hands-on. Along with artists and teachers, students are given the opportunity to experiment with various media and techniques.

One especially popular series is the Art Makes You Smart program for preschoolers. Once a month, children 3 to 5, along with their adult companion, are invited to explore the museum with the assistance of an early childhood educator. They tour the facility, hear stories, sing songs, play games, and make art.

At various times of the year, the museum sponsors festivals that celebrate specific cultures and exhibits and offers performances, tours, and hands-on activities for children.

This is only the tip of the iceberg, so be sure to call for currently scheduled programs and events for youngsters and details about any scholarships that might apply.

Williamsburg Regional Library
515 Scotland Street
(757) 259-4050

7770 Croaker Road
(757) 259-7720
www.wrl.org

When the lights are on, and they're open for business, both locations of the Williamsburg Regional Library provide services for children from birth through high school. Programming is designed to promote the love of reading

i Ring, ring.... Santa's calling! A couple weeks before Christmas, the James City County Parks and Recreation Department offers a Santa Calling Program—a direct line to Mr. Claus himself. Registration forms are available at local schools and community centers, and must be submitted at least a week before the designated call day. To obtain a form, dial (757) 259-3200.

and to increase language skills among children. It includes story time for preschoolers and early elementary school children, author visits, children's theater groups, professional storytellers, puppet theaters, and assorted workshops. In addition to the summer reading incentive program for young readers, special kids' programs are offered throughout the week. Puppets, crafts, story times, and the

"Catch a Dragon by the Tale" reading adventure are just a few of the activities featured. Older children can also get involved in several library events, including the popular Teen Volunteer Program. Most programs are offered free of charge. For more information call the numbers listed above.

Williamsburg Symphonia
312 Waller Mill Road
(757) 229-9857
www.williamsburgsymphonia.org
The Williamsburg Symphonia offers twenty in-school programs and several youth concerts annually in addition to its regular subscription series. Reservations are on a first-come, first-served basis. Information on the concerts can be obtained from the symphonia at the above number. Find out more about the symphonia in The Arts chapter.

PARKS AND RECREATION

While you may be on the road, if you're willing to carve out the time, you can still enjoy physical activity beyond historic site tours and thrill rides. If it's leisure activities you miss, we'll help you find just about anything you want. Williamsburg area localities take recreation seriously and offer residents myriad options, which they'll gladly share with you.

Most of the organized sports and recreation activities take place through the parks and recreation departments of the local governments. The sports leagues for enthusiasts of all ages and skills are too numerous to list; their organizers are volunteers, so the contacts change frequently. Anyone interested in sports and recreation information should consult the *Virginia Gazette*'s sports section, which gives extensive coverage to local sports. Another good source of information is the James City County (JCC) Parks and Recreation's comprehensive seasonal publication, which is available at the JCC-Williamsburg Community Center, listed later in this chapter, and at other sites. Both the Williamsburg and York County parks and recreation departments also publish lists of recreational opportunities.

For those of you hoping to hit the links during your stay, please turn to the Golf chapter for information on area courses.

PARKS DEPARTMENTS

James City County Parks and Recreation
5249-C Olde Towne Road, Williamsburg
(757) 259-4200
www.james-city.va.us/recreation
This department oversees a wide range of recreation programs throughout the county including those at the James City County–Williamsburg Community Center, the James

River Community Center, Little Creek Reservoir, Mid County Park, and Upper County Park. Office hours are 8:00 a.m. to 5:00 p.m. Monday through Friday.

Williamsburg Parks and Recreation Department
202 Quarterpath Road, Williamsburg
(757) 259-3760
www.ci.williamsburg.va.us
Numerous recreation programs are available through this department, which also oversees Quarterpath Park, Waller Mill Park, and Kiwanis Park. The department's regular office hours are 8:00 a.m. to 5:30 p.m. Monday through Friday, although someone is on duty whenever the recreation center is open.

York Parks & Recreation
100 County Drive, Grafton
(757) 890-3500
www.yorkcounty.gov/parksandrec/
Located at the York County operations center off Goodwin Neck Road, the office of York Parks & Recreation oversees the operation of six parks, the Yorktown Beach waterfront, and county public boat landings at various sites. The offices are open 8:15 a.m. to 5:00 p.m. Monday through Friday, except on holidays.

PARK LOCATIONS AND ACTIVITIES

Back Creek Park
Goodwin Neck Road, Seaford
(757) 890-3850
A free boat-launching facility keeps this twenty-seven-acre York County park hopping year-round. It is a U.S. Tennis Association award-winning park that also features a picnic area, restrooms, and six lighted tennis courts.

Charles Brown Park
Route 238, Lackey
(757) 890-3500
Named in memory of a Lackey resident and
York County educator who demonstrated a
keen interest in youth, this ten-acre park
includes a baseball field, two basketball
courts, two tennis courts, picnic shelter,
playground area, and restrooms. A 3,000-
square-foot community center on-site
includes two small meeting rooms, one large
meeting room, restrooms, and a small
kitchen.

Chisman Creek Park
Wolf Trap Road, Grafton
(757) 890-3500
This thirteen-acre park was reclaimed from a
fly ash site in 1991. It has two lighted softball
fields, restrooms, and a parking lot. It includes
skinned infields and irrigated outfields. It is
used primarily for York County's adult softball
program in the spring and summer and is
used in the fall for youth soccer.

College Landing Park
South Henry Street, Williamsburg
(757) 259-3760
This small park on the southern edge of town
off South Henry Street is always open. It is
built alongside a marsh and has picnic areas,
a boat ramp, and a quiet boardwalk. It is
wheelchair accessible.

Diascund Reservoir
US 60 West, Toano
(757) 259-4200
This James City County reservoir, operated
jointly with Newport News and the Division of
Game and Inland Fisheries, is open to the
public for boating and fishing. Public boat-
landing hours are one hour before dawn to
one hour after sunset. Electric trolling motors
are the only ones allowed on the reservoir.

The Greensprings Trail
Route 5, behind Jamestown High School,
Williamsburg
(757) 259-4200

The 4.7-mile Greensprings Trail is a soft-
surface hiking trail that consists of three inter-
connecting loops through rural landscapes. It
includes a boardwalk over a beaver pond. It
can be reached by parking at the tennis
courts at Jamestown High School and following the dirt road to the left of the courts.

James City County District Park
Sports Complex
Off Centerville Road, Williamsburg
(757) 259-4200
This new 675-acre park being built by James
City County is under development; plans call
for numerous trails for hiking, biking, and
horseback riding. It will also have picnicking
facilities as well as tennis, basketball, and
volleyball courts. Long-range plans include
an outdoor education center and an
indoor/outdoor pool. The project is ongoing.

Kiln Creek Park
Kiln Creek Subdivision, Yorktown
(757) 890-3500
Located in the Kiln Creek community, this
twenty-one-acre York County park opened in
1999. The park features a lighted soccer field,
lighted baseball field, youth softball/baseball
field, two outdoor basketball courts, a playground, a picnic shelter, parking, and restrooms. The park is used primarily for the Little
League baseball program and the youth soccer program.

Kiwanis Municipal Park
123 Longhill Road, Williamsburg
(757) 259-3760
Little League baseball fields, basketball
courts, lighted tennis courts, a picnic shelter,
and a playground and playground equipment
make this Longhill Road park a local favorite.
Besides a convenient location and many
leisure activities, the park offers tennis classes
(see the entry under Tennis for further information on this park).

Little Creek Reservoir Park
180 Lakeview Drive, Toano
(757) 566-1702

Located off Forge Road, this park is a fisherman's paradise featuring year-round fishing and boating on the 996-acre reservoir, which is stocked with largemouth bass, bluegill, crappie, stripers, walleye, perch, pickerel, and a variety of sunfish and catfish. If you don't have a boat, you can rent one here, by the hour, and choose among jon boats with or without motors, kayaks, canoes, and paddleboats, or you can use the fishing pier, for which there's no charge. Use of the boat ramps costs a nominal amount. All fishermen must have a Virginia fishing license. The park is a nice place for a picnic, too, and offers a concession facility and shelter with grills. It's open daily March through November from 7:00 a.m. until sunset (6:00 a.m. until sunset on weekends and holidays) and 7:00 a.m. to 5:00 p.m. on weekends only from December through February. (See also the entry for Little Creek Reservoir in this chapter's Fishing and Hunting section.)

Mid County Park
3793 Ironbound Road, Williamsburg
(757) 229-1232

Fitness trails, soccer, baseball, basketball, softball, tennis, and volleyball are a few of the recreational activities available at this James City County park, which is open daily from sunrise to dusk. Located off Route 199, Mid County also offers picnic shelters and Kidsburg, an all-volunteer, community-built children's play area, parts of which are modeled on area attractions. For more on Kidsburg, see the Kidstuff chapter.

New Quarter Park
Lakeshead Drive, York
(757) 890-3500

Near the Queens Lake area of Williamsburg, this 545-acre York County park is especially good for group activities. Family reunions, company picnics, business meetings, and the like often take place here, where people can enjoy boating, hiking, fishing from the piers, playing horseshoes, and picnicking in the pavilions. The park is open May through October,

ber, 8:00 a.m. to dusk, and 10:00 a.m. to 5:00 p.m. in other months.

Powhatan Creek Access
Jamestown Road at Powhatan Creek
Williamsburg
(757) 259-4200

Listed on the Natural Resources Inventory, this facility provides access to Jamestown Island and the James River. It consists of a small-boat and canoe launch with parking for twenty vehicles.

Quarterpath Park and Recreation Center
202 Quarterpath Road, Williamsburg
(757) 259-3760

This park is home to some huge area sports leagues, and for good reason. Its facilities include free tennis and basketball courts (which are being renovated), an outdoor pool that's open through Labor Day, three softball fields, a playground, and indoor courts for basketball or volleyball. Fitness classes are offered for a fee.

Upper County Park
180 Leisure Road, Toano
(757) 566-1451

This James City County facility is open from Memorial Day to Labor Day and boasts an outdoor pool, bathhouse, community room, picnic shelters, and playground. Entrance to the park is free, although use of the pool costs $2.50 per day for resident adults, $3.50 for nonresidents, $2.00 for resident children, and $3.00 for nonresidents. Children 5 and younger are admitted free. Local families can purchase season pool passes for $70. The park is open from 11:00 a.m. to 7:45 p.m. daily.

Waller Mill Park
Airport Road (Route 645)
Williamsburg
(757) 259-3778

On Route 645 west of Williamsburg, Waller Mill is the place to go for a picnic or a lazy paddle around the lake. Open from sunrise to sunset year-round, Waller Mill offers shelters, tables, nature trails, jogging and fitness trails, a 5.5-mile mountain bike trail, and fishing, plus canoe, rowboat, and pedal-boat rental (boat rates range from $4 to $8 per hour). Boats for fishing rent for $5 per licensed angler per day. For a nominal fee you can launch your own fishing boat at the boat ramp. There's also a walking course for senior citizens. (See also the entry under the Fishing and Hunting section.)

Williamsburg Indoor Sports Complex
5700 Warhill Trail, Williamsburg
(757) 253-1947
www.thewisc.com

This 50,000-square-foot indoor sports facility is owned by the Williamsburg Indoor Sports Complex, a private organization that went into partnership with James City County. The complex sits on county park property. The Williamsburg Indoor Sports Complex, or WISC as it is known, offers camps for soccer (see more about soccer a little later in this chapter), in-line hockey, field hockey, basketball, gymnastics and cheerleading, fitness, and lacrosse. Call or check the Web site for the current class schedule and fees. The organization also hosts a variety of activities including parties, dances, and open skate times. There are sports activities throughout the year and no residence restrictions.

Wolf Trap Park
Wolftrap Road, Grafton
(757) 890-3500

This twenty-eight-acre park hosts the Yorktown United Soccer Club's matches. It features four soccer fields, restrooms, and a parking lot. Two ponds also are located here. It is home, too, to the York County Memorial Tree Grove, which provides an opportunity for friends, relatives, and organizations to commemorate deceased local citizens.

York River State Park
5526 Riverview Road, Williamsburg
(757) 566-3036

The Virginia Department of Conservation and Recreation operates this 2,505-acre tract of land year-round. The park lies alongside the York River, which is formed by the joining of the Pamunkey and Mattaponi Rivers at West Point. On the park property is Croaker Landing, an archaeological site listed on the National Register of Historic Places. The park is on what was once Taskinas Plantation. In the 17th and 18th centuries, it was the site of a public tobacco warehouse, where local planters stored their crops to be shipped. Remnants of wooden "corduroy" roads dating from the period can still be seen at low tide.

York River State Park opened in 1980 and is a great place to see firsthand the rare and delicate coastal estuarine environment, where freshwater and salt water merge to create a habitat rich in marine and plant life. You'll find excellent outdoor opportunities here, including 25 miles of hiking, biking, and horseback-riding trails through the park's diverse natural areas. The 1.75-mile Taskinas Creek Trail gives hikers a fascinating look at the Chesapeake Bay estuary. The Taskinas Creek area is one of four sites along the York River designated as a Chesapeake Bay Estuarine Research Reserve site. The park also has excellent picnicking facilities, with three shelters that overlook the scenic marsh or York River. The shelters, which have grills, picnic tables, and access to restrooms and the playground, may be reserved by calling the state park reservation office at (800) 933–PARK. In addition to the shelters, the park has forty picnic tables that are available first-come, first-served.

York River State Park offers many interpretive programs, including pontoon boat tours, guided canoe trips on the Taskinas Creek, night canoe trips, ranger-guided programs, ghost night hikes, Junior Rangers, fossil hikes, wildlife observations, nature hikes, and campfire programs in the fall, as well as environmental education programs for groups of ten or more. The guided canoe trips are provided May to October. Some programs do involve extra fees and require reservations.

The park has an interesting equipment rental policy: Once you pay the rental fee, you can swap equipment, which includes bikes, canoes, paddleboats, jon boats, and kayaks, as well as horseshoes, volleyballs, Frisbees, and badminton equipment. Rental equipment is available May through October.

While the park hours are 8:00 a.m. to dusk, the visitor center, park office, and gift shop are open from 8:00 a.m. to 6:00 p.m. during the week and 10:00 a.m. to 6:00 p.m. on Saturday and Sunday. The gift shop sells snacks, drinks, and ice cream. There are also primitive group tent camping sites available for up to forty-eight people. At York River there are three areas to fish; take your pick: freshwater, salt water, or brackish water. A valid fishing license is required (see the entry in this chapter under Fishing and Hunting).

York River State Park hosts several events through the year, including Harvest Day at the end of October. Admission is regular price, though some events may cost extra. During this festivity the park offers colonial and American Indian games, arts and crafts, old-fashioned games, such as the potato sack race and three-legged race, hayrides, and a maze for the children to wander through.

Located about ten miles west of Williamsburg on Riverview Road (also known as Route 606), York River State Park can be reached by taking the Croaker exit 231B off of Interstate 64.

Yorktown Waterfront
U.S. Route 17 and Water Street
Yorktown
(757) 898-3500
This two-acre beachfront is open to the public year-round free of charge. However, there are no lifeguards on duty. Water lovers can swim, fish, and boat here and even take a shower afterwards. Restrooms are located on-site. Showers and restrooms are open April 1 to mid-October.

RECREATION

Greater Williamsburg Family YMCA
630 South Henry Street, Williamsburg
(757) 258-3830
This small but active center is the first foray of the YMCA into Greater Williamsburg. Before- and after-school programs and a summer camp program are held in this building, located across from the Marshall Wythe School of Law of the College of William and Mary on South Henry Street.

The center operates a state-licensed before- and after-school program open to all students 6 to 12. Students participate in various activities, including fitness, homework time, free play, multicultural projects, character-building programs, and nature studies. The YMCA also offers a variety of summer camps for children 5 to 12 and a Neighborhood Basketball League.

James City County–Williamsburg Community Center
5301 Longhill Road, Williamsburg
(757) 259-4200
This large facility has just about anything a person could want in recreation: a gymnasium with two basketball courts, four volleyball courts, a two-lane indoor suspended track, a 25-meter-by-25-yard swimming pool with three lap-lanes, locker rooms with showers and saunas, racquetball courts, a whirlpool for sixteen people, and a fitness room with free weights, two circuits of Cybex, and twenty-three pieces of cardiovascular equipment. There's also a teen area equipped with TV and games, and a senior area with pool table and game table. The center also

i The temperate climate that makes outdoor life so enjoyable for humans also spawns a variety of tiny wildlife that can get you itching and scratching. This includes mosquitoes, ticks, and spiders, among others. Use a bug repellent for comfort and safety when spending time outdoors.

has a craft room, a kiln and pottery wheels, and a dance and aerobics room. Hours of operation are Monday through Friday 6:00 a.m. to 9:00 p.m., Saturday 9:00 a.m. to 6:00 p.m., and Sunday 1:00 to 6:00 p.m.

The center offers senior activities provided in conjunction with the Historic Triangle Senior Center and rehabilitation and health education programs in conjunction with Williamsburg Community Hospital. Also, trainers are on-site to offer fitness assessments and personal fitness training.

A notary public is on site 8:00 a.m. until 5:00 p.m. Monday through Friday.

The Greater Williamsburg Branch YMCA provides child care for children 6 months through 10 years in the Community Center while their parents are using the facility. Reservations may be made by phone or in person up to one week in advance and must be made at least twenty-four hours in advance.

Patron services include orientation on weight equipment, on-site registration for division-wide programs and services, rentals for picnic shelters, soccer and softball field rentals, and corporate passes for local businesses.

Family and individual membership fees are based on a member's age and income, call for more information. The center closes for Labor Day, Thanksgiving, Christmas, New Year's Day, Easter, and the Fourth of July.

James River Community Center
8901 Pocahontas Trail, Williamsburg
(757) 887-5810
The center includes a gymnasium, a multipurpose room with game tables and large-screen TV, a glass-backed racquetball court, fitness room, table tennis and pool table, three tennis courts, basketball courts, a sand volleyball court, soccer field, softball field, and a nature trail. The fitness room is equipped with a circuit of Cybex equipment, dumbbells, a weight bench, and a pull-up dip station. Patrons have access to a cafeteria and kitchen area.

The multipurpose rooms, cafeteria, and gym are available for rent for small parties or large gatherings. Patron services include ori-

entation on weight equipment, on-site registration for division-wide programs and services, rentals for picnic shelters, soccer and softball field rentals, and corporate passes for local businesses. A notary public is on-site noon until 8:00 p.m. Monday through Friday. The center also offers a wide variety of classes, such as karate, CPR, tennis, and oil painting.

The center is open Monday through Thursday from noon to 9:00 p.m., Friday noon to 8:00 p.m., weekends 1:00 to 6:00 p.m., and closed on major holidays. One-year resident access passes cost $35 for adults, $50 for families, $25 for seniors, and $15 for youth. All resident patrons without a monthly access pass must purchase a $5 access pass to use the center.

ACTIVITIES

Biking
Many visitors enjoy biking through the Historic Area, especially on quiet and picturesque back streets where the illusion of a return to the past is most complete. Bikes are available from the following private businesses.

Bikes Unlimited
759 Scotland Street, Williamsburg
(757) 229-4620
Near both the college and the west end of the Historic Area, this company offers complete biking services. Hours are 9:30 a.m. to 6:30 p.m. Tuesday through Friday, 10:00 a.m. to 5:00 p.m. Saturday, and noon to 4:00 p.m. Sunday (April through October). The store is closed Monday.

i A favorite biking trip is the 23-mile Colonial Parkway, which passes through various landscapes and provides wonderful views without the heavy traffic of local streets and highways. Observe Virginia biking laws, which require bikers to ride in the same direction as the flow of traffic at all times.

Bikesmith of Williamsburg
515 York Street, Williamsburg
(757) 229-9858

The Bikesmith sells, rents, services, and repairs bicycles near the east end of the Historic Area. The store is closed on Sunday, and opens at 10:00 a.m. all other days. It is open until 6:00 p.m. on Monday, Tuesday, Thursday, and Friday; 5:00 p.m. on Saturday; and 1:00 p.m. on Wednesday. Call ahead if you're visiting off-season.

Williamsburg Area Bicyclists
Williamsburg
www.wabonline.org

If you bring your bike to town and are looking for companions to ride with, check out this club, which encourages the use of the bicycle for recreation, fitness, and transportation, while also encouraging the development of facilities for bicycling on public lands. A calendar of rides is kept up to date on its Web site and provides phone numbers for ride leaders. Scheduled rides vary from the casual ride that is good for beginners and families to more advanced. Annual membership is $15; $20 for families. Riders are required to wear helmets for all rides.

Bowling

AMF Williamsburg Lanes
5544 Olde Towne Road, Williamsburg
(757) 565-3311

Regular hours here are 9:00 a.m. to midnight Sunday through Thursday, 9:00 a.m. to 2:00 a.m. Friday and Saturday. Colorful excitement is offered in the form of the Xtreme Bowl Package, usually held Friday and Saturday nights. During these events regular lighting is turned off, the music is turned up, and black lights provide special effect lighting on the pins, which glow in the dark. Three times a year Williamsburg Lanes hosts tournaments, which may make getting a lane difficult. The Virginia Women's Tournament takes place over several weeks in October and November. Colonial Virginia's Men's Tournament comes along during March and April. During the Colonial Virginia's Mixed Tournament in June, July, and August, they really mix it up. Special rates are offered to children, senior citizens, and groups. This is an excellent spot for a child's birthday party since they offer special packages.

Fishing and Hunting

Water surrounds the Historic Triangle—rivers, tributaries, lakes, ponds, wetlands, estuaries, and the Bay. A complete guide to area fishing would require a hefty volume. Here we offer merely some local fishin' holes and information about licenses. If you're a die-hard angler, check with the Department of Game and Inland Fisheries in Richmond, (804) 367-1000, for a copy of its annual state fishing guide and the facts on seasons and creel limits, etc. Or call (800) 986-2628 to purchase Virginia licenses by phone.

Used to be you could toss your line in the ocean or Chesapeake Bay for free, but since 1992 a license for fishing in salt water is required for all those between 16 and 65. The cost is $30 for residents. A freshwater license is required for those 16 and older all over the state of Virginia, and the Tidewater area is no exception. A statewide freshwater license is $18. Licenses are valid for the calendar year during which they are bought and are available at local bait and tackle shops, marinas, sporting goods counters of larger stores, and county circuit court clerks. Licenses can also be purchased online with a credit card at www.dgif.state.va.us. For more information on fishing licenses or for boat licenses, contact the Department of Game and Inland Fisheries.

If hunting is your sport, you'll need a license, too. Hunters 16 and older who have previously had a license can purchase one valid in Virginia by phone through Bass Pro Shops at (800) 986-2628. If you've never had a hunting license before or are between 12 and 15, you must first take a hunter safety course to obtain a Virginia hunting license. These courses are given by the state for free. Again, contact the Department of Game and Inland Fisheries.

Little Creek Reservoir
180 Lakeview Drive, Toano
(757) 566-1702

Little Creek Reservoir in Toano, covering 996 acres, has a boat ramp, a dock, and a fishing pier. You can also fish from the shore. Crappie, largemouth bass, pickerel, bluegills, stripers, and walleye can be hooked here. Little Creek is open daily March through November; December through February it opens weekends only, weather permitting. Season passes are available for $60 a year. Children younger than 16 fish for free. Boat rentals for pleasure riding range from $4 to $8 per hour or $20 per hour with motor and battery. This wonderful, practically secret lake is a bit hard to find: From US 60 in Toano, take Route 610 (Forge Road) 2 miles to the first left, which is Lakeview Drive. (See also the Little Creek Reservoir Park entry in this chapter under Park Locations and Activities.)

Powhatan Creek Access
Jamestown Road at Powhatan Creek
Williamsburg
(757) 259-4200

Listed on the Natural Resources Inventory, this simple facility provides access to Jamestown Island and the James River. It consists of a small-boat and canoe launch with parking for twenty vehicles. It is located along Jamestown Road across from Cooke's Greenhouse.

Waller Mill Park
Airport Road (Route 645)
Williamsburg
(757) 259-3778

For freshwater fishing, try Waller Mill Park, which has one of the area's deepest lakes, known for large striped bass, crappie, largemouth bass, perch, pickerel, and channel catfish. There is no charge to fish from the pier. The fee to rent a boat is $5 per day per person. That charge includes fishing privileges. For more information on Waller Mill, see the earlier entry under Park Locations and Activities.

York River State Park
5526 Riverview Road, Williamsburg
(757) 566-3036
www.dcr.state.va.us/parks/yorkrive.htm

The Virginia Department of Conservation and Recreation operates this large tract 10 miles west of Williamsburg off I–64 and adjacent to the York River. Here you'll find excellent fishing and boat ramps. A broad spectrum of fish are here for the catch, including saltwater fish (croaker, spot), brackish-water fish (largemouth bass, sunfish, spot, croaker), and freshwater fish (primarily bluegill, largemouth bass, and catfish). The park is open from 8:00 a.m. to dusk. There is a $2 parking fee per car, and a variety of boats are available for rental.

Horseback Riding

Carlton Farms
3516 Mott Lane, Williamsburg
(757) 220-3553

Carlton Farms offers lessons, boarding, summer camp, and sales, and has an indoor, lighted arena. It specializes in hunter horses and has a special package for beginning riders. Instructors at the farm suggest that beginning riders have at least three private lessons to get used to being on a horse.

Cedar Valley Farm
2016 Forge Road, Toano
(757) 566-2621

Off Lightfoot Road, Cedar Valley Farm gives private lessons to groups or individuals in English riding. Summer camps are offered sometimes, and horse owners can obtain permission to ride at the farm. Cedar Valley Farm also runs the College of William and Mary riding program and equestrian show team.

Jogging and Running

Joggers will find that many area parks offer some kind of fitness path. Waller Mill Park offers four trails—its mile-long trail is one of the best—and the trail at the James City County–Williamsburg Community Center is also very popular. But Insiders love running along the Colonial Parkway best of all.

James City County–Williamsburg Community Center
5301 Longhill Road, Williamsburg
(757) 259-4200
The center includes a two-lane indoor suspended track. The inside lane is reserved for walking and is also accessible to wheelchairs and canes. The outside lane is reserved for joggers and speed walking. The facility also has 2 miles of walking and bicycling paths on the grounds.

Waller Mill Park
Airport Road (Route 645)
Williamsburg
(757) 259-3778
This park offers a wide range of trails for the jogger, walker, and bicyclist. All of them wind through a wooded setting. The mile-long Fitness Trail is especially popular because it features fitness stops along the way for different exercises. The other trails include the 1.5-mile Bayberry Nature Trail; the 3-mile Lookout Tower Trail; the 5.5-mile Dogwood Trail, which is used by joggers and bicyclists; and the 1-mile senior walking course.

Soccer

The sport of soccer is thriving here, with the number of youth soccer clubs on the increase.

James City County Division of Parks and Recreation Youth Soccer League
5249 Olde Towne Road, Williamsburg
(757) 259-4200
James City County offers a youth soccer league in the spring and fall for school-age boys and girls and a special program in fall for preschoolers. This program is for fun and educational purposes and is noncompetitive.

Virginia Legacy Soccer Club
(757) 253-1947
www.williamsburgsoccer.com
In 2006 the Virginia Legacy Soccer Club came to be as the merger of the Williamsburg Soccer Club and the Colonial Football Club. It's the largest soccer club in the Williamsburg area and offers a wide range of packages, lessons, and leagues. Its premier team is the Williamsburg Legacy, a United Soccer League affiliate.

Williamsburg Indoor Sports Complex
5700 Warhill Trail, Williamsburg
(757) 253-1947
www.thewisc.com
This private facility on county land is operated by Chris Haywood, a former collegiate All-American and professional soccer player and a Lafayette High School boys soccer coach. He started the Colonial Football Club, which operates out of the Williamsburg Indoor Sports Complex (WISC). The sports complex offers numerous sports activities, including soccer.

York County Division of Parks and Recreation
100 County Drive, Grafton
(757) 890-3500
Boys and girls in kindergarten through twelfth grade from York County can participate in the Youth Soccer Program sponsored by York County Division of Parks and Recreation. There are spring and fall programs. Practices take place at area elementary and middle schools and county parks. Registration begins at the end of August and February. Fees vary, so call for details. Coach certification programs are also offered. A weather hotline at (757) 890-3501 keeps participants informed of weather cancellations.

Tennis
Public Courts
Back Creek Park
3000 Goodwin Neck Road, Seaford
(757) 890-3850
This twenty-seven-acre United States Tennis Association award-winning tennis facility, accessible year-round, features six lighted tennis courts. Fees are charged when the park is staffed—on weekends in the spring

through late November. Players can use the courts for free from the end of November through late March. Courts can be reserved up to a week in advance by calling the park. Lessons are available in the spring, summer, and fall.

Charles Brown Park
Route 238, Lackey
(757) 890-3500
This ten-acre park has two tennis courts, open year-round. There is no fee for using these courts.

Kiwanis Municipal Park
123 Longhill Road, Williamsburg
(757) 259-3776
Kiwanis Municipal Park has seven hard-surface courts that are free, but call for availability. Tennis lessons are offered in the spring, summer, and fall.

Mid County Park
3793 Ironbound Road, Williamsburg
(757) 229-1232
and
Quarterpath Park
202 Quarterpath Road, Williamsburg
(757) 259-3200
There are three asphalt surface courts at both Mid County Park and Quarterpath Park, which are used at no charge on a first-come, first-play basis.

Semiprivate Courts

Kingsmill Tennis Club
931 Kingsmill Road, Williamsburg
(757) 253-3945
The Kingsmill Tennis Club, which was recently voted a top-seventy-five worldwide tennis resort by tennisresortsonline.com, has fifteen courts, thirteen clay and two hard surface. The courts are free for guests at all times. Nonguests pay $16 a person per day for courts, or $8 after 4:00 p.m. Reservations are recommended. Regular tennis shoes, not running shoes, must be worn.

The Williamsburg Inn
136 East Francis Street, Williamsburg
(757) 220-7794
Colonial Williamsburg provides Colonial Williamsburg hotel guests with access to tennis courts on the property of the Williamsburg Inn near Providence Hall. Memberships for area residents are available.

Health and Fitness Clubs

Iron Bound Gym
1228 Richmond Road, Williamsburg
(757) 229-5874
This coed fitness center, located behind Williamsburg Crossing Shopping Center's Food Lion, features free weights, Nautilus equipment, cardio equipment, treadmills, bikes, and steppers, as well as a sauna, an outdoor pool, a Jacuzzi, and a tanning bed. Guest rates are $5 a day. The center is open 5:30 a.m. to 11:30 p.m. Monday through Thursday, 5:30 a.m. to 9:00 p.m. Friday, and 9:00 a.m. to 5:00 p.m. on weekends.

GOLF

Williamsburg continues its growth as one of the premier golf destinations on the Eastern Seaboard. More than twenty courses are now available in the area, and that number continues to grow because the region's temperate weather allows virtually year-round play.

By far, the biggest draws are the championship tournaments at Kingsmill. Previously home to the Professional Golf Association (PGA) Michelob Championship every October, Kingsmill now hosts the Ladies Professional Golf Association (LPGA) Michelob ULTRA Open in early May, with the inaugural event held in 2003. The first year attracted forty-nine of the country's fifty top women golfers with a $1.6 million purse.

The nationally acclaimed Golden Horseshoe Golf Course in Colonial Williamsburg, designed by the venerable Robert Trent Jones, has been renovated by his son Rees. The multimillion-dollar effort has only improved what was already a jewel of a layout. Greens, bunkers, and cart paths have been upgraded, but rest assured, the changes remain faithful to the elder Jones's original design.

Many of the courses cater heavily to the communities with which they are associated, as well as the growing local retired population and visitors looking for an alternative to touring or shopping. Insiders have become accustomed to the pricey greens fees, but they also know there are some good bargains out there. (Check the sports pages of the local newspapers for discount coupons.) They also know to make tee times in advance. In this chapter we give you an overview of the courses, including greens fees, yardages (from the men's tees), and directions. Greens fees include cart unless otherwise noted. Reduced rates, based on time of year, time of day, etc., are available at most of the courses. We've also tried to let you know when carts are a must for a particular course. The growing trend requiring soft spikes is pervasive, so be sure to ask when you call for tee times.

THE COURSES

The Colonial Golf Course
8281 Diascund Road, Lanexa
(757) 566-1600, (800) 566-6660
www.golfcolonial.com
Designed by Lester George (with the help of PGA pro Robert Wrenn) and opened in 1995, this course is situated in Lanexa, on Diascund Road (which is off U.S. Route 60, 7 miles west of the Williamsburg Pottery). It is a daily-fee course, carved out of dense woods and wetlands, with several holes overlooking the Chickahominy River. The daunting par 3 sixth hole is all carry over marshland to an elevated green. This championship course plays to a par 72 and is 6,886 yards long. Unique features include a three-hole practice course ($18, with cart and practice balls) and the Teaching Center and Golf Academy. Different rates apply for the various teaching and clinic packages, and reservations are appropriate. A round with cart (a must) ranges from $42 (weekday afternoons) to $70 (weekend mornings). Call for details.

Ford's Colony Country Club
240 Ford's Colony Drive, Williamsburg
(757) 258-4130, (800) 334-6033
www.fordscolony.com/golf
Fifty-four holes, designed by Dan Maples, are set on verdant hills with water, water everywhere at Ford's Colony. Here, you will find four nine-hole layouts that can be played in a number of combinations.

Opened in 1999, the Blackheath course plays 6,146 yards. With undulating greens and water on seven holes, it is a real challenge.

Other options are the Marsh Hawk (6,230 yards for eighteen holes), and the eighteen-hole Blue Heron (6,290 yards). Greens fees at Ford's Colony vary seasonally, so inquire about fees when calling for a tee time. Lessons are available, and guests of the Manor Club, a time-share resort, can purchase golf packages at a discounted rate. The clubhouse facilities are first-rate, and after your round, world-class dining awaits.

The Golden Horseshoe Golf Course
South England Street, Williamsburg
(757) 220-7696
www.goldenhorseshoegolf.com

You can choose from three beautiful, challenging courses here. Robert Trent Jones designed the Gold Course, which opened in 1963. A spectacular multimillion-dollar renovation by Rees Jones was completed in 1998. Nationally renowned, the course features numerous elevation changes, tight fairways, and plenty of water. Its signature hole, the par 3 sixteenth, boasts the first island green ever built in America. Playing to a par of 71, the 6,248-yard layout's five closing holes are a test for any golfer. The Golden Horseshoe—known locally as "the Shoe"—offers full clubhouse amenities, including a pro shop, locker rooms, and a lounge.

The Rees Jones–designed Green Course, which opened in 1991, is a 6,244-yard, par 72 course where mounds abound and the par 5 eighteenth hole requires a 200-yard carry off the tee. More wide open than its sister course, this design still offers a stiff test for hackers of all levels. Like the Gold Course, the Green features a first-class clubhouse, pro shop, and restaurant.

After designing the Gold Course, the senior Jones took the time to create the Spotswood Course. Its executive-length design allows golfers to get around its nine holes in quick order, perfect for a late afternoon of fun.

Fees range from $50 to more than $150 in peak season. Lessons are available.

Kingsmill Golf Club
100 Golf Club Road, Williamsburg
(757) 253-1703
www.kingsmill.com

The three courses at this golf club have something to satisfy every golfer. Kingsmill on the James, a planned community, and Kingsmill Resort surround the courses. But the wide, exceptionally well-landscaped vistas and breathtaking views of the James River remove you from any sense of encroachment. Kingsmill is home to the Michelob ULTRA Open, a tournament event on the LPGA tour in early May.

The River Course is the crown jewel. Designed by the legendary Pete Dye, the par 71, 5,001-yard course is both challenging and scenic. Holes four, eight, ten, and sixteen are bears, but your reward is the par 3, which overlooks the historic James River. In recent years changes to several holes have toughened up the layout.

The Plantation Course, par 72, is a 5,503-yard Arnold Palmer design. Undulating greens make for a putting challenge, and a couple of the par 4s will test you off the tee. In 1993 the eighteenth hole was redesigned to feature a new fairway and green.

Lastly there is the Woods Course, designed by Tom Clark and two-time U.S. Open Champion pro Curtis Strange. East of the other courses, this 6,030-yard achievement looked like a course that had cured for twenty years on the day it opened. It features its own clubhouse with all the amenities you would expect at a world-class resort such as Kingsmill.

The courses are open to the public. Greens fees range from $45 to $150, depending on the season and which course you play. A nine-hole par 3 is complimentary for resort guests. All fees include the mandatory golf cart. Lessons are available. Visitors can reserve a tee time twenty-four hours in advance.

Traditions Golf Club at Kiskiack
8104 Club Drive
(757) 566-2200, (800) 989-4728

This John LaFoy–designed course was created from woodlands and rolling terrain and has

Many area accommodations offer special deals for golfers. To find out what vacation packages may be available during your visit, call the Williamsburg Hotel & Motel Association at (800) FOR-GOLF.

quickly become a favorite among local golfers. Ten minutes west of Williamsburg, at the Croaker Road exit on Interstate 64, this 6,405-yard, par 72 layout is a treat. The par 3 eleventh hole, requiring a hefty carry over water, is easily the signature hole. Greens fees, including cart, range from $63 to $85, and getting a tee time in advance is a must.

Newport News Golf Club at Deer Run
Newport News Park
901 Clubhouse Way, Newport News
(757) 886-7925
www.nngolfclub.com

Insider golfers looking for a lower-cost day on the links often take advantage of Deer Run. The par 72 courses offer 5,863 yards on the Cardinal Course and 6,324 yards on the Championship Course. Greens fees with cart start at $30, a bargain in the immediate Williamsburg vicinity. The course is an easy fifteen-minute drive east on I–64 at the Fort Eustis exit.

Royal New Kent
Route 155, Providence Forge
(804) 966-7023, (866) 284-6534

The second Legends course to open in the Williamsburg area is an unusual one, unlike any other on this side of the Atlantic. Instead, it has been compared to Ballybunion and Royal County Down in Ireland, two of the world's greatest links courses. Among other things, it features stone walls, hidden greens, and blind fairways, giving this course a particularly natural setting. This par 72 course is 6,200 yards long. Greens fees with a cart, which we recommend, range from $85 to $100. Soft spikes are required. Call ahead for

tee times and golf packages. The course is about thirty minutes west of Williamsburg; follow I–64 to exit 214 (Providence Forge). Take Route 155 south 2.5 miles to the course entrance.

Tradition Golf Course at Stonehouse
Route 30, Williamsburg
(757) 566-1138, (888) 2-LEGENDS

This course has generated more comment than any other in recent years. Located about fifteen miles west of Williamsburg near Toano, Stonehouse is said to be one of the most beautiful mountain courses in the Mid-Atlantic region. It features beautiful, deep bunkering; awesome vistas; and undulating, fast greens comparable to Cypress Point in Pebble Beach, California. Some greens sit atop cliffs, while others meander along spring-fed creeks. The par 71 design measures 6,111 yards. Greens fees range from $45 in the winter to $100 in high season weekends. Lesson costs vary. We strongly recommend a cart. Call the toll-free number for tee times. The quickest route to the course is via I–64 west to exit 227. The entrance is a half-mile north on the right.

Williamsburg National Golf Club
3700 Centerville Road, Williamsburg
(757) 258-9642, (800) 859-9182
www.wngc.com

Club Development Associates of Pinehurst developed the Williamsburg National just east of Williamsburg near the intersection of Route 5 and Centerville Road. Within the developing Greensprings neighborhood, this 6,951-yard course is open to the public and offers eighteen holes designed by Jack Nicklaus's Golden Bear Associates. The golf course is designed for both the low and high handicapper. For example, the fourth hole lets golfers play a shot over wetlands, but there is a safe area to the left for the high handicapper.

The $60 to $90 fees include cart, which you will definitely need. Lessons are available, and weekly clinics and a summer Junior Camp are also offered.

THE ENVIRONMENT

We all know there are a lot of people on this Earth vying for their little corner of the world. Indeed, in 2007 the population of good old planet Earth was calculated to be a whopping 6.6 billion. More than 7 million of that total live in the commonwealth of Virginia, including more than 120,000 in Williamsburg, James City County, and York County.

It's an unfortunate fact of life that people generate pollution. As the population climbs, so does the congestion on our streets, the litter on our sidewalks, and the garbage in our landfills. The Chesapeake Bay—the landmark body of water in this region—has been particularly vulnerable to population growth in the eastern United States. Over the last several decades, this magnificent 200-mile-long estuary—which is fed by the James, York, and Chickahominy Rivers of the Historic Triangle—has watched its vast numbers of oysters, crabs, and finfish decline.

Year after year, the population explosion around the Bay continues at a staggering pace. The Chesapeake Bay Foundation estimates that every hour development consumes another ten acres of land in the Cheapeske Bay region. And each new person who comes to live in the Bay watershed generates about 50,000 pounds of waste annually.

SOME BAY BASICS

To better understand what has been happening to the Bay, it helps to know a little bit more about this amazing body of water. It may surprise you to know that the Chesapeake Bay, formed 12,000 years ago, is the largest and most biologically productive estuary in North America, home to more than 2,700 species of plants and animals. (An estuary is an area where freshwater and salt water mix.) While this long stretch of water averages 15 miles across, its depth averages a mere 21 feet. Other facts about the Bay, compiled by the Chesapeake Bay Foundation, follow:

- The Bay covers 2,500 square miles and holds 18 trillion gallons of water.
- Flowing into the Bay are 49 rivers with 102 branches and tributaries. These can be navigated for 1,750 miles.
- There are more than 17 million people living in the Bay's watershed, which includes Virginia, Maryland, West Virginia, Pennsylvania, Delaware, New York, and the District of Columbia.
- The Bay's blue-crab harvest annually represents more than half of our country's total catch.
- The Bay is the winter home for about 500,000 Canada geese and 40,000 whistling swans.
- The Bay has more than 5,600 miles of shoreline, but only 2 percent of it is accessible to the public. The rest is privately owned.
- Amazingly, if you reduced the Chesapeake Bay to the scale of a football field, its average depth would equal three dimes. The bay's shallowness makes it vulnerable to pollution because ample water is not available to absorb toxins, nutrients, and sediment.
- Archaeological records reveal that the Chesapeake Bay watershed has been inhabited by humans since 8000 B.C.
- The name Chesapeake is derived from the Native American word Tschiswapeki, which means "great shellfish bay."

TROUBLE IN PARADISE

Population growth has been only one part of the problem facing the Bay. The lifestyles, business practices, and environmental nonchalance of most of the twentieth century have merely added insult to injury. One of the most recent blows came in the spring of 1999, when the Bay—from the Maryland border to the York River—was added to the Environmental Protection Agency's list of polluted Virginia waterways.

Despite that announcement, numerous organizations and thousands of people are continuing strenuous efforts to clean up the Bay. And it seems—at least in some small measure—that their years of vigilance are beginning to pay off. Bay watchers will be happy to learn that there have been some positive developments in the past decade.

For example, in its 2006 State of the Bay Report, the Chesapeake Bay Foundation (CBF) noted that the health of the Bay had improved slightly, but there is still much work to be done if the Bay is to be taken off the nation's list of "dirty waters" by 2010, as pledged by local politicians and environmentalists. In 1999, Foundation President William C. Baker noted that "water pollution from excessive nitrogen and phosphorus remains the Bay's most serious problem, and it will continue to be until there is a long-term, Baywide trend toward reduced levels of these polluting nutrients." Pollution from pipes and smokestacks has been reduced, and the Bay's overall decline has slowed; CBF also says there have been small positive changes, providing hope for the future of this great natural resource.

The State of the Bay Report was first issued by the Foundation in 1998 as a way to assess the Bay's health through an analysis of thirteen factors: oysters, shad, underwater grasses, wetlands, forested buffers, toxic substances, water clarity, dissolved oxygen, crabs, striped bass, resource lands, phosphorus, and nitrogen. And while the report did note the positive findings above, the Bay, says Baker, "remains a system dangerously out of balance. Key systems are distressed, and it operates at barely more than one-quarter of its historical potential."

CONCERN ABOUT CRABS

The Chesapeake Bay blue crab—the tasty crustacean we raved about in the chapter on Regional Cuisine and Wines—has been one of the main victims of both the Bay's failing health and overzealous harvests by fishermen.

The crab industry, typically an $88-million-a-year trade in Virginia, suffered through one of its most dismal seasons ever during the winter of 1998. Indeed, some watermen said it was the worst winter crab-dredging harvest they had experienced in two decades—calling the reduction in their catch "devastating" and the lack of crabs "ridiculous."

The blue crab needs several different types of aquatic habitats during its lifespan, and the Chesapeake Bay Foundation blames reduced amounts of underwater grasses and low levels of oxygen in the summer for the reduced populations of these crabs. The annual blue-crab advisory report of the Chesapeake Bay Stock Assessment Committee called the current situation "risky" and warned that the population could be in danger of a collapse. The catch in 2003 of 48 million pounds was below the average of 75 million. The stock assessment report concluded that there has been a declining trend in reproduction in recent years, and that the spawning stock has decreased since the mid-1990s. The committee recommended a 15 percent reduction in fishing activity over three years to protect the crab population. Both Virginia and Maryland have moved toward that goal.

OYSTER ANXIETY

The crab's compatriot, the tasty bay oyster, is having a tough time of its own. In fact, in recent years the decline in the numbers of this shellfish has been dramatic. The harvest of market-size oysters dropped from about 25 million pounds in the mid-1950s; now, the oyster population is a mere 2 percent of that historic level. It is estimated that in the late

ℹ️ If you want to catch a few crabs off a local pier, keep these pointers in mind. Recreational fishermen do not need a license to use a dip net or two crab pots to catch their crustaceans, which must measure at least 5 inches across. No more than one bushel of hard crabs per person, please. Because of ongoing protection and restoration efforts, regulations change often. For the most current information, call the Virginia Marine Resources Commission at (757) 247-2200, or visit their Web site at www.state.va.us/mrc/ for a summary of regulations.

1800s, more than 6,000 shell fishermen plied the Chesapeake Bay using tongs—two shafts fastened together like scissors—to pull 18 million bushels of oysters out of the water in a single season!

Researchers have been looking for ways to revive the Bay's ailing oyster population. One of the most recent studies was done by the Virginia Institute of Marine Science at Gloucester Point (VIMS), just across the York River from Yorktown. Marine scientists at VIMS placed experimental Japanese oysters in a variety of habitats throughout the Bay to see how well they grew in those foreign environments and if they were immune to the diseases that have decimated native oyster populations. While the same species of oyster already had been introduced in Europe, the Pacific Northwest, and Chile, VIMS scientists found that they did not grow as well as native ones in Bay waters.

Another area of research is the oyster habitat. Over thousands of years oysters and their shells accumulated to form extensive reefs and bars. The existence of these reefs is critical to oyster development. Unfortunately, during the past 300 years, the reefs have been harvested to the point of depletion. As a way to help the ailing oyster population by providing a high-quality habitat, reefs are being built of shell, concrete, and

coal ash in the lower Chesapeake Bay and elsewhere.

VIMS doesn't restrict its aquatic research to oysters. Chartered in 1940 as an arm of the College of William and Mary, VIMS is the largest marine center in the nation focused on coastal ocean and estuarine research. Because of its groundbreaking work, the Institute is recognized internationally as a world leader in marine science. In the recent past researchers have helped establish hard clam and soft-shell crab aquaculture in the state and have done considerable research on the bay scallop. VIMS also has launched a new aquaculture genetics and breeding center to step up the pace of its seafood-farming research.

While the fate of many types of shellfish remains iffy, one species of aquatic life that appears to be making a comeback is the striped bass, more commonly known as rockfish to local anglers. Rockfish live all along the East Coast but primarily spawn in the Bay and were plentiful in area waters during the 1960s and early 1970s. Continued heavy fishing drove populations to all-time lows, and stringent restrictions were placed on rockfishing in the early 1980s. Indeed, in 1989 Virginia banned commercial striped-bass fishing in order to replenish declining populations. Those efforts, perhaps aided by a cyclical resurgence of the species, have paid off. Rockfish are once again plentiful in the Bay and neighboring waters, and restrictions have been eased considerably.

WATER WOES AND WONDERS

While many species of fish and shellfish are suffering, the bodies of water that sustain them have their own set of problems.

The York River, for instance, has low dissolved-oxygen counts, indicating large amounts of waste discharge and sluggish flushing action. Some shellfish grounds have been condemned in recent years as a consequence of these conditions. The James River has recuperated from Kepone (a highly toxic

ℹ️ From the 1600s to 1950 (about 350 years), approximately 1.7 million acres of the Bay's forests, wetlands, and farmland were depleted by development. Between 1950 and 1980 an additional 2.7 million acres of open space and farms in the Bay watershed were lost to further development and poor land-use planning.

insecticide) contamination since the Kepone ban was established in the 1970s, but sewage overflows from Richmond plague the river, as do industrial discharges and agricultural runoff. Although the latter two problems have improved somewhat in recent years, shellfish grounds here, too, have been condemned in various areas due to contaminants.

One local body of water that teems with life is the Chickahominy River, which extends from western Henrico County, northwest of Richmond, to the James River just upstream of The Governor's Land at Two Rivers subdivision in James City County. Named after the Native American people who still live in the area, the word Chickahominy means "coarse-pounded corn people." To this day the Chickahominy remains one of the cleaner tributaries to the Chesapeake Bay, providing homes for herons, egrets, and bald eagles in its marshes, swamps, and surrounding land. Rare plant species such as swamp pink and yellow cowlily can be found in the middle and lower sections of the watershed, and even freshwater mussels, highly sensitive to any disturbances in the environment, make their home in Chickahominy tributaries. But an influx of development around the cities of Richmond and Williamsburg has raised concerns about the watershed's future. In an effort to prevent new problems from developing and old ones from escalating, a comprehensive effort is under way to document the watershed's resources and to learn more about how the health of its wetlands and waterways are related to the use of surrounding land.

THE AIR WE BREATHE

Air quality in the Historic Triangle is affected not so much by industrial discharges as by automobile emissions and the area's proximity to the urban centers of Richmond and Hampton Roads. When it comes to cars, the main culprit is nitrogen oxides, which, together with the hydrocarbons emitted by vehicles, combine with sunlight to produce ozone. It is this lower-atmosphere ozone that can cause respiratory problems in people.

To keep future highway plans from violating federal clean-air laws, the region may have to give up a few of its larger road projects and consider using cleaner fuels and stricter emissions testing. However, analyses indicate that the region's road plans through the year 2010 are very close to meeting federal standards, and data from the last fifteen or so years suggest that ozone levels continue to drop in the region. All indications are that the region should be able to comply with current federal smog standards for the next decade through the continued use of cleaner-burning gasoline and compliance with new federal regulations on paints and other products. That doesn't mean the area is completely out from under a dark cloud, however, as there are rumblings that the federal government will tighten air pollution rules in the not-too-distant future.

FRIENDS OF THE ENVIRONMENT

While we tend to focus on the problems we have in taking care of our environment, the news on the local "green" front is getting better all the time. Throughout Williamsburg and the rest of the Peninsula, individuals and groups work together to make the area a better place in which to live. Earth Day activities abound across the region every April and have included tree plantings at York River State Park and a March for Parks—part of a nationwide program to raise money for America's parks—at the Yorktown battlefield. And, Virginians continue to show support for the environment through the purchase of Friend

Cleanup Crusader

Back in the 1980s Robert Dean was a recreational boater who liked to motor on the Chesapeake Bay and its many tributaries. What he noticed on his pleasure trips soon appalled him.

"I saw the garbage everyone was throwing into the waterways," says Dean, who lives in Virginia Beach. "People are using the Earth as a trash dump."

Dean got busy. In 1989 he organized the very first Clean the Bay Day, an all-volunteer effort to get people out to pick up every can, bottle, or plastic container they came across as they walked the shore. That year about 2,000 people carted away thirty tons of trash from 52 miles of coastline—trash that not only was unsightly but also endangered marine wildlife, especially birds, sea turtles, and fish.

After such an auspicious beginning, the cleanup effort continues to grow. In 2003, more than 4,500 volunteers removed more than 145,000 pounds of debris from 197 miles of waterways during the annual cleanup. On the Peninsula, coastal areas of the York, James, and Chickahominy Rivers, and Buckroe and Grandview beaches in Hampton have been cleaned. In recent years cleanup efforts have been expanded into Pennsylvania, Maryland, Delaware, and Washington, D.C., and now include underwater cleanup, done by volunteer scuba divers from the civilian and military community.

With assistance from the Ocean Conservancy (formerly the Center for Marine Conservation), which is based in Washington, D.C., but operates a field office in Virginia Beach, the cleanup effort has become fairly stream-lined. Volunteers are now given data cards listing the categories of items that most frequently turn up on the beaches, along with information on how the data card is used to compile an assessment of beach debris.

"Since 1989, we've picked up more than 3.3 million pounds of debris," says Dean. "When you consider that 52 percent is plastic, it's an incredible volume because plastic is so lightweight."

Another big offender is cigarette butts. "If you look at our major highway intersections, you'll see hundreds of cigarette butts where people have dumped their ashtrays," says Dean. "When it rains, they get washed into our storm water and eventually reach the Bay." He further points out that contrary to what many people think, it takes six to seven years for a single cigarette filter to break down in the environment.

There often are surprises during the annual cleanup. In 1998 members of a Boy Scout troop cleaning an area of Long Creek in Virginia Beach found a man's wallet that had been lost twenty-one years earlier during a boat explosion. The Scouts returned the wallet to its owner at a special presentation during a regular troop meeting. Also during the 1998 Virginia Beach cleanup, volunteer divers brought up two empty safes—both thought to be from local robberies. And a 2,100-pound tandem truck axle—complete with four tires and rims—was floated to the surface of London Bridge Creek in Virginia Beach using air bags during that same year's cleanup.

continued

As Clean the Bay efforts become more widespread, education has become a key component of the program. Research data, a public speakers' bureau, and videos directed at children and adults now are available. The Clean the Bay Day annual poster and T-shirt theme is reproduced as a Scout patch that can be earned by participating scouting groups. Still, despite the scope of the program, it relies almost exclusively on volunteer involvement.

That involvement hasn't gone unrecognized. In recent years Clean the Bay Day has been a first-place winner of numerous environmental awards, including Take Pride in America, Keep America Beautiful, and the Governor's Award for Volunteering Excellence.

Despite years of collecting mountains of trash, Dean sees no end in sight to the need for this extensive grassroots effort. Indeed, he has observed little improvement in peoples' habits over the past dozen years or so. "We haven't seen any dramatic changes at all," he laments. "When I started this project, I thought that, in four or five years, we wouldn't need it anymore. But if it weren't for all the volunteers who pick up garbage along the beaches and the streets, our cities would look like trash dumps."

If you'd like to join the Mud Rats in their annual cleanup crusade, keep in mind that Clean the Bay Day typically is held from 9:00 a.m. to noon on a Saturday in early to mid-June. For more information call (800) SAVEBAY or check out the calendar on the Chesapeake Bay Foundation's Web site: www.cbf.org/calendar/ctbd.htm.

of the Chesapeake license plates, which sport a blue crab on a seagrass background. Each time a set of plates is purchased, a donation is deposited into a Chesapeake Bay restoration fund.

And to make environment-friendly habits easier to establish in the region, the Virginia Peninsulas Public Service Authority (VPPSA), the organization that oversees recycling in Williamsburg, York, and James City Counties, has expanded its recycling program in recent years to include mixed paper—a broad category that covers everything from cereal boxes and computer paper to magazines and telephone books. The VPPSA also has begun periodic collections of hazardous household chemicals to give residents an alternative to dumping them down the drain or stashing them in trash bins.

Environmental Groups

Residents interested in trying to eliminate the region's environmental problems can begin by contacting a number of local, state, and national organizations, including the following.

Williamsburg Land Conservancy
5000 New Point Road, Suite 3101,
Williamsburg, VA 23188
(757) 565-0343
www.williamsburglandconservancy.org
Founded in 1990 as the Historic Rivers Land Conservancy, this private, nonprofit land trust is dedicated to promoting the preservation and protection of significant natural, scenic, and historic lands in the Historic Triangle area. To achieve this goal, the conservancy supports education about and scientific study of the area's ecology and encourages innovative

methods of conservation and environmentally sound land use. The conservancy also strives to protect the environment through land acquisition, conservation easement, and other management practices.

The Alliance for the Chesapeake Bay
P.O. Box 1981, Richmond, VA 23218
(804) 775-0951
www.acb-online.org

This nonprofit environmental organization is a coalition of environmentalists, business-people, governmental officials, scientists, farmers, sports enthusiasts, and others who are working together to protect the Bay through habitat restoration projects, field trips, special cleanup days, and educational programs aimed at improving stewardship of the Bay. Formed in 1971, the alliance also provides the public with information and opportunities to become involved in Bay activities. A wealth of information is available on the alliance Web site, which is noted above. The Alliance publishes a monthly newsletter, the Bay Journal, with informative articles about the Chesapeake Bay and the environmental issues involved.

Chesapeake Bay Foundation (CFB)
142 West York Street, Suite 318, Norfolk, VA 23510
(757) 622-1964

Virginia State Office
1108 E. Main Street, Suite 1600, Richmond, VA 23219
(804) 780-1392
www.cbf.org

With more than 110,000 members, the foundation is the largest nonprofit conservation group working to save the Bay. Each year foundation educators go out into the marshes and open waters in workboats and canoes to provide tens of thousands of students with in-the-field environmental education. A foundation lands program works to manage growth and development in the Bay watershed.

The foundation takes seriously the challenge to restore the habitat, increase the number of fish, and stop pollution of the Chesapeake Bay. In its protection and restoration efforts, the foundation enlists volunteers to help plant, map, and identify underwater grasses in the Chesapeake Bay. Other volunteers participate in oyster restoration by helping with distribution of oyster seed and roundup of grown oysters, moving oysters from the CBF's oyster farm near Gloucester to sanctuary reefs in various rivers or by making shell bags. Volunteers also help monitor forest buffer and wetland sites that have been restored. Visit the Chesapeake Bay Foundation's Web site for information about volunteer opportunities, events, facts about the Bay, updates on the condition of the Bay, environmental bills before Congress, and even suggestions for the best environmental practices in boat operation.

Chesapeake Bay National Estuarine Research Reserve in Virginia
P.O. 1346, Gloucester Point, VA 23062
(804) 684-7135
www.vims.edu/cbnerr

Managed by and operated out of the Virginia Institute of Marine Science, the reserve was started in 1991 as part of the U.S. Coastal Zone Management Act. Currently, there are twenty-five reserves nationally, all of which were formed to provide outdoor laboratories for research and education in support of coastal resource management. The best place to view the ongoing work of the reserve is at Taskinas Creek at the York River State

---

i To prevent erosion when you landscape your yard, make sure you plant plenty of vegetation and place splash blocks at your downspouts. To hold soil in place and for wildlife habitat, plant native trees and shrubs. And, to help protect the environment, please refrain from over-fertilizing your lawn or garden.

The James River from Colonial National Historic Park. JESSI DICK

Park on Riverview Road in Croaker. At the park, a trail winds through the edge of the marsh. Vigilant (and quiet) visitors can spy ospreys, bald eagles, fiddler crabs, and other wildlife all along the trail.

Chickahominy Watershed Alliance
P.O. Box 70321, Richmond, VA 23255
(804) 730-9363
As part of The Alliance for the Chesapeake Bay, this coalition of concerned citizens and environmental groups works to help maintain the high quality of the Chickahominy watershed and to preserve its multitude of natural resources. The Alliance sponsors field trips and educational meetings as well as restoration projects and welcomes all volunteers to join its efforts.

James River Association
P.O. Box 909, Mechanicsville, VA 23111
(804) 730-2898
www.jamesriverassociation.org
The members of this group work together to promote conservation of the natural and historic resources of the James River watershed. The association's goals include supporting creative land-use policies through the watershed and educating the public so that it can better appreciate the resources of the James River. Its accomplishments include getting 25 miles of the James River designated as a Historic River, producing a complete inventory of natural and cultural resources along the river, planting 25,000 trees to support the river, and developing a Watershed Resources Management plan and videotape.

People for the Ethical
Treatment of Animals (PETA)
501 Front Street, Norfolk, VA 23510
(757) 622-PETA
www.peta.org

Although this group has a different mission from the others we have discussed, it is mentioned here because it's large, it's often controversial, and its U.S. headquarters are in Norfolk. Formed in 1980, PETA has more than a half-million members worldwide who are dedicated to establishing and protecting the rights of all animals. The PETA principle is basic: Animals are not ours to eat, wear, experiment on, or use for entertainment. In addition to numerous campaigns against the use of animals in laboratory testing and in the fur industry, PETA staff members regularly speak to student groups across the country. The PETA Web site provides news releases, action alerts, vegetarian recipes, and an online store that sells everything from T-shirts to stickers aimed at promoting animal rights.

Events

Clean the Bay Day
Various locations
(800) SAVEBAY, (757) 622-1964
www.cbf.org

On the annual Clean the Bay Day in early to mid-June, volunteers collect tons of trash from beaches around Jamestown and Yorktown as well as the rest of Hampton Roads. The purpose of this one-day effort is not only to enlist the help of citizens to spruce up beaches and shorelines, but also to quantify and document the types of litter found. Check out the Close-up in this chapter for more information or contact the Chesapeake Bay Foundation, listed earlier.

International Coastal Cleanup Day
Various locations
(800) 519-1541, (202) 429-5609
www.oceanconservancy.org

Volunteers arm themselves with trash bags the third Saturday in September and patrol area beaches on International Coastal Cleanup Day, organized by the Ocean Conservancy (formerly the Center for Marine Conservation) in Washington, D.C., which operates a regional office in Virginia Beach. The event began in Texas in 1986 and expanded its reach across the nation within two years. In 2005, 450,000 volunteers removed 8.2 million pounds of debris from coasts worldwide. In recent years the City of Hampton has become particularly active in this effort, as more than 200 volunteers annually collect fast-food wrappers, disposable coffee cups, and other trash from the twenty or so waterfront sites throughout the city.

Estuaries Day
York River State Park,
Route 606, Croaker
(757) 566-3036

Another way to get acquainted with environmental groups and projects in the region is to participate in Estuaries Day, which typically is held the last Saturday in September. Hosted by York River State Park, Estuaries Day offers guided wetland hikes, canoe trips, pontoon boat trips, a fossil hike for the children, live-animal demonstrations, hayrides, and a number of exhibits on environmental quality issues. Estuaries Day is free with park admission. Preregistation is required. Because York River encourages carpooling, no car pays more than $5 to get in, no matter how many passengers.

Recycling

Virginia Peninsulas Public Service
Authority (VPPSA)
Williamsburg
(757) 259-9850

James City County
(757) 565-4000

York County
(757) 890-3780

Residents of Williamsburg, James City County, and York County are served by the Virginia Peninsulas Public Service Authority (VPPSA). Residents of each of these communities have curbside recycling as a weekly service. Residents may recycle newspaper, glass, aluminum, bimetal, No. 2 plastics, corrugated cardboard, brown grocery bags, steel paint cans (washed and without lids), and empty aerosol cans (no lids). Residents may also recycle mixed paper, including magazines, catalogs, telephone books, junk mail, computer paper, stationery, school paper, envelopes, and single-layer cardboard.

Jolly Pond Convenience Center
1204 Jolly Pond Road
James City County
(757) 565-4000
www.james-city.va.us/recycling/index.html
One of three recycling centers run by the county, Jolly Pond is the only location that accepts materials that are not included as part of the curbside recycling program. These items include antifreeze, used motor oil, automotive batteries, and large appliances that do not require a cooling element. The center is open from 7:00 a.m. to 5:00 p.m., seven days a week. The county also offers a detailed

phone message on the various components of its recycling program when you call the number above, or visit the Web site for a detailed list.

York County Recycling Center
145 Goodwin Neck Road, Yorktown
(757) 890-3780
This drop-off facility accepts antifreeze, used oil, automotive batteries, and scrap metals. It is open 8:00 a.m. to 4:00 p.m. Monday through Saturday.

York Waste Composting Facility
145 Goodwin Neck Road, Yorktown
(757) 898-5012
If you live in York County (or nearby Poquoson) and have spent the day doing yard work, you can drop off your grass, leaves, and brush at this composting facility between the hours of 8:00 a.m. and 4:00 p.m. Monday through Saturday. Compost and mulch also are available for sale here at various times, with quantity discounts offered.

RELOCATION

The Williamsburg area's natural beauty, vibrant culture, and small-town ambience make it an extremely attractive area for relocation. So attractive, in fact, that housing prices have skyrocketed over the past few years, rising nearly as high as prices in the Washington, D.C., metro area. Families value the area's strong public school systems—some of which offer a choice of schools specifically focused on fine arts and math and science. Many retirees have flocked here from northern cities for the milder winters and coastal atmosphere. And others are drawn to the area's rich history.

The City of Williamsburg, in particular, retains the spirit of the small colonial capital city it was prior to and after the American Revolution. It's still a safe place to live with a distinct identity. Nonetheless, the population in our immediate vicinity continues to grow and neighborhoods proliferate, adding to this ambience the feel of a more contemporary, energetic community.

Residents of the Williamsburg area often receive special discounts and privileges when visiting many of the area's historic sites and theme parks. For instance, all residents of York County, James City County, and Williamsburg are entitled to free admission to Jamestown Settlement and Yorktown Victory Center (proof of address is required). There's also a Good Neighbor Pass that gives residents discounts to all the Colonial Williamsburg attractions.

Those looking for a home in the greater Williamsburg area have many options, and not surprisingly, many modern-day neighborhoods have a colonial theme. In keeping with the era, designs are often faithfully symmetrical, with high pitched roofs, neat porches, tall windows with shutters, small outbuildings (some of which serve as modern-day garages), long walks, formal gardens, and other amenities that were in fashion 200 years ago.

Of course, not everyone fancies traditional design. Luckily, local builders have found great success by offering myriad designs—including transitional and contemporary homes with the latest in modern amenities.

Neighborhoods are springing up all over the Historic Triangle, though some are limited by the nature of the area's topography. The York River to the north and the James River to the south have blocked growth in those directions, while providing some of the most beautiful scenery we could desire. To the east, the federal properties of the Colonial National Historical Park with its Colonial Parkway, Fort Eustis, Naval Weapons Station, and Camp Peary form a band that effectively keeps us from being absorbed into the explosive growth of the cities on the lower part of the Peninsula. Only the beautiful woodlands and farmlands to the west of the city remain available for growth, and it is there that you'll find many of the new developments in James City County and western York County.

The Virginia Peninsula in general is a fairly transient area, with many military families coming and going on assignment and young businesses bringing in people who later move on to other locations. However, the population in James City County and western York County continues to grow. The last two decades have seen the appearance of many new neighborhoods.

We counted more than 150 neighborhoods and condominium and apartment complexes in preparing for this chapter, and we are sure we overlooked some of the newer or smaller ones. Home prices range from about $50,000 to more than $2.5 million, with everything in between available. Generally the pricey homes are on the waterfront, in the city of Williamsburg, or in planned communities such as Kingsmill on the James, Ford's Colony, and The Governor's Land at Two Rivers. Lower-cost homes are in the older neighborhoods and the small, new developments tucked along the roads of James City and York Counties.

The Williamsburg area is a very active real estate market. If you are looking for a residence in the area, our Insiders' suggestion is that you check out the real estate sections of the local newspapers and drive around back streets and roads to find areas that appeal to you. Then you can contact one of the real estate agencies listed in this chapter for a closer look, other options, and more specifics about your choices. Our best discoveries have been the accidental ones we just happened to drive past one day.

If you're looking for a bargain or would prefer to operate independently of a real estate agent, occasionally one can find a home for sale by owner in the classified section of the *Virginia Gazette,* which hits the streets each Wednesday and Saturday. Several free real estate tabloids come out with frequency and can be found at the entrances of most of the supermarkets in the area. They list both homes and land for sale in the area, including many for sale by owner.

NEIGHBORHOODS

Adam's Hunt

This subdivision off Centerville Road, about midway between U.S. Route 60 and Longhill Road, features modest homes on good-size lots in heavily wooded, rolling terrain. The one- and two-story houses are in a mixture of styles. It is a good beginner neighborhood for people interested in getting into the single-family housing market.

i All residents are eligible for Good Neighbor passes from Colonial Williamsburg. These $10 tickets entitle them to admissions, bus service, and shopping discounts in Colonial Williamsburg's properties. They can purchase admission tickets for up to ten guests each year at a 40 percent discount, and holders receive a helpful newsletter published seasonally by Colonial Williamsburg.

Banbury Cross

About 5 miles west of Williamsburg, this lovely, sprawling neighborhood is accessible by Interstate 64, exiting at Route 646 north. Large lots, mostly an acre or more, are the rule here. An abundance of natural woods with tall pines, oaks, and mountain laurel make this an ideal setting for those interested in living near town but beyond the suburbs of Williamsburg. Homes are large, colonial or transitional in style.

Baron Woods

Offered by Sash Digges, a prominent local builder, this property proved so popular that lots sold about as fast as they could be subdivided. The charming neighborhood features modest homes on small lots with many tall trees. It's on Ironbound Road, just north of Route 5 at Five Forks.

Berkeley's Green

Proving to be one of the area's most popular subdivisions, Berkeley's Green is off Route 5 and Greensprings Road. Tucked discreetly behind a facade of tall oaks and pines, this neighborhood features several carefully executed home designs, colonial as well as transitional.

Birchwood Park

Birchwood is one of Williamsburg's established neighborhoods, located off Route 199.

Its modest homes, many of them ranch style, have landscaped yards and established gardens. It is especially accessible to shopping and schools, as well as I–64.

Brandon Woods

Located on John Tyler Highway (Route 5) in Five Forks, this subdivision is characterized by rolling, wooded home sites on tree-lined streets and easy, quick access to shopping and services. Home styles are transitional, and have either brick or "hardy plank" low-maintenance exteriors. These single-family detached homes are condominium ownership, which means the homeowner's association is responsible for all exterior maintenance, including roofs, and the upkeep of all common areas.

Canterbury Hills

Also an established, small neighborhood, this charming area boasts winding roads shaded by large, old trees, neatly tended yards, and larger, well-maintained homes. Off Route 5 and very accessible to the Williamsburg Crossing Shopping Center, it is bounded by Indigo Park and Mill Creek Landing.

Chanco's Grant

A few years ago this neighborhood began as a two-street, starter-home subdivision with low-priced homes on small lots. It proved so vastly popular that it has developed by leaps and bounds to include an abundance of attractive colonial-style homes on several well-tended streets. It is on Ironbound Road, midway between Route 5 and Jamestown Road, close to Clara Byrd Baker Elementary and convenient to shopping.

Chickahominy Haven

Chickahominy Haven started out as a recreational community with small summer homes tucked away on the river from which it gets its name. Now it boasts numerous year-round residents who have built a mix of large and small transitional or contemporary homes interspersed among the summer cottages. It's

a drive back through the James City County woods to get there, but take Forge Road off US 60 west, keep bearing right, and wind your way to the river.

Cobble Creek

Located in York County, immediately off the Colonial Parkway and near Queens Lake, is this relatively new community close to shopping and convenient to I–64. Single-family homes are transitional in style, though some offer traditional colonial floor plans and exteriors. Some homes feature vaulted ceilings, kitchen islands, Jacuzzis, and other amenities. All have fireplaces. This community offers a choice of floor plans in new construction, and here you'll find an updated version of the traditional split-level concept. A choice of ravine lots or level tracts give this wooded community visual appeal.

The Coves

Off South Henry Street, after it winds its way past the College of William and Mary's Marshall-Wythe School of Law, is this pristine little subdivision along two short lanes. Most homes here are masterpieces, custom-designed and meticulously maintained by their owners. Every once in a while, someone will put a lot up for sale in this extremely desirable location, but not very often—and they are pricey when they do become available. But its location—within walking distance of Colonial Williamsburg, Merchants Square, the college, and more—is ideal. It also offers easy access via Route 199 to I–64.

Cromwell Ridge

One of several new condominium communities that have emerged in the greater Williamsburg area, Cromwell Ridge is part of the Powhatan Secondary complex, situated just a short walk from the Monticello Marketplace. The three-bedroom condos here feature private garages, first-floor master suites, 9-foot ceilings on the first floor, and fireplaces.

Druid Hills

An established neighborhood off Jamestown Road, Druid Hills features a mix of large and small homes—two-story colonials as well as contemporary ranches—on winding lanes shaded by old trees. Because of its proximity to the campus of the College of William and Mary, many professors, students, and their families live here.

Fernbrook

Large, heavily wooded lots in James City County's Fernbrook development off Greensprings Road will appeal to families seeking to locate within ten minutes of the heart of Williamsburg. Colonial and transitional homes populate the area.

Fieldcrest

This upscale neighborhood offers luxurious living in a country setting. Large, new homes line its wide streets. Old, stately trees shade Greensprings Road as it leaves Route 5 and leads to the entrance of this lovely subdivision. Homes are primarily transitional in style and usually brick.

Ford's Colony

If you're looking for an elegant home in a gated community replete with golf, lighted tennis courts, fine dining, and one of the state's most extensive wine lists (turn to the Restaurants chapter for details about The Dining Room and The Grille), this expansive planned community is for you. The homes are large and luxurious; the condominiums, townhomes, and cluster homes are equally elegant. The two golf courses here are outstanding and will provide continual challenges (see the Golf chapter for more information). Ford's Colony is a gated community of 2,500 acres on Longhill Road, a couple of miles west of the Historic Area. Lots run in size from a third-acre to a half-acre.

Fox Ridge

Still one of the most affordable subdivisions in the greater Williamsburg area, Fox Ridge is off Centerville Road between Longhill Road and US 60. Charming, smaller homes are interspersed among tall trees, dogwoods, and mountain laurel on rolling hills.

The Governor's Land at Two Rivers

This is, without reservation, the most elegant subdivision in western James City County. Smaller than Kingsmill but no less impressive in its amenities and terrain, this developing subdivision offers large home sites, many along the river's edge. Off Route 5 at the confluence of the James and Chickahominy Rivers, it offers the last riverfront acreage in the county. A professional golf course, beach facilities, nature trails, a swimming pool, and tennis courts are in place, and the clubhouse offers all one could wish to complete the high quality of the neighborhood.

Graylin Woods

Understated is the best description of this charming, elegant, albeit small subdivision off Route 5 between Route 199 and Five Forks. Large, stately homes on modest, lovely wooded lots and rolling hills give this neighborhood charm and character.

Greensprings Plantation

Williamsburg's newest golfing community is an excellent option for anyone, but especially the golf enthusiast looking for a home-based golfing community. Lots range in size from a third-acre to a half-acre, sometimes a bit larger. Homes in the wooded hills are adjacent to the Williamsburg National Golf Club, an eighteen-hole championship golf masterpiece designed by Jack Nicklaus's Golden Bear Associates. In addition to the wonderful golfing, amenities include a full-size pool, tennis courts, a recreational center, and two children's play areas.

Heritage Landing

This elegant subdivision off Route 5 west of Five Forks features large brick and wood custom homes on large lots. Rolling hills, winding lanes, and flowering trees and shrubs make this an exquisite venue just far enough out of town to make you feel like you're on vacation.

Holly Hills of Williamsburg

Upper-end new property within the city limits is at a premium. Holly Hills on Jamestown Road is the last development to serve the city market. It is located on nearly 300 acres of heavily wooded property just a mile from the Historic Area and the College of William and Mary. Home sites range in size from just under half and acre to two acres. Strict architectural guidelines ensure that the appearance and value of properties will remain high.

Hunter's Creek

This family-oriented subdivision is small but attractive with its modest colonial homes and well-tended gardens. Off US 60 west of Williamsburg on the edge of Toano, it offers easy access to I-64.

Indigo Park

One of the Route 5 area's earlier developments, Indigo Park has endured as a charming neighborhood of well-maintained homes along rolling, winding lanes shaded by large, old trees. A family-oriented neighborhood with a private pool for residents, Indigo Park is within a five-minute drive of Williamsburg Crossing Shopping Center and schools, as well as Williamsburg's Historic Area and other shopping areas. Two-story ranch homes in brick or wood are a good buy.

Kingsmill on the James

One of Williamsburg's most prestigious neighborhoods, this multifaceted development of 2,900 acres includes everything from sprawling estates to tidy condos on the edge of its PGA golf course. Kingsmill residents enjoy several recreation areas, a world-class eighteen-hole golf course, several superb restaurants, an outstanding recreation and conference center, a private marina, dry-dock facilities, and a riverside beach. Developed by the Anheuser-Busch

i Williamsburg enjoys small-town charm along with a sophistication that's not common in most small towns. Home to a nationally esteemed college and world-renowned living-history museum, the arts and intellectual pursuits flourish.

Corporation, it also features a twenty-four-hour private security force and limited-access entrances. Prices vary widely.

Kingspoint

This quiet, established neighborhood is tucked away at the foot of South Henry Street just across Route 199. Bounded by the Colonial Parkway on one side and College Creek on the other, it is a wide, tree-covered peninsula. Kingspoint is noted for its friendliness as well as its convenience to the heart of town via Henry Street. It also offers quick access via Route 199 to other parts of James City County and the interstate. You'll find an eclectic mix of sizes, styles, and ages from 1960s to new construction.

Kingswood

Conveniently located off Jamestown Road, about halfway between Merchants Square and the Jamestown Ferry, this idyllic, quiet neighborhood is the choice for those seeking convenience and solitude. Well-tended yards and an assortment of older contemporary and traditional homes line the area's streets and lanes. The neighborhood has a private pool that is open for a fee each summer to guests from nearby developments as well.

Kristiansand

The Norwegian name pays tribute to the town of Norge, which is adjacent to this small subdivision. Off US 60 west, it is just down the road from the Williamsburg Pottery Factory. It offers quick and easy access to Ewell Station Shopping Center and I-64 as well as local schools.

Lake Toano

If you don't mind driving about fifteen minutes west of Williamsburg along US 60 west, you can find this subdivision situated in a heavily wooded area surrounding a quiet reservoir in the Toano area. Large and small homes, both contemporary and traditional, line the streets and cul-de-sacs that make up this country neighborhood. It is just minutes from the I–64 exit for Toano.

Landfall at Jamestown

Talk about a lush setting! This upscale subdivision is located on prime real estate, off Jamestown Road, about half a mile from the James River. Some lots sit amid meandering streams and creeks; others front the James River. New construction includes transitional and contemporary as well as traditional colonial design, most with brick exterior.

Longhill Gate

Located on Longhill Road just before the entrance to Ford's Colony, these attached homes range in size from moderate to fairly large. Sidewalks, manicured landscapes, and winding streets are indicative of the low-key family ambience that sets the tone of this charming neighborhood.

The Meadows

Looks are deceiving as you approach this small community of small- to moderate-size homes, between Strawberry Plains and Ironbound Roads. At the back edge of a wide-open field, the streets of this neighborhood dip and wind, curve and wander. Neatly kept yards and pristine houses characterize this subdivision, halfway between downtown Williamsburg and Jamestown via Sandy Point Road.

Mill Creek Landing

Without a doubt, this elegant subdivision of custom-built homes (nearly all of them brick) situated around a seven-acre fish-stocked pond is one of the area's best-kept secrets. Limited in size, it is off Route 5 and Stanley Drive. It offers a country setting less than 2 miles from Williamsburg's Historic Area, with easy access to schools, Williamsburg Crossing Shopping Center (which is within walking distance), and I–64.

Mirror Lake Estates

About fifteen minutes west of the Historic Area, this inviting neighborhood features small, moderate, and larger starter homes, all built fairly recently. It can be reached via Richmond Road or from I–64, which is less than a mile from the entrance of the subdivision.

North Cove

Off Route 646 in York County, this large-lot subdivision features rolling hills, large homes, lots of trees, and quick access to I–64. About ten minutes west of Williamsburg, it is a charming setting that seems far removed from the bustle of downtown. It is also near York River State Park and a public boat ramp on the York River. You'll find homes in brick, cedar, and stucco.

Peleg's Point

Conveniently located off Neck-O-Land Road in James City County, this relatively new neighborhood features larger homes, many brick, in colonial, transitional, and contemporary styles. It is only a few miles from downtown Williamsburg, but also offers proximity to the James River and Colonial Parkway.

Piney Creek Estates

Two of the area's most renowned builders, Ronald T. Curtis and Joel S. Sheppard, offer owners a prime city address—and low taxes. This new development is within a mile of the James City County–Williamsburg Community Center and Kiwanis Park, and it's a short drive from all area attractions and shopping.

Poplar Hall

About 8 miles east of downtown Williamsburg, this meandering neighborhood is tucked discreetly away from the traffic of US 60 east, off of which it is located. This subdivision offers a variety of sizes and styles and boasts both older and new homes. It is mid-way between two I–64 interchanges and is just minutes from Busch Gardens and the Anheuser-Busch brewery.

Port Anne

One of the last subdivisions in the city where you can still purchase land and build a custom house, this neighborhood is for the discerning homeowner in search of an idyllic setting above College Creek. Large, custom-designed homes on smaller lots provide the perfect place to settle down in style. A clubhouse, tennis courts, and pool are among other amenities. It offers quick access to I–64 and is within biking and walking distance of the city's Historic Area.

Powhatan Crossing

One of the developing moderate-income neighborhoods in James City County, this small but charming subdivision is just east of Route 5 at Five Forks. It features affordable, small to moderately sized homes along a cozy lane that stretches into the woodlands. Residents enjoy easy access to downtown Williamsburg or I–64 via Route 5.

Powhatan Place

Located near Monticello Marketplace off News Road, this three-bedroom luxury townhome community offers excellent location and all amenities. Two floor plans are offered. The 2,700-square-foot end units feature first-floor master suites. The 2,500-square-foot interior units feature master bedrooms with spacious his/her master baths. All units feature gas heat and hot water, as well as gas-log fireplaces, single-car garages, and laundry rooms. All units are prewired for security systems.

Powhatan Secondary of Williamsburg

On the site of the early-17th-century Powhatan Plantation off Ironbound Road at Mid County Park, this popular and growing subdivision offers choice wooded home sites at reasonable prices. The attractive, custom-built homes are a mix of contemporary and

i Over the years some land in James City County has tested positive for hydric soil (water-soaked soil with a tendency to shift). This is no big deal provided your builder knows about it and takes precaution when doing the foundation of a new home. If you're buying an existing home, you'll want to have a "shrink-swell" test to find out if the land is hydric. If it tests positive, have a home inspector make sure this was taken into account when the home was built.

traditional styles, all meticulously maintained and landscaped. The community includes forty-five acres of recreational land and lakes for homeowners to enjoy. Buyers can choose from a variety of floor plans from nine quality builders.

Powhatan Shores

While most neighborhoods offer some attractive amenities to their homeowners, this charming family neighborhood has them all, especially for the boating enthusiast. Most lots have private access via a creek to the James River. It is just a few minutes from the city's Historic Area and is close to Route 199 and I–64.

Queens Lake

This stately, established neighborhood, bounded by Queens Creek and the Colonial Parkway, is one of the most prestigious neighborhoods in the greater Williamsburg area. Tennis courts, a pool, a recreation center, and a marina are among the amenities. Some of the area's loveliest homes are situated on the rolling, wooded lanes of this charming subdivision. It offers country living just minutes from I–64, Colonial Williamsburg, and area schools.

Queenswood

Off Hubbard Lane, this family-oriented neighborhood features newer homes on moderate-size lots away from the activity of downtown

Williamsburg and major roads. Ranches and two-story colonials are the norm here, and meticulously landscaped and maintained home sites are typical. It is within minutes of Colonial Parkway, James York Plaza Shopping Center, and Route 143, which leads to I–64.

Richmond Hill

This is a small, high-end neighborhood in the city limits very close to the Historic Area. All brick homes are federal architectural designs similar to those on Richmond's Monument Avenue. Three golf courses, indoor tennis, and the shopping and dining of Colonial Williamsburg are all within walking distance.

Rolling Woods

Lovely midrange homes with brick, vinyl, and cedar exteriors tucked away under stately oaks and pines make this hilly subdivision much sought after. Off Lake Powell Road in James City County, it offers seclusion just minutes from the congestion of downtown Williamsburg. It is near Route 199 and I–64.

Seasons Trace

One of the most popular planned communities in the area is this neighborhood with its neatly maintained townhomes, condos, cluster homes, and small private homes. Off Longhill Road, adjacent to Lafayette High School and across the road from the Windsor Forest subdivision, Seasons Trace features winding lanes and a pond stocked with fish and populated with ducks. Also offered are such amenities as a pool, tennis courts, a basketball court, and dry-dock storage for boats and RVs.

Settler's Mill

Off Jamestown Road approximately halfway between Route 199 and Jamestown, Settler's Mill has emerged as a very popular development. Located in a heavily wooded community, it features a lake, ponds, and rolling hills. It is a joint venture of four of the most prestigious names in residential building and development in the area: Larry McCardle, Sterling

Nichols, Joel Sheppard, and Ron Curtis. Homes feature a variety of traditional and transitional styles.

Skimino Hills

Developed in the late 1970s and early 1980s, this large subdivision is situated on gently rolling hills in western York County. Off I–64 at Route 646, it offers large lots with trees and lush growths of mountain laurel and dogwood. A mix of large and small contemporary and traditional homes lines its narrow streets.

Skimino Landing Estates

Large lots—from an acre up—and lots of trees, including hardwoods, characterize this subdivision in upper York County. The neighborhood features a boat ramp with access to the York River. Construction reflects a mix of styles, many transitional, most with brick facades.

Skipwith Farms

This was the City of Williamsburg's first real subdivision, built in the 1950s and 1960s, and it features modest single- and two-story homes. Few areas are more centrally located or offer easier access to shopping, recreation, and area schools. It is off Richmond Road, less than 3 miles from the heart of the city's Historic Area.

St. George's Hundred

One of the area's most popular, family-oriented neighborhoods, St. George's is off Route 5 about 5 miles west of Williamsburg. Charming homes, mostly colonial style, line the streets. Established more than two decades ago, this neighborhood continues to grow. In addition to its easy access to area shopping and schools, it features a recreation area with picnic tables, basketball courts, and a softball field.

Stonehouse

Located along the I–64 corridor in both James City and New Kent Counties is Stonehouse, a 5,700-acre development that offers homeowners an all-digital residential community in a beautiful natural setting. A joint venture of the real estate divisions of Dominion Resources Inc. and Chesapeake Corp., Stonehouse is offering large single-family homes, golf villas on the Legends of Stonehouse Golf Course, patio homes, and town houses. The project includes lots ranging in size from a third of an acre to more than an acre. Stonehouse homeowners have access to a variety of technological services, from digital TV with more than 200 audio and video channels to state-of-the-art security systems and high-speed Internet service. The community is being developed on a twenty-five-year plan and eventually will offer an aquatic and sports center, retail shops, churches, offices, grocery stores, movie theaters, and more. More than 50 percent of the property will remain in its natural state. For more information visit the Web site at www.stonehouseva.com.

The Vineyards of Williamsburg

Off Neck-o-Land Road, this subdivision of large, stately homes is quickly becoming one of Williamsburg's most prestigious addresses. Larger houses are the rule, but there are a few areas offering smaller, exquisitely constructed dwellings. Most are tucked away discreetly among old shade trees. Breezes from the nearby James River and proximity to both Jamestown Road and the Colonial Parkway make this a much-sought-after location.

Westgate at Williamsburg

In a community where condominiums are quickly catching a foothold, this complex is one of the most reasonably priced options. Located off US 60 just west of the Prime Outlets, it's convenient to Williamsburg and I–64. Placed along quiet streets, the charming two- and three-bedroom condos here are large, measuring about 1,600 square feet. They feature natural gas heat and water, vaulted ceilings, walk-in closets, and lofts. Some have gas fireplaces and sunrooms. The community also offers owners use of a pool and cabana.

Westmoreland

Off Olde Towne Road near its intersection with Long Hill Road, this small development currently has fifteen single-family lots on richly wooded property developed by the Hornsby family (relations of Bruce Hornsby). Convenient access to shopping and amenities on the Richmond Road side of town, proximity to the Historic Area (a ten-minute drive), and convenient access to I–64 are strong advantages to this neighborhood.

Westray Downs

Rolling hills, winding lanes, and charming homes characterize this relatively new neighborhood off Route 5 in James City County. Ranch-style homes, traditional two-story homes, and some charming colonial-style homes add interest to the landscape. It is minutes from the county's Law Enforcement Center and Fire Station on Route 5 and offers quick, easy access to Williamsburg Crossing Shopping Center, Five Forks, the Jamestown Ferry, and I–64 via Route 199.

Windsor Forest

Before Ford's Colony joined the ranks, this was the most upscale subdivision on the northeast side of James City County. It is off Longhill Road, and large homes—some contemporary, most traditional colonial-style—are the norm here. Amenities include a community pool. Nearby are the county recreation center and lots of shopping. There is easy access to I–64 via Airport Road, and the city's Historic Area is just a few miles away.

i Thinking about building in greater Williamsburg? Think you've narrowed your list of potential builders? Before selecting, make a call to the Peninsula Housing & Builders Association, (757) 595-1600 (or go to www.penhousing .com). They can discuss each builder's track record—and perhaps save you some money in the long run.

Close-up

The Williamsburg Land Conservancy

In the late 1920s, when John D. Rockefeller Jr. decided to bankroll restoration of the Williamsburg Historic Area, the tiny college town, once capital of the Virginia Colony, revived. In fact, it grew by leaps and bounds. Adjacent, primarily rural and agricultural James City County, however, didn't follow suit. Then fifty years later something happened: Anheuser-Busch built a theme park and an upscale housing subdivision on a historic site in James City. Afterward, other businesses, including several plants and shopping malls, opened and—boom—James City since has experienced phenomenal growth.

Along with the rampant growth has come a host of related problems, not the least of which is suburban sprawl. As development has grown rapidly, so has a groundswell of frustration, giving voice to a population reluctant to give up the quiet, rural character of their county.

Enter the Williamsburg Land Conservancy. Founded in 1990 as the Historic Rivers Land Conservancy, and renamed in 1997, the nonprofit group has come a long way in a short time. Once an all-volunteer organization, it now has a permanent office and a staff. Its mission is to protect and preserve significant scenic, historic, and natural lands in the watershed of the York and James Rivers. As such, the conservancy acts in the present to preserve the past for the future.

In order to achieve its goals, the conservancy has identified three objectives: to encourage appropriate methods of land conservation and use, to increase public understanding and appreciation of land conservation, and to preserve land by promoting partnerships among like-minded entities. These objectives assume that neither a no-growth policy nor unbridled growth serves the best interest of the community. Instead, it recognizes that protection of natural resources is symbiotic with well-planned economic growth.

The conservancy, which now numbers more than 600 individuals, families, and businesses, takes its role seriously. In 1999 members teamed with

The Woods

This handsome, upscale subdivision is quickly establishing itself as one of distinction. Large, stately homes are situated on rolling hills amid lush woods and tall, old oaks and pines. Off Jamestown Road and within a brisk walking distance of the city's Historic Area, this fine subdivision offers easy access to just about everything, including I–64 via Route 199.

Yorkshire

Nothing short of elegant is this small albeit stately subdivision, located conveniently off Jamestown Road near the Route 199 intersection. Large custom homes are located on quiet meandering streets and cul-de-sacs set inside rolling hills and woodlands. The neighborhood is less than a mile from the city's Historic Area and is located within the city limits.

representatives of James City County to pot 10,600 seedlings to be planted along roads leading into Williamsburg.

The challenges are simple in concept, not so simple in reality. The office daily works at finding funding for ongoing programs, for development, and for contracts for specific professional services. Since its inception the conservancy has granted protection for more than 3,000 acres of local lands. In the meantime, it applies for grants to help underwrite costs associated with its mission.

Having Grammy Award–winning entertainer Bruce Hornsby on the advisory board has helped considerably. In conjunction with the celebration of Williamsburg's 300th anniversary in 1999, he held three concerts, donating more than $93,000 in proceeds to the conservancy to help purchase its first major tract: Mainland Farm, a 215-acre property that has been farmed continuously since the 17th century.

In the fall of 1999, the conservancy campaigned to raise the remainder of the $2.2 million needed to buy the property, asking the community to support its cause. James City County intervened in the deal and helped arrange an installment plan for the conservancy to purchase the Mainland Farm tract, so all the money need not be raised at one time.

The Mainland site is called the "Governor's Land" because Royal Governor Yeardly in 1618 had more than 3,000 acres of land set aside as his preserve, and to this day, much of it has not been developed, having been kept intact because of its rich archaeological value. Mainland Farm, while used as an operating farm for many years, was part of that land holding.

As word of the conservancy's mission gains notoriety, others have been inspired to help it achieve its goals. A 1.39-acre site near Jamestown was given to the organization. The tract contains archaeological evidence that it was the site of the 1750 Mainland Church.

For more information on the work of the Williamsburg Land Conservancy, or to make a tax-deductible contribution, call (757) 565-0343 or write to 5000 New Point Road, Suite 3101, Williamsburg, VA 23188. The Land Conservancy's Web site is at www.williamsburglandconservancy.org.

REAL ESTATE COMPANIES

It stands to reason that there are plenty of realtors to bring housing seekers and sellers together, and there are. We have listed below a sample of some of the area realtors. (All realtors are located in Williamsburg unless otherwise noted.)

Abbitt Realty Company Inc.
104 Bypass Road
(757) 827-6995, (800) 969-3003
www.abbittrealty.com
Established in 1946, Abbitt Realty is a recognized leader in the Peninsula real estate market, with five offices, one in the Williamsburg area.

ℹ Looking for a reputable real estate company and agent? Call the Williamsburg Area Association of Realtors at (757) 253-0028 or visit www.waarealtor.com.

Coldwell Banker Professional Realtors
312-A Lightfoot Road
(757) 564-9595
www.coldwellbanker.com

This firm, one of the area's largest with twenty-five realtors, represents buyers and sellers throughout the greater Williamsburg market.

Executive Homes Realty
124 Quaker Meeting House Road
(757) 565-1963
www.ehrc.com

Executive Homes Realty handles properties in prestigious golf, waterfront, and gated communities surrounding historic Williamsburg. Their specialty is buyer representation while purchasing a home site or an existing home as well as buyer representation during the construction of a new home.

GSH Real Estate, Williamsburg Office
1312 Jamestown Road
(757) 253-2442
www.gsh.com

GSH has a major presence in the Tidewater area and is heavily involved in commercial real estate and property management. The local office provides full and expert representation in commercial, residential, and land transactions. They've been in business for more than fifty years.

Hornsby Real Estate Co.
4732 Longhill Road, Suite 1101
(757) 565-1234
www.realhornsby.com

This is a long-established (more than fifty years) and highly respected company handling commercial, residential, and land transactions throughout the greater Williamsburg area. The firm recently developed the

upscale Westmoreland subdivision off Olde Towne Road.

Kingsmill Realty Inc.
15 John Jefferson Road
(757) 253-3933, (800) 392-0026
www.kingsmill.com

While other companies represent properties in Kingsmill, Kingsmill Realty is an obvious option for those seeking to own in the Kingsmill on the James planned community. On top of what's available as well as what's coming onto the market in all of Kingsmill's neighborhoods, the company's agents can help clients find the ideal location.

Long & Foster Realtors
4655-101 Monticello Avenue
(757) 229-4400
www.williamsburgvahomes.com

Associated with the company that's been selling real estate since 1968 in the Washington, D.C., area, this full-service office has had a presence in the Williamsburg area for more than a decade.

Prudential McCardle Realty
4135 Ironbound Road
(757) 253-5686
7405 Richmond Road
(757) 565-4696

9701 Mill Pond Run (Toano)
(757) 234-5000

3449 John Tyler Highway
(757) 220-9500
www.mccardlere.com

This independent, locally owned company

ℹ While homes in the City of Williamsburg aren't as plentiful as in James City or upper York Counties, they are available. In addition to closer proximity to downtown, homes in the city are taxed at a lower rate than those located in the counties. This will directly impact your monthly house payment.

became affiliated with Prudential in early 1999 and has expanded to four offices in the Williamsburg area that handle commercial, residential (new and resale), and land sales.

**William E. Wood
& Associates Realtors**
1326 Jamestown Road
(757) 229-0550

926-A J. Clyde Morris Boulevard
Newport News
(757) 599—8449, (800) 866—3201

907 Richmond Road
(757) 253-8150

William E. Wood is one of the community's largest and longest-established companies, with numerous offices in the Tidewater area that handle commercial, residential, and land sales.

Williamsburg Realty Inc.
811 Richmond Rd.
(757) 564-0988
www.williamsburgrealtyinc.com
Jerry and Pam McCardle, the owners of Williamsburg Realty, have more than thirty years of local real estate experience. He knows his territory well. Before selling homes, Jerry McCardle helped build 300 of them in the Williamsburg area.

RETIREMENT

The Historic Triangle continues to grow in popularity as a retirement destination, drawing older Americans from across the nation. Why? Well, for starters, our temperate climate is a significant draw. We enjoy four distinct seasons, yet winters here generally are mild and short. The brunt of wintry weather doesn't begin until mid-December and is over by late February or early March. Snow may fall, but it rarely lingers. Ice may form, but it quickly melts. Colorful redbud and dogwood are harbingers of spring, which often arrives early. Summers can be sultry, but elongated falls, replete with nearly summerlike weather well into October, make the impending winter easier to swallow.

People retiring from military service in the Hampton Roads area are familiar with the area's amenities, and many settle here. The cost of living is relatively low when compared to many other parts of the country, particularly Northeast urban centers. There are numerous recreational opportunities and good health care options. And, as a college town, Williamsburg offers a broad spectrum of generally inexpensive cultural activities senior citizens can enjoy. There are several new housing developments in the area exclusively for the 55-and-older crowd.

According to the most recent U.S. Census Bureau figures for the Historic Triangle, nearly 2,000 seniors 60 and up live in the City of Williamsburg, while more than 10,000 live in James City County and another 7,300 in York County. Obviously, such a large population group has a need for special services, and rightly deserves special privileges.

Seniors also are eligible for discounts at many area attractions, including Busch Gardens and Water Country USA. Perhaps the most important contact point for seniors here is the Historic Triangle Senior Center, located in the James City County–Williamsburg Community Center. The center, open to persons 50 and older, is a meeting and greeting place, the site of special events and many regularly scheduled monthly events, and the starting point for varied trips for seniors. Additionally, the center offers billiards, line dancing, sewing circles, fitness classes, Scrabble, bridge, movies, canasta, and other activities for interested seniors.

The center also offers free health care screenings, workshops, and Wellness Days programs, which focus on such topics as maintaining good health through smart physical activity, risk factors for coronary artery disease, and what to expect when you undergo joint replacement surgery. Many of these programs are offered in conjunction with Williamsburg Community Hospital's home health care program. For a current calendar, go to the center's Web site, www.theseniorcenter.org, or call (757) 259-4187.

Additional courtesies abound in the Historic Triangle for its seniors. Senior Times, published monthly, is a good place to look for current discount information. CVS and Berkeley pharmacies offer senior discounts, as do all the local movie theaters and some area apartment complexes. Real bargain hunters will be pleased to know that the Williamsburg Pottery Factory also offers a 10 percent discount to seniors every Monday through Thursday.

Discounts are abundant for visiting seniors as well; you just have to do a little asking around. We suggest that when making reservations or inquiries at area hotels, restaurants, and attractions, you always ask if there are reduced rates or special offerings for seniors.

The Web site of the National Council of Senior Citizens, at http://seniorjournal.com, links to senior-friendly businesses and discounts.

Whether you're here for a few days, or a few years, this area has a lot to offer. (All services are based in Williamsburg unless otherwise noted.)

ACTIVITIES

Active seniors interested in participating in social, civic, and special-interest activities don't have to look very far. The College of William and Mary sponsors concert series, theater productions, exhibits, and gallery talks, usually for a small admission fee or no charge at all. We describe some of these in The Arts chapter. Call (757) 221-4000 for details. What follows is a list of some of the more active clubs and programs in this area.

The Christopher Wren Association for Lifelong Learning
College of William and Mary
(757) 221-1079
www.wm.edu/cwa/
No report on retired living in the Historic Triangle would be complete without mention of The Christopher Wren Association for Lifelong Learning, an innovative educational program begun at the College of William and Mary in 1991. Any Williamsburg area resident of retirement age who loves learning is welcome to take part in this course of study. Don't worry, there are no grades or tests here, though intellectual challenge is amply present.

The association, founded by retired college professors Ruth and Wayne Kernodle, is peer run and peer taught. By tapping the area expertise of local retirees, the college has offered a wide variety of classes in history, technology, art, and many other fields. For a $75 membership fee, lifelong learners can enroll in twelve weeks of classes. The association also sponsors social events, brown-bag lunches, and day trips for its members. Another option, the associate

i One of the best-kept secrets in Williamsburg is the Earl Gregg Swem Library at the College of William and Mary. Senior citizens are welcome to use the materials found here on the premises, including copies of most major American newspapers. In addition, here you'll find more than one million books, even more microforms, and a half million items in the government publications collection. For more information call (757) 221-4636 or go to www.swem.wm.edu.

membership, is $25. It's designed for those interested in receiving the newsletter, attending the convocation, and participating in trips, retreats, or bag lunches, but not in taking classes. For a complete schedule and registration instructions, call or go to the Web site listed above.

Historic Triangle Senior Center
5301 Longhill Road
(757) 259-4187
This is perhaps the most popular meeting place for local senior citizens. With its convenient location in the James City County–Williamsburg Community Center on Longhill Road, the center serves as a clearinghouse for social activities designed with the senior citizen in mind. It offers everything from weekly and monthly social events and special activities, special health and wellness programs, computer literacy training, special lunch programs, fitness classes, workshops, medical transportation, and much, much more. The center also publishes a monthly newsletter updating senior citizens on upcoming programs and events as well as specially scheduled trips.

The Meetin' & Movin' Fifty Plus Group
P.O. Box BB, Williamsburg, VA 23187
(757) 229-1771
This ecumenical program, sponsored by Williamsburg United Methodist Church, is open to all interested persons 50 and older.

i Retired military officers and their families can keep abreast of what's happening through the Virginia Peninsula Chapter, Retired Officers Association. This organization puts out a monthly newsletter, holds local chapter meetings, and enjoys social events. To learn more about this special group, call (800) 234-6622.

The group meets once a month and undertakes church-related social and fund-raising projects, trips, and more.

Retired & Senior Volunteer Program (RSVP)
12388 Warwick Boulevard, Suite 201
Newport News
(757) 595-9037
www.rsvpvapeninsula.org

RSVP responds to community needs through a network of senior citizen volunteers that recruits and places people 55 and older who are interested in providing community service. Volunteers give their time to more than 250 places such as Meals on Wheels, non-profit agencies, convalescent centers, and hospitals in the area.

Senior Center of York
5314 George Washington Highway
Yorktown
(757) 898-3807
www.theseniorcenter.org

This growing center offers myriad activities for citizens 55 and up. Here seniors can participate in such activities as ceramics, quilting, dominoes and bridge, line dancing, a computer club, and more. A free monthly calendar, available at the center, lists scheduled activities and events, including special senior citizen trips.

Town and Gown Brown Bag
College of William and Mary
(757) 221-2640

One popular activity is the Town and Gown luncheon and lecture series, sponsored by the College of William and Mary and usually held in the Campus Center. This program attracts many area retirees, who gather when the college brings in speakers from near and far to give informal talks after a catered luncheon on topics of sometimes general, sometimes specialized, interest. The series is open only to regular and associate members of The Christopher Wren Association. (If you would like to become a member, look for more information about the association in its entry earlier in this section.) Since this is a popular event, reservations are necessary so that adequate seating may be provided.

WJC Retired Teachers Association
(757) 220-2662

This group meets the first Wednesday of each month, except January, April, and October, for a luncheon and business meeting at the Holiday Inn Downtown on Capitol Landing Road. In November the meeting is at a local school. The group is open to all senior citizens who are retired from the field of education.

SERVICES

Catholic Charities of Hampton Roads
1300 Jamestown Road
(757) 253-2847

Catholic Charities' services for senior citizens include a fix-it force, bill paying and transportation program, telephone reassurance and friendly visitor programs, and elder care consultation and referral. There is also a caregivers support group and a bereavement support group in Williamsburg.

Computer Literacy Training
Historic Triangle Senior Center
5301 Longhill Road
(757) 259-4181
www.theseniorcenter.org

The center offers various computer literacy classes for seniors 55 and up, including Internet skills and word processing. Volunteer instructors will assist seniors, provide access to computers for practice, or arrange a self-paced course between the instructor and the pupil. Call for a schedule of classes.

Meals on Wheels
227 Richmond Road
(757) 229-9250
www.wmbgmealsonwheels.com
Everyone gets into the act here! Seniors help serve other seniors and others who are either homebound or too elderly or infirm to cook for themselves on a regular basis. Operated out of an office in the Williamsburg Baptist Church, this volunteer group serves more than one hundred local senior citizens a nutritionally balanced, hot meal prepared from Monday through Friday. Recipients are charged on a sliding-scale, ability-to-pay basis. Anyone wishing to call should use the number listed above. Those who prefer to write for more information can send their inquiry to Meals on Wheels, P.O. Box 709, Williamsburg, VA 23187.

Medical Escort Service
Historic Triangle Senior Center
5301 Longhill Road
(757) 259-4187
Thanks to the generosity of the Williamsburg Community Health Foundation and other local funding, the Historic Triangle Senior Center provides transportation Monday through Friday, if arranged twenty-four hours in advance, to doctors' appointments, the hospital, clinics, and the Olde Towne Medical Center.

Peninsula Agency on Aging (PAA)
739 Thimble Shoals Boulevard, Suite 1006
Newport News
(757) 873-0541
www.paainc.org
The PAA is the central source of information on services for senior citizens throughout the entire area. This office provides services and programs covering needs such as housing, health, income or financial aid, community services, adult day care, legal services, nutrition and meal programs, transportation, recreation, in-home support, and social services.

Riverside Adult Daycare Center
3635 John Tyler Highway
(757) 565-5305

1000 Old Denbigh Boulevard
Newport News
(757) 875-2033
www.riverside-online.com
This organization operates a day-care center for seniors with physical limitations and mental disorders such as Alzheimer's disease. Active programs include outings, guest speakers, singing, current events discussion, crafts, and exercise.

Williamsburg Community
Sentara Home Care Services
1100 Professional Drive
(757) 259-6251
www.sentara.com/homecare/
This service, provided through the local hospital, provides home nursing care, companions, sitters, and social services for the elderly. The hospital offers case management for twenty-four-hour care, whether or not the principal caregiver lives in the area.

PUBLICATIONS

Williamsburg Regional Library
515 Scotland Street
(757) 259-4070

7770 Croaker Road
(757) 259-4040
Williamsburg Regional Library and the satellite library in upper James City County keep on file a variety of published resources of interest to senior citizens. These resources include publications especially for older Americans, such as Modern Maturity, which is the magazine published monthly by the American Association of Retired Persons (AARP).

Senior Times
James City County–Williamsburg
Community Center
5301 Longhill Road
(757) 259-4187
This newsletter, published monthly by the Historic Triangle Senior Center, lists all activities and programs for senior citizens, 50 and up,

at the center and beyond. Nearly 1,000 copies are mailed each issue, and others are distributed at the center.

Services for Citizens 55 and Older
James City County
Social Services Office
5249 Olde Towne Road
(757) 259-3100
James City County's older residents can pick up Services for Citizens 55 and Older, a free guide on local resources that is provided by James City County Social Services. It contains information about recreation, medical emergencies, day care, and support services. The office is open Monday through Friday from 8:00 a.m. to 5:00 p.m.

RESIDENTIAL LIVING

While many seniors choose to live in conventional, mixed-age neighborhoods, others prefer the more exclusive, secure, or convenient atmosphere of the retirement community. Currently, Williamsburg can provide several such options for retirees in search of a community lifestyle.

Brookdale at Chambrel at Williamsburg
3800 Treyburn Drive
(757) 220-1839
www.brookdaleliving.com
Located across the street from Williamsburg Community Hospital, active seniors can choose from a number of lifestyle options, including apartments or cottage homes. In addition, Brookdale offers assisted living in both efficiencies and full-size garden apartment arrangements. Brandon House and York Manor are the special-care needs section of Brookdale. This assisted-living option provides services tailored to the specific needs of each resident.

Dominion Village
4132 Longhill Road
(757) 258-3444
Many seniors in need of long-term, assisted-

i Fore! If you're a golfer, you're really in luck. With more than 15 golf courses in the Historic Triangle, golfers have a grand selection of links from which to choose. Better yet: Most offer senior citizen discounts. Call ahead and inquire about discounts and reservations at the same time.

living care opt for this facility, conveniently located about 5 miles from the city's Historic Area across Longhill Road from the entrance to Ford's Colony. It provides permanent and short-term residence options in private and semiprivate rooms.

Patriots Colony
6000 Patriots Colony Drive
(757) 220-9000, (800) 716-9000
www.patriotscolony.com
Retired military officers and their spouses are welcomed to this gated, continuing-care retirement community. Patriots Colony offers residences and a community center featuring fine dining, a fitness and wellness center, and recreational areas. Long-term health care options, which are open to seniors without military ties, include assisted living, assisted living for residents with Alzheimer's disease and other dementia, and a convalescent care center.

Ruxton Health of Williamsburg
1235 Mount Vernon Avenue
(757) 229-4121
This established facility, part of the Genesis Eldercare System, offers long-term and skilled nursing and respite care, varied activities, and physical, occupational, respiratory, and speech therapies.

Tandem Health Care at Williamsburg
1811 Jamestown Road
(757) 229-9991
www.tandemhealthcare.com
One of the newest senior nursing-care facilities in the area, this center's design features a

number of living areas and courtyards, as well as spacious dining and activity rooms. The center offers three levels of care: intermediate, skilled, and Alzheimer's.

Williamsburg Landing
5700 Williamsburg Landing Drive
(757) 565-6505, (800) 554-5517
www.williamsburglanding.com
At this upscale, gated community, seniors can choose home or apartment independent living and can take advantage of health services that range from a minimal wellness program to licensed nursing-home care. The Landing also offers on-site banking, gift shopping, library, computer room, woodworking shop, billiards room, health spa, outdoor pool, tennis court, and more. The adjacent Woodhaven Hall health care complex offers rehabilitative and other health services.

HEALTH CARE H

Health care, in some ways, has come full circle since colonial times. The use of natural remedies and some noninvasive treatments popular in the 18th century—such as the use of leeches—are once again being employed by people who opt for alternative and holistic healing.

In other ways, of course, medical care has made breathtaking advances. It's come a long way since the days when doctors, trained in the medical practices of the times, worked to keep soldiers alive on the battlefields of the American Revolution. In recent years a revolution of sorts has taken place in the Williamsburg health care community, where area hospitals have expanded and broadened services. Simultaneously, alternative health care options—and not just old-fashioned ones—also are proliferating.

Perhaps the most significant newcomer to the medical horizon in recent years is the Williamsburg Community Health Foundation. Founded in 1996, the foundation supports the hospital and works to continuously improve health in our community. Since 1997 the foundation has awarded more than $25 million to more than 150 groups, large and small. For information on the organization or its grant application process, call (757) 345-0912.

One of the fastest-growing organizations in the area is the Williamsburg AIDS Network. It began in the early 1990s as a small, understaffed agency, working out of a single room and reliant completely on volunteers. Today it is a professional, full-service organization working to improve the quality of life through support for persons living with AIDS and education about HIV/AIDS. For more information on the group, call (757) 220-4606 or go to www.williamsburgAIDSnetwork.org.

The health care community in the Williamsburg area offers virtually every medical service available in major metro areas. Through partnerships with regional facilities, local patients can access physicians as well as diagnostic tools and treatments they once had to travel great distances to find. This is no accident. The growing local population, a large retirement community, and the influx of millions of visitors each year have made the community a good place for the development of medical facilities and practices.

The centerpiece of medical services is the expanded Williamsburg Community Hospital, which has the fierce loyalty of area citizens and provides high-quality care for nearly all medical needs. An oncology center, located directly across the street from the hospital, is a tangible sign of the commitment the local medical community has made to better serve the community's needs. The hospital's emergency room is among the best in the region. In addition, several professionally staffed urgent-care centers are strategically located around town.

Needs that can't be met in Williamsburg are provided at other regional hospitals.

Dial 911 for medical emergencies in any Historic Triangle location. This number puts you in immediate touch with a trained professional who will take information about your location and the nature of your problem before dispatching the appropriate police, fire, rescue, or ambulance services to assist you.

EMERGENCY HEALTH CARE

Medical emergencies can be treated at several locations around Williamsburg. The most complete treatment is available at Williamsburg Community Hospital Emergency Care

i Nightingale Air Ambulance flies patients out for emergency care at regional centers more advanced in treatment for certain disorders, such as head trauma or severe heart complications. The main heliport is across Mount Vernon Avenue from Sentara Williamsburg Community Hospital.

Center, of course, but minor and immediate-attention emergencies can be handled at the other care providers listed.

First Med of Williamsburg
312 Second Street
(757) 229-4141
On the side of the city closest to Busch Gardens and Water Country USA, this clinic offers a broad range of emergency services with X-ray and laboratory support on the premises.

Riverside Urgent Care Centers
Williamsburg Crossing Shopping Center
5231 John Tyler Highway
(757) 220-8300
Riverside provides quick, efficient service and is particularly convenient to the Jamestown Road side of town and the Route 5 corridor. Most X-ray and laboratory requirements can be handled on-site.

Sentara Williamsburg Community Hospital Emergency Care Center
301 Monticello Avenue
(757) 259-6000
The city is justly proud of the role that Community Hospital plays in serving local patients as well as visitors to the Historic Area. A highly qualified staff of certified emergency care physicians and medical professionals gives careful attention to patients, and patients who arrive at the ER but are deemed nonemergency cases are triaged and then directed by the nursing staff to the hospital's Convenient Care Center.

GENERAL HEALTH CARE

In recent years the number of health care facilities in the greater Williamsburg area has grown significantly. Although Williamsburg Community Hospital remains the largest and most extensive medical facility in the community, the lower

Peninsula has seen the construction of several smaller facilities designed to provide many medical services once offered only at the hospital.

Colonial Services Board
Mental Health Center
1657 Merrimac Trail
(757) 220-3200
www.colonialcsb.org
This agency offers crisis services twenty-four hours daily. Normal operating hours are 8:30 a.m. to 5:00 p.m. Monday through Friday, but an answering service can put emergency callers in touch with professional counselors at all other times. Evening appointments also are available.

First Med of Williamsburg
312 Second Street
(757) 229-4141
Opened in 1984, this facility is the oldest private freestanding medical center in the greater Williamsburg area. Services include family practice, internal medicine, occupational medicine, and primary care. On the side of the city closest to Busch Gardens and Water Country USA, this clinic has X-ray and laboratory on the premises. It is open 9:00 a.m. to 6:00 p.m. Monday through Friday and 9:00 a.m. to 1:00 p.m. Saturday. It's closed on Sunday. No appointment is necessary. Credit cards and personal checks are accepted.

New Horizons Family Counseling Center
Jones Hall, W&M School of Education, Campus Drive
(757) 221-2363
www.wm.edu/education/newhorizons/

This educational and training project in the School of Education at the College of William and Mary provides counseling services at several school sites as well as the campus center. It provides free family counseling to any family with a child in a Peninsula regional public school who is referred by their school (there may be waiting lists for these services). Staff work with children who have problems related to school performance, communication, and behavior. Counseling hours are seasonal.

Olde Towne Medical Center
5249 Olde Towne Road
(757) 259-3258
Located on U.S. Route 60 west of Williamsburg, Olde Towne Medical Center is a nonprofit health center that provides comprehensive primary health and dental care for patients who are low-income or have no medical insurance, with fees based on a sliding scale. Staffed by volunteer doctors and nurse practitioners, it is subsidized by the City of Williamsburg and James City and York Counties. The hours are 7:00 a.m. to 7:00 p.m. Tuesday, 8:00 a.m. to 8:00 p.m. Thursday, and 8:30 a.m. to 5:00 p.m. Monday, Wednesday, and Friday. Appointments are required.

Sentara Williamsburg
Community Hospital
301 Monticello Avenue
(757) 259-6000
www.sentara.com/williamsburg
Established in 1961 and the major medical facility in the area, Williamsburg Community in partnership with Sentara is a full-service, nonprofit health organization. Primary care and physician services include convenient care from the hospital and medical staff and the Williamsburg Community Medical Group. Acute-care services include cardiology, cardiac catheterization, emergency care, maternity care, intensive care, medical/surgical care, pediatrics, progressive care, respiratory services, surgery, inpatient rehabilitation services, and more. Ambulatory and diagnostic services include a Coumadin clinic, diagnostic centers, endoscopy services, MRI, mammography, nuclear medicine, ultrasound imaging, lab services, lithotripsy, neurodiagnostics, occupational health, outpatient surgery center, pain clinic, pulmonary lab, sleep disorders clinic, vascular lab, and radiation therapy center. Visiting hours are 8:00 a.m. to 9:00 p.m. on regular floors and noon until 8:00 p.m. in the Family Maternity Center.

The Williamsburg Center
1235 Mount Vernon Avenue
(757) 229-4121
This center offers physical, occupational, respiratory, and speech therapies as well as long-term comprehensive health and nursing care. The large staff demonstrates affection and concern for individual residents, and the social and entertainment programs are top-notch. The community takes an active interest in the center, with organizations volunteering a variety of services and activities. Hours are 8:00 a.m. to 8:00 p.m. daily. Appointments are recommended.

REFERRAL SERVICES

Williamsburg Community Hospital provides a Physician Referral Service at (757) 229-4636. The hospital also will advise on home health care at this number.

The Olde Towne Medical Center also can provide additional helpful information. In Williamsburg, James City County, and York County, call (757) 259-3252.

CRISIS AND SUPPORT GROUPS

Al-Anon/Alateen
(888) 425-2666
www.va-al-anon.org
There are dozens of Al-Anon and Alateen meetings held each week at churches and community centers in the Williamsburg area. For a complete listing, go to the Web site or call the number above.

Alcoholics Anonymous (AA)
(757) 253-1234
www.alcoholics-anonymous.org
Numerous AA meetings are held each week on the Peninsula, including more than twenty in greater Williamsburg, sponsored by the Williamsburg Area Intergroup. For specific times and locations, call the number above.

Alzheimer's Association
263 McLaws Circle, Suite 203
(757) 221-7272
This association provides information and education to families of Alzheimer's patients, sponsors an ID bracelet program, support groups, respite care, provides education to the public through a Speaker's Bureau, and promotes local and national research projects.

Arthritis Support Group
(757) 259-6777
Sponsored by the Williamsburg Sentara Hospital and the Arthritis Foundation, this group meets each month at the hospital.

Avalon, A Center for Women and Children
(757) 258-5051 (hotline)
(757) 258-5022 (office)
www.avaloncenter.org
This group has served Williamsburg, James City County, and York County for more than twenty-five years. In addition to immediate shelter, it offers a twenty-four-hour women's help line, rape crisis intervention, legal and housing aid, and support groups. The group has built a complex, including a shelter and transitional apartments, serving women and families in crisis.

Breastfeeding Support Class
(757) 259-4233
Sponsored by the Family Maternity Center at Williamsburg Sentera Hospital, this one-time class costs $35 and is open to all new parents. The hospital also operates a breastfeeding support hotline for mothers who delivered at the hospital, (757) 984-7299.

i Every spring since 1994 the College of William and Mary's law school has sponsored a bone marrow drive to identify potential donors. It is the second-largest annual drive in the United States. The college also hosts several fundraisers, such as a 5K run/walk and poker tournament, to raise money for cancer research.

Catholic Charities of Hampton Roads
1300 Jamestown Road
(757) 253-2847
This nonprofit, United Way agency offers support and counseling in a variety of areas, including support for caregivers and people who are divorced, separated, or pregnant. It also sponsors a bereavement support group, offers free depression screening, and runs the Community Assistance and Resource for Seniors (CARES) program. Call for more information on other programs and services from 8:30 a.m. to 5:00 p.m. Monday through Friday.

Children and Family Connection
(757) 229-7940
www.ctrchildfamilyservices.org
This nonprofit United Way resource and referral agency is dedicated to quality child care and other family issues. It's a lifeline of information about local childcare providers, services for military families, early childhood education, and support groups for stay-at-home moms and other groups.

The Diabetes Education Program
(757) 259-4225
The Sentara Williamsburg Community Hospital offers Diabetes education and support classes at the James City County–Williamsburg Community Center, 5301 Longhill Road. Call for specific times and dates.

Domestic Violence Hotline
(757) 723-7774
This hotline, sponsored by the Virginia Peninsula Council on Domestic Violence, is staffed around the clock.

Fibromyalgia Syndrome Support Group
(757) 229-4636
The Sentara Williamsburg Community Hospital hosts free information and support classes for persons suffering with this muscle and joint condition.

Hospice Support Care of Williamsburg
(757) 253-1220
www.williamsburghospice.org
This agency provides professional and volunteer services to terminally ill patients at home or in a hospital or nursing home located in Williamsburg, James City County, or York County. Time out for caregivers and patient care supplies and equipment also are available to those who need them. Bereavement support and cancer support programs and related consultation and referral services also are offered. The agency is supported by the Greater Williamsburg United Way, so there are no charges for goods or services provided by this group.

Narcotics Anonymous
(757) 875-9314
www.peninsulana.com
The regional chapter offers numerous meetings in the area for individuals with addictions to drugs.

Prostate Cancer Support Program
(800) 827-2438
Sentara Williamsburg Community Hospital offers support groups in both Wiliamsburg and Hampton for this condition. Call for specific dates and times.

Stroke Information & Support Group
(757) 345-4490
This group provides support and education for stroke survivors and family members. It meets monthly at the Rehab Department, Sentara Geddy Outpatient Center, 6601 Mooretown Road, in Williamsburg. Call for specific dates and times.

United Way Community HelpLine
(757) 229-2222
www.uwgw.org
This resource and referral crisis line is answered twenty-four hours a day. It connects those in need with appropriate agencies that provide for needs such as child care, clothing, housing, medication, mental health services, and other forms of assistance.

Williamsburg AIDS Network
(757) 220-4606
www.willamsburgaidsnetwork.org
This local organization, funded in part by the Greater Williamsburg United Way, serves as a resource, referral, and support group for persons with HIV infection or AIDS, as well as their families. The group provides comprehensive case management services and offers a bimonthly support group. Case management services include assistance in accessing medical care, medications, financial assistance, and information and referral to other services in the area. In addition, the group provides HIV-prevention education speakers for local schools, churches, and community groups.

Williamsburg Self Help for Hard of Hearing (WISHHH)
(757) 229-3272, (757) 564-3795
Williamsburg Self Help for Hard of Hearing people meets at the James City County Library on Croaker Road. Hearing-assistance devices are set up during the meeting. The group also publishes a monthly newsletter and brochures of help to the hearing disabled. There is no cost to attend.

ALTERNATIVE HEALTH CARE

At present, the alternative health care options locally include several types of services, from

i If you're interested in nontraditional medicine, you'll find lots of choices here. New options continue to appear, attesting to the growing popularity of alternative health care in the Williamsburg area.

holistic care and chiropractic to acupuncture, massage, meditation, and variations on more traditional medical treatments.

The range of services provided by individual practitioners and chiropractic centers varies, so we urge you to call and ask questions before making an appointment. Area therapists must be licensed by the state and certified by the locality in which they practice.

Acupuncture ChiroCare Plus
3204 Ironbound Road
(757) 565-7776
Dr. Dennis Gesualdi, an acupuncturist, uses this ages-old form of therapy to relieve chronic pain and provide relief for other maladies. Chiropractic services are also provided.

Integrative Chiropractic and Acupuncture
1318 Jamestown Road, Suite 102
(757) 229-4450
www.integrativechiropractic.com

This is a physical medicine and wellness center that integrates several alternative-care practices with an eye toward total well-being. Formerly known as Physmed, the services include chiropractic, acupuncture, massage, and rehabilitative treatments to help facilitate each patient's overall good health.

Phoenix Rising Yoga Therapy
12 Canterbury Lane
(757) 229-2482
www.pryt.com
Practitioner Quinn Sale is a trained psychotherapist and licensed professional counselor who combines the ancient wisdom of yoga with nondirective dialogue techniques. Through a sequence of carefully assisted yoga postures and breathing tailored to each client's individual needs, this therapy provides the opportunity for release of habitual holding patterns from specific areas of the body. Most sessions are one-on-one; sessions with couples and women's groups also are offered. No previous experience with yoga is necessary.

EDUCATION AND CHILD CARE

Anyone who's visited the Williamsburg area within the last couple of years can confirm that the area is experiencing a growth phenomenon unlike anything since the founding of the colonial capital city in 1699. And with the influx of new homes and businesses come children—in all developmental stages and grade levels. Area public and private schools have had to expand to accommodate a growing population.

This chapter offers information on options for families with children of all ages. We begin with an overview of the local public school systems, of which there are two—Williamsburg–James City County and York County—followed by a listing and update on the area's private schools. But we don't stop after high school graduation!

For those of you who are interested in furthering your education, we also include a section on the colleges and universities nearby. The Old Dominion boasts many fine public and private colleges, several in or near the Historic Triangle, and we tell you how to find out all you need to know about each institution.

Since the topics seem to go hand in hand, the second half of the chapter is devoted to child care for those who plan to live in the area, live elsewhere but work here, or just need a night away from the little ones while on vacation.

EDUCATION
Public Schools

The Williamsburg–James City County Public Schools division is a unified system that serves the majority of students in the area from kindergarten through high school. The York County school system serves the balance of students from families living in the northern and eastern portions of the Historic Triangle.

The community is very actively involved in the two public school systems. In addition to the parent board associated with each school, local businesses, museums, historic sites, military bases, local governments, and the Williamsburg Area Chamber of Commerce are active participants offering opportunities for education, advancement, and fun for students.

Williamsburg–James City County Public Schools

This combined school division serves more than 10,000 students in fifteen schools: three high schools, three middle schools, seven elementary schools, and an alternative school. Each school has a character and atmosphere all its own, one that reflects the taste and interests of its administration, faculty, staff, and student body. Students are assigned to schools through a districting formula that is revisited regularly to ensure enrollment balance for each school.

A seven-member school board governs the system, which is run by a superintendent and staff. The five representatives of James City County are elected, while the two city representatives are appointed to the school board. All public meetings of the school board are televised on the W-JCC Schools cable channel.

The system is fully networked and computerized, with each school sporting a Web site all its own. More importantly, interested individuals can access information on anything from curriculum, the school calendar, block scheduling, sporting events, and teacher evaluations from the Web site, www.wjcc.k12.va.us. There are links to each

Williamsburg–James City County Public Schools

HIGH SCHOOLS

Jamestown High School
3751 John Tyler Highway
Williamsburg 23185
(757) 259-3600

Lafayette High School
4460 Longhill Road
Williamsburg 23188
(757) 565-0373

Warhill High School
4615 Opportunity Way
Williamsburg 23188
(757) 565-4615

MIDDLE SCHOOLS

Berkeley Middle School
1118 Ironbound Road
Williamsburg 23185
(757) 229-8051

James Blair Middle School
117 Ironbound Road
Williamsburg 23188
(757) 229-1341

Center for Educational Opportunities
(Grades six through twelve)
4610 Ironbound Road
Williamsburg 23188
(757) 565-0373

Toano Middle School
7817 Richmond Road
Williamsburg 23188
(757) 566-4251

ELEMENTARY SCHOOLS

Clara Byrd Baker Elementary School
3131 Ironbound Road
Williamsburg 23185
(757) 221-0949

D. J. Montague Elementary School
5380 Centerville Road
Williamsburg 23188
(757) 258-3022

James River Elementary School
8901 Pocahontas Trail
Williamsburg 23185
(757) 887-1768

Matoaka Elementary School
4001 Brick Bat Road
Williamsburg 23188
(757) 564-4001

Matthew Whaley Elementary School
301 Scotland Street
Williamsburg 23185
(757) 229-1931

Norge Elementary School
7311 Richmond Road
Williamsburg 23188
(757) 564-3372

Rawls Byrd Elementary School
112 Laurel Lane
Williamsburg 23185
(757) 229-7597

Stone House Elementary School
3651 Rochambeau Drive
Williamsburg 23188
(757) 566-4300

ℹ️ Williamsburg–James City County Public Schools operates a Youth Services Coalition, which is provided in conjunction with agencies and institutions in the community at large. Services include such things as a "Dare to Prepare" program for at-risk fifth graders with the potential to be the first in their families to attend college. Other programs touch on behavior, substance abuse, family and peer relationships, academic achievement, and career exploration.

school Web site, all administrators, and allied organizations such as parent organizations, scholarship groups, and more.

One of the most important online features of W-JCC Schools is its twenty-four-hour Information Hotline, which also can be accessed by calling (757) 259-4154. Here parents and students can get up-to-the-minute information on school closings, school-related announcements and, of special interest to students, birthday listings. Student birthdays also are televised on the W-JCC Schools cable channel.

Options for high school students include advanced-placement courses, vocational education, technology education, business, practical nursing, and fine arts sequences.

For information on specific schools, you can call the school directly or visit each school's Web site, which is accessed through the Web address listed earlier.

The local teacher's association, the Williamsburg–James City County Education Association, advocates for high-quality public education. It supports rigorous standards and seeks to develop, maintain, and strengthen meaningful partnerships between parents, the community, and educators. It is a local affiliate of the Virginia Education Association and the National Education Association. WJCEA is governed by an executive board, which is elected each year by the membership.

York County Public Schools

The York County school system is a large division that covers a vast area. It includes the territory bounded by Hampton on the south and east and Newport News and James City on the western and northern perimeters, and encompasses several military installations such as Langley Air Force Base, Cheatham Annex, the Yorktown Coast Guard Station, and Yorktown Weapons Station.

The system operates twenty-one schools, including seven high schools, four middle schools, and ten elementary schools. It is a large system, governed by a five-member school board and run by a superintendent and staff. One member represents each of the county's five election districts. The board meets monthly, usually on the fourth Monday of each month, for its regular meeting. The public is welcome to attend; the meetings are also televised on local cable television. The York County schools have been honored by several private entities for students' academic achievement. In 2007, for the fifth consecutive year, all York County School Division schools earned Virginia's highest accreditation rating based on results of its state assessment, Standards of Learning (SOL).

While there are more than 12,000 students who attend York public schools, the vast majority of them matriculate outside of the greater Williamsburg area. Residents of upper York County near Williamsburg enjoy a zoning plan designed to let children attend the schools that are closest to their homes. The system has a large, easily accessible Web site, http://yorkcountyschools.org, where you can access administrators and learn about each school and the vast array of special programs. For information on registration call the school board office, located at 302 Dare Road, at (757) 898-0300. For information on specific schools, go to the Web site or call or write the schools directly at the addresses and phone numbers provided in the sidebar.

York County Public Schools

HIGH SCHOOLS

Bruton High School
185 East Rochambeau Drive
Williamsburg 23185
(757) 220-4050

Grafton High School
403 Grafton Drive
Yorktown 23692
(757) 898-0530

School of the Arts
185 East Rochambeau Drive
Williamsburg 23185
(757) 220-4095

Tabb High School
4431 Big Bethel Road
Yorktown 23693
(757) 867-7400
http://yorkcountyschools.org/ths/

Virtual High School
The YCSD Virtual School offers high
school courses for homebound and
alternative education students working
toward a standard diploma.

York High School
9300 George Washington Highway
Yorktown 23692
(757) 898-0354

York River Academy
9300 George Washington Highway
Yorktown 23692
(757) 898-0516

MIDDLE SCHOOLS

Grafton Middle School
403 Grafton Drive
Yorktown 23692
(757) 898-0525

Queens Lake Middle School
124 West Queens Drive
Williamsburg 23185
(757) 220-4080

Tabb Middle School
300 Yorktown Road
Yorktown 23692
(757) 898-0320

Yorktown Middle School
11201 George Washington Highway
Yorktown 23692
(757) 898-0360

ELEMENTARY SCHOOLS

Bethel Manor Elementary School
1797 First Street
Langley AFB 23665
(757) 867-7439

Coventry Elementary School
200 Owen Davis Boulevard
Yorktown 23692
(757) 898-0403

Dare Elementary School
300 Dare Road
Yorktown 23692
(757) 898-0324

Grafton-Bethel Elementary School
410 Lakeside Drive
Yorktown 23692
(757) 898-0350

Magruder Elementary School
700 Penniman Road
Williamsburg 23185
(757) 220-4067

Mt. Vernon Elementary School
310 Mt. Vernon Drive
Yorktown 23693
(757) 898-0480

Seaford Elementary School
1105 Seaford Road
Seaford 23696
(757) 898-0352

continued

Tabb Elementary School
3711 Big Bethel Road
Yorktown 23692
(757) 898-0372

Waller Mill Elementary
Fine Arts Magnet School
314 Waller Mill Road
Williamsburg 23185
(757) 220-4060

Yorktown Elementary Math, Science
and Technology Magnet School
131 Siege Lane
Yorktown 23692
(757) 898-0358

Private Schools

More than 1,000 children in the Williamsburg area attend private schools. These include the oldest private school—Walsingham Academy—and two other private institutions, one local, the other on the Lower Peninsula.

Neither Williamsburg Christian Academy nor Walsingham Academy provide transportation for students. Hampton Roads Academy, about 25 miles east, does have bus service available for students in the Williamsburg area.

Walsingham Academy
1100 Jamestown Road
(757) 229-6026, (757) 229-2642
www.walsingham.org

Established in 1948 and directed by the Sisters of Mercy in partnership with a lay faculty, Walsingham emphasizes the education and development of the whole person through a caring, value-centered, high-standard curriculum. This independent, coeducational institution offers an elementary as well as a college preparatory high school, and while it is a Catholic academy, it is open to students of various faiths. The student/teacher ratio is 18 to 1. Enrollment is limited and we recommend applying early: for the Lower School, when students are a year or two out; for the Upper School, at the end of the year prior to the fall in which they wish to attend. This fully accredited school recently completed a multimillion-dollar sports facility and indoor gym complex

for the Upper School and a $1 million renovation of the Lower School.

Williamsburg Christian Academy
101 Schoolhouse Lane
(757) 220-1978
www.wcanet.org

Opened in 1978, this school focuses on Christian values and biblical viewpoints. The academy, which in 1992 became an independent, interdenominational Christian school with no church affiliation, offers pre-kindergarten through twelfth grade. Tuition ranges from $5,300 to more than $8,000 each year.

Hampton Roads Academy
739 Academy Lane, Newport News
(757) 884-9100
www.HRA.org

Founded in 1959, Hampton Roads Academy, or HRA as it's referred to locally, enrolls more than 500 students in grades six through twelve, many of whom commute 30 miles from the Greater Williamsburg area. From its inception HRA has stood for excellence in college preparatory education and has earned the designation as a "Blue Ribbon School" from the U.S. Department of Education. Hampton Roads Academy is fully accredited by the Virginia Association of Independent Schools. HRA appeals to a wide cross-section of students because of its broad-based athletics, arts, and music programs; commitment to community service; small class size; active

Honor Council and honor code; and reputation for sending many of its graduates to four-year colleges and universities. It offers bus service from Williamsburg. HRA recently completed a $2 million wing that houses a new library, computer center, and classrooms.

Colleges and Universities

A number of colleges and universities serve the Historic Triangle and surrounding communities. Whether high school graduates are seeking to further their education or older residents are looking to obtain advanced degrees, technical certifications, or new spheres of knowledge, there's an institution of higher learning sure to offer a curriculum geared to each individual's particular interest.

A two-year community college and four-year colleges and universities with advanced graduate level programs in a variety of disciplines are all located within a 30-mile radius of Williamsburg.

College of William and Mary
Richmond Road, Williamsburg
(757) 221-4000
www.wm.edu
William and Mary is one of the nation's oldest public institutions and is nationally recognized for its excellent educational offerings. King William III and Queen Mary II granted the charter in 1693, making the college the second institution of higher learning in the new country.

Often referred to as a "public ivy," William and Mary is a state-supported, four-year university that offers its students the diverse resources of a large institution with the community atmosphere of a smaller school.

William and Mary students walking to class near the Wren Building. JOETTA SACK

ℹ️ The College of William and Mary offers a youth enrichment program each summer. The Center for Gifted Education at the School of Education runs the activity for two sessions of weeklong courses in July. Gifted and talented students in pre-kindergarten through twelfth grade are eligible for classes. Call (757) 221-2362 for more details.

Today's 7,500 students can explore a broad curriculum in the schools of Arts and Sciences, Business Administration, Education, Law, and Marine Sciences. The Marshall-Wythe School of Law, ranked as a top law school in the nation by *U.S. News and World Report,* awards the juris doctor degree. The School of Marine Science/Virginia Institute of Marine Science—the third-largest marine research and education center in the country—offers both master's degrees and doctorate programs.

Most students live on campus, though a few commute, and most matriculate directly out of high school, so the student population is young.

Residents as well as visitors can take advantage of numerous cultural events and opportunities sponsored by the College of William and Mary (see The Arts chapter). Local citizens are offered special rates if they want to attend William and Mary's Alumni College, a four-day course offered each June to explore complex issues, such as modern technology. Call (757) 221-1174 for details. The Christopher Wren Association, a lifelong-learning program in which retirement-age citizens with a field of expertise share their knowledge with fellow retirement-age community members, has become a big hit at the university. (See the Retirement chapter for more details.) Call (757) 221-1079 for information.

The Wendy and Emery Reves Center for International Studies was established at the college to foster broader understanding of global issues at the university, across the nation, and throughout the world. At William and Mary, the center supports and integrates international programs in the arts and sciences, professional schools, and inter-disciplinary programs. It coordinates six undergraduate degree programs in international relations and area studies, administers study abroad programs for William and Mary undergraduates, and supports international studies on campus. The center also promotes faculty research and sponsors lectures, colloquia, workshops, and symposia on many issues of global concern.

Student-led tours of the college campus for prospective students are available throughout the year. For information on tours call (757) 221-4223. For other information about the college, see the Attractions chapter profile or call (757) 221-4000.

Christopher Newport University (CNU)
1 University Place, Newport News
(757) 594-7000
www.cnu.edu

Once the two-year branch of the College of William and Mary, CNU became independent in 1977 and since has developed an identity of its own. Now a four-year institution, it is located on a verdant, 125-acre campus about 25 miles southeast of Williamsburg in Newport News and offers a wide variety of undergraduate and graduate courses and degrees.

"We are a young university on the move that enjoys a growing reputation for really caring about students, great teaching, small classes, and having Virginia's safest campus," says CNU President Paul S. Trible, a former U.S. senator.

CNU offers more than eighty undergraduate and graduate programs in business, science, technology, education, government, and the performing arts to 4,800 students.

The Students-First Academic Program includes the Presidential Leadership Program, a minor in leadership studies; and the Presidential Scholars Program, a recognition program for students that provides annual scholarships ranging from $1,000 to $5,000.

CNU's performing- and fine-arts programs are showcased in the Ferguson Center for the Arts, which opened in 2004 and was designed by the world-renowned architectural firm of Pei Cobb Freed & Partners. The college's Freeman Center, a sports and convocation center, serves as a gathering place for sports, entertainment, and civic events. CNU's intercollegiate sports program includes NCAA Division III contests in eighteen sports including a twelve-time national championship women's track and perennial nationally ranked men's basketball team.

Christopher Newport University has many recent high school grads but also draws a contingent of older students who return to school after working for a few years. Most CNU students commute, though some live in dorms on campus.

Thomas Nelson Community College (TNCC)
Historic Triangle Center,
161-C John Jefferson Square
(757) 253-4300
www.tncc.cc.va.us

Thomas Nelson Community College, based in Hampton, opened its Historic Triangle satellite campus in the spring of 1999 in order to provide a full range of classes to residents in the Williamsburg–James City County–York County area. Located in John Jefferson Square in the Busch Corporate Center off U.S. Route 60 near Busch Gardens, the office provides one-stop admissions, registration, academic assessment, counseling, and book ordering, so students do not have to go to the Hampton campus, about 30 miles away, for any services. (For more information on the Hampton campus, see its entry under Education in the Newport News and Hampton chapter.)

The new location allows TNCC to offer classes at the Historic Triangle location on both day and evening schedules. Additional evening courses are offered at Lafayette High School and Jamestown High School and on the campus of the College of William and Mary. Students also are able to enroll in a growing number of distance learning courses the college now offers via television and the Internet. Many courses can transfer to other colleges and universities.

Another activity of the college in the Historic Triangle is dual enrollment arranged through the high schools, allowing students in certified high school courses to take those courses for college credit. Senior citizens may take courses at TNCC on a space-available basis without paying tuition under a program the college offers.

Along with credit courses at the locations listed above, TNCC provides credit-free courses in computing topics at its Greater Williamsburg Computer Training Center on Jamestown Road.

Hampton University
Hampton, VA 23668
(757) 727-5000
www.hamptonu.edu

Privately supported Hampton University celebrated its 140th anniversary in 2008. When it opened its doors on April 1, 1868, it was known as the Hampton Normal and Agricultural Institute, which had a few buildings on 120 acres of land, little equipment, two teachers (who earned $15 a month), fifteen students, and a dormitory retrofitted from a converted hospital barracks.

General Samuel Chapman founded the school with a plan to educate the newly emancipated African Americans. Today Hampton University is one of the most popular historically black colleges in America, boasting a student population of more than 5,000.

Hampton has a $180 million endowment, state-of-the-art facilities, a distinguished faculty, and an innovative curriculum. It offers a variety of programs including especially strong ones in science, engineering, pharmacy, business (including an MBA degree), architecture, and nursing.

Hampton offers an exceptional athletic program as well, including a men's and women's sailing team.

The university, which stresses the importance of leadership through its Leadership

Institute, also reaches out to the community with its A Plus (A+) Summer Program for Pre-College Students. The monthlong program for 13- to 15-year-olds offers everything from mentoring and mathematics to art and scuba diving.

Listed among famous graduates is Booker T. Washington, class of 1875, who took what he learned here south, where he founded Tuskegee Institute.

CHILD CARE

The busy pace of life, especially for single-parent families and for those with two working parents, creates a need for safe, dependable child care. While word of mouth remains one of the best ways to find good child care, newcomers may not be sure whose recommendations to trust. The majority of child care centers are licensed by the state, and there are two ways to get current information about providers in whom you have an interest. Several options for finding local care providers are available as parents begin their search. In the Williamsburg area Child and Family Connection is your best bet for accurate, up-to-date information on daily child care or babysitting services. A locally based research and referral agency, it maintains a list of commercial and private day-care providers. Of course, you can also contact the National Association for the Education of Young Children, which also can provide information on child care options.

The National Association for the Education of Young Children
(800) 424-2460
www.naeyc.org
This national organization, known for high standards, is a source of information on child care. Guidelines from this group can be picked up locally at the Virginia Social Services Department, which can be reached by calling (757) 594-7594.

Child and Family Connection
312 Waller Mill Road, Suite 500
(757) 229-7940
www.ctrchildfamilyservices.org
This nonprofit organization is a resources and referral service funded primarily through the United Way. Here, parents are provided with assistance finding licensed, home-based care providers. A computerized directory of area day-care centers and information concerning all local child care options, including nanny services, aids the search. In addition, the Connection maintains a resource library of books and videos pertaining to many aspects of parenting, including immunizations and health care. It offers support services to parents, newsletters, and many other classes.

Child Development Resources
150 Point of Woods Road, Norge
(757) 566-3300
http://cdr.org/
Parents of children with special needs or of kids who might benefit from early evaluation and intervention can contact this nationally recognized organization, based in Norge, about 10 miles west of Williamsburg. Professionals here offer testing, information, advice, referrals, and support for families with children who have special needs, particularly those faced with out-of-the-ordinary needs.

Babysitting Services for Visitors

With so many families visiting the area, there are frequent inquiries about the babysitting services available to nonresidents.

While area hotels and motels once routinely offered sitting services for their guests,

i The local fire departments offer classes in CPR and basic babysitting skills for area teenagers. When you hire sitters, inquire whether they have taken the course or if they are trained in emergency first aid and CPR.

that's no longer the case. Typically, they still can arrange for babysitting, but need to know well in advance. They make the connection between sitter and family, but it's up to the family to make their own arrangements in reference to times and pay scale.

If you would consider leaving your child with a sitting service or private individual, it is critical for you to have references and to know if the sitter is bonded, what first-aid and medical training the sitter has, and if the care will be provided in your lodging or elsewhere. You must be sure to give the sitter your evening's itinerary, including phone numbers. Be prepared to pay a premium—up to $10 an hour—if you are visiting.

Another referral service is the Child and Family Connection, (757) 229-7940, discussed earlier in this chapter. This nonprofit group keeps a list of College of William and Mary students looking to earn extra money as babysitters. (Obviously, sitters may be in short supply in summer months when school is out.) The fee for sitting is negotiable between the student and the family seeking babysitting services.

MEDIA

Williamsburg relies heavily on print and broadcast media based elsewhere, including daily newspapers and national television network affiliates in the Richmond and Hampton Roads areas. The exceptions to the rule are a couple of local radio stations and newspapers and two good, informative, competitive magazines—one published monthly, the other three times a year—which offer locals as well as visitors a good overview of what's new and what's up and coming on the tourism scene. Both *Williamsburg Magazine* and *The Official Williamsburg/Jamestown/Yorktown Visitors Guide* are published locally. Both are extremely popular and have a tendency to disappear from the stands quickly once they hit the streets. When you see a copy, grab it fast and hold on to it!

NEWSPAPERS

Virginia Gazette
216 Ironbound Road, Williamsburg
(757) 220-1736, (800) 944-6908
www.vagazette.com
If you want to know what's really happening around the greater Williamsburg area, including Jamestown and Yorktown, this is the place to look. The *Virginia Gazette*, a twice-a-week newspaper, covers only local news—but they do it with a vengeance. First published in the colonial capital city in 1736, and with the exception of a few stops and starts during its early years, it is the oldest continuously published newspaper in the commonwealth. It hits the streets each Wednesday and Saturday.

It's a gold mine for information on attractions, local restaurants, places to stay, and what special events are on tap during your stay in the area.

York Town Crier/Poquoson Post
4824 George Washington Memorial Highway, Yorktown
(757) 898-7225
www.yorktowncrier.com
The *York Town Crier,* published weekly on Wednesday, covers York County events, including updated information on Yorktown area attractions, and serves as a useful tool when touring this restored riverside town and its battlefields. You'll also find some coverage on major issues affecting the parts of York County contiguous with Williamsburg and James City County. If you're planning a trip to Langley Air Force Base or the Peninsula NASA Langley facility, you'll find articles and information on these installations and other military-related attractions in this paper, too.

Daily Press
7505 Warwick Boulevard, Newport News
(757) 247-4800, (757) 247-4600
www.dailypress.com
The *Daily Press* is owned by the Tribune, a multimedia company that owns publishing and broadcast properties in major markets throughout the United States. The newspaper maintains a branch office at 201 Bypass Road in Williamsburg with a local news team. The *Daily Press* also operates the 1-Line, a free twenty-four-hour information telephone service that lets callers access the latest information on news, sports, local attractions, weather, and entertainment. That number, for touch-tone phone users, is (757) 928-1111.

Richmond Times-Dispatch
401 Duke of Gloucester Street Williamsburg
(757) 229-1512
www.timesdispatch.com

The Richmond paper, owned by Media General, maintains a Williamsburg bureau that covers significant local issues as well as stories in Richmond and on the national and international scene. Look for information on area attractions, tourism-related issues, and money-saving coupons to Williamsburg area attractions as well. It also carries news of special events of interest to visitors, such as entertainment news, and reviews of local restaurants and movies showing in town.

Virginian-Pilot
150 West Brambleton Avenue, Norfolk
(757) 446-2000, (800) 446-2004
www.pilotonline.com
Owned by Landmark Communications, Inc., the *Pilot* (as locals call it) is the largest daily newspaper in Virginia. It covers all of Hampton Roads and offers a zoned North Carolina section that covers the northeastern portion of that state. There is no home delivery to Williamsburg or other parts of the Peninsula, but the *Pilot* can be purchased from boxes or at newsstands throughout the greater Williamsburg area. The *Pilot* also offers a free telephone information service for twenty-four-hour updates to news, weather, sports, and entertainment. To access the service dial (757) 640-5555 from a touch-tone phone.

William and Mary News
College of William and Mary
P.O. Box 8795, Williamsburg, VA 23187
(757) 221-2639
www.wm.edu/news
If you want to know what's happening on the campus of the College of William and Mary, pick up a copy of the *William and Mary News,* published every other Thursday during the school year and once a month during the summer. Copies are available across the campus. The *William and Mary News* is aimed at faculty and staff as well as townspeople. You'll find a schedule of lectures, programs, and concerts going on around campus as well as college-related news and information, including job listings.

Flat Hat
College of William and Mary
P.O. Box 8795, Williamsburg, VA 23187
(757) 221-3281
www.flathatnews.com
The *Flat Hat,* the college's student paper, is published each Friday during the regular academic year. It's a quintessential student newspaper, expounding on events useful and controversial from the student perspective. There's always a listing of upcoming performances, lectures, and programs presented by faculty, students, national performing troupes, and artists, as well as by myriad local organizations.

MAGAZINES

Williamsburg Magazine
216 Ironbound Road, Williamsburg
(757) 220-1736
www.williamsburgmag.com
This lively, informative magazine and Web site includes close-ups on tourist attractions, people who are shakers and movers in the tourism industry, what's new and what's timely, as well as details on when attractions open and close, special events, operating hours, and ticket prices. It is free and extremely popular—if you see one, grab it. They can be found at the entrances to many supermarkets and convenience stores, gas stations, restaurants, hotels, and motels. They hit the streets right around the first of each month year-round.

The Official Williamsburg/Jamestown/ Yorktown Visitors Guide
1915 Pocahontas Trail, Suite E-3
Williamsburg
(757) 229-8508

i *Williamsburg Magazine,* which comes out around the first of each month, is loaded with coupons. If you see one, grab it. Chesapeake Publishing, which also owns the *Virginia Gazette,* puts out this immensely popular magazine.

Also helpful and readily available, especially in area hotels and motels, is this free, full-color magazine designed with visitors in mind. Published by the Williamsburg Area Hotel & Motel Association, it comes out three times a year with timely articles and updates on what's new at local attractions. The photos are crisp, the information is useful, and the advertising is especially helpful when you're looking for something specific.

RADIO STATIONS

There are three radio stations originating in Williamsburg, including the campus station for William and Mary. Residents also can pick up stations broadcast from quite a number of other cities, including Norfolk, Portsmouth, Virginia Beach, Hampton, and Richmond. The following is a sampling of what you'll find when you scan the dial.

.These university stations play an eclectic mix of news, views, and tunes, everything from classical music to the latest popular hits:
WCWM-FM 90.7 (College of William and Mary)
WHOV-FM 88.3 (Hampton University)
WNSB-FM 91.1 (Norfolk State University)

If you are more in tune to the oldies, now called "classic rock," put the dial on these Norfolk goodies:
WAFX-FM 106.9
WFOG-FM 92.9

Country fans have several selections, including:
WCMS-FM 100.5
WGH-FM 97.3
WKHK-FM 95.3

Norfolk is the place to be for rock options with:
WNOR-FM 98.7
WROX-FM 96.1

The adult contemporary crowd looks to Hampton for:
WWDE-FM 101.3

For oldies from the 1940s and 1950s:
WMBG-AM 740

For school closings, the best stations for information are:
WROX-FM 96.1
WOWI-FM 102.9
WWDE-FM 101.3

National Public Radio broadcasts out of Norfolk on two stations:
WHRO-FM 90.3
WHRV-FM 89.5

Then there is the PBS station in Richmond:
WCVE-FM 89.9

If you have a sports fan who doesn't want to miss out on the action, several stations carry live broadcasts of games:
WTAR-AM 850
WBYM-AM 1490
ESPN-AM 1310
WRNL-AM 910
WHKT-AM 1650

TELEVISION STATIONS

Williamsburg, James City County, and upper York County residents pick up a variety of local channels from Newport News, Portsmouth, Norfolk, Gloucester, and Richmond.

The Vacation Channel (TV4), an independent cable channel, is available in most hotels and motels in the Williamsburg area. The format is a continuous broadcast of available recreational activities, shopping, and dining.

Listed here are some of the main channels.
WTKR Channel 3 (CBS), Norfolk
WTVR Channel 6 (CBS), Richmond
WRIC Channel 8 (ABC), Richmond
WAVY Channel 10 (NBC), Portsmouth
WWBT Channel 12 (NBC), Richmond
WVEC Channel 13 (ABC), Norfolk
WHRO Channel 15 (PBS), Norfolk
WCVE Channel 23 (PBS), Richmond
WVBT Channel 14 (FOX), Portsmouth
WGNT Channel 27 (UPN), Portsmouth
WPXV Channel 49 (PAX), Virginia Beach

WORSHIP

Early English settlers in Jamestown brought organized religion to Virginia, and many of those traditions continue today. They met each day to "have Prayer with a Psalme," a tradition that is continued by volunteers who, at noon each Sunday April through October, weather permitting, lead a ten-minute prayer service in the Old Church on Jamestown Island. (Call 757-229-1733 to double-check the time before you go.) Prayers dating from 1603, 1610, and 1638 from *The Order for Noonday Prayer* are invoked, giving visitors a feel for the way early settlers worshipped here. This prayer service is a joint program of Bruton Parish Church and the Association for the Preservation of Virginia Antiquities, which owns the church and twenty-two surrounding acres.

Although the Virginia Colony wasn't founded for wholly religious purposes, religion was of primary importance in the lives of settlers, who claimed their new home for their church, the Church of England, as well as for their king. Everywhere they moved, they built churches. These churches were nothing fancy, but they were more ambitiously conceived than the settlers' dwellings. By the time Jamestown was three years old, its church had two bells in the steeple, cedar pews, and windows.

In addition to the Jamestown Island church, which is mostly in ruins, several other colonial-era churches still stand and welcome visitors for tours. They include four significant edifices: Bruton Parish Church in Williamsburg's Historic Area, Hickory Neck Episcopal

Church on U.S. Route 60 in Toano, Grace Episcopal on Church Street in Yorktown, and Westover Church, the Byrd family church, located along Route 5 in Charles City County. (For information on historic churches, please turn to the Attractions chapter.)

The Church of England dominated religious life in the Virginia Colony. Church attendance was mandatory in colonial Virginia—twice a day every day of the week in some settlements. Delinquents spent the night in the Guardhouse or were fined in pounds of tobacco. Keeping the Sabbath holy was a serious preoccupation for early courts: Pity poor Thomas Scully who, in 1624, was ordered to pay "5 pounds sterling in good tobacco" for "going a hunting" on a Sunday.

Witch trials didn't occur only in the New England colonies. Jamestown is where the first charge of witchcraft in British North America was recorded in 1626. Colonial Williamsburg now periodically presents "Cry Witch," an audience-interactive dramatization of the 1706 trial of a well-known Virginia witch accused of, among other things, shrinking herself and sailing to North Carolina on an eggshell. In later years other religious non-conformists in the colony, notably the Quakers, faced persecution, even banishment.

As dissent fomented in England, diversity and a bit of tolerance spread to America. Presbyterian, Methodist, and Baptist churches were founded here by the end of the colonial era. Presbyterians organized in Williamsburg in 1765. Williamsburg Presbyterian Church at one time met on the Palace Green on a lot bought from the College of William and Mary in 1885. In 1930, during the restoration of the Palace Green area, that property was sold; the new edifice at 215 Richmond Road was completed in 1931. The

i Tourists pour into area churches on Sunday. Insiders know to arrive earlier than usual in season to ensure both parking and seating.

Williamsburg Places of Worship

Ascension of Our Lord Byzantine Catholic Church, 114 Palace Lane,
   Williamsburg, (757) 253-5641

Bruton Parish Church, Duke of Gloucester Street, Williamsburg,
   (757) 229-2891

Chickahominy Baptist Church, 631 Chickahominy Road, Toano,
   (757) 566-8330

Christian Life Center, 4451 Longhill Road, Williamsburg, (757) 220-2100

Colonial Church of Christ, 301 First Street, Williamsburg, (757) 565-5669

Church of God, 209 Longhill Road, Williamsburg, (757) 229-9433

Church of Jesus Christ of Latter Day Saints, 2017 Newman Road, Williamsburg, (757) 564-1933

Faith Baptist Church, 4107 Rochambeau Drive, Williamsburg, (757) 566-0456

First Baptist Church, 727 Scotland Street, Williamsburg, (757) 229-1952

First Church of Christ Scientist, 620 Jamestown Road, Williamsburg,
   (757) 229-3820

Grace Baptist Church, 1013 Penniman Road, Williamsburg, (757) 229-2232

Grace Covenant Presbyterian Church, 1677 Merrimac Trail, Williamsburg,
   (757) 220-0147

Grace Episcopal Church, 111 Church Street, Yorktown, (757) 898-3261

Greensprings Chapel, 3687 Ironbound Road, Williamsburg, (757) 253-2270

Grove Christian Outreach Center, 16401 Chickahominy Bluff Road, Williamsburg, (757) 565-3142

Heritage Free Will Baptist Church, 1042 Penniman Road, Williamsburg,
   (757) 220-2038

Hickory Neck Episcopal Church, 8300 Richmond Road, Toano, (757) 566-0276

James River Baptist, 4931 Centerville Road, Williamsburg, (757) 258-0303

Jamestown Christian Fellowship, 5306 Olde Towne Road, Williamsburg,
   (757) 229-1993

Jamestown Presbyterian Church, 3287 Ironbound Road, Five Forks,
   (757) 229-5445

King of Glory Lutheran Church, 4897 Longhill Road, Williamsburg,
   (757) 258-9701

Kingdom Hall of Jehovah's Witnesses, 5731 Richmond Road
   Williamsburg, (757) 565-1571

Little Zion Baptist Church, 8625 Pocahontas Trail, Williamsburg,
   (757) 229-9788

Mt. Calvary Seventh Day Adventists, 200 Railroad Street, Williamsburg,
   (757) 229-3926

Mt. Gilead Baptist Church, 8660 Pocahontas Trail, Williamsburg,
   (757) 229-4654

Mt. Pleasant Baptist Church, 4002 Ironbound Road, Williamsburg,
   (757) 220-0934
Olive Branch Christian Church, 7643 Richmond Road, Williamsburg,
   (757) 566-8077
Our Savior's Lutheran Church, 7479 Richmond Road, Norge, (757) 564-3745
Smith Memorial Baptist Church, 6515 Richmond Road, Lightfoot,
   (757) 565-0476
St. Bede Catholic Church, 3686 Ironbound Road, Williamsburg, (757) 229-3631
St. John Baptist Church, 1397 Penniman Road, Williamsburg, (757) 229-0759
St. Martin's Episcopal Church, 1333 Jamestown Road, Williamsburg,
   (757) 229-1111
St. Olaf Catholic Church, 104 Norge Lane, Williamsburg, (757) 564-3819
St. Stephen Lutheran Church, 612 Jamestown Road, Williamsburg,
   (757) 229-6688
Stonehouse Church of the Nations, 8824 Richmond Road, Toano,
   (757) 566-8590
Temple Beth El, 600 Jamestown Road, Williamsburg, (757) 220-1205
Walnut Hills Baptist Church, 1014 Jamestown Road, Williamsburg,
   (757) 220-5900
Wellspring United Methodist Church, 4871 Longhill Road, Williamsburg,
   (757) 258-5008
Williamsburg Assembly of God, 5232 Longhill Road, Williamsburg,
   (757) 253-2990
Williamsburg Baptist Church, 227 Richmond Road, Williamsburg,
   (757) 229-1217
Williamsburg Christian Church, 200 John Tyler Highway, Williamsburg,
   (757) 253-2506
Williamsburg Church of Christ, 227 Merrimac Trail, Williamsburg,
   (757) 253-5662
Williamsburg Community Chapel, 3899 John Tyler Highway, Williamsburg,
   (757) 229-7152
Williamsburg Mennonite Church, 7800 Croaker Road, Williamsburg,
   (757) 566-3026
Williamsburg Presbyterian Church, 215 Richmond Road, Williamsburg
   (757) 229-4235
Williamsburg Seventh Day Adventists, 3989 John Tyler Highway, Williams-
   burg, (757) 220-3795
Williamsburg Unitarian Universalists, 3051 Ironbound Road, Williamsburg,
   (757) 220-6830
Williamsburg United Methodist Church, 500 Jamestown Road, Williamsburg,
   (757) 229-1771
York River Baptist Church, 8201 Croaker Road, Williamsburg, (757) 566-3030

church now serves a congregation of more than 1,400.

During colonial times, the Williamsburg Baptist Church, 227 Richmond Road, met in members' homes and in the Powder Magazine, which later was remodeled into a church and housed the congregation until Colonial Williamsburg's restoration began. Chartered in 1828, the church moved to the current building in 1935.

Church building first flourished during the 18th and early 19th centuries. A more recent resurgence in church construction began in the late 1980s and continues today. As the Williamsburg area continues to grow and prosper, so does its religious community. Existing congregations have grown significantly, with members and visitors filling edifices to capacity.

Many long-standing churches locally have had to expand, and congregations have split their populations between two or more churches. For example, St. Bede Roman Catholic Church, located on Richmond Road adjacent to the College of William and Mary's Alumni House, lists nearly 2,000 member families. Some split off with the emergence in recent years of St. Olaf, another Catholic parish in upper James City County. At present both of these churches are in the midst of capital campaigns with an eye toward building new, larger churches. In June 2001 St. Bede broke ground on its new $10 million church on Ironbound Road across from Mid County Park. St. Olaf's members hope to first pay off their current church, which, when the new church is built sometime down the road, will be transformed into a parish center.

At the same time, new and diverse congregations are opening with amazing regularity. Route 5 is quickly becoming a "church row" of sorts, with numerous new churches sprouting up between the city and county line at the confluence of the James and Chickahominy Rivers.

Once-tiny church communities, such as the Ascension of Our Lord Byzantine Catholic Church, are gaining members weekly. The church, located at 114 Palace Lane, off Bypass Road, holds several liturgies on Sunday and others during the week. The liturgy is offered in English, with much of it sung, and it retains much of the pomp and circumstance lost in the Roman liturgy since Vatican II.

The Jewish community, once a tiny group, has grown tremendously in recent years, as has the Unitarian Universalist congregation, which has opened an exquisite and expanded edifice on Ironbound Road between Jamestown Road and John Tyler Highway.

As the faith community grows, so does the scope of programs and services provided by different congregations. Several offer babysitting during services; one has opened a community child care center. The First Church of Christian Science offers a reading room at 626 Jamestown Road, across from the campus of the College of William and Mary. Of particular interest to the hearing impaired, York River Baptist signs its services. And if you're a pet lover, you'll be glad to hear that Bruton Parish Church holds a special Blessing of the Animals liturgy each spring that over the years has drawn some unusual creatures.

Easter is a special time everywhere, but in Williamsburg a very special service is held. A consortium of religious leaders representing various faiths leads a "sunrise service," usually beginning at 7:00 a.m., at the historic cross on Jamestown Island. Check the religion pages of the *Virginia Gazette* to get specifics each Easter.

The above list is not an exhaustive compilation of Historic Triangle churches, but an overview. We recommend that readers seeking information concerning worship services and times call the church they wish to attend for exact information. Another source for current listings of religious observances held around the Historic Triangle is the *Saturday Virginia Gazette*.

NEWPORT NEWS AND HAMPTON

Want to take in all the rich history and diversity the Virginia Peninsula has to offer while you're in Williamsburg? Then head southeast on Interstate 64 and check out Newport News and Hampton, adjacent cities that truly are one of a kind. If the ocean depths fascinate you, you can submerge yourself in the sights at the Mariners' Museum in Newport News, one of the largest and most comprehensive maritime museums in the world. If you're more given to far-flung flights of fancy, the Virginia Air and Space Center in Hampton is a must-see. But, even if you're a bona fide landlubber who likes to keep both feet planted firmly on Mother Earth, these two Virginia Peninsula cities offer a variety of cultural and recreational resources that are more than worth a detour south for a day or two.

In this chapter we provide you with an overview of each city, thoroughly explore the region's main attractions, offer insights into recreation, and direct you to the best places to dine and rest your weary head before venturing out for another day of sightseeing. Because Hampton and Newport News are next-door neighbors—and you pretty much get to each city the same way—we've combined much of our information. For convenience and ease of planning, however, we've kept listings of the attractions, restaurants, accommodations, shopping, and recreation in each city separate.

NOTES ON NEWPORT NEWS

Newport News's somewhat curious name has an intriguing origin. It was Captain Christopher Newport who guided the *Susan Constant* and her two sister ships *Discovery* and *Godspeed* as they carried settlers to Jamestown and the rest of the New World in 1607. After his initial voyage the good captain continued to make the trek between England and America, carting supplies, additional colonists, and word from home to the struggling Jamestown residents. To say the settlers awaited his arrival with great anticipation probably would have been the understatement of the 17th century.

Indeed, Captain Newport became quite beloved, and the sight of his boat in the lower reaches of the James was very good news to all those living in the rugged New World. So good, in fact, that Newport's name became linked with the idea of news from home, both forming the moniker for the city that eventually grew along these shores. Even so, Newport News wasn't much of a town until 1882, when Collis P. Huntington brought the C&O railroad to the body of water called Hampton Roads, a superb natural harbor formed at the joining of the James, York, Elizabeth, and Nansemond Rivers. (Today the term Hampton Roads also is commonly used to refer to all of southeastern Virginia, embracing the Virginia Peninsula to the northwest and south Hampton Roads cities and counties across the James River. See the Getting Here, Getting Around chapter for a more detailed explanation.)

A few years later Huntington created the Newport News Shipbuilding and Drydock Company, and the city's fortunes took off like a speedboat on smooth water. Shipbuilding booms spurred by the World Wars, along with the establishment of Fort Eustis and other military bases, spawned greater economic expansion. A former subsidiary of Tenneco Inc., the shipyard now steers its own course into the future as a separate, independent company with its own publicly traded stock and board of directors. Despite the changes and a long wave of layoffs caused by U.S. Department of Defense belt tightening, the yard still ranks as one of Virginia's largest private employers with approximately 18,000 workers.

A glance at a current map shows that Newport News—home to more than 200,000—is a long, narrow city, covering 69.2 square miles from the James City County line to the mouth of the James River. The city also boasts an amazing 30 miles of coastline, most of it along the James and Warwick Rivers. With so much shore at its disposal, it's not surprising that Newport News has one of the finest natural harbors in the world. In fact, Newport News Marine Terminal—part of the successful Hampton Roads port system—is here. Studies have shown that the port creates more than 6,000 jobs locally and generates more than $45 million in taxes each year for the city of Newport News alone. Newport News has relied on its port connections, a modernized airport, and the Monitor-Merrimac Memorial Bridge-Tunnel spanning the James River to help bring in industry and carve out a more diverse economic base.

A number of international businesses have been attracted to Newport News and its sister municipalities on the Virginia Peninsula over the past decade, including Canon Virginia, a major manufacturer of copy machines; Muhlbauer Inc., the American arm of a German-based company that makes high-speed machines for producing "smart cards," such as prepaid telephone cards and credit cards that contain computer chips; and the Thomas Jefferson National Accelerator Facility, a cutting-edge physics research lab that has made Newport News a familiar name in scientific circles. The park also is home to the seven-story Applied Research Center, site of ongoing research and development by local colleges and universities.

But, as they say, progress has its price. Continued residential growth and the influx of new industry have further burdened the city's major highways. While work continues on widening I–64 in upper Newport News,

motorists are advised to avoid this area during the late afternoon and early-morning rush hours. (And don't expect relief anytime soon. The multimillion-dollar project to eventually widen I–64 to eight lanes on the Peninsula likely will span this entire decade.)

SAY HELLO TO HAMPTON

Neighboring Hampton prides itself on being a city of "firsts." Settled in 1610, it is the oldest continuous English-speaking settlement in America. Our nation's first free education has its roots in the city, which was also the site of America's first Christmas. And the list continues. The city also was the site of the nation's first formal trading post, first continuous Anglican church, first national seafood festival, and the first site for the National Advisory Committee for Aeronautics, the precursor of the National Aeronautics and Space Administration (NASA, for short).

Hampton's NASA Langley Research Center actually was established in 1917 to advance the nation's airplane research. Proponents of the center say the work done there in the 1930s on the design of advanced airplane wings gave the United States and its allies the advantage that made them World War II victors. It wasn't until the late 1950s and early 1960s that NASA established the Space Task Force and located its office at Langley. While engineers and scientists in that group worked on America's original manned space program, today Langley is moving more toward the aeronautics research of its younger days.

Because of this research, the NASA Langley Research Center was singled out by former Vice President Al Gore in 1997 for its contributions to airline safety, including technology that visually updates pilots on weather patterns and a system that offers pilots an electronic liquid-crystal display of any airport they are approaching, showing them locations of active runways, ground traffic, and how close they are to the airport surface. The latter technology debuted in the summer of 1998 at Hartsfield-Atlanta International Airport.

Despite these and other success stories, there is some doubt about the future of NASA Langley, which has suffered spending cuts and a somewhat diminished stature as space exploration continues to take precedence over the less glamorous aeronautical research conducted here.

Hampton may have been "first to the stars," as city promoters like to say, but it also boasts a rich—and rather bloody—seafaring history. It was in Hampton in 1718 that the freshly severed head of Blackbeard the pirate was stuck on a stick and left at the harbor entrance. And during the Civil War, the iron-clads *Merrimac* and *Monitor* battled it out in the Hampton harbor, exchanging futile cannon fire over this Confederate stronghold.

Throughout the centuries Hampton has proved itself a city of resolute spirit, having survived shelling during the Revolutionary War and twice enduring devastating fire—first during the War of 1812, and next during the Civil War, when Hampton citizens set fire to their homes rather than see the city fall to Union forces. Today's Hampton is a vibrant and colorful city where commercial fishing, military installations, and aeronautic enterprises, along with smaller businesses and industries, sustain a population of more than 150,000. A revitalized downtown area with dozens of attractions has at its nucleus the captivating Virginia Air and Space Center. In recent years new shops and restaurants have opened and a rejuvenated nightlife has blossomed. Downtown's Mill Point Park, bordering the Hampton River, is the site of numerous festivals and after-work parties, and Queen's Way, a cobblestone downtown street, is the scene of popular Saturday night block parties.

Queen's Way is also the setting—or at least the focal point—for Hampton's major annual bash known as Bay Days. This celebration, held the second weekend of September, pays homage to the bounty of the Chesapeake Bay with marine-life displays, water conservation tips, and educational materials and activities for both the young and old. But Bay Days also is a festival, complete with all the celebratory trappings. Once you're there, you can't help but be hooked by the arts and crafts, the rides, the vast array of food, and the live entertainment that runs continuously on a number of stages throughout the festival grounds.

Hampton also is home to Hampton University, the nation's largest historically black private university. Each June the college, together with the city, sponsors the renowned Hampton Jazz Festival, which brings popular entertainers such as B. B. King, Aretha Franklin, and Kenny G. and thousands of jazz fans to the city for three days of soulful sounds and rousing good times. (For more on Bay Days and the Hampton Jazz Festival, turn to the Annual Events chapter.)

The southernmost city on the Peninsula has its own share of highway headaches, but the city recently completed widening its main commercial artery, Mercury Boulevard, which has helped. For more on Hampton's history, geography, and demographics, visit www.hampton-development.com.

GETTING STARTED

In planning your day trip to the middle and Lower Peninsula, there are a few logical places to start. We've listed these fonts of information here.

Newport News Convention and Visitors Bureau
Fountain Plaza, 700 Town Center Drive, Suite 320
(757) 926-1400, (888) 493-7386
www.newport-news.org
Another place to obtain a current visitor guide or other information is this downtown

i If you're headed from Hampton to Norfolk or Virginia Beach, you can avoid traffic at the Hampton Roads Bridge-Tunnel by taking the Monitor-Merrimac Memorial Bridge-Tunnel via I-664.

Emancipation Oak

Its low branches stretch impossibly wide, creating a cool canopy over the hot, flat landscape of Hampton, Virginia. It was here, under the sturdy limbs of what is now called the Emancipation Oak, that residents of Hampton first learned of their emancipation from slavery in 1863. This was the site of the first Southern reading of President Abraham Lincoln's Emancipation Proclamation, according to historians at Hampton University.

The peaceful shade of the Emancipation Oak, located at the entrance to Hampton University, also served as the first classroom for newly freed men and women eager for an education. It had already been a classroom for slaves: Before the Civil War, Mary Peake, a prominent educator who was the daughter of a free colored woman and a Frenchman, broke the law to teach classes to slaves and free blacks under this tree.

Ninety-eight feet in diameter, the Emancipation Oak is designated as one of the Ten Great Trees of the World by the National Geographic Society. A live oak, the tree's foliage remains green year-round.

Emancipation Oak. LYNN ZELEM

office. Since it's a bit off the beaten path, your best bet is to check the Web site or call and ask to have what you need mailed to you.

Hampton Visitor's Center
Hampton History Museum
120 Old Hampton Lane
(757) 727-1102, (800) 800-2202
www.hamptoncvb.com
Stop here for brochures on everything from restaurants and accommodations to walking tours and citywide attractions. This also is the place to purchase tickets for a Hampton waterfront cruise, which departs from docks right at the center.

Once you get your bearings, it's time to start exploring. For the sake of convenience, we've divided our listings under separate city headings, when appropriate. We've also included phone numbers so that you can call ahead and organize your stops for optimum enjoyment.

GETTING THERE

Both cities are a straight shot from Williamsburg east on I-64. The interstate runs through the northern half of Newport News before practically bisecting Hampton from end to end and crossing over and under the water to Norfolk via the Hampton Roads Bridge-Tunnel. While traffic congestion can be troublesome from 4:00 to 6:00 p.m. in the eastbound lanes, there's a chronic traffic problem westbound between the J. Clyde Morris Boulevard and Jefferson Avenue exits, where three lanes bottleneck into two. We have to admit this area is almost always backed up, but it gets worse around rush hour, so plan your trip accordingly. If the interstate is clear, it should take you about fifteen or twenty minutes to get to Newport News, thirty to forty minutes for the trip to Hampton.

An alternate route is to take U.S. Route 60/Warwick Boulevard from Williamsburg to the attractions located in the northern end of Newport News.

Seafaring tourists also can set sail for the Lower Peninsula and tie up at the Downtown Hampton Public Piers outside the Radisson Hotel. Showers, restrooms, Dumpsters, telephones, and pump-out facilities are available along the downtown waterfront.

In Newport News many of the attractions you'll be interested in are concentrated near the intersection of J. Clyde Morris and Warwick Boulevards. To reach that part of the city, exit the interstate at J. Clyde Morris (exit 258A), and follow the highway to its endpoint at Warwick. The quickest route to lower Newport News is to follow I-64 to Interstate 664 south (exit 264) and then take exit 5. In Hampton the main focus is downtown, also accessible by interstate exits that are clearly marked. But if your interests lie elsewhere or you're just the exploring type, you'll want to venture onto other highways and byways. Since both cities cover a decent amount of square mileage, your best bet is to contact your destination and get specific directions. Don't be shy when making your requests. Traffic can get to be a headache—particularly in Newport News, where Jefferson Avenue and Warwick Boulevard are the major north-south arterials—and you'll want to know the best time to venture off the interstate into the hinterlands.

ATTRACTIONS
Newport News

Nowhere is the old adage "geography is destiny" truer than in Newport News. The long, narrow shape of the city has given rise to some distinct neighborhoods with very different identities. One of the fastest-growing is Denbigh, near the northern tip of the city. Home to the bustling Patrick Henry Mall, the ever-expanding Yoder Farms Shopping Center, the Newport News/Williamsburg International Airport, and some of the city's most popular eateries, in recent years Denbigh has become the commercial center of the Lower Peninsula. An influx of young professionals in the 1980s spurred construction, with new housing developments and shopping centers shooting up practically overnight. All of this growth has created its own set of problems: Road construction hasn't kept pace with the population explosion, and traveling in Denbigh on Jefferson Avenue anywhere near rush hour can generate a major migraine. But once the five o'clock whistle is a distant memory, this is a great place to venture out for a night on the town.

Head toward the southern end of the city, and you'll stumble upon Hilton Village, a charming enclave that contrasts nicely with the newness of Denbigh. Hilton, whose 500 English cottage–style homes were erected in 1918 to provide housing for shipyard employees, has evolved into one of the most desirable addresses on the Peninsula. The local elementary school is first-rate, and the shopping district, blessed with wide brick sidewalks, beautiful landscaping, and shade trees, offers everything from gift and antiques shops to a vintage playhouse and one-of-a-kind ice-cream parlor.

The downtown waterfront—in the southernmost part of the city—is home to Northrop Grumman Newport News, one of the largest private employers in the state of Virginia, and the Newport News Marine Terminal of the Port of Hampton Roads.

Endview Plantation
362 Yorktown Road (exit 247 off I-64)
(757) 887-1862
www.endview.org

Since 1996 the Virginia War Museum has been hard at work developing Endview Plantation in northern Newport News as an adjunct to the War Memorial property. The plantation, which was built around 1760 by the Harwood family, briefly served as a Confederate field hospital during the Civil War. Endview also was used as either a resting place or campground on September 28, 1781, by 3,000 Virginia militia on their way to Yorktown and the climactic battle of the Revolutionary War. During the War of 1812, Endview had passed on to the Curtis family and was at that time the home of Confederate Captain

Humphrey Harwood Curtis, commander of the 32nd Virginia Regiment.

Today, Endview is a living-history museum with both Confederate and Union camps represented. A variety of programs and events are scheduled throughout the year, including a weekend devoted to outdoor cooking in the 19th century, and others on the art of blacksmithing and medical practices during the Civil War. Ghost walks are held in October, and the house is decorated with greenery and period decorations during December. Endview Plantation's annual Civil War reenactment is in March.

Regular admission is $6 for adults, $5 for seniors, and $4 for children 7 through 18. Some programs may cost extra. Endview is open 10:00 a.m. to 4:00 p.m. Monday and Thursday through Saturday and 1:00 to 5:00 p.m. Sunday. It is closed on Tuesday year-round, and on Wednesday January through March.

Fort Fun at Huntington Park
(off Warwick Boulevard)
(757) 886-7912

Head south on Warwick toward downtown Newport News and, about a mile past Main Street, you'll come to another favorite spot. The 13,500-square-foot Fort Fun is a great place for kids to work off pent-up energy. This playground, on a bluff overlooking the James River, features a multilevel wooden structure that provides a maze, fun house, haunted castle, tightrope, bucking bronco, fire pole, sandbox, slides, swings, tunnels, balancing beams, and much more.

While you're there, take along a picnic lunch and some fishing poles and try out the children's fishing pier on nearby Lake Biggins. The park is open from sunrise to sunset.

i Newport News is the site of the nation's most powerful continuous electron beam accelerator, located at the Thomas Jefferson National Accelerator Facility.

Lee Hall Mansion
163 Yorktown Road (exit 247 off I–64)
(757) 888-3371
www.leehall.org

Restored by the City of Newport News and opened as a historic house museum, Lee Hall gives visitors a glimpse of the life of a wealthy family before the Civil War. The Italianate mansion also served as a Confederate headquarters during the 1862 Peninsula campaign, during which the Union attempted to capture Richmond via the Virginia Peninsula. Built around 1850 by wealthy Warwick County landowner Richard Decauter Lee, Lee Hall is one of the last surviving antebellum homes in the region.

When you visit you will see a ladies' parlor, dining room, music room, and two bedrooms that have been restored to their 1862 splendor, as well as the room used as Magruder's headquarters. An exhibit gallery features artifacts from the Peninsula campaign, including a tablecloth from the USS *Monitor* and items recovered from a nearby battle site.

Lee Hall Mansion is open Monday and Thursday through Saturday from 10:00 a.m. to 4:00 p.m. and Sunday from 1:00 to 5:00 p.m. It is closed on Tuesday year-round and Wednesday from January through March. Admission is $6 for adults, $5 for seniors 62 and older, and $4 for children 7 and older.

Mariners' Museum
100 Museum Drive (exit 258A off I–64)
(757) 596-2222, (800) 581-SAIL
www.mariner.org

If the ships that once plied the world's oceans set your imagination sailing, you can explore U.S. maritime history with a visit to this world-renowned museum, which boasts the nation's most extensive international marine collection. Founded in 1930, the museum has preserved and interpreted the culture of the sea for millions of visitors over the decades. Its collection contains more than 35,000 maritime treasures including ship models, scrimshaw, maritime paintings, decorative arts, carved figureheads, navigational instruments, and working steam engines.

In 1997 the museum unveiled the National Maritime Museum Initiative, a cooperative venture with the New York–based South Street Seaport Museum, which has the largest privately maintained fleet of historic vessels. The alliance allows the two museums to exchange exhibits, share educational programs, link Web sites, and offer reciprocal memberships. The Mariners' Museum now has more than a dozen permanent galleries, ranging from displays of miniature ships to a 26-foot antique boat.

Among the Mariners' permanent exhibits is "Defending the Seas," where visitors can walk among re-creations of the most important ships in our navy's history. In addition, ongoing dive expeditions to the USS *Monitor* wreck continue to bring unusual and fascinating artifacts from the famous ironclad to the museum, which has been named the national repository for these objects.

Perhaps one of the museum's biggest treasures is its research library and archives, home to more than 78,000 maritime holdings. In fact, there is no other American institution that can match the library for the size, scope, and depth of its maritime collection, which include more than 650,000 photographs and negatives, 5,000 nautical charts and maps, nearly 50,000 plans to build craft from warships to pleasure boats, and thousands of other archival items, including Mark Twain's pilot license. In 2001 the Mariners' Museum received a grant from the Institute of Museum and Library Services to rehouse and conserve 1,290 of its maps dating from 1573 to 1899. The library will move to a new, 23,000-square-foot facility at Christopher Newport University in the fall of 2008; until then, visits can be arranged by appointment.

After visiting the museum, explore the 550-acre Mariners' Museum Park on the Noland Trail, a 5-mile amble around Lake Maury featuring fourteen pedestrian bridges, or have lunch in shady picnic areas. The park also features bike trails and boat rentals for fishing.

The museum is at the end of J. Clyde Morris Boulevard and is open Monday through Saturday from 10:00 a.m. to 5:00 p.m. and Sunday noon to 5:00 p.m. Current admission prices are $12.50 for adults and $7.25 for any student 6 to 17. Children under 5 are admitted free.

Matthew Jones House
Harrison Road, Fort Eustis
(757) 878-4123, (888) 493-7386

While you're visiting Fort Eustis, stop by this restored Virginia Historic Landmark, which originally was designed as an architectural museum house exposing three historic periods. The Matthew Jones House boasts ninety architectural features that are labeled as teaching points. A tour booklet keyed to the numbers helps you identify each feature. In-house collections highlight the history of Mulberry Island and the Jones and Webb families, who lived there for a span of 275 years. It's generally open 1:00 to 4:00 p.m. Saturday and Sunday June through Labor Day and by arrangement for tours. Admission is free, but donations are accepted. For more information on visiting hours, your best bet is to contact the visitor center at (757) 886-7777.

The Newsome House
Museum and Cultural Center
2803 Oak Avenue (exit 3 off I–664)
(757) 247-2360, (757) 247-2380
www.newsomehouse.org

Built in 1899, the Newsome House is a modified Queen Anne structure that was home to Joseph Thomas Newsome, one of the first black attorneys to argue before the Virginia Supreme Court. Newsome also was the editor of a black newspaper, cofounded a Newport News church, and formed the Colored Voters League of Warwick County. His home, on Oak

i The major industries in Virginia include manufacturing, exports, tourism, high technology, and agriculture. Virginia's tourism continues to increase, accounting for $17.6 billion in 2006.

Avenue in the city's East End, houses an exhibit on the Newsome family and extensive archives on the African-American community in Newport News. Hours are from 10:00 a.m. to 4:00 p.m. Monday and Wednesday through Saturday, and 1:00 to 5:00 p.m. Sunday. It is closed on Tuesday. Admission is free. Donations are accepted.

The Peninsula Fine Arts Center
101 Museum Drive (exit 258A off I–64)
(757) 596-8175
www.pfac-va.org

Just across from the Mariners' Museum is Newport News's fine-arts center, which offers changing exhibits that showcase works by outstanding artists to help promote education and an appreciation of the visual arts. Exhibitions change every eight to ten weeks and feature art of regional and national interest, juried exhibitions, student shows, and touring collections of historical and contemporary works. The museum continues to enjoy growing popularity, thanks in part to the attention it is paying to all the budding artists out there. The center's Hands On for Kids Gallery features activities and exhibits that involve visitors in active learning about art. There is also a gallery gift shop. Admission to the Fine Arts Center is $5 for adults; $4 for seniors, students, and military; and $3 for children 4 to 15. Hours are Tuesday, Wednesday, Friday, and Saturday from 10:00 a.m. to 5:00 p.m., Thursday from 9:00 a.m. to 8:30 p.m., and Sunday from 1:00 to 5:00 p.m. Free docent-led tours are available for school and community groups.

Peninsula SPCA Petting Zoo
523 J. Clyde Morris Boulevard
(exit 258A off I–64)
(757) 595-1399
www.peninsulaspca.com/zoo.html

Lions and leopards and llamas...oh my! That's what you'll find at this popular SPCA zoo, which attracts 80,000 visitors a year. Inside, of course, there are all sorts of cats and dogs that need good homes, and outdoors you'll find a unique petting zoo for kids. The menagerie features everything from goats and turkeys to otters and an ostrich. There also are a number of jungle cats, a kangaroo, a peacock, a bald eagle, and a dozen or so alligators and crocodiles. (But they, of course, are not for petting!) Hours are Monday through Friday 10:00 a.m. to 5:00 p.m. and Saturday 10:00 a.m. to 4:30 p.m. Cost is $4 for adults and $2 for children 3 through 12.

U.S. Army Transportation Museum
Building 300/Besson Hall
Fort Eustis (exit 250A off I–64)
(757) 878-1187
www.transchool.eustis.army.mil/museum/museum.html

At this museum on an active military base, visitors can explore more than 200 years of army transportation history including miniatures, dioramas, experimental models, and exhibits focusing on the personal stories of army personnel during Operations Desert Storm and Desert Shield. Kids will enjoy seeing a truck and a jeep that flies. There also are four outdoor parks where more than one hundred types of aircraft, trains, ships, land craft, and jeeps are on display. The museum, located just 11 miles south of Williamsburg, is open daily from 9:00 a.m. to 4:30 p.m. It is closed Monday and federal holidays. Admission is free, but donations are accepted.

Victory Arch
West Avenue and Twenty-Fifth Street
(exit 6 off I–664)
(757) 247-8451, (888) 493-7386

Since Hampton Roads was the World War II port of embarkation, the Victory Arch greeted our nation's armed forces during their jubilant homecoming. Its eternal flame serves as a memorial for all of the troops lost in battle. The arch was originally built of wood in 1919 and reconstructed in granite in 1962. Its inscription reads: "Greetings with love to those who return: a triumph with tears to those who sleep."

Virginia Living Museum
524 J. Clyde Morris Boulevard
(757) 595-1900
www.thevlm.org

Take a walk on the wild side at the fascinating Virginia Living Museum. The museum is an intriguing hybrid: part zoo, part botanical gardens, part observatory and planetarium, with native bird and aquatic life exhibits thrown in for good measure. Opened in May 1987, this multifaceted center is devoted to the preservation and study of Virginia and Eastern coastal plains wildlife and flora. Inside the museum you'll find a 60-foot living reproduction of the James River, fossil exhibits, a touch-tank for hands-on learning about marine life, and a two-story glass aviary with native songbirds. Outside, a half-mile boardwalk winds through a nature preserve where animals—everything from regal bald eagles to coyotes—can be viewed in their natural habitats. In the Coastal Plain Aviary, a net canopy encloses a marshy ecosystem for herons, egrets, ducks, pelicans, cormorants, and other birds, as well as turtles and a variety of plants indigenous to wetland areas.

Back indoors, the Living Museum's state-of-the-art planetarium is your ticket to the greater universe, featuring multi-image shows and telescope observation.

The Living Museum has concluded a $22.6 million expansion, which includes a new 62,000-square-foot exhibits building that opened in spring 2004. Visitors can now virtually walk into a Chesapeake Bay deep-water aquarium, walk through a Shenandoah Valley cave, and explore the natural environments of an Appalachian cove and cypress swamp. The Coastal Plain Aviary and the half-mile boardwalk trail with larger animal habitats is part of this expansion.

Adults pay $13 to enter the museum, and children 3 to 12 enter for $10. Children 2 and younger are admitted free, but are only allowed to specific showings in the planetarium.

Hours are 9:00 a.m. to 5:00 p.m. daily from Memorial Day through Labor Day. In the off-season, hours are Monday through Saturday

9:00 a.m. to 5:00 p.m. and Sunday noon to 5:00 p.m. Planetarium shows are offered every day.

Virginia War Museum
9285 Warwick Boulevard
Huntington Park
(757) 247-8523
www.warmuseum.org

This museum, administered by the Historic Services Division of the city's Department of Parks and Recreation, offers a detailed look at U.S. military history from 1775 to the present. There are more than 60,000 artifacts on exhibit, including an 1883 brass Gatling gun, a World War I Howitzer tank, and a Civil War blockade-runner's uniform. Most aspects of America's military heritage are well represented in the museum's many galleries. Priced at $6 per adult, $5 for seniors, and $4 per child 7 to 18, this is a great stop for families interested in American history. The Virginia War Museum is open Monday through Saturday from 9:00 a.m. until 5:00 p.m. and Sunday from 1:00 to 5:00 p.m.

Hampton

Downtown Hampton enjoyed glory days in the 1940s and 1950s, but the 1960s brought the stagnation of Old Hampton—as the downtown area is called—when businesses yanked up their roots and headed out to Mercury Boulevard, to an area now called Coliseum Central. In recent years, city officials have struggled long and hard to turn around the fortunes of Old Hampton. The city's first luxury hotel sprang up on the waterfront with a lighthouse-inspired visitor center next door. A fourteen-story office tower has given downtown a legitimate claim to a skyline, and new restaurants, antiques shops and museums, outdoor cafes, attractive murals, a pedestrian walkway winding along the Hampton River, and a park featuring a restored 1920 carousel have contributed to the area's rejuvenation.

In 1996 the Downtown Hampton Development Partnership was formed to help revitalize the heart of the city. Its efforts were so successful that the National Civic League designated Hampton an "All-America City." The city has also embarked on a $200 million project that includes a new convention center, site improvements and new parking facilities around the Hampton Coliseum, and new shopping and dining areas. Already, many new hotels and restaurants have opened near the convention center.

On the outskirts of downtown, a new library has opened, and the former library next door was transformed into the city's first arts center. The Casemate Museum on the grounds of Fort Monroe traces that army installation's colorful history, while the Hampton University Museum showcases an outstanding collection of African- and Native American art. Hampton also is home to Langley Air Force Base, where our nation's Air Combat Command is headquartered. In addition, the city boasts its own public beach, which is a less-crowded alternative to Virginia Beach. And Phoebus, a tightly knit community at Hampton's eastern tip, is a must-see with its plethora of antiques shops, fine restaurants, and a newly restored 1908 theater.

Whether you're here for a day or plan to stay longer, this section will help you find your way around. There's usually plenty of public parking and most attractions are within walking distance.

Air Power Park
413 West Mercury Boulevard
(757) 727-1163

One place for the kids to work off a little energy is Air Power Park, which houses one of the largest civilian-owned collections of aircraft and missiles in the nation, with more than fifty exhibits, some of which have been recently renovated. Outdoors, surrounding the park's information center, are aircraft from various service branches, including a Nike surface-to-air missile and an F-100D Super Sabre, the first Air Force fighter with true supersonic performance. The park is open daily from 9:00 a.m. to 4:30 p.m. Admission is free.

The American Theatre
125 East Mellen Street, Phoebus
(757) 722-2787
www.theamericantheatre.com

Although not an attraction per se, this refurbished theater is an important part of the Peninsula's arts landscape. Built in 1908 as a vaudeville and movie house, the theater underwent several transformations before closing in the 1990s. In recent years it has undergone renovations and now offers live theater, concerts, classic movies, and children's programs.

Bluebird Gap Farm
60 Pine Chapel Road
(757) 727-6739

Not only is the sixty-acre Bluebird Gap Farm a great retreat for the younger set, it's also free. About a ten-minute drive from downtown, Bluebird Gap Farm is home to numerous animals, including pigs, deer, goats, sheep, cows, chickens, ducks, and an occasional horse. A playground area is perfect for picnicking, and public restrooms and vending machines are available. The park is open Wednesday through Sunday from 9:00 a.m. to 5:00 p.m. Bluebird Gap Farm is closed Thanksgiving, Christmas, New Year's Day, and Wednesday when a major holiday falls on a Monday or Tuesday. Admission is free, but you may want to bring a couple of quarters in your pocket to plunk into food machines to feed the animals. Do not bring your own food to feed the animals; it might upset their diets.

Casemate Museum
Grounds of Fort Monroe
(757) 788-3391

Fort Monroe, which serves as headquarters for the U.S. Army Training and Doctrine Command, holds the title of the largest stone fort ever built in America and gives visitors a feel of life inside a fort. Within its walled core you'll find the Casemate Museum, which chronicles the history of the fort and the Coast Artillery Corps. During your tour of the museum, you will see the cell in which captured Confederate President Jefferson Davis was imprisoned, as well as weapons, uniforms, Frederick Remington drawings, and other military artifacts. You also will learn how "Freedom's Fortress" helped shelter thousands of slave refugees. Other nearby points of interest include Robert E. Lee's quarters, now a private residence, seacoast batteries, and the Old Point Comfort Lighthouse. The Casemate Museum is open daily, with no admission charge, from 10:30 a.m. to 4:30 p.m.

Charles H. Taylor Arts Center
4205 Victoria Boulevard
(757) 727-1490
www.theamericantheatre.com

On historic Victoria Boulevard, where grand old homes dominate the landscape, sits the Charles H. Taylor Arts Center. Housed in Hampton's 1926 library, where Victoria intersects Kecoughtan Road, the center displays the work of local artists and photographers as well as traveling exhibitions. The center also is home to the Hampton Arts Commission, which stages the highly acclaimed Great Performers Series at the American Theatre. If you stop in, pick up a copy of the organization's newsletter, *Hampton Arts Calendar,* which gives a comprehensive rundown of arts activities on the Peninsula. The center is open Tuesday through Friday from 10:00 a.m. to 6:00 p.m. and Saturday and Sunday from 1:00 to 5:00 p.m. Admission is free.

Cousteau Society
710 Settlers Landing Road
(757) 722-9300
www.cousteau.org

Known internationally for pioneering underwater exploration, photography, and conservation, the Cousteau Society opened an attraction on the downtown Hampton waterfront in 2003. The waterfront gallery showcases the undersea endeavors of Jacques-Yves Cousteau using photography, artifacts, ship models, and film footage. Visitors can see world-renowned underwater photography, models of the research vessels *Calypso* and *Alcyone,* and diving equipment from the past and present. Artifacts from Cousteau's expeditions are also on display, including a hovercraft in which guests can sit and have their pictures taken. The attraction is free and open from 10:00 a.m. to 4:00 p.m. daily.

Hampton Carousel Park
602 Settlers Landing Road
(757) 727-0900

Pony up a dollar and take a ride on Hampton's beautifully restored 1920s carousel. Housed in a weather-protected pavilion along the city's downtown waterfront, it is one of only about 170 antique wooden merry-go-rounds still existing in the United States. Hampton's carousel was originally built in 1920 by the Philadelphia Toboggan Company, once the premier manufacturer of both merry-go-rounds and roller coasters in the United States. Its stately chariots and prancing steeds were hand carved and carefully painted by German, Italian, and Russian immigrants. The carousel was delivered to Buckroe Beach Amusement Park in 1921, where it delighted thousands of visitors until the park closed in the 1980s. The city bought the carousel and had it painstakingly restored. You can take a spin on one of its prancing steeds from noon to 5:00 p.m. Monday through Wednesday and noon to 7:00 p.m. Thursday through Sunday in the summer. The carousel is closed mid-December through March.

Hampton History Museum
120 Old Hampton Lane
(757) 727-1610
www.hampton.va.us/history_museum/

The Hampton History Museum, which opened in 2003, showcases the city's heritage as the nation's oldest continuous English-speaking settlement. Nine permanent galleries are organized as follows: Native American, 17th Century, Port Hampton, 18th Century, Antebellum, Civil War, Reconstruction, Late 19th Century, and Modern Hampton. The museum is open Monday through Saturday from 10:00 a.m. to 5:00 p.m. and 1:00 to 5:00 p.m. Sunday. Admission is $5 for adults and $4 for active military, seniors, and children 4 to 12. The Hampton Visitor's Center is at the same location.

Hampton University Museum
Huntington Building, Frissell Avenue
(757) 727-5308
www.hamptonu.edu/museum/

Founded in 1868, the Hampton University Museum is the second-oldest museum in the Old Dominion. It contains more than 9,000 objects and works of art from cultures and nations worldwide. Among the works housed at the museum are nine paintings by the renowned African-American artist Henry O. Tanner.

The museum is housed in a beautiful, expanded facility—a former Beaux Art–style library, which includes a Fine Arts Gallery; the African Gallery, with objects from nearly one hundred ethnic groups and cultures; the Native American Gallery, with its vast collection of American Indian artifacts including everything from basketry to beadwork; the Hampton History Gallery, which traces the university's own historical contributions; plus galleries devoted to changing exhibits by contemporary artists, the Harlem Renaissance, and a studio gallery that showcases the works of Hampton's students. The museum is open Monday through Friday from 8:00 a.m. to 5:00 p.m. and Saturday from noon to 4:00 p.m. It is closed on major holidays and campus holidays. Admission is free, and tours can be arranged. In addition to the museum, the university also is the site

i Hampton Roads is rich in African-American history, culture, and heritage. The region has served as the backdrop for a people's rise from enslavement to equality, and many sites and events bring to life that journey. Call (800) 767-8782 for an African-American Heritage brochure to guide your way.

of six National Historic Landmarks, including the Emancipation Oak, where President Abraham Lincoln's Emancipation Proclamation was first read to the slaves of Hampton in 1863 (see the Close-up in this chapter).

Miss Hampton II Harbor Cruise
764 Settlers Landing Road
(757) 722-9102, (888) 757-2628
www.misshamptoncruises.com

One of the advantages of visiting a waterfront town is the opportunity to scope out the place aboard a boat. From April through October the 65-foot *Miss Hampton II* departs from the visitor center for a three-hour tour, voyaging out of the Hampton River into the Hampton Roads harbor. The cruise sails past Fort Monroe and docks at Fort Wool for a guided walking tour. Construction of this pre–Civil War fort, built on a fifteen-acre man-made island, was supervised by then Lieutenant Robert E. Lee. The fort was active during the battle of the *Monitor* and *Merrimac* and was used to guard the entrance to the harbor during the Civil War and both World Wars.

After completing your tour of Fort Wool, you'll see the 2-mile waterfront of the Norfolk Naval Base before heading home. Times of the cruises vary depending on the season, so call ahead. Fares are $21 for adults, $10 for children 6 through 12, and $19 for seniors and military. Reservations are recommended, and group rates are available.

St. John's Episcopal Church
100 West Queens Way
(757) 722-2567
www.stjohnshampton.org

Away from the waterfront on downtown's Queens Way sits St. John's Church, the oldest continuous English-speaking parish in the United States. The church was built in 1728, but it is the fourth site of worship of Elizabeth City Parish, which was established in 1610. The tree-lined churchyard holds graves dating from 1701, including a memorial to Virginia Laydon, one of the first persons to survive an arduous birth in the New World. Communion silver made in London in 1618 and a stained-glass window depicting the baptism of the Indian princess Pocahontas are among the church's most prized possessions. The church is open weekdays from 9:00 a.m. to 3:30 p.m. and on Saturday from 9:00 a.m. to noon. There are no tours at St. John's on Sunday because of services. Guided tours may be arranged by calling the church office, and admission is free.

Virginia Air and Space Center
600 Settlers Landing Road
(757) 727-0900, (800) 296-0800
www.vasc.org

After working off your sea legs, why not flap your wings a little. After all, the Virginia Air and Space Center is just a short stroll along the waterfront, and as you approach the glass, brick, and steel structure, you'll notice that, appropriately enough, the stunning architecture does resemble a bird in flight. This museum, which is designated the official NASA Langley Visitors Center, is considered the pièce de résistance of Hampton's revitalization.

Inside, the museum features changing exhibits relating to its "from the sea to the stars" theme. Artifacts on display include the *Apollo 12* command module, an astronaut's suit, a meteor from Mars, and a three-billion-year-old moon rock. In the 300-seat giant-screen IMAX theater, which is specially equipped with technology for the hearing impaired, visitors can watch dramatic films.

As you walk through the museum, note the nineteen vintage U.S. aircraft that hang from the 94-foot ceiling, including a Corsair F-106B Delta Dart struck nearly 700 times by lightning while flying through storms as part of NASA lightning research. A gantry that rises three stories takes visitors up for closer inspection. Why not pause and launch a rocket to new heights as part of an interactive, hands-on exhibit that allows you to master the steps of mission control. Or perhaps you might prefer to hop on board a space shuttle, assume the controls, and attempt to land the vehicle. (We guarantee after one attempt, you will understand why astronauts must train extensively to execute a perfect landing!)

A permanent exhibit called "Wild, Wild Weather" looks at everything from hurricanes to tornadoes and how all types of weather affect our daily lives.

"Space Station" is an interactive exhibit that focuses on the process of design and construction required to build the first international space station. The "Ham Radio" exhibit takes visitors from the past into the future in a world-class, fully automated, digital amateur radio satellite station.

The center also offers summer camp programs for children and provides live science demonstrations.

Summer hours of operation are Monday through Wednesday 10:00 a.m. to 5:00 p.m., Thursday through Saturday 10:00 a.m. to 7:00 p.m., and Sunday from noon to 7:00 p.m. Winter hours are Monday through Saturday 10:00 a.m. to 5:00 p.m. and Sunday from noon to 5:00 p.m. Admission prices vary depending on whether you want to take in a film while you're at the museum. For the exhibit only, tickets are $9 for adults, $8 for seniors and military, and $7 for children 3 to 11. Call or go to the Web site for combination ticket prices.

RESTAURANTS

All this sightseeing is bound to stir up a hearty appetite. Lucky for you, there's a bounty of choices in both Hampton and Newport News. Pretty much all the bases are covered—from the ever popular seafood and Italian eateries to those serving Japanese or Vietnamese fare. To better acquaint you with this Peninsula smorgasbord, we've pulled together a sampling of our favorites.

Price Guidelines

The following code indicates the average price of two entrees—without appetizer, dessert, beverages, tax, or gratuity. Rates may be higher in season (generally from mid-March to November and again during the winter holidays).

$.	**Less than $20**
$$	**$21 to $35**
$$$	**$36 to $50**
$$$$	**More than $50**

Newport News

Al Fresco $$$
11710 Jefferson Avenue, Oyster Point
(757) 873-0644
Dining at this Italian restaurant is, indeed, a pleasant change of pace. The indoor "garden" atmosphere is the perfect setting for a variety of chicken, veal, shrimp, and pasta entrees. The restaurant is open for lunch and dinner Monday through Friday and dinner only on Saturday. It is closed Sunday.

Boulevard Restaurant and Tavern $$
11135 Warwick Boulevard
(757) 599-6003
This eatery offers plenty of atmosphere—twinkling lights, a bubbling fountain, and plenty of privacy—and a menu featuring steak, pork, and seafood dishes. Keep in mind that items on the menu are seasonal—the rack of lamb with its bourbon sauce you enjoyed in blustery January might not be available when you return in the heat of July. Our advice: If you see something that piques your appetite, enjoy it while you can! Lunch and dinner are served seven days a week.

Crab Shack on the James $$
7601 River Road,
Foot of James River Fishing Pier
(757) 245-2722
When we have guests in town who demand seafood, this is where we take them. Not only is the food good—we especially like the blue crabs, lightly fried shrimp, and crab cakes—but the view of the James River is incomparable. When you arrive and give your name to the hostess, be sure to ask to dine on the deck. It's all very casual, so there's no need to dress up.

Danny's Deli Restaurant $
10838 Warwick Boulevard
(757) 595-0252
If you're a sandwich lover, you're in luck. This busy lunch spot offers just about any combination your heart desires, and all are served up with an endless supply of crunchy sliced dill pickles. Danny's is open for lunch Monday through Saturday and dinner Monday through Friday. It is closed on Sunday.

Das Waldcafe $$
12529 Warwick Boulevard
(757) 930-1781
This longtime Peninsula favorite prepares authentic German cuisine (from the Rhineland region) including Wiener schnitzel, bratwurst, knockwurst, and noodle dumplings. A variety of more obscure dishes rounds out the menu. Specialty sausages are from New York, and the beers are German imports. Das Waldcafe serves lunch and dinner Tuesday through Sunday.

El Mariachi $$
660 J. Clyde Morris Boulevard
(757) 596-4933
We were in Mexican heaven when we discovered this authentic eatery. Don't fill up on the chunky salsa and chips, as here you can custom order all the traditional Mexican dishes you have come to love in just about any combination, with a sparkling margarita on the side. But be aware: Since reservations aren't accepted, on weekends you'll probably have to wait. Don't worry; service is swift, and lines move fast at both lunch and dinner.

Kyung Sung Korean Restaurant $$
13748 Warwick Boulevard
(757) 877-2797
One of only a handful of Korean restaurants on the Peninsula, the Kyung Sung prepares inexpensive and spicy food and serves it in an unadorned setting. The house specialty is beef boolgogi, a Korean-style barbecue, but the menu also includes chop suey, several teriyaki variations, shrimp tempura, some stir-fried dishes, soups, and noodle dishes. If you like food with a kick, try a side order of kim chee, a spicy Korean cabbage. Both lunch and dinner are available daily.

Luigi's Italian Restaurant $$
15515 Warwick Boulevard
(757) 887-0005
The operative word here is Italian. The marinara sauce is to die for (try it over mussels as an appetizer), and the pasta dishes are classic. We enjoy the veal and spaghetti with a red shrimp sauce, but our friends rave about the manicotti, ravioli, and lasagna. Portions are huge, and dinners are served with warm and delicious garlic knots. Luigi's is closed on Monday.

Mama Lina's Ristorante $$
14346 Warwick Boulevard
(757) 872-6547
If you like home-style Italian cooking, a visit to the newly expanded Mama Lina's is in order. You'll find everything from foccacia and white pizza to a wide variety of pasta dishes here. Chicken, seafood, and veal dishes round out the menu. And, for those of us who like to be well taken care of as we dine, the wait staff here is particularly courteous. Mama Lina's is open for lunch and dinner Tuesday through Saturday and dinner only on Sunday.

Mike's Place $
458 Warwick Village Shopping Center
(757) 599-5500
Locals—especially the guys—like to gather in this neighborhood tavern, which offers crab cakes, prime rib, and daily specials in sports-pub-like environs. Popular items include the Big O Burger and crab cakes. An Irish theme prevails and, needless to say, the place is packed on St. Paddy's Day. Four wide-screen televisions ensure you won't miss weekend football games. The restaurant is open for lunch and dinner.

Nara of Japan $$
10608 Warwick Boulevard
(757) 595-7399

If you like to be entertained while you dine, grab a few friends and head over to the Nara for dinner. At this lively Japanese restaurant, your waiter prepares your food right at your table. Nara specializes in hibachi steak, chicken, and seafood seasoned with lemon juice, soy sauce, pepper, and sesame seeds. Soup, salad, and appetizer are included with your meal. This is a great place to enjoy a birthday celebration. Nara does not serve lunch.

99 Main Street Restaurant $$$
99 Main Street
(757) 599-9885

Located in the charming Hilton Village neighborhood, this sophisticated addition to the local culinary scene offers a diverse menu featuring both the traditional and exotic. The often French-inspired cuisine includes everything from a simple and flavorful roasted chicken or your choice of grilled fish to Moroccan-style lamb shanks and filet mignon with oysters and crab. Portions are large, so come hungry and save room for homemade dessert. Bon appetit! Closed Sunday and Monday.

Port Arthur $$
11137 Warwick Boulevard
(757) 599-6474

Housed in an impressive brick structure with elegant Oriental touches, Port Arthur is one of the Peninsula's most enduring Chinese restaurants. The eatery first opened in downtown Newport News in 1934, before moving to its current site in 1974. Mandarin and Szechuan specialties are featured along with a complete menu of beef, poultry, seafood, and pork preparations. Sodium-free dishes are available upon request. Port Arthur serves lunch and dinner daily.

Sushi Yama Japanese Restaurant $
11745-2 Jefferson Avenue
(757) 596-1150

If you love sushi, you can order from the traditional (tuna, salmon, and shrimp) to the exotic (squid and eel) here. The ingredients are always fresh and the careful attention paid to craftsmanship shows. Other traditional Japanese dishes also are available. Lunch is offered Monday through Friday and dinner Monday through Saturday.

Hampton

Golden Palace $$
2234 Cunningham Drive
(757) 825-1900

The specialty of this 300-seat restaurant with its colorful, inviting decor is a buffet including sushi, available for both afternoon and evening patrons. The offerings on the a la carte menu are fresh and appealing.

Good Fortune $$
225 D-1 Fox Hill Road
(757) 851-6888

At Willow Oaks Shopping Center, Good Fortune has a varied menu of traditional Chinese dishes. You may think once you've tasted one wonton soup, you've tasted them all, but Good Fortune's is especially delicious. A lunch buffet is a filling midday repast. A dinner buffet is offered on Friday and Saturday.

Goodfella's $$
13 East Queens Way
(757) 723-4979

In its easily accessible downtown digs, Goodfella's serves up reasonably priced pasta, seafood, beef, and pizza. Live music on weekend nights pulls in the crowds. Outdoor patio dining is available in warm-weather months. Enjoy Goodfella's family atmosphere during lunch or dinner.

The Grate Steak $$
1934 Coliseum Drive
(757) 827-1886
http://thegratesteak.com/

Just minutes from Hampton Coliseum, this extremely popular steak house adds a new twist to dining. Beef-eaters have the opportunity to select the steak of their choice and prepare it themselves on a huge grill in the center of the restaurant. Steaks come in three cuts: petite, restaurant, and owner's. If you select the owner's cut, you get to peruse the refrigerated display case and come away with the steak of your choice. All steaks are served with salad and potato bar as well as all the garlic bread you can eat. The menu also offers prime rib (it's delicious), poultry, and seafood dishes. The Grate Steak serves dinner daily and lunch and dinner on Sunday.

Harpoon Larry's Oyster Bar $$
2000 North Armistead Avenue
(757) 827-0600

This is the kind of restaurant you'd expect to find at the beach. Its long wooden tables, massive bar, and casual atmosphere all make it a favorite after-work spot for locals. The menu includes all types of "killer" seafood prepared just about any way you can imagine. If you don't like crowds, come for lunch when the lines are shorter, but the food is just as good!

Mongolian Bar-B-Q Restaurant $$
1118 West Mercury Boulevard, Riverdale Plaza
(757) 838-3638

If you like an incredible amount of food and enjoy watching while it's cooked (it's actually part of the fun), check out this popular Hampton eatery. This is where you heap your plate with seasonal vegetables, meats ranging from beef to lamb, and a variety of sauces that include lemon, garlic, oyster, hot oil, and barbecue. There's also an accompanying salad and hot foods bar, where you can fill up on any number of Chinese entrees being offered that night. Soup, sesame bread, steamed rice, and light desserts are also part of the package. The food is excellent, and the price is more than reasonable.

Oasis Restaurant $
3506 Kecoughtan Road
(757) 723-5736

For a reasonably priced home-style meal any time of day, this long-established eatery is

the place. Popular with locals, there's everything from grits and eggs to creamed chipped beef for breakfast, a variety of seafood dishes and specialty sandwiches for lunch, and daily lunch and dinner specials. We particularly like the roasted chicken and the chicken and dumplings. Oasis closes at 8:00 p.m. Monday through Friday and 2:00 p.m. on Saturday and Sunday.

Oyster Alley $
700 Settlers Landing Road
(757) 727-9700

This casual outdoor restaurant is in downtown's Radisson Hotel and overlooks a marina. Sandwiches, salads, and seafood appetizers are featured. Oyster Alley is open late April through October, daily from 7:00 to about 10:00 p.m., depending upon the weather.

Pho 50 $
1109-C North King Street
(757) 728-9788

A mile or so north of downtown, this small Vietnamese restaurant is the place to come for lunch. Try Vietnamese soups chock-full of beef, chicken, noodles, and herbs. It's open every day except Wednesday.

Tommy's Restaurant $
3406 West Mercury Boulevard
(757) 825-1644

Although located a few miles from downtown Hampton, it is worth the drive if you're looking for a delicious, filling, and inexpensive breakfast or lunch. Insiders know this as the place for breakfast, so they don't mind lining up at the door and waiting their turn for a table. For breakfast try the combination or any of the omelets. For lunch, the chicken and dumplings and pepper steak are exceptional. Tommy's does not serve dinner.

Win Wok Buffet $
2082 Nickerson Boulevard
(757) 851-8089

If you're touring downtown Hampton, a detour to the eastern side of the city brings

i America's first seven astronauts trained at NASA Langley Air Force Base in Hampton.

you to this very popular Chinese restaurant. It offers a lunch and dinner buffet that has everything from mussels, steamed shrimp, and crab legs to steamed dumplings, garlic string beans, and delicate spring rolls. A sushi bar, Mongolian barbecue, and a fresh fruit and salad bar are all part of the offerings.

ACCOMMODATIONS

If you've decided there's too much to see and do in one day in Hampton and Newport News, spend the night and devote another twenty-four hours to your local explorations. There are plenty of options should you decide to rest your weary head on a Lower Peninsula pillow. The facilities we've listed below are well run and offer the modern conveniences you've come to expect when you're spending a night on the road. We have included 800 numbers when available, but be aware that many are for central reservation offices and will not connect you directly to the hotel.

Price Guidelines

We offer the following price code as a general guide. The figures indicate an average charge for double occupancy during peak season.

$. . . . . Less than $50
$$ . . . . $51 to $75
$$$ . . . . $76 to $125
$$$$ . . . . $126 to $175
$$$$$ . . . . More than $175

Newport News

The Boxwood Inn $$$$
10 Elmhurst, Lee Hall Village
(just off US 60 near Old Virginia Route 238)
(757) 888-8854
www.boxwood-inn.com
This bona fide bed-and-breakfast inn is run by Barbara and Bob Lucas. Built in 1896, the inn

originally was the home of Simon Curtis, once considered the "boss man" of Warwick County. It also has served as the Warwick County Hall of Records, a general store, a post office, and a hotel for soldiers during World Wars I and II. Items found in the home's spacious attic have been used to decorate the house and its three rooms and one suite, each of which has a private bath. In addition to breakfast, the Boxwood Inn also has its own tearoom. High tea is offered from 2:00 to 4:00 p.m. by reservation only. Lunch is served 11:00 a.m. to 2:00 p.m. Tuesday through Friday and dinner is served on Friday at 7:00 p.m. by reservation only. Groups are welcome with advance reservation. The inn cannot accommodate children, and smoking is not permitted.

Throughout the year Boxwood hosts special "Dinnertainments," where costumed entertainers perform during a four-course meal. Past events have included a Murder Mystery Evening, Pirates of the Peninsula, RMS *Titanic*, and the Dickens Christmas Dinner. Call ahead to find out what's happening during your visit to the area.

Comfort Inn $$$
12330 Jefferson Avenue
(757) 249-0200, (800) 368-2477
Adjacent to Patrick Henry Mall in Denbigh, Comfort Inn has 124 rooms, each equipped with coffeemaker, iron, and ironing board. There's also an outdoor pool, and guests have free access to a local fitness club. A continental breakfast is included in the price of a night's stay, and room service is provided by the Outback Steakhouse. A free shuttle service is offered to the Newport News/Williamsburg International Airport.

Hampton Inn & Suites $$$$
12251 Jefferson Avenue
(757) 249-0001, (800) HAMPTON
Across from the Patrick Henry Mall, this hotel, built in 1995, marked the Hampton Inn chain's first foray into the suite business. The Newport News property has 90 guest rooms, 30

suites, a small weight room, and an outdoor pool. Guests also enjoy a free continental breakfast, HBO, and free access to a local health club. Room service is provided by the Outback Steakhouse.

Holiday Inn Newport News $$$
943 J. Clyde Morris Blvd.
(757) 596-6417
This 122-room hotel gets rave reviews for its accommodating service and first-rate amenities. About a half-mile from downtown, it's adjacent to the city center complex. It has an indoor pool, fitness center, business center, and high-speed Internet available to all guests.

Kiln Creek Golf and Country Club $$$$
1003 Brick Kiln Boulevard
(757) 874-2600
www.kilncreekgolf.com
This attractive hotel is actually part of a golf and country club. Its sixteen rooms overlook a golf course. A restaurant is on-site, and a swimming pool and fitness center, complete with a Jacuzzi, steam and sauna rooms, and locker facilities, are available. The hotel also offers an indoor tennis "bubble" and a refrigerator, a coffeemaker, and a small safe in each room, plus patios or balconies overlooking the putting green. If you're an avid duffer, ask for details on the special golf packages Kiln Creek offers.

Marriott at City Center $$$$
740 Town Center Drive
(757) 873-9298
www.marriott.com
The Newport News Marriott is a full-service hotel and conference center offering top-of-the-line service and amenities for both leisure and business travelers. It's located in city center, close to retail stores, restaurants, and offices.

Mulberry Inn $$$
16890 Warwick Boulevard
(757) 887-3000
www.mulberryinnva.com

This hotel's 102 guest rooms include some efficiencies and connecting rooms. All rooms have refrigerators. Amenities include a fitness center, guest laundry, a pool, terrace, and a free continental breakfast.

Omni Newport News Hotel $$$$
1000 Omni Boulevard
(757) 873-6664, (800) 843-6664
This AAA Three Diamond Oyster Point hotel has 183 rooms, including four suites. Mitty's, an Italian restaurant, is on the premises. Other amenities include a nightclub, piano bar, indoor pool, and health club with whirlpool and sauna.

Point Plaza $$$–$$$$$
960 J. Clyde Morris Boulevard
(757) 599-4460
The 219 guest rooms feature work areas, clock radios, and individual temperature controls. A restaurant is on the premises. The hotel also has an indoor fitness center and heated pool.

Hampton

Clarion Hotel $$$
1809 West Mercury Boulevard
(757) 838-5011, (800) 562-8090
Located a stone's throw from the city's main business district, this Clarion Hotel has 189 guest rooms (including thirty-four suites), an indoor swimming pool, and a restaurant and lounge. Early check-in and checkout and free room upgrades are available. Pets are permitted for an extra $25 nonrefundable charge.

Comfort Inn $$$–$$$$
1916 Coliseum Drive
(757) 827-5052, (800) 835-7629
One of a bevy of Coliseum-area hotels and motor inns, the five-story, sixty-six-room Comfort Inn is convenient to the Coliseum Central commercial district. The inn has four whirlpool rooms, which are available for an extra charge. Amenities include a pool, free breakfast, extended cable TV, and free local telephone. A restaurant is within walking distance.

Country Inn & Suites by Carlson $$$
1551 Hardy Cash Drive
(757) 224-9994

This newcomer to the Hampton scene caters to families and offers a complimentary hot breakfast each morning, indoor pool and fitness center, a game room, and 52-inch plasma television (with cable, of course!) in each room.

Courtyard by Marriott $$$–$$$$
1917 Coliseum Drive
(757) 838-3300, (800) 321-2211

A moderately priced motor inn next door to the Hampton Coliseum, Courtyard by Marriott has 146 rooms, including twelve suites, a pool, a whirlpool, a mini-gym, and a restaurant and lounge.

Embassy Suites Hampton Road
Convention Center $$$$
1700 Coliseum Drive
(757) 827-8200
www.embassysuiteshampton.com

The Embassy Suites Hampton features spacious two-room suites with a complimentary cooked-to-order breakfast every morning and a nightly Manager's Reception with cocktails and hors d'oeuvres. Enjoy a relaxing day in the indoor heated pool, whirlpool, sundeck, or fitness center, or rejuvenate at the Spa Botanica day spa. Lunch or dinner is available in the Cyprus Grille. The hotel is connected to the Hampton Roads Convention Center.

Hampton Inn $$
1813 West Mercury Boulevard
(757) 838-8484, (800) HAMPTON

Near an I-64 exit, the Hampton Inn has 131 rooms and pool privileges at the nearby Holiday Inn. Teens stay free with their parents, and a complimentary continental breakfast is served each morning. Rooms are outfitted with irons, ironing boards, and hair dryers. Pets weighing less than twenty-five pounds are permitted for no additional charge.

Holiday Inn Hampton $$$
1815 West Mercury Boulevard
(757) 838-0200, (800) 842-9370
www.ichotelsgroup.com

One block from the Hampton Coliseum and within walking distance of a number of shopping centers, this Holiday Inn has 320 guest rooms (each equipped with coffeemaker, iron, and ironing board), indoor and outdoor pools, a fitness center, and a gift shop. An open atrium area features a restaurant and lounge. Pets twenty-five pounds and under are permitted for an extra fee of $25.

La Quinta Inn $$
2138 West Mercury Boulevard
(757) 827-8680, (800) 221-4731

This budget-friendly, 129-room facility offers a pool, in-room coffeemakers and video game rentals, free breakfast, and free local phone calls. Pets are permitted, and there is a restaurant nearby.

Radisson Hotel Hampton $$$$
700 Settlers Landing Road
(757) 727-9700, (800) 333-3333

The Radisson is on the waterfront overlooking the Hampton River. All 172 guest rooms have floor-to-ceiling windows—a big plus for water views. Amenities include a seafood restaurant and raw bar, outdoor rooftop pool and Jacuzzi, a lounge, health club, and complimentary covered parking.

SHOPPING

A little bit of this, a little bit of that . . . that just about sums up the shopping experience on the Peninsula. To make it a little easier to find your way around, we've divided our entries geographically: The two main shopping areas in Newport News are Hilton Village, a charming enclave to the south, and Denbigh, a rapidly developing neighborhood to the north.

In Hampton there's Old Hampton (or downtown), the old-fashioned community of Phoebus, and the bustling Coliseum Central corridor along recently widened Mercury Boulevard.

Newport News

Hilton Village

This charming residential area in lower Newport News features a number of quaint shops stretching from Warwick Boulevard to the James River. The village was transformed with an updated streetscape that included brick-patterned sidewalks and lush landscaping. Some of the shops you will find nestled amid the splendor are listed below.

Beecroft & Bull Ltd.
10325 Warwick Boulevard
(757) 596-0951
This long-established store is the last word in fine men's clothing and accessories. Beecroft & Bull also has a shop in Williamsburg.

Hilton Village Goldsmith
10345 Warwick Boulevard
(757) 599-6300
www.hvgjewelry.com
With a registered jeweler and a master craftsman on staff, this jeweler is the place to go for that one-of-a-kind, custom-designed ring, brooch, pendant, or bracelet. The knowledgeable staff even provides you with a "diamond lesson" before you leave the store with your precious purchase.

Plantiques—Hilton Village
10377 Warwick Boulevard
(757) 595-1545
This gift shop sells a little bit of everything—antiques, small collectibles, candles, pewter, stained glass, sailing ship models, silk flowers and wreaths, Christmas items, skin-care products...well, you get the idea.

Silverman Furs
10301 Warwick Boulevard
(757) 595-5514
This Hilton institution has been in business since 1938, specializing in furs, leathers, and outerwear. Silverman also does repairs, cleaning on-site, and storage.

Village Stitchery
97 Main Street
(757) 599-0101
http://villagestitchery.tripod.com/
Just around the corner from most of our Warwick Boulevard establishments, the Village Stitchery sells everything you need for cross-stitch and other creative needlework. Custom framing is available.

Denbigh

As we mentioned in the introduction to Newport News, the Denbigh area—particularly along Jefferson Avenue—has been growing like dandelions in the spring sunshine. It has become somewhat of a retail mecca in this long, slender city, sprouting entire new shopping centers seemingly overnight. It is also home to Patrick Henry Mall, easily accessible off I–64. We'll start there to give you our rundown.

Patrick Henry Mall
12300 Jefferson Avenue
(exit 255A off I–64)
(757) 249-4305
www.shoppatrickhenrymall.com
Anchored by Dillard's and Macy's, Patrick Henry also is home to American Eagle Outfitters, Casual Corner, The Sports Fan, Spencer Gifts, Bath & Body Works, Victoria's Secret, Radio Shack, and dozens of other shops. If you work up an appetite while shopping, check out one of the eateries in the food court or dine at A&W or Ruby Tuesdays. The mall also has a movie theater. It's twenty minutes from Colonial Williamsburg.

Yoder Farms Shopping Center
Jefferson Avenue and Oyster Point Road
(no phone)
Yoder Farms gets its name from—what else—a long-lived dairy farm that stood on the property. Just a short distance down Jefferson Avenue from Patrick Henry Mall, this 400,000-square-foot strip houses Barnes & Noble, Circuit City, PetSmart, Target, Bed Bath and Beyond, and OfficeMax stores.

Hampton

Old Hampton

If you're looking for ambience while you browse, stroll along the quaint brick, tree-lined streets in Old Hampton. Here you will find dozens of specialty shops selling everything from British imports to elaborate doll collections. Our favorites are listed below. For more information on downtown shopping, check out the Web site www.downtownhampton.com.

Benton-Knight Ltd.
28 South King Street
(757) 723-0521
Fine high-quality men's clothing—ranging from casual to formal—is sold at this downtown Hampton landmark. Service is superb.

Blue Skies Gallery
26 King Street
(757) 727-0028
http://blueskiesart.com/
This popular gallery offers 5,000 square feet of creative work by more than one hundred established artisans. Its selection includes sculpture, paintings, clothing, and crafts in silver, acrylic, wood, fiber, fabric, paper, and glass. You can even browse among some selections of antiquarian books and furniture.

The Brass Shop
197 West Queen Street
(757) 723-4523
www.brassshop.com
Don't miss this excellent shop where thousands of brass items are deeply discounted. This is a great place to stop for brass lamps, candlesticks, brass frames, and trivets. The Brass Shop is closed Sunday and Monday.

Camera City Inc.
101 South Armistead Avenue
(757) 722-2511
www.cameracity.com
Just half a block from the back side of the Brass Shop is this gem of a store, which stocks hard-to-find camera equipment for novice and expert photographers alike.

i The four-day Hampton Jazz Festival in June has emerged as one of the nation's premier jazz and pop extravaganzas. Performers have included many of the greats: Anita Baker, Ray Charles, Al Jarreau, George Benson, and the Duke Ellington Orchestra. Call (757) 838-4203 for information after April 1.

La Bodega Hampton
22 Wine Street
(757) 722-8466
This delightful addition to the downtown Hampton scene sells glassware, linens, gourmet foods, gift items, a variety of freshly made sandwiches and salads, many unusual beers, and shelves and shelves of wine. The staff is knowledgeable and helpful. Grab a quick lunch and browse to your heart's content.

Shabby Chic
47 East Queens Way
(757) 727-0100
If it's old, you'll find it here. This fun and eclectic shop stocks everything from vintage furniture and iron fencing gates to decorative arts and dried flowers.

The Virginia Store
555 Settlers Landing Road, Suite L
(757) 727-0600, (800) 633-2203
If you want something that screams Virginia to give the folks back home, this is the place to stop. True to its name, the Virginia Store carries Old Dominion gift baskets, wines, hams, peanuts, pottery, jewelry, and books.

Phoebus

While you're in the neighborhood, you might want to make a quick detour down Settlers Landing Road to Phoebus, a quaint waterfront community that was incorporated into the City of Hampton in 1952. Visiting Phoebus is like a trip back in time, when malls were unheard of and Main Street was where everything happened. The two major streets in Phoebus—Mallory and Mellen—intersect one another and are home to a number of inter-esting shops and restaurants. Ongoing streetscape work is transforming both streets with rebuilt sidewalks, new trees, and updated utilities. The former New American Theatre, a movie house and restaurant, has been refurbished by the Charles H. Taylor Arts Center Foundation and Hampton Arts Commission and transformed into the city's only performing arts hall. For general information or brochures about Phoebus, contact the Phoebus Improvement League at (757) 727-0808. Some of the more unusual stores in Phoebus are listed below.

Electric Glass Co.
1 East Mellen Street
(757) 722-6200
www.electricglass.com
This attractive and unique shop carries an astonishing array of stained-glass lamps and crystal chandeliers. (We guarantee, however, that after one glance in the window, parents of small children will silently recite that old quip, "Beautiful to look at, nice to hold, but if you break it, consider it..." well, you get the idea.)

Free City Traders
22 East Mellen Street
(757) 722-3899
This two-story antiques mall displays the merchandise of thirty-six antiques dealers. We made one of our favorite finds here—an antique oak pedestal mirror that once graced the inside of a department store.

Mugler's of Phoebus
123 East Mellen Street
(757) 723-6431
http://muglers.com/
Established in 1898, this shop carries men's clothing, uniforms, and accessories in more than 150 sizes.

Phoebus Auction Gallery
16 East Mellen Street
(757) 722-9210
www.phoebusauction.com

While not actually a shop, per se, this popular gallery pulls in big crowds every two weeks or so for its Sunday auction of fine art, antique furniture, rugs, and advertised items and collectibles. Special holiday auctions are held on New Year's Day, Memorial Day, Labor Day, and Thanksgiving. The gallery often is open for browsing before each auction. Call ahead or check the Web site to see what's on the agenda when you plan to be in town.

Snow's Bicycle Shop
133-135 East Mellen Street
(757) 723-1011
www.rfsnowbike.com
A veritable institution in Phoebus, you can buy new or gently used bikes here or bring yours in for a quick repair.

Coliseum Central

For all intents and purposes, this is the main business district in Hampton. Located on either side of recently widened Mercury Boulevard, the area is named after the Hampton Coliseum, just off Mercury, a highly visible landmark from I–64, as well as the Coliseum Mall, on the other side of the boulevard. In 1997 an ambitious improvement plan was released for Coliseum Central, calling for more green and open spaces; the transformation of a part of the boulevard into "Mercury Mile," with bus shelters, better lighting, and water icons at key areas celebrating Hampton's connection to its natural environment; and a new visitor center and community building near the intersection of Mercury Boulevard and Coliseum Drive, considered the primary gateway to this important business district. In 1999, as part of this plan, a three-quarter-mile stretch of median in this area was widened by about 20 feet and dozens of trees were planted. Other changes are in the works but won't occur overnight. The Coliseum Central master plan is a twenty-year blueprint for redevelopment that will be done in more manageable phases throughout the next two decades.

What you'll see right now is a busy thoroughfare crowded with stores, chain restaurants, movie theaters, and some hotels. To make it easier for you to locate a store, we've divided the entries by mall or shopping center. Since most of these stores will be familiar to you, we've listed rather than described them and provided central phone numbers, when available. The area also harbors a freestanding Super Wal-Mart, Pier 1 Imports, Walgreens drug store, and a Target department store.

Coliseum Crossing
2100 through 2159 Coliseum Drive
(odd numbers only)
(no phone)

The Crossing is a popular, fast-growing strip center that not only offers stores galore but also has plenty of restaurants and services, including banks, a dry cleaner, and a one-hour photo outlet. The main stores here include Bottom Dollar Grocery, Marshalls (discount clothing), A&N Stores, Dollar Tree, Red Wing Shoes, and Boater's World, a discount marine center that stocks everything from deck shoes and snorkels to wet suits and water skis.

Peninsula Town Center
1800 West Mercury Boulevard
(757) 838-1505
www.coliseummall.com

This mall, formerly known as Coliseum Center, is undergoing a major renovation, including a name change. It's anchored by a Macy's, JCPenney, Barnes & Noble, Steve & Barry's sporting goods, and a Burlington Coat Factory department store and also offers more than fifty smaller stores and restaurants.

Coliseum Square
2040 Coliseum Drive
(no phone)

Stores in this shopping center, located across Coliseum Drive from the mall, include Boston Market, Ames Tuxedos, and A & N, which carries inexpensive casual clothing, workout wear, and shoes.

ℹ️ If you're going to an event at the Hampton Coliseum and don't want to pay to park, leave your car at the Coliseum Mall—it's only about 3 blocks away.

Riverdale Plaza
1044 through 1118 West Mercury Boulevard (even numbers only)
(757) 838-5605

Big and Tall Men's Shop, Goodman & Sons Jewelers, Office Depot, Advance Auto, a Virginia ABC store, and a post office outlet are among the major stores in this strip center. Restaurants in and around the plaza include Pizza Hut, Red Lobster, Andreas Pizza, and Mongolian Bar-B-Q.

RECREATION

Beaches

Newport News

Huntington Park Beach
5500 West Mercury Boulevard
(foot of James River Bridge)
(757) 886-7912

Newport News also has its own free public beach, located in the same park that is home to Fort Fun and the James River Fishing Pier (see Fishing later in this chapter). The sandy strip fronts the James River, of course, and is open from sunrise to sunset. Lifeguards are on duty from 11:00 a.m. to 7:00 p.m. daily during the summer, but at other times you're allowed to swim at your own risk. There's a nice little snack bar with a deck and picnic tables, and restrooms are available. Two swing sets and a few volleyball nets offer a couple of other diversions.

Hampton

Buckroe Beach
End of Pembroke Avenue at First Street
(757) 850-5134, (757) 727-8311

If you're interested in a day at the beach, there's no reason to trek all the way to the Virginia Beach resort strip. Hampton's own Buckroe Beach is an ideal spot for a little family

R&R. Bordering the Chesapeake Bay, Buckroe's gentle surf and sandy shore are perfect for family frolicking and castle building. A paved boardwalk attracts strollers and cyclists, while an outdoor pavilion is the setting for plenty of warm-weather entertainment. A bustling resort back in the 1930s, Buckroe Beach's fortunes declined when the 1957 opening of the Hampton Roads Bridge-Tunnel provided easier access to ocean attractions. In the late 1980s the city invested millions to build Buckroe Park, complete with a stage, picnic shelters, and public restrooms. During the summer the beach pavilion frequently is the scene of free concerts on Sunday, while family movies are shown on a big outdoor screen on Tuesday evenings. Films start at sundown but there is prefilm entertainment at 7:00 p.m. Lifeguards are on duty at the beach from 10:00 a.m. to 6:00 p.m. from Memorial Day to Labor Day.

To get to the beach, take the last Hampton exit from I-64 before the bridge-tunnel (exit 268). Turn left on Mallory Street. Follow it to its end, then turn right on Pembroke Avenue. The beach will be right in front of you. There's a small parking lot next to the beach, but on hot summer days, it typically is full. Paid parking is available in makeshift lots on fields across the street.

Fishing

If you want to get an angle on some outdoor fun, toss a line off one of the Peninsula's many fishing piers. Depending on the time of year, you'll probably pull out spot, croaker, flounder, bluefish, and an occasional trout. No license is needed for fishing at any of these piers (it's included in the fee), and equipment rentals are available at most of them. One of the best places for your hook, line, and sinker is listed here.

Newport News

James River Fishing Pier
Huntington Park,
5500 West Mercury Boulevard
(757) 247-0364

This popular fishing pier is located at the foot of the James River Bridge. To fish the waters beneath will cost adults $8 and seniors and children 7 through 12, $6. Nearly a mile long, this is a great place to fish for croaker and spot. During the right season, you might even land striped bass, flounder, gray trout, or red drum. There also is a bait shop on hand that will provide you with the necessities: snacks, bait, and some tackle. If all that casting and reeling works up an appetite—or if the fish aren't biting and you have a hankering for some fresh seafood—The Crab Shack restaurant, (757) 245-2722, is located at the entrance to the pier. Here you can get everything from soft-shell crabs to shrimp at reasonable prices.

Golf

While the fishermen troll the waters in pursuit of the big one, golfers might want to shoulder their clubs and tee off at one of the area's public courses.

Newport News

Newport News Golf Club at Deer Run
901 Clubhouse Way, Newport News Park
(exit 250B off I-64)
(757) 886-7925
www.nngolfclub.com
Test your skills at the Deer Run Golf Course, a challenging eighteen-hole course located in the 8,000-acre Newport News Park. The clubhouse has a snack bar and restaurant, driving range, putting greens, and pro shop. The city's Department of Parks and Recreation manages the course. Whether you tackle Ed Ault's 7,206-yard wooded course or opt for the middle-length 6,645-yard links (this one is really suited to all levels of play), the greens fees are the same. Eighteen holes and a cart run about $32, depending on the course and the day of the week. For more information on this club and duffers' havens closer to Williamsburg, turn to the Golf chapter.

Hampton

The Hamptons
320 Butler Farm Road
(757) 766-9148
www.hampton.va.us/thehamptons/
This meticulously maintained twenty-seven-hole championship course (three different nine-hole courses) is set in a combination of woods, wildflowers, waterfalls, and lakes. There's a large practice putting green and driving range, and the clubhouse offers a full-service restaurant, snack bar, and pro shop. Greens fees are about $30 for eighteen holes on weekdays and $32 for eighteen holes on weekends, including the cart. Senior rates are nearly half off. At those prices, you could play every day. Look out, Tiger Woods!

The Woodlands
9 Woodland Road
(757) 727-1195
Located 25 minutes south of Williamsburg, this 5,400-yard regulation par 69 course has bentgrass greens, Bermuda fairways and roughs, and fifty-two sand bunkers to test your skills. The clubhouse features a pro shop with a full line of golfing apparel, a full-service restaurant, and a practice putting green. Seven tennis courts also are available. Greens fees for eighteen holes during the week are $17. Weekends, as is par for the course, will cost a few extra dollars and run $19, and carts are another $11. There are good discounts for seniors.

Parks

Newport News

Newport News Park
13560 Jefferson Avenue
(exit 250B off I–64)
(757) 886-7912, (800) 203-8322
www.nnparks.com
This beautiful oasis in the northern tier of the city—the second-largest municipal park in the United States—has more than 8,000 acres of woodlands and two freshwater lakes. While entrance to the park is free, 188 individual campsites are available for rent. A primitive area also is available for Boy Scout troops only. Each of the standard campsites includes a picnic table and charcoal grill, twenty-four-hour registration, and security. Heated restrooms with hot showers, a laundry room, pay phones, sewage dumping station, playground equipment, ice, general store, and water and electrical hookups also are available. The 188 campsites are open year-round. A five-star archery range located near the campsites is open to the public. To use this facility you must furnish your own bows and arrows and successfully complete a free archery safety class.

The park also offers 20 miles of hiking trails, a 5.3-mile mountain bike trail, and a variety of trails that serve as bridle paths. Bicycles and helmets may be rented on a daily basis. While exploring the park, keep a sharp eye out for the many species of birds, flowers, trees, plants, and animals that inhabit the park. You may be rewarded by the sight of a bluebird that has nested in one of the houses erected by the Hampton Roads Bird Club.

For the angler in the family, there are two reservoirs stocked with bass, pickerel, pike, bluegill, perch, and crappie. Boats are available for rent for an entire day of fishing fun (bring sunscreen). Make sure you have a valid fishing license before you cast your line for the first time.

One of the highlights in the park is the eighteen-hole disk golf course, one of the first of its kind in Virginia. The championship range will have you sailing your disk 5,450 yards, while the regulation, or white, course is 4,165 yards.

For history buffs, Dam No. 1, Confederate gun positions, and remaining Union trenches are evidence of the area's involvement in the 1862 Peninsula campaign. The park's visitor center interprets the action that took place there and offers a free park map and literature on other sites nearby. Across from the Dam No. 1 Bridge is the park Discovery Center, which displays flora and fauna exhibits as well as Civil War artifacts.

The park also hosts the annual Fall Festival in October and is the site of Celebration in Lights during the holiday season. For more information on these and other nearby festivals, turn to the Annual Events chapter.

Hampton

Grandview Nature Preserve
Intersection of Beach Road and
State Park Drive
(757) 850-5134
Another place sure to please the outdoor enthusiast is the Grandview Nature Preserve in northeast Hampton, with its 578 acres of marshland and beach area. Grandview is home to endangered species of birds and wildlife. It's the perfect place to stroll a 2-mile stretch of bayfront beach to observe all of nature's glory. Off the beaten path a bit, you get to Grandview by taking Mercury to Fox Hill. Travel Fox Hill for a few miles—past the Willow Oaks development—and turn left onto Beach Road. You'll find Grandview just where you would expect—at the end of Beach. No admission fee is charged.

Sandy Bottom Nature Park
1255 Big Bethel Road
(757) 825-4657
Hampton's public park has 456 acres of woodland, two lakes, play and picnic areas, walking and interpretive trails, a wildlife area, nature center, paddleboats, and concessions. Built almost entirely by volunteers, this park has room for overnight guests, too. There also are two primitive group sites (popular with Boy Scout troops) and four tent cabins. The park also offers environmental education programs and special programming in astronomy, wildlife observation, and environmental field testing. To get to the park, take exit 261A off I–64 and follow Hampton Roads Center Parkway to Big Bethel Road. The park entrance will be on your left. Admission to the park is free.

EDUCATION

There are forty public schools in Newport News, including two high schools that opened in the fall of 1996. In Hampton, thirty-four schools—including four high and six middle schools—serve the needs of the population.

In the area of higher education, the Peninsula has two four-year institutions and a two-year community college. We have listed these here. For more detailed information on learning opportunities in and around Williamsburg, turn to the chapter on Education and Child Care.

Christopher Newport University (CNU)
1 University Place, Newport News
(757) 594-7000
www.cnu.edu
This state-supported, four-year school offers more than eighty different majors and concentrations to its 4,800 full- and part-time students. It has master's programs in applied physics and education. CNU also operates SEVAnet, a nonprofit online education center that has been working to set up electronic commerce and data interchange in partnership with a number of businesses, including Newport News Shipbuilding. The Ferguson Center for the Arts, which was designed by the world-class architectural firm founded by I. M. Pei, opened in 2004.

Hampton University
East Hampton off Settlers Landing Road
(757) 727-5000
www.hamptonu.edu
The country's largest historically black college offers thirty-eight bachelor's degree programs and fourteen master's degree programs in fields such as architecture, business, and art to its more than 5,700 full- and part-time students. The college also has Ph.D. programs in physics, nursing, physical therapy, and pharmacy. Hampton University achieved a long-

time goal in 1995, when its endowment money topped the $100 million mark and now exceeds $200 million.

From a historical standpoint, Booker T. Washington is one of the university's most famous graduates. A former slave who later became a determined student and gifted leader, Washington graduated in 1875 and later moved to Alabama to launch what eventually would become the prestigious Tuskegee Institute. On Marshall Avenue on the university campus stands a statue of Booker T. Washington. In the midst of a memorial garden, the statue serves as a reminder of one man's inspiring accomplishments. The works of another Hampton University graduate, famed artist Dr. John Biggers, can be seen in the William R. and Norma B. Harvey Library on campus.

Thomas Nelson Community College (TNCC)
99 Thomas Nelson Drive, Hampton
(757) 825-2700
www.tncc.cc.va.us
Thomas Nelson Community College in Hampton has a reputation for quality-year associate degree programs. The college, established in 1967, grants associate degrees in thirty-eight fields and more than forty certificates in career-related areas, including administrative support technology, automotive career studies, and information systems technology. Some credits are transferable to a four-year college. Recently, the college expanded its involvement with local businesses, frequently tailoring training programs for industries located on the Peninsula and offers dual enrollment classes to high school students. (TNCC also offers classes at a satellite facility in the Williamsburg area. See the Education and Child Care chapter for more on the Williamsburg site.)

INDEX

ABOUT THE AUTHORS

MARY ALICE BLACKWELL

Mary Alice Blackwell is a native Virginian who has enjoyed a writing career as a newspaper reporter and editor; she is coauthor of a guide to Virginia's Blue Ridge. Over the years, Mary Alice has collected some twenty-five-plus awards for writing and editing from the Virginia Press Association, the West Virginia Press Association, and Virginia Press Women. She lives in Charlottesville, Virginia.

ANNE PATTERSON CAUSEY

Anne Patterson Causey grew up in the Tidewater area and has worked as a newspaper reporter and editor, a publicist and event management consultant, and a library research assistant. She lives in Charlottesville, Virginia.

JOETTA SACK

Joetta Sack is a writer and editor for the National School Boards Association, which publishes *American School Board Journal,* a national magazine, and several other award-winning publications. She is a graduate of the University of Maryland's school of journalism and lives in Arlington, Virginia, with her husband (and two cats).